NATCHITOCHES
1800-1826

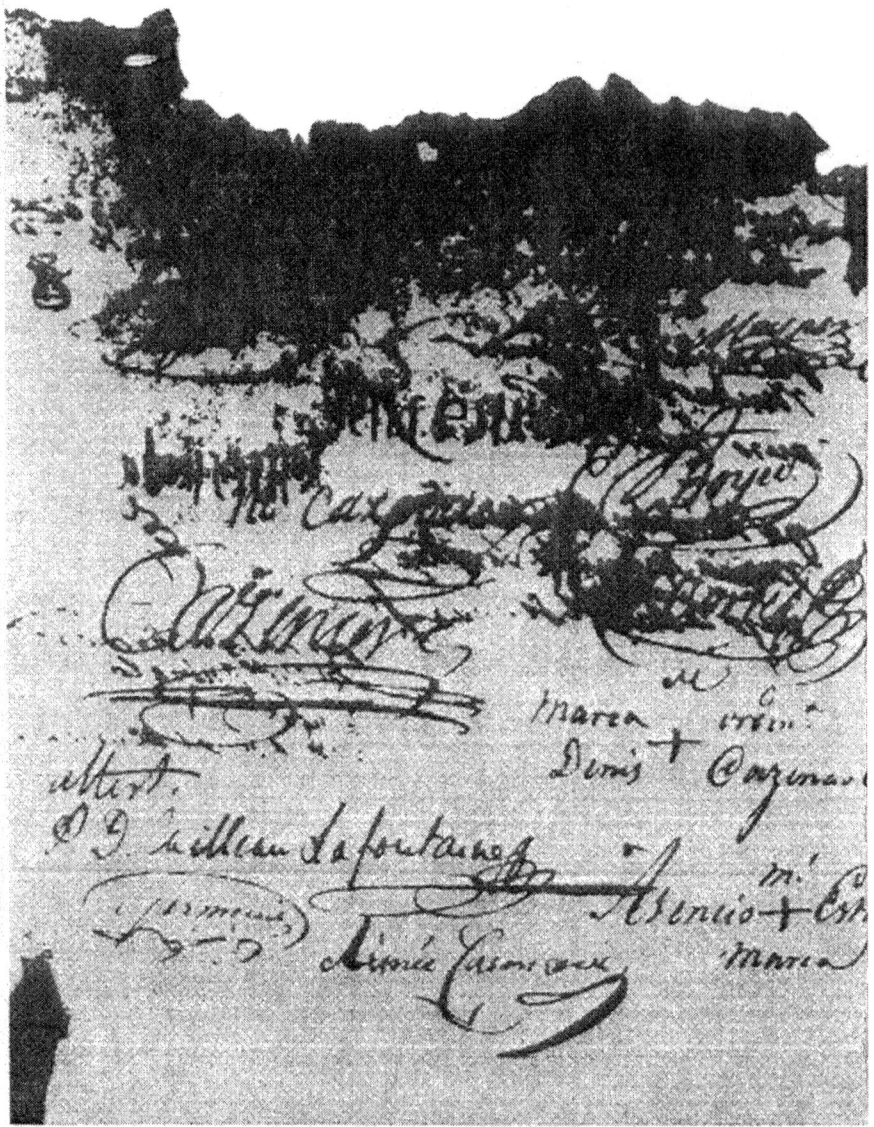

Register 5, page 268
Marriage of Joseph [—?—] to [—?—] Casenave

This document illustrates the deplorable condition of many crumbling pages within the fire-damaged Register 5. In 1978, before using the register to prepare this volume of translated abstracts, Mills deacidified and encapsulated the fragments of each page in archival Mylar; the register was then rebound by the parish. Some of the abstracts that follow contain data from transcriptions Mills made about 1970, when those entries were somewhat more intact.

NATCHITOCHES

Translated Abstracts
of
Register Number Five
of the
Catholic Church Parish
of
St. François des Natchitoches
in
Louisiana

1800—1826

Elizabeth Shown Mills

HERITAGE BOOKS
2007

HERITAGE BOOKS
AN IMPRINT OF HERITAGE BOOKS, INC.

Books, CDs, and more—Worldwide

For our listing of thousands of titles see our website
at
www.HeritageBooks.com

Published 2007 by
HERITAGE BOOKS, INC.
Publishing Division
65 East Main Street
Westminster, Maryland 21157-5026

Copyright © 1980 Elizabeth Shown Mills

Other books by the author:

Natchitoches, 1729-1803

Natchitoches Church Marriages, 1818-1850: Translated Abstracts from the Registers of St. Francios des Natchitoches Louisiana

Tales of Old Natchitoches
Elizabeth Shown Mills and Gary B. Mills

All rights reserved. No part of this book may be reproduced or transmitted in any form or by any means, electronic or mechanical, including photocopying, recording or by any information storage and retrieval system without written permission from the author, except for the inclusion of brief quotations in a review.

International Standard Book Number: 978-1-58549-925-0

To
MOTHER

Other Books in This Series

Vol. 1
CHAUVIN dit CHARLEVILLE

Vol. 2
NATCHITOCHES, 1729–1803:
Abstracts of the Catholic Church Registers
of the French and Spanish Post of
St. Jean Baptiste des Natchitoches in Louisiana

Vol. 3
TALES OF OLD NATCHITOCHES

Vol. 5
NATCHITOCHES COLONIALS:
Censuses, Military Rolls, and Tax Lists, 1722–1803

Vol. 6
NATCHITOCHES CHURCH MARRIAGES, 1818–1850
Translated Abstracts from the Registers of
St. François des Natchitoches, Louisiana

TABLE OF CONTENTS

	Page Nos.
The Ministers	vi
Index to Sacraments	vii
Introduction	viii
Sacramental Entries	3
Appendix: Supplemental Extracts from Register 19	383
Index	405

> NOTE: The abbreviations (s) and (x) which appear in various entries indicate whether individuals signed or made their marks of a cross.

MINISTERS SERVING THE PARISH OF ST. FRANÇOIS DES NATCHITOCHES

Name	Station	Period	Entry Nos.
Pierre Pavie	Natchitoches	Sept 1801–Sept 1806	1-213 1703-1732 1811-2014
Louis Buhot	Opelousas	August 1807	214-232 2015-2036
Vicente Simon Gonzales de Cosco	Durango	Sept 1808	233-248 2037-2046
Louis Buhot	Opelousas	Nov-Dec 1809	249-322 2047-2087
José Maria de Jesus Huerta	Nacogdoches	Sept 1810	324-326
Louis Buhot	Opelousas	Dec 1810	2764
Louis Buhot	Opelousas	Aug 1811	327-347, 2089-2095
Jose Mariano Sosa	Nacogdoches	Sept 1811	348-352
Louis Buhot	Opelousas	Aug-Dec 1812	353-391 2096-2099
Francisco Magnes	Nacogdoches	Dec 1812-Feb 1813	393-406 2100-2108
	Natchitoches	April 1813-Sept 1822	407-1576 2109-2757, 2765-2936 1652-1700, 1804-1808
Bishop Louis Dubourg	New Orleans	Nov 1821-Aug 1822 Oct 1825 May 1826 July 1826	1577-1631 1632-1650 1651

INDEX TO SACRAMENTS

Entry Nos.

Baptisms

1801-April 1813	white and f.p.c.	1-412
January 1802	white	1811
September 1808	white	2037-2038
April 1813-March 1816	white and f.p.c.	421-719
January 1802-August 1807	slave and f.p.c.	1809-2036
May 1818-September 1822	slave and f.p.c.	1065-1577
November 1821-August 1822	slave and f.p.c.	1652-1700
December 1821	slave and f.p.c.	1804-1808
October 1825-July 1826	slave and f.p.c.	1577-1651

Burials

January 1802-August 1815	white and f.p.c.	800-945
April 1802-September 1806	slave and f.p.c.	1703-1732
June 1813-August 1822	slave and f.p.c.	1733-1801
September-December 1815	white	413-420

Marriages

January 1802-1816	white and f.p.c.	946-1064
1816-September 1818	white and f.p.c.	720-799

INTRODUCTION

The first quarter of the nineteenth century was, assuredly, the most turbulent era in the history of Natchitoches. Within the first three years of that century, the Louisiana colony passed from Spanish to French to American control; but the frontier that Natchitoches embraced was doomed to suffer from political instability for decades to come as the new American regime fought a diplomatic battle with neighboring Spanish Texas over the boundary that should lie between them. Natchitoches, for the most part, lay within the disputed territory; and more than once, along this frontier, the cold war threatened to erupt into open military action.

Meanwhile, migrants from the older American states, as well as immigrants from the British Isles, poured by the thousands into the new territory of Louisiana, bringing with them a strikingly alien culture that challenged the Latin, Roman Catholic way of life. Within the span of years embraced by Register 5, the "Anglo" newcomers achieved political dominance in the new civil parish of Natchitoches, a "county" that embraced all ten-thousand square miles of northwest Louisiana.

Register 5 of the Catholic Parish of St. François des Natchitoches reflects many of the changes that occurred within this period. Students of history who have already scrutinized the earlier registers of the parish[*] will note the significant changes that occur in the ethnic origins of the population during the period covered by this present register. Even during the Spanish regime in Louisiana, the *habitans* of Natchitoches had remained almost entirely French; yet in the second decade of the 1800s, the increasing anarchy created by American migrants into Spanish Texas drove many Spanish settlers across the Sabine to Natchitoches -- and Register 5 reveals a greater

---

[*]See Elizabeth Shown Mills, *Natchitoches 1729-1803; Abstracts of the Catholic Church Registers of the French and Spanish Post of St. Jean Baptiste des Natchitoches in Louisiana* (New Orleans: Polyanthos, Inc., 1977).

increase in the Spanish population at Natchitoches than that which occurred at any other time.

To some extent this register also reflects the increased anglicization of the parish, and the extent to which the contrasting Catholic-Protestant cultures met and melded on this frontier. While most migrants from across the Mississippi, and from the British Isles, remained staunchly Protestant, a surprising percentage renounced the faith of their childhood in favor of Catholicism. Significantly, those who did included, by and large, the new "Anglo" leadership of the parish.

The transfer of Louisiana from European to American control also created additional problems for the Catholic population of Natchitoches. The religious orders of France and Spain were no longer responsible for providing clergy to Louisiana, and the Roman Catholic Church in America lacked the additional personnel necessary to minister to the many thousands of new Catholics now added to their ranks. For fourteen years, the vast Catholic territory of Louisiana had no bishop of its own -- instead it was assigned to the distant diocese of Baltimore under Bishop Carroll. In 1806, the French pastor of Natchitoches was recalled, and the parishioners of St. François were left with no spiritual leader at all. Throughout the next seven years, their sacramental needs were served, very sporadically, by visiting priests from Opelousas, Nacogdoches, and Durango.

In 1813, the Nacogdoches pastor Francisco Magnes was reassigned by the Mexican Church to foreign duty at Natchitoches, but the rapidly changing character of the frontier flock proved a difficult challenge. Eight years after Magnes' arrival, on March 22, 1821, Bishop Louis Dubourg of New Orleans paid his first pastoral visit to Natchitoches and recorded there the discouragement that he felt. The church itself, Bishop Dubourg wrote, was in a ruinous state. "I saw with sorrow the decadence of everything pertaining to religion. . . . Faith turned cold . . . . these deplorable ills are the result of an unfortunate litigation which has robbed the church of all her properties, and lack of instruction which for more than fifteen years afflicts this parish."[*]

The bishop's discouragement proved contagious, and affairs within the parish deteriorated to a new nadir.

---

[*]Monsignor Henry F. Beckers et al, *A History of Immaculate Conception Catholic Church* (privately printed, 1973), unnumbered page.

Father Magnes left St. François six months later in the midst of a new legal dispute over property ownership which had been initiated against the church by the recently incorporated town of Natchitoches. Early in the next spring, March 29, 1823, the delapidated remains of the church building and sixty-five surrounding homes and businesses went up in flames as a result of a fire that originated in the church. Blame was cast upon its beadle of twenty years, identified by history only as "the Negro Joe" who allegedly was drunk during a storm and failed to notice high winds that blew the curtains of the church into the candles he had lit. Again, the wardens of the impoverished parish of St. François found themselves in court, as a damage suit was filed against them by a prominent but non-Catholic victim of the fire.

The last priest whose name appears in Register 5 is Bishop Dubourg himself. In 1825 Dubourg returned to the parish to find an unexpected, inexplicable, renewal of faith; and this time he recorded the fervor with which the ladies of St. François had prepared for his arrival. Meeting in a public hall, the Bishop and his assistant, Father Anduze, baptized three hundred and fifty infants,* catechized numerous youth, and "rehabilitated" many marriages that Catholic parishioners had been forced to contract before a civil judge in the years they had been without a priest.

With the close of Register 5, the parish of Natchitoches entered a new era. The Louisiana legislature, on February 27, 1826, authorized the parish to conduct a lottery to raise as much as $20,000 for the purpose of rebuilding their church, and the imposing, twin-towered brick edifice that was to rise on the corner of Church and Second Streets symbolized the renewed faith and the new, long awaited stability that was at last being achieved on this frontier of Louisiana.

In yet one other way, Register 5 graphically symbolizes the maladies that Catholicism suffered in this quarter century at Natchitoches. A small portion of the heart of this book has been destroyed, and periphereal pages have been irrevocably lost -- the victim of fire and the corrosive acid that formed the very substance of the book's paper and ink. Yet, even this void has not been hopelessly permanent. Like the church which created

---

*The majority of these baptisms were recorded in Register 6 rather than in the present register.

it, the damaged portions of this book have been somewhat reconstructed.

In 1977, with the authorization of Bishop Lawrence P. Graves of the Diocese of Alexandria who has been greatly interested in the preservation of the Catholic records under his charge, this editor had the opportunity to perform restoration work that will hopefully salvage the extant portions of Register 5 and delay further ravages of time. Through the auxiliary use of other church and civil records, it has also been possible for this editor to reconstitute many of the damaged or destroyed entries. While the total loss could never be completely reversed, that loss has been significantly minimized.

In using the translated abstracts that follow, the researcher may rest assured that all data of genealogical and historical importance has been incorporated into this work. There are, additionally, several other points which this editor feels should be called to the attention of those researchers who have not had the opportunity to do extensive personal research in the Natchitoches registers.

1. The original entries are recorded, intermittently, in both French and Spanish. Moreover, the names of the Catholic parishioners who received these sacraments are also rendered in both French and Spanish. Even those parishioners of "Anglo" birth frequently appear in this register under the French or Spanish equivalents of their names. Researchers who are not familiar with the French, Spanish, and English equivalents of given names will find a helpful conversion table on pages 420-423 of the aforementioned *Natchitoches 1729-1803*, in which the previous registers of the parish (Books 1 through 4-B) were published by this editor in translated form.

2. As with the preceding registers -- in fact, even more so -- the careful researcher will be alert to unusual variant spellings of both given and family names that have resulted from the different and conflicting cultures and from the lack of a permanent priest, in certain periods, who might otherwise become familiar with the names and families of the Natchitoches region. The name Chelette, for example, is spelled within Register 5 in seventeen different ways, ranging from such unexpected variants as Eslect to Slyder.

3. The researcher should also be aware that the records which comprise this register do not represent ALL the sacramental entries recorded at Natchitoches

in the years 1800-1826. Those who have already done research in these registers (or consulted my preceding volume of translations) are undoubtedly familiar with the degree to which the various registers overlap each other chronologically and the extent of chronological disorganization that exists even within a given register. For additional records of this period, the researcher is referred to the following registers that are not yet available in translated, indexed, and published form:

    Baptisms (white and f.p.c.) 1817-40   Register 6
    Baptisms (slave and f.p.c.) 1826-31   Register 7
    Marriages (white and f.p.c.) 1818-37   Register 11

4. Finally, the editor is compelled to repeat one paragraph from the preface which accompanied the previous volume of translated registers, for its importance cannot be too strongly emphasized:

"The editor has sought to provide for researchers a usable, accessible, and accurate rendition of these invaluable but sometimes barely legible records. However, she is still human and subject to human imperfection. In cases where contradictions exist, or should any entry raise questions in the minds of any researcher, the editor encourages the researcher to examine the original himself [or at second best to submit an interlibrary loan request to Northwestern State University that will enable him to obtain and examine the microfilmed copy made of the register prior to restoration.] The editor also encourages the reader to supplement the entries in these registers with research in all available source materials for the area. Her own comparisons of church, civil, and miscellaneous records have convinced her that ANY original document well might contain error. Officials of yesteryear were human also. Only by gathering, scrutinizing, and comparing a variety of records on any individual can a researcher 'rest easy' with the 'facts' he has collected."

Certified copies of any entry in this volume may be obtained at a nominal fee by addressing a brief, written request to the Secretary of the Church of the Immaculate Conception, Post Office Box 13, Natchitoches, LA 71457. Please provide a stamped, self-addressed return envelope with your request.

§ § § §

Once again, and with even deeper gratitude, I want to acknowledge the assistance of those dedicated men and women, both within the Church and outside of it, who have made this work possible: Bishop Lawrence P. Graves of the diocese of Alexandria. . . the Reverend Father Frank S. Foret, former pastor of Immaculate Conception Church, under whose ministry this work was performed . . . Mesdames Suzanne Williams, Cissy Cunningham and Shelby Nealy, the parish secretaries who are so responsive to the pleas for help that they receive from so many family historians . . . Natchitoches Parish Clerk of Court Irby L. Knotts and his efficient deputies . . . Donald N. MacKenzie, Director, Northwestern State University of Louisiana, who has taken such a personal interest in the preservation of the area's religious records . . . and finally, but by no means last in my heart, my husband, critic, and occasional colleague, Dr. Gary B. Mills, and our children Clayton, Donna, and Danny, whose ties to Natchitoches I hope, in this small way, to help preserve.

E. S. M.

NATCHITOCHES
1800 - 1826

REGISTER 5

NOTE: Marginal notation which appears in the original register beside the first entry below indicates that it was the 31st entry recorded in the year 1801. Apparently the earlier entries have been lost. See Appendix.

The first number that appears beside each entry below is the Entry Number assigned by the Editor. The number which appears in parenthesis, below the Entry Number, is the page number of the original register on which the entry appears.

1. JEAN BAPTISTE /PALVA/DOS
(1) /Entry badly torn -- date illegible/. Baptism of an infant at Bayou Pierre, with permission of the pastor of Nacogdoche who has jurisdiction over that region. Infant is legitimate son of Jean Pal/vados/ and /entry torn -- name should be Eleanor Tessier/. Paternal grandparents: /torn/; maternal grandparents: Pierre Texier and Magdalena /torn/. Godparents: Jean Baptiste Plaisance and Marie D'aragon. Priest: P. Pavie.

2. GEUFROI DUPRE
(1) 20 September 1801, baptism of an infant born 21 June 1799 in this post, legitimate son of Pierre Dupre and Francoise Lecour. Grandparents: Joseph Dupre, Marie Derbanne; Louis Lecour, Jeanne Leroi. Godparents: Jacques Lacase and Marie Lecour. Priest: P. Pavie.

3. CHARLES LACASE
(1) 26 October 1801, baptism of an infant born 5th of the previous month, legitimate son of Etienne Lacase and Dorothée Massip. Grandparents: Charles Lacase, Felicité Langlois; Jean Massip, Marie /illegible, but should be Marie Louise LeMoine/. Godparents: Charles /illegible/ and /illegible/. Priest: P. Pavie.

NOTE: one complete entry, which should appear here, is torn from the top of page 2 of present register.

4.   ETIENNE MAXIMILIEN OUALES /WALLACE/
(2) /torn/ December 1801, baptism of an infant born 12
     October last in this post, legitimate son of Etienne
     Maximien /"Macquen" has been written over this name
     in the same handwriting/ Ouales and of Hiacinthe
     Gagne. Grandparents: Joseph Ouales and Denée
     Bertrand; Etienne Gagne and Louise Bertrand. God-
     parents: Pierre Ternié and Anne Gagné. Priest:
     P. Pavie.

5.   MARIE CELESTE DUROQUE
(2) 11 December 1801, baptism of an infant born 1 No-
     vember last, legitimate daughter of Nicolas Du-
     roque and Marie Manuel Rosse, living at the vache-
     rie of Marie Brevel, widow of deceased Grillet, in
     the jurisdiction of the post of Nacogdoches. Pére
     Caiton, pastor of said post, has given his consent.
     Grandparents: Pierre Duroque, Marie Dalbarcq?;
     Joseph Rosse, Barbe Corde. Godparents: Jean Bap-
     tiste Theodule Grillet and Marie Marguerite Prud-
     homme. Priest: P. Pavie.

6.   HONORE FRAIDIEU
(3) 27 December 1801, baptism of an infant born 4 Oct-
     ober last in this post, legitimate son of Augustin
     Fraidieu and of Marie Jeanne Sorel. Grandparents:
     Augustin Fraidieu, Angelique Claire; Pierre Sorel,
     Marie Rose Bossalié. Godparents: Manuel Rachal
     and Marie Louise Rachal. Priest: P. Pavie.

7.   ANTOINE JARRI /MICHEL-ZORICHE/
(3) 2 January 1802, baptism of an infant born 22 Sep-
     tember last, in this post, legitimate son of Pierre
     Jarri and Celeste Dupre. Grandparents: Michel
     Jarri, Marie Amien; Robert Dupre, Manon Cavé.
     Godparents: Antonio Lainoir, Catherinne Brosset.
     Priest: P. Pavie.

8.   MARIE FRANCOISE ASELLI BUART
(3) 23 January 1802, baptism of an infant born 27 Sep-
     tember, 1801, legitimate daughter of Denis Buart
     and Marie Victoire Poissot. Grandparents: Gabriel
     Buart, Marie Roussot; Remis Poissot, Marie Louise
     Ca/vé/. Godparents: Francois Rouquier, Marie
     Francoise Malbert. Priest: P. Pavie.

9.   MARIE ASPASIE THIERRY (QUIERE)*
(3-4) 7 February 1802, baptism of an infant born 24 Oct-
      ober last, legitimate daughter of Pierre Queri and
      Marie Rosalie Frederic, living in this post.

Grandparents: /illegible/ Query, Francoise Beque; Philippe Frederik, Catherinne Sauvage. Godparents: Jean Baptiste Armand and Marie Catherinne Frederic. Priest: P. Pavie.

*Marginal notation records this name as "Thierry." Text repeatedly reads "Queri." "Queri," "Querry" and "Kerry" are the usual spellings of this family name at Natchitoches.

10. VALERI LEMOINE
(4) 12 February 1802, baptism of an infant born 1 December last, legitimate son of Jean Baptiste Lemoine and Felicité Lacase, habitants of this post. Grandparents: Charles Lemoine, Elisabeth Dupre; Charles Lacase, Felicité Langlois. Godparents: Remi Lambre, represented by Rosaimon Chamart, and Catherinne Lambre. Priest: P. Pavie.

11. MARIE ARCISE* /GRAPPE/
(4) 28 February 1802, baptism of a quadroon born 18 October last, natural daughter of Felicité, a free mulatress residing at this post, and of a father unknown. Godparents: Manuel Triche and Pelagie Grape. Priest: P. Pavie.

*This name is also spelled in text "Arches."

12. MARIE MARGUERITE CHRISTII /TIHOUA/*
(5) MARIE DENEIGE CHRISTII /TIHOUA/*
10 March 1802, baptism with consent of Reverend Father Joseph Manuel Caitan, pastor of the church of Notre Dame La pilard de la Nacodoche, of two natural daughters of Magdeleine Christi by father unknown*. The first child, born 15 November 1799, the second born 15 August 1801 "at Tapatcat of the post of Nacotdoche". Godparents of Marie Marguerite: Jacques Terrié and Marie Margueritte Duval. Godparents of Marie Deneige: Ignace Maiou and Marie Cicile Maiou. Priest: P. Pavie.

*See entry 960.

13. MARIE DELPHINE POISSOT
(5) MARIE FIRMIN POISSOT
14 March 1802, baptism of a girl, aged three years, and a boy (Marie Firmin) born 25 September last, both legitimate children of Marie Athanasse Poissot and Marie Louise Heleine Pavie, living at this post. Grandparents: Athanase Poissot, Marie Soto; Etienne Pavie and Marie Thérèse Buart. Godparents of Marie Delphine: Julien Besson and

Marie Soto. Godparents of Marie Firmin: Silvestre Poissot and Marie Elisabeth Metoyer. Priest: P. Pavie.

14. JEAN BAPTISTE NEUVILLE /LE COURT/*
(5-6) 4 April 1802, baptism of an infant born 25 September last, son of Marie Ursule, a free *metive*, and of a father unknown.* Godparents: Jean Baptiste Florentin /Conant/, free mulatto, and Pelagie, free quadroon. Priest: P. Pavie.

*Numerous civil and church records of the parish, in later years, identify this child as the son of Barthelemy Le Court.

15. MARIE GENEVIEVE LEVASSEUR
(6) 4 April 1802, baptism of an infant born 9 March in this post, legitimate daughter of Simeon Levasseur and Marie Joseph Ulalie Mercie. Grandparents: Francois Levasseur, Marie Jeanne Mader; Louis Mercier, Marie Louise Lefevre. Godparents: Louis Levasseur, Felicite Adelaide Mercier. Priest: P. Pavie.

16. PLACIDE RABALE
(6) 10 April 1802, baptism of an infant born 8 November last, in this post, legitimate son of Joseph Rabalé and Marie Joseph Bontems. Grandparents: Joseph Rabale and Anne Barbé; Maternal grandfather unknown, maternal grandmother: Marie Anne Bontems. Godparents: Placide Bossié and Marguerite Denis. Priest: P. Pavie.

17. JEAN BAPTISTE ANTI
(6) 11 April 1802, baptism of an infant born 24 September last, legitimate son of Jean Baptiste Anty and Marie Cypriene Derbane, living in this post, Grandparents: Jean Baptiste Anti, Catherinne Gallien; Pierre Derbane, Marie Francoise Brevel. Godparents: Joseph Derbane, Louise Rachal. Priest: P. Pavie.

18. JEAN BAPTISTE MARIE FRANCOIS HERRIE
(7) 12 April 1802, baptism of an infant born 25 February last, legitimate son of Jacques Herrié and Marie Anastasie Maiou, living in this post. Grandparents: Jacques Herrié, Genevieve Vige; Ignace Maiou, Therese Philipot. Godparents: Jean Marie Francois Rouquier, represnted by Francois Rouquier his father, and Marie Joseph Henriette Rouquier. Priest: P. Pavie.

19.   ETIENNE DAVION
(7)   16 April 1802, baptism of an infant born 20 January
        last, legitimate son of Dominique Davion and Pe-
        lagie Gagné. Grandparents: Jean Baptiste Davion,
        Marie Hiacinthe Triche; Etienne Gagné, Marie
        Louise Bertrand. Godparents: Jean Baptiste Da-
        vion, Anne Gagné. Priest: P. Pavie.

20.   JEAN BAPTISTE FAUSTIN PLAISANCE
(7)   17 April 1802, baptism of an infant born the first
        of this month, legitimate son of Bertrand Plai-
        sance and Marie Barbe Grillé. Grandparents: Bap-
        tiste Plaisance, Margueritte Totin; Marin Grillé
        Marie Louise Brevel. Godparents: Jean Lalande,
        Adelaide Vercher. Priest: P. Pavie.

21.   JOSEPH JEROME TORRES
(7-8)   8 May 1802, baptism of an infant born 28 February
        1801, son of Marie Gertrude Torres, living in this
        post, and of a father unknown. Godparents: Rose-
        mon Chamart and Marie Antoine Torres. Priest: P.
        Pavie.

22.   STEPHANIE SOREL
(8)   19 May, 1802, baptism of an infant born 10 April
        last, legitimate duaghter of Dominique Sorel and
        Marie Marthe Fort. Grandparents: Pierre Sorel,
        Marie Rose Bosselié, Jacques Fort, Marie Francoise
        Malbert. Godparents: Luc Sorel and Marie Fran-
        coise Malbert. Priest: P. Pavie.

23.   MARIE SUSANNE /METOYER/
(8)   26 June 1802, baptism of an infant mulatress, na-
        tive of this parish, aged 9 months, legitimate
        daughter of Dominique /Metoyer/, a free mulatto,
        and Marguerite /LeComte/, a free mulatress. Pa-
        ternal grandmother: Marie Therese Coincoin. Ma-
        ternal grandmother: Marie, Negress slave of Widow
        LeComte. Godparents: Nicolas Augustin /Metoyer/,
        a free mulatto, and Marie Louise /Mariotte/, a free
        Negress, uncle and aunt of the infant. P. Pavie.

24.   MARIE PELAGIE ELOISE DAVID
(8)   4 July 1802, baptism of infant of 10 months, born
        in this post, daughter of Elisabeth David and a
        father unknown. Godparents: Francois Grape and
        Pelagie Grape. Priest: P. Pavie.

25.   ANTOINE BROSSET
(9)   18 July 1802, baptism of infant born 12 September
        last in this post, legitimate son of Pierre Bro-

sset and Marie Joseph Grillé. Grandparents: Jean Brosset, Jeanne Rutin; Marin Grillé, Marie Louise Brevel. Godparents: Jean Renau and Marie Luce Rachal. Priest: P. Pavie.

26. MARIE ROSELIE MASSIP
(9) 8 August 1802, baptism of infant born 22 October last, in this post, legitimate daughter of Jean Massip and Marie Lemoine. Grandparents: Pierre Massip and Jeanne Lafont; Charles Lemoine and Elisabeth Dupre. Godparents: Jean Baptiste Rachal, Marie Pelagie Brevel. Priest: P. Pavie.

27. MARIE MODESTE GONIN
(9) 15 August 1802, baptism of infant born 17th of the previous month in this post, legitimate daughter of Francois Gonin and Marie Barbe Frederik. Grandparents: Jean Baptiste Gonin and Manuel Riche; Philippe Frederik and Anne Barbe Cheletre. Godparents: Francois Lestage and Marie Pelagie Frederik. Priest: P. Pavie.

28. EUPHROSINE BAUDOUIN
(9-10) 12 September 1802, baptism of child born 26 February 1800, legitimate daughter of Jean Pierre Baudouin and Anne Robin, living in this post. Grandparents: Francois Baudouin and Marie Anne Bontems; Michel Robin and Marie Louise Boulet. Godparents: Jean Baptiste Denis and Lucide Denis. Priest: P. Pavie.

29. MARIE SUSANNE /METOYER/
(10) 19 September 1802, baptism of a mulatress born 4 July last, in this post, legitimate daughter of Antoine Joseph /Metoyer/, a free mulatto, and of Pelagie /Le Court/, a free quadroon. Godparents: Louis Cesair /Le Court/, free quadroon, and Marie Jeanne, free Negress. Priest: P. Pavie.

30. MARIE DELPHINE DUBOIS
(10) 19 September 1802, baptism of infant born 9 June last, in this post, legitimate daughter of Francois Dubois and Heleonoris Ris. Grandparents: Jean Baptiste Dubois and Marie Joseph Clermont; Jean Ris and Marie Jeanne Chagneau. Godparents: Jean Baptiste Adelet and Sophie Olié. Priest: P. Pavie.

31. MICHEL GASPART BODIN
(11) 22 September 1802, baptism of infant born 5 April last, legitimate son of Gaspar Bodin and Marie

Louise Villefranche /"Le Duc" is inserted above the last name/, residents of this post. Grandparents: Jean Laurent Bodin and Marie Rosalie La croix; Jean Baptiste Villefranche and Marie Anne Guedon. Godparents: Michel Chamart and Marie Rose Malige. Priest: P. Pavie.

32. PELAGIE LEMOINE
(11) 26 September 1802, baptism of infant born 28 September 1801, legitimate daughter of Charles Lemoine and Jeanne Lebrun, living in this post. Grandparents: Charles Lemoine and Elisabeth Dupre; Guillaume Lebrun and Marie Louise Totin. Godparents: Philippe Brosset, Marie Jeanne Melanie Rachal. Priest: P. Pavie.

33. MARIE LANGLOIS
(11) LOUIS LANGLOIS
16 October 1802, baptism of two infants, the first born 23 November 1799 and the other born last 9 December, legitimate children of Louis Langlois and Celeste Vergé. Grandparents: Augustin Langlois and Marie Louise Riché; Etienne Vergé and Marie Francoise Dupre. Godparents of Marie: Pierre Dupre and Marie Rose Dupre. Godparents of Louis: Jacques Lacasse and Marie Francoise Dupre. Priest: P. Pavie.

34. ANDRE ISAAC HECER /HESSER/
(12) 17 October 1802, baptism of infant born 16th of last month, baptized privately in danger of death, legitimate son of Christiane Hecer and *Adelaide Rambin. Grandparents: Frederic Hecer and Catherine Bull; André Rambin and Catherinne Buart. Godparents: André Rambin and Marie Rouquié. Priest: P. Pavie.

*Notation by P. Pavie adds "Marie Francoise" in front of the name "Adelaide."

35. AURESILE ANTI
(12) 24 October 1802, baptism of infant born 7 July of previous year, at this post, legitimate daughter of Louis Anti and Marie Jeane Crete. Grandparents: Ignace Anti, Catherinne Guerin; Pierre Cret, Marie Louise Vergé. Godparents: Silvestre Anti and Marie Euphrosine Rachal. Priest: P. Pavie.

36. MARIE MERANDI POISSOT
(12) 25 October 1802, baptism of infant born 25 November last, legitimate daughter of Paul Poissot and Marie Louise Anti. Grandparents: Remi Poissot

and Marie Cavé; Jean Baptiste Anti and Catherinne Gallien. Godparents: Louis Anti, represented by Francois Rouqui é, and Heleine Gallien, represented by Aimé Rouqui é. Priest: P. Pavie.

37. MARIE ADELAIDE RACHAL
(13) 31 October 1802, baptism of infant born in this post last 13 August, legitimate daughter of Julien Rachal and Marie Louise Brevel. Grandparents: Louis Rachal and Marie Louise Deroi /Le Roy/; Jean Baptiste Brevel and Marie Francoise Poissot. Godparents: Jean Baptiste Rachal and Victoire Brevel. Priest: P. Pavie.

38. FRANCOIS CELESTAIN TAUSIN
(13) 28 November 1802, baptism of infant born 24 September last, legitimate son of Joseph Tausin and Marie Chamart. Grandparents: Girard Tausin and Jeanne Bartheau; Louis Chamart and Catherinne Bardon. Godparents: Barthelemis Chabus and Marie Rose Malige. Priest: P. Pavie.

39. LOUIS RACHAL
(13) 8 January 1803, baptism of infant born last October 26, in this post, legitimate son of deceased Louis Rachal and Marie Joseph Laberi. Grandparents: Louis Rachal and Marie Louise Leroi; Jean Baptiste Laberi and Jeanne Guedon. Godparents: Bernard Guissarnat and Marie Jeanne Melanie Rachal. Priest: P. Pavie.

40. MARIE CARMELITE FRANCOISE CHABUS
(14) 9 January 1803, baptism of infant born 23 December last, legitimate daughter of Francois Chabus and Marie Jeanne Malige, residents of this post. Grandparents: Jean Francois Chabus and Marie Anne Charpenel; Joseph Malige and Marie Anne Bardon. Godparents: Marie Anne Bardon, grandmother of the infant. Priest: P. Pavie.

41. MANUEL BERNARD PIERRE GONSALEZ
(14) 15 January 1803, baptism of infant born first of this month, legitimate son of Pierre Gonsalez and Catherinne Bonnet. Grandparents: Bernard Gonsalez and Catherinne Lamougne; Jean Bonnet and Antoinette Gastille. Godparents: Pierre Cheletre and Margueritte Reine Pievert?. Priest: P. Pavie.

42. JEAN PIERRE ROSALIE GAGNE
(14) 15 February 1803, baptism of infant born last August 9, in this post, legitimate son of Pierre

Gagné and Marie Lalande. Grandparents: Pierre Gagné and Marie Louise Davion; Jean Lalande and Catherinne Dupre. Godparents: Jean Pierre La lande and Susanne Gagné. Priest: P. Pavie.

43. JEAN NICOLAS BODIN
(15) 19 February 1803, baptism of infant born last 26 May, legitimate son of Jean Laurent Bodin and of Marie Modeste, a Canneci Indian, residents of this post. Paternal grandparents: Laurent Bodin and Michel Rosalie Crous. Maternal grandparents: Pierre and Marie Magdeleine. Godparents: Jean Nicolas and Marie Ursule. Priest: P. Pavie.

44. MANUEL HILAIRE BORDELON
(15) 20 February 1803, baptism of infant born last 11 October, legitimate son of Hipolite Bordelon and Marie Therese Triche, residents of this post. Grandparents: Nicolas Bordelon and Andrienne Rondeau; Manuel Triche and Marie Louise Grape. Godparents: Manuel Triche and Marie Felicité Modeste Triche. Priest: P. Pavie.

45. MARIE BONNE CHELETRE
(15) 21 February 1803, baptism of infant born last 5 August, legitimate duaghter of Barnabé Cheletre and Marie Jeanne Gonin. Grandparents: Michel Cheletre and Anne Barbe /Metz/; Jean Baptiste Gonin and Manuele Riché. Godparents: Placide Bossie and Marie Jeanne Cheletre. Priest: P. Pavie.

46. FRANCOIS LAVESPERE
(16) 3 April 1803, baptism of infant born 23 October last, legitimate son of Francois Lavespere and of Marie Louise Derbanne, residents of this post. Grandparents: Jean Lavespere and Magdeleine Augeraut*. Godparents: Gaspard Roubieu and Catherinne Brosset. Priest: P. Pavie.

*Correction by priest at bottom of entry adds: "name of maternal grandmother, Marie Lecler" However, the priest still failed to enter the name of the grandfather, Pierre Derbanne.

47. MARIE ARCENE TRICHE
(16) 3 April 1803, baptism of infant born last 22 December, native of this post, legitimate daughter of Jean Baptiste Triche and Marie Modeste Fonteneau. Grandparents: Jean Baptiste Triche and Marie Anne Daublin; Louis Fonteneau and Pelagie Grape. Godparents: Gilbert Closeau and Pelagie Grape. Priest: P. Pavie.

48. MODESTE LACASE
(16) 10 April 1803, baptism of child aged four years, native of this parish, legitimate daughter of Etienne Lacase and Dorotée Massip. Grandparents: Charles Lacase and Felise Langlois; Jean Massip and Marie Lemoine. Godparents: Jacques Lacase, Stephalie Lambre. Priest: P. Pavie.

49. JACQUES /CECILE/
(17) 10 April 1803, baptism of a mulatto born last 25 December in this post, son of Cecile, a free mulatress, and of a father unknown. Godparents: Pierre /Metoyer/ a free mulatto and Marie Louise /Mariotte/ a free mulatress. Priest: P. Pavie.

50. CELESTE /CECILE/
(17) 10 April 1803, baptism of a mulatress born 11 October 1801 in this post, daughter of Cecile, a free mulatress, and of a father unknown. Godparents: Jean Baptiste Lecomte and Elisabeth Rachal. Priest: P. Pavie.

51. FELISE ST. ANDRE*
(17) 16 April 1803, baptism of infant born 8 July 1801 in this post, legitimate daughter of Andre Saint André and of Marie Rachal, residents of this post. Grandparents: Jacques Saint André and Marie Anne Picard; Jacques Rachal and Ursule Castel. Godparents: Jean Joseph Rachal and Marie Joseph Laberi. Priest: P. Pavie.

*The name "Botien" was added in Father Pavie's handwriting, at an apparent later date, in the margin beneath the name "St. Andre."

52. CHRISOSTOME VASCOCU
(17-18) 28 April 1803, baptism of infant born last 27 March in this post, legitimate son of Louis Vascocu and Magdeleine Pereau. Grandparents: Antoine Vascocu, Marie Barbe Toups; Francois Pereau, Marie Catherinne Dupre. Godparents: Michel Barberou and Modeste Vascocu. Priest: P. Pavie.

53. MARIE ARTHEMISE CHAMART
(18) 23 May 1803, baptism of infant born last 2 March in this post, legitimate daughter of Michel Chamart and Marie Louise Euphrosine Rambin, residents of this post. Grandparents: Louis Charles Chamart and Marie Catherinne Bardon; Andre Antoine Rachal and Marie Catherinne Buart. Godparents: André Antoine Rambin and Marie Catherinne Bardon. Priest: P. Pavie.

54. ROSALIE BOSSIE
(18) 4 June 1803, baptism of infant born last 27 February in this post, legitimate daughter of Francois Bossié and Catherinne Pelagie Lambre. Grandparents: Francois Bossié, Rosalie Baré; Jean Baptiste Lambre and Marie Jeanne Levasseur. Godparents: Jean Baptiste Buart and Marie Aspasie Bossié. Priest: P. Pavie.

55. EDOUARD RACHAL
(18-19) 20 August 1803, baptism of infant born 27 October of the past year, in this post, legitimate son of Jean Baptiste Barthelemi Rachal and Marie Pelagie Brevel. Grandparents: Barthelemi Rachal and Marie Lamalathie; Jean Baptiste Brevel and Marie Francoise Poissot. Godparents: Antoine Barthemi Rachal and Marie Louise Rachal. Priest: P. Pavie.

56. MARIE PALVADOS
(19) 21 August 1803, baptism, with consent of Reverend Joseph Modeth Puelles, pastor of Nacogdoches, of an infant born last 2 April at Baiou au Pierre, legitimate SON of Jean Palvados and Heleonore Tecier, residents of Baiou au Pierre. Grandparents: Francois Palvados and Jeanne Bernard; Pierre Tecier and Magdeleine Turpain. Godparents: André Valentin and Angeline Malige. Priest: P. Pavie.

57. MANUEL DERBANE
(19) MARCELITTE DERBANE
28 August 1803, baptism of two infants born 20 August of last year in this post, legitimate son and daughter of Gaspart Derbane and of Marie Joseph Perau. Grandparents: Gaspart Derbane and Marie Vergé; Francois Perau and Catherinne Dupre. Godparents of Manuel: Manuel Triche and Marie Felicité Chrisostomé /Pereau/; godparents of Marcelitte: Louis Clauseau and Margueritte Totin. Priest: P. Pavie.

58. MARIE AGLAE
(20) 11 September 1803, baptism of a quadroon born 12 December last, daughter of Pelagie, free mulatress, and of a father unknown. Godparents: Arnaud Lauvé and Sophie Olié. Priest: P. Pavie.

59. LUDGER RACHAL
(20) 18 September 1803, baptism of infant born last 22 March in this post, son of Barthelemi Rachal and Magdeleine Grillé. Grandparents: Barthelemi Rachal and Marie Francois Lamalathi; Marin Grillé

and Marie Louise Brevel. Godparents: Louis Derbanne and Marie Francoise Rachal. Priest: P. Pavie.

60. JEAN LOUIS VERCHER
(20) 18 September 1803, baptism of infant born 12 May last, in this post, legitimate son of Jacques Querin Vercher and Marie Jeanne Euphrosine Gallien. Grandparents: Nicolas Gallien and Marie Antoine Lecourt; Louis Vercher and Marie Louise Grillé. Godparents: Nicolas Gallien and Marie Louise Grillé. Priest: P. Pavie.

61. LESSEIN /ONESIME/ LUDGER LEVASSEUR
(21) 18 September 1803, baptism of infant born the last day of last July in this post, legitimate son of Manuel Levasseur and Marie Joseph Mercié. Grandparents: Francois Levasseur and Marie Jeanne Mader; Louis Mercié and Marie Louise Lefevre. Godparents: Jean Levasseur and Marie Therese Eugenie Buart. Priest: P. Pavie.

62. ANTOINE NEUVILLE PRUDHOMME
(21) 25 September 1803, baptism of infant born last 1 May in this post, legitimate son of Antoine Prudhomme and Marie Lambre. Grandparents: Jean Baptiste Prudhomme and Henriette Colantin; Jacques Lambre and Marie Anne Poissot. Godparents: Jean Jacques Lambre and Henriette Rouquié. Priest: P. Pavie.

63. MARIE DELPHINE LAMBRE
(21) 4 October 1803, baptism of infant born last 20 April in this post, legitimate daughter of Remi Lambre and Susanne Prudhomme. Godparents: Jacob Lambre and Marie Anne Poisseau; Jean Baptiste Prudhomme and Henriette Colantin. Godparents: Francois Rouquié and Aimé Rouquié. Priest: P. Pavie.

64. MARIE CELESTE RABALLE
(22) 29 October 1803, baptism of infant born 4 May last, legitimate daughter of Joseph Raballe and Marie Bontems. Paternal Grandparents: Joseph Raballé and Anne Barbe; maternal grandmother: Marie Anne Bontems /maternal grandfather not named/. Godparents: Jean Baptiste Varangue and Marie Celeste Baudouin.

65. JEAN ELOY RACHAL
(22) 6 November 1803, baptism of infant born last 9

August, in this parish, legitimate son of Dominique Rachal and Rosalie Vercher. Grandparents: Barthelemi Rachal and Marie Francois Lamalathie; Louis Vercher and Marie Louise Grillé. Godparents: Jean Lalande, Felicité Chrisostomé /Pereau/. Priest: P. Pavie.

66. JOSEPH DERBANE
(22) 20 November 1803, baptism of infant aged 22 months, born in this post, son of Pierre Derbanne and of Marie Francoise Brevel. Grandparents: Pierre Derbane, Manon Claire /LeClerc/; Jean Baptiste Brevel and Marie Francoise Poissot. Godparents: Pierre Derbane and Marie Joseph Melanie Rachal. Priest: P. Pavie.

67. LOUIS SIMEON RACHAL
(22-23) 20 November 1803, baptism of infant born last 26 December in this parish, legitimate son of Simeon Rachal and Marie Magdeleine Laberi. Grandparents: Louis Rachal and Marie Louise Leroi; Jean Baptiste Laberi and Jeanne Guedon. Godparents: Louis Rachal and Marie Rachal. Priest: P. Pavie.

68. BERNARD BARTHELEMY RACHAL
(23) 3 December 1803, baptism of infant aged 2 months, legitimate son of Barthelemi Rachal and of Francoise Laberi, natives of this post. Grandparents: Louis Rachal and Marie Louise Leroi; Jean Baptiste Laberi and Jeanne Guedon. Godparents: Bernard Guisarnat and Marie Robt? Rachal. Priest: P. Pavie.

69. MARIE LOUISE ADELINE /RACHAL/*
(23) MARIE LOUISE ADELAIDE /RACHAL/*
4 December 1803, baptism of twins born 5 February 1801 in this post, daughters of Dorothée /Monet/* Indian of the Canneci nation and of a father unknown. Godparents of Marie Louise Adeline: Louis Monet and Marie Louise LeComte, represented by Pierre Joseph Maës and Marie Genevieve Agathe Maës; godparents of Marie Louise Adelaide: Pierre Joseph Maës and Marie Genevieve Agathe Maës. Priest: P. Pavie.

*Doc. 2838, Colonial Archives, Office of the Clerk of Court, Natchitoches, identifies Dorothée as daughter of Louis Monet. Numerous later church records indicate that her twin daughters used the surname Rachal (i.e. Register 6 (1838) #82) although none have been found to date which identify their father. Note that in entry 311 of this present register, a sister of the above twins is identified as daughter of Etienne Rachal.

70. LOUIS /MONET/
(23) 4 December 1803, baptism of infant born 15 February last, in this post, son of Dorothée /Monet/, Indian of the Canneci nation and of a father unknown. Godparents: Nicolas Martin and Marie Louise Clement. Priest: P. Pavie.

71. JEAN BAPTISTE NARCISSE THIERRY /QUIERRY/
(24) 11 December 1803, baptism of infant born last 20 October, legitimate son of Pierre Quieri and of Marie Joseph Frederic, residents of this post. Grandparents: Antoine Quieri and Francoise Bequer; Philippe Frederic and Catharinne Sauvage. Godparents: Jean Baptiste Buart and Marie Magdeleine Frederic. Priest: P. Pavie.

72. JOSEPH LAURENT TORRES
(25) 11 December 1803, baptism of a child aged three years on August 12, native of this post, legitimate son of Joseph Marie Torre and Susanne /no last name/. Paternal Grandparents: Joseph Torre and Marie Jeanne Deroi. Maternal grandmother: Marie Barbe Joseph Legrand /Varangue/; Maternal grandfather: unknown. Priest: P. Pavie.

73. AZENOR GABRIEL TORRES
(25) 11 December 1803, baptism of infant born 10 March of the previous year, legitimate son of Joseph Marie Torres and Susanne /no last name/. Paternal grandparents: Joseph Torre and Marie Jeanne Deroi; maternal grandmother: Marie Barbe Legrand /Varangue/; maternal grandfather: unknown. Godparents: Andre Chamart and Marie Pelagie Cheletre. Priest: P. Pavie.

74. PIERRE ERRIE /HERRIE/
(25) 20 December 1803, baptism of infant born 16 August last, in this parish, legitimate son of Jacques Errié and Anastasie Maillou. Grandparents: Jacques Errié and Genevieve Viger; Ignace Maillou and Therese Flibot. Godparents: Pierre Dolé and Marie Cecile Maillou. Priest: P. Pavie.

75. MARIE GIROU
(25) 8 January 1804, baptism of infant born last 18 December, legitimate daughter of Francois Girou and Marie Anne Couia, residents of this parish. Grandparents: Louis Girou and Marie Joseph

Leonard; Gracia Couia and Marie Louise Courteri. Godparents: Francois Perau and Marie Felicité Perau. Priest: P. Pavie.

76. NICOLAS DAMIEN DUROQUE
(25) 8 January 1804, baptism, with permission of Rev. M. J. Puelli, pastor of Nacogdoches, of an infant born 22 November of last year, legitimate son of Nicolas Duroque and Marie Manuel Rosse, living on the vacherie of Widow Grillé in the post of Nacogdoche. Grandparents: Pierre Duroque and Marie Holbarcq; Joseph Rosse and Barbe Corde. Godparents: Antoine Grillet and Marie Felicité Chrisostomé Perau. Priest: P. Pavie.

77. JEAN BAPTISTE BOSSIE
(26) 29 January 1804, baptism of infant aged 18 months, born in this post, legitimate son of Soulange Bossié and Heléonore Himel. Grandparents: Francois Bossié and Marie Charlote Baré; Antoine Himel and Marguerite Cheletre. Godparents: Jean Baptiste Buart and Marie Therese Eugenie Buart. Priest: P. Pavie.

78. JOSEPH JEAN BAPTISTE PRUDHOMME
(26) 2 March 1804, baptism of infant born 13 February of this year, legitimate son of Jean Baptiste Prudhomme and Rosalie Malige. Grandparents: Bastien Prudhomme and Marie Jeanne Chevert; Joseph Malige and Marie Anne Bardon. Godparents: Joseph Malige, grandfather of infant, and Marie Louise Prudhomme. Priest: P. Pavie.

79. EDOUARD PLAISANCE
(26) 25 March 1804, baptism of infant born 5 January of this year, legitimate son of Bertrand Plaisance and Marie Barbe Grillet, residents of this post. Grandparents: Jean Baptiste Plaisance and Marguerite Totin; Marin Grillet and Marie Louise Brevel. Godparents: Jean Baptiste Theodore Grillet and Marie Louise Rachal. Priest: P. Pavie.

80. LOUIS GASPARD DERBANE
(27) 1 April 1804, baptism of infant born 20 November 1802 in this post, legitimate son of Jean Baptiste Derbane and Marie Heleine Brevel. Grandparents: Gaspart Derbane and Marie Vergé; Jean Baptiste Brevel and Marie Francoise Poissot. Godparents: Louis Derbanne and Marie Francoise Rachal. Priest: P. Pavie.

81. JEAN BAPTISTE LACOUR
(27) 1 April 1804, baptism of infant born last August 1 in this post, legitimate son of Gaspar LaCour and Felicité Brevel. Grandparents: Pierre La Cour and Marie Louise Vergé; Jean Baptiste Brevel and Francoise Poissot. Godparents: Jean Baptiste Derbanne and Modeste Anti. Priest: P. Pavie.

82. MANUEL
(27) 1 April 1804, baptism of a child aged 3 years on the past October 1, native of this post, a son of Marie Louise, a Canneci Indian, by an unknown father. Godparents: Manuel Rachal and Marie Victoire Brevel. Priest: P. Pavie.

83. MARIE ZELINE
(28) 1 April 1804, baptism of an infant born last 3 October in this post, daughter of Marie Louise, a Canneci Indian, by an unknown father. Godparents: Julien Rachal and Marie Rosalie Larenaudiere. Priest: P. Pavie.

84. MERANTE AGENT /ARAGON/
(28) 1 April 1804, baptism of infant born 15 February 1803 in this post, legitimate daughter of Jean Baptiste Agent /Aragon/ and Marie Gertrude Torres. Grandparents: Michel Agent /Aragon/ and Thereze Cigouielle; Joseph Torres and Marie Jeanne Deroi. Godparents: Barthelemi Rachal and Marie Euphrosine Philipe. Priest: P. Pavie.

85. MARIE ARCENE /LE COURT/
(28) 12 May 1804, baptism of infant born 8 February last, daughter of Marie Ursulle, free mulatress,* and of a father unknown /Barthelemy Lecourt/. Godparents: Jean Baptiste, free mulatto; and Marie Louise /LeCourt/, sister of the infant.

*According to the earliest entries that have been found on this Marie Ursulle, she was actually a Caddo Indian. (See Mills, *Natchitoches 1729-1803* Entry 2255 (1796) for example.) Other entries such as 3096 in this same work and No. 14 of the present register, identify her as a *metive*. See note accompanying Entry 2837 in *Natchitoches 1729-1803*.

86. JOSEPH FRANCOIS CHABUS
(28) 19 May 1804, baptism of infant born last 28 April, legitimate son of Francois Chabus and Marie Jeanne Malige. Grandparents: Jean Francois Chabus and

Marie Anne Charpanee; Joseph Malige and Marie Anne Bardon. Godparents: Joseph Malige, grandfather of the infant and Marie Catherine Bardon, aunt of the infant. Priest: P. Pavie.

87. JEAN BAPTISTE ARMANT
(29) 7 June 1804, baptism of infant born 26 April of this year, legitimate son of Jean Baptiste Armant and Marie Catherinne Frederik. Grandparents: Joseph Armant and Therese Legros; Philippe Frederik and Marie Catherinne Sauvage. Godparents: Pierre Cheletre and Marie Therese Victoire Aillot St. Anne. Priest: P. Pavie.

88. MAXIMILIEN LARENAUDIERE
(29) 17 June 1804, baptism of infant born 24th of last November in this post, legitimate son of deceased Pierre Larenaudiere and Jeanne Laberi. Grandparents: Charles Larenaudiere and Jeanne Delerio; Jean Baptiste Laberi and Jeanne Guedon. Godparents: Bertrand Plaisance and Marie Joseph Totin. Priest: P. Pavie.

89. HENRI PROVOT
(29) 24 June 1804, baptism of an unmarried male, aged 28, born in the Indian nation of <u>Ecasse?</u> and living since the age of fifteen in the Indian nation of Marcisogne, son of deceased Henri Provot and of Marie Halein. Paternal grandfather: Henri Provot; maternal grandmother: name unknown. No maternal grandparents named. Baptism administered after Provot was instructed in the principles of the Catholic faith at the Natchitoches post. Godparents: Jean Mounneron and Marie Jeanne Melanie Rachal. Priest: P. Pavie.

90. JEAN BAPTISTE VALERI
(30) 27 June 1804, baptism of child born 21 October 1801 at Couteille /Cotile/ of the post of Rapides, in absence of a priest at that post, legitimate son of Jean Baptiste Valeri and Marie l'Assumption Torres. Maternal grandmother: Marie Barbe Legrand /Varangue/; Maternal grandfather unknown.* Maternal grandparents: Joseph Torres and Marie Jean Deroi. Godparents: Joseph Latie and Marie PElagie Cheletre.

*According to testimony of Bret LaCour in Land Claim #4459, Representatives of Jean Baptiste Vallery (National Archives, Washington, DC)

Marie Barbe Joseph Legrand Varangue, or "Madame Babé" as she was known in the Cotile neighborhood, "was what is called an Egyptian /and she/ often told deponent that one of the Indian men was her husband and the father of her children."

91. MARCEL VALERI*
(30) 27 June 1804, baptism of child born 20 November 1802 at Couteille /Cotile/ in the post of Rapides, since the priest of that post is absent. Infant is legitimate son of Jean Baptiste Valeri and Marie l'Assomption Torres. Paternal grandmother: Marie Barbe*; paternal grandfather unknown. Maternal grandparents: Joseph Torres and Marie Jeanne Deroi. Godparents: Antoine Himel and Marie Francoise Himel. Priest: P. Pavie.

*See note accompanying previous entry.

92. JACQUES VALERI*
(30) 27 June 1804, baptism of infant born 5 January of the current year at Couteille /Cotile/, post of Rapides, the priest of that post being absent, legitimate son of Jean Baptiste Valeri and Marie l'Assomption Torres. Paternal grandfather: unknown; paternal grandmother: Marie Barbe*; maternal grandparents: Joseph Torres and Marie Jeanne Deroi. Godparents: Jacques Valeri, uncle of the infant, and Marie Joseph Cheletre. Priest: P. Pavie.

*See note accompanying entry 90.

93. EUSEBE HISSOURA
(31) 20 August 1804, baptism of infant born 14 May 1802 in this post, legitimate son of deceased Bernard Hissouri and of Margueritte Grillé. Grandparents: Jean Hissoura, Bernarde Detchou; Marin Grillé, Marie Louise Brevel. Godparents: Remi Totin and Marie Joseph Honoré Totin, brother and sister of infant on maternal side. Priest: P. Pavie.

94. ADONIS ISIDORE HISSOURA
(31) 20 August 1804, baptism of infant born 4 April of this year, legitimate son of deceased Bernard Hissoura and Marguerite Grillé. Grandparents: Jean Hissoura and Bernarde Detchou; Marin Grillé, Marie Louise Brevel. Godparents: Bertrand Plaisance and Marie Euphrosine Rachal. Priest: P. Pavie.

95. MARIE FRANCOISE TOMACIN [THOMASSINO]
(31) 9 September 1804, baptism of child born 2 November 1802 in this post, legitimate daughter of Louis Tomacine and Catherinne Latié. Grandparents: Louis Tomacine and Therese Solé; Joseph Latié and Anne Vergé. Godparents: Pierre Charlot and Marie Francoise Malbert. Parents were residents of Couteille in the post of Rapides but had not carried infant there to be baptized since there was no priest at that post. Priest: P. Pavie.

96. HELEINE REED
(32) ANNE REED
10 September 1804, baptism of two children born at Natchée, on 3 March 1801 and 21 October 1803, legitimate daughters of David Reed of the Presbyterian faith and of Margueritte Uuily [Euly? Wiley?] of the Roman Catholic faith, both Americans. Grandparents: Samuel Reed and Lidy Musgrove; Jacque Uuily and Heleine Layly. Godparents of Heleine: Edouard Morphil and Elisabeth Buart. Godparents of Anne: Joseph Malige and Eulalie Malige. Priest: Pierre Pavie.

97. MARIE EUPHROSINE POISSOT
(32) 12 September 1804, baptism of infant born last February in this post, legitimate daughter of Antoine Poissot and Silvie Goutier. Grandparents: Remi Poissot and Louise Cave; Michel Goutiere and Marie Ines [Duplessis]. Godparents: Cesair Fonteneau and Marie Pompose Benoist [Montenary]. Priest: P. Pavie.

98. MARCELITTE JEAN RIS
(32) 12 September 1804, baptism of infant born last 26 July in this post, legitimate daughter of Joseph Jean Ris and of Francoise Vascocu. Grandparents: Jean Ris and Marie Jeanne Chagneau; Antoine Vascocu and Marie Barbe Toups. Godparents: Louis Vascocu and Genevieve Jean Ris. Priest: P. Pavie.

99. MARIE ROSE SOPHRONIE GRAPE
(33) 12 September 1804, baptism of infant born 17 April 1801 in this parish, legitimate daughter of Jean Baptiste Grape and Genevieve Sorel. Grandparents: Alexis Grape and Marie Louise Guedon; Pierre Sorel and Marie Rose Boisselie. Godparents: Hypolite Bordelon and Marie Perau. Priest: P. Pavie.

100. MARIE DENEIGE
(33) 12 September 1804, baptism of a mulatress born last 6 November, daughter of Magdeleine, free mulatress of this post, and of a father unknown. Godparents: Joseph /Metoyer/, mulatto, and Marie Susanne /Metoyer/, mulatress. Priest: P. Pavie.

101. FRANCOIS ABRAHAM GONIN
(33) 7 October 1804, baptism of infant born 6th of last month, legitimate son of Francois Gonin and Marie Barbe Frederick, residents of this post. Grandparents: Jean Baptiste Gonin and Manuel Riché; Philippe Frederik and Anne Barbe Cheletre. Godparents: André Frederik and Marie Rose Cadet Lestase. Priest: P. Pavie.

102. AVIT JEAN DAVION
(33) 7 October 1804, baptism of infant born last 17 June in this post, legitimate son of Dominique Davion and of Pelagie Gagne. Grandparents: Jean Baptiste Davion and Marie Hiacinthe Triche; Etienne Gagne and Marie Louise Bertrand. Godparents: Louis Clauseau and Francoise Triche. Priest: P. Pavie.

103. MARIE POMPOSE /METOYER/
(34) 7 October 1804, baptism of a free mulatress born in this post 19 September 1802, legitimate daughter of Augustin /Metoyer/, free mulatto, and Marie Agnes /Poissot/, free mulatress. Godparents: Athanase, free negro and Susanne /Metoyer/, free mulatress. Priest: P. Pavie.

104. MARIE ANASTHASIE /METOYER/
(34) 7 October 1804, baptism of a mulatress born last 24 May in this post, legitimate daughter of Joseph /Metoyer/, free mulatto, and Pelagie /Le Court/ free mulatress. Godparents: Augustin /Metoyer/, free mulatto and uncle of the infant, and Magdeleine, mulatress slave of Mr. Ambroise LeComte. Priest: P. Pavie.

105. MARIE MARCELITE PERAU
(34) 7 October 1804, baptism of infant born "9 January of the year in this post" /sic/, legitimate daughter of Jean Chrisostome Perau and of Marie Louise Salvant. Grandparents: Francois Perau and Catherinne Dupre; Jean Salvant and Marie Louise Lambre. Godparents: Antoine Grillé and Marie Joseph Gagné. Priest: P. Pavie.

106. THEOPHILE EVARISTE TAUSIN
(34) 7 October 1804, baptism of an infant born last
      6 February in this post, legitimate son of Joseph Tausin and Marie Chamart. Grandparents:
      Girard Tausin and Jeanne Bartheau; Louis Chamart
      and Catherine Bardon. Godparents: Evariste
      Tausin and Matilde Celeste Tausin, brother and
      sister of the infant. Priest: P. Pavie.

107. MELANIE LEMOINE
(35) 14 October 1804, baptism of a child aged two
      years this past June 17, born in this post, legitimate daughter of Jean Antoine Lemoine and
      Genevieve Bellegarde. Grandparents: Charles Lemoine and Elisabeth Dupré; Jean Baptiste Bellegarde and Magdeleine Monpierre. Godparents:
      Jean Baptiste Lemoine and Marie Joseph Rachal.
      Priest: P. Pavie.

108. MARIE ADELE PRUDHOMME
(35) MARIE ADELINE PRUDHOMME
      14 November 1804, while on visit to Isle a Brevel, as authorized by Msgr. Leveque, Reverend
      P. Pavie baptized two young daughters of Manuel
      Prudhomme and Catherinne Lambre. Both were aged
      four years and had been baptized privately while
      ill. Grandparents: Jean Baptiste Prudhomme and
      Marie Joseph Colentin; Jacques Lambre and Marie
      Poisseau. Godparents of Marie Adele: Jean Baptiste Prudhomme, her brother, and Marie Anne
      Lambre; godparents of Marie Adeline: Louis Prudhomme, her brother, and Marie Anne Prudhomme.

109. MARIE CIDRE BREVEL
(35-36) 15 November 1804, while on visit to Isle a Brevel, as authorized by Msgr. Leveque, Reverend P.
      Pavie baptized at the home of Michel Jarri an
      infant born in this post on November 3, 1803,
      the legitimate daughter of Jean Baptiste Brevel
      and Melanide Derbane. Grandparents: Jean Baptiste Brevel and Francoise Poisseau; Jean Baptiste Derbanne and Therese Roi. Godparents:
      Louis Derbane and Francoise Rachal.

110. PHILIPE BERNARD BOSSIE.
(36) 15 November 1804. While on visit to Isle a Brevel, as authorized by Msgr. Leveque, Reverend P.
      Pavie baptized at the home of Michel Jarri an
      infant of three months, born in this post, legitimate son of Soulange Bossié and Heleonore Himle. Grandparents: Francois Bossié and Char-

lotte Barré; Antoine Himle and Marguerite Cheletre. Godparents: Philipe Brosset and Silvie Brosset.

111. CATHERINE JARRI /MICHEL-ZORICHE/
(36) 15 November, 1804, while on visit to Isle a Brevel, as authorized by Msgr. Leveque, Rev. P. Pavie baptized at the home of Michel Jarri an infant born in this post on last 25 March, legitimate daughter of Michel Jarri and Cecile Robert /Dupre/. Grandparents: Michel Jarri and Marie Brianne; Robert Dupré and Manon Cavé. Godparents: George Petre ?Riche and Euphrosine Pommier.

112. MARIE SUSANNE /METOYER/
(37) 15 November 1804, while on visit to Isle a Brevel, as authorized by Msgr. Leveque, Rev. P. Pavie baptized at the home of Pierre Jarri an infant mulattress born 15 June in this post, legitimate daughter of Pierre /Metoyer/, a free mulatto, and of Marie Perine /LeComte/, a free mulattress. Godparents: Augustin /Metoyer/, free mulatto, and Margueritte /LeComte/, a free mulattress.

113. MARIE PIERRE /METOYER/
(37) 15 November 1804, while on visit to Isle a Brevel, as authorized by Msgr. Leveque, Rev. P. Pavie baptized at the home of Pierre Jarri an infant mulattress born 19 April 1803 in this post, legitimate daughter of Dominique /Metoyer/, free mulatto, and of Marguerite /LeComte/, a free mulattress. Godparents: Pierre /Metoyer/, free mulatto, and Perine /LeComte/, mulattress.

114. JEAN BAPTISTE /MARIOTTE/
(37) 16 November 1804, while on visit to Rivière aux Cannes, with permission of Msgr. Leveque, Rev. P. Pavie baptized at the home of Ambroise Le Comte an infant quadroon of three months, native of this post, natural son of Adelaide /Mariotte/ a free mulattress, and of a father unknown. Godparents: Jean Baptiste LeComte and Marie Francoise LeComte.

115. MANUEL MARCEL COUTI
(38) 16 November 1804, while on visit to Rivière aux Cannes, with permission of Msgr. Leveque, Rev. P. Pavie baptized an infant of 17 months, native of this post, legitimate son of Paul Couti and Mari Joseph Corré Torre. Grandparents: Jean

Couti and Marie Olivie; Joseph Corretant Torre and Marie Jeanne Deroi. Godparents: Francois Davion and Marguerite Cloutié.

116. MARIE ROSALIE GALLIEN
(38) 16 November 1804, while on visit to Rivière aux Cannes, with permission of Msgr. Leveque, Rev. P. Pavie baptized an infant of two years and 6 months, native of this parish, legitimate daughter of Nicolas Gallien and deceased Marie Lecour. Grandparents: Noel Gallien and Marie Rachal; Matthias Lecour and Jeanne Leroi. Godparents: Jacques Vercher and Marie Jeanne Euphrosine Gallien.

117. JEAN LOUIS BAUDOUIN
(38) 16 November 1804, while on visit to Rivière aux Cannes, with permission of Msgr. Leveque, Rev. P. Pavie baptized an infant of one year, a native of this parish, legitimate son of Pierre Baudouin and Anne Robin. Paternal grandparents: Francois Baudouin and Louise Bontems. Maternal grandparents not named. Godparents: Silvestre Anti and Jeanne Celeste Anti.

118. AMBROISE /CECILE/
(39) 18 November 1804, while on visit to Rivière aux Cannes, with permission of Msgr. Leveque, Rev. P. Pavie baptized an infant mulatto born last 15 August, son of Cecile, a free mulattress, and of a father unknown. Godparents: Joseph Dupre and Marie Louise Lecomte, the widow of Monet.

119. ATHANASE DUPRE.
(39) 19 November 1804, while on a visit to Rivière aux Cannes, with permission of Msgr. Leveque, Rev. P. Pavie baptized in the home of Jean Baptiste Cloutier at Ecord* an infant of two years, native of this parish, legitimate son of Athanase Dupre and Cecile Lecour. Grandparents: Joseph Dupre and Marie Derbanne; Louis Lecour and Jeanne Leroi. Godparents: Louis Lambre and Francoise Lecour.

120. ASELIE DUPRE
(39) 19 November 1804, while on a visit to Rivière aux Cannes, with permission of Msgr. Leveque, Rev. P. Pavie baptized in the home of Jean Baptiste Cloutier at Ecord* a child of 4 years, native of this post, legitimate daughter of

*This region is now known as Monette's Ferry.

Athanase Dupré and Cecile Lecour. Grandparents: Joseph Dupré and Marie Derbane; Louis Lecour and Jeanne Leroi. Godparents: Barthelemi Lecour and Marie Anne Dupré.

121. MARIE LOUISE ST. ANDRE
(40) 19 November 1804, while on a visit to Rivière aux Cannes, with permission of Msgr. Leveque, Rev. P. Pavie baptized in the home of Jean Baptiste Cloutier at Ecord* a child aged two years this past May, legitimate daughter of André St. André and Marie Rachal. Child is a native of this parish. Grandparents: Jacques St. André and Marie Anne Picard; Jacques Rachal and Ursul Castel. Godparents: Jean Pierre Cloutier and Adrienne St. André.

122. ANDRE ST. ANDRE
(40) 19 November 1804, while on a visit to Rivière aux Cannes, with permission of Msgr. Leveque, Rev. P. Pavie baptized in the home of Jean Baptiste Cloutier at Ecord* a child born last 4 October, legitimate son of André St. André and Marie Rachal. Grandparents: Jacques St. André and Marie Anne Picard; Jacques Rachal and Ursule Castel. Godparents: Athanase Dupre and Marie Salvant.

123. MARIE AURORE CLOUTIE
(40) 19 November 1804, while on a visit to Rivière aux Cannes, with permission of Msgr. Leveque, Rev. P. Pavie baptized in the home of Jean Baptiste Cloutié at Ecord* a child aged two years this past June, native of this parish, legitimate daughter of Jean Pierre Cloutié and Marie Salvant. Grandparents: Alexis Cloutier /Sr./ and Marie Rachal; Jean Salvant and Marie Louise Lambre. Godparents: Alexis Cloutier /Jr./ and Heleine+ Cloutié.

+In recent years, the name "Zeline" has been erroneously pencilled above the name of Heleine Cloutié.

124. JEAN BAPTISTE CLOUTIE
(41) MARIE LUCE CLOUTIE
19 November 1804, while on a visit to Rivière aux Cannes, with permission of Msgr. Leveque, Rev. P. Pavie baptized in the home of Jean Baptiste Cloutié at Ecord* two infants born last

* Ecord ("the Bluff") is the region now known as Monette's Ferry.

17 October in this post, legitimate children of Jean Pierre Cloutié and Marie Salvant. Grandparents: Alexis Cloutié /Sr./ and Marie Rachal; Jean Salvant and Marie Louise Lambre. Godparents of Jean Baptiste: Jean Baptiste Leconte and Marie Louise Leconte; godparents of Marie Luce: Ambroise Leconte and Francoise Leconte.

125. PIERRE EDOUARD FRAIDIEU
(41) 22 November 1804, while on a visit to Isle a Brevel home of Jean de cadot, with permission of Msgr. Leveque, Reverend P. Pavie baptized an infant born "23rd of the year past" /sic/ in this post, legitimate son of deceased Augustin Fraidieu and Marie Anne Sorel. Grandparents: Augustin Fraidieu and Angelique Claire; Pierre Sorel and Marie Rose Bosselie. Godparents: Pierre Zarik /Pierre Michel-Zoriche/ and Marie Louise Massip.

126. PIERRE CLEMENT DUPRE /LEMANT CHALER/
(41) 22 November 1804, while on a visit to Isle a Brevel home of Jean de cadot, with permission of Msgr. Leveque, Reverend P. Pavie baptized an infant born 4 August 1800, native of this post, son of deceased Marie Dupre and a father unknown. Godparents: Jacques Lacasse and Marcelitte Dupre.

127. FRANCOIS TERENCE DUPRE /TERENCE CHALER/
(42) 22 November 1804, while on a visit to Isle a Brevel home of Jean de cadot, with permission of Msgr. Leveque, Rev. P. Pavie baptized an infant born 25 December 1801, son of deceased Marie Dupre and a father unknown. Godparents: Jacques Lacasse and Marcelite Dupre.

128. MARIE LAMBRE
(42) 23 November 1804, while on a visit to Isle a Brevel home of Remi Lambre, with permission of Msgr. Leveque, Rev. P. Pavie baptized a child born in this post on 23 April 1801, legitimate daughter of Remi Lambre and Susanne Prudhomme. Grandparents: Jacques Lambre and Marie Poisseau; Jean Baptiste Prudhomme and Marie Joseph Colentin. Godparents: Dominique Prudhomme and Anne Prudhomme.

129. JEAN BAPTISTE LAMBRE
(42) 23 November 1804, while on a visit to Isle a

Brevel home of Remi Lambre, with permission of Msgr. Leveque, Rev. P. Pavie baptized an infant of eight days, legitimate son of Remi Lambre and Susanne Prudhomme. Grandparents: Jacques Lambre and Marie Poissau; Jean Baptiste Prudhomme and Marie Joseph Colentin. Godparents: Jean Baptiste Prudhomme, Jr. and Marie Therese Victoire /Ailhaud St. Anne/.

130. MARIE ARAGON
(43) 23 November 1804, while on a visit to Isle a Brevel home of Remi Lambre, with permission of Msgr. Leveque, Rev. P. Pavie baptized an infant of two years, native of this parish, leigitimate daughter of Santo Aragon and Clara Maria Balbo, living on the vacherie of Mr. Remi /Lambre/. Grandparents: not identified. Godparents: Antoine Prudhomme and Marie Lambre.

131. MARIE AIMEE CASSENAVE
(43) 10 February 1805, baptism of an infant born 27 September 1804, native of this parish, legitimate daughter of Michel Denis Aimé Cassenave and Marie /Jean/ Ris. Grandparents: Bernard Cassenave and Felicité Renée Clavau; Jean Ris and Marie Jeanne Chag/neau/. Godparents: Gilbert Clausau and Francoise Triche. Priest: P. Pavie.

132. URSIN GRILLET
(43) 2 March 1805, baptism of infant born 29 January, legitimate son of Antoine Grillet and Marie Felicité Chrisostome Perau. Grandparents: Marin Grillet and Marie Louise Brevel; Chrisostomé Perau and Marie Louise Salvant. Godparents: Chrisostomé Perau and Marie Francoise Grillet. Priest: P. Pavie.

133. MANUEL ULGER LANGLOIS
(44) 5 March 1805, baptism of infant born 24 April 1804, legitimate son of Louis Langlois and Marie Celeste Vergé. Grandparents: Augustin Langlois and Marie Louise Riché; Etienne Vergé and Marie Francoise Dupré. Godparents: Manuel Rachal and Marie Deneige Dolet. Priest: P. Pavie.

134. MARIE VICTOIRE POISSOT
(44) 15 March 1805, with permission of Rev. Puelles, pastor of Nacogdoche, baptism of an infant born at Baiou aux Pierre of the Post of Nacogdoches on 31 June 1804, legitimate daughter of Athanase Poissot and Marie Louise Heleine Euphrosine

Pavie. Grandparents: Athanase Poissot and Marie Manuel Soto: Etienne Pavie and Marie Therese Buart. Godparents: Charles Pavie, cousin of the infant on the paternal /sic/ side and Marie Victoire Aillot de St. Anne, also a cousin on the maternal side. Priest: P. Pavie.

135. JOSEPH MARIE BOITE LAFITE
(44-45) 21 March 1805, with permission of Rev. Pouelles, pastor of the church at Nacogdoches, baptism of an infant born 24 March 1804 at baiou aux pierres in the parish of Nacogdoche, legitimate son of Pierre Boite la fitte and of Ursule Gagné, living at Baiou aux pierres. Grandparents: Paul Boite Lafite and Magdeleine Grape; Etienne Gagné and Marie Louise Bertrand. Godparents: Francois Grape and Pelagie Gagné. Priest: P. Pavie.

136. JACQUES DERBANE
(45) 13 April 1805, baptism of infant born last 6 February in this parish, legitimate son of Jean Baptiste Derbane and Marie Heleine Brevel. Grandparents: Gaspart Darbane and Marie Verge; Jean Baptiste Brevel and Francoise Poissau. Godparents: Jacques Lacasse and Marie Louise Dupre. Priest: P. Pavie.

137. MELECE ANTI
(45) 14 April 1805, baptism of an infant born 8 Septempber last, legitimate son of Jean Baptiste Ignace Anti and Marie Ciprienne Derbane; child is a native of this parish. Grandparents: Baptiste Anti and Marie Catherinne Gallien; Pierre Derbanne and Francoise Brevel. Godparents: Pierre Derbanne and Marie Celeste Anti. Priest: P. Pavie.

138. ANTOINE
(46) 15 April 1805, baptism of an Indian of five years, native of this parish, son of Marie Jeanne, an Indian of the Natchitoches Nation who is not baptized. Godparents: Manuel Triche and Marie Felicité Triche. Priest: P. Pavie.

139. MARIE LOUISE
(46) 15 April 1805, baptism of an Indian of one year, native of this parish, daughter of Marie Jeanne, an Indian of the Natchitoches nation who is not baptized. Godparents: Manuel Triche and Louise Agathe Laberi. Priest: P. Pavie.

140. ANDRE RAIMOND VASCOCU
(46) MARIE AIME VASCOCU
28 April 1805, baptism of two infants born last 20 March, legitimate son and daughter of André Vascocu and Marie Magdeleine Raimond. Grandparents: Antoine Vascocu and Marie Barbe Toups; Pierre Raimond and Marie Francoise /no last name/. Godparents of André Raimond: Baptiste André Vascocu, his brother, and Marie Thérèse Vascocu, his sister; godparents of Marie Aimé: Joseph André Vascocu, her brother, and Marie Aimé Perau. Priest: P. Pavie.

141. JOSEPH DUPRE
(46) 4 May 1805, baptism of infant born 1 March 1804, legitimate son of deceased Pierre Dupre and Marie Francoise Lecour. Grandparents: Joseph Dupre and Marie Derbane; Louis lecour and Jeanne Leroi. Godparents: Joseph Dupré and Marie Robain. Priest: P. Pavie.

142. MARIE CHAMART
(47) 10 May 1805, baptism of infant born last 4 January, legitimate child of Michel Chamart and Marie Louise Euphrosine Rambin. Grandparents: Louis Charles Chamart and Marie Catherinne Bardon; André Antoine Rambin and Catherinne Buart. Godparents: Louis Charles Chamart and Marie Adelaide Rambin. Priest: P. Pavie.

143. LOUIS TIHOUA
(47) 16 May 1805, baptism of an Indian of the Natchitoches nation, aged 30 years, living at Atacalpa of the post of Nacogdoche, natural son of Tihoua and of Nahueriet, Indians of the Natchitoches nation. Rev. Puelle, pastor of Nacogdoche, has given his consent. Godparents: Louis Chamart and Catherine Bardon. Priest: P. Pavie.

144. PIERRE GEOFROI BORDELON
(47) 2 June 1805, baptism of infant aged 6 months, legitimate son of Hipolite Bordelon and Catherinne Trichel, natives of this post. Grandparents: Nicolas Bordelon and Adrienne Rondeau; Manuel Trichel and Marie Louise Grape. Godparents: Pierre Triche and Marie Cilesie Trichel. Priest: P. Pavie.

145. PHILIPPE VALERIEN GUISARNAT
(47-48) 2 June 1805, baptism of an infant born 28 Jan-

uary in this parish, legitimate son of Bernard
Guisarnat and Marie Louise LaRenaudiere. Grandparents: Jean Guisarnat and Catherinne Borée;
Pierre La Renaudiere and Jeanne Laberi. Godparents: Philipe La Renaudiere and Marie Rosalie Larenaudiere. Priest: P. Pavie.

146. MARIE PELAGIE BREVEL
(48) 2 June 1805, baptism of an infant aged two mos.,
legitimate daughter of Jean Baptiste Brevel and
Melanie Derbane. Grandparents: Jean Baptiste
Brevel and Francois Poissot; Jean Baptiste Derbane, Therese Leroi. Godparents: Pierre Lacour
and Marie Aspasie Derbanne. Priest: P. Pavie.

147. JACQUES MARCELLIN VERCHER
(48) 2 June 1805, baptism of infant born 30 March in
this parish, legitimate son of Jacques Therin
Vercher and Marie Jeanne Euphrosine Gallien.
Grandparents: Louis Vercher and Marie Louise
Grillé; Nicolas Gallien and Marie Lecour.
Godparents: Louis Gallien and Marie Rosalie
Vercher. Priest: P. Pavie.

148. MARIE PELAGIE
(48) 2 June 1805, baptism of a mulattress of three
months, daughter of Pelagie, a free mulattress,
and of a father unknown. Godparents: Pierre
Trichel and Marie Pompone Montanari. Priest:
P. Pavie.

149. LOUISE /GRAPPE/
(49) 2 June 1805, baptism of a mulattress born 25
October 1804 in this parish, daughter of Felicité /Grappe/, free mulattress, and of a father
unknown. Godparents: Jean Baptiste, Negro
slave of Aillot de St. Anne, and Marie Louise,
a free mulattress. Priest: P. Pavie.

150. MARIE JEANNE
(49) 2 June 1805, baptism of a mulattress born 20
October 1804, daughter of Margueritte, a free
mulattress, and of a father unknown. Godparents: Nicolas, free Negro, and Marie Jeanne,
free Negress. Priest: P. Pavie.

151. FREDERIK FELIX HESSER
(49) 16 June 1805, baptism of an infant born last 30
April, legitimate son of Christiane Hesser and
Marie Francoise Adelaide Rambin. Grandparents:
Frederik Hesser and Catherinne Boull; Antoine

Rambin and Catherine Buart. Godparents: Francois Augustin Rambin and Marie Louise Euphrosine Rambin. All are residents of this post. Priest: P. Pavie.

152. EUPHROSINE ASELIE* RACHAL
(50) 14 July 1805, baptism of infant born 22 May in this parish, legitimate daughter of Barthelemi Rachal and Magdeleine Grillet. Grandparents: Barthelemi Rachal and Marie Francoise Lamalati; Marin Grillé and Marie Louise Brevel. Godparents: Antoine Rachal and Marie Euphrosine Rachal. Priest: P. Pavie.

*Name appears as Aselie in text and as Amelie in marginal notation. Aselie is correct.

153. EDOUARD DUBOIS
(50) 16 July 1805, baptism of an infant born 17 July 1804, at Couteille /Cotile/ in the post of Rapides, legitimate son of Jean Baptiste Dubois and Rose Cheletre. Grandparents: Jean Baptiste Dubois and Marie Jeanne Clairmont; Michel Cheletre and Anne Barbe Pommier. Godparents: Nicolas Lauve and Marie Genevieve Dubois. Since no priest was stationed at the Rapides post, the infant was carried to Natchitoches for baptism. Priest: P. Pavie.

154. JEAN BAPTISTE ALEXANDRE TEEL
(50) 11 August 1805, baptism of infant born 12 November 1804 in this parish, legitimate son of Jacques Teel and Marie Rose Seideik, living in this post. Grandparents: Edouard Teel and Rebecca Dejones; Pierre Clavis Seideik and Ursule Cheletre. Godparents: Cesair Morphil and Marie Aspasie Morphil. Priest: P. Pavie.

155. MARIE ULALIE DETUIL
(51) 19 August 1805, baptism of infant born 8 September 1803, daughter of Catherinne Detuil and of a father unknown. Godparents: Marie Nicolas Zosime Demesiere and Marguerite Detuil. Priest: P. Pavie.

156. AURORE BOUET LAFITTE
(51) 1 September 1805, baptism of infant born 13 August in this parish, legitimate daughter of Paul Boüet Lafitte and Marie Anne Soto, living at Baiou au pierre. Paternal Grandparents: Boite Lafitte and unknown; maternal grandparents:

Manuel Soto and Marie Deneige St. Denis. Priest: P. Pavie.

157. MARIE ADELINE THIERRY [QUERI]
(51) 1 September 1805, baptism of infant born 20 June legitimate daughter of Pierre Queri and Marie Rosalie Frederik. Grandparents: Antoine Queri and Francois Bequete; Philippe Frederik and Marie Catherinne Sauvage. Godparents: Pierre Victorin Metoié and Marie Therese Elisabeth Metoié. Priest: P. Pavie.

*Name appears as "Thierry" in margin and as "Quieri" in text.

158. JEAN BAPTISTE TRICHE
(52) 8 September 1805, baptism of infant born 22 June in this parish, legitimate son of Jean Baptiste Triche and Marie Modeste Fonteneau. Grandparents: Jean Baptiste Triche and Marie Anne Daublin; Louis Fonteneau and Pelagie Grape. Godparents: Louis Clauseau and Marie Francoise Triche. Priest: P. Pavie.

159. PELAGIE
(52) 29 September 1805, baptism of Indian of the Canneci Nation, born in this post, aged 7 years, daughter of Marie Jeanne, Indian of the Canneci Nation who has never been baptized. Godparents: Louis Clausau and Francoise Triche. Priest: P. Pavie.

160. MARIE EUPHROSINE LEMOINE
(52) 12 October 1805, while on pastoral visit to Isle a Brevel, as authorized by Msgr. Leveque, baptism of infant born 6 June, legitimate daughter of Jean Baptiste Lemoine and Felicité Lacase. Grandparents: Charles Lemoine and Elisabeth Dupre; Charles Lacase and Felicité Langlois. Godparents: Silvestre Rachal and Marie Denise Lemoine. Priest: P. Pavie.

161. MARIE LEMOINE
(53) 12 October 1805, during course of a pastoral visit to Isle a Brevel, authorized by Msgr. Leveque, baptism of an infant born 6 June, legitimate daughter of Jean Baptiste Lemoine and Felicité Lacasse. Godparents: Charles Lemoine and Elisabeth Dupré; Charles Lacase and Felicité Langlois. Godparents: Silvestre Rachal and Marie Denise Lemoine.

162. PIERRE DERBANNE
(53) 13 October 1805, baptism at Rivière aux Cannes
of an infant born 1 March 1804 at Rivière aux
Cannes, legitimate son of Manuel Derbanne and
of Margueritte Denis. Grandparents: Pierre Derbane, Marie LeClerc; Jean Baptiste Denis and
Elisabeth Bontems /Baudouin/. Godparents:
Pierre Baudouin and Marie Denis. Priest: P.
Pavie.

163. JOSEPH RABALAI
(53) 13 October 1805, baptism at Rivière aux Cannes
of an infant born 20 July last, legitimate son
of Joseph Rabalai and Marie Bontems. Paternal
Grandparents: Joseph Rabalai and Anne Barbe;
maternal grandparents: /grandfather not named/
and Marie Anne Bontemps. Godparents: Manuel
Derbanne and Francoise LeComte. Priest: P. Pavie.

164. JEAN BAPTISTE SEVERE ARAGON
(54) 13 October 1805, baptism at Rivière aux Cannes
of an infant born 18 February last in this post,
legitimate son of Jean Baptiste Aragon and Marie
Gertrude Torres. Grandparents: Michel Argin
and Therese Aciguirie; Joseph Torres and Marie
Anne Deroi. Godparents: Jean Baptiste Cloutié
and Marie Davion. Priest: P. Pavie.

165. MARIE JOSEPH COUTI
(54) 13 October 1805, baptism at Rivière aux Cannes
home of Ambroise LeComte of an infant of two
months, legitimate daughter of Paul Couti and
Marie Joseph Torre. Grandparents: Jean Couti
and Marie Olivie; Joseph Torre and Marie Jeanne
Deroi. Godparents: Jean Baptiste Lecomte and
Marguerite Cloutié. Priest: P. Pavie.

166. MARIE AURORE DUPRE
(54) 13 October 1805, baptism at Rivière aux Cannes
home of Ambroise Leconte, of an infant born 14
December 1801 in this post, legitimate daughter
of deceased Pierre Dupré and Marie Francoise Le
Cour. Grandparents: Joseph Dupré, Marie Derbane; Louis Lecour and Jeanne Leroi. Godparents:
Jean Baptiste Varangue and Marie Marcellite Dupré. Priest: P. Pavie.

167. VALERI BAUDOUIN
(55) 13 October 1805, baptism at Rivière aux Cannes
home of Ambroise Leconte, of an infant born 4
August 1801 in this post, son of Nicolas Bau-

douin and Marie Deneige Malbert, whose marriage is not recognized. Grandparents: Francois Baudouin and Marie Bontems; Jean Baptiste Malbert and Jeanne Vergé. Godparents: Jean Baptiste Rachal and Marie Francoise Baudouin. Priest: P. Pavie.

168. ANTOINE DENIS BAUDOUIN
(55) 13 October 1805, baptism at Rivière aux Cannes home of Ambroise Leconte, of an infant born in this post in the month of July 1803, son of Nicolas Baudouin and Marie Deneige Malbert, whose marriage is not recognized. Grandparents: Francois Baudouin and Marie Bontems; Jean Baptiste Malbert and Jeanne Vergé. Godparents: Antoine Bergeon and Marie Zenir Baudouin. Priest: P. Pavie.

169. JOSEPH BAUDOUIN
(55) 13 October 1805, baptism at Rivière aux Cannes home of Ambroise Leconte, of an infant born 1 April in this post, son of Nicolas Baudouin and Marie Deneige Malbert, whose marriage is not recognized. Grandparents: Francois Baudouin and Marie Bontems; Jean Baptiste Malbert and Jeanne Vergé. Godparents: Joseph Dupré and Margueritte Denis. Priest: P. Pavie.

170. JOSEPH EMMANUEL TORRES
(56) 16 October 1805, baptism at Ecords* home of Antoine Rachal of infant born in this post three months earlier, legitimate son of Joseph Marie Torres and Susanne /Vallery/. Paternal grandparents: Joseph Torre and Marie Jeanne Deroi. Maternal grandmother: Marie Barbe /Varangue/ Maternal grandfather unknown**. Godparents: Silvestre Rachal and Andriene de St. André. Priest: P. Pavie.

    **See note accompanying Entry 90.

171. MARIE THERESE ROSALIE /MONET/
(56) 17 October 1805, baptism at Ecorts* home of Widow Monet of an Indian born 6 July in this post, daughter of Dorothée /Monet/, Indian of the Canneci nation, and of a father unknown. Godparents: Jacques, a quarter-Indian /Jacques Le Comte?/ and Marie Archange, Indian of the Canneci nation. Priest: P. Pavie.

*Ecords (var. Ecorts) is the region of Natchitoches Parish now known as Monette's Ferry.

172. **MARIE DENEIGE**
(56) 17 October 1805, baptism at Ecort* home of Widow Monet, of a mulattress born 15 August, daughter of Marie, a mulattress slave of Widow Monet who declares the infant to be free; father of child unknown. Godparents: Ambroise Lecomte and Louise Lecomte, widow Monet. Priest: P. Pavie.

173. **JUDITH LEMOINE**
(57) 17 October 1805 at Ecorts* home of Widow Monet, baptism of an infant born 28 May in this parish legitimate daughter of Antoine Lemoine and Genevieve Bellegarde. Grandparents: Francois Lemoine and Elisabeth Dupré; Jean Baptiste Bellegarde and Magdeleine Montpierre. Godparents: Diegue Rami and Marie Olivié. Priest: P. Pavie.

174. **JEAN BAPTISTE DENIS**
(57) 17 October 1805, baptism at Rivière aux Cannes home of Alexis Cloutier, of an infant born 7 January in this post, son of Lucide Euphrosine Denis and of a father unknown. Godparents: Jean Baptiste Denis and Marie Zemire Baudouin. Priest: P. Pavie.

175. **NARCISSE /METOYER/**
(57) 19 October 1805, baptism at Isle a Brevel home of Pierre Jarri, of a free mulatto born 25 February in this post, legitimate son of Dominique /Metoyer/ a free mulatto, and of Marie Louise /Marguerite LeComte/, a free mulattress. Godparents: Louis /Metoyer/, a free mulatto, and Therese /LeComte/, a free mulattress** uncle and aunt of the infant. Priest: P. Pavie.

> **According to numerous records such as the marriage of Therese and Louis Metoyer in Register 4-B (see Mills, *Natchitoches, 1729-1803*, Entry 3448) Therese was actually of Canneci Indian rather than Negro ancestry.

176. **CONSTANCE BENOITE** LEFEVRE**
(58) 27 November 1805, baptism of infant born last 25 October in this parish, legitimate daughter of Augustin Lefevre and Victoire Constance Le Maitre. Grandparents: Pierre Lefevre and Marie Claire; Francois Lemaitre and Louise LeDuc Ville Franche. Godparents: Francois Grape and

*This area is now known as Monette's Ferry.

Louise Le Duc Villefranche. Priest: P. Pavie.

**Infant's middle name appears as "Benoite" in the margin and as "Benedic" in the text.

177. MARIE DOE GONSALEZ
(58) 1 December 1805, baptism of infant born 11 November, legitimate daughter of Pierre Gonsalez and Catherinne Bonnet. Grandparents: Bernard Gonsalez and Catherinne Lamougne; Jean Bonnet and Antoinette Gastille. Godparents: Charles Pavie and Josephine Maes. Priest: P. Pavie.

178. REMI GAGNE
(58) 7 December 1805, baptism at Camté of infant born 18 January, legitimate son of Pierre Gagné and Marie Lalande. Grandparents: Pierre Gagné and Marie Louise Davion; Jean Lalande and Catherinne Dupre. Grandparents: Remi Perau and Marie Joseph Gagné. Priest: P. Pavie.

179. MARIE STEPHALIE
(59) 7 December 1805, baptism at Camté of a mulattress born 25 November, daughter of Magdeleine, a free mulattress. Godparents: Jean Baptiste, free mulatto, and Marie Hortance, free mulattress. Priest: P. Pavie.

180. MARIE AURORE ARCINE PERAU
(59) 8 December 1805 at Camté, baptism of an infant born 7 October, legitimate daughter of Jean Chrisostomé Perau and Marie Louise Salvant. Grandparents: Francoise Perau and Catherinne Dupré, Jean Salvant and Marie Louise Lambre. Godparents: Julien Francois Besson and Marie Felicité Triche. Priest: P. Pavie.

181. MARIE SUZANNE DUBOIS
(59) 8 December 1805, baptism of infant born 5 April 1804 in this parish, legitimate daughter of Francois Dubois and Heleonore Jean Ris. Grandparents: Jean Baptiste Dubois and Marie Joseph Clairmont; Jean Ris and Marie Jeanne Chagneau. Godparents: Jean Baptiste Dubois and Marie Aspasie Dubois. Priest: P. Pavie.

182. AURELIE AURORE DUBOIS
(60) 27 February 1806, baptism of infant born 13 January 1806 in this post, legitimate daughter of Antoine Dubois and Marie Joseph Malige. Grandparents: Jean Baptiste Dubois and Marie Joseph

Clairmont; Joseph Malige and Marie Antoinette Lebrun. Godparents: Francois Grape and Pelagie Marie Deneige Adelet. Priest: P. Pavie.

183. MARIE PAULA FOLSOM
(60) 27 February 1806, baptism of infant born 1 December in this post, legitimate daughter of Mo̲i̲s̲e̲? Folsom and Marie Magdeleine Lair. Grandparents: Israel Folsom and Marie Chaimbre; George Lair and Charlotte Guymley. Godparents: Jean Baptiste Pereau and Marie Agathe Laberi. Priest: P. Pavie.

184. JACQUES PARET
(60) 28 February 1806, baptism of infant aged two months, born in this parish, son of Laigné Paret and Marie Couart. Paternal grandparents: name not given to priest. Maternal grandparents: Adouen /?Edwin/ Couart and Marie Hossop. Godparents: Denis Etienne Cassenave; Victoire Constance Lemaitre. Priest: P. Pavie.

185. MARGUERITE DUROQUE
(61) 5 March 1806, baptism of infant aged 1 month, a native of this parish, legitimate daughter of Nicolas Duroque and Marie Manuel Rasse. Grandparents: Pierre Duroque and Marie Halbarcq; Joseph Rasse and Pierre Conde. Godparents: Denis Cassenave and Marie Euphroisine Morvant. Priest: P. Pavie.

186. MARIE EGILDE ADELET
(61) 16 March 1806, baptism of infant born 3 December in this post, legitimate daughter of Jean Adelet and Marie Victoire Brevel. Grandparents: Jean Adelet and Marie Genevieve Dubois; Jean Baptiste Brevel and Francoise Poissot. Godparents: Valentin Adelet and Marie Dolet /Lolette/ Rachal. Priest: P. Pavie.

187. JEAN BAPTISTE DAMAS POISSOT
(61) 22 March 1806, baptism of infant born last November in this post, legitimate son of Paul Poissot and Marie Louise Anti. Grandparents: Remi Poissot and Marie Louise Cavé; Jean Baptiste Anti and Catherinne Gallien. Godparents: Jean Baptiste Buart and Marcelite Poissot. Priest: P. Pavie.

188. SUSANNE BUART
(62) 22 March 1806, baptism of infant born last 18

December in this parish, legitimate daughter of Jean Baptiste Buart· and Marie Louise Poissot. Grandparents: Gabriel Buart and Marie Anne Roussau; Remi Poissot and Marie Louise Cave. Godparents: Louis Buart and Marie Louise Cavé.
Priest: P. Pavie

189. GEORGE MACTAER
(62) 27 March 1806, baptism of infant born last January 11, legitimate son of George Mactaer and Marie Louise Maiou. Grandparents: Jean Mactaer and Jeanne Futertan; Ignace Maiou and Therese Philibot. Godparents: Antoine Lenouart and Marie Julien Rondain. Priest: P. Pavie.

190. MARIE LOUISE THEODORE /CHAGNEAU/ *
(62) 30 March 1806, baptism of a quadroon born 11 January, in this parish, daughter of Felicité /Grappe/, a free mulattress, and of a father unknown. Godparents: Jacques, a free mulatto, and Francoise, a free mulattress. Priest: P. Pavie.   *See Register 11, page 68.

191. MARIE HENRIETTE AZELIE PRUDHOMME
(63) 5 April 1806, baptism of infant born 4th of last January, in this parish, legitimate daughter of Antoine Prudhomme and Marie Lambre. Grandparents: Jean Baptiste Prudhomme and Henriette Colentin; Jacques Lambre and Marie Anne Poissot. Godparents: Jean Baptiste Prudhomme and Marie Therese Victoire Aillot de St. Anne. Priest: P. Pavie.

192. GUILLAUME HOY
(63) 6 April 1806, baptism of an infant aged six weeks, born in this parish, son of Dorset Hoy and Marie Anne Lemaitre. Grandparents: Sabert Hoy and Eliabeth Globert; Francois Lemaitre and Marie Louise Vilfranche. Godparents: Louis Fonteneau and Genevieve Ris. Priest: P. Pavie.

193. THEODORE CLEMENT RACHAL
(63) 6 April 1806, baptism of infant born last November 22, legitimate son of Louis Barthelemi Rachal and Marie Francoise Grillet. Grandparents: Barthelemi Rachal and Marie Lamalatie; Marin Grillet and Marie Louise Brevel. Godparents: Louis Rachal and Marie Luc Rachal. Priest: P. Pavie.

194. ANDRE LESTAN RAMBIN
(64) 20 April 1806, baptism (with consènt of Rev. Puelle, pastor of Nacogdoges) of an infant born

last Nov. 14 at Baiou au Pierre, post of Nacogdoche, legitimate son of Michel Rambin and of Therese Maiou. Grandparents: André Rambin and Francoise Clairmont; Ignace Maiou and Therese Philibot. Godparents: Silvestre Poissot and Sophie Haulie. Priest: P. Pavie.

195. JOSEPH CHELETRE
(64) 21 May 1806, baptism of infant born at Couteil /Cotile/ on 3rd of last February, legitimate son of Barnabé Cheletre and Marie Joseph Gonin. Grandparents: Michel Cheletre and Anne Barbe Pomié; Jean Baptiste Gonin and Manuel Riché. Godparents: Joseph Lambre and Francoise Cheletre. Priest: P. Pavie.

196. EUGENIE LAURANCE
(65) 22 May 1806, baptism of child born 8 April 1803, at Ouachita, legitimate daughter of Alexandre Laurance and Susanne Uueb /Webb/. Grandparents: Jean Laurance and unknown; Leonard Uueb /Webb/ and Jeanne Helbeuf /Le Boeuf/. Godparents: Rosaimon Chamart and Marie Louise Maiou. Priest: P. Pavie.

197. ALEXANDRE LAURANCE
(65) 22 May 1806, baptism of child of one year, a native of Ouachita, legitimate son of Alexandre Laurance and Susanne Uueb /Webb/. Grandparents: Jean Laurance and unknown; Leonard Uueb /Webb/ and Jeanne Helbeuf /Jeanette Le Boeuf/. Godparents: Antoine Lenoir and Marie Julien Ronde. Priest: P. Pavie.

198. MARIE LOUISE DESIREE RACHAL
(65) 24 May 1806, baptism of infant born last 4 March in this parish, legitimate daughter of Jean Baptiste Rachal and Pelagie Brevel. Grandparents: Barthelemi Rachal and Marie Francoise Lamalatie; Jean Baptiste Brevel and Francoise Poissot. Godparents: Jacques Lacas and Marie Louise Dupré. Priest: P. Pavie.

199. VICTOR DAMAS RACHAL
(66) 25 May 1806, baptism of infant born last 8th of March, son of Dominique Rachal and Rosalie Vercher. Grandparents: Barthelemi Rachal and Marie Francoise Lamalatie; Louis Vercher and Marie Louise Grillé. Godparents: Jean Baptiste Theodore Grillé and Honorine Totin. Priest: P.Pavie.

200. MARIE NITE* LANGLOIS
(66) 28 Mary 1806, baptism of infant born last 24 April in this parish, daughter of Marie Therese Langlois and a father unknown. Godparents: Rosaimond Chamart and Marie Marguerite Prudhomme. Priest: P. Pavie.

*Name appears as <u>N</u>ite in margin and <u>R</u>ite in text.

201. MARIE DESNEIGES /METOYER?7
(66) 1 June 1806, baptism of a mulattress born last 2 March in this parish, legitimate daughter of Joseph, a free mulatto and Marie Therese, a free mulattress. Godparents: Athanase, free Negro, and Marie Ursule, a free mulatto.* Priest: P. Pavie.

*See note accompanying Entry 85.

202. MARIE LOUISE CELINE PLAISANCE
(67) 8 June 1806, baptism of infant born last March 14 in this parish, legitimate daughter of Bertrand Plaisance and Marie Barbe Grillet. Grandparents: Jean Baptiste Plaisance and Margueritte Totin; Marin Grillé and Marie Louise Brevel. Godparents: Pierre Dolet and Marie Louise Gagnon. Priest: P. Pavie.

203. CHARLES EMMANUEL GRENAU
(67) 24 July 1806, baptism of infant born at Opeloussas on 1 June 1804, legitimate son of deceased Emanuel Grenau and Victoire Emerante Bossié, living in this parish. Grandparents: Simon Grenau and Marie Anne Langlois; Francois Bossié and Rosalie Charlotte Baré. Godparents: Charles Pavie and Emeranciane Grenau. Priest: P. Pavie.

204. MICHEL LATIE
(67) 26 July 1806, baptism of infant born 24 April 1804 at Couteil /Cotile/ a dependency of Rapides, legitimate son of Joseph Latié and Francoise Cheletre. Grandparents: Joseph Latié and Anne Vergé; Michel Cheletre and Anne Barbe Pommier. Godparents: Francois Latié and Anne Marguerite Cheletre. Priest: P. Pavie.

205. MARIE MIRAMIE VASCOCU
(68) 27 July 1806, baptism of infant born last 17 March, legitimate daughter of Louis Vascocu and Magdeleine Perau. Grandparents: Antoine Vas-

cocu and Marie Barbe Toups; Francois Perau and Catherinne Dupré. Godparents: Gilbert Clauseau and Marie Catherine Marcelite Perau. Priest: P. Pavie.

206. JEAN BAPTISTE NARCISSE FREDERIK
(68) 28 July 1806, baptism of infant born last 26 February, legitimate son of Jean B̶a̶p̶t̶i̶s̶e̶ [sic] Francois Frederik and Marie Felicité Lavespere. Grandparents: Philipe Frederik and Marie Catherinne Sauvage; Francois Lavespere and Marie Louise Derbanne. Godparents: Jean Baptiste Frederik and Marie Melanide Lavespere. Priest: P. Pavie.

207. FRANCOIS VALERI
(68) 3 August 1806, baptism of infant born at Couteil [Cotile] on 3 February 1805, legitimate son of Jean Baptiste Valeri and Marie Assencion Torres. Paternal grandmother: Marie Barbe Joseph Varangue; paternal grandfather not named*. Maternal grandparents: Joseph Torres and Marie Jeanne Deroi. Godparents: Joseph Dupré and Marie Luce Rachal. Priest: P. Pavie.

208. MARIE DES NEIGES VALERI
(69) 3 August 1806, baptism of an infant born at Couteil [Cotile] on 2nd of last May, legitimate daughter of Jean Baptiste Valeri and Marie Assention Torres. Paternal grandmother: Marie Barbe Joseph Varangue; paternal grandfather not named*. Maternal grandparents: Joseph Torres and Marie Jeanne Desroi. Godparents: Jean Baptiste Lecomte and Marie Marcelite Rouquié. Priest: P. Pavie

*See note accompanying Entry 90.

209. MARIE LOUISE LACOUR
(69) 24 August 1806, baptism of infant born last 11 March, in this parish, legitimate daughter of Gaspart Lacour and Felicité Brevel. Grandparents: Pierre Lacour and Marie Louise Vergé; Jean Baptiste Brevel and Francoise Poissot. Godparents: Francois Davion and Margueritte Cloutié. Priest: P. Pavie.

210. FRANCOIS DUBOIS
(69) 24 August 1806, baptism of infant born last 5 June in this post, legitimate son of Francois Dubois and Heleonore Jean Ris. Grandparents:

Jean Baptiste Dubois and Marie Joseph Clairmont; Jean Ris and Marie Jeanne Chagneau. Godparents: Manuel Levasseur and Heleine Vascocu. Priest: P. Pavie.

211. MARIE HENRIETTE LAMBRE
(70) 7 September 1806, baptism of infant born last July 1, legitimate daughter of Remi Lambre and Susanne Prudhomme. Grandparents: Jacques Lambre and Marie Anne Poissot; Jean Baptiste Prudhomme and Henriette Joseph Colantin. Godparents: Jean Baptiste /Le/ Comte and Marie Anne Stephalie /Cephalide/ Lambre. Priest: P. Pavie.

212. MARIE JOSEPH ADELAIDE BAUDOUIN
(70) MARIE THECLE BAUDOUIN
21 September 1806, baptism of infants born 24 December 1805, legitimate daughters of Jean Pierre Baudouin and Anne Robin. Grandparents: Francois Baudouin and Marie Anne Bontems; Michel Robin and Marie Louise Boulai. Godparents of Marie Joseph Adelaide: Bertrand Mailloche and Marie Joseph Grillé; grandparents of Marie Thecle: Charles Lemoine and Jeanne Lebrun. Priest: P. Pavie.

213. MARIE EUPHROSINE JARRI   /MICHEL-ZORICHE/
(70) 21 September 1806, baptism of infant born 15 last May, legitimate daughter of Pierre Jarri and Cecile Dupre. Grandparents: Michel Jarri and Marie Amien; Robert Dupré and Manon Cavé. Godparents: Jean Baptiste Lemoine and Marie Euphrosine Frederick. Priest: P. Pavie.

214. SOPHIE GONIN
(71) 9 August 1807, baptism of infant born 25 August 1806, legitimate daughter of Francois Gonin and of Marie Barbe Frederik. Godparents: Barnabé L'Estage and Dame Sophie Hollier. Priest: Louis Buhot of Opelousas.

215. HONORINE RACHAL
(71) 9 August 1807, baptism of infant born 27 last May, legitimate daughter of Barthelemi Rachal and Marie Madeleine Grillé. Godparents: Bertrand Plaisance and Marie Honorine Tottin. Priest: Louis Buhot of Opelousas.

216. MARIE AZELINE GRILLETTE
(71) 9 August 1807, baptism of infant born 24 last March, legitimate daughter of Antoine Grillette and of Marie Felicité Peraut. Godparents: Jn.

Bte. Théodore Grillette and Marie Honorine Tottin. Priest: Louis Buhot of Opelousas.

217. MARIE LOUISE LATTIER
(72) 9 August 1807, baptism of infant born 18 last May, legitimate daughter of Francois Lattier and Marie Pelagie Schlette. Godparents: Jn. Bte. Lattier and Marie Reine Frederick. Priest: Louis Buhot of Opelousas.

218. GENNEVIEVE AMELIE /LE/ VASSEUR
(72) 9 August 1807, baptism of infant aged 8 months, legitimate daughter of Manuel Vasseur and Gennev. Gonin. Godparents: Antoine Vascocu and Pelagie Adelette. Priest: Louis Buhot of Opelousas.

219. LAZARE COLEAU
(72) 9 August 1807, baptism of infant born 15 June 1806, legitimate son of Lazare Colau and Julie Duval. Godparents: Julie /sic/ Duval and Marie Louise Laberie. Priest: Louis Buhot of Opelousas.

220. MARIE FANNY BEAULIEU
(73) 9 August 1807, baptism of child aged 4 years, legitimate daughter of Pierre Beaulieu and Marie Therese Baudouin. Godparents: Louis Rachal and Marie Frosine Rachal. Priest: Louis Buhot of Opelousas.

221. MARIE PELAGIE BEAULIEU
(73) 9 August 1807, baptism of infant aged 4 months, legitimate daughter of Pierre Beaulieu and Marie Therese Baudouin. Godparents: André Frederick and Marie Pelagie Frederick. Priest: Louis Buhot of Opelousas.

222. ALEXIS BORDELON
(73) 9 August 1807, baptism of infant born last 29 March, legitimate son of Hippolite Bordelon and Marie Therese Trichel. Godparents: Alexis Trichel and Celeste Bordelon. Priest: Louis Buhot of Opelousas.

223. PIERRE HELIE (ELIE)* /BERNARD/
(74) 10 August 1807, baptism of infant aged 9 months, legitimate son of Jean Pre. Elie and Marie Derbonne. Godparents: Joseph Helie and Melanie Trichel. Priest: Louis Buhot of Opelousas.

*Name is spelled Helie in margin and as both

Helie and Elie in text. Family surname sometime appears as "Bernard" in these records.

224. MICHEL VASCOCU
(74) 11 August 1807, baptism of infant born last 10 April, legitimate son of André Vascocu and Marie Anne Raimond. Godparents: Michel Chamart and Marie Louise Agathe Laberie. Priest: Louis Buhot of Opelousas.

225. CHARLES LEMOINE
(74) 15 August 1807, baptism of infant born 5 March 1804, legitimate son of Jean Baptiste Lemoine and Felicité Lacasse. Godparents: Pre. Massip and Jeanne LeBrun. Priest: Louis Buhot of Opelousas.

226. PLACIDE BREVEL
(75) 15 August 1807, baptism of infant born 20 March 1806, natural son of Baltazar Brevel and Marie Louise Rachal. Godparents: Placide Boissier and Marie Louise Massip. Priest: Louis Buhot of Opelousas.

227. JULES VICTOR BOISSIER
(75) 16 August 1807, baptism of infant born 30 June 1806, legitimate son of Francois Boissier and Catherine Pelagie Lambre. Godparents: Alexandre Hildebert Boissier and Elisabeth Buhart. Priest: Louis Buhot of Opelousas.

228. JEAN FRANCOIS ADELET
(76) 16 August 1807, baptism of infant born 21st of last April, legitimate son of Jean Bte. Adelet and Marie Victorine Brevel. Godparents: Francois Adelet and Marie Louise Rachal. Priest: Louis Buhot of Opelousas.

229. MARIE LOLETTE BOISSIER
(76) 16 August 1807, baptism of infant aged 6 months, legitimate daughter of Soulange Boissier and Eleonore Himmel. Godparents: Jn Pre. <u>Slyder?</u>*
and Eulalie Bossier. Priest: Louis Buhot of Opelousas.

*Possibly this should be Jn. Pre. Chelette, variously spelled Schlet and Schlettre, who was the husband of Eulalie Bossier, the godmother of the child above.

230. LOUIS SOREL
(76) 16 August 1807, baptism of infant born last 14

June, legitimate son of Dominique Sorel and of Euphrosine David. Godparents: Louis David and Sophronie Grape. Priest: Louis Buhot of Opelousas.

231. FRANCOIS PRUDHOMME
(76) 16 August 1807, baptism of infant born last 1 March, legitimate son of Baptiste Prudhomme and Rose Malige. Godparents: Francois Chabus and Catherine Chamart. Priest: Louis Buhot of Opelousas.

232. MARIE TERNIER
(77) 16 August 1807, baptism of infant born last 8 March, legitimate daughter of Pierre Ternier and Marie Francois Ganier. Godparents: Francois Rouquier, Jr. and Margueritte Prudhomme. Priest: Louis Buhot of Opelousas.

233. TRANQUILINA SUSANA PAILLETT
(77-78) 11 September 1808, baptism of infant (performed without holy oils, since there were none in the parish), who was born last 6 July at 3 p.m., the legitimate daughter of Juan Santiago Paillette, first justice of the peace of this town (son of Susana Le Roy and Pedro Jorge Paillette) and Victoria Poisont*(daughter of Luisa Cabet and Remi Poisont). Godparents: Eduardo Cesar Morphy (s/ Dourd Cezair Murphy), Merchant, and Manuela Puaso. Witnesses: Bta. Buard (s), Juan Bta. Arman, and Jose Tausin (s/ Teuzin), elder of this church. Priest: Vicente Simon Gonzales de Cosco, of the Cathedral Church in the city of Durango, Kingdom of New Spain.

*Note, an alteration in a different ink and penmanship changes "Poisont" to "Pöisot".

234. JOSEFA MARCELINA ARMAN
(78-79) 27* September 1808, baptism of infant born last 30 July, legitimate daughter of Juan Bta. Arman (son of Jose Armand and Teresa Legros) and Catalina Federico (daughter of Felipe Federic). Godparents: Jose J. /sic/ Paillette (s/ Paillette) "ingeniero primero" /first engineer/ and Ermete Estete. Witnesses: Jose Paillete and Bapta. Buard (s). Priest: Vizente Simon Gonzales de Cosco, of the Cathedral Church in the city of Durango, Kingdom of New Spain.

*In view of the dates on subsequent entries by Padre Gonzales, it appears this entry should have been dated 17 September instead of 27 September.

235. MARIA AZELIA DAVINPORT
(79-80) 17 September 1808, baptism of infant born 30 December 1807, legitimate daughter of Samuel Davinport (son of Guillę Davinport and Ana Davidson) and Maria Louisa Gagnon (daughter of Pedro Gagnon and Maria Teresa Valentino. Godparents: Eduardo Cezard Murphy and Maria Francisca Eugenia /Murphy/. Witnesses: Louis Bmy. Rachal, Arnardo Lauve and Louis Lamalati. Priest: Vizente Simon Gonzales. (See Entry 233.)

236. PAUL RACHAL
(80) 17 September 1808, baptism of infant born last 23 May, legitimate son of Dominigue Rachal (son of Bartholome Rachal and Maria Lamalaty) and of Maria Rosalia Vercher (daughter of Louis Vercher and Maria Louisa Grillet). Godparents: Bertrand Plasencia and Maria Barbo Grillet. Witnesses: Bte. Trichel, Pedro Maillou, and Theodore Grillet. Priest: Vizente Simon Gonzales (see Entry 233).

237. JEAN BAPTISTE VALSIN* GRILLET
(81) 17 September 1808, baptism of infant born 31 December 1807, legitimate son of Theodore Grillet (son of Marin Grillet and Maria Louisa Brevel) and Maria Catharina Peraux (dau of Fco. Peraux and Maria Louisa Agatha Labery). Godparents: Louis Derzilin Peraux and Maria Rosalia Vercher. Witnesses: Arnaldo Lauve, Louis Lamalaty and Bta. Trichel. Priest: Vizente Simon Gonzales (see Entry 233).

*This name appears as Valsin in margin and under the Spanish version, Valcino, in the text.

238. MARIE EMILIE TRICHEL
(81-82) 17 September 1808, baptism of infant born 22 October 1807, legitimate daughter of Jn. Bautista Trichel (son of Jn Bta Trichel and Mariana Doblin) and Maria Modesta Fontenaux (daughter of Louis Fontenaux and Pelagia Grappa). Godparents: Fco. Louis Fontenaux and Maria Thereza Constansa Fontenaux. Witnesses: Evaristo Lauve, Louis Lamalaty and Pedro Maillou. Priest: Vizente Simon Gonzales (see Entry 233).

239. JEAN BAPTISTE MACTIER
(82-83) 17 September 1808, baptism of infant born last 24 January, legitimate son of George Mactyer (son of Jn. Mactyer and Juana Fulerton) and Maria Mayou (daughter of Ygnacio Mayou and Theresa Filibot). Godparents: Pedro Mayou and Maria Modesta Vascocu. Witnesses: E^{to} Lauve, P^{de} Bossier and F^{co} Bossier. Priest: Vizente Simon Gonzales (see Entry 233).

240. MARIE ERNESTINE BARBAROUS
(83-84) 20 September 1802, baptism of infant born 30th September 1807, legitimate duaghter of Miguel Barbarous (son of Guillermo Barbarous and Maria Juana Chagnaux) and Nanetta Gagnier (daughter of Esteban Gagnier and Maria Louisa Bertrand). Godparents: Guillermo Barbarous and Maria Juana Chagnaux. Witnesses: Jn Adley, E^{te} Lauve, Andres Rambino. Priest: Vizente Simon Gonzales (see Entry 233).

241. MARCELLIN TAUZIN
(84) 20 September 1808, baptism of infant born 24 October 1807, legitimate son of Jose Tausin and Maria Chamart. Godparents: Eugene Tauzin and Euphrosina Tauzin, representing Maria Tauzin. Witnesses: Francisco Laurenco /Llorens/, Francisco Montuco, Rosemond Chamart. Priest: Vizente Simon Gonzales (see Entry 233).

242. THEOPHILE EGGLESTONE COBBS
(85) 18 September 1808, baptism of infant born last 3 June, legitimate son of Samuel Cobbs (son of Jn. C. Cobbs and Rachal /blank/) and Marguerita Leonardo (daughter of Jn. Bta. Leonardo and Lucia Bonnet). Godparents: Francisco Neuman & Barbarita Rouquillo /?Troquillo/. Witnesses: E^{te} Lauve (s), F^{o} Brunet (s), and Jn Adle (s). Priest: Vizente Simon Gonzales (see Entry 233).

243. SYLVESTRE POISSOT
(85-86) 23 September 1808, baptism of infant born last 2 January, legitimate son of Paul Poissot (son of Remy Poissot and Louisa Cabet) and Maria Louisa Anty (daughter of Bauptista Anty and Cathalina Cloutier /Gallien/). Godparents: Arnaldo Lauve and Mariana Buard. Witnesses: J.J. Paillette (s), Pre. Bossier (s), E^{te} Lauve (s). Priest: Vizente Simon Gonzales (see Entry 233).

244. PLACIDE BUARD
(86-87) 23 September 1808, baptism of infant born 9 November 1807, legitimate son of Jn. Luis Buard (son of Louis Buard and Maria Rosa Lambre) and Eulalia Bossier (daughter of F^{co} Bossier and Pelagia Lambre). Godparents: P^{de} Bossier (s) and Maria Aspasia Bossier. Witness: E^{te} Lauve (s), Bta. Buard (s), Arn^{do} Lauve (s). Priest: Vizente Simon Gonzales (see Entry 233).

245. JUAN FRANCISCO CRISOSTOME PEROT
(87) 26 September 1808, baptism of infant, [no birth date], legitimate son of Juan Crisostomo Piero and Maria Luisa Clavens [Salvant]. Godparents: Juan Frco. Crisostomo [Perot] and Juana Regina Perau?. Priest: Vizente Simon Gonzales (see Entry 233).

246. PRUDENCIO HOY
(88) 14 September 1808, baptism of infant [no birth date], son of David Hoy and Maria Ant^{a} Lemetre. Godparents: Cade Sotenel and Felisite Lemetre. Priest: Vizente Simon Gonzales (see Entry 233).

247. MARIA LUISA LEFEVRE
(88) 25 September 1808, baptism of infant [no birth date], daughter of Agustin Lefevre and Victoria Constansa Lemetre. Godparents: Migel Casenave and Maria Ris. Priest: Vizente Simon Gonzales (see Entry 233).

248. ANTONIO BLASA GONZALEZ
(89) 17 September 1808, baptism of infant born last 3 February at 2 o'clock in the afternoon, legitimate son of Pedro Gonzales (son of Bernardo Gonzales and Catarina Lemuno) native of Sta. Maria Blimeda, district of Obiede in Spain) and of Catarina Bonete (native of New Orleans, daughter of Juan Bonete and Antonia Reimund Garcia). Godparents: Jose Bonete and Mariana Ruquie. Priest: Vizente Simon Gonzales (see Entry 233).

249. LOUIS NARCISSE PRUDHOMME
(90) 3 November 1809, baptism of infant born 19 September 1807, legitimate son of Narcisse Prudhomme and Therese Elisabeth Metoyer. Godparents: Pre. Metoyer and Cath^{ne} Lambre. Priest: Louis Buhot of Opelousas.

250. MARIE ANTOINETTE PRUDHOMME
(90) 7 December 1809, baptism of infant born last 15

September, legitimate daughter of Antoine Prudhomme and Marie Lambre. Godparents: Jn. Fcois. Hertzog and Marie Anne Desirée Prudhomme. Priest: Louis Buhot of Opelousas.

251. PIERRE PRUDHOMME
(90-91) 7 December 1809, baptism of infant born 24 June 1807, legitimate son of Emmanuel Prudhomme and Catherine Lambre. Godparents: N. Maës and Mad^e Pavie née Rouquier. Priest: Louis Buhot of Opelousas.

252. EMERANTE LAMBRE
(91) 7 December 1809, baptism of infant born 15 May 1808, legitimate daughter of Remi Lambre and Susanne Prudhomme. Godparents: Jean Jacques Lambre and Marie Aurore Lambre. Priest: Louis Buhot of Opelousas.

253. MARIE PELAGIE RACHAL
(91) 7 December 1809, baptism of infant aged 18 months, legitimate daughter of Jean Bte. Rachal and Pelagie Brevel. Godparents: Jn. Bte. Prudhomme and Susanne Prudhomme. Priest: Louis Buhot of Opelousas.

254. JEAN EMMANUEL PRUDHOMME
(92) 8 December 1809, baptism of infant born 14 July 1807, legitimate son of Jean Bte. Prudhomme and Marie Therese Victoire Aillaud de Ste. Anne. Godparents: Emmanuel Prudhomme and Louise Buart. Priest: Louis Buhot of Opelousas.

255. GABRIEL PRUDHOMME
(92) 8 December 1809, baptism of infant born 24 September 1807, legitimate son of Jean Bte. Prudhomme and Marie Therese Victoire Aillaud de Ste. Anne. Godparents: Jean Bte. Ailhaud de Ste. Anne and Catherine Lambre. Priest: Louis Buhot of Opelousas.

256. GUILLEAUME LESTAGES
(92-93) 10 December 1809, baptism of infant aged two years, legitimate son of Barthelemi Lestages and Marie Pelagie Frederic. Godparents: Jn Bte. Lestages and Rosalie Lestages. Priest: Louis Buhot of Opelousas.

257. FRANCOIS LATTIER
(93) 10 December 1809, baptism of infant born last 2 October, legitimate son of Francois Lattier and

Marie Pelagie Schlater. Godparents: Jn. Pre. Schlater and Marie Jeane Schlater. Priest: L. Buhot of Opelousas.

258. MARIE FELONISE LATTIER
(93) 10 December 1809, baptism of infant aged two years, legitimate daughter of Francois Lattier and Marie Pelagie Schlater. Godparents: Pre. Schlater and Felicite Destouches/De Louche/ Priest: Louis Buhot of Opelousas.

259. JAMES MCMICHEL
(94) 10 December 1809, baptism of infant aged 1 year, son of a father unknown and of Sarah McMichel. Godparents: Gaspart Philibert and Marie Anne LeMaitre. Priest: L. Buhot of Opelousas.

260. ELOISE DELFINE LAMBRE
(94) 10 December 1809, baptism of infant aged 14 months, legitimate daughter of Josef Lambre and Eugenie Roquigni. Godparents: Fois. Rouquier and Elisabeth Buart. Priest: L. Buhot of Opelousas.

261. VALENTIN ADLE
(94-95) 10 December 1809, baptism of infant born 2 December 1808, legitimate son of Valentin Adlé and Silesie Brossé. Godparents: Pierre Brossé and Gennevieve Dubois. Priest: L. Buhot of Opelousas.

262. MARIE ADELISE PALVADO
(95) 11 December 1809, baptism of infant aged eight months, legitimate daughter of Jean Palvado and Leonor Tessier. Godparents: André Valentin and Pompose Benoit /Montenary/. Priest: L. Buhot of Opelousas.

263. MARIE BARBE RISSE
(95) 11 December 1809, baptism of infant aged 13 months, legitimate daughter of Jos. Risse and Francoise Vascocu. Godparents: Vital Louis Vascocu and Marie Celeste Risse. Priest: L. Buhot of Opelousas.

264. AMBROISE LECONTE
(96) 11 December 1809, baptism of infant born 11 June 1807, legitimate son of Jean Bte. Le Conte and Marie Anne Lambre. Godparents: Ambroise Le Conte and Susanne Prudhomme. Priest: L. Buhot of Opelousas.

265. LOUIS /JULIEN/ RACHAL
(96) 12 December 1809, baptism of infant born last 15 May, legitimate son of Julien Rachal and Marie Lavispere. Godparents: Sebastien Compere and Lolette Rachal. Priest: L. Buhot of Opelousas.

266. MANUEL TRICHE
(97) 14 December 1809, baptism of infant born 8 December 1808, son of a father unknown and of Lolette Trichel. Godparents: Fois. Durie and Marie Mel. Trichel. Priest: L. Buhot of Opelousas.

267. MARIE LOUISE BORDELON
(97) 14 December 1809, baptism of infant born last 18 August, legitimate daughter of Hippolite Bordelon and of Marie Therese Trichel. Godparents: N^{as} Bordelon and Fois. Trichel. Priest: L. Buhot of Opelousas.

268. MARIE VASCOCU
(97-98) 14 December, 1809, baptism of infant born last 6 March, legitimate daughter of André Vascocu and Marie Madel. Raymond. Godparents: Henry Trichel and Marie Anne Rouquier. Priest: L. Buhot of Opelousas.

269. FRANCOIS HENRY TRICHE
(98) 15 December 1809, baptism of infant born last 7 August, legitimate son of Manuel Trichel and of Louise Euphrosine Prudhomme. Godparents: Fois. Prudhomme and Francoise Trichel. Priest: L. Buhot of Opelousas.

270. JEAN BAPTISTE HELIE /BERNARD/
(98) 15 December 1807, baptism of infant born last 12 October, legitimate son of Pierre Helie and of Marie Derbonne. Godparents: Fois. Rouquier and Marie Derbonne. Priest: L. Buhot of Opelousas.

271. FIRMIN LACOUR
(99) 17 December 1809, baptism of infant born 16 September 1808, legitimate son of Gaspart Lacour and Felicité Brevel. Godparents: Ant^e Rachal and Marie Derbanne. Priest: L. Buhot of Opelousas.

272. FRANCOIS POIRIER
(99) 17 December 1809, baptism of infant born 4 November 1806, legitimate son of Francois Poirier and Therese Thomassie. Godparents: Jos. Vercere and Lise Berzot. Priest: L. Buhot of Opelousas.

273. ANTOINE POIRIER
(99-100) 17 December 1809, baptism of infant aged 10 mos., legitimate son of Fois. Poirier and Therese Thomasie. Godparents: Louis Thomassie and Pelagie Adlé. Priest: L. Buhot of Opelousas.

274. JOSEF VICTORIN BARBEROUSSE
(100) 17 December 1809, baptism of infant aged 11 mos., legitimate son of Michel Barberoux and Manette Ganié. Godparents: Josef Riesse and Pelagie Gagne. Priest: L. Buhot of Opelousas.

275. ALFREDE BUARD
(100) 17 December 1809, baptism of infant born last 29 June, legitimate son of Jn. Bapte. Buard and Aspasie Boissier. Godparents: Jn. Louis Buard and Eulalie Boissier. Priest: L. Buhot of Opelousas.

276. MARIE BAUDOUIN
(101) 17 December 1809, baptism of infant born 16 last October, legitimate daughter of Pierre Baudouin and Anne Robin. Godparents: Josef Derbonne and Cathe. Brossé. Priest: L. Buhot of Opelousas.

277. MARIE LOUISE FREDERIC
(101) 17 December 1809, baptism of infant born 13 January 1808, legitimate daughter of Fois. Frederic and Felicité Lavispere. Godparents: Pierre Shlater and Marg^{tte} Frederic. Priest: L. Buhot of Opelousas.

278. CECILE ARMAND
(101) 17 December 1809, baptism of infant born 26 June 1808, legitimate daughter of Jean Armand and Aspasie Mayou. Godparents: Ignace Mayou and Pelagie Riesse. Priest: L. Buhot of Opelousas.

279. JULIE BUARD
(102) 17 December 1809, baptism of infant born last 3 September, legitimate son [sic] of Jean Louis Buard and Eulalie Boisier. Godparents: Jn Bte. Buard and Eugenie Buard. Priest: L. Buhot of Opelousas.

280. MARIE IRENE DERBANNE
(102) 17 December 1809, baptism of infant born 1 November 1808, legitimate daughter of Jean Bte. Derbanne and Marie Helene Brevel. Godparents: Jn. Ch. Pavie and Marie Anne Rouquier. Priest: L. Buhot of Oeplousas.

281. CONSTANT FREEMAN (BUCLEY)
(102-3) 22 December 1809, baptism of infant born last 30 October, son of James Bucley and of Mary Lane. Godparents: "the colonel Constant Freeman" and "his wife Marg^tte Cox." Priest: Louis Buhot of Opelousas.

282. DANIEL SPADE
(103) 22 December 1809, baptism of infant born last 3 January, son of John Spade and Mahala McKafe. Godparents: Col. Constant Freeman and Mag^tte Cox. Priest: L. Buhot of Opelousas.

283. EVARISTE LAUVE
(103) 23 December 1809, baptism of infant born last 26 November, legitimate son of Evariste Lauve and Euphrosine Celeste Brunet. Godparents: Nicolas Lauve and Marg^tte Desbordes. Priest: L. Buhot of Opelousas.

284. PLACIDE TEAL
(104) 23 December 1809, baptism of infant born 1 February 1808, son of James Teal and Rose Saidec. Godparents: Placide Boissie and Eugenie Buard. Priest: Louis Buhot of Opelousas.

285. MARIE AURORE BESSON
(104) 23 December 1809, baptism of infant aged 2 years, legitimate daughter of Jean Bte. Besson and Marie Jeane Frederic. Godparents: Josef Risse and Marie Peraut. Priest: L. Buhot of Opelousas.

286. MARIE LOLETTE VASCOCU
(104) 23 December 1809, baptism of infant born 27 February 1808, legitimate daughter of Louis Vascocu and Mad. Peraut. Godparents: Louis Closau and Marie Peraut. Priest: L. Buhot of Opelousas.

287. FRANCOIS VASCOCU
(105) 23 December 1809, baptism of infant aged 2 years, legitimate son of Louis Vascocu and Mad. Peraut. Godparents: Fois. Peraut and Denize Christi. Priest: L. Buhot of Opelousas.

288. ADELAIDE FULSON
(105) 23 December 1809, baptism of infant born 23 March 1808, daughter of Isen? Fulson and Mary Lair. Godparents: Louis Closau and Marie Aimée Peraut. Priest: L. Buhot of Opelousas.

289. MARIE LOUISE MARCELITTE CORTES
(105) 24 December 1809, baptism of infant born 19 Oct.,

1808, legitimate daughter of Jean Cortes and Marcelite Rouquier. Godparents: Fois. Rouquier and Marie Louise Prudhomme. Priest: L. Buhot of Opelousas.

290. MARIN GRILLETTE
(106) 24 December 1809, baptism of infant born 29 of last month, legitimate son of Antoine Grillette and Felicité Peraut. Godparents: Josef Peraut and Marie Aimée Peraut. Priest: L. Buhot of Opelousas.

291. MARIE ADELAIDE GANIE
(106) 24 December 1809, baptism of infant born 16 April, legitimate daughter of Pierre Ganier and Marie Anne Lalande. Godparents: Josef Ganier and Adel. Verchere. Priest: L. Buhot of Opelousas.

292. EUGENIE DENAIN
(106) 24 December 1809, baptism of an adult, aged 14 years, daughter of Jean Bte. Denain. Godparents: Amb. Sompayrac and Adelaide Tauzin. Priest: L. Buhot of Opelousas.

293. MARCELITTE LEFEVRE
(107) 25 December 1809, baptism of infant aged 6 mos., legitimate daughter of Louis Lefevre and of Victoire Lemaitre. Godparents: Fois. Rouquier, Jr., and Marie Anne Rouquier. Priest: L. Buhot of Opelousas.

294. FRANCOIS JEAN BAPTISTE FONTENOT
(107) 26 December 1809, baptism of infant born last 28 November, legitimate son of Jean Bte. Fontenot and Marie Pompose Lafitte. Godparents: Fois. Grappe and Pelagie Grappe. Priest: L. Buhot of Opelousas.

295. EUSEBE CASE
(107) 26 December 1809, baptism of infant born last 28 November, legitimate son of David Case and Marie Marg^{tte} Prudhomme. Grandparents: Colonel Constant Freeman and Marg^{tte} Cox. Priest: L. Buhot of Opelousas.

296. AMBROISE VALEIN TAUZIN
(108) 27 December 1809, baptism of infant born last 26 July, legitimate son of Josef Tauzin and Marie Chamart. Godparents: Ambroise Sompayrac and Marcellitte Poisseau. Priest: L. Buhot of Opelousas.

297.
(108)
MARIE DELPHINE DERBANNE
28 December 1809, baptism of infant born last 23 January, legitimate daughter of Jean Bte. Derbanne and Marie Dupré. Godparents: Jacques Lacasse and Francoise LeCourt. Priest: L. Buhot of Opelousas.

298.
(109)
FRANCOIS HUBERT FREDERIC
28 December 1809, baptism of infant born last 6 December, legitimate son of Fois. Frederic and Felicité Lavespere. Godparents: Jn Bte. Lattier, Jr. and Marie Eloise Lattier. Priest: L. Buhot of Opelousas.

299.
(109)
MICHEL LEMOINE
28 December 1809, baptism of infant born last 17 October, legitimate son of Bte. Lemoine and Felicité Lacasse. Godparents: Gme. Bernard and Carol Lemoine. Priest: L. Buhot of Opelousas.

300.
(109)
MARIE ZELINE AGUESSE
28 December 1809, baptism of infant aged eight months, legitimate daughter of Jean Renaud Aguesse and Marie Louise Massipi. Godparents: Pre. Massipe and Frosine Rachal. Priest: L. Buhot of Opelousas.

301.
(110)
MARIE DIVINE LANGLOIS
28 December 1809, baptism of infant born 28 July 1808, legitimate daughter of Augustin Langlois and Marie Verger. Godparents: Jacques Langlois and Frosine Frederic. Priest: L. Buhot of Opelousas.

302.
(110)
MARIE SUSANNE RACHAL
28 December 1809, baptism of infant born 11 May 1808, legitimate daughter of Julien Rachal and Marie Lavespere. Godparents: Hilaire Lavespere and Marie Aimée La Vespere. Priest: L. Buhot of Opelousas.

303.
(110)
ZULIME RACHAL
28 December 1809, baptism of infant aged 9 mos., legitimate daughter of Jean Bte. Rachal and Rosalie Derbanne. Godparents: Julien Rachal and Ositte Rachal. Priest: L. Buhot of Opelousas.

304.
(111)
DENIZE POISSEAU
28 December 1809, baptism of infant aged 4 days, legitimate daughter of Paul Poisseau and Marie

Anti. Godparents: Jean Jq. Paillet and Denize Buart. Priest: L. Buhot of Opelousas.

305. MARIE THERESE
(111) 28 December 1809, baptism of Indian of five years, daughter of Madel., Indian. Godparents: the Negroes Gme. and Therese. Priest: L. Buhot of Opelousas.

306. JEAN PIERRE CLOUTIER
(112) 29 December 1809, baptism of infant born 28 January 1808, legitimate son of Jn. Pierre Cloutier and Marie Salvan. Godparents: Jn. Bte. Severe Cloutier and Marie Luce Rachal. Priest: L. Buhot of Opelousas.

307. SIMPHORIEN DERBANE
(112) 29 December 1809, baptism of infant born 11 August 1808, legitimate son of Pre. Derbane and Anastasie Davion. Godparents: Fcois. Davion and Fcoise. Brevel. Priest: L. Buhot of Opelousas.

308. JEAN BAPTISTE LEMOINE
(112) 29 December 1809, baptism of infant born 26 August 1808, legitimate son of Antoine Lemoine and Genev^{ve} Bellegarde. Godparents: A^{ne} Rachal and Fcois. Marie Osite Dupre. Priest: L. Buhot of Opelousas.

309. MARIE ROSE RABALAIS
(113) 29 December 1809, baptism of infant born last 8 April, legitimate daughter of Josephe Rabalais and Marie Baudouin /Bontems/. Godparents: Athanas Lecourt and Marie Robin. Priest: L. Buhot of Opelousas.

310. PHILIPPE BAUDOIN
(113). 29 December 1809, baptism of infant born 26 October 1807, legitimate son of N^{las} Baudouin and Marie Malbert. Godparents: Ch^{le} Philippe Larnaudiere and Margeritte Raballais. Priest: L. Buhot of Opelousas.

311. MARIE CELINE RACHAL
(113) 29 December 1809, baptism of child aged two and a half years, daughter of Etiéne Rachal and Dorothé Monet. Godparents: Jacques St. André and Adelaïde Bricou. Priest: L. Buhot of Opelousas.

312. MARIE SUSANNE GUILLERIE
(114) 29 December 1809, baptism of a child of four years, legitimate daughter of Ls. Guillerie and Rosalie. Godparents: Jn. Baptiste and Marie Lse. Adele /Rachal/. Priest: L. Buhot of Opelousas.

313. MARIE DENIZE WALLETTE
(114) 29 December 1809, baptism of infant of one year, legitimate daughter of Germain Wallette and Marie Antoine. Godparents: Jean Josef Rachal and Marie Rachal. Priest: L. Buhot of Opelousas.

314. MANUEL VERCHERE
(114) 29 December 1809, baptism of child of three years, legitimate son of Josef /Jacques Therin/ Verchere and Marie Jeane Gallien. Godparents: Josef Verchere and Marie Celeste Anty. Priest: L. Buhot of Opelousas.

315. VICTOR VERCHERE
(115) 29 December 1809, baptism of infant aged ten months, legitimate son of Jacques Verchere and Marie Jeanne Gallien. Godparents: Neuville Gallien and Farosine Gallien. Priest: L. Buhot of Opelousas.

316. JOSEF DERBANNE
(115) 29 December 1809, baptism of infant of 4 months, legitimate son of Manuel Derbanne and Marg^{tte} Denis. Godparents: Josef Dupré and Zemire Baudouin. Priest: L. Buhot of Opelousas.

317. MARIE FRANCOISE WELL*
(115) 29 December 1809, baptism of infant born October 28, 1808, daughter of Simon Well* and Nanette Denis. Godparents: Pre. Brossé and Marie Jos. Rachal. Priest: L. Buhot of Opelousas.

*This name is written very distinctly, in text and in margin, as "Well". However, in Entry 520 the name is written as "Grey" or "Guey."

318. JOSEPH EVARISTE WELL*
(116) 29 December 1809, baptism of infant aged four months, legitimate son of Simon Well* and Nanette Denis. Godparents: Manuel Derbanne and Marguerite Denis. Priest: L. Buhot of Opelousas.

319. JOSEF BONNET
(116) 29 December 1809, baptism of infant aged nine months, legitimate son of Jean Bte. Bonnet and Lucide Denis. Godparents: Jn Bte. Bonnet, Sr. and Marie Louise Baudouin. Priest: Louis Buhot of Opelousas.

320. MARIE LISE GALLIEN
(116) 29 December 1809, baptism of infant born last 18 January, legitimate daughter of Louis Gallien and Marie Celeste Anty. Godparents: Alexis Cloutier and Marie Jeane Craite. Priest: L. Buhot of Opelousas.

321. MARIE ZELIME MORIN
(117) 29 December 1809, baptism of infant aged 14 mos. legitimate daughter of Bte. Morin and Lucile Const. Toue? Godparents: Pre. Michel and Marie Rose Michel. Priest: L. Buhot of Opelousas.

322. JACQUES VALCOUR LECONTE
(117) 29 December 1809, baptism of infant aged nine months, legitimate son of Jacques Leconte and Marie Silvie Brossé. Godparents: Ambroise Le Conte and Helene Cloutier. Priest: L. Buhot of Opelousas.

323. MARIE ANNE FRANCOISE LEFEVRE
(117) NOTE: This entry consists only of a note to the effect that the registration of the baptism of Marie Anne Francoise Lefevre is found in Folio 63. Marginal notation indicates that mother's surname was Charrio. This entry was then voided by the priest with a series of diagonal lines.

324. MARIE ASPASY LAUVE
(118) 12 September 1810, baptism of an infant born 15 of last February, legitimate daughter of Arnaldo Lauve and Maria Elisabeth Murphy. Godparents: Nicolas Lauve and Maria Elisabeth Buard. Priest: José Maria de Jesus Huerta, pastor of the town of Nacogdoches.

325. MARIE OPHELIE PHIBERT
(118-19) 12 September 1810, baptism of infant born last 18 July, legitimate daughter of Gaspard Philibert and Felicidad Theophille. Godparents: Jn Pre Mie. Dubois and Maria Louise Lemaitre. Priest: José Maria de Jesus Huerta, pastor of the town of Nacogdoches.

326. JUAN LOUIS TRICHEL
(119) 12 September 1810, baptism of infant born last 11 February, legitimate son of Bautista Trichel and Modesta Fonteneau. Godparents: Manuel Trichel and Francisca Trichel. Priest: José Maria de Jesus Huerta, pastor of the town of Nacogdoches.

327. EUPHEMIE ROUBIEU
(119) 22 Aug. 1811, baptism of infant born 23 October 18__ /entry torn/* natural daughter of Aug^{te} Roubieu and Marie Judith Le Vas____*/entry torn/ Godparents: Fcois. Roubieu and Adelaide Buart. Priest: Louis Buhot of Opelousas.

*An abstract of this entry was made in 1973 by this editor, before the document was damaged. That abstract indicates that child was born in 1809 and the mother's complete surname was Levasseur.

328. MARY ANNE FRANKLIN
(120) 4 Aug. 1811, baptism of child aged three years, daughter of Lisky Franklin and Mary Uigangham. Godparents: Robert Douty and Sarah Rosse. Priest: Louis Buhot of Opelousas.

329. JEAN FRANCOIS LEVASSEUR
(120) 4 August 1811, baptism of infant born 29 July 1810, legitimate son of Jean Francois LeVasseur and of Marie Francoise Trische. Godparents: Gilbert Clauso and Francoise Trische. Priest: L. Buhot of Opelousas.

330. LOUIS VERCHAIR
(120) 7 August 1811, baptism of infant born 27 October 1810, legitimate son of Jean Pre. Verchaire and Marie Emil Schleter. Godparents: Jn Bte. Verschair and Marie Louise Schleter. Priest: L. Buhot of Opelousas.

331. MARIE AIMEE LESTAGE
(121) 13 August 1811, baptism of infant of 18 months, legitimate daughter of Barthelemi Lestage and Marie Pelagie Frederic. Godparents: André Frederic and Marie Philippe /Frederic/. Priest: L. Buhot of Opelousas.

332. MARIE LOLETTE RACHAL
(121) 11 August 1811, baptism of infant born 5 June 1810, legitimate daughter of Louis Julien Rachal and of Marie Reine Thomassi. Godparents: Jq. Porter and Marie Lolette Rachal. Priest: L. Buhot of Opelousas.

333. JOSEFINE LAMBRE
(121) 11 August 1811, baptism of infant born last 25 September, legitimate daughter of Josef Lambre and Eugenie Roquigni. Godparents: Cesair Murphy, Adelphe Lambre. Priest: L. Buhot of Opelousas.

334. MARIE AURORE GONIN
(122) 11 August 1811, baptism of infant aged 14 months, legitimate daughter of Fcois. Gonin and Marie Barbe Frederic. Godparents: Philippe Frederic and Marie Eugenie Buart. Priest: L. Buhot of Opelousas.

335. MARIE ELISABETH KOB (COBB)
(122) 11 August 1811, baptism of infant aged 1 year, legitimate daughter of Samuel Kob and Marg$^{tte}_{e}$ Leonard. Godparents: Michel Chamart and Marie Anne Rouquier. Priest: L. Buhot of Opelousas.

336. JACQUES TRANQUILLEN /LE/ COMTE
(122) 13 August 1811, baptism of infant born last 23 March, legitimate son of Jacques Comte and Silvie Brossé. Godparents: Charles Noyrit and Marcellitte Rouquier. Priest: L. Buhot of Opelousas.

337. MARIE FRANCOISE HERTZOG
(123) 8 August 1811, baptism of infant born last 27 December, legitimate daughter of Jean Fois. Hertzog and Marie Anne Prudhomme. Godparents: Ant^e Prudhomme and Marie Lambre. Priest: L. Buhot of Opelousas.

338. MARIE BOISSIER
(123) 11 August 1811, baptism of infant aged 5 months, legitimate daughter of Soulange Boissié and Eleonor Himmel. Godparents: Cesaire Boissié and Marie Su____ /torn/ Boissié.

339. JAMES (JOHN)* MILLER
(123) 14 August 1811, baptism of infant born 29 December 1809, legitimate son of James Miller and Euphrosine Pommier. Godparents: Louis Pommier and Felicité Pommier. Priest: L. Buhot of Opelousas.

*Text gives name as John. Marginal entry gives name as James.

340. HENRIETTE ARMAND
(124) 15 August 1811, baptism of infant born last 28 October, legitimate daughter of Jean Baptiste Armand and Cath. Frederic. Godparents: Jean Bte. Armand, Jr. and Marguerite Frederic. Priest: L. Buhot of Opelousas.

341. MARIE LOUISE LION
(124) 15 August 1811, baptism of infant aged 1 month, legitimate daughter of Jean Lion and Marie Mercie. Godparents: Ignace Mayou and Euphrosine Perraut. Priest: L. Buhot of Opelousas.

342. MARIE ANNE ARTHEMISE HOY
(124) 15 August 1811, baptism of infant aged 1 year, legitimate daughter of Dorsett Hoy and Marie Anne Lemaitre. Godparents: Gaspar Bodin and Pompose Montanari. Priest: L. Buhot of Opelousas.

343. MARIE REINE ROGER
(125) 16 August 1811, baptism of Marie Reine, born 30 of last September, legitimate daughter of Fois. Roger and Marie Pelagie Adlé. Godparents: Dr. John Sibley and Marie Ge. Dubois. Priest: L. Buhot of Opelousas.

344. AURORE RACHAL
(125) 17 August 1811, baptism of an infant born last 3 October, legitimate daughter of Julien Rachal and Melanie LaVespere. Godparents: Hilaire Rachal and Carmelitte Langlois. Priest: L. Buhot of Opelousas.

345. MARIE ANNE FRANCOISE LEFEVRE
(125) 18 December 1811, baptism of infant born last 3 October, legitimate daughter of Jean Bapte. Le fevre and Marie Louise Victoire Charrié. Godparents: Jean Cortes and Marie Anne Rouquier. Priest: L. Buhot of Opelousas.

346. JEAN JACQUES WILLIAM PAILLETTE
(126) 19 August 1811, baptism of infant born last 10 January, legitimate son of Jean Jacques Paillette, a native of Normandy, senior captain of the artillery, and justice of the peace at Natchitoches, and Victoire Poissot. Godparents: Wm. Murray (s) and Marianne Buart (s). Priest: L. Buhot of Opelousas.

347. MARIE LEOCADIE BUARD*
(127) 19 August 1811, baptism of infant born 19 March, 1806, natural daughter of Jean Btte. Buard and Marie Françoise Himel. Godparents: Antoine Himel and Leoneur Himel. Priest: Louis Buhot of Opelousas.

348. MARIE MODESTE LEVASSEUR*
(127) 13 September 1811, baptism of infant born 20 October 1808, legitimate daughter of Manuel Levasseur and Genoveva Gonet. Godparents: Francisco Vascocu, Jr., and Marie Silbye Plesans. Priest: Jose Mariano Sosa, pastor of Natchitoches /Nacogdoches/.

349. MARIANO DEL REFUGIO TOTIN*
(128) 13 September 1811, baptism of infant born 10 October, 1810, legitimate son of Remy Totin and Maria Teresa Bascocu. Godparents: Jn. Bautista Plesans and Morine Totin. Priest: Rev. Mariano Sosa, pastor of Nacogdoches.

350. MARIA CELESTINA TOUTIN /?TEAL/
(129) 13 September 1811, baptism of infant born 14 May 1810, daughter of Santiago Toutin and Maria Rosa Saibuck? /Saideck?/. Godparents: Pedro Suibuck? and Maria Sora LaLanda. Priest: Josef Mariano Sosa of Nacogdoches.

> NOTE: The family surname is clearly written Toutin. The mother's maiden name, and godfather's surname appears to be Saibuck. The editor has not been able to locate any Santiago or Jacques Toutin at Natchitoches, nor a Saibuck family. However, there was a Jacques (James) TEAL with a wife Marie Rose Saideck, whose father and brother were both named Pierre (Pedro).

351. MARIA RYSSE
(129) 13 September 1811, baptism of infant born 14 February, 1808, daughter of Guillermo /Illegible word/ Ris and Maria Abransa. Godparents: Juan Hyistimin and Maria Lajbache. Priest: Josef Mariano Sosa of Nacogdoches.

352. TOMAS
(129) ROSSE
13 September 1811, baptism of Tomas & Rosse, born 9 November /no year -- no further information in entry/. Priest: Josef Mariano Sosa, Nacogdoches.

*These three entries were recorded by Rev. Francisco Magnes of Nacogdoches, based upon information provided him by godparents and witnesses.

353. FRANCOIS SEVERE LATTIER
(130) 23 August 1812, baptism at Rivière aux Cannes of infant born last 17 May, legitimate son of F^{ois} Lattier and Marie Pelagia Schleter, habitants of Natchitoches. Godparents: Jn Bte. Lattier and Marie Louise Schleter. Priest: Louis Buhot of Opelousas.

354. MARIE JEANE HERTZOG
(130) 27 November 1812, baptism of infant born last 26 September, legitimate daughter of Jean F^{ois} Hertzog and Marie Anne Prudhomme. Godparents: Sebastien Compère and Jeane Lartigue. Priest: Louis Buhot of Opelousas.

355. MARIE CONSTANCE LEVASSEUR
(130-131) 26 November 1812, baptism of infant born last 6 October, legitimate daughter of Jean F^{ois} LeVasseur and Marie F^{oise} Trische. Godparents: Manuel Vasseur and Marie Modeste Fontenot. Priest: Louis Buhot of Opelousas.

356. EUGENIE MCTYRE
(131) 26 November 1812, baptism of infant aged 7 weeks, legitimate daughter of George McTyre and Marie Louise Mayoux. Godparents: Ignace Mayoux and Euresime Pereaut. Priest: Louis Buhot, Opelousas

357. AMELIE RACHAL */VERCHER/
(131) 26 November 1812, baptism of infant born last 4 March, legitimate daughter of Jean Pre Rachal* and Marie Emelie Schleter. Godparents: Jean Bte. Schleter & Agathe Rachal. Priest: Louis Buhot of Opelousas.

*/This name should be VERCHER, not Rachal. Jean Pierre VERCHER was husband of Marie Emelie Schlater (Chelette), as evidenced by their marriage -- Entry # 999. No Jean Pierre Rachal existed at the Natchitoches post prior to the Civil War. Apparently the recorder of this document confused the name of the father with that of the godmother/

358. MARIE JOACHINE LATTIER
(132) 26 November 1812, baptism of infant born last 8 October, legitimate daughter of F^{ois} Lattier and Marie Pelagie Schleter. Godparents: Jn Bte Schleter and Cathe. Lattier. Priest: Louis Buhot of Opelousas.

359. ADELAIDE LEFEVRE
(132) 26 November 1812, baptism of infant aged 3 months,

legitimate daughter of Auguste Lefevre and Victoire Lemaitre. Godparents: Alexis Dubois and Felicité Peraut. Priest: Louis Buhot, Opelousas.

360. MARIE AGLAE PRUDHOMME
(132) 26 November 1812, baptism of infant born last 26 March, legitimate daughter of Narcisse Prudhomme and Marie Therese Metoyer. Godparents: P^{re} Victorin Metoyer and Marie Therese Aillotte /Ailhaud Ste. Anne/. Priest: Louis Buhot of Opelousas.

361. MARIE CEPHALINE PRUDHOMME
(133) 26 November 1812, baptism of infant born 30 August 1810, legitimate daughter of Narcisse Prudhomme and Marie Therese Metoyer. Godparents: Emmanuel Prudhomme and Therese Buard. Priest: Louis Buhot of Opelousas.

362. VALERI ANTI
(133) 30 November 1812, baptism of infant born 18 August 1810, legitimate son of Valeri Anti and Marie Aspasie Derbanne. Godparents: Jean Bte. Anti and Marie F^{oise} Brevel. Priest: Louis Buhot of Opelousas.

363. HILAIRE LEFEVRE
(133) 30 November 1812, baptism of infant born last 4 September, legitimate son of Jean Bte. Lefevre and Marie Louise Charier. Godparents: Emmanuel Rachal and Elisabeth David. Priest: Louis Buhot of Opelousas.

364. JEAN RENÉ AGUESSE
(134) 30 November 1812, baptism of infant aged 3 months, son of Jean Renould Aguesse and Perine Olivier. Godparents: F^{ois} Massippe and Marie Aguesse. Preist: Louis Buhot of Opelousas.

365. JACQUES AGUESSE
(134) 30 November 1812, baptism of infant born 3 March 1811, son of Jean Renaud Aguesse and Perine Olivier. Godparents: Jques Lacasse and Marie Roset Massippe. Priest: Louis Buhot of Opelousas.

366. MARIE LANGEVIN
(134) 30 November 1812, baptism of child aged 9 years, daughter of Louis Langevin and Sarah Langevin. Godparents: Josef Brandt and Elisabeth David. Priest: Louis Buhot of Opelousas.

367. MARCELITE POISSEAU
(135) 1 December 1812, baptism of infant born last 25 March, legitimate daughter of Paul Poisseau and Marie Louise Anti. Godparents: Jn Cortes and Therese Benitte. Priest: Louis Buhot of Opelousas.

368. MARGUERITTE BERNARD
(135) 1 December 1812, baptism of infant aged 1 year, legitimate daughter of Celestin Elie Bernard and Silesie Trische. Godparents: Henry Trische and Felicité Triche. Priest: Louis Buhot, Opelousas.

369. PIERRE JEAN JOSEPH SOMPEYRAC
(135) 2 December 1812, baptism of infant born 4 November 1811, legitimate son of Ambroise Sompayrac (s) and Josefine Briand. Godparents: Jean Josef Bauvant St. Amand and Marie Mad. Appart, his wife. (s/ Bauvard St. Amand). Priest: Louis Buhot of Opelousas.

370. MARIE CAROLINE BOUCHER
(136) 2 December 1812, baptism of infant born 1 June 1811, legitimate daughter of Jean Boucher and Marie Anne Durand de St. Romes. Godparents: Charles Pavie and Marcelite Rouquier. Priest: Louis Buhot of Opelousas.

371. LEONARD FAUSTIN PERAUT
(136) 2 December 1812, baptism of infant born 6 October 1811, legitimate son of Faustin Peraut and Celeste Bordelon. Godparents: Hippolite Bordelon and Marie Therese Trische. Priest: Louis Buhot of Opelousas.

372. LUCE MARG^{TTE} GRILLETTE
(136) 2 December 1812, baptism of infant born 13 November 1811, legitimate daughter of Ante. Grillette and Felicité Peraut. Godparents: Isebe Issoura and Marie Adeline Issoura. Priest: Louis Buhot of Opelousas.

373. JEAN FRANCOIS CORTES
(137) 4 December 1812, baptism of infant born 26 January 1811, legitimate son of Jean Cortes and Marie Josef. Rouquier. Godparents: Judge John C. Carr and Marie Anne Rouquier. Priest: Louis Buhot of Opelousas.

374. MARIE JOSEF HENRIETTE CARR
(137) 4 December 1812, bpatism of infant born 25 January 1810, legitimate daughter of John C. Carr and Henriette Rouquier. Godparents: Fois. Rouquier and Marie Louise Prudhomme. Priest: Louis Buhot of Opelousas.

375. MARIE HERMINIA CARR
(137) 4 November [sic] 1812, baptism of infant born last 5 September, legitimate daughter of John C. Carr and Henriette Rouquier. Godparents: Ch. Pavie and Aimée Bludworth. Louis Buhot of Opelousas.

376. MARIE CEPHALINE GALLIEN
(138) 5 December 1812, baptism of infant born 20 October 1811, legitimate daughter of Louis Gallien and Marie Celeste Anti. Godparents: Louis Neuville Gallien and Marie Helene Anti. Priest: Louis Buhot of Opelousas.

377. VICTORINE MAYOUX
(138) 5 December 1812, baptism of infant born last 31 March, legitimate daughter of Laurent Mayoux and Margtte. Duval. Godparents: Fois. Serpentini and Cecile Mayoux. Priest: Louis Buhot, Opelousas.

378. MARIE CAROLINE PHILIBERT
(138) 5 December 1812, baptism of infant born last 23 February, legitimate daughter of Gaspart Philibert and Felicité Lemaitre. Godparents: Dr. Jn. Sibley and Marie Anne Lemaitre. Priest: Louis Buhot of Opelousas.

379. JAMES EDWARD CASE
(139) 6 December 1812, baptism of infant born 14 January 1812, legitimate son of David Case and Marie Margtte. Prudhomme. Godparents: John Cortes and Marie Josephine Rouquier. Priest: Louis Buhot of Opelousas.

380. WILLIAM JAMES LINNARD
(139) 6 December 1812, baptism of infant born last 31. October, legitimate son of Thomas M. Linnard and Adelaïde Tauzin. Godparents: Josef Tauzin and Marie Chamart. Priest: Louis Buhot, Opelousas.

381. ELISABETH SIBLEY
(139) 6 December 1812, baptism of infant born 22 December 1811, legitimate daughter of Samuel Hopkins Sibley and Margtte. McDonald. Godparents: Thos. M. Linnard and Adelaide Tauzin. Priest: Louis Buhot of Opelousas.

382.   MARIE EUPHROSINE LESTAGES
(140) 6 December 1812, baptism of infant aged 9 months, legitimate daughter of Barth. Lestages and Marie Pelagie Frederic. Godparents: Fois Gonin and Marie Barbe Frederic. Priest: Louis Buhot of Opelousas.

383.   MARIE DESIRÉE ELIE /BERNARD/
(140) 6 December 1812, baptism of infant aged 1 month, legiimate daughter of Pierre Elie and Marie Derbanne. Godparents: Jean Bte. Derbanne and Marie Derbanne. Priest: Louis Buhot of Opelousas.

384.   SEVERE LAFITTE
(140) 6 December 1812, baptism of infant aged 4 years, son of Pre. Lafitte and Ursule Gagnié. Godparents: Pre. Ternier and Marie Josef Palvado. Priest: Louis Buhot of Opelousas.

385.   MARIE CEPHALIDE TERNIER
(141) 6 December 1812, baptism of infant born last 4 February, legitimate daughter of Pre. Ternier and Marie Gagnié. Godparents: Fois. Prudhomme and Pelagie Gagnié. Priest: Louis Buhot, Opelousas.

386.   ETIENNE RACHAL
(141) 6 December 1812, baptism of infant born 15 October 1811, legitimate son of Jean Bte. Rachal and Pelagie Brevel. Godparents: Hilaire Rachal and Agathe Rachal. Priest: Louis Buhot of Opelousas.

387.   EDOUARD FREDERIC
(141) 6 December 1812, baptism of infant born last 23 January, legitimate son of François Frederic and Felicité La Vespere. Godparents: Hilaire La Vespere and Françoise Armand. Priest: Louis Buhot of Opelousas.

388.   MARIE AGATHE DE PORCUNA
(142) 6 December 1812, baptism of infant born 15 November 1811, legitimate daughter of Pre. Nolaso de Porcuna and Madeleine Laberie. Godparents: Francisco Llorens and Marie Agathe Laberie. Priest: Louis Buhot of Opelousas.

389.   LOUIS ALEXANDRE BUART
(142) 6 December 1812, baptism of infant, legitimate son of Jean Louis Buart and Eulalie Boissié. Godparents: Hildebert Boissié and Elisabeth Buart. Priest: Louis Buhot of Opelousas.

390. MARIE DES NEIGES FONTENOT
(142) 8 December 1812, baptism of infant born last 5
January, legitimate daughter of Jn Bte. Fontenot
and Marie Lafitte. Godparents: Cesair Fontenot
and Marie desNeiges Lafitte. Godparents: Louis
Buhot of Opelousas.

391. FELIX LANGLOIS
(143) /The following entry was inserted at this point
on an unspecified date by Rev. Francisco Magnes
of the parish of Nacogdoches, based upon information provided him by the godparents and witnesses./

11 December 1812, baptism of infant born 28 February 1811, legitimate son of Augustin Langlois
and Ma. Celeste Berger /Verger/. Godparents:
Miguel Cazenave and Maria Ris. Priest: Louis
Buhot of Opelousas.

392. VICTORIO MADISON DESPALLION
(144) 31 January 1813, baptism of infant, aged 1 month,
12 days, legitimate son of Bernardo Despalier and
Candida Grande. Godparents: Josiah J. Johnston
and Ana Elisa Sibley. Priest: Franco. Magnes of
Nacogdoches.

393. PEDRO NOLASCO HAYS
(144) 31 January 1813, baptism of infant born 4 July
1811, legitimate son of Guillermo Hays and Margarita Roberson. Godparents: Polinario Marmela
and /godmother not named/. Priest: Franco.
Magnes of Nacogdoches.

394. FRANCISCO VALENTIN
(144) 2 February 1813, baptism of infant born 14 August
1812, legitimate son of Jose Valentin and Maria
Prudhomme, residents of Bayou Pierre. Godparents:
Juan Cortes and Eulalia Malige. Priest: Franco.
Magnes.

395. MARIA CANDELARIA CHAZMAN
(145) 2 February 1813, baptism of infant aged 2 years
and 1 month, natural daughter of Nansi Chazman.
Godparents: Juan Bautista Chirino and Maria Antonia Yudd. Priest: Franco. Magnes.

396. REMIGIO CASIMIRO PEROT
(145) 5 February 1813, baptism of child of 4 months and
20 days, legitimate son of Casimiro Pero and Damasena Puessot /Poissot/. Godparents: Atanasio
Puesot and Maria Agata Laveri /La Berry/. Priest:
Franco. Magnes.

397. AMILIA BLUDWORTH
(145) 6 February 1813, baptism of child born 16 May 1809, legitimate daughter of Santiago Bludworth and Amada Rouquier. Godparents: Franco. Rouquier, the infant's uncle, and Maria Luisa Rouquier. Priest: Franco. Magnes.

398. ANA JULIANA BLUDWORTH
(146) 6 February 1813, baptism of child born 12 January, 1811, legitimate daughter of Santiago Bludworth and Amada Rouquier. Godparents: Fran^{co} Rouquier and Ana Bludworth. Priest: Franco. Magnes.

399. MARIA ELIZA BLUDWORTH
(146) 6 February 1813, baptism of infant born 19 December 1812, legitimate duaghter of Santiago Bludworth and Amada Rouquier. Godparents: Franklin T. Bludworth and Mariana Ruquier. Priest: Franco. Magnes.

400. FRANCISCO ROUQUIER
(146) 7 February 1813, baptism of infant born 4 December 1812, legitimate son of Francisco Rouquier and Isavela Buard. Godparents: Luis Buard and Maria Luisa Prudhomme. Priest: Franco. Magnes.

401. ALEXANDRO MONVIL BUARD
(147) 7 February 1813, baptism of infant born 2 November 1812, legitimate son of Juan Bautista Buard and Aspasie Bossie. Godparents: Hildebert Bossie and Maria Teresa Buard. Godparents: Franco. Magnes.

402. EUFROSINA MANUELA CHILETTRE
(147) 9 February 1813, baptism of infant born 25 December 1812, legitimate daughter of Juan Bautista Chilettre and Eufrosina Rachal. Godparents: Pedro Chilettre and Maria Francesca Grillet. Priest: Franco. Magnes.

403. ELIZA VICTORINA KEISER
(147) 9 February 1813, baptism of child of 14 years, legitimate daughter of Jacobo Keiser and Margarita Davemport. Godparents: Fran^{co} Bossier and Mariana Victoriana Merenciana Bossier. Priest: Franco. Magnes.

404. PELAGIA PROCELA KEISER
(148) 9 February 1813, baptism of child of 10 years, legitimate daughter of Jacovo Keiser and Marga-

rita Davemport. Godparents: Juan Cortes and
Maria Catalina Pelagia Lambre. Priest: Franco.
Magnes.

405. MANUEL SAMUEL KEISER
(148) 9 February 1813, baptism of child of 8 years, legitimate son of Jacobo Keiser and Margarita Davemport. Godparents: Miguel Arnmega and Mariana Rosalia Grenau. Priest: Franco. Magnes.

406. MARIA MARGARITA KEISER
(148) 9 February 1813, baptism of child of 6 years, legitimate daughter of Jacobo Keiser and Margarita Davemport. Godparents: Samuel Davenport and Mariana Rosalia Aurora Bossier. Priest: Franco. Magnes of Nacogdoches.

/Note: between February and April 1813, apparently, Rev. Magnes was transferred from Nacogdoches to Natchitoches./

407. JOSE MIGUEL BENSAN
(149) 6 April 1813, baptism of child of 5 years, natural child of Miguel Bensan and a Cado Indian named Nagueney. Godfather: Marcelo Soto, resident of Bayupier who has adopted the boy. Godmother not named. Priest: Franco. Magnes.

408. MARIA ANTONIA MORBAN /MORVANT/
(149) 6 April 1813, baptism of child of 5 years, natural daughter of Franc^{co} Morban and an Indian of the Cado people named Nachus?. Godparents: Francisco Rambin and Maria Dolores Soto. The child is adopted by Marcelo Soto, resident of Bayu pier. Priest: Franco. Magnes.

409. JOSE OLIBIE /OLIVIER/
(149) 15 April 1813, baptism of child of 6 years, 11 months, and 21 days, son of a father unknown. Mother not named. Godparents: Pedro Lafita, who has adopted him for a son, and Maria Soto. Priest: Franco. Magnes.

410. JOSE ANTONIO LAFITA
(150) 15 April 1813, baptism of a child of 3 years, 11 days, legitimate son of Jose Sever? Lafita and Beise Leton. Godfather: Pedro Lafita. Godmother: not named. Priest: Franco. Magnes.

411. REMIGIO LAFITA
(150) 15 April 1813, baptism of child of 2 years, 7

months, 17 days, legitimate son of José Sévère? Lafita and Beise Liton. Godparents: Silvestre Pueso /Poissot/ and /godmother not named/. Priest: Franco. Magnes.

412. MARIANA LAFITA
(150) 15 April 1813, baptism of child of __ years, 11 months, 4 days, legitimate daughter of Jose Severe? Lafita and Beise Leton. Godparents: Vicente Rolan and Maria Hortans Beltran /Bertrand/. Priest: Franco. Magnes.

413. MARIA CONSTANCE MEILL/EUR/
(151) 5 (or 25) September 1815. Burial in the parish Cemetery of Maria Constance Meill/eur/, 54 years of age, widow of Francois /Landreaux/ natives "de la Luciana en Orleans". Died of fever leaving __ son and 1 daughter. Priest: Franco. Magnes /entry is badly torn/

414. SEPHALIN /LESTAGE/
(151) 1815. Burial in parish cemetery of Sephalin, aged 9 months, child of /Barthele/my Lestaze and Pelagy /Frederic/. Priest: Franco. Magnes. /Entry is badly torn/

415. CLAUDE /THOMAS PIERRE METOYER/
(151) /October/ 1, 1815. Burial in parish cemetery of Mr. Claude /Thomas Pierre Metoyer/ native of La Rochel . . . widower of Mda. /Marie Therese Eugenie Buard/, a native of this post. Deceased left 2 sons and 1 daughter, died of fever. Priest: Franco. Magnes. /Entry is badly torn. According to Metoyer's gravemarker in the American cemetery at Natchitoches, he died on September 30, 1815./

416. UNKNOWN
(151) 1815 burial in parish cemetery, corpse of Dlle. M____, aged 28 /entry is almost completely illegible./

417. UNKNOWN
(151- /Torn/."...nio, leaving 2 sons and 8 daughters...
152) dropsy... Priest: Franco. Magnes /entry is almost completely illegible/

418. MARIANNE SCHELLETTRE LESTAGE
(152) 14 December 1815, burial of corpse of Mda. Mari.. 25 years, native of this post . . . Sr. Btte. Lestage . . . 20 days old. Priest: Franco. Magnes. /Entry is almost completely illegible. Ap-

arently the wife of Baptiste Lestage died leaving
a 20 day old infant./

419. FRANCOIS GONET LAFERET? /BOUET LAFITTE?/
(153) 17 December 1815, burial in cemetery . . . of
Francois . . . post . . . three /sons or daugh-
ters/ . . . /entry is almost completely torn away/

420. UNKNOWN
(153) 27 December 1815. Burial. /Entry is almost completely destroyed./

This series of burial entries continues
with Entry 2644.

421. ZELEDINA RUBLO
(154) 15 April 1813, baptism of child of 4 years, 1 mo.
and 4 days, legitimate daughter of Pedro Rublo
and Magdalena Pruddeau /Prudhomme/. Godparents:
Vicente Rolan and Dna. Andres Valentin. Priest:
Franco. Magnes.

422. DAMASIA RUBLO
(154) 15 April 1813, baptism of child of 2 years, 4
mos., 4 days. legitimate daughter of Pedro
Rublo and Madalena Prudeau. Godparents: Silbestre Pueso /Poissot/ and Maria Hortans Beltrans
/Bertrand/. Priest: Franco. Magnes.

423. MARIA DOLORES RAMBEN
(154) 17 April 1813, baptism of child of 2 years, legitimate daughter of Miguel Ramben and Teresa Mayu.
Godparents: Juan Baptista Prudeaon /Prudhomme/
Godmother: not named. Priest: Franco. Magnes.

424. MARIA JOSEFA DUI BUA /DU BOIS/
(154) 17 April 1813, baptism of child of 3 years, legitimate daughter of Antonio Dui Bua and Maria Josefa Malis /Malige/. Godfather: Antonio Dui Bua
and /godmother not named/. Priest: Franco Magnes.

425. JOSE CYPRIANO LUC
(154) 18 April 1813, baptism of infant aged 1 month,
legitimate son of Cypriano Luc and Rosalia Guey.
Godparents: Remigio Joacen and Teresa Andre.
Godparents: Franco. Magnes.

426. MARIA ROSALIA PRUDDUON /PRUDHOMME/
(154) 4 May 1813, baptism of infant aged /blank/, legi-

timate daughter of Jean Baptiste Prudduon and Josefa Malis /Malige/. Godparents: Nuel Malis and Maria Ruquier. Priest: Franco. Magnes.

427. **FRANCISCO DAVIER GONNE**
(155) 9 May 1813, baptism of Infant of 4 months, legitimate son of Franco. Gonne and Maria Barbara /no last name given -- should be Frederic/. Godparents: Franco. Gonne and Maria Emanuel /no last name given/. Priest: Franco. Magnes.

428. **MARIA ELEISA RACHAL**
(155) 9 May 1813, baptism of infant of 4 months, legitimate daughter of Luis Rachal, Jr. and Maria Luisa Chelaitre. Godparents: Luis Rachal, her grandfather, and Margarita Feve /Lefevre/. Priest: Franco. Magnes.

429. **JUAN BAUTISTA PEDRO CHALAITRE**
(155) 16 May 1813, baptism of child of /torn/, legitimate son of Juan Pedro Chelaitre and Ulalia Sulans Boussie. Godparents: Alexandro Hilaris /Hildebert/ Baussie and Margarita Raine /no last name-- should be Frederic/. Priest: Franco. Magnes.

430. **JUAN BAUTISTA FRANCISCO PLAISANCE***
(156) 16 May 1813, baptism of infant of 1 year, natural son of Margarita Bastien* /father not named/. Godparents: Juan Baptista Plesanns and Maria Felicité Peraut. Priest: Franco. Magnes.

*/The surname Plaisance appears as the child's surname in the marginal guide but not in the text. Bastien, the surname given for the mother above, is frequently used during this period as the surname of one branch of descendants of Bastien Prudhomme./

431. **FRANCISCO OSCAR RUBIEU**
(156) 28 May 1813, baptism of infant born 28 December 1812, legitimate son of Francisco Oscar Rubieu and Mariana Laferne.* Godparents: Agustin Rubieu and Maria Laferne. Priest: Franco. Magnes.

*/Mariana Laferne, erroneously given above as wife of François Oscar Roubieu, was actually his mother. Roubieu's wife was Marie Ausite Rachal./

432. **FRANCISCO SUMOBIL DERBANNE**
(156) 13 June 1813, baptism of infant born 25 August 1812, legitimate son of Juan Bautista Derbanne and Marie Mercelite DiuPre. Godparents: Franco.

Derbanne and Osite Dupre. Priest: Franco Magnes.

433. **VICTORIANA AMEDI SONS** /JOHNSON/
(157) 20 June 1813, baptism of infant born 11 <u>September</u>? 1811, legitimate daughter of Juan Sons and Francisco Grano /Greneaux/. Godparents: Carlos Manuel Grano and Rosalia Grano. Priest: Franco. Magnes.

434. **URSEN GRILLET**
(157) 12 July 1813, baptism of infant aged 1 month and 20 days, legitimate son of Teodoro Grillet and Maria Pero. Godparents: Beltran Plesans, Eufrasine Celeste /torn/. Priest: Franco. Magnes.

435. **JUAN BAUTISTA BESANNT** /BESSON/
(157) 27 July 1813, baptism of infant born 18 January 1813, legitimate son of Juan Bautista Besannt and Mariana Pievert. Godfather: Juan LaLandre and Felicite Trist /Triche/. Priest: Franco. Magnes.

436. **ROGUE ISIDORO PLESANNS**
(158) 3 October 1813, baptism of infant born 17 August 1813, legitimate son of Beltran Plesans and Maria Barbara Grillet. Godparents: Bertelmil Rachal and Juana Perau. Priest: Franco. Magnes.

437. **MARIA ANGELA FLORES**
(158) 4 October 1813, baptism of infant aged 4 days, natural daughter of Encarnacion Flores. Godparents: Franco. Menchaca and Justa? Rosina Casanova. Priest: Franco. Magnes.

438. **MARIA CATARINA DAMASIA RAMBEN**
(158) 14 October 1813, baptism of infant aged /torn/ legitimate daughter of Franco. Rambin and Maria Damasia Soto. Godparents: Andres Rambin and Maria Dolores Soto. Priest: Franco. Magnes.

439. **MARIA ANTONIA PRADO**
(159) 25 October 1813, baptism of a Spanish infant of 1 month, legitimate daughter of Jose Prado and Maria Jetrudis Soto, residents of Bexar. Godparents: Edmon Chamard and Catarina Berdon. Priest: Franco. Magnes.

440. **MARIA TRANQUILINA RACHAL** /LE COURT/*
(159) 30 October 1813, baptism of infant of 2 years, 3 months, legitimate daughter of Bertelmil Rachal and Mda. Suil. Godparents: Pedro Brosset and

Fansonet LeCour. Priest: Franco. Magnes.

*/The priest erred in recording this entry. There was no Marie Tranquilline Rachal in this period. The baptized infant was Marie Tranquilline LECOURT, daughter of Barthelemy LeCourt and Marie Ursulle (Suil) a Caddo Indian. The godfather, Pierre Brosset, was the infant's brother-in-law, and the godmother, Fanchonette LeCourt, was her aunt./

441. JOSE MARIO DEL PILAR MATA MEDINA
(159) 31 October 1813, baptism of infant of 20 days, legitimate son of Juan Jose Mata Medina and Maria Josef Elde. Godparents: Damian Arocha and Antonia Flores. Priest: Franco. Magnes.

442. PEDRO TERNIER
(160) 1 November 1813, baptism of infant born 2 July 1813, legitimate son of Pedro Terniée and Rosa Gagnée. Godparents: Juan Bautista Gagnée and Modesta Proudhomme. Priest: Franco. Magnes.

443. MARIA ISABEL DE JESUS GONSALEZ* (HIDALGO)
(160) 2 November 1813, baptism of infant of 1 year and 4 months, legitimate daughter of Jose Franco. Gonzalez Idalgo* and Maria Isabel Corona. Godparents: Mario Carrasco and Maria Josefa de Landa. Priest: Franco. Magnes.

*/Marginal reference gives only "Gonzales" as the family name. Text identifies father as Gonzales Idalgo. Since *idalgo* or *hidalgo* is spanish for "nobleman" it is possible that the word "Idalgo" following "Gonzales" is a title. However, no comma separates "Gonzales" from "Idalgo." It should also be noted that entry 571 identifies this family name only as "Idalgo" with no reference to "Gonsalez"./

444. LUIS RAMON ACOSTA
(160) 14 November 1813, baptism of infant of 2 months, legitimate son of Jose Acosta and Maria de la Cruz. Godparents: Ignacio de los S^{tos} /Coy/ and Maria Jetrudis Chirino, both natives of Nacogdoches. Priest: Franco. Magnes.

445. MARGARITA LIS PLESANNS
(161) 14 November 1813, baptism of infant born 29 August, 1813, legitimate daughter of Margarita /sic/ Plesanns and Maria Josefa Balbado /Palvados/. Godparents: Beltran Plesanns and Adelay Balbado. Priest: Franco. Magnes.

446. ZEFERINO /SEPHERIN/ TRICHEL
(161) 14 November 1813, baptism of infant born 16 August 1813, legitimate son of Juan Bautista Trichel and Modesta Fonteneau. Godparents: Juan Bautista Fonteneau and Felise /La Fitte/. Priest: Franco Magnes.

447. SESER /CESAIRE/ FONTENEAU
(161) 14 November 1813, baptism of infant born 15 December 1812, legitimate son of Seser Fonteneau and Felicite Lafitte. Godparents: Juan Bautista Fonteneau and Pelagia Grap. Priest: Franco. Magnes.

448. MARIA ROSALIA DOMINGUEZ
(162) 1 December 1813, baptism of infant aged 2½ months, legitimate daughter of Jose Ypolito Dominguez and Maria Jetrudis Medina, Spaniards. Godparents: Juan de Mora and Maria Jacinta Castro. Priest: Franco. Magnes.

449. CARLOS GRADOS BERNARDO
(162) 5 December 1813, baptism of infant born 21 December 1812, legitimate son of Guillom Bernardo and Franca. Labauf. Godparents: Remigio Albre and Felicite Lacasa. Priest: Franco. Magnes.

450. JUAN LUIS CONELTIN /QUINNELTY/
(162) 18 December 1813, baptism of infant born 11 March 1812, legitimate son of Santiago Coneltin and Marie Manuela Chelte /Chelette/. Godparents: Juan Luis Buard and Rosalia Lestas. Priest: Franco. Magnes.

451. BENJAMIN VALCOUR CORTES
(163) 25 December 1813, baptism of infant born 18 July 1813, legitimate son of Juan Cortes D'artheits, native of _etcharry /torn/ in "Navarra Basa" of the Kingdom of France and Josefina Marcelita Rouquier, native of Natchitoches in Louisiana. Grandparents: Pedro Cortes D'Artheits and Maria Claverie Dassou, natives of the same "Navarra Basa;" and Franco. Rouquier, native of Tuy Leveque in Department of Lot, in France, and Maria Luisa Prudhomme, native of this post of Natchitoches. Godparents: Franco. Rouquier, Maria Aimée Rouquier. Priest: Franco. Magnes.

452. CARLOS EMILIANO SOMPAYRAC
(163) 25 December 1813, baptism of infant born 23 September 1813, legitimate son of Ambrosio Sompayrac, native of Castros /Castres/, Department of Tarn,

in France; and Francisco Briant and Maria Elisabeth Mozar, both natives of Paris, France. Godparents: Carlos Noyrit and Josefina Marcelita Ruquier. Priest: Franco. Magnes.

453. FRANCISCO JOSE ELISEO HOY
(164) 26 December 1813, baptism of infant born 15 August 1813, legitimate son of Docit Hoy and Mariana Lemarttre /Le Maitre/. Godparents: Luis Tauzin and Euphrasin Tauzin. Priest: Franco. Magnes.

454. MARIA ELEYSA LAMBRE
(164) 3 January 1814, baptism of infant born 5 February 1813, legitimate daughter of Remigio Lambre and Susana Prudhomme. Godparents: Pedro Phanor Prudhomme and "Madaimousel" Maria Josefa Prudhomme. Priest: Franco. Magnes.

455. FRANCISCO AQUILAIN LEFEBVRE
(164) 16 January 1814, baptism of infant born 23 August 1813, legitimate son of Agustin Lefebvre and Victoria Constance LeMaitre. Godparents: Juan Bautista Bell and Aimée Perou. Priest: Franco. Magnes.

456. ANTONIO SAYDECK
(165) 23 January 1814, baptism of infant born 28 February 1813, legitimate son of Pedro Saydeck and Susana Teel. Godparents: Eduardo Bibis and Maria Rutch. Priest: Franco. Magnes.

457. GUILLERMO ETTREDGE
(165) 23 January 1814, baptism of infant born 20 July 1813, legitimate son of Guillermo Ettredge and Maria Teel. Godparents: Pedro Saydeck and Susana Teel. Priest: Franco. Magnes.

458. MARIA TOMASA
(165) 29 January 1814, baptism of infant /document torn/ legitimate daughter of Domingo /illegible/ and Maria Dolores Sa_hez /torn/ Godparents: _____ Acosta and Maria Jetrudis Sanchez. Priest: Franco. Magnes.

459. MARTIN CHAVANA
(165) 15 February 1814, baptism of infant /birthdate torn/, legitimate son of Lino Chavana and Barbara Chabes. Godparents: Rosemond Chamard and Maria Jetrudis Alamillo. Priest: Franco. Magnes.

460. AGUSTIN GILIBERTO PHILIBER
(166) 5 February 1814, baptism of infant aged 19 days, legitimate son of Gaspar Philiber and Felicité Teofille /Le Maitre/ Godparents: Francisco Wliam. Murray and Maria Magdalena Garaud Bauvard de St. Amans. Priest: Franco. Magnes.

461. **MARIA PHILOE ADLE**
(166) 7 February 1814, baptism of infant aged 4 months, legitimate daughter of Valentin Adley and /torn/. Godparents: Juan Bautista Ad/torn/ and Pelagia Adlay. Priest: Franco. Magnes.

462. **MARIA GAVINA JOSEFA ARTEMICE MARTINES**
(166) 21 February 1814, baptism of infant born "diez y ____" /torn/ of that same month /10th through 19th of February/ legitimate daughter of _____ /torn/ and Maria Daria Castro. Godparents: Rosemond Chamart and /torn/. Priest: Franco. Magnes.

463. **MARIA /torn/ SANCHEZ**
(167) 3 March 1814, baptism of infant of 6 months, legitimate daughter of Jose Le_____ Sanchez and Maria Casimire Garza. Godparents: Jose Antonio Gonsalez and Josefa Paloma. Priest: Franco. Magnes.

464. **REMIGIO JOSE GOMEZ**
(167) 3 March 1814, baptism of a child aged $2\frac{1}{2}$ months, natural son of Juan Gomez and Maria Messier. Godparents: Manuel Levasseur and Maria Luisa Bastian /Prudhomme/. Priest: Franco. Magnes.

465. **MARIA DEL CARMEN MORA**
(167) /torn/ 1814. Baptism of infant /birthdate torn/, child of Estevan Mora and Maria Jetru/torn/. Godparents: Santiago LaCase and Maria Luisa Dupre. Priest: Franco. Magnes.

466. **MARIA DEL CARMEN ROZALES?**
(168) 15 March 1814, baptism of infant aged 10 days, legitimate daughter of Julien Rosalez? and Agustina Alamillo?* Godparents: Juan Joval and Maria Teresa Rodriguez. Priest: Franco. Magnes.   *Mamello?

467. **MARIA ANTONIA CLEMENCIA CARO**
(168) 20 March 1814, baptism of infant aged 3 months, legitimate daughter of Pedro Sote Caro and Maria Micaella Equis. Godparents: Ponciano Ybarbo and Maria Petra Padilla. Priest: Franco. Magnes.

468. **JOSE FELIS**
(168) 2 April 1814, baptism . . . legitimate . . . /almost all of entry has been destroyed/

469. **FRANCISCO PERAU**
(168) 19 June 1814, baptism of infant of $2\frac{1}{2}$ months, legitimate son of Luis Perau and Maria Melani Trischelle. Godparents: Enrique Trichelle and Maria Agata Laveri. Preist: Franco. Magnes.

NOTE: original numbering system indicates that sixteen etries for the year 1814 are missing. See appendix.

470. MARIA _____ LESTAGE
(169) 2 June, 1814, baptism of infant born 7 November 1812, legitimate daughter of Juan Bautista Lestase and Maria Juana Cheletre. Godparents: Franco. _____ /illegible/ and Margarita Ren Federick. Priest: Franco. Magnes.

471. JUAN WASHINGTON HERKHAM
(169) 2 June 1814, baptism of infant born 18 April 1813, legitimate son of Santiago Herkham and Isabel Herkham. Godparents: Pedro los fuertes and Margarita Roverson. Priest: Franco. Magnes.

472. MARIA DEL _____
(169) 8 June 1814, baptism of infant born 13 of . . . /remainder of entry is torn/

473. CATARINA SURIGNI
(170) 12 June 1814, baptism of child of 7 years and 1 month, legitimate daughter of Luis Surigni and Margarita Bonne. Godparents: Jose Nepomanceno Arocha and Adelayde Palvado. Priest: Franco. Magnes.

474. JOSE MANUEL RODRIGUEZ
(170) 18 June 1814, baptism of infant aged 3 days, legitimate son of Cypriano _____tin Rodriguez and Maria Matiana Dias. Godparents: Silvestre _____ and Felicite Teofil Lemettere. Priest: Franco. Magnes. /entry torn/

475. UNKNOWN
(170) /entry has been completely destroyed/

476. JOSE POLICARPIO FLORES
(171) 21 June 1814, baptism of infant born 6 January 1814, legitimate son of Vital Flores and _____ /torn/ Mora. Godparents: Luis Procela and Maria Dolores Soto. Priest: Franco. Magnes.

477. JUAN JOSE CESARIO YBARBO
(171) 21 June 1814, baptism of infant born 25 February 1814, legitimate son of Jose Ignacio Ybarbo and Cleta Flores. Godparents: /Pon/ciano Ybarbo and Trinidad Flores. Priest: Franco. Magnes.

478. JUAN ANTONIO CASTAÑEDA
(171) 24 June 1814, baptism of infant aged 11 days, natural son of Maria Josefa Castañeda. Godparents: Teodoro Grillet and Juana Perau. Priest: Franco. Magnes.

479. JUAN ANTONIO CASTAÑEDA
(172) /duplicate of above entry/

480. ISIDORO SESER FREDIU
(172) 26 June 1814, baptism of infant born 15 May 1814, legitimate son of ____ ser _____ u and Rosa _____. Godparents: Santiago _edride and Juana Perau? Priest: Franco. Magnes. /Entry is badly torn. Other records in this volume indicate that Sr. Augustin Caesar Fredieu was the husband of Marie Rose Derbanne. It is probable that they are the parents in the above entry./

481. MARIA JUANA NARCISA PERAUT
(172) 26 July /sic/ 1814, baptism of infant born 14 December 1813, legitimate daughter of Jose Peraut and Polonia Fredue. Godparents: Seser Fredieu and Maria Modesta Peraut. Priest: Franco. Magnes.

482. MARIA PAMEDA FOSTON /JOHNSON/
(173) 28 June 1814, baptism of infant born ___ /date torn/ of January, 1814, legitimate daughter of Juan Foston and Francisca Grenoble. Godparents: Stephen Brown and Mariana Grenoble. Priest: Francisco Magnes.

483. JOSE MARICO ANDRES RAICHAL
(173) 9 July 1814, baptism of infant born 30 November 1813, legitimate son of Estevan Raichal and _____lise Ramon. Godparents: _____ and _____Beille /entry is badly torn/. Priest: Franco. Magnes.

484. JUAN FERMIN QUESADA
(173) 18 July 1814, baptism of infant born 17 July 1814, legitimate son of Jose Cayetano Quesada and Maria Rosa la Cerda. Godparents: Teodoro Grillet and Maria Crisostome /Pereau/. Priest: Franco. Magnes.

485. ETIENNE BREVIL ESLECT /CHELETTE/
(174) 20 July 1814, baptism of infant born /torn/ legitimate son of Juan Btta. Eslect and Maria Frosin Rachal. Godparents: Juan Pedro Eslect and Maria Lana Rachal. Priest: Franco. Magnes.

486. JOSE FACUNDO SANTOS
(175) 23 July 1814, baptism of male . . ./rest of entry torn/

487. ELEYSA VICTORIA PAILLET
(174) 24 July 1814, baptism of infant born 23 June 1814, the legitimate daughter of Juan Santiago Paillette, native of Harque, a town in France, retired captain of the artillery in the old government and member of the legislature of the state of Louisiana, and Victoria Poissot. Paternal grandparents: Maria Pedro Jorge Paillette and Juana LeRoy, natives of France; maternal grandparents: Remigio Poissot and Luisa Cave, habitants of this district. Godparents:

Alexis Cloutier, church elder, and his spouse. Priest:
Franco. Magnes.

488. FRANCISCO FIRMIN TOVAR
(175) 14 August 1814, baptism of infant, 7 days old, legitimate
son of Juan Tovar and Teresa Rodriguez. Godparents: Jose
Castrier and Gertrudis Procela. Priest: Franco. Magnes.

489. MARIA ISABEL HARMON
(175) 27 August 1814, baptism of child born "in Kintock," aged 9
years, legitimate daughter of Worner Harmon and Susana Owens.
Godparents: Apolinario Mamela and Isabel Nelson. Priest:
Franco. Magnes.

490. JUAN BAUTISTO DERVANNE
(175) 28 August 1814, baptism of infant of 2 months and 6 days,
legitimate son of Pierre Dervanne and Maria Anastasia /no
last name given -- should be Davion/. Godparents: Juan
Btta. Conde and Celetin Cloutier. Priest: Franco. Magnes.

491. MARIA PAULA /CHAVINDA/
(176) 1 September 1814, baptism of Indian girl born 15 January
1814, natural child of Luis Chavinda, Indian, and Maria Magdalena Snt. Cristin /Christy/. Godparents: Juan Jose Rosas
and Maria Lena Padilla. Priest: Franco. Magnes.

492. JOSE CANDIDO SNT. CARQUIER
(176) 5 Sept. 1814, baptism of infant aged 2 days, legitimate son
of Pedro Snt. Carquier and Maria fina Mamillo. Godparents:
Gaspar Philiver and Jetrudis Mora. Priest: Franco. Magnes.

493. PEDRO EMILIANO BESSON
(176) 7 September 1814, baptism of infant born 25 November 1813,
natural son of Francisco Besson, "_____nada" and of Denise
Snt. Cristin /Christy/. Godparents: Ignacio Mayou and
Maria Magdalena Snt. Cristin. Priest: Franco. Magnes.

494. MARIA DEL PILAR HORTIZ
(177) 15 September 1814, baptism of infant born ____ _____mbre,
1813, son of ___aum___ Hortiz and Maria Santos Aragon.
Godparents: Hilario Cirrasco and Maria Jesusa Servantes.
Priest: Franco. Magnes.

495. MARIA CELESTE
(177) 14 October 1814, baptism of infant of a month and a half,
legitimate daughter of _____ /left blank on entry/ and
Maria Luisa Tibodo. Godparents: Eduardo Roverson and
Eulalia Malige. Priest: Franco. Magnes.

496. ANA MARIA GUIN
(177) 2 October 1814, baptism of infant of 6 months and 7 days,

legitimate daughter of Miguel Guin and Celeste Cheredem
/Sheridan/. Godparents: Francisco Dill and Layla Dill.
Priest: Franco. Magnes.

497. IGNACIO ARMANT
(178) 18 October 1814, baptism of infant born 27 October 1813 /or
1811? - entry is torn/ legitimate son of Juan Btta. Arman
and Maria Anastasia Maiou. Godparents: Andres Miguel Ramben and Maria Felicite Perau. Priest: Franco. Magnes.

498. PEDRO NAYSA LATTIER
(178) 26 October 1814, baptism of infant of 6 months, legitimate
son of Francisco Lattiere and Maria Pelagia Chelte. Godparents: Carlos Lemoint and Juana Levron /LeBrun/. Priest:
Franco. Magnes.

499. FRANCISCO LEOPOLD LEFEVRE
(178) 31 October 1814, baptism of infant aged 34 days, legitimate
son of Agustin Lefebre and Victoria Constancia Lemetre.
Godparents: Francisco Vienne and Magdalena Garo. Priest:
Franco. Magnes.

500. ENRIQUE CUERCA /QUIRK/
(179) 20 November 1814, baptism of infant born /torn/ legitimate
son of Guillermo Cuerca and Maria Nores. Godparents: Polinario Marmela and Margarita Roverson. Priest: Franco.
Magnes.

501. MARIA TRINIDAD MARINEZ
(179) 6 December 1814, baptism of infant aged 11 days, legitimate
daughter of Dolores Marinez and Manuela Gomez. Godparents:
Manual Cedena and Maria Ignacia Soto. Priest: Franco.
Magnes.

502. MARIA VIRGINIA PROUDHOMME
(179) 22 December 1814, baptism of infant aged 1 years, legitimate
daughter of Narciso Proudhomme and Maria Teresa Isavel Metoyem. Godparents: Jn. Btta. Proudhomme and Maria Adelle,
"her uncle and aunt." Priest: Franco. Magnes.

503. ARNAUD LOUVE
(180) 25 December 1814, baptism of infant aged 9 months and /torn/
days, legitimate son of Arnaud Louve and Marie Elisavet Aspasi Morphy. Grandparents: Nicolas Louve and Catalina
Coulret, natives of New Orleans; Eduardo Morphy, native of
"Doublin in Yrlanda" and Maria Elisavet Buard, native of
this post. Godparents: Eduardo Seser Morphy, his uncle,
and Catalina Coulret, his grandmother. Priest: Franco.
Magnes.

504. EDUARDO CESER MORPHY
(180) 25 December 1814, baptism of infant born 12 August 1814, legitimate son of Eduardo Seser Morphy and Adelay Buard. Grandparents: Eduardo Morphy, native of Dublin, Ireland, and Maria Elisavet Buard, native of this post; Juan Deni Buard and Victoria Poissot, natives of this post. Godparents: Santiago Pallet and Maria Elisavet Buard. Priest: Franco. Magnes.

505. MARIA ADELY ARMANT
(181) 31 December 1814, baptism of infant born 18 May 1814, legitimate daughter of Juan Btta. Arman and Maria Catalina Fredderick. Godparents: Juan Btta. Lattiere and Maria Pelagia Federick. Priest: Franco. Magnes.

506. LUICE DELZIE VERCHER
(181) 9 January 1815, recording of baptism administered 8 December 1812 to an infant born 5 November 1812, legitimate daughter of Joseph Vercher and Marie Luice Ber_____ /torn/. Godparents: Beroni /Beloni/ Vercher and Louce Rachal. Officiating Priest: Louis Buhot of Opelousas. Witnesses: Jn Vercher and E. Cr. Morphy. Recording priest: Franco. Magnes.

507. MARIANA FELONY BOUDOIN
(181) 30 January 1815, baptism of infant born 10 March 1813, legitimate daughter of Pierre Boudouin and Anna Rovin. Godparents: Jn. Btta. Brosay and Louise Boudoin. Priest: Franco. Magnes.

508. MARIE ASELY RACHAL
(182) 30 January 1815, baptism of infant aged 7 months, legitimate daughter of Luis Rachal and Maria Luisa Chelecttre. Godparents: Alexi Cloutierre and Luz Rachal. Priest: Franco. Maynes.

509. JUAN BAUTISTA ANTY
(182) 31 January 1815, baptism of infant aged 1 year, 10 and a half months, legitimate son of Valery Anty and Maria Despasy Dervanne. Godparents: Miguel Dervanne and Arselina Cloutierre. Priest: Franco. Magnes.

510. MARIA LUISA AGATA VERCHER
(182) 31 January 1815, baptism of infant aged 3 months, legitimate daughter of Santiago Bercher and Maria Jacoba Froiasin Galien. Godparents: Benoni /Belony/ Bercher and Maria Adelayde Bercher. Priest: Franco. Magnes.

511. ATANASIO ALFRED BROSEAY /BROSSET/
(183) 31 January 1815, baptism of infant born 20 August 1814, legitimate son of Felipe Brosseaey and Maria Teresa Brebel /Brevel/. Godparents: Atanacio Brosseay and Janette Le

Brun. Priest: Franco. Magnes.

512. ATANASIO BONET
(183) 31 January 1815, baptism of infant aged 7 months, legitimate son of Juan Bautista Bonet and Froisina Denys. Godparents: Atanacio Denys and Maria Celesta Boudoin. Priest: Franco. Magnes.

513. JUAN PIERRE (PEDRO) LARNAUDIERRE
(183) 31 January 1815, baptism of infant aged 6 months, legitimate son of Juan Bautista Larenaudierre and Ma. Franca. Baudoin. Godparents: Pedro Boudoin and Ana Rovin. Priest: Franco. Magnes.

514. MICHEL ANTY
(184) 31 January 1815, baptism of infant aged 24 days, legitimate son of Silbestre Anty and Maria Boudoin. Godparents: Nicolas Gallien and Ana Rovin. Priest: Franco. Magnes.

515. ROSELIN OLIS ARNAUDIERRE /La Renaudiere/
(184) 1 Feb. 1815, baptism of infant aged 1 year, legitimate son of Felipe Arnaudierre and Denis de Eny?. Godparents: Jn Btta Anty and Rosalia Arnaudierre. Priest: Franco. Magnes.

516. JOSEPHA ONORÉ SARNAC /CHARNAC?/
(184) 1 February 1815, baptism of infant aged 1 month and 4 days, legitimate daughter of Francisco Sarniac and Magdalena Arnaudierre /La Renaudiere/. Godparents: Jose Sarniac and Louise Arnaudierre. Priest: Franco. Magnes.

517. CURANY POIRRIER
(185) 1 February 1815, baptism of infant born 22 December 1813, legitimate son of Francisco Poirrier and Teresa Lestasy /Thomassie/. Godparents: Jose Tomasy and Maria Francisca Tomasy. Priest: Franco. Magnes.

518. JUAN BTTA. POIRRIER
(185) 1 February 1815, baptism of infant born 4 July 1811, legitimate son of Francisco Poirrier and Teresa Lestasy Tomasi. Godparents: Cesaire Tomassy and Maria Rin /Reine/ Tomassy. Priest: Franco. Magnes.

519. MARIE ARSEN DERVANNE
(185) 1 February 1815, baptism of infant born 4 July 1814, legitimate daughter of Manuel Dervanne and Marguerite Deny. Godparents: Louis Frua /Geofrois/ Dupre and Francisca Brevel. Priest: Franco. Magnes.

520. LOUIS BALSEM GUEY*
(185) 1 February 1815 Baptism of infant born 27 June 1814, legitimate son of Simon Guey and Nanet Denay. Godparents:

Gradas Duprée and Marie Rovin. Priest: Franco. Magnes.
/*See note accompanying Entry 318/

521. FRANCISCO XAVIER DE JESUS ARRIOLA
(186) 15 February 1815, baptism of infant aged 2 months, legitimate son of Eduardo Ariola and Maria Candelaria Richal, Spaniards. Godparents: Marcelo Soto and Juana Peraut. Priest: Franco. Magnes.

522. MARIA MARTINA IGNACIA RIOS
(186) 15 February 1815, baptism of infant aged 15 days, legitimate daughter of Jose Ignacio Rios and Maria Paula Bargas. Godparents: Jose Cipriano de la Garza and Maria Damascena Varrera. All are Spaniards. Priest: Franco. Magnes.

523. MARIE MARCELITE CELESTE LAUVE
(186) 13 /sic/ February 1815, baptism of infant born 15 December 1814, legitimate daughter of Evariste Lauve and Euphroisine Celeste Brunet. Godparents: A^S Sompayrac, representing Maria Bienvenu Brunet, and Marie Marcelite Rouquier Cortes. Priest: Franco. Magnes.

524. JOSE FRANCISCO ALAMILLO
(187) 15 February 1815, baptism of infant aged 4 days, legitimate son of Juan Jose Alamillo and Maria Paul Pina. Godparents: Francisco Bienne /Vienne/ and Eloyse Brom. Priest: Franco. Magnes.

525. JOSE GUADALUPE SAMUEL
(187) 17 February 1815, baptism of infant aged 2 months and 6 days, legitimate son of Santiago Samuel and Maria Josefa Mora, Spaniards. Godparents: Miguel Delgado and Maria Candida Delgado. Priest: Franco. Magnes.

526. JOSE DE JESUS VIMENEZ (XIMINES?)
(187) 18 February 1815, baptism of infant aged 4 months, legitimate son of Francisco Vimenes and Maria Albina Posos. Godparents: Asencio Estrada and Maria del Rosario Dominguez. Priest: Franco. Magnes.

527. MARIA ASENCIA PINSOUNEAU
(188) 27 February 1815, baptism of infant aged 1 month and 5 days, legitimate son of Toussaint Pinsouneau and Maria Josefa Gagner. Godparents: Josef Gagner and Maria Teresa Davion. Priest: Franco. Magnes.

528. MARIE ODIS GUALLET /WALLET/
(188) 27 February 1815, baptism of infant born 4 October 1813, legitimate daughter of Luis Guallet and Maria Angela Gagne. Godparents: Julian Gagner and Maria Josefa Gagner. Priest: Franco. Magnes.

529. JUAN BAUTISTA /unknown/
(188) 5 March 1815, baptism of infant aged 2 /number is written, but then erased/ months and /blank/ days, legitimate son of /end of entry/.

530. ADELAYDE MARCELITE VERCHERE
(189) 15 March 1815, baptism of infant born 17 December 1814, legitimate daughter of Pierre Verchere and Marie Emely Slecttre /Chelette/. Godparents: Narciso Rachal and Susichet Rachal. Priest: Franco. Magnes.

531. FELICIANO VENJAMIN METOYEM
(189) 17 March 1815, baptism of infant born 9 June 1814, legitimate son of Francois Venjamin Metoyem and Marie Orror Lambret. Grandparents: Pierre Claut Tomas Metoyem, native of "Rosail" /La Rochelle/ in France and Terese Buard; Remy Lambret and Susana Proudhomme, all of this post. Godparents: his grandfather, Pierre Metoyem, and his grandmother, Susanne Proudhomme. Priest: Franco. Magnes.

532. MARIA DE LOS DOLORES DEL RIO
(189) 28 March 1815, baptism of infant aged 4 days, legitimate daughter of Anto. del Rio and Maria Jetrudis Carmona. Godparents: Antonio Polierre and Maria Jetrudis Alamillo. Priest: Franco. Magnes.

533. HENRY JOSEPH BIAYS LENNARD
(190) 2 April 1815, baptism of infant born 13 December 1814, legitimate son of Thomas M. Lennard and Adelayde Tauzin. Godparents: Louis Tauzin and Celeste Tauzin. Priest: Franco. Magnes.

534. JOSE PEDRO DOLORES LOPEZ
(190) 4 April 1815, baptism of infant aged 1 year, legitimate son of Jose Dionisio Lopez and Guadalupe Cordova. Godparents: Juan Soto and Jetrudis Hibarbo. Priest: Franco. Magnes.

535. MARIE FELICITÉE CHRISTIN
(190) 5 April 1815, baptism of infant aged 6 months, legitimate daughter of Remy Christin and Ludi Veve /Beebe/. Godparents: Jose Christin and Maria Josefa Delgado. Priest: Franco. Magnes.

536. JOSE ALEXOS ANTONIO DE LOS DOLORES GUTIERREZ
(191) 9 April 1815, baptism of infant born 10 July 1814, legitimate son of Bernardo Gutierrez and Maria Josefa Urive. Godparents: Francois Grappe and Marie Pelagie Grappe. Priest: Franco. Magnes.

537. MARIE FRANCOISE SELIMA LEVASEUR
(191) 9 April 1815, baptism of infant born 29 December 1814, legit-

imate daughter of François Levaseur and Marie Françoise Triches. Godparents: Louis Clauseu and Felicite Tris /Trichel_7. Priest: Franco. Magnes.

538. CIRIACO FONTENEAU
(191) 9 April 1815, baptism of infant born 17 October 1814, legitimate son of Ceser Fonteneau and Marie Felicite Laffit. Godparents: Jn. Btte. Trichel and Marie Pompose Laffit. Priest: Franco. Magnes.

539. FRANCOIS OCTAVE ROYER
(192) 9 April 1815, baptism of infant born 16 June 1814, legitimate son of Pierre Vital Royore, native of Beaumon, department of Vocluse /Vaucluse_7 en Provence, France, and of Felicite Elisabette Bavé, native of New Orleans. Grandparents: Pierre Royere and Françoise Aslau; Richard Bavé and Felicite Duverné. Godparents: François Saucier and Henriette Saucier. Priest: Franco. Magnes.

540. FRANCOIS FLEMING
(192) 9 April 1815, baptism of child born 5 May 1812, legitimate son of Bertelmis Fleming and Marie Terese Constance Fonteneau. Godparents: François Grape and Pelagie Grappe. Priest: Franco. Magnes.

541. EMILY LAIESA FLEMING
(192) 9 April 1815, baptism of infant born 26 August, 1814, legitimate daughter of Bertelmis Fleming and Marie Terese Constance Fonteneau. Godparents: Jn. Btte. Fonteneau and Marie Modeste Fonteneau. Priest: Franco. Magnes.

542. CARLOS WALTHER
(193) 13 April 1815, baptism of child born 16 June 1799, who has been instructed and examined in the Christian Doctrine and the Catholic, Apostolic, and Roman Religion, legitimate son of Federico Walther and Chareté Shilé. Godparents: Santiago Lacasse and Marie Louise Dupré. Priest: Franco. Magnes.

543. MARIE CELESTE WALTHER
(193) 13 April 1815, baptism of child aged 13 years, who has been examined in Christian Doctrine and the Catholic, Apostolic, and Roman Religion, legitimate daughter of Federico Walthere and Charité Shilé. Godparents: Santiago LaCasse and Marianne Dupré. Priest: Franco. Magnes.

544. MARIE ELAYSA BULLET
(193) 17 April 1815, baptism of child born 25 December,

1812, legitimate daughter of Benjamin Bullet and
Marie Ferguson. Godparents: D. McClellan and
Anne Keisem. Priest: Franco. Magnes.

545. MARCELITE LOUCIANA BULLET
(194) 17 April 1815, baptism of infant born 25 October,
1813, legitimate duaghter of Benjamin Bullet and
Marie Ferguson. Godparents: James Smith and Marcelite Cortes. Priest: Franco. Magnes.

546. MARIA GENOBEVA CELESTE MEDRANO
(194) 17 April 1815, baptism of infant aged 1 month,
legitimate daughter of Jose Maria Medrano and Maria
Eudona Cortinas. Godparents: Enry Tris /Trichel7
and Genoveva Ris. Priest: Franco. Magnes.

547. CELESTIN AGAPITO BERNARD
(194) 24 April 1815, baptism of infant aged 1 month, legitimate son of Celestin Bernard and Marie Celeste
Tris /Trichel7. Godparents: Andre Bernard and
Marie Celeste Bourdeleau. Priest: Franco. Magnes.

548. BERNARD THEOFILE HENRY HERTZOG
(195) 29 April 1815, baptism of infant born 15 August
1814, legitimate son of Jn. Fs. Hertzog and Marianne Proudhomme. Grandparents: Henry Mathieu Hertzog, native of Francfort on the Maine and Marie
Jeanne Lartigue, native of Bordeaux; Antonio Proudhomme and Marie Lambre, natives of this parish.
Godparents: Bernard Teofile Lafont and Susanna
Proudhomme. Priest: Franco. Magnes.

549. MARIA MAGDALENA ALEXANDRA MAY
(195) 1 May 1815, baptism of infant born 18 January 1815,
natural daughter of Juana Baptista May. Godparents:
James Smith and Maria Magdalena Garo. Priest:
Franco. Magnes.

550. LOUIS SOCIER
(195) 1 May 1815, baptism of infant born 16 December
1814, legitimate son of Louis Socier and Marie Du
Rosé. Godparents: Beltrand Plesans, and Marie
Louise Victoire Socier. Priest: Franco. Magnes.

551. JOSE MARIA MALLOUD
(196) 4 May 1815, baptism of infant born 12 February
1815, legitimate son of Lorenzo Malloud and Marguerite Duval. Godparents: Jose Maria Carrier
and Maria Luisa Victoria Charier. Priest: Franco.
Magnes.

552. JOSE BENIGNO SANTOS
(196) 6 May 1815, baptism of infant born 13 February 1815, legitimate son of Manuel Santos and Maria Guadalupe Lucia Chirino. Godparents: Jose Encarnacion Chirino and Maria Candida Delgado. Priest: Franco. Magnes.

553. SANTIAGO OCONÓ [O'CONNOR]
(196) 7 May 1815, baptism of infant aged 13 months, legitimate son of Henry Ocono and Hister Hoffman. Godparents: Pierre David Cailleu Lafontaine and Famy Mekam. Priest: Franco. Magnes.

554. CARLOS DAVID YEWELL RICHEY
(197) 7 May 1815, baptism of child aged 3 years, legitimate son of Ben Richey and Hister Hoffman. Godparents: Carlos Slocum and Margarita Robertson. Priest: Franco. Magnes.

555. JUAN BAUTISTA DESIR LENOIR
(197) 13 May 1815, baptism of infant born 17 April 1814, legitimate son of Antonio Lenoir and Maria Denis Dervan, natives of this parish. Godparents: Jn. Btte. Dervan and Jeanne Peraut. Priest: Franco. Magnes.

556. ALEXOS LY [LEE]
(197) 4 June 1815, baptism of child aged 5 years, legitimate son of Cristofor Ly and Maria Louise Esprink. Godparents: Bernard Guisarnac and Maria Louise Richal. Priest: Franco. Magnes.

557. BENJAMIN BAYLES
(197) 4 June 1815, baptism of infant of 2 months, legitimate son of Benjamin Bayles and Marie Louise Bodo. Godparents: Bernardo Guisarnac and Ana Maria Ly. Priest: Franco. Magnes.

558. MARIE LY [LEE]
(198) 4 June 1815, baptism of child of 9 years, legitimate daughter of Cristofo Ly and Maria Louise Esprink. Godparents: Eduardo Roverson and Maria Louise Bodo. Priest: Franco. Magnes.

559. MARIE ENCARNATION CRUZ
(198) 11 June 1815, baptism of infant born "25 of the year 1814," legitimate daughter of Pedro Cruz and Juana Maria Amador, Spaniards. Godparents: Jn. Btte. Lattierre and Catarina Brosser. Priest: Franco. Magnes.

560. MARIE SOPHY BROSSET
(198) 11 June 1815, baptism of infant born 15 of _____
/blank/, 1813, legitimate daughter of Philipe Brosset and Marie Terese Vrevel /Brevel/. Godparents: Jn. Btte. Anty, Jr. and Marie Cyprianne Dervanne. Priest: Franco. Magnes.

561. JN. BTTE. BENJAMIN BOUDOIN
(198) 11 June 1815, baptism of infant born 3 November 1814, legitimate son of Nicolas Boudoin and Marie Malbere. Godparents: Jn. Btte. /blank/ and Marie Boudoin. Priest: Franco. Magnes.

562. MARIE PERIN ROVALY /RABALAIS/
(199) 12 June 1815, baptism of infant born 1 May 1813, legitimate daughter of Jose Rovaly and Marianne Boudoin /Bontemps/. Godparents: Vital Arbau and Marie Rose Forg. Priest: Franco. Magnes.

563. CESERE ABBLÉE BROSÉE
(199) 12 June 1815, baptism of infant born 13 June 1814, legitimate son of Cesere Brossee and Marie Louise LeCour. Godparents: Louis Cesere /Le Court/ and Marie Celesy Brossée. Priest: Franco. Magnes.

564. GASPAR LE COUR /LA COUR/
(199) 12 June 1815, baptism of infant born 25 October, 1813, legitimate son of Gaspar LeCour and Maria Felicite Brevel. Godparents: Michel Dervanne and Marie Denis Clouttiere. Priest: Franco. Magnes.

565. MARIE DAMASCENNE GALLIEN
(199) 12 June 1815, baptism of infant born 25 January 1815, legitimate daughter of Louis Gallien and Marie Celeste Anty. Godparents: Louis Manuel Gallien and Maria Orory /Aurora/ Anty. Priest: Franco. Magnes.

566. JOSE MARZELO COUTY
(200) 13 June 1815, baptism of child born 16 March 1810, legitimate son of Juan Paul Couty and Marie Josephe Torres. Godparents: Jacobo St. Andres and Marie Adelayde Pastio. Priest: Franco. Magnes.

567. MARIE DAMASCENA COUTY
(200) 13 June 1815, baptism of infant aged 3 years, legitimate daughter of Jean Paul Couty and Marie Joseph Torres. Godparents: Pierre Michel Sarry /Michel dit Zoriche/ and Marie Rose Michel Sarry. Priest: Franco. Magnes.

568. MARIE *SEOSY COUTY /*JESSY?7
(200) 13 June 1815, baptism of infant aged 1 year, legitimate daughter of Jean Paul Couty and Marie Josefa Torres. Godparents: Pierre Michel Sory /Michel dit Zoriche7 and Maria Magdalena Lavery. Priest: Franco. Magnes.

569. JEAN BTTE. WALLET
(200) 13 June 1815, baptism of child born 31 March 1811, legitimate son of Charles Wallet and Maria Antonia Flores. Godparents: Pierre Nolasco de Porcuna and Maria Magdalena Lavery. Priest: Franco. Magnes.

570. MARCELINA DE JESUS VOLTARIS
(201) 16 June 1815, baptism of infant aged 8 days, natural daughter of Eligio Voltaris and Encarnacion Flores. Godparents: Jose Teal and Maria Soto. Priest: Franco. Magnes.

571. JOSE FRANCO. YDALGO
(201) 29 June 1815, baptism of infant aged 7 months, legitimate son of Franco. Ydalgo and Maria Isavel Corona. Godparents: Jose Roblai and Maria Josefa de Landa. Priest: Franco. Magnes.

572. ANDRES SNT. CHARMENT /ST. GERMAINE7
(201) 30 June 1815, baptism of infant aged 18 days, legitimate son of Franco. San Charment and Ma. Drienne Ste. Andre. Godparents: Andres Ste. Andre and Ma. Luisa Lemoin. Priest: Franco. Magnes.

573. FRANCO. BOUDRY
(201) 30 June 1815, baptism of child aged 4 years, legitimate son of Franco. Boudry and Ma. Victoria Ste. Andre. Godparents: Alexim /Onesime called "Lezime"7 Ste. Andre and Celin Dupre. Priest: Franco. Manges.

574. MARIA ZEPHALY BOUDRY
(202) 30 June 1815, baptism of infant aged 1½ years, legitimate daughter of Franco. Boudry and Ma. Victoria Ste. Andre. Godparents: Juan Bauptista Cloutierre and Ma. Luis Ste. Andre. Priest: Franco. Magnes.

575. JUAN BAPTISTA FEDERIQ WALTEHER
(202) 30 June 1815, baptism of child aged 9 years, legitimate son of Fred. Walteher and Charite Chifilef. Godparents: Atanasio Dupre and Mariana Dupre. Priest: Franco. Magnes.

576. ADOULFO DUPREZ
(202) 30 June 1815, baptism of child of 3 years, legitimate son of Atanacio Dupre and Secilia Le=cour. Godparents: Atanacio Dupre and Celin Dupre. Priest: Franco. Magnes.

577. SILBESTRE LEMOINE
(202- 30 June 1815, baptism of infant born 17 August 1814,
203) legitimate son of Anto. Lemoin and Xambiez Velgarda /Bellegarde/. Godparents: Anto. Rachal and Ma. Luisa Lemoin. Priest: Franco. Magnes.

578. MARIA AIMÉE LEMOIN
(203) 30 June 1815, baptism of child born 17 January 1812, legitimate daughter of Anto. Lemoin and Xambiez Velgarda /Bellegarde/. Godparents: Anto. Lemoin, her brother, and Ma. Rosa Richel. Priest: Franco. Magnes.

579. MAGDALENA GILLARD
(203) 1 July 1815, baptism of infant born 2 February 1813, legitimate daughter of Joseph Gillard and Petronile Le=Cour. Grandparents: Joseph Gillard, native of Croisie in France, Department of Nantes, and Margarita Sarde, native of Orleans; Nicola Le=Cour, native of Pointe Coupée and Magdalena Arman, native of "Luis Bourd" /Louisburg, Nova Scotia/. Godparents: Leandro Le=Cour and Ma. Luisa Gillard. Priest: Franco. Magnes.

580. MARGARITA GILLARD
(203- 1 July 1815, baptism of infant born 23 December
204) 1814, legitimate daughter of José Gillard and Petronile Le=Cour. Grandparents: Joseph Gillard, native of Croisie in France, Department of Nantes, and Margarita Sarde, native of Orleans; Nicolas Le=Cour, native of Pointe Coupée and Magdalena Arma, native of Luis-Bourd /Louisburg, Nova Scotia/. Priest: Franco. Magnes.

581. MAGDALENA GILLARD
(204) 1 July 1815, baptism of child born 15 January 1811, legitimate daughter of Juan Bautista Gillard and Cesilia La=Cour. Grandparents: "same as those above." Godparents: Jose Gillard and Petronila La=Cour. Priest: Franco. Magnes.

582. JUAN BAPTISTA GILLARD
(204) 1 July 1815, baptism of infant born 23 February 1814, legitimate son of Juan Baptista Gillard and Secilia La=Cour. Grandparents: "Same as those

above." Godparents: Juan Maria La=Cour and Josefina Gillard. Priest: Franco. Magnes.

583. **JUAN MARIA LACOUR**
(204) 1 July 1815, baptism of child born 15 October 1811, legitimate son of Leandro La=Cour and Ma. Luisa Gillard. Grandparents: Nicolas La=Cour, native of Pointe Coupée and Magdalena Arman, native of Luis-bourd /Louisburg, Nova Scotia/, Canada; Jose Gillard, native of Croyine in France, Department of Nantes and Margarita Sarde, native of Orleans. Godparents: Juan Maria Le=Cour and Secilia Le=Cour. Priest: Franco. Magnes.

584. **MA. LUISA LACOUR**
(205) 1 July 1815, baptism of infant born 6 February 1814, legitimate daughter of Leandro La=Cour and Ma. Luisa Gillard. Grandparents: "Same as those above." Godparents: Juan Baptista Gillard and Petronila La=Cour. Priest: Franco. Magnes.

585. **MARGARITA LACOUR**
(205) 1 July 1815, baptism of infant born 15 May 1815, legitimate daughter of Leandro La=Cour and Ma. Luisa Gillard. Grandparents: "Same as those above." Godparents: Agustin Ballou /Baillio/ and Felonie Lesard. Priest: Franco. Magnes.

586. **JUAN MA. LACOUR**
(205) 1 July 1815, baptism of infant born 5 March 1814, legitimate son of Juan Ma. La=Cour and Josefina Gillard. Grandparents: "Same as those of his brother Leandro." Godparents: Leandro La=Cour and Ma. Luisa Gillard. Priest: Franco. Magnes.

587. **MARIA LAYSA LANGOIS**
(206) 2 July 1815, baptism of infant born 1 March 1815, legitimate daughter of Agustin Langois and Ma. Selene /Celeste/ Vercher /Verger/. Godparents: Jose Lattiere, Jr. and Ma. Asely Langois. Priest: Franco. Magnes.

588. NOTE BY F. MAYNES: The following white children
(206) were baptized at "Coutey" /Cotile/ and at Rapides while on visit there with the order and permission of the Vicar General of Louisiana, residing in New Orleans:

589. **DENIS ESLECT /CHELETTE/**
(206) 3 July 1815, baptism of child born 11 February 1812, legitimate son by marriage of Vernave

/Bernabé/ Eslect and Ma. Josefa Gonet of Cotile.
Godparents: Agustin Bailio and Ma. Elenna Eslect.
Priest: Franco. Magnes.

590. MIGUEL NEGLIGEN /MC GLOTHEN/
(206) 3 July 1815, baptism of child born 10 January 1812,
"legitimate son by contract"* of Moris Megligen and
Franca. Eslect /Chelette/. Godparents: Joseph
Eslect and Ma. Elenne Eslect, all of Cotile.
Priest: Franco. Magnes.

*Note the wording of this entry as compared to
preceding entry which states "legitimate son by
MARRIAGE." The McGlothen-Eslect marriage was a
CIVIL one, not recognized by the church, according to the terminology used. However, no civil
marriage contract is on file for the couple at
Natchitoches. Possibly it occurred at the post
of Rapides, whose records for this period have
been destroyed.

591. JOSEPH GREGORIO NEGLIGEN /MC GLOTHEN/
(207) 3 July 1815, baptism of child born 12 March 1814,
legitimate son by contract* of Moris Megligen and
Franca. Eslect. Godparents: Junian de la Garza
and Ma. Joseph Gonet, all of Cotile. Priest:
Franco. Magnes.   *See above note.

592. MARIA NANSI CONELTY /QUINNELTY/
(207) 3 July 1815, baptism of child born 10 January 1815,
legitimate daughter by marriage of Denis Conelty
and Ma. Elenna Eslect /Chelette/. Godparents:
Juan Luis Baillio and Elena Baillio, habitants of
Cotile. Priest: Franco. Magnes.

593. MARIA ROSA SARVOUNAU (CHARBAUNAU)*
(207) 3 July 1815, baptism of infant born 20 January,
1814, "legitimate daughter by contract"** of
Joseph Luis Sarvounau and Ma. Balty Dubois. Godparents: Eduardo Dubois and Ma. Elenna Eslect
/Chelette/, habitants of the village of the Apalaches. Priest: Frnaco. Magnes.

*This name was originally written as SArvounau in
both margin and text. The marginal notation has
been changed to CHARbounau.

**See explanatory note accompanying Entry 590.

594. JOSEPH LUIS CHARBONEAU
(207- 3 July 1815, baptism of child born 25 January 1812,
208) "legitimate son by contract** of Jose Luis Char-

bounau and Ma. Balty Dubois. Godparents: Jose Miguel Charvounau and Ma. Oror /Aurore/ Dubois, habitants of the village of the Apalaches. Priest: Franco. Magnes.

595. MARIA CLARA* ESLECT /CHELETTE/
(208) 3 July 1815, baptism of infant born 28 February, 1815, natural daughter of Maria Arsen Eslect. Godparents: Juan Baptista Balery /Valery/ and Ma. Barbara Josefa Barranco /Varangue/.

*This infant used the name Clarisse as an adult. Family tradition, as later related by her son Napoleon Basco, holds that Clarisse's father was one Frank O'Neal.

596. URSULA DE LOUEX /DE LOUCHE/
(208) 3 July 1815, baptism of infant born 23 April 1813, natural daughter of Felicite de Louex. Godparents: Julien de Louex and Nanet de Loux. Priest: Franco. Magnes.

597. MARIANNE BAILLIO
(209) 3 July 1815, baptism of infant born 14 November, 1814, legitimate daughter of Agustin Bailliou and Felonis Lexar /Layssard/. Godparents: Juan Louis Bailliou and Elenné Bailliou, residents of Cotile. Priest: Franco. Magnes.

598. MARIA ASCENCION VALLERY
(209) 3 July 1815, baptism of child born 1 January 1813,* legitimate daughter of Juan Baptista Valery and Maria Ascencion de Torres, residents of the Apalache Village. Godparents: Juan Baptista Gillard and Cesilia LaCour. Priest: Franco. Magnes.

*The birthdates of Maria Ascencion and her brother Antonio are written very legibly on the original documents and the dates are exactly as they appear in these abstracts. However, one is obviously in error.

599. ANTONIO VALERY
(209) 3 July 1815, baptism of child born 22 May 1813* legitimate son of Juan Baptista Balery and Maria Ascencion Torres, residents of the Apalache Village. Godparents: Antonio Fernandez and Felonis Lexar /Layssard/. Priest: Franco. Magnes.

*See note accompanying previous entry.

600. MARIA REINE TORRES
(209) 3 July 1815, baptism of child born 7 January 1812,

legitimate daughter of Jose Maria Torres and Susanne Valery, residents of the Apalache Village. Godparents: Juan Andres and Felonis Lexar /Layssard7. Priest: Franco. Magnes.

601. MARCELINA TORRES
(210) 3 July 1815, baptism of infant of 1 year and 4 months, legitimate daughter of Jose Maria Torres and Susanne Valery. Godparents: Jose Lattier and Elenna Bailliou. Priest: Franco. Magnes.

602. FELONIS BORNÉ
(210) 3 July 1815, baptism at Cotile of a child of 14 years, legitimate daughter of Juan Borné and Lucia Ebrom /?LeBrun7. Godparents: Agustin Bailliou and Felonis de Lexar /Layssard7. Priest: Franco. Magnes.

603. MARIE BORNÉE
(210) 3 July 1815, baptism at Cotile of child of 12 years, legitimate daughter of Juan Bornée and Lucia E Brom /?LeBrun7. Godparents: Louis Baillio and Elenne Baillio. Priest: Franco. Magnes.

604. JUILINO ESCOFIE
(210) 3 July 1815, baptism at Cotile of child of 14 years, legitimate son of Juan Francois Escofie and Marie Francoise Lamot. Godparents: Alexandro Enery and Elenne Baillio. Priest: Franco. Magnes.

605. MARCELA RACHAL
(210) 3 July 1815, baptism at Cotile of infant born 8 July 1813, "legitimate daughter by contract"* of Francois Rachal and Marie Povarrier /Poirrier7. Godparents: Remy Rachal and Anne Pouarrier. Priest: Franco. Magnes.

*See note accompanying Entry 590.

606. MARIE FELESY LABERRY /LAPRERY -- LA PRAIRIE7*
(211) 3 July 1815, baptism at Cotile of child born 15 December 1812, natural daughter of Margarita Laprery*. Godparents: Jose Lattierre and Marie Francoise Deloux. Priest: Franco. Magnes.

*This name originally appeared in both margin and text as Laprery. The marginal note was changed, apparently in same ink, to Laberry.

607. MARIA ADELINE BROM
(211) 5 July 1815, baptism at Rapides of infant born 22 November 1814, legitimate daughter of John

Brom and Clere Lesar /Layssard/. Godparents: Louis Baillio and Delin Lesar. Priest: Franco. Magnes.

608. JULIEM GRADNER
(211) 5 July 1815, baptism at Rapides of infant born /Illegible day/ of April 1814, legitimate son of Santiago Gradner and Artemise Andreson, spouses by contract*. Godparents: George Andreson and Delsir Bolom Lesar /Layssard/. Priest: Franco. Magnes.

*See note accompanying Entry 590.

609. MARIA ANTONIO EMILY ALVARADO
(211- 5 July 1815, baptism at Rapides of infant aged "1
212) year and months", legitimate daughter of marriage of Mateo Albarado and Cataranina de Cor. Godparents: Silvesto Bailio and Emily LaCour. Priest: Franco. Magnes.

610. MARIE ADELLE BAILLIO
(212) 5 July 1815, baptism at Rapides of infant born 15 February 1814, natural daughter* of Louis Bailio and Marie Constans Lesar /Leyssard/. Godparents: Julien Escophiée and Amely Bailio. Priest: Franco. Magnes.

*Entry originally read "legitimate daughter" but this was erased and the word "natural" inserted. by Father Magnes.

611. JUAN GUILSCEM /?WILSON/
(212) 5 July 1815, baptism at Rapides of infant born 31 May 1815, legitimate son of Juan Guilscem and Nanet Hodman, spouses by contract.* Godparents: Rovert Frayar and Barvaire /Barbary/ Hodman. Priest: Franco. Magnes.

*See note accompanying Entry 590.

612. YSABEL HUPER
(212) 5 July 1815, baptism at Rapides of infant born 23 April 1814, natural daughter of Thomas Huper and Celeste Lesar /Layssard/. Godparents: Louis Bailio and Louise Lesar. Priest: Franco. Magnes.

613. NICOLAS VAILAIN
(212- 5 July 1815, baptism of infant born 30 March 1814,
213) legitimate son of Nicolas Vailaim and Celeste Bailio. Godparents: Pierre Bailio and Emery LaCour, maternal grandparents of the infant. Priest: Franco. Magnes.

614. ROSE POUARRET /POIRRIER/
(213) 5 July 1815, baptism at Rapides of infant born 30

August 1814, natural daughter of Joseph Pouarret and Rosaly Laprery. Godparents: Pierre Bailio and M/ar/ianne. Pouarret. Priest: Franco. Magnes.

615. JEANN TABITHA WAS BROM
(213) 5 July 1815, baptism at Rapides of infant born 8 July 1814, legitimate daughter by marriage of Louis Was Brom and Maria Jetrudis Soli Bellas. Godparents: R. C. Cuny and Tabitha, his wife. Priest: Francisco Magnes.

616. MARIE LOUISE WAS BROM
(213) 5 July 1815, baptism at Rapides of infant born 24 January 1813, legitimate daughter by marriage of Estevan Louis Was Brom and Marie Jetrudis Soli Bellas. Godparents: Estevan Cuny and Editha /No last name -- apparently the wife of Cuny/. Priest: Franco. Magnes.

617. MARIE JOSEPHINE POUARRET /POIRRIER/
(213) 5 July 1815, baptism at Rapides of infant born 14 September 1814, natural daughter of Joseph Pouarret and Marie Guet. Godparents: Andres Sanson and Josephin Remira. Priest: Franco. Magnes.

618. ISABEL WELLS
(214) 5 July 1815, baptism of child of 10 years, at Rapides, legitimate daughter of Oliviet Wells and Betsy Calvit. Godparents: Jose Calvit and Amely Bailio. Priest: Franco. Magnes.

619. CLARA GUET
(214) 5 July 1815, baptism at Rapides of child of 12 years, legitimate daughter by contract of Louis Guet and Marie Magdalenne Cruz. Godparents: Andres Renua and Clara LaCour. Priest: Franco. Magnes.

620. LOUIS GUET
(214) 5 July 1815, baptism at Rapides of child aged 5* years, legitimate son by contract of Louis Guet and Maria Madalenne Cruz. Godparents: Louis Bailio and Chatalina Renua. Priest: Franco. Magnes.

*See note accompanying Entry 622.

621. MARIE DENIS GUET
(214) 5 July 1815, baptism of child aged 6 years, legitimate daughter by contract of Louis Guet and Maria Madalenne Cruz. Godparents: Andres Sansom and Francisca Renua. Godparents: Franco. Magnes.

622. MARGARITA GUET
(214) 5 July 1815, baptism of child of 5* years, legiti-

mate daughter by contract of Louis Guet and Maria Madalenne Cruz. Godparents: Jean Kerkly and Josephin Renua. Priest: Franco. Magnes.

*In this entry and in entry 620, the words "5 years" have been very legibly written by Father Maynes. Apparently, one of these was written in error or else Margarita and Louis were twins.

623. APOLONIO GUET
(215) 5 July 1815, baptism of child of 9 years, legitimate child by contract of Louis Guet and Maria Madalenne Cruz. Godparents: Francois Guet and Amely Bailio. Priest: Franco. Magnes. At Rapides.

624. MARIE FELICITE DUVIL*
(215) 5 July 1815, baptism of infant of 20 months, legitimate daughter of Balentin Duvil and Margarite Devil, married by the church. Godparents: Juan Btte. Belgar and Felicite Chanot. Priest: Franco Magnes. At Rapides.

*No family name was originally entered in the margin for this child, only in the text. At a later date, someone with similar ink but a different handwriting, inserted in the margin what appears to the the surname David. In the text the names Duvil and Devil appear very legibly as shown in the above abstract.

625. CAROLINE LAMOT
(215) 6 July 1815, baptism of child born 14 March 1808, legitimate daughter of Policarpio Lamot and Editha Wells. Godparents: Santiago Lamot and Maria Franca. LeDoux. Priest: Franco. Magnes. At Rapides.

626. BELONY LAMOT
(215) 6 July 1815, baptism of child born 17 April, 1812, legitimate son by marriage of Policarpio Lamot and Editha Wells. Godparents: Cesar Cuny and Emely Ledoux. Priest: Franco. Magnes. At Rapides.

627. SAMUEL LAMOT
(215) 6 July 1815, baptism of child at Rapides, born 15 February 1810, legitimate son by marriage of Policarpio Lamot and Editha Wells. Godparents: Samuel Cuny and Signy Wells. Priest: Franco. Magnes.

628. MARIE DAGUES LAMOT
(216) 6 July 1815, baptism at Rapides of child born 14 April 1814, legitimate daughter by marriage of

Policarpio Lamot and Editha Wells. Godparents: Estivin Cuny and Sophar Lamot. Priest: Franco Magnes.

629. ESTEVAN CRUZ
(216) 6 July 1815, baptism of child "of year and a half" legitimate son by contract of Joseph Cruz and Marie Laprery. Godparents: Agusto Onil and Susanne Rosée. Priest: Franco. Magnes. At Rapides.

630. MARIE CELESTE CRUZ
(216) 6 July 1815, baptism of child aged 3 years, legitimate daughter of Joseph Cruz and Maria Laprery. Godparents: Jn. Btte. Velgar /Bellegarde/, Jr., and Celeste Cruz. Priest: Franco. Magnes. At Rapides.

631. FELIPE CRUZ
(216) 6 July 1815, baptism at Rapides of child of 1 year, legitimate son by contract of Joseph Cruz and Marie Laprery. Godparents: Jacobo Col and Marie Chaconil /?O'Neal?/. Priest: Franco. Magnes.

632. THOMAS VELGARA /BELLEGARDE/
(216) 6 July 1815, baptism of infant of 16 months, legitimate son of Jn. Btte. Velgara and Marie Devil, married in the church. Godparents: Louis Hodman and Louise LePrery. Priest: Franco. Magnes. At Rapides.

633. AGUSTO ONIL
(217) 6 July 1815, baptism of child at Rapides, 11 mos., legitimate son by contract of Agusto Onil and Dorotee Velgara /Bellegarde/. Godparents: Jn Bte Chanot and Dolory Velgara. Priest: Franco Magnes.

634. FRANCOIS BLONDE
(217) 6 July 1815, baptism of child, at Rapides, born 4 April 1815, legitimate son by contract of Guillom Blonde and Elisabet Hodman. Godparents: Jn. Btte. Valery and Marie Hodman. Priest: Franco. Magnes.

635. MANUEL SAMUEL CHAQUET
(217) 6 July 1815, baptism at Rapides of child of 2 years and 5 months, legitimate son by contract of Robin Chaguet and Marianne Pourrait /Poirrier/. Godparents: Apolinario Bailio and Josephine Renuat. Priest: Franco. Magnes.

636. ROVIN CHAQUET
(217) 6 July 1815, baptism at Rapides of child of 3

months, legitimate son by contract of Robin Chaguet and Marianne Pourrait /Poirrier/. Godparents: Agusto Larnodierre and Marie Larnodiere. Priest: Franco. Magnes.

637. MARIE DILIA MILLAR
(217) 7 July 1815, baptism at Rapides of infant born 15 March 1814, legitimate daughter of Guillermo Millar and Ursula Meullion. Godparents: Emmanuel Millar and Louise Millar. Priest: Franco. Magnes.

638. MARIE JEANNE LAPRERY
(218) 7 July 1815, baptism of infant aged 1 year and 9 months, legitimate daughter by marriage of Michel Laprery and Magdalene Rogé. Godparents: Joseph Pouarret /Poirrier/ and Emery LeDoux. Priest: Franco. Magnes.   At Rapides.

639. EVARISTE ARCHINARD
(218) 9 July 1815, baptism at Rapides of child born 10 February 1809, legitimate son of Jeann Archinard and Louise Rapicault. Godparents: Cesar Archinard and Maria Clara LaCour. Priest: Franco. Magnes.

640. SAMUEL ARCHINARD
(218) 9 July 1815, baptism at Rapides of child born 10 August 1811, legitimate son of Jeann Archinard and Louise Rapicault. Godparents: Francois Archinard and Melizet Le Doux. Priest: Franco. Magnes.

641. MARIE DESIRÉE ARCHINARD
(218) 9 July 1815, baptism of infant born 10 September 1814, legitimate daughter of Jeann Archinard and Louise Rapicault. Godparents: Rosemond Archinard and Lolete Le Doux. Priest: Franco. Magnes.
At Rapides.

642. NOTE BY FRANCISCO MAYNES: The following Indians
(219) were baptized at the Apalache village, while on visit there with the order and permission of the Vicar General of Louisiana, residing at New Orleans:

643. FRANCOIS FORTUNE
(219) 2 July 1815, baptism at Apalache of an infant of 4 years, natural son of Chen /Etienne/ and Marianne. Godparents: Alexandro and Catalina. Priest: Franco. Magnes.

644. FRANCOIS
(219) 2 July 1815, baptism at Apalache of a child of 7

years, natural son of Echem /Etienne/ and Marianne. Godparents: Jn Btte. Valery and Victoria. Priest: Franco. Magnes.

645. ETIENNE
(219) 2 July 1815, baptism at Apalache of child of 2 years, natural son of Echem /Etienne/ and Marianne. Godparents: Jose Lattierre and Ascension Torres. Priest: Franco. Magnes.

646. JOSE ASENOR
(219) 2 July 1815, baptism at Apalache of child of 5 years, natural son of Echem /Etienne/ and Marianne. Godparents: Asenor and Petronila Torres. Priest: Franco. Magnes.

647. CRISOSTOMO
(219) 2 July 1815, baptism at Apalache of child of 3 years, natural son of Josph. Jouafa and Francisca. Godparents: Jn Btte. Valery, Jr. and Marie Denis Valery. Priest: Franco. Magnes.

648. CARLOS
(219) 2 July 1815, baptism at Apalache of child of 18 months, natural son of Joseph Joufa and Francisca. Godparents: Carlos Michel and Rose Eslecctre /Chelette/. Priest: Franco. Magnes.

649. JN. BTTE.
(220) 2 July 1815, baptism at Apalache of child of 3 years, natural son of Joseph Jouafa and Francoise. Godparents: Louis Bailio and Juana Paurriere. Priest: Franco. Magnes.

650. JEANN PIERRE
(220) 2 July 1815, baptism at Apalache of child of 7 years, natural son of Joseph Jouafa and Francoise. Godparents: Agusto Bailio and Bersy Pouarret /Poirrier/. Priest: Franco. Magnes.

651. MARIE JEANNE /ACOYE/
(220) 2 July 1815, baptism at Apalache of child of 7 years, natural daughter of Louis Acoye and Felicite. Godparents: Pierre Valery and Felicité De Loux. Priest: Franco. Magnes.

652. LORENZO ACOYE
(220) 2 July 1815, baptism at Apalache of child of 3 years, natural son of Louis Acoye and Felicite. Godparents: Jn. Btte. Valery and Ascension Torres. Priest; Franco. Magnes.

653. JOSEPH GRAHAM
(220) 2 July 1815, baptism at Apalache of child of 3
years, natural son of Antonio Charlé and Margarite
Nicolase. Godparents: Thomas Graham and Marianne
Dupre. Priest: Franco. Magnes.

654. JOSEPH ANTONIO
(220) 2 July 1815, baptism at Apalache of child of 1
year, natural son of Antonio Charle and Margarite
Nicolas, Indians. Godparents: Antonio Fernandez
and Barvara Valery. Priest: Franco. Magnes.

655. MARIE CELESTE
(221) 2 July 1815, baptism at Apalache of child of 3
years, natural daughter of Joseph Folocque and Marie Louise Nicolas, Indians. Godparents: Louis
Baillio and Susanne Solmon. Priest: Franco.
Magnes.

656. FRANCOIS PANCHO
(221) 2 July 1815, baptism at Apalache of child of 2
years, natural son of Louis Nicolas and Marie,
Indian. Godparents: Pierre Valery and Susanne
Solomon. Priest: Franco. Magnes.

657. JOSEPH /LAYSSARD/
(221) 2 July 1815, baptism at Apalache of child of 2
years, natural son of Andres Marafret /Layssard/
and Nanet, Indian. Godparents: Jose Maria Torres
and Felicite De Loux. Priest: Franco. Magnes.

658. MANUEL
(221) 2 July 1815, baptism at Apalache of child of 3
years, natural son of Joseph and Catarine Thomas,
Indians. Godparents: Marcelo Valery and Josephe
Thomas. Priest: Franco. Magnes.

659. ANTONIO FONTENEAU
(221) 2 July 1815, baptism at Apalache of child of 1½
years, natural son of Joseph and Chatarine Thomas,
Indians. Godparents: Louis Bailio and Marie
Thomas. Priest: Franco. Magnes.

660. ROSE
(221) 2 July 1815, baptism at Apalache of child of 2
years, natural daughter of Crisostome and Margarite Btte., Indians. Godparents: Jose Ma. Torres
and Felicite De Loux. Priest: Franco. Magnes.

661. CARLOS
(221) 2 July 1815, baptism at Apalache of child of 3

years, natural son of Marté and Ma. Concepcion, Indians. Godparents: Carlos Nicolas and Tonton Celestin. Priest: Franco. Magnes.

662. ESTEVAN
(222) 2 July 1815, baptism at Apalache of child of 6 months, natural son of Marté and Ma. Concepcn. Godparents: Echén and Susanne Solmon. Priest: Franco. Magnes.

663. CRISOSTOMO
(222) 2 July 1815, baptism at Apalache of child of 3 years, natural son of Anto. Btte. and Louise Torro, Indians. Godparents: Crisostomo and Margarite Btte. Priest: Franco. Magnes.

664. MARIE ROSE
(222) 2 July 1815, baptism at Apalache of child of 1 year, natural daughter of Antonio Btte. and Louise Toro. Godparents: Joseph Lorenzo Torres and Me. Rose Torres. Priest: Franco. Magnes.

665. MARIE CELESTE
(222) 2 July 1815, baptism at Apalache of child of 9 years, natural daughter of Charlo and Souly, Indians. Godparents: Alexandro and Victoria Crisostomo. Priest: Franco. Magnes.

666. ATANASIO PALIER
(222) 2 July 1815, baptism at Apalache of child of 12 years, the natural son of Carlo and Souly, Indians. Godparents: Atanasio Guany and Francisca Nicolas. Priest: Franco. Magnes.

667. MARIE SEPHALY
(222) 2 July 1815, baptism at Apalache of child of 3 years, natural daughter of Charlo and Souly, Indians. Godparents: Atanasio Guany and Francisca Nicolas. Priest: Franco. Magnes.

668. FRANCOIS
(222) 2 July 1815, baptism at Apalache of child of 5 years, natural son of Carlo and Souly, Indians. Godparents: Louis and Margarite Nicolas. Priest: Franco. Magnes.

669. ETIEM
(223) 2 July 1815, baptism at Apalache of child of 5 years, natural son of Michel Tensá and Marie, Indians. Godparents: Jose Maria Torres and Susanne Solmon. Priest: Franco. Magnes.

670. ALEXI
(223) 2 July 1815, baptism at Apalache of child of 5
years, natural son of Michel Tensa and Marie, Indians. Godparents: Thomas Graham and Anton____
/document tor_n_7 and Celestin. Priest: Franco Magnes.

671. ELENNE
(223) 2 July 1815, baptism at Apalache of child of 2
years, natural daughter of Michel Tensa and Marie,
Indians. Godparents: Jn Btte. Dubois and Tonton
Celestin. Priest: Franco. Magnes.

672. PIERRE NOLASCO BENGE
(223) 2 July 1815, baptism at Apalache of child of 6
months, natural son of Benge and Susanne Michel.
Godparents: Pierre Nolasco de Porcuna and Marie
Barvara de Barange /Varangu_e_7. Priest:Franco. Magnes.

673. JOSEPH RESIT
(223) 2 July 1815, baptism at Apalache of child of 1
year, natural son of Estevan Toró and Francisca
Matheo, Indians. Godparents: Jn. Btte. Valery
and Francois Bornée. Priest: Franco. Magnes.

674. MARIE SUSANNE
(223) 2 July 1815, baptism at Apalache of child of 3
years, natural daughter of Jn Btte and Francoise
Magdalenne, Indians. Godparents: Antonio Charles
and Susanne Pierro. Priest: Franco. Magnes.

675. PIERRE
(223) 2 July 1815, baptism at Apalache of child of 1
year, natural son of Nicolas Apalas and Me. Louise,
Indian. Godparents: Jn. Btte. Croux and Dolory
Velgara /Bellegard_e_7. Priest: Franco. Magnes.

676. JOSEPH TOUAZIN
(223) 2 July 1815, baptism at Apalache of child of 13
months, natural son of Pierre Tensa and Marie,
Indian. Godparents: Louis Bailio and Nanet De
Loux. Priest: Franco. Magnes.

677. FRANCOIS CHARNAC
(224) 2 July 1815, baptism at Apalache of child of 10
years, natural son of Pierre Tensa and Marie,
Indian. Godparents: Louis Bailio and Belony
Bornée. Priest: Franco. Magnes.

678. FRANCOIS DORSINO
(224) 2 July 1815, baptism at Apalache of child of 5
years, natural son of Nicolas La Palaches and

Francisca, Indians. Godparents: Francisco Rachal and Maria Pouarret /Poirrier/. Priest: Franco. Magnes.

679. JOSE TENSA
(224) 2 July 1815, baptism at Apalache of child of 2 months?, natural son of Michel Tensa and Maria, Indians. Godparents: Jose Dionisio Procela and Maria Estefania Padilla. Priest: Franco. Magnes.

680. LOUIS ACOYÉ
(224) 2 July 1815, baptism at Apalache of child of 10 years, son of Louis Acoye and Felicite Guary, Indians. Godparents: Louis Charvaneau and Marie Balsy Dubois. Priest: Franco. Magnes.

681. BALCOUR /VALCOUR/
(224) 2 July 1815, baptism at Apalache of child of 2 years, natural son of Meson Blans and Tamonet? Acoye, Indian. Godparents: Francois Valery and Catarine Jouafa. Priest: Franco. Magnes.

NOTE: Eighteen entries at this point have been destroyed for 1815. By a comparison of extant entries with the abbreviated copies that were later made in Book 19, all of these entries can be accounted for except one. See Appendix.

682. JOSEPH SORVIC VERCHER
(225) 14 October 1815, baptism of infant born 19 November 1814, legitimate son of /torn/* Vercher and Marie Luz Verchor. Godparents: Jose Tauzin and Susanne Rachal. Priest: Franco. Magnes.

*Entry is badly torn. Name of father is missing. Other records at the Natchitoches post indicate that parents of Joseph Sorvic Verchere were Joseph Louis Vercher and Marie Luce Verger (also variously spelled Vergau, Berzot and Berjiou).

683. PLACIDO BERTIL DERVAN
(225) 22 October 1815, baptism of child born 14 May, 1815, legitimate son of Juann Btta. Dervan and Lucie Plesans. Godparents: *_____ Dervan and Susanne Plesans. Priest: Franco. Magnes.

*Entry is badly torn.

684. PELAGY BUARD
(225) 22 October 1815, baptism of infant born *____ber 1814, daughter of Jeann Louis Buard and _____. Godparents: Onesim Buard and _____. Priest:

Franco. Magnes.

*Entry is badly torn.

685. AMBROSIO BERNARDO THEOPHILE SOMPAYRACT
(225) 29 October 1815, baptism of infant born 7 March 1815, legitimate son of Ambrosio Sompayract and Josefa Briant. Father is a native of Castros, Department of Tarn in France; mother is a native of Ernery in "el Guarico", France. Grandparents: Ambrosio Sompayract and Suzette Bassinure; Franco. Briant and Maria Elisabet Mauzard, both natives of Paris. Godparents: Bernardo Thofilo Lafon and Maria Desiré Proudhomme. Priest: Franco. Magnes.

686. MARIA ADELIN GRILLET
(225) /Torn/ November, 1815, baptism of infant born 13 September 1814, legitimate daughter of Antonio Grillet and Maria Felicite Crisostomo Peraut. Godparents: Hypolito Bordeleau, Jr. and Suset Rachal. Priest: Franco. Magnes.

687. JOSE MAXIMO COMPERE
(225) *____ November 1815, baptism of infant born 29 May 1815, legitimate son of Pedro Sebastian Compere and Marie Lulette Rachal. Godparents: G. B. Ste. Amant and Josefa Briant. Priest: Franco Magnes.

*Entry is badly torn.

688. JUAN FRANCISCO DE LOS DOLORES TOVAL
(225) 23 December 1815, baptism of infant aged /torn/ and 1 month, son of Juan Toval and Ma. Teresa /Rod/riguez. Godparents: Joseph Carrier and Jetrudis Procela. Priest: Franco. Magnes.

689. MARIE ZEPHELIN PERAUT
(225) 24 December 1815, baptism of infant born 11 September, 1814, legitimate daughter of Casimiro Peraut and Maria Delphin Poissot. Godparents: Firme Poissot and Marie Zeline Poissot. Priest: Franco. Magnes.

690. JOSEPH VICTOR PERAUT
(226) 24 December 1815, baptism of infant born _____ * legitimate son of Jose Cris/o/stome Peraut/ and _____ _____ olefi Fredieu. Godparents: ____ and Maria Marcelite Peraut. Priest: Franco. Magnes.

*Entry is badly torn

691. EUGENIO MANUEL HOYE*
(227) 1 January 1816, baptism of child born 3 September
1813, son of /Dorset David/ Hoy and Marianne Artemisse LeMaitre. Godparents: Juan Eugenio Michamps and Francisca Vachon. Priest: Franco. Magnes.

692. MARIE CLISTA BOSSIERRE*
(227) 13 January 1816, baptism of child born ____ 1815,
legitimate daughter of Soulangeo /Bossier/ and Leonore Ymblee /Himel/. Godparents: ____ Bossierre
and Marie ____. Priest: Franco. Magnes.

693. MARIE EMELY CHAMARD*
(227) 30 January 1816, baptism of infant aged 30 days
/legitimate daughter of Andre Chamard and Felicite
Saucier. Granddaughter of/ Louis Chamard and Marie Chata/rine Bardon/; Henry Sausc/ier/ and ____,
natives of ____. Godparents: ____ and
Anriette Sausciere. Priest: Franco. Magnes.

694. _____*
(228) __ February 1816, baptism of a girl aged 5 months,
legitimate daughter of Jose Manuel ____ and
Getrudis Gomes. Godparents: ___dres Rambin and
Anarietta ____. Priest: Franco. Magnes.

695. JUAN BAUTISTA VERCHER*
(228) _____, 1816, baptism of a child aged 3½
months, son of Velony Vercher and Marie /Orezine/
Gallien. Godparents: Jacques Vercher and Marie
Luz Rachal. Priest: Franco. Magnes.

696. _____ ANTY*
(228) __ February 1816, baptism of child born 20 ____,
legitimate daughter of Valery /Anty/ and /Marie
As/pasy Dervan. Godparents: ____ Cloutier and
Marie ____. Priest: Franco. Magnes.

697. VICTOR RACHAL*
(228) 16 February 1816, baptism of child born ____,
1814, legitimate son of Julian Rachal and Marie
Melanie Lavespere/. Godparents: ____ Lavespere
and Elen ____. Priest: Franco. Magnes.

698. MARIE CLYSIN RACHAL*
(228) 16 February 1816, baptism of child born ____
December, 1815, /legitimate child of Julien Rachal/
and Melany /Lavespere/. Godparents: _____.
Priest: Franco. Magnes.

*These entries are badly torn. See duplicates
in appendix.

699. HILARIO VALIER RACHAL*
(229) 16 February 1816, baptism of child born ___ September 1815, son of Berthelmy Rachal, Jr. and _____. Godparents: Hilario _____ and Margarite Federic. Priest: Franco. Magnes.

700. EDUARDO PONTHIEU*
(229- 16 February 1816, baptism of child born January,
230) 18___, legitimate son of _____ Ponthieu and Margarite _____. Priest: Franco. Magnes.

/This entry also contains the fragments "___toro Bossie" and "___rore Lambre," although it is not possibly to supply identifying information from the fragments that remain./

701. MARIA ANTONIA INICULINA RUIZ*
(230) _____ 1816, baptism of child born 7 November 1815, daughter of Santiago Ruiz and Juana Rosa _____. Godparents: Manuel Gonzalez and _____lla. Priest: Franco. Magnes.

702. _____*
(230) _____, baptism of the legitimate son of _____ and Josefa Sanches. Godparents: _____ Sepulveda? and _____. Priest: Franco. Magnes.

703. JUANA MARIA RUDERINDA CASTRO*
(230) ____ March 1816, baptism of child of 1 day, natural daughter of Maria Jetrudis Castro. Godparents: Juan Jose Mariana Acosta (represented by _____) and _____idad Sanches. Priest: Franco. Magnes.

704. FRANCISCA DE LOS DOLORES TOVAL*
(230) _____ 1816, baptism of a child of 1 month and 13 days, child of Maria Antonio _____ and Maria Telesfora _____. Godparents: Jn Btta Chirino and _____. Priest: Franco. Magnes.

705. _____ SEPULVEDA - MARIA GRA_____
(231) /Rest of entry is destroyed./

706. MARIE CLARE SCHAMPS
(231) /Rest of entry is destroyed./

707. LOUIS_____
(231) /Rest of entry is destroyed./

*These entries are badly torn. See duplicates in appendix.

708. MARIE AGLANTINE ANTY*
(231) 13 ____ 1816, baptism of infant born ____ November 1815, /legitimate daughter of Valery/ Anty and Marie As/pasie Derbanne/. Godparents: Alexy _____ and Estase Davion. Priest: Franco. Magnes.

709. _____*
(232) /Only remaining portion of this entry contains the names "____ino de Sose" and "_____riguez."

710. _____*
(232) /No names remain on the extant scrap of this entry./

711. MARIA ELISA? BOSSIERRE?*
(232) _____, baptism of an infant born 14 March ____, child of _____ Bossierre and _____. Godparents: Nemesi _____ and _____lete Bossierre. Priest: Franco. Magnes.

712. _____LY CHAMARD*
(232) _____, baptism of legitimate daughter of Andres Chamard and /Felic/ite Saucierre. Paternal grandparents: /Louis Chamar/d, native of Poittou in France and /Cathar/ine Bardeau; maternal grandparents /Henry Sau/cier and Elisabett Barrette, /native of New Or/leans. Priest: Franco. Magnes.

713. ENTRY MISSING
(233)

714. JOS____ CHAVA____* /CHAVANA?/
(233) _____, baptism of the legitimate son of Ramon Chav_____ and _____. Godparents: Jose _____ and Berenciana Sta. Cruz. Priest: Franco. Magnes.

715. _____RACHAL*
(233) 1 _____, 1816, baptism of child born 7 of _____, legitimate son of Jn. Btta. /Barthelemy Rachal, Jr./ and Marie Lemoin. Godparents: _____ Rachal and _____. Priest: Franco. Magnes.

716. _____*
(233- _____1816, baptism of infant born 26 ____
234) /181/5, legitimate son of Alexandre _____, native of Bordeau and Mar_____ _____hnson, native of Opelousas. Godparents: Jean Jacques _____ and _____. Priest: Franco. Magnes.

*These entries are badly torn. See duplicates in appendix.

111.

717.   _____*
(234) /Only remaining names on this torn fragment appear
       to be those of the godparents, _____ Rac_____
       and _____ Federic./ Priest: Franco. Magnes.

718.   JUANA MARIA CASTRO*
(234) _____, baptism of the natural daughter of
       _____. Godparents: _____ and Maria
       _____. Priest: Franco. Magnes.

719.   MARIA ANTONIA HERNANDEZ*
(234) 1 March 1816, baptism of natural daugher of ____
       Hernandez. Godparents: _____ and Jetrudis
       Chirino. Priest: Franco. Magnes.

*The remainder of 1816 baptisms have been destroyed. See
appendix for duplicates extracted from the abbreviated copies of these entries that a later priest recorded in Register 19.

720.   JEAN BAPTISTE AUGUSTIN METOYER*   (s)
(235) MARIE SUSANNE METOYER /ANTY/   (x)
       _____, 1816, marriage of Jean Baptiste
       Augustin Metoyer, free mulatto, aged 19, legiti-
       mate son of Augustin Metoyer and Me. Agnes /Pois-
       sot/, also free mulattoes . . . and . . . Susanne
       Metoyer /Anty/ aged /17**/ years, natural daughter
       of Susanne Metoyer, a free mulattress /all natives
       of this post**/. Signed: J. Bte. Metoyer, fils
       Aug^{tin}, m.l. (s); Pre. Charnau (s); /J. B./ Anty
       (s); Jn Bte Florentin /Conant/ (s); Louis Metoyer,
       m.l. (x); Joseph Metoyer, m.l. (x); Auguste fils
       Aug^{tin} Metoyer, m.l. (s); Agustin Metoyer (x);
       Marie Agnes (x); Susanne Metoyer, m.l. (x).

**Information thus marked was extracted from this
entry by this editor in 1973, at which time the
entry was somewhat less damaged. Bracketed information without asterisks is supplied by editor and
based upon data found in other church and civil
records identified in Gary B. Mills, *The Forgotten
People; Cane River's Creoles of Color* (LSU Press,
1977).

721.   JN. BTTE. FLORANTIN METOYER /Conant/* (s)
(236) MARIE LOUISE METOYER   (x)
       _____1816, marriage of Jn. Btte. Florantin
       Metoyer /Conant/, a free mulatto of /21/ years,
       natural son of /Susanne/ Metoyer, free mulatto
       . . . and . . . Marie Louise Metoyer, free mulat-
       to, aged 17 years /legitimate daughter of Nicolas

*These entries are badly torn

Augustin Metoyer and Marie Agnes Poissot/. Signed: Jn. Baptis Florantin Metoyer, m.l. (s); /J.B./ Anty (s); Juan Jose Medina (s); Jn. Bte. Metoyer, fils Augtin (s); Dominique Metoyer (x); Luis Metoyer (x); Jh. Lavigne (x); Me. Louise Metoyer (x); Agustin Metoyer (x); Marie Agnes (x); Susanne Metoyer (x); Maxle. Metoyer (s).

/See note accompanying Entry 720/

722. _____ DAVION? (x)
(237) PELAGIE GAGNE? (x)
Marriage. Only signatures remain for this entry. The names _____vion (x) and Pelagie Gagne (x) appear in position where bride and groom usually sign. Other signatures were: B. _____(s); Ely Bernard (x); Louis Vascocu (s); Jn Peraux (s); Henry Trichel (s); Jn. V. Vacocu (s); Louis Geoffrois (s); Jn. Landreaux (s).

723. JEAN PIERRE BODOUN /BODIN/ (x)
(238) ME. FRANCISCA BEVE? (x)
Marriage, ca. 1816. Entry is completely destroyed except for signatures. Jn. Prer. Bodoun (x) and Me. Francisca Beve (s) appear in position where bride and groom usually sign. Other signatures are: Jeann Boudoin (x); Me. Gualthemam (x); Jose Luis De la Bega (s); Gaspar Boudin (x); Diego Gonsalez (x).

724. RENE ROCHETTED?
(239) MARIE _____
1817 Marriage. Only a scrap of the marginal notation remains and this is extremely illegible.

725. /UNKNOWN/
(240) 1817. Marriage. Only an unfathomable scrap remains of this entry.

726. ANDRÉ CHAMARD (s)
(241) FELICITE SAUCIER (s)
1816 or 1817 marriage. A scrap which appears to belong to this entry indicates that the groom was from _____ Orleans, 33 years, and legitimate son of _____. Bride was 16 years, legitimate daughter of _____ and Elisabet Baré. Other signatures which definitely go with this entry are: Catherin Chamard (s); Theodore Deterville (s); Jh. Tauzin (s); Elizabeth Baré (s); Michel Chamard (s). Priest: Franco. Magnes.

113

727. /FRANCOIS/ VIENNE (s)
(242) MARIE ANNE BUARD (s)
  1816 or 1817 marriage. A scrap which appears to
  go with this entry indicates that the groom was
  25. The bride was legitimate daughter of Jn Btte
  Bu/ard/ and Louise Poissot. Extant signatures:
  Ve Buard (s); Paillette (s); Manuel Rachal (s);
  Buard (s); Rouquier (s); E. C^r Murphy (s).
  Priest: Franco. Magnes.

728. BENJAMIN DRANGUET (s)
(243) MATHILDE CELESTE TAUZIN (s)
  1816. Marriage. Groom is native of _____ in-
  ferieur in /France/, legitimate son of Charles
  Antoine? Dranguet and Marie Anne ____ Mais.
  Bride is native of this post, aged 1_?, legitimate
  daughter of Mar. Joseph Tauzin and Marie Chamard.
  Signed: Jh. Tauzin (s); Marie Chamard Tauzin (s);
  Catherine Chamard (s); Bouvard De St. Amans (s);
  E. Cr. Murphy (s); A. Sompayrac (s); Felix Trudeau (s); Michel Chamard (s); Thomas M. Linnard
  (s). Priest: Franco. Magnes. Entry is badly torn.

729. /BERNARD THEOPHILE/ LAFON (s)
(244) SUSANNE PROUDHOMME (s)
  ca. 1816 marriage. Groom is native of France,
  son of _____ and Marie _____. Bride is
  daughter of Antonio Proudhomme and Marie /Lambre/.
  Signed: Marie Prudhomme (s); Prudhomme (s) Bn
  Metoyer (s); Jn. Cortes (s); Jn? Prudhomme (s);
  J. F. Hertzog (s); M. A. Gauvain? (s). Priest:
  Franco. Magnes. Entry is badly torn.

730. VALERY _____ (s)
(245) ADELEYDA PALVADO (x)
  1816 or 1817 marriage. Entry is almost completely
  destroyed. Remaining signatures are: Malige (s);
  Marianne Bardon Malige (s); Jh. Tauzin (s); Aé.
  Chamard (s); Ma. Chavus (x); Carmelite Chabus (s);
  B. D. St. Amans (s); Francois Chabus (s). Priest:
  Franco. Magnes.

731. /JEAN BAPTISTE DOMINIQUE/ METOYER (s)
(246) /ADELAIDE RACHAL/ *
  1816 or 1817 marriage. Entry is almost completely
  destroyed. Remaining signatures are: J. Bte.
  Metoyer, fils Aug^{tin} (s); Pre. Metoyer (s); Maxlle.
  Metoyer, fils Augustin (s); Dominique Metoyer (x);
  Jn. Bte. Rachal (x); Auguste Metoyer, fils (s);
  Jn. Bte. Metoyer fils Louis (s); Juan Jose Medina (s).

*Bracketed information was copied by editor in 1974 at which time this entry was slightly less damaged. To complete the information in this document, researchers are referred to the civil marriage contract on file in the Natchitoches Courthouse in *Books 2 & 3, Marriages & Miscellaneous*, Document No. 23.

732. JEAN CRISOSTOME PERAUT (x)
(247) MARIE SUSANNE RACHAL (x)
No date. Marriage entry is completely destroyed except for signatures. Below those of the bride and groom there appears the signature of D. Rachal (s) ⟦father of the bride⟧. In the column where witnesses' signatures appear, there are the names: Pre. Gagone (s); Jn. Egne. Michamps (s); Jh. Vercher (s), and one illegible signature.

733. LOUIS GEOFFROIS (s)
(248) MARIE THERESE DAVION (x)
No date. Marriage entry is completely destroyed except for signatures. Below those of the bride and groom there appear the signatures of Pelagie Gagné (x) and Jn. Btte. Davion (x). Those signing as witnesses were: Pre. Ternié (s); Bte. Trichel (s); Louis Vascocu (s); Jn Peraux (s); Jh. Vacocu (s); Alexis Trichel (s); and Henry Trichel (s). Priest: Franco. Magnes.

734. LOUIS LAFFITTE (x)
(249) MARIA ANTONIA FLORES? (x)
Marriage, ca. 1816. Nothing remains of entry but the signatures. The two above names appear in location where bride and groom usually sign. Remaining signatures are: Denis Laffitte (x); Francois Prudhomme (s); Jose Flores (s); Jn. Btte. Arce (x); P_____ ____ologo Flores (s); Franco. Gueraco (s); Felipe de Jesus Flores (s). Priest: Franco. Magnes.

735. FR⟦ANCOIS S⟧COPINE (x)
(250) _____NE PERRAUT (s)
Marriage, ca. 1816. Nothing remains of this entry but the signatures. The two above names appear in the location where bride and groom usually signed. Other signatures are: J. ⟦Ba⟧tt. Pereaux (s); Frs. Perot, Jr. (s); Bte. Trichel (s); Athanase Trichel (s); P.E. LeBrun dit Dagobert (s); Pre. Ternié (s); Henry Trichel (s); Boyer (s). Priest: Franco. Magnes.

736. JOSE MA. CASTRO? (x)
(251) MARIE LOUISE MASIPPI (x)
Marriage, ca. 1816. Nothing remains of this entry but signatures and a portion of marginal notation showing the surname of the bride to be Masippi. The signature of Jose Ma. Castro appears just under that of Marie Louise Masippi in the location usually reserved for bride and groom. Other signatures are: Jean Masippe (x); Pierre Masippi (x); _____ Compere (s); Desiree Hertzog ne Prudhomme (s); Jean Franco. Hertzog. Priest: Franco Magnes.

737.
(252) _____ DUPRE
Marriage, ca. 1816. Nothing remains but signatures and a portion of marginal notation identifying bride's surname. Signature where groom usually signed is almost completely torn; remainder is illegible and reveals only that he made his mark. Below this signature, in position where bride usually signed, appears: V^e /Widow/ Francoise LeCour (x)*. Other signatures are: Pierre De Loux (x); Pierre Dolet (s); Francois Lattier (x); Jose Luis de la Bega (s); Athanase LeCour (x). Priest: Franco. Magnes.

*Possibly the bride in this entry is Françoise LeCour whose first husband Pierre Dupre died between 1804 and 1806.

738. MATHEO RICHARD (x)
(253) MARIANNA LEMETTRE (x)
Marriage, ca. 1816. Nothing remains but signatures. The two above names appear in location where bride and groom usually sign. Other signatures are: P. D. Caillebeau LaFontaine (s); and Manuel ___ Hoffman (s). Priest: Franco. Magnes.

739. JN. PRE. GRAPPE (s)
(254) FELICITE PERAUX (s)
Marriage, ca. 1816. No identification remains except for signatures at bottom of entry. The two above names appear in location where bride and groom usually sign. Other signatures are: Chs. Perot (s); Jn Perot, Jr. (s); Fcois Grappe (s); Boyer (s); Jn. V. Vacucu (s); Pre. Ternié (s); Henry Trichel (s); Louis Perot (s); and Pierre Laffitt (s). Priest: Franco. Manges.

740. JN JOSEPH NASARIO GUILLERMO (x)
(255) MARIE ARZELE GRAPPE (x)
Marriage, ca1816. Entry is almost entirely des-

troyed. Only a portion of marginal notation remains, along with the signatures of bride, groom, family and witnesses. Signatures, in addition to those of bride and groom, are: Felicite Grappe (x); Fcois Grappe (s); Jn. Pereau (s); P. E. Le Brun (s); Bart. Fleming (s); Henry Trichel (s); Julien Perot (s); Jn. Pre Grappe (s); Charle Dortolant (s); Paul Cazenave (s). Priest: Franco. Magnes.

741. JOSE MALBOURG? (s)
(256) MA. ANTONIA? PROCELLA (x)
Marriage, ca. 1816. Entry is almost entirely destroyed. Signatures remain but they are extremely faded. The two above signatures appear in location where bride and groom usually sign. Other legible signatures are: Joseph Ma. Procela (x); Fer____ Juan Isidro Artz? (s); Joseph Duret (s); Manuel Busta (s); Juan Marmelo? (s). Priest: Franco. Magnes.

742. _____ JO (or SO)_____
(257) MARIE VICTOIRE ____O____ /POISSOT?/
Marriage, ca 1815-16. Nothing remains of entry except a small portion of marginal note and most of the signatures. Groom's signature is torn. Other signatures are: Felix Trudeau (s); Jh. Tauzin (s); Metoyer (s); Narcisse Prudhomme (s); Ch. Noyrit (s); Attanasse Poisot (s); Helene Pavie (s); _____ St. Amans (s); Firmin Poissot (s); Mc. Sompayrac (s); E. C. Murphy (s). Priest: Franco. Magnes.

743. ATHANAS BROSSET (s)
(258) Marie /CELESTE BEAUD/OIN (x)
Marriage, ca 1816. Nothing remains except signatures. The two names above appear in location where bride and groom usually signed. Other signatures were: Pierre Baudoin (x); Pierre Brosset (x); Jose Luis de la Bega (s); James Smith (s); Julien /De/Louche (s); Gisarnac (s); Cazenave (s); Joseph Lattier (s); Gisarnat, Jr. (s); Louis Fort (s). Priest: Franco. Magnes.

744. FRA_____ LANDREAUX (s)
(259) MARIE MARCELITE POISSOT (s)
Marriage, 1816. Nothing remains of this entry except a portion of marginal note and most of the signatures. The two names above appear in location where bride and groom usually signed and the remaining fragments of marginal notation indicate that they are the spouses. Remaining signatures

are: Ve. Buard (s); Louis Buard (s); Jh. Tauzin (s); Jn. Landreaux (s); E. Cr. Murphy (s); Jques. Landreaux (s); Paul Poissot (s); Paillette (s); Ls. Tauzin (s); O. Buard (s). Priest: Franco Magnes.

745. ⟨UNKNOWN⟩
(260) 1816 marriage. Nothing remains of entry except signature of two witnesses: P. Cailleau Lafontaine (s) and Gd. Philibert (s).

746. ATH⟨ANASE⟩ DE⟨NIS⟩ (x)
(261) MARIE MODESTE BOUDOIN (x)
1816 marriage. Nothing remains of entry except a portion of marginal note and most of the signatures. Family and witnesses who signed were: Pierre Baudoin (x); Jn Btte. Denis (x); James Smith (s); Cazenave (s); Juan Jose Medina (s); Gisarnat, Jr. (s). Priest: Franco. Magnes.

747. JN. BTTE. PROUDHOMME (x)
(262) MA. _____ YBARBO (x)
ca1816 marriage. Nothing remains of this entry except signatures. The two above names appear in location where bride and groom usually signed. Other signatures are: Felipe Moro (x); Ma. Denis Laffitte (x); Manuel Trichel (x); Pierre Dolle (x); Andres Adley (x); Pre. Ternié (s); Aé. Chamard (s). Priest: Franco. Magnes.

748. JOSE LUIS DE LA BEGA
(263) MARIA GUADALUPE PROU (?PROCELLA) (x)
1816 marriage. Little remains of entry except periphereal words. It's length indicates that unusual circumstances were involved. The word *padrinos* (godparents) appears, which was not customary in these marriage entries. The word "affinity" also appears, indicating that a dispensation was obtained from the impediment of affinity. Witnesses were few: James Smith (s); Joseph Carriere (s); B. Gisarnat (s); Antonio Pru (x) and Jose Acosta (s).

749. FRANCISCO _____ (x)
(264) ME. M _____ GONSALEZ? (x)
ca1816 marriage. Nothing remains of entry except a few periphereal words of text and the signatures. The two rather illegible signatures above are entered in the location where bride and groom usually signed. Other legible signatures are: B. Gisar⟨nac⟩ (s); James Smith (s); Paul Cazenave (s); _____ Millikin (s): Jose Acosta (s): A. B. Gisarnat, Jr. (s).

750.   JEANN PIERRE DOLLE (x)
(265) MARIE POMPOSE PROUDHOM (x)
       1816, marriage. Nothing remains of entry except
       signatures and almost all of the marginal notation
       identifying the parties. Family and witnesses who
       signed were: Marie De_____ Proudhom (x); Pierre
       Dolet (s); Chamard Tauzin (s); Jh. Tauzin (s);
       Chs. Noyrit (s); Pre. Ternié (s); A. L. Deblieux
       (s); H. E. Tauzin (s); Juan Mora (s). Priest:
       Franco. Magnes.

751.   FRANCISCO CARDENA (x)
(266) MARIA MARTINA PRADO (x)
       ca1816, marriage. Nothing remains of entry except
       a few periphereal words and the signatures. The
       two names above appear in location where bride and
       groom usually signed. Other signatures were:
       Joseph Martin Prado (x); B. Gisarnat (s); Gisarnat,
       Jr. (s); Juan de Dios Perez (s). Priest: Franco
       Magnes.

752.   JOSEPH ANTONIO CARO (s)
(267) MARGARITE CELESTE ROSAS (x)
       1816, marriage. Nothing remains of this entry ex-
       cept marginal identification of bride and groom
       and the signatures. Others who signed were Michaele
       Equis (x); Maria Manuella Sanches (x); Jose Luis
       de la Bega (s); Juan Mora (s); Felise Estrada (s);
       Jn. Btte. Procela (x). Priest: Franco. Magnes.

753.   JOSEPH _____
(268) _____CAZANAVE
       ca1816, marriage. Little remains of the text of
       this entry. The above are the only legible names.
       Their respective position in the text, in relation
       to other extant words, indicate that they are
       bride and groom. Signatures are complete, but
       bride and groom did not sign in usual location.
       Signatures are: Felis Estrada (s); M. Cazenase (s);
       Boyer (s); Cazenave (s); Jn. Cortes (s); Denis
       Cazenave (x); P. D.Cailleau Lafontaine (s); Ger-
       maine (s); Aimée Casenave (s) and Arcencio Estrada
       (x). Priest: Franco. Magnes.

754.   EDWARD KIRKLAND (s)
(269) CELESTE BAILLIO VILLIAN (s)
       1817. Marriage. Nothing remains of entry except
       marginal identification of bride and groom, a few
       periphereal words of text, and signatures. Those
       who signed were: P. Baillio (s); Emelie Lacour (s);
       Stephen _____(s); _____Layssard (s); Sauztaine

A. Baillio (s); James Fortchuse? (s); John Brown (s); John Martin (s). Priest: Franco. Magnes.

755. JNO. M. CANNON (s)
(270) ADELINNE LAYSARD (x)
ca1817. Marriage. Nothing remains of entry except signatures and a few periphereal words of text. The latter includes the word "Rapides" and the name "Laysard." The signatures of the two parties above appear in location where bride and groom usually signed. Other signatures are: _____ Layssard (s); P. Baillio (s); John Brown (s); Malafrete Layssard (s); John Martin (s) and James Fortchuse (s). Priest: Franco. Magnes.

756. LEON BRUNET TOTIN (x)
(271) MARIE M_____ITE POISOT (x)
ca1817. Marriage. Nothing remains of entry except a portion of marginal notation identifying the bride and the majority of the signatures. The two above names appear in location where bride and groom usually sign. Other signatures include Marguerite Griete (x) ⟦Grillet?⟧; Marie Louise Untiel (x); _____hy (s); Gd. Philibert (s); Ls Tauzin (s) and Frs. Perot, Jr. (s). Priest: Franco. Magnes.

757. _____ (s)
(272) SUSANNE NORRIS (x)
ca1817. Marriage. Nothing remains of entry except a few periphereal words, including the name "Ramon" in position where bride's parents are usually identified, and the majority of the signatures. Almost all of the groom's signature is destroyed; what remains indicates only that he signed rather than merely making his mark. Other signatures were: Jn. Egne Michamps (s); Migu___ (s); Miguel Leal (x); Juan Procela (x). Priest: Franco. Magnes.

758. JOSEPH CLETO? TORRES
(273) MARIA DEL PILAR ACOSTA
ca1817. Marriage. Nothing remains of entry except marginal notation identifying bride, a few periphereal words, and the signatures. The two above names appear in location where bride and groom usually signed and marginal notation verifies this identity of the bride. Other signatures were: Pedro _____ (x); Jose Acosta (s); and Juan De Dios Peres (s). Priest: Franco. Magnes.

759. _____ BOUDOIN
(274)
ca1816. Marriage. Nothing remains of entry except a few periphereal words which yield only the above name, and its position in text does not conclusively indicate whether this is the bride or the groom. A portion of signatures also are extant. In position where bride and groom usually sign appear the names: Pier Boudoin (x) and _____ _____elous_____ (x). Other signatures are: Silvestre Anty (x) Me. Angelle Poun_____ (x); Nicolas Boudoin (x). Priest: Franco. Magnes.

760. JN. BTTE. LESTAGE (s)
(275) MARIE LEOCADY SOULANGE BOSSIER (s)
1817. Marriage. Little remains of this entry except marginal identification of bride and groom, a few periphereal words (including *vuido* or widower in position where information is usually given on groom) and signatures. These include: Soulange Bossie (s); P. N? Bossier (s); _____ Buard (s); Bte. Armant (s); _____ Callaghan (s); Cezer Bossier (s); Ete. Bossier (s). Priest: Franco. Magnes.

761. JULIEN DESLOUCHE (s)
(276) MARIE OSITTE DUPRE (x)
ca1817. Marriage. Little remains of this entry except periphereal words which include "native of this /parish/" and "legitimate son of Jn Bte" in section where information on groom is recorded. Below this appears "legitimate daughter of Pier Du_____" and then "LeCourt." Signatures include the two names first given above, in position where bride and groom usually signed, and: Francoise LeCourt (x); J. Bte. Lecomte (s); Brd. Mtin Despallier (s); Ls Derbanne (s) and Francois Lattier (s). Priest: Franco. Magnes.

762. JN BTTE /ESPALLIER/ RACHAL (x)
(277) MARIE SUSANNE METOYER (x)
1817. Marriage. Little remains of this marriage of free people of color except marginal notation identifying bride and groom, a few periphereal words, and signatures. These include: Julien Delouche (s); Antoine Coindet (s); M. Prevost Dupre (s); and Dominique Metoyer (x).

NOTE: The civil marriage contract filed by this couple in the Natchitoches courthouse identifies bride's parents as Dominique and Marguerite Metoyer and the mother of the groom as Françoise, f.w.c. The succession opened at the death of the groom (#927, Natchitoches Courthouse Estate sale dated 2-27-1855) identifies the father of the groom as Jean Baptiste Barthelemy Rachal, Sr.

763. LOUIS SOLASTIE RACHAL (s)
(278) ME. HELOISE ST. ANDRE (x)
ca 1817. Marriage. Little remains of entry except marginal notation identifying surname of bride, a few periphereal words (indicating that groom was legitimate and 25 years old) and the following signatures: Narcisse Rachal (s); Onezime St. André (s); Francois Baudry (x); Antonio Rachal (x); Andre Ste. Andres (x); Silvestre Rachal (s). Priest: Franco. Magnes.

NOTE: In 1971 this editor made an earlier abstract of the above entry, at which time the original document was somewhat more complete. Additional information abstracted at that time identified the bride as "aged fourteen" and the legitimate daughter of André St. André and Marie Jacob Rachal.

764. MAGSIME AGUILLON (x)
(279) MARIA REFUGIA CORTINAS (x)
1817. Marriage. Little remains of entry except marginal notation identifying bride and groom, a few periphereal words, and signatures, which include: Cayetano Arreñago (x); Pedro Nolasco de Porcuna (x); Jas. F. Porter (s); Manuel Laserda (x). Priest: Franco. Magnes.

765. J. ANTONIO SEPULVEDA (s)
(280) MARIA GUADALUPE CHAVANA (x)
ca1817. Marriage. Little remains of entry except signatures and periphereal words. The latter indicates that groom's mother was Polonia _____ and that bride was a native of Texas. Position of the signatures of the two individuals above indicate that they were probably the bride and groom. Other signatures are: Ramon Chevana (x); Jose Luis de la Bega (s); Miguel _____ (s); Jose Flores (x); Manuel Bustante (s). Priest: Franco. Magnes.

766. JACQUE PAUL (s)
(281) MARIA DOLORES BERGARD /BELLEGARDE?7 (x)
1817. Marriage. Nothing remains of entry except

marginal notation identifying spouses, and the
following signatures: Jh. Lattier (s); Adam
Huffman (s); <u>Michal?</u> (s); Jn. Btte. Bergard (x).
Priest: Franco. Magnes.

767. JOHN COMPTON (s)
(282) AMELIE BAILLIO (s)
ca1817. Marriage. Nothing remains of entry except the marginal note identifying groom, a few
periphereal words and signatures. The name Amelie Baillio appears in position where bride usually signs. Other signatures include: Emelie
Lacour (s); P. Baillio (s); _____ Murray (s);
Vtin. Layssard (s); Edward Kirkland (s). Priest:
Franco. Magnes.

768. FRANCISCO <u>MARIA?</u> <u>ESTRADA?</u> (x)
(283) MARIA R_____ A CARO (x)
1817. Marriage. Nothing left of entry except
marginal reference, which partly identifies bride
and groom, and most of the signatures. Others
who signed, in addition to spouses, were Joseph
Caro (x); Joseph Cordova (x); Samuel Norris (s);
Encarnasion Chirino (s); Miguel Delgado (x); and
Jn. Btte. Procela (x). Priest: Franco. Magnes.

769. ATHANASE RACHAL (x)
(284) 1817. Marriage. Nothing remains of entry except a
few periphereal words and the signatures. Others
who signed were B. Dranguet (s); A. L. DeBlieux
(s); Henry Trichel (s); and Mda. Jacqe. Laveseur
(s).

NOTE: More complete information on this couple
may be obtained from the Civil Records of the
Parish, *Marriage Book 6*, p. 227.

770. SAMUEL NORRIS (s)
(285) _____ POIRIET (x)
ca1817. Marriage. Nothing remains of this entry
except a portion of the signatures. The two above
signatures appear in the location where bride and
groom usually signed. Other remaining signatures
are: J. Poirier (s); Nathaniel Norris (s); Jh.
Lattier (s); Julien Delouche (s); P____ Poirier
(x). Priest: Franco. Magnes.

NOTE: Entry 57, *Marriage Book I*, Parish of St.
John the Baptist, Cloutierville, indicates that
wife of Samuel Norris was ANNA Poirier.

771. NATHANIEL NORRIS (s)
(286) /JUANA/ POIRRIET (x)
ca1817. Marriage. Nothing remains of this entry
except a few periphereal words and the signatures.
The two above names appear in the location where
bride and groom usually signed, although only a
portion of the bride's name is extant. Other signatures are: Jn. Btte. Besson (x); _____ Baillio
(s); J. Poirier; Julien Delouche (s); Samuel Norris (s). Priest: Franco. Magnes.

NOTE: Carolyn Reeves Ericson, *Nacogdoches, Gate-
way to Texas; A Biographical Directory, 1773-1849*
(Fort Worth: Arrow/Curtis Printing Company, 1974)
p. 109 identifies bride as "Juana Puarie."

772. _____ITE (s)
(287) _____BEAUDOIN?
ca1817. Marriage. Nothing remains of this entry
except signatures. Those of the bride and groom
are almost entirely destroyed. The signature of
Nicolas Baudoin (x) appears just under that of the
bride and groom, a spot usually reserved for close
family members, and more often for a father. Under the column labelled "witnesses" there appear
the following signatures: Michel Carlos Mere____n
(x); Athanas LaCour (x); Pier Baudoin (x); M. Prevost Dupré (s); Pre. Charnau (s); Bte. Cheval (s).
Priest: Franco. Magnes.

773. MAXILLE METOYER (s)
(288) MARIE ASPASY METOYER /ANTY/ (x)
1817. Marriage. Nothing remains of this entry
but periphereal words and the signatures. The two
signatures above appear in location where bride
and groom usually signed. Other signatures were
Augustin Metoyer (x) /groom's father/; Susanna
Metoyer (x) /bride's mother/; _____ Metoyer (x);
Jen Batite (s); Jean Baptiste Metoyer (s); J. Bte.
Florantin /Conant/ (s); Metoyer (s); Juan Jose
Medina (s). Priest: Franco. Magnes.

NOTE: The civil record of this marriage is still
extant in the Natchitoches Parish Courthouse.

774. HILAIRE RACHAL (s)
(289) MARIE LOUISE AIMEE LEVASSEUR (x)
1817. Marriage. Nothing is extant but marginal
notation identifying bride and groom, a few periphereal words, and signatures. Others who signed
were: Me. Therese Grillet (x); P. Compere (s);
Lambre (s); Btte. Adlé (s); Baltasard Brevelle (s).
Priest: Franco. Magnes.

775. MICHEL DERBANNE (x)
(290) MARIE CLEMIRE ANTY (x)
ca1817. Marriage. Nothing remains of entry but periphereal words which partially identify bride and groom and the following additional signatures: Jh. Derbanne (s); Jacque Verchere (s); Baltazard Brevel (s); Jn. Pe. Me. Dubois (s); /Le/ Comte, fils (s). Priest: Franco. Magnes.

776. JOSEPH LAFLEUR (x)
(291) MARIA _ GRACIA PROCELA (x)
1817. Marriage. Nothing remains of entry except marginal note identifying bride and groom, a few periphereal words, and signatures. Juan Btta. Procela (x) signed immediately under bride and groom in position where a parent usually signed. In column labelled "witnesses," there appear the signatures: Manuel Prou (x); Francois Fabro (x); Joseph Tauzin (s); A. L. Deblieux (s). Priest: Franco. Magnes.

777. /MARC/ SOMPAYRAC (s)
(292) /ZELINE/ CLOUTIER (x)
ca1817. Marriage. Nothing remains of this entry except a few periphereal words which contain partial identification of the groom, and the signatures. Those signing immediately below the bride and groom were Alexoy Cloutier (x); A. Sompayrac (s). Those signing under the heading "witnesses" were _____ /Pre/vost Dupre (s); Paillette (s); Bmin. Metoyer (s); Fs. Roubieu (s). Priest: Franco. Magnes.

778. CORNELIUS VIA
(293) MARIE _____
ca1817. Marriage. Nothing remains of this entry except the marginal note giving name of groom and a portion of the bride's name. Signature of the bride has been destroyed and only the groom's last name remains of his signature. Immediately following the signatures of the spouses, where parents usually sign, there appears: Me. Jeanne Lavery (x). Witnesses were: P. S. Compere (s); Felipe Federic (x); Jn. Btte. Larnodier (x). Priest: Franco Magnes.

779. _____ (x)
(294) ISAVEL LETHON (x)
ca1817. Marriage. Nothing remains of this entry except a portion of the signatures. That of the groom is destroyed except for the notation that he made his mark of a cross. Witnesses were: P. D.

/̲C̲a̲i̲l̲l̲e̲a̲u̲/ Lafontaine (s); Felix Trudeau (s); Ae. Chamard (s). Priest: Franco. Magnes.

780. GERMIN SPARTRATTE? PAILLETTE (s)
(295) DENIS BUARD (x)
November 20, 1817. Marriage. Entry partially destroyed. In section where information on groom is recorded there appear the fragments "of the age of 23 years" and /̲n̲a̲t̲i̲v̲e̲ ̲o̲f̲/ the "department of S̲_̲_̲_̲_̲ ̲_̲nferior in Fr/̲a̲n̲c̲e̲/, legitimate son of Mr. Geo̲_̲_̲_̲_̲_̲_̲_̲_̲_̲aillette and Mda. He̲_̲_̲_̲_̲_̲_̲_̲." Bride is identified as legitimate daughter of the deceased Mr. Denis Buard and Victoria Poissot. 3 bans. Signatures include: Victoire Poissot Paillette (x); /̲J̲e̲a̲n̲ ̲J̲a̲c̲q̲u̲e̲s̲/ Paillette (s); J. Landreaux; E. Cr. Murphy (s); Prudhomme (s); Fs. Vienne (s); Mc. Sompayrac (s); and Lafon (s). Priest: Franco. Magnes.

781. PIERRE BENIOL (s)
(296) ANNE MERCHIOL (s)
12 December /̲1̲8̲1̲7̲/. Marriage. Entry badly torn. Groom: native of Leon, France, legitimate son of ̲_̲_̲_̲_̲_̲ Boniol and Francoise ̲_̲_̲_̲_̲_̲_̲_̲d. Bride: native of ̲_̲_̲_̲_̲_̲_̲_̲, France, aged ̲_̲3 years, widow of Michel Ry̲_̲_̲_̲_̲olf, and legitimate daughter of Franco. Merchiol and Ana Cho̲_̲_̲_̲_̲_̲_̲. Witnesses: ̲_̲eneuil (s); André Sanson (s); Evariste? Villand (s); P. Baillio (s); Sauzthaine A. Baillio (s). Priest: Franco. Magnes.

782. JN. BTTE. CORT̲_̲_̲_̲
(297) MARIA CRUZ RODRIGUEZ (x)
1817. Marriage. Entry is entirely destroyed except for marginal note which identifies the spouses and the year, and except for the signatures: Immediately following that of the bride and groom is the signature of Juan Toval (s). Witnesses were: Domingo Lestage? (x); M̲_̲_̲_̲uel Crux (x); Martin Prada (s); Felix Trudeau (s); Juan de dios Perez (s). Priest: Franco. Magnes.

783. PIERRE MICHEL ZORICHE
(298) MARIE ADEL RACHAL
ca1817. Marriage. Entry is destroyed except for periphereal words and some of the signatures. Those who signed, in addition to bride and groom, were: Fs. Roubieu(s); Silvestre Rachal (s); Pre. ̲_̲_̲ Gagnon (s); ̲_̲_̲_̲_̲_̲_̲/̲A̲/dlé (s); Baltazard Brevell (s); Jn. Bte. Lattier, fils (s); Narcisse Rachal (s). Priest: Franco. Magnes.

784. PIERRE METOYER (s)
(299) HENRIETTE /CLOUTIER/ (x)
   8 January 1818. Marriage. Entry partially destroyed. Groom: native of this post, a free man of color and widower of Marie Perinne /LeComte/. Bride: native of this post, aged 18 years, natural daughter of Dorotea /Monet/, also a free woman of color. Signatures of witnesses are: Jn. Bte. Metoyer, fils Aug^{tin} (s); E (or C?) Grilliet (s); Maxille Metoyer (s); Jn Bte Florantin /Conant/; Jn Bte. Dominique /Metoyer/ (s); Augte. Metoyer, fils (s). Priest: Franco. Magnes.

   NOTE: For more complete information on spouses, researchers are referred to Gary B. Mills, *The Forgotten People; Cane River's Creoles of Color* LSU Press, 1977).

785. MANUEL LLORENS (s)
(300) MARIE ARSENE ANTY (x)
   29 January 1818. Marriage. Groom: aged 28, native of New Orleans, free man of color, natural son of Francisco Llorens /white/ and Francisca Nivette. Bride: 15, native of this post, free woman of color, natural daughter of Jn Btte. Anty /white/ and Susanne Metoyer. Signatures of witnesses are: Susanne Metoyer (x); Agustin Metoyer (x); Pierre Metoyer (s); Jn Bte. Metoyer, fils Aug^{tin} (s); Maxlle. Metoyer (s); Augte. Metoyer (s); J. Bte. Metoyer fils de Louis (s); J. Bte. Dominique /Metoyer/, fils (s); Florantin Conant (s); Francisca Nivette (x). Priest: Franco. Magnes.

786. CYPRIAN RACHAL (x)
(301) EUPHROSINNE RACHAL (x)
   28 March 1818. Marriage. Groom: 19 years of age, native of this post, legitimate son of Julian Rachal and Marie Louise Brevel. Bride: 13, native of this post, legitimate daughter of Berthelemy Rachal and Magdalene Grillet. 3 bans. Spouses are related by blood in the third degree. Witnesses: Magdalenne Grillet (x); P. S. Compere (s); Ls. Derbanne (s); J. F. Hertzog (s); Pre. Michel, fils (s); Fs. Roubieu (s); Auguste Langloi (s). Priest: Franco. Magnes.

787. JEAN VITAL VASCOCU (s)
(302) MARIE FELICITE SOREL (x)
   6 April 1818. Marriage. Groom: 25, native of this post, legitimate son of Louis Vascocu and Marie Magdalenne Peraut. Bride: 22, native of this post, legitimate daughter of Dominique Sorel and

Marie David, all residents of this parish. 3 bans. Witnesses: Louis Vacocu (s); Dominique Sorel (x); Chs. Noyrit (s); De la Baume (s); Jeann La Land (x); Joseph Jean Ris (x); Remy Perot (s). Priest: Franco. Magnes.

788. JEAN EUGENE MICHAMPS
(303) MARIE DENIS SHALERE
25 April 1818. Marriage. Groom: aged 36, native of Paris, legitimate son of Eugenio Mechamps and a mother not known, widower of Rosa Vachon who died in this parish leaving no children from their marriage. Bride: 23 years and 7 years [sic], native of this parish, legitimate daughter of Pier Shalere, native of New Orleans, and of Maria Victoria Dervan, a native of Natchitoches. 3 bans. Witnesses: Jh. Derbanne (s); Jn Pe. Me. Dubois (s); Bmin. Metoyer (s); [Le] Comte, fils (s); Fcois Frederic (s); Pre Charnau (s). Priest: Franco. Magnes.

789. PIERRE DELOUX
(304) FELICITE POMIER
5 May 1818. Marriage. Groom: aged 27 years 9 months and 20 days, native of this parish, legitimate son of Juan Deloux and Maria Ursula Boule, both deceased. Bride: aged 18 years, native of this parish, legitimate daughter of Jean Pomier and Marie Dupre, both deceased. 3 bans. Witnesses: Francois Slettre (x); Jn Bte. Lattier, fils (s); [Le] Comte, fils (s); J. F. Hertzog (s); M. Prevost Dupré (s). Priest: Franco. Magnes.

790. JACQUES LACASSE (x)
(305) MARIE PHONISSE MASIPPE (x)
28 May 1818. Marriage. Groom: 53 years old, widower of Marie Louise Dupre. Bride: 19 years, native of this parish, legitimate daughter of Jeann Masipe and Marie Lemoin, all residents of this post. Witnesses: Jas. Miller (s); Pierr Chellettre (x); Francois Challer (x); Francois Chelectre (x). Priest: Franco. Magnes.

791. FRANCOIS RUELLE (s)
(306) MARIE LISE LAMBRE (s)
11 June 1818. Marriage. Groom: bachelor, aged 28, native of Serres, Department of "Altes Alpes" [Hautes-Alpes] in France, legitimate son of Antonio Ruelle and Louise Cloden Harman, both deceased. Bride: native of this parish, 17, legitimate daugh-

ter of Remy Lambre and Susanne Proudhomme, both deceased. 3 bans. Witnesses: Bmin. Metoyer (s); J. F. Hertzog (s); Metoyer (s); V. Rouquier(s); Prudhomme (s); J. Lauve (s); Lafon (s); <u>Mal. Morin?</u> (s); F. Vienne (s); O. Buard (s); /Le/ Comte, fils (s); Marie Prudhomme (s); Aurore Metoyer (s). Priest: Franco. Magnes.

792. HILARIO CARRASCO (x)
(307) MARIE CELESTE WALTHER (x)
    25 June 1818. Marriage. Groom: 29 years, bachelor, legitimate son of Geraldo Carrasco and Matilda Flores, all natives of "Guilemer," province of Chihuahua in Mexico. Bride: 17 years, native of New York, legitimate daughter of Federic Walther, a native of "Olanda" and Charity Lely, a native of New York. 3 bans. Witnesses: Jose Ma. Cortinas (x); Jose Simon Montalvo (x); Thos. Graham (s); Charles F. Walthers (s). Preist: Franco. Magnes.

793. ATHANISIT DUPRE (x)
(308) MARIE HORROR /AURORE/ DUBOIS (x)
    25 June 1818. Marriage. Groom: aged 15 years, native of the Rigolet de Bon Dieu, a bachelor, legitimate son of Athanas Dupre and Cecile LeCour, both natives of the post of Natchitoches. Bride: 17, native of the parish of Rapides, legitimate daughter of Jn. Btte. Dubois and Rosse Slecttre. 3 bans. Witnesses: Athanas Dupre (x); Jn. Btte. Dubois (x); Thos. Graham; Charles F. Walthers (s); Valentine Dubois (s); Jean Baptis Dubois (s). Priest: Franco. Magnes.

794. ANTOIN RACHAL (x)
(309) FRANCOISE RACHAL (x)
    30 June 1818. Marriage. Groom: 22, native of this jurisdiction, legitimate son of Antonio Rachal and Maria Luisa Lemoin, a bachelor. Bride: 17 years, native of this jurisdiction, legitimate daughter of Berthelmy Rachal and Francisca Lavery, all residents of this jurisdiction. 3 bans. Signatures: Berthme. Rachal (x); Me. Louis Lemoine (x); Silvestre Rachal (s); Mc. Sompayrac (s); Jn. Bte. Cazenave (s); Nicola Gracia (s); Bte. Lemoine (x). Priest: Franco. Magnes.

795. JEAN BAPTISTE GAGNE (x)
(310) MARIE JOSEPHE HONORINE TOTIN (s)
    2 August 1818. Marriage. Groom: 26 years, native of this parish, legitimate son of Etien Gagne and Marie Louise Bertran. Bride: 27, native of this

parish, legitimate duaghter of Remy Totin and Margarite Grillet. Dispenation granted from bans. Signed: Bertrand Plaisance (x); T. E. Grilliet (s); A. Sompayrac (s); Fs. Vienne (s); Callaghan (s). Priest: Franco. Magnes.

796. JULIO ESTRADA (s)
(311) MARIE ADELISE /BERNA7RDO PANTALEON (s)
9 September 1818. Marriage. Groom: 27, native of province of Monterrey in Boca Leones, legitimate son of Enrique Estrada and Margarita Romero, both natives of Mexico. Bride: 17, native of this parish, legitmate daughter of Bernardo Pantaleon and Margarite Grillet. 3 bans. Signed: Vuida Pantaleon (x); E. Grilliet (s); Josef Arocha (s); Germeuil (s); Rouquier, fils (s); ____ Torres (s); ____ Carr (s); Chs. Noyrit (s); A. Grillet (s); Bernar Pantalon (s) and one illegible signature. Priest: Franco. Magnes.

797. JEAN BAPTISTE ROBINSON (x)
(312) MARIE MANUEL GONÉE /GONIN7 (x)
15 September 1818. Marriage. Groom: bachelor, 27, native of this parish, legitimate son of Peigee Rovertson and Marie Martin. Bride: 17, native of this parish, legitimate daughter of deceased Francisco Gonée and Marie Barbare Federic. 3 bans. Signed: Marie Barbe Frederick (x); Litch Page Robinson (x); Jean Bte. Lestage (x); André Frederick (x); Barthelemy Lestage (x); Phillipe Frederick (x); A. L. Deblieux (s); Francois Serpentini (s). Priest: Franco. Magnes.

798. FELIPE FLORES (s)
(313) MARIE SUSETTE ROBLO (x)
22 September 1818. Marriage. Groom: 22, bachelor, native of Nacogdoches, legitimate son of Jose Flores and Ana Maria Guerrero. Bride: 16, native of Bayou Pierre, legitimate daughter of Pier Raublaut and Magdaline Prudhomme. 3 bans. Signed: Pier Raublau (x); Jh. Tauzin (s); B. Dranguet (s); Francois Serpentini (s); Michel La____n (s). Priest: Franco. Magnes.

799. JEANN PREVOT
(314) MARIANNE GRENAUX (s)
22 September 1818. Marriage. Groom: 24, bachelor, native of Cause, department of "Cherantte Enferior" /France7, legitimate son of Louis Prevot and Marie David. Bride: 22, native of Apelusas, legitimate daughter of Emmanuel Greneaux and

Victoroire Emerante Bossier. 3 bans. Signed:
Veuve Grenaux (s); C. Eml. Grenaux (s); Jn Bte.
Lestage (x); Andre Frederic (x); Antoine Adlé (x);
O. Buard (s); D. Bossier (s). Priest: Franco Magnes.

800. FRANCOIS LAPLANTE
(315) 18 January 1802, burial in cemetery of this parish
of the corpse of Francois Laplante, aged 30 years,
native of St. Louis in Illinois, who died suddenly
without making his confession or testament or receiving the sacraments. Priest: P. Pavie.

801. MARIE GREGOIR DELACROIX
(315) 6 February 1802, burial in cemetery of this parish
of the corpse of Marie Gregoire de la Croix, aged
62 years, native of the Adaille, wife of deceased
Francois Langlois. Death occurred after the receipt of the sacraments of penance and extreme unction, but without having made a confession.
Priest: P. Pavie.

802. MARIE JEANNE GRILLET
(315) 8 March 1802, burial in cemetery of this parish of
the corpse of Marie Jeanne Grillet, wife of Francois Levasseur. Death occurred the preceding day
at the age of 40 years, after receiving the sacraments of penance and extreme unction, but without
having made her confession. Priest: P. Pavie.

803. LOUIS FONTENEAU
(315) 18 March 1802, burial in cemetery of this parish
of the corpse of Louis Fontineau, native of Opeloussas and husband of Pelagie Grape. Death occurred the preceding day at the age of about 45
years, after receipt of the sacraments of penance
and extreme unction, and after having made his
confession. Priest: P. Pavie.

804. JOSEPH MARIE TRICHE /MARIE JOSEPHE TRICHE7
(316) 1 June 1802, burial in cemetery of this parish of
the corpse of Joseph Marie Triche, native of this
parish, daughter of Manuel Triche and Marie Louise
Grape. Death occurred the preceding day at the
age of 26 years, after receiving all the sacraments but without having made a confession. Priest:
P. Pavie.

805. J. B. ARMAND
(316) 1 June 1802, burial in cemetery of this parish of
a newborn infant who died after being privately
baptized, son of Jean Baptiste Armant and Marie

Catherinne Frederick. Priest: P. Pavie.

806. **JEAN DENIS BUART**
(316) 4 June 1802, burial in cemetery of this parish of corpse of Jean Denis Buart, native of this parish, husband of Victoire Poissot. Buart died suddenly at the age of about 30 years, without receiving the sacraments or making his confession. Priest: P. Pavie.

807. **JEAN FRANCOIS ANTOINE GONSALES**
(316) 5 June 1802, burial in cemetery of this parish of the corpse of an infant who died the preceding day at the age of 7 months, son of Francois Gonsalez and Maria Apolonie Daragon. Priest: P. Pavie.

808. **MARIE GENEVIEVE LEVASSEUR**
(316) 2 July 1802, burial in cemetery of this parish of corpse of a child who died the preceding day at the age of 4 months, daughter of Simon Levasseur and Marie Joseph Ulalie Mercier, residents of this parish. Priest: P. Pavie.

809. **JEAN BAPTISTE ETIENNE PAVIE**
(317) 31 July 1802, burial in cemetery of this parish of a youth of about 16 years, native of this parish, who died the preceding day after having made his confession and received general absolution (there not being sufficient time to administer the other sacraments since Pavie died so suddenly). Priest: P. Pavie.

810. **MARIE ANNE GRAPPE (DAUBLIN)***
(317) 25 July 1802, burial in cemetery of this parish of corpse of a woman aged 58 years, widow of Manuel Triche, who died after receiving the sacraments of penance and extreme unction. Her malady did not permit her to receive the viaticum (holy communion) nor did she make her confession. Priest: P. Pavie.

*In both the text and in the marginal reference, the surname of the deceased is first written as "Grappe." This is marked through and replaced by the name "Daublin."

811. **PRUDHOMME**
(317) 27 September 1802, burial in cemetery of this parish of the corpse of an infant of Antoine Prudhomme who died the preceding day after having been baptized privately. Priest: P. Pavie.

812. MARIE FRANCOISE ASELLE BUART
(318) 2 October 1802, burial in cemetery of this parish of corpse of a child of 8 months who died the preceding day, daughter of deceased Denis Buart and Marie Victoire Poissot. Priest: P. Pavie.

813. LOUIS RACHAL
(318) 19 December 1802, burial in cemetery of this parish of the corpse of Louis Rachal, a resident of this post who died suddenly the preceding day without the administration of the sacraments. Deceased was about 50 years of age and the husband of Marie Joseph Laberi. Priest: P. Pavie.

814. LOUIS MARGUERITE DERBANNE
(319) 30 December 1802, burial in cemetery of this parish of the corpse of Louise Marguerite Derbanne, native of this parish, aged 73 years, widow of deceased Louis Saint Denis. Death occurred the preceding day after receipt of the sacraments of penance, communion and extreme unction, and after having made her confession. Priest: P. Pavie.

815. PHILIPPE FREDERIK
(319) 13 January 1803, burial in cemetery of this parish of the corpse of Philippe Frederik, spouse of deceased Barbe Cheletre, a native of this colony who died preceding day at 51 years. Sacraments were administered and confession made. Priest: P. Pavie.

816. MARIE SUSANNE /METOYER/
(319) 28 February 1803, burial in cemetery of this parish of the corpse of a child of 8 months who died the preceding day, daughter of Antoine Joseph /Metoyer/, a free mulatto and of Pelagie /Le Court/ a free mulattress. Priest: P. Pavie.

817. MERCIÉ
(319) 12 March 1803, burial in cemetery of this parish of the corpse of an infant of 4 days, who died after having been privately baptized, legitimate son of Louis Mercié and Louise Lefevre. Priest: P. Pavie.

818. GUISARNAT
(320) 9 May 1803, burial in cemetery of this parish of the corpse of an infant of 1 month who died after having been privately baptized, legitimate son of Bernard Guisarnat and Marie Louise Larenaudiere. Priest: P. Pavie.

819. GRAPPE
(320) 11 June 1803, burial in cemetery of this parish of
the corpse of an infant who died after having been
privately baptized, legitimate son of Jean Baptiste
Grape and Genevieve Sorel. Priest: P. Pavie.

820. JEAN GAUSÉ
(320) 15 July 1803, burial in cemetery of this parish of
corpse of Jean Gausé *dit* Jourdin, who died the preceding day at the home of Mr. Morphil. Deceased
was a native of Paris, aged 34 years, and the legitimate son of Jean Charles Gausé and Magdeleine
Pieret. Priest: P. Pavie.

821. JEAN JOSEPH GUIRINE /CHIRINO/
(320) 23 July 1803, burial in cemetery of this parish of
the corpse of Jean Joseph Guirine, a native of
Nacogdoche, aged 20 years, son of Barthelemi Guirine and Joseph Ariole, who died at the home of
Mr. Bossié. Priest: P. Pavie.

822. SOREL
(320) 30 September 1803, burial in cemetery of this parish of the corpse of an infant aged 10 days, son
of Dominique Marli Sorel *dit* Marli /sic/ and of
Marie Marthe Fort who were not able to carry him
to the church for baptism. Priest: P. Pavie.

823. EUPHROSINE ANTI
(320) 6 October 1803, burial in cemetery of this parish
of corpse of Euphrosine Anti, who died the preceding day at the age of 10 years, daughter of Jean
Baptiste Anti and Francoise Levasseur. Priest:
P. Pavie.

824. PRUDHOMME
(320) 6 October 1803, burial in cemetery of this parish
of the corpse of an infant who died after having
been privately baptized, legitimate son of Manuel
Prudhomme and Catherine Lambre. Priest: P. Pavie.

825. PIERRE LARENAUDIERE
(320) 24 December 1803, burial in cemetery of this parish of the corpse of Pierre Larenaudiere, who died
the preceding day, at age 40, after receiving the
sacraments. Spouse was Jeanne Laberi. Priest:
P. Pavie.

826. MARIE JOSEPH MERCIÉ
(320) 12 January 1804, burial in cemetery of this parish
of Marie Joseph Mercié who died the preceding day

at the age of about 20 years, the deceased wife of Manuel Levasseur. Received all the sacraments. Priest: P. Pavie.

827. MAGDELEINE ROBERT
(320) 14 January 1804, burial in cemetery of this parish of the corpse of Magdeleine Robert, an Indian of the Caneci nation who died the preceding day at the home of Jean Baptiste Barcas without having received the sacraments. Deceased was about 18 years of age and daughter of Charlotte, a Caneci Indian. Priest: P. Pavie.

828. MICHEL DUFY
(320) 24 January 1804, burial in cemetery of this parish of corpse of Michel Dufy, master surgeon, native of Ireland, who died the preceding day at about the age of 36. Received all the sacraments. Priest: P. Pavie.

829. LOUIS ALEXANDRE GUERBOIS
(321) 12 February 1804, burial in cemetery of this parish of the corpse of Louis Alexandre Guerbois, native of Rouen, France, husband of Elisabeth Trepanié. Guerbois died the preceding day at this post, at the age of about 56, after receiving the sacrament of extreme unction. Priest: P. Pavie.

830. MARIE FORT SOREL
(321) 17 February 1804, burial in cemetery of this parish of the corpse of Marie Marthe Fort, wife of Pierre Sorel, a native of this post, who died the preceding day at the age of about 25 years, after receiving the sacraments. Priest: P. Pavie.

831. JACQUES ERRIÉ
(321) 19 March 1804, burial in cemetery of this parish of the corpse of Jacques Errié, native of New Orleans, husband of Anasthasie Maillou. Errié died the preceding day at the age of about 45 years, after receiving all the sacraments. Priest: P. Pavie.

832. MARIE ELISABETH DENES
(321) 2 July 1804, burial of Marie Elisabeth Denis, a native of Hennebout in Lower Brittany, diocese of Nante, France. Deceased was daughter of Jean Baptiste Denes and Elizabeth Dumont, and was widow of Louis Caser Bormee. She died suddenly the preceding day at the age of about 72 years. Priest: P. Pavie.

833. PAUL MARCOLLAY
(321) 18 July 1804, burial in cemetery of this parish of the corpse of Paul Marcollay, native of La Rochelle, legitimate son of Pierre Marcollay, merchant, and of Catherinne Gobin. Died the preceding day at the age of $59\frac{1}{2}$ years, after making confession and receiving all the sacraments. Priest: P. Pavie.

834. ANGELIQUE
(322) 16 September 1804, burial in cemetery of this parish of the corpse of an Indian of the Canneci nation, who died suddenly at this post at the age of about 50 years, without receiving the sacraments. Priest: P. Pavie.

835. MARIE JOSEPH MELANIE RACHAL
(322) 17 October 1804, burial in cemetery of this parish of the corpse of Marie Joseph Melanie Rachal, 18 year old daughter of Louis Rachal and Marie Joseph Laberi, who died suddenly the preceding day without the administration of sacraments. Priest: P. Pavie.

836. POISSOT
(322) 24 October 1804, burial in cemetery of this parish of an infant who died after having been privately baptized, legitimate son of Paul Poissot and Marie Louise Anty. Priest: P. Pavie.

837. CHARLOTTE MERCIÉ
(322) 27 October 1804, burial in cemetery of this parish of Dame Charlotte Mercié, native of Carcassone in France, aged about 50 years, wife of Sieur Joseph Capuran. She died the preceding day after making her confession. Priest: P. Pavie.

838. FRANCOIS
(322) 3 November 1804, burial in cemetery of this parish of an Indian named Francois, native of Mobile, of the Ansa nation, who died suddenly the preceding day. Priest: P. Pavie.

839. MARIE JEANNE TOTIN
(323) 9 November 1804, burial in cemetery of this parish of Marie Jeanne Totin, aged 45 years, wife of Guillaume Chevert, who died the preceding day after receiving all the sacraments and making her confession. Priest: P. Pavie.

840. GONSAQUE /GONSALEZ/
(323) 30 December 1804, burial in cemetery of this parish

of the corpse of an infant who died after being
privately baptized, son of Pierre Gonsaque and
Catherinne Bonnet. Priest: P. Pavie.

841. ANTOINE VASCOCU
(323) 15 January 1805, burial in cemetery of this parish
of the corpse of Antoine Vascocu, aged 50 years,
who died the preceding day after having received
all the sacraments and made his confession. Deceased was a native of this post and husband of
Genevieve Gonin. Priest: P. Pavie.

842. RACHAL
(323) 5 February 1805, burial in cemetery of this parish
of the corpse of a child who died immediately after birth, after having been privately baptized.
Infant was daughter of Jean Baptiste Barthelemi
Rachal and Pelagie Brevel. Priest: P. Pavie.

843. PASCHAL TURJON
(324) 4 May 1805, burial in cemetery of this parish of
corpse of Paschal Turjon, a native of Quebec,
Canada, aged about 75 years, who died the preceding day without having received the sacraments
since he was not forewarned of his illness.
Priest: P. Pavie.

844. PAILLET
(324) 18 September 1805, burial in cemetery of this parish of an infant aged 10 days who died after being
privately baptized, legitimate son of Jean Baptiste Jacques Paillete and Marie Victoire Poissot.
Priest: P. Pavie.

845. MARIE ARCENE TRICHE
(324) 20 November 1805, burial in cemetery of this parish of the corpse of Marie Arcene Triche, aged 3
years or about, daughter of Jean Baptiste Triche
and Marie Modeste Fonteneau. Priest: P. Pavie.

846. PIERRE BADIN
(325) 29 December 1805, burial in cemetery of this parish of Pierre Badin, who died the preceding day
after receiving the sacraments. Deceased was 80
years old, a native of Thorigne in the diocese of
Poitier, France, and widower of Marie Anne Serpault. Priest: P. Pavie.

847. JEAN BAPTISTE BREVEL
(325) 26 April 1806, burial in cemetery of this parish
of Jean Baptiste Brevel, native of this parish,

this parish, who died the preceding day at the age of 76 years, after having received the sacraments. Brevel was the widower of deceased Marie Francoise Poissot. Priest: P. Pavie.

848. JULIEN BESSON
(325) 3 May 1806, burial in cemetery of this parish of Julien Besson, native of this post, who died the preceding day at the age of 58 years after having received the sacraments. Deceased was husband of Marie Perau. Priest: P. Pavie.

849. JOHN JONES
(325) 24 May 1806, burial in cemetery of this parish of "an American named John Jones" who died the preceding day after having been carried sick to this post. Deceased received the sacraments, but priest was not given the name of his parents nor his birthplace. Priest: P. Pavie.

850. MAIOU
(325) 27 May 1806, burial in cemetery of this parish of an infant of Laurent Maiou who died the day of his birth, after having been baptized privately. Priest: P. Pavie.

851. FRANCOIS LACASE
(325) 4 June 1806, burial in the cemetery of this parish of the corpse of Francois Lacase, master surgeon, native of Aignant, diocese of Auche in France, who died the preceding day at the age of about 75. Priest: P. Pavie.

852. TAUSIN
(326) 20 June 1806, burial in cemetery of this parish of an infant of Joseph Tausin who died after having been privately baptized. Priest: P. Pavie.

853. JOSEPH LEMOINE
(326) 18 July 1806, burial in cemetery of this parish of Joseph Lemoine, native of Montreal, Canada, who died suddenly at this post at the age of about 50 years. His parents are not known. Priest: P. Pavie.

854. GASPART DERBANE
(326) 10 July 1806, burial in cemetery of this parish of Gaspart Derbanne who died without receiving the sacraments, not having been aware of his malady. Deceased was husband of Marie Joseph Perau. Priest: P. Pavie.

855. MARIE AURORE PERAU
(326) 29 August 1806, burial in cemetery of this parish of the 10 month old daughter of Chrisostome Perau and Marie Louise Salvant. Priest: P. Pavie.

856. MAIOU
(326) 13 September 1806, burial in cemetery of this parish of twin infants who died the day of their birth, after having been privately baptized. They were daughters of Marie Anastasie Maiou, widow of Jacque Herrié. Priest: P. Pavie.

857. BLUDWORD
(327) 20 August 1807, burial in cemetery of this parish of an infant of Mr. Bludword, aged 15 days. Priest: Louis Buhot of Opelousas.

858. LOUISE CAVE POISSEAU
(327) 23 August 1807, burial of Louise Cave, widow of Remi Poisseau who died without the sacraments at the age of about 60 years. Priest: Louis Buhot of Opelousas.

859. N. MAYOU
(327) 9 December 1809, burial of Sieur N. Mayou, aged about 60 years, who died without the sacraments. Priest: Louis Buhot of Opelousas.

860. MARIE TERESA BUARD
(328) 6 February 1813, burial in cemetery of this parish of Marie Teresa Buard, aged 70 years, widow in first marriage of Estevan Pavie by whom she had a daughter. By her second marriage the deceased was wife of Pedro Metoyer, by whom she had 2 sons and a daughter. Priest: F. Magnes, curé of Nacogdoches.

861. SILVESTRE BUARD
(328) 7 June 1813, burial in cemetery of this parish of Silvestre Buard, native of Natchitoches, aged 30 years, legitimate son of Luis Buard and Maria Rosa Lambre. The deceased, a bachelor, died of fever. Priest: F. Magnes, curé of Natchitoches.

862. MARIA MAGDALENA PERAUT
(329) 19 July 1813, burial of Maria Magdalena Peraut, aged 45 years, wife of Louis Vascocu by whom she left /torn/ sons and 2 daughters. Deceased received all the last sacraments, died in virtue, and was buried in the lot of her house at Campti, in this jurisdiction, close to the "Lac aux Murs."

Priest: F. Magnes.

863. PEDRO VIMENEZ
(329) 2 September 1813, free burial of Pedro Vimenez, native of Spain, who died at the age of 72 years, a widower who left a son in the colony of Nuevo Santander in the Kingdom of Mexico. Viminez died of a sudden illness and for this reason did not receive the sacrament or make his confession. "His burial was one of charity, for he was very poor." Priest: F. Magnes.

864. FRANCISCO TREVINO
(329) 11 September 1813, free burial in cemetery of this parish of a native of Besar, aged 58 years, husband of Maria Josefa de la Garza by whom he left 2 married sons. Deceased died of fever and received all the sacraments, but was not able to speak and could not make his confession. Priest: F. Magnes.

865. JUAN JOSE VELA
(329) 23 September 1813, free burial of a Spaniard of the kingdom of Mexico, aged 36 years and a native of Serralbo, legitimate son of Salvado Vela and Ana Maria Ramos. Deceased left a widow, Maria Josefa Mendez. He made his confession but received none of the sacraments, having died almost suddenly of the fever. Priest: F. Magnes.

866. VICTORIANO RAMOS
(330) 27 September 1813, burial in cemetery of this parish of a Spaniard of the Kingdom of Mexico, aged about 60 years and a widower who had lived many years in Apelusa. The deceased made no confession and received no sacraments since he died very suddenly of exhaustion. Priest: F. Magnes.

867. ANTONIO BADEN
(330) 2 October 1813, burial in cemetery of this parish of A. Baden, native of Bordeaux, France, aged 28 years and a bachelor. He did not make his confession or receive any of the sacraments, being unconscious from his illness. Cause of death: putrid fever. Priest: F. Magnes.

868. MARGARITA VICTORIA PRUDHOMME GRENOBLE
(330) 3 October 1813, burial in cemetery of this church of the corpse of Marg. Victoria Prudhomme, widow in first nuptials of Mr. Tristan and in second nuptials of Etienne Ternier by whom she left one

son, and in third nuptials of Pierre Durranton. Deceased received the sacraments. Priest: F. Magnes.

869. APOLINARIO LAUVE
(331) 10 October 1813, burial in cemetery of this church of a child of 4 days "who had received only the baptismal water," legitimate son of Evariste Lauve and Eufrosina Cte. Bruna. Death was caused by epilepsy. Priest: F. Magnes.

870. FERNANDO MENCHACA
(331) 20 October 1813, burial in cemetery of this church of a Spaniard, native and resident of Besar, aged about 35 years, leaving a widow, Tomasa de Vimenez, and two sons and one daughter. He did not receive any of the sacraments nor make a confession since he was unconscious with putrid fever. Priest: F. Magnes.

871. FACUNDO DEL RIO
(331) 21 October 1813, burial in cemetery of this church of a Spaniard, native of Nacogdoches, 16 years old and a bachelor, legitimate son of Ficente del Rio and Feliciana Cruz. Deceased did not receive any of the sacraments nor make a confession since he was unconscious with putrid fever. Priest: F. Magnes.

872. IGNACIO PEÑA
(332) 23 October 1813, burial in cemetery of this parish of a 40-year old native of Besar in the province of Texas, who died leaving a widow Maria de la Luz Nararrete, a resident of Bexar, and one son. Deceased did not receive the sacraments nor make a confession since he was unconscious with putrid fever. Priest: F. Magnes.

873. MARIA ANASTASIA MAILLIUD & ARMAN
(332) 27 October 1813, free burial in cemetery of this parish of Madama Maria Anastasia Mailliud y Arman, widow by first nuptials with Santiago Eheer /Herrié7, by whom she left two sons, and by second marriage with Juan Harman by whom she left 3 daughters and 2 sons. Deceased received no sacraments nor made her confession since she died suddenly of the putrid fever which rendered her unconscious. Priest: F. Magnes.

874. MARCELO SERVANTES
(332) 10 November 1813, free burial in the cemetery of

this church of a Spaniard of 40 years "who left a widow, Juan Bta. Martinez," with four adult sons and three daughters. He received the sacraments but did not make a confession since he died of the fever. Priest: Franco. Magnes.

875. MARIA TERESA SANCHEZ
(333) 1813. Burial entry. Almost completely destroyed. Remains indicate that deceased left a husband Jose _____ and died of the fever. Free Burial. Priest: F. Magnes.

876. JOSE ESTEVAN BORREGO
(333) 24 December 1813. Free burial in cemetery of this parish. Deceased was 30 years old, a bachelor, and legitimate son of Ma_____ _____nego and Maria Anta. Encarnacn. Acosta, both residents of Besar in province of Texas. Borrego received the sacraments of penitence and extreme unction but made no confession as he died of the fever. /Entry is partially destroyed.7. Priest: F. Magnes.

877. JUAN MORALES
(333) 27 December 1813, burial in cemetery of this parish of a Spaniard of 35 years, a bachelor and native of Sn. Antonio de Besar in the Province of Texas, legitimate son of Alberto Morales and Maria Jetrudis Orosco. Deceased received the sacraments of penitence and extreme unction but did not make confession since he died of fever. Free burial. Priest: F. Magnes.

878. UNKNOWN
(334) December 1813 or January 1814. Entry is almost entirely destroyed. Deceased was married, received the sacraments, and died of asthma. Priest: F. Magnes.

879. JOSE LUIS DURAN
(334) 2 (or 3) January 1814, free burial in cemetery of this parish of a Spaniard, native of Besar, aged 35 years, a widower by his first nuptials with Mauricia Sosa, by whom he had 2 sons, and by his second nuptials with Guadalupe Traviso. Deceased received the sacrament of extreme unction and died of a pain. Priest: F. Magnes.

880. MARIA JETRUDIS SOTO
(334) 29 January 1814, burial in cemetery of this parish of a native of Nacogdoches, aged 30 years, who left a widower Felipe Mora, by whom she left one

daughter and an older son. From her single years she left two sons. Deceased received the sacraments of penitence and extreme unction but did not make a confession. She was buried at public expense. Priest: F. Magnes.

881. MARIA SERRIA?
(335) 1814. Burial. Entry almost completely destroyed. Remains yield the partial name "Miguel Plo_____," which appears to be that of her husband, and indicates that she was a Spaniard, received the sacraments, and was buried at public expense. Priest: F. Magnes.

882. JUAQUIN MURQUIZ
(335) 12 February 1814, burial in cemetery of this parish of a Spaniard of about 50 years, resident of Besar, who died leaving a widow named Margarita _____ /blank/ and a son. Deceased received the sacraments of penance and extreme unction but did not confess. Burial at public expense. Priest: F. Magnes.

883. MARIA FRANCISCA MALBER y FORCH /FORT/
(335) 12 March 1814, burial in cemetery of this parish of Madama Maria Francisca Malber, aged 50 years, widow of /torn/ and native of this post. She received none of the sacraments. Priest: F. Magnes.

884. FRANCISCO RODRIQUEZ
(335) 22 March 1814, burial in cemetery of this parish of a Spaniard, aged 62 years, widower by first nuptials with _____ na Travieso, by whom he left 2 daughters, and who was now married with Maria Ruiz by whom he leaves 2 sons and 1 daughter. Deceased did not confess and received only the sacrament of extreme unction since he died suddenly of a pain. Priest: F. Magnes.

885. UNKNOWN
(336) 1814. Burial. Entry almost completely destroyed. Deceased was aged 35, a native of Mon_____ /Montreal?/ in Canada, received none of the sacraments and did not make a confession since he died suddenly. Priest: F. Magnes.

886. JOSE PABLO MONTOYA
(336) 19 April 1814. Free burial of a Spaniard, native of Besar, province of Texas, aged 34 years, who left a widow, Maria Concepcion Cruz, but no chil-

dren. He received the sacraments of penance and extreme unction, but did not make a confession. Death caused by a pain. Priest: F. MAgnes.

887. MARIA _____
(336) ___ May 1814. Burial. Entry badly torn. Deceased was a child of 6 years, legitimate daughter of _____ and Maria Gertrudis Carmona, Spaniards. Burial by public alms. Priest: F. Magnes.

888. FRANCISCO GULLYM
(337) 14 J/une/ 1814. Burial. Entry badly torn. Deceased was "aged forty _____," did not receive any of the sacraments or make a confession since he died very suddenly. Priest: F. Magnes.

889. JUAN BAUTISTA GRAPPA
(337) 21 June 1814, burial in cemetery of this parish of Juan Bautista Grappa, a native of this parish, 18 years old, bachelor, and legitimate son of Juan Bautista Grappa and Genoveva Sorel. Deceased did not receive any of the sacraments or make a confession; died of fever. Priest: F. Magnes.

890. ISIDORO HERNANDEZ
(337) 6 July 1814. Free Burial. Entry almost completely destroyed. Deceased was 30 years old and left "two _____ /sons or daughters?/. Priest: F. Magnes.

891. JUAN BTTA. DAVION
(337) 8 July 1814, burial. Entry almost completely destroyed. The name "Marie Jacinta" appears on a bottom fragment. Priest: F. Magnes.

892. LEFEBRE
(338) 1814. Burial. Entry almost completely destroyed. Deceased apparently was a child of ____ months and 8 days, son of _____ LeFebre and died of the fever. Priest: F. Magnes.

893. ANDRES ANTONIO RAMBEN
(338) 10 July 1814. Burial in cemetery of this parish of Mr. Andres Antonio Ramben, aged 64 years, native of New Orleans, widower of Mda. Maria Catalina Buard by whom he left 2 sons and 2 daughters. He made no confession but received sacrament of extreme unction. Priest: F. Magnes.

894. MARIA _____
(338) 1814. Burial. Entry almost entirely destroyed.

The name "Maria" and the word "daughter" are the only revealing words. Priest: F. Magnes.

895. UNKNOWN
(338) 1814. Burial. Entry almost entirely destroyed. Deceased was 25 years old and a native of Leon. Priest: F. Magnes.

896. JOSEF BOC_____ /BOCANEGRA?/
(339) Entry completely destroyed except for marginal notation with name followed by word "Negr___". It is possible that the indiviual was Jose Bocanegra. Burial. Priest: F. Magnes.

897. SIMON LOPES
(339) Entry completely destroyed except for marginal notation. Burial. Priest: F. Magnes.

898. UNKNOWN
(339) /A half page of burial entries are destroyed at this point./

899. _____ GARCIA
(340) Burial entry destroyed except for this one word.

900. UNKNOWN
(340) /Three-fourths page of burial entries are destroyed at this point./

901. UNKNOWN
(341) 1814. Burial. Entry destroyed except for one fragment. Deceased was aged ____ years and 7 months, child of _____polier and d_____. Death by fever. Priest: F. Magnes.

902. JOSE FRANCISCO ALAMILLA
(341) 29 _____ 1814. Burial. Entry almost entirely destroyed. Remaining fragment indicates that deceased was from "Bajas" and the legitimate son of _____. Priest: F. Magnes.

903. MARIA O_____ FILIBERT
(341) 2 October 1814. Burial. Entry almost completely destroyed. Child was apparently aged 4 years and 3 /months or days/. Priest: F. Magnes.

904. MARIA ASPASI ___RFIL _____ /MURPHY/
(341) 3 October 1814. Burial. Entry almost entirely destroyed. Remaining fragments indicate that deceased was a native of this post, widow of Mr. A_____. Deceased left "_____ and one son."

(By her second marriage?) Deceased was legitimate daughter of Mr. Eduardo _____. Death caused by fever. Priest: Franco. Magnes.

905. UNKNOWN
(342) Entry destroyed except for inconsequential fragment.

906. UNKNOWN ⟦CHELETTE or BUARD⟧*
(342) 1814. Burial. Entry almost entirely destroyed. Remaining fragment indicates deceased was legitimate son of _____ and Eulalia Bossie. Priest: F. Magnes.

*Eulalie Emelie Bossier, fille Soulange, was the wife of Jean Pierre Chelette. Eulalie Bossier fille François was the wife of Jean Louis Buard.

907. UNKNOWN
(342) 1814. Burial. Entry almost entirely destroyed. Remaining fragments indicate deceased was a woman, a native of this post, a widow who left an indiscernable number of sons, and did not receive any of the sacraments. Priest: F. Magnes.

908. _____ YEPER
(342) ___ October 1814. Burial. Entry almost entirely destroyed. Remaining fragment indicates deceased was 28 years old, the legitimate son of Luis Yeper and Guana, of _____ rales de Guanajuato in ____. Death caused by fever. Sacraments were administered. Priest: Franco. Magnes.

909. MARIA FANI ARMAN
(343) 1814. Burial. Entry largely destroyed. Remains indicate that deceased was aged 15, legitimate daughter of ⟦Jean Baptiste⟧ Arman and Catalina Phelipa ⟦Frederic⟧ and died of dropsy without receiving the sacraments. Priest: F. Magnes.

910. JOSE FRANCISCO BELOZ
(343) 5 November 1814, burial in the cemetery of this parish of the 5 year old legitimate son of Juan Diego Beloz and Maria Francisca de Cardenes, Spaniards and natives of Parras, who died of epilepsy. Free burial. Priest: F. Magnes.

911. BERTELMIL RACHAL
(343) 13 November 1814, burial in cemetery of this parish of Mr. Bartelmil Rachal, son of Bartelmil Rachal, native of this parish, aged about 40 years, husband of Maria Magdalena Grillet by whom he left

one son and ____ daughters. Death by vomiting
/and apparently without benefit of the sacraments
due to the nature and degree of his illness./
Priest: F. Magnes.

912. CIRIAN VERGER /VERCHER/
(343) ___ November 1814, burial in cemetery of this
parish of a child of 4 or 5 years, legitimate son
of Juan Pedro Verger and Maria Emeli Eslect /Che-
lette/. Death by fever. Priest: F. Magnes.

913. UNKNOWN
(344) 1814. Burial. Entry almost completely destroyed.
Entry appears to have been begun, but not finish-
ed, by F. Magnes.

914. SARA DANALLE y _____
(344) 7 December 1814. Burial of Sarah Donalle, native
of Riche? Burd,* widow of Morico Richal by whom she
left 2 sons and 1 daughter. Death caused by
jaundice. Sacraments were administered. Priest:
F. Magnes.

*"Burd" was F. Magnes' phoenetic spelling of
"bourg."

915. ANTONIO /DE/ MESSIER
(344) ___ December 1814, burial in cemetery of this
parish of Antonio Mesierre, native of this post,
aged 52 years, who left a widow, Candida Rio__,
a native of Havadia, by whom he left no children.
Priest: F. Magnes.

916. _____ CHEZ
(345) November 1814. Burial. Entry almost completely
destroyed. Deceased was aged 35, a native of
Besar, and left a widow named ____ a Rodriguez
and two sons. /Possibly left daughters also. Entry
is torn at this point./ Priest: F. Magnes.

917. JOSE ____
(345) 1814. Burial. Entry almost completely torn.
Deceased was a Spaniard. The name "___rcelo
Bor____," also appears on the line following his
name, and "residents of" appears on the next line.
Priest: F. Magnes.

918. UNKNOWN
(345) /Two entries at this point are completely destroyed./

919. TOUSSAINT SINEGAL
(345) 2 January 18__. Burial. Entry almost completely
destroyed. Deceased was ___ and seven years of
age, and left a widow named _____ Osilinue by
whom he left /number of children is no longer ex-
tant_7. Priest: F. Magnes.

920. JOS. LUIS DUR_____
(346) 3 January? 18__. Burial. Rest of entry destroyed.

921. UNKNOWN
(346) /Two entries at this point are destroyed._7

922. BERNARDO DES/PALLIER_7
(347) ca1814. Burial. Entry is almost completely destroyed. Remaining fragment mentions a widow,
Candida Grande. Priest: F. Magnes.

923. JOSE FRANCISCO ALAMILLO
(347) __ September 1814. Burial. Entry is almost completely destroyed. Deceased was aged ". . . año
y *once meses*" /apparently 1 year and eleven months_7
and the legitimate son of _____ Alamillo and Paula
Pena. Priest: F. Magnes.

924. MARIA _____
(347) ca1814. Burial. Entry is almost completely destroyed. Remaining fragment indicates only that
deceased was wife or widow "of Mr. _____" and
that she died of fever. Priest: F. Magnes.

925. UNKNOWN
(347) Burial entry is almost completely destroyed.

926. UNKNOWN
(347) Burial entry completely destroyed.

927. UNKNOWN
(348) Burial entry almost completely destroyed. Remaining fragment indicates deceased was probably a son
or daughter of Mda. Mariana Bar_____.

928. PLACIDE BUARD
(348) 5 October 18__. Burial. Entry is almost completely destroyed. Remains indicate that deceased was
son of Luis Buard and died of intestinal worms.
Priest: F. Magnes.

929. MARIA LUISA GRILLET y BERGER /VERGER_7
(348) 15 October _____. Burial. Entry is destroyed except for word "two" in the approximate position

where number of surviving sons and daughters is usually recorded. Priest: F. Magnes.

930. JOSE _____
(348) 20 _____. Burial. Entry completely destroyed except for fragment yielding first name and day of the month. Priest: F. Magnes.

931. JETRUDIS MONTES
(349) 25 December 1814, burial of Spaniard, a native of Besar, wife in first nuptials of Guillermo Casanova, by whom she had 1 son, and wife in second nuptials of Portuges _____ /blank/, by whom she had another son. Deceased received the sacraments and died of fever. Priest: F. Magnes.

932. MARGARITA RINN CHELECTTRE
(349) 5 January 1815, burial in cemetery of this parish of a woman of 48 years, native of this post, who left a husband, Pedro Chelesettre, by whom she left 2 sons and 4 daughters. Last sacraments were administered and death was caused by dropsy. Priest: F. Magnes.

933. PIERRE MALLOUD
(349) 24 January 1815, burial in cemetery of this parish of a man of 35 years, native of this post, a bachelor and the legitimate son of Ignacie Malloud, a native of Canada, and Teresa cu Filibot, native of Ilinua. Death was sudden and caused by dropsy. Priest: F. Magnes.

934. MARIE JOSEPH ARMAN
(350) 20 February 1815, burial in cemetery of this parish of Marie Joseph Armant, aged about a hundred years, native of Metz in Lorraine, France. He left a widow, Teresa Latamdres /LeGros/ by whom he also left one daughter and 3 sons. Of his first marriage, he left 2 sons and 3 daughters. Deceased received the sacraments and died of fever. Priest: F. Magnes.

935. SUSANNE PROUDHOMME LAMBRE
(350) 10 April 1815, burial in cemetery of this parish of a native of this post, aged about 40 years, who left a widower, Remy Lambre, by whom she also left 2 sons and 8 daughters. Death was "almost sudden" and no sacraments were administered. Priest: F. Magnes.

936. DORSET HOY
(350) 12 April 1815. *Burial of Dorset Hoy, aged about 40, of the American nation. He left a widow, Marianne Artemisse Lamaitre, by whom he also left "daughters and sons" /exact number not specified7. Sacraments were administered; death caused by dropsy. Priest: F. Magnes.

*Cemetery not identified.

937. CHARLES TAUDEM
(351) 24 April 1815, burial in cemetery of this parish of a native of Paris, parish of St. Pier? Dumond, aged 57 years. Sacraments were administered. Death by dropsy. Priest: F. Magnes.

938. MARIE LOUISE BREVEL RACHAL
(351) 29 April 1815, ecclesiastical burial administered to Mda. Marie Louise Brevel, native of this parish, aged about 50 years, widow of Mr. Julian Rachal by whom she left 5 sons and 4 daughters. Death caused by dropsy. Priest: F. Magnes.

939. JUAN NEPOMANO CEVALLOS
(351) 20 June 1815, burial in cemetery of this parish of a native of Havadia, aged 51 years, who left a widow, Maria de los S^{tos} /Santos7 and two daughters. Deceased received the sacraments and died of fever. Priest: F. Magnes.

940. MARIE PERIN /LECOMTE7
(351) 11 July 1815, burial in cemetery at Riviera Ocan /Riviere aux Cannes7* of Marie Perin, a free mulattress, aged 28 years. Deceased was the wife of Pierre Metoyer, a free mulatto, by whom she left one daughter and two sons. Death caused by fever. Priest: F. Magnes.

*This cemetery is known today as "Shallow Lake" Cemetery and lies on the riverbank, west of Hwy. 1, between Cloutierville and Derry. Few markers remain.

941. MARIE LOUISE AGATE LAVERY
(352) 10 August 1815, burial in the cemetery of this parish of Marie Louise Agate Lavery, aged 50 years, who left a husband, Francois Peraut, 3 sons, and 3 daughters. Death caused by dropsy. Priest: F. Magnes.

942. MICAELA ROSALIA /STA. CRUZ7 BOUDIN
(352) 18 August 1815, burial in cemetery of this parish

of Micaela Rosalia Baudin Cruz, aged 60 years, widow of Lorens Boudin, by whom she left 3 sons and 1 daughter. Deceased received the sacrament and died of fever. Priest: Franco. Magnes.

943. MARIA LUISA MORALES
(352) 28 August 1815, burial in cemetery of this parish of a native of Nacogdoches, aged 29, never married. Deceased succumbed to fever and died without receiving the sacraments. Priest: F. Magnes.

944. MARIA VLCIANE /FELICIANE/ LESTAS
(352) 28 August 1815, burial in cemetery of this parish of a child of 22 months, legitimate daughter of Jn. Btte. Lestas and Marianna Chlettre. Death by fever. Priest: F. Magnes.

945. GEORGE GUASINTON /WASHINGTON/ GUES /CASE/
(352) 30 August 1815, burial in cemetery of this parish of a child of 18 months, legitimate son of David Gues and Maria Proudhomme. Death by fever. Priest: F. Magnes.

/This series of burials continues with Entry 413./

946. PIERRE /METOYER/
(353) PERINE /LECOMTE/
1802. Marriage entry. Partially torn. Groom: son of Therese Coincoin, a free Negro. Bride: a free woman of color, daughter of Francoise, mulattress slave of _____ Lecomte, all natives of this parish. Witnesses: Jerome Frederik; Augustin /Metoyer/, free mulatto; Dominique /Metoyer/ free mulatto, and both brothers of the groom; and Ma_____ and Gaspart Bodin. Priest: P. Pavie.

947. GASPART BODIN
(353) MARIE LOUISE /LE DUC dit/ VILLEFRANCHE
22 September 1802. Marriage, after 3 bans. Groom: native of this parish, legitimate son of deceased Laurens Bodin and Marie Rosalie La Croix /Sta. Cruz/. Bride: Widow of Francois Lemaitre and legitimate daughter of deceased Jean Baptiste Villefranche and Marie Anne Guedon. Sacrament of penance administered prior to the marriage. Witnesses for groom: Louis Chamart, Paul Marcolet. Witnesses for bride: Joseph Marie Armant and Louis Totion. Priest: P. Pavie.

948. JOSEPH DERBANNE
(353- *⟨CATHERINE⟩ BROSSET
354) 22 November 1802. Marriage, after 3 bans. Groom: native of this parish, legitimate son of Pierre Derbanne and Marie LeClerc. Bride: native of this parish, legitimate daughter of P⟨ierre -- document torn⟩ Brosset and Marie Joseph Grille. Witnesses: Jean Baptiste Anty; Remi Lambre; Bernard Vissoura ⟨Hissoura⟩; Barthelemi Rachal. Priest: P. Pavie.

*The bride's name is torn from the above record. However, the second marriage of her husband -- recorded in *Register 11* under date 11 April 1831 -- identifies him as the widower of "deceased CATHERINE Brosset."

949. AUGUSTIN LEFEVRE
(354) VICTOIRE LEMAITRE
4 February 1803. Marriage, after 3 bans. Groom: native of Quebec, aged 29 years, legitimate son of Pierre Lefevre and deceased Marie Leclerc, now living in this post. Bride: legitimate daughter of deceased Francois Lemaitre and Marie Louise Ville-franche, native of this parish and now living here. Witnesses: Michel Chamart; Louis Berthelemieu; Augustin Roubieu; Jacques Herrier. Priest: P. Pavie.

950. ANTOINE GRILLET
(354- MARIE FELICITÉ PEROT
355) 15 February 1803. Marriage, after 3 bans. Groom: native and resident of this parish, legitimate son of deceased Mavin Grillet and Marie Louise Brevel. Bride: Native and resident of this post, legitimate daughter of Chrisostome Perot and Marie Louise Salvant. Witnesses: Jean Baptiste Anti; Dominique Rachal; Joseph Tauzin; and Paul Marcollay. Priest: P. Pavie.

951. JEAN BAPTISTE PRUDHOMME
(355) ROSALIE MALIGE
18 April 1803. Marriage, after 3 bans. Groom: native of this parish, legitimate son of deceased Bastien Prudhomme and Marie Jeanne Chevert. Bride: native of New Orleans, legitimate daughter of Joseph Malige and Marie Anne Bardon. Witnesses: Remi Lambre; Francois Rouquié; Charles Chamart; Joseph Tausin. Priest: P. Pavie.

952. LUC PERÉ
(355) MARIE LALEMAND
13 November 1803. Marriage, after 3 bans. Groom: native of the town of "Sta. Crux in Canarie," legitimate son of deceased Antoine Peré and Francoise Capite. Bride: natural daughter of Pierre Lallemand and Therese Langlois, all living in this post. Witnesses for groom: Joseph Marie Armand and Francois Grape. Witnesses for bride: Joseph Triche and Francois Rouquier. Priest: P. Pavie.

953. JEAN BAPTISTE JACQUES PAILLETTE
(356) MARIE VICTOIR POISSOT
21 November 1803. Marriage, after bans. Groom: native of Heugueville in France, "department of Seine-Inferieure," legitimate and major son of George Pierre Paillete and Susanne Leroy, now a resident of this post. Bride: Widow of Denis Buart, legitimate daughter of deceased Remis Poissot and Marie Louise Cavé. Witnesses: Manuel Prudhomme; Francois Rouquié, syndic; Louis Buart; Jean Baptiste Buart. Priest: P. Pavie.

954. MANUEL DERBANNE
(356) MARGUERITE DENIS
2 February 1804. Marriage, after bans. Groom: native of this parish, legitimate son of deceased Pierre Derbanne and Marie Leclerc. Bride: daughter of Jean Baptiste Denis and deceased Elibeth Bontems, a native and resident of this parish. Witnesses: Nicolas Lauve, Jr.; Guillaume Barre; Edouart Morphil; Jean Baptiste Théodore Grillet; Francois Levasseur. Priest: P. Pavie.

955. JEAN BAPTISTE BESSON
(357) MARIE JEANNE PIEVER
2 June 1804. Marriage, after 3 bans. Groom: native of this parish, son of Julien Besson and Marie Perot. Bride: native of this parish, daughter of Francois /Frederic dit/ Piever and Marie Jeanne Chagneau. Witnesses for groom: Louis Lamalathie; Francois Grape; Francois Perot. Witnesses for bride: Joseph Jean-Ris; Michel Chagneau. Priest: P. Pavie.

956. FRANCOIS COINCOIN /METOYER/
(357) MARGUERITE /LA FANTASY/*
23 July 1804. Marriage after 3 bans. Groom: a free mulatto, native and resident of this parish, son of Marie Therese Coincoin, a free Negress. Bride: a free mulatress, living at this post,

daughter of deceased Francoise, Negro slave of Pi=
erre Derbanne. Witnesses for groom: Augustin
Coincoin /Metoyer7, a free mulatto and his brother;
Dominique Lambre, a free mulatto. Witnesses for
bride: Louis and Joseph Coincoin /Metoyer7 also
free mulattoes. Priest: P. Pavie.

*See Gary B. Mills, *The Forgotten People: Cane
River's Creoles of Color* (LSU Press, 1977), 83.

957. FRANCOIS POIRIER
(358) THERESE THOMACIN /THOMASSIE7
9 October 1804. Marriage, after 3 bans. Groom:
native of this parish, son of deceased Vincent
Poirié and Jeanne Riché. Bride: legitimate daughter of Louis Thomacine and Catherine Latier, native
of this post and living at Couteille /Cotile7 in
post of Rapides where there is no priest. Witnesses: Pierre Cheletre; André Frederic; Paul Himel;
Jean Baptiste Armand. Priest: P. Pavie.

958. JEAN FRANCOIS FREDERIC
(358) MARIE FELICITÉ LAVESPERE
4 April 1804. Marriage, after 3 bans. Groom: a
native of Rapides, living in this post, legitimate
son of Philipe Frederik and Marie Catherine Sauvage. Bride: native of this parish and living
here, legitimate daughter of Francois Lavespere
and Marie Louise Derbane. Witnesses: Louis Derbane; Joseph Tausin; Pierre Cheletre; Arnau Lauve.
Priest: P. Pavie.

959. DOMINIQUE SOREL
(359) MARIE EUPHROSINE MATHURIN DAVID
6 May 1805. Marriage, after bans. Groom: widower of Marie Marthe Fort, legitimate son of deceased
_____ Sorel /sic7 and Rose Bauchellié /Boisselier7
and living now in this post. Bride: legitimate
daughter of deceased David Mathurin /sic7 and Marie
Anne Lamalati. Witnesses: Louis David Mathurin
/sic7; Paul Poissot; Antoine Barthelemi Rachal;
and Louis Charles Chamart. Priest: P. Pavie.

960. LOUIS TIHOUA
(359) MARIE JOSEPH MAGDELEINE CHRISTI
16 May 1805. Marriage performed with consent of
Rev. Father Puelles, pastor of Nacogdoches, and
Msgr. Leveque de Montairai, bishop of the province
of Thécle /Texas7 and after dispensation of bans.
Groom: an Indian of the Natchitoches nation who
was baptized this same day, natural son of Tihoua

and Nahouet, Indians of the Natchitoches nation
living at Tapalca in the parish of Nacogdoches.
Bride: also a resident of Catapalca /sic/ in parish of Nacogdoches, legitimate daughter of Jacques
Christi and Marianne Dorotheé Perau. Four children of the couple were thereby legitimized: Marie Euphrosine, born 12 June 1798; Marie Marguerite,
born 15 November 1799; Marie Deneige, born 15 August 1801; and Cesair, aged 2 years or about. Witnesses: Louis Chamart; Joseph Tausin; Remis Christi; and Henri Meneust. Priest: P. Pavie.

961. JEAN BAPTISTE ADELET
(360) MARIE VICTOIRE BREVEL
22 July 1805, marriage, after 3 bans. Groom: a
native of this parish and living here, legitimate
son of Jean Adelet and Marie Genevieve Dubois.
Bride: native and resident of this post, legitimate daughter of Jean Baptiste Brevel and deceased
Marie Francoise Poissot. Witnesses: Arnau Lauve;
François Grape; Antoine Grille; Barthelemi Rachal.
Priest: P. Pavie.

962. JEAN BAPTISTE PRUDHOMME
(360) MARIE THERESE VICTOIRE AILHAUD STE. ANNE
10 October 1805, marriage, after bans. Groom:
minor and legitimate son of Emmanuel Prudhomme and
Catherinne Lambre. Bride: legitimate daughter of
Jean Baptiste Ailhaud Ste. Anne and Marie Louise
Buard, all natives and residents of this post.
Witnesses for groom: Antoine Prudhomme, his uncle; Remi Lambre, also his uncle on the maternal
side. Witnesses for bride: Pierre Metoier and
Jean Baptiste Buart, also her uncles on the maternal side. Priest: P. Pavie.

963. PIERRE ELIE BERNARD
(361) MARIE DERBANNE
11 January 1806. Marriage, after 3 bans. Groom:
native and resident of this post, legitimate son
of Elie Bernard and Heleonore Chagneau. Bride:
native and resident of this post, legitimate daughter of Gaspar Derbane and Marie Joseph Perau.
Witnesses: Francois Dubois; Michel Barberoue;
Francois Perau and Elie Bernard. Priest: P. Pavie.

964. BARTHELEMI LESTASE
(361) MARIE PELAGIE FREDERIK
17 February 1806, marriage. after 3 bans. Groom:
native and resident of this post, legitimate son
of Guillaume Lestase and Manuel Riche. Bride:

native and resident of this post, legitimate daughter of deceased Philippe Frederic and Marie Barbe /Chelette/. Witnesses: Francois Gonin; Jean Baptiste Lestase; André Frederik; and Jean Baptiste Armand. Priest: P. Pavie.

965. MANUEL LEVASSEUR
(362) GENEVIEVE GONIN
17 February 1806. Marriage, after publication of bans. Groom: native and resident of this parish, widower of Marie Joseph Mercier, legitimate son of Francois Levasseur and deceased Marie Josephe Mader. Bride: widow of Antoine Vascocu, native and resident of this post also, legitimate daughter of Jean Baptiste Gonin and Marie Riché. Witnesses: Francois Gonin; Louis Levasseur; Jean Baptiste Lestase; and Francois Adelet. Priest: P. Pavie.

966. MARIE ADELET
(362) 16 March 1806, baptism of infant born 3 December 1805, legitimate daughter of Jean Baptiste Adelet and Marie Victoire Brevel. Godparents: Valentin Adelet and Marie Dolet Rachal. Grandparents: Jean Adelet and Marie Genevieve Dubois; Jean Baptiste Brevel and Francoise Poissot. Priest: P. Pavie.

967. PIERRE NOLASCO PORCUNA
(363) MAGDELEINE LABERI
19 March 1806. Marriage, after publication of bans. Groom: native of Trise, province of Andalousia in Spain, legitimate son of Juan Manuel de Porcuna and Antoinette Muños. Bride: widow of Simeon Rachal, legitimate daughter of Jean Baptiste Laberi and Jeanne Guedon. Witnesses: Bernard Guisarnat; Louis Chamart; Francois Bardon; André Chamart. Priest: P. Pavie.

968. JEAN BAPTISTE MORIN
(363) MARIE CONSTANCE LUGUE
19 May 1806. Marriage, after 3 bans. Groom: native of Comarasca, diocese of Quebec, Canada, legitimate son of deceased Jean Marie Morin and Marie Saucié. Bride: native of Ouachitas, legitimate daughter of deceased Jean Lugue and Anne Olivie. Witnesses: Jacques St. André, Pierre Blese *dit* St. Germain; Francois Latié; and Jean Louis Baiou. Priest: P. Pavie.

969. GERMAIN OUAILETTE /WALLETTE/
(364) MARIE ANTOINETTE TORRES
19 May 1806. Marriage, after 3 bans. Groom: na-

tive of parish of Camarasca in diocese of Quebec, Canada, legitimate son of André Ouailette and Joseph Coté, and now a resident of this post. Bride: legitimate daughter of Joseph Torres and Marie Le Roi /Maria Juana de los Reyes/. Witnesses for groom: Francois Latié and Jean Louis Baiou. Witnesses for Bride: Pierre Blese *dit* St. Germain and Jacques St. André. Priest: P. Pavie.

970. JEAN BAPTISTE COMTE
(364) MARIE STEPHALIE /CEPHALIDE/ LAMBRE
9 June 1806. Marriage, after publication of bans. Groom: native and resident of this post and minor son of Ambroise Comte and Heleine Cloutier. Bride: also a native and resident of this post, legitimate daughter of Remi Lambre and Susanne Prudhomme. Witnesses: Jean Baptiste Anti; Jean Baptiste Buart; Louis Derbanne; Francois Belar. Dumas; Jean Baptiste Paillet; Felix Trudeau. Priest: P. Pavie.

971. JEAN BAPTISTE THEODORE GRILLET
(365) MARIE CATHERINE MARCELITE PERRAU
11 August 1806. Marriage, after publication of bans. Groom: native and resident of this parish, legitimate son of deceased Marin Grillet and Marie Louise Brevelle. Bride: also a native and resident of this parish, legitimate daughter of Francois Peraux and Marie Louise Agathe Laberri. Witnesses: Renaud Lauve; Dominique Rachal; Jean Pierre Lalande; Francois Grape; Nicolas Lauve. Priest: P. Pavie.

972. FRANCOIS LATIE
(365) MARIE PELAGIE CHELETRE
12 August, 1806. Marriage, after publication of bans. Groom: native of this parish, legitimate son of Joseph Latie and deceased Anne Verge. Bride: legitimate daughter of Pierre Cheletre and Marie Reine Frederick. All live in this parish. Witnesses: Jean Baptiste Paillette; Bertrand Mailloche; Jean Francois Frederik; Pierre Lacour. Priest: P. Pavie.

973. FRANCOIS MAURICE MELON
(366) MARIE LOUISE /RACHAL/*
26 August 1806. Marriage, after 3 bans. Groom: a free mulatto, native of New Orleans, son of deceased Felicité, a free Negress, and of a father unknown. Bride: a free mulattress, native of this parish, daughter of a father unknown* and of Francoise, slave of Baptiste Rachal. Witnesses:

Dominique /Metoyer/; Antoine Joseph /Metoyer/;
Baltasar /Monet/ and Philippe Daunois, all free
mulattoes. Priest: P. Pavie.

*See Gary B. Mills, *The Forgotten People: Cane
River's Creoles of Color* (LSU Press, 1977).

974. LOUIS NARCISSE PRUDHOMME
(366) MARIE THERESE ELISABETH METOYER
23 September 1806. Marriage, after publication of bans. Groom: Native of this parish, legitimate son of Manuel Prudhomme and Catherine Lambre. Bride: native also of this parish, daughter of Pierre Metoyer and Therese Buart. All are residents of this post. Witnesses: Antoine Prudhomme; Remi Lambre; Francois Rouquiér; Jean Baptiste Buart; Edouart Morphil. Priest: P. Pavie.

975. CHARLES ROQUE PAVIE (s)
(367) MARIE ANNE ROUQUIER (s)
8 August 1807. Marriage. Groom: Native of Bordeaux and resident of this post, legitimate son of Jean Baptiste Pavie and Anne Bernard. Bride: native of this parish, legitimate daughter of Francois Rouquier and Marie Louise Prudhomme. Signed: C. Pavie (s); Tonton Rouquier (s) /Bride/; Jh. Tauzin (s); Proudhomme (s); Rouquier (s); Rouquier, fils (s); Nlas. Lauve (s); Ete. Lauve (s). Priest: Louis Buhot, pastor of Opelousas.

976. JEAN BAPTISTE FONTENOT (s)
(368) MARIE POMPOSE LAFITTE (x)
10 August 1807. Marriage. Groom: native of this parish, legitimate son of deceased Louis Fontenot and Pelagie Grappe. Bride: Also a native of this parish, legitimate daughter of Paul Boué Lafitte and Marie Anne De Soto. Signed: Bte. Trichel; Ete. Lauve (s); A. Lauve (s); Cazenave (s); Louis Vacocu (s): Priest: Louis Buhot of Opelousas.

977. REMI TOTTIN
(369) MARIE THERESE VASCOCU
13 August 1807. Marriage, after one ban. Groom: native and resident of this parish, legitimate son of deceased Remi Tottin and Marguerite Grillette. Bride: Native of this post, daughter of André Vascocu and Madeleine Remond. Signed: Fois. Vascocu (x); Rouquier, fils (s); Michel Chamard (s); A. Grilliet (s). Priest: Louis Buhot of Opelousas.

978. ARNAULD LAUVE
(370) MARIE ELISABETH ASPASIE MURPHI

3 August 1807. Marriage, after 1 ban. Groom: native of New Orleans and resident of this parish, son of Nicolas Lauve and Catherine Couterette. Bride: native of this parish, legitimate daughter of Edouard Murphi and Marie Elisabeth Buard. Signed: Bellabre Dumas (s); Cazenave (s); Bte. Trichel (s); Nlas. Lauve (s). Priest: Louis Buhot of Opelousas.

979. FIERRE DERBONE (x)
(371) MARIE ASTASIE DAVION (x)
17 August 1807. Marriage. Groom: native and resident of this parish, legitimate son of Pierre Derbonne and Marie Francoise Brevel. Bride: native of this parish, legitimate daughter of Francois Davion and Margte. Cloutier. Signed: Fois. Davion (x); Bte. Trichel (s). Priest: Louis Buhot of Opelousas.

§ NOTE: Marriages from August 1807 to December 1809 are no longer extant. In 1973, before this portion of the register crumbled, the editor extracted the following note from these now-destroyed records:

JEAN BAPTISTE JULIEN RACHAL
MARIE ROSALINE DERBANNE
16 November 1807. Marriage. Groom: son of Julien Rachal and Marie Louise Brevel. Bride: daughter of Jn. Bte. Derbanne and Therese Roy.

980. JEAN FRANCOIS HERTZOG (s)
(372) MARIE ANNE DESIRÉE PRUDHOMME (s)
7 December 1809. Marriage. Groom: native of Bordeaux, legitimate son of Henry Mathieu Hertzog and Jeanne Lartigue. Bride: native of this parish, legitimate daughter of Antoine Prudhomme and Marie Lambre. Signed: Prudhomme (s); Prudhomme fils (s); Remy Lambre (s); Compere (s). Priest: Louis Buhot of Opelousas.

981. VALENTIN ADLÉ (s)
(373) MARIE SILESIE BROSSÉ (x)
10 December 1809. Marriage. Groom: native of this parish, legitimate son of Jean Bte. Adlé and Genevieve Dubois. Bride: native of this parish, legitimate daughter of Pierre Brossé and Marie Josef Grillie. Signed: Pierre Brosset (x); A. Lauve (s); Ete. Lauve (s); Amb. Duval (s). Priest: Louis Buhot of Opelousas.

982. LOUIS FONTENOT (x)
(374) MARIE JOSEF PALVADO (x)
10 December 1809. Ratification of civil marriage.
Groom: native of this parish, legitimate son of
deceased Louis Fontenot and Pelagie Grappe. Bride:
native of this parish, legitimate daughter of Jn.
Palvado and Eleonor Tessier. Signed: Louis Fontenot (x); Marie Josef Palvado (x); Bte. Trichel
(s); Manuel Rachal (s); Durey (s); Ete. Lauve (s);
Priest: Louis Buhot of Opelousas.

983. JULIEN RACHAL (x)
(375) MARIE /MELANIE/ LAVESPAIR (x)
12 December 1809. Marriage. Groom: native of
this parish, legitimate son of Julien Rachal and
Marie Louise Brevel. Bride: native of this parish, legitimate daughter of Francois Lavespair
and Marie Louise Derbanne. Signed: Lavespere (s);
Cezair Murphy (s); A. Lauve (s). Priest: Louis
Buhot of Opelousas.

984. FRANCOIS ROGER (s)
(376) PELAGIE ADLE (s)
13 December 1809. Marriage after ordinary publication of bans. Groom: native of Havre de Grace,
legitimate son of Jn. Bte. Roger and Marie Elisabeth Julie. Bride: Native of this parish, legitimate daughter of Jean Etienne Adlé and Genevieve
Dubois. Signed: A. Lauve (s); Fcois. Grappe (s);
Jn. Ls. Buard (s); C. Bossier (s). Priest: Louis
Buhot of Opelousas.

985. DORSETTE HOY (x)
(377) MARIE ANNE LE MAITRE (x)
17 December 1809. Marriage. Groom: native of
Ireland, legitimate son of Sibert Hoye and Elisabeth Glover. Bride: native of this parish, daughter of Francois Le Maitre and Marie Louise Villefranche. Signed: M. Barberous (s): Henry Trichel
(s). Priest: Louis Buhot of Opelousas.

986. MICHEL BARBEROUSSE (s)
(378) NANETTE GANIER (x)
17 December 1809. Marriage. Groom: native of
this parish, son of Gme. Barberousse and Marie
Jeanne Chaniot. Bride: native of this parish,
daughter of Etienne Ganier and Marie Louise Bertrand. Signed: Henry Trichel; Bte. Triche (s).
Priest: Louis Buhot of Opelousas.

987. JEAN FRANCOIS LEVASSEUR (s)
(379) MARIE FRANCOISE TRICHEL (s)
     17 December 1809. Marriage. Groom: native of
     this parish, legitimate son of Francois LeVasseur
     and Marie Jeanne Matere. Bride: native of this
     parish, legitimate daughter of Jn. Bte. Trichel
     and Marie Anne Daublin. Signed: Bte. Trichel (s);
     A. Sompayrac (s); Ete. Lauve (s). Priest: Louis
     Buhot of Opelousas.

988. JEAN CORTES   (s)
(380) MARCELLITTE ROUQUIER (s)
     23 December 1809. Ratification of a marriage con-
     tracted civilly on 16 January 1808. Groom: Jn.
     Cortes Dartheils, native of Etcharry, district of
     Basses-Pyrénées, France, legitimate son of deceas-
     ed Pre. Cortes and deceased Marie Claray y Cassau.
     Bride: native of this parish, legitimate daughter
     of deceased Fcois. Rouquier and Marie Louise Prud-
     homme. Signed: Maës, fils (s); James Carr (s);
     C. Pavie (s); V. Rouquier (s); Rouquier, fils (s);
     Priest: Louis Buhot of Opelousas.

989. JOHN C. CARR (s)
(381) MARIE JOSEPH HENRIETTE ROUQUIER (s)
     23 December 1809. Ratification of civil marriage.
     Groom: native of Liverpool, legitimate son of Theo-
     phile Carr and Margtte. Cath. Rowen Boyd. Bride:
     native of this parish, legitimate daughter of
     Fois. Rouquier and Marie Louise Prudhomme. Signed:
     Jn Cortés (s); V. Rouquier (s); C. Pavie (s);
     Rouquier, fils (s); Maës, fils (s). Priest: Louis
     Buhot of Opelousas.

990. AMBROISE SOMPAYRAC   (s)
(382) JOSEPHINE BRIAND   (s)
     23 December 1809, ratification of civil marriage
     contracted at New Orleans. Groom: native of Cas-
     tres in Albigeois, legitimate son of Amb. Sompay-
     rac and Susanne Gassignau. Bride: native of St.
     Dominigue, legitimate daughter of Fois. Briand
     and Marie Elisabeth Mozard. Signed: Jn. Pe. Mie.
     Dubois (s); J. F. Hertzog (s); Rouquier, fils (s);
     Maës, fils (s). Priest: Louis Buhot of Opelousas.

991. GASPARD PHILIBERT (s)
(383) FELICITE THEOPHILE LEMAITRE   (x)
     25 December 1809, ratification of civil marriage.
     Groom: native of Marseille, legitimate son of
     Augustin Philibert and Marie Anne Richard. Bride:
     native of Natchitoches, daughter of N. Lemaitre

and "Mde. N." Signed: Louis Tauzin (s); Jn. The. Lemonnser Duparig? (s). Priest: Louis Buhot, Opelousas.

992. MICHEL SIMONS (x)
(384) ROSALIE VINCENT (x)
25 December 1809. Ratification of civil marriage. Groom: native of Canada, son of Jean Simons and Margtte. Trichette. Bride: native of this parish, daughter of Michel Vincent and Helene Roubleau. Signed: Louis Tauzin (s); Hippolite Bouregart (x). Priest: Louis Buhot, Opelousas.

993. JEAN BTE. MORANTI (MAURANTI) (x)
(385) MARIE MADEL. EUPHRASIE FREDERIC (x)
28 December 1809. Marriage. Groom: native of "Ajation in Corse," legitimate son of Jean Bte. Moranti and Marie Vangile Moreau. Bride: native of this parish, legitimate daughter of deceased Philippe Frederic and Marie Catherine Sauvage. Signed: Jh. Tauzin (s); Jn Pe. Mie. Dubois (s); Fs. Roubieu (s). Priest: Louis Buhot, Opelousas.

994. JEAN RENAUD AGUESSE (x)
(386) MARIE LOUISE MASSIPPE (x)
28 December 1809. Marriage. Groom: Native of this post, legitimate son of Jn. Agaesse and Perine Olivier. Bride: Native of this parish, legitimate daughter of Jean Massippe and Marie Lemoine. Signed: Jn. Bte. Derbanne (x); Jacques LaCasse (x); Jh. Tauzin (s); Priest: Louis Buhot, Opelousas.

995. ANTOINE RACHAL (x)
(387) MARIE ASTASIE DERBANNE (x)
28 December 1809. Marriage. Groom: native of this parish, legitimate son of Barthelemi Rachal and Marie Francoise Lamalati. Bride: native of this parish, legitimate daughter of Jean Bte. Derbanne and Marie Helen Brevel. Signed: L. B. Rachal (s); Jh. Tauzin (s); Ls. Derbanne (s); Jn. Pe. Mie. Dubois (s). Priest: Louis Buhot, Opelousas.

996. ALEXIS CLOUTIER (x)
(388) MARIE LUCE RACHAL (x)
28 December 1809. Marriage. Groom: resident of the parish of Natchitoches. Son of Alexis Cloutier and Marie Rachal. Bride: Native of this parish, legitimate daughter of Louis Rachal and Marie Francoise Grillette. Signed: Ml. Prevost Dupré (s); L. B. Rachal (s); Jh. Tauzin (s); Jn. Pre. Mie. Dubois (s). Priest: Louis Buhot, Opelousas.

997. LOUIS GALLIEN (x)
(389) MARIE CELTESTE ANTY (x)
29 December 1809. Marriage. Groom: Native of this parish, legitimate son of Nlas. Galien and Marie Antoine Lecourt. Bride: Native of this parish, legitimate daughter of Louis Anty and Marie Jeanne Checte /Crete7. Signed: Jh. Tauzin (s); Jn. Pe. Mie. Dubois (s); Ete. Lauve (s). Priest: Louis Buhot of Opelousas.

998. JACQUES LECOMTE (x)
(390) MARIE SILVIE BROSSE (x)
29 December 1809. Marriage. Groom: native of this parish, son of Amb. LeComte and Therese, Indian. Bride: native of this parish, legitimate daughter of Pre. Brosse and Marie Joseph Grillette. Signed: Comte, fils (s); Jh. Tauzin (s); Jn. Pe. Mie. Dubois (s); Ete. Lauve (s). Priest: Louis Buhot of Opelousas.

999. JEAN PIERRE VERCHER (x)
(391) MARIE EMELITTE SHLETER (x)
_____ 1811. Marriage. Entry badly torn. Ratification of a civil marriage performed 11 April _____. Parental information destroyed. Signed: Louis Tauzin (s); Chs. Noyrit (s); Pierre Mailliud (s); Jh. Tauzin (s). Priest: Louis Buhot of Opelousas.

1000. JEAN BAPTISTE BARTHELEMI RACHAL (x)
(392) MARIE DENIZE LEMOINE (x)
8 August 1811. Marriage Entry badly torn. Groom: native of this parish, legitimate son of Jn. Bte. Barthelemi Rachal and /Marie Pelagie7 Brevel. Bride: parental information destroyed. Signed: Jn. Bte. Lemoine (x); Bte. Adlé (x); Chs. Noyrit (s); Priest: Louis Buhot of Opelousas.

1001. LOUIS JULIEN RACHAL(x) - MARIE REINE THOMASSIE (x)
(393) 30 December 1809. Entry partially torn. Marriage at Riviere aux Cannes. Groom: native of this parish, legitimate son of Julien Rachal and Marie Louise /Brevel7. Bride: native of this parish, legitimate daughter of /Louis Thomassie7 and of /Catherine Lattie7. Signed: Alexis Cloutier (x); Louis Thomassi (x); Nicolas Gallien (x). Priest: Louis Buhot of Opelousas.

1002. FRANCOIS BESSON (x)
(394) DENIZE CHRISTI (x)
11 August 1811. Marriage. Groom: native of

Canada, legitimate son of Antoine Besson and Marie __urrvre. Bride: Native of this parish, legitimate daughter of Jacques Christi and Dorothée Perrault. Signed: Jean Bte. Besson (s); Pier Maulliou (s); Felix Flotroiz (s); Remi Christi (x); Priest: Louis Buhot, Opelousas.

1003. THOMAS M. LINNARD (s)
(395) ADELAIDE TAUZIN (s)
12 August 1811. Ratification of civil marriage. Groom: Native of Philadelphia, legitimate son of William Linnard and Susanna Linnard. Bride: native of this parish, legitimate daughter of Joseph Tauzin and Marie Chamart. Signed: Louis Tauzin (s); Jh. Tauzin (s). Priest: Louis Buhot, Opelousas.

1004. PIERRE CHARNAU (s)
(396) MARGUERITTE RABALAIS (s)
13 August 1811. Marriage. Groom: native of Saiyon in Saintonge, France, legitimate son of Pierre Charnau and Susanne Maitter. Bride: native of this parish, legitimate daughter of Josef Rabalais and Marie Louise Malbert. Signed: Chs. Noyrit (s); Ls. Derbanne (s). Priest: Louis Buhot, Opelousas.

1005. FRANCOIS ROUQUIER (s)
(397) MARIE ELISABETH BUART
15 August 1811. Ratification of civil marriage. Groom: native of Natchitoches, legitimate son of Fois. Rouquier and Marie Louise Prudhomme. Bride: Native of Natchitoches, legitimate daughter of Louis Buart and deceased Marie Rose Lambre. Signed: Chs. Noyrit (s); A. Sompayrac (s). Priest: Louis Buhot, Opelousas.

1006. JN. BTE. SHLETER /Chelette/ (x)
(398) MARIE EUPHROSINE RACHAL (x)
29 November 1812. Ratification of civil marriage. Groom: native of this parish, legitimate son of Pre. Schleter and Marie Reine Frederic. Bride: legitimate daughter of Louis Barthel. Rachal and Francoise Grillette. Signed: Chs. Noyrit (s); A. Somayrac (s). Priest: Louis Buhot, Opelousas.

1007. JEAN BAPTISTE VERCHER (x)
(399) MARIE ORESILLE GALLIEN (x)
29 November 1812. Marriage. Groom: legitimate son of Louis Verschere and Marie Louise Grillette. Bride: legitimate daughter of Nicolas Gallien and Marie LeCourt. Signed: Chs. Noyrit (s); A. Sompayrac (s). Priest: Louis Buhot, Opelousas.

1008. LOUIS RACHAL (x)
(400) MARIE LOUISE SCHLETER /CHELETTE/ (x)
29 November 1812. Marriage. Groom: legitimate
son of Louis Barth. Rachal and Foise. Grillette.
Bride: legitimate daughter of Pre. Schleter and
Marie Reine Frederic. Signed: Chs. Noyrit (s);
A. Sompayrac (s). Priest: Louis Buhot, Opelousas.

1009. THEODORE GRILLET (s)
(401) MARIE AIMEE PERAUT (x)
29 November 1812. Marriage. Groom: legitimate
son of Marin Grillette and Marie Louise Brevel.
Bride: legitimate daughter of Chrisosthome Peraut
and Marie Louise Salvan. Signed: Chs. Noyrit (s);
A. Sompayrac (s). Priest: Louis Buhot, Opelousas.

1010. CELESTIN ELIE BERNARD (x)
(402) CELESIE TRISCHE (x)
1 December 1812. Marriage. Groom: Resident of
Natchitoches, legitimate son of Elie Bernard and
Eleonore Chaniot. Bride: native of Natchitoches,
legitimate daughter of Manuel Trische and Marie
Louise Grappe. Signed: Henry Trichel (s); Francois Dubois (x); Chs. Noyrit (s); A. Sompayrac (s);
Priest: Louis Buhot, Opelousas.

1011. JEAN BOUCHER (s)
(403) MARIE ANNE DURAND DE ST. ROMES (s)
30 November 1812. Marriage. Groom: native of La
Rochelle, son of Bernard Boucher and Margueritte
Maltete. Bride: Native of Port au Prince, legitimate daughter of Charles Durand, Chevalier de St.
Louis, and of Dme. Therese Chevalier. Signed: Joseph Carriere (s); Cazenave (s). Priest: Louis
Buhot, Opelousas.

1012. CELESTIN FAUSTIN PERROT (s)
(404) CELESTE BORDELON (s)
2 December 1812. Marriage. Groom: native of
Natchitoches, legitimate son of Crisosthome Peraut
and deceased Marie Louise Salvan. Bride: Native
of Natchitoches, legitimate daughter of Hippolite
Bordelon and Marie Therese Trische. Signed: Chs.
Noyrit (s); A. Sompayrac (s). Priest: Louis Buhot, Opelousas.

1013. JEAN BTE. PLAISANCE (x)
(405) MARIE JOS. PALVADO (x)
2 December 1812. Marriage. Groom: native of this
parish, legitimate son of deceased Bte. Plaisance
and Margtte. Tauttin. Bride: native of this

parish, legitimate daughter of Jean Palvado and Leonor Tessier. Signed: Chs. Noyrit (s); A. Sompayrac (s). Priest: Louis Buhot, Opelousas.

1014. LOUIS PERAUT (x)
(406) MELANIE TRISCHE (x)
2 December 1812. Marriage. Groom: native of this post, legitimate son of Fois. Peraut and Marie Louise Labairie. Bride: native of this parish, legitimate daughter of Henri Trische and Gennev. Riesse. Signed: Chs. Noyrit (s): Henry Trichel (s); Cazenave (s); A. Sompayrac (s). Priest: Louis Buhot, Opelousas.

1015. NEVILLE GALLIEN (x)
(407) MARIE ELOISE LATTIER (s)
5 December 1812. Marriage. Groom: legitimate son of Nicolas Gallien and Marie LeCour. Bride: legitimate daughter of Jean Bte. Lattier and Marie Pelagie Frederic. Signed: Marie deloyse Lattier (s) /bride7; Chs. Noyrit (s); Ls. Derbanne (s); Cauranson (s). Priest: Louis Buhot, Opelousas.

1016. CESAIR MURPHI (s)
(408) ADELAIDE BUARD (x)
5 December 1812. Ratification of civil marriage. Groom: legitimate son of Edouard Murphi and Elisabet Buard. Bride: legitimate daughter of Denis Buart and Victoire Poissot. Signed: Ed. Cr. Murphy (s); Adelaite Buard (x); A. Sompayrac (s); Narcisse Prudhomme (s). Priest: Louis Buhot, Opelousas.

1017. NARCISSE RACHAL (x)
(409) MANETTE RACHAL (x)
6 December 1812. Marriage. Groom: legitimate son of Antoine Rachal and Marie Louise LeMoine. Bride: legitimate daughter of deceased Julien Rachal and Marie Louise Brevel. Signed: Compere (s); Chs. Noyrit (s); Fs. Roubieu (s). Priest: Louis Buhot, Opelousas.

1018. CASIMIRO PERO (x)
(410) DAMASENA PUESO /POISSOT7 (x)
5 February 1813. Ratification of civil marriage. Groom: Native of Natchitoches, legitimate son of Crisostomo Pero and Maria Luisa Salban. Bride: native of this same post, legitimate daughter of Atanasio Pueso and Maria Elena Pavi. Signed: Cazenave (s); A. Sompayrac (s). Priest: Franco. Magnes, pastor of Nacogdoches.

1019. DR. JOHN SIBLEY (s)
(411) EULALIE MALIGE (s)
12 February 1813. Marriage. Groom: native of the state of "Massasuchit," widowed for about two years from his second wife, Maria Winslow. Bride: not previously married. Aged 25 years, native of New Orleans, legitimate daughter of Josef Malige and Mariana Bardon, who give their consent to the marriage. Signed: Jh. Malige (s); Wm. N. Emery (s); Jn. Cortes (s); Thomas M. Linnard (s). Priest: Franco. Magnes, pastor of Nacogdoches.

1020. FRANCISCO RAMBIN
(412) MARIA DAMASIA DE SOTO
6 April 1813. Ratification of civil marriage. Groom: native of Natchitoches, legitimate son of Andres Antonio Rambin and Ma. Catalina Buard. Bride: native of Bayou Pierre, legitimate daughter of Marcelo De Soto and Maria Bayou /Baillio7. Signed: André Rambin (s); Marcel Desoto (s); Martin Cruz (x); Jose Cruz (x). Priest: Franco. Magnes.

1021. JUAN BAUTISTA ADLEY (x)
(413) MARIA DENISE DOLLE (x)
6 April 1813. Ratification of civil marriage. Groom: native of Natchitoches, a bachelor, legitimate son of Juan Adley and Genoveva Duvois. Bride: native of Bayou Pierre, legitimate daughter of Pedro Dolle and Maria Rosa Diuprae. Signed: Btte. Adley "for his father and mother" (s); Etin. Adlé (s); Martin Cruz (x); Jose Cruz (x). Priest: Franco. Magnes.

1022. JUAN BAUTISTA TIMOTEO ADLEY (x)
(414) MARIA DENEIGE PRUDHOMME (x)
6 April 1813. Ratification of civil marriage. Groom: native of Natchitoches, legitimate son of Juan Adley and Genoveva Duvois. Bride: legitimate daughter of Franco. Prudhomme and Maria Barbara Rambin. Signed: Btte. Adley "for his father and mother" (s); Andres Balentin (x); Martin Cruz (x). Priest: Franco. Magnes.

1023. PEDRO SEVASTIAN COMPERE
(415) MARIA LOLETTE RACHAL
6 May 1813. Ratification of civil marriage. Groom: native of Bordeaux, legitimate son of Roverto Compere and Magdalena Duguillen. Bride: native of Natchitoches, legitimate daughter of Julian Rachal and Maria Luisa Brevel. Signed:

Cazenave (s); A. Sompayrac (s). Priest: Franco. Magnes.

1024. JUAN BAUTISTA DERBANNE
(416) LUCIA PLAISANCE
20 May 1813. Marriage. Groom: native of this parish, legitimate son of Gaspar Derbanne and Maria Josefa Perau. Bride: native of this parish, legitimate daughter of Beltran Plaisance and Maria Barbara Grillet. Signed: Cazenave (s); Chs. Noyrit (s); Ls. Davenport (s). Priest: Franco. Magnes.

1025. FRANCISCO ROUBIEU
(417) MARIA OSITE RACHAL
28 May 1813. Ratification of civil marriage. Groom: native of "Islas Negras" /Illinois/, legitimate son of Gaspar Roubieu and Marianna Laferne. Bride: native of Natchitoches, legitimate daughter of Julian Rachal and Maria Luisa Brevel. Signed: /J. J./ Pailette (s); Chs. Noyrit (s); A. Sompayrac (s). Priest: Franco. Magnes.

1026. AGUSTIN /CEZER/ FREDIEU (s)
(418) MARIA ROSA DERVANN (s)
1 June 1813. Ratification of civil marriage. Groom: legitimate son of Agustin Fredieu and Mariana Sorel. Bride: legitimate daughter of Gaspar Derban and Maria Josefa Perou. Signed: Cezer Fredieu (s) /groom/; Bossie (s); P. D. Cailleau Lafontaine (s). Priest: Franco. Magnes.

1027. FRANCISCO BENJAMIN METOYER (s)
(419) MARIA AURORA LAMBRE (s)
17 June 1813. Ratification of civil marriage. Groom: /legitimate son of Pierre Metoyer and Marie Thereze Eugenie Buard/*. Bride: daughter of Remigio Lambre and Susana Prudhomme. Signed: /Pierre/ Metoyer (s); Remy Lambre (s); Cazenave (s); S. Davenport (s). Priest: Franco. Magnes.

1028. ANDRES ADLEY (x)
(420) MODESTA PRUDHOMME (x)
1 July 1813. Ratification of civil marriage, Groom: /legitimate son of Jean Adley and Marie Genovieve Dubois/*. Bride: native of Bayou Pierre, legitimate daughter of Franco. Prudhomme and Maria Barbara Rambin. Signed: John Sibley (s);

*Entries partially destroyed.

Btte. Adle (s); Cazenave (s); Vtin. Adle (s).
Priest: Franco. Magnes.

1029. JOSE CRISOSTOME PERRAULT (x)
(421) MARIA OLIMPE FREDIEU (x)
11 July 1813. Ratification of civil marriage.
Groom: native of Natchitoches, legitimate son of
Crisostome Peiraut and /blank/. Bride: native of
Natchitoches, legitimate daughter of Agustin Fre-
dieu and Mariana Sorel. Signed: Malige (s); Noel
Malige (s); Cazenave (s). Priest: Franco. Magnes.

1030. TOMAS WALES /WALLACE/
(422) MARIA HORTENSE BERTRAND
9 August 1813. Ratification of civil marriage.
Groom: native of Apelussas, legitimate son of
Jose Wales and Linée Bals__en. Bride: legiti-
ate daughter of Luis Bertrand and Ysabela Dabion,
native of this parish. Signed: Luis Bertrand (x);
Jh. Tauzin (s); Cazenave (s). Priest: Franco Magnes.

1031. REMIGIO SN. CRISTIN /CHRISTY/ (x)
(423) LORETA JULI OCONOR (x)
11 September 1813. Ratification of civil marriage.
Groom: son of Santiago Sn. Cristin and Mariana
Dorotea Pero, native of this parish. Bride: native of /torn/, legitimate daughter of Pier Oconor
and Margarita B_____. Signed: Michel Chamard
(s); Ls. Tauzin (s); Rozamond Chamard(?) (s); Cazenave (s). Priest: Franco. Magnes.

1032. SILVESTRE RACHAL (s)
(424) MARIE ROSE MICHEL (s)
23 September 1813, ratification of civil marriage.
Groom: native of this parish, legitimate son of
Antonio Rachal and Maria Luisa Lemoine. Bride:
native of this parish, legitimate daughter of Pe-
dro Michel and Cecilia Dupre. Signed: Antoine
Rachal (x); Pier Michel (x); Comte, fils (s);
Lambre, fils (s); Pre. Compere (s); Jn. Pre. Mie.
Dubois (s). Priest: Franco. Magnes.

1033. JOSE MIGUEL LEAL (x)
(425) MARIA ALEXANDRA SN. MIGUEL (x)
5 October 1813. Ratification of civil marriage.
Groom: native of Besar in the Kingdom of Mexico,
aged 20 years, a bachelor, and legitimate son of
Franco. Leal and Franca. Vimenez. Bride; native
of the same Besar, aged 17 years, single, legitimate daughter of Nepomaceno Sn. Miguel and Mariana de Luna. Signed: Pier Longert? "for the fath-

ers of the interested parties," (s); Franco. Menchao (s); Gavino Delgado (s); Josef Mig. Flores (s). Priest: Franco. Magnes.

1034. PIERRE BROSSET (x)
(426) MARIA LUISA LECOUR (x)
30 October 1813. Ratification of civil marriage. Groom: native of this post, legitimate son of Pierre Brosset and Maria Josefa Grillet. Bride: native of this parish, legitimate* daughter of Bertelmil Lecour and Maria Siul /Ursulle7. Signed: Cazenave (s); Lezime St. André (s); Lafon (s); priest: Franco. Magnes.

*The baptismal entry of this female identifies her as a "natural" child. (See Mills, *Natchitoches 1729-1803*, Register 4, Entry 2255.) No record of the marriage of her parents has been found and as late as 1809 children of her parents were being baptized under the designation "natural". (See Entry 2080 of present volume.)

1035. FRANCISCO SAN GERMAN (x)
(427) ADRIANA SANT ANDRE (x)
30 October 1813. Ratification of civil marriage. Groom: native of Canada, legitimate son of Miguel San Germain and Margarita San Miguel. Bride: native of this parish, legitimate daughter of Dn. Andres Sant Andre and Maria Rachal. Signed: Lafon (s); Cazenave (s); Lezime St. André (s). Priest: Franco. Magnes.

1036. SESER FONTINEAU (s)
(428) FELICITE BOUET LAFITTE (x)
15 November 1813. Ratification of civil marriage. Groom: native of this post, legitimate son of Luis Fonteneau and Pelagia Grap. Bride: Felicite Bouet Lafitte, native of Bayou Pierre, legitimate daughter of Pablo Bouet Lafitte and Maria Ysabel Soto. Signed: Caizere Fontenau (s); Henry Trichel (s); Cazenave (s); B. St. Amans (s). Priest: Franco. Magnes.

1037. JUAN BAUTISTA BARTOLOME RACHAL (s)
(429) MARGARITA FREDERIC (x)
5 January 1814. Ratification of civil marriage. Groom: Widower in first nuptials of Maria Pelagia Brebel. Bride: Widow in frist nuptials of Francisco Adley. Signed: A. Sompayrac (s); Bertehelmil Rachal (x); Ls. Derbanne (s); C. Grilliet (s). Priest: Franco. Magnes.

1038. LUIS BACOSCIU /VASCOCU/ (x)
(430) MARIA CELESTE RICE /RIS/ (x)
 21 February 1814. Ratification of civil marriage.
 Groom: native of this parish, a bachelor, legitimate son of Luis Vascoscu and Maria Magdalena Peraut. Bride: Native of this parish, single, and legitimate daughter of Juan Rice and Maria Francisca Bacoscu. Signed: Juan Rice (x); Vital Vacocu "for my father" (s); F. Vienne (s); Bmin. Metoyer (s); Juan Bte. Derbanne (x). Priest: Franco. Magnes.

1039. HILARIO CARRASCO
(431) MARIA DE JESUS SERVANTES
 12 April 1814. Ratification of civil marriage.
 Groom: a bachelor, native of Tulimes in province of Chihuaqua, aged 27 years, legitimate son of Geraldo Carrasco and Matilda Gonzalez. Bride: a Spaniard, aged "17 or 18 years," native of Sn. Antonio de Bejar, Province of Texas; single and legitimate daughter of Marzelo Servantes and Juana Martinez, residents of Bejar. Signed: B. Gisarnat (s); Cayssetano de la Garza (s); Jose Luis de la Bega, (s). Priest: Franco. Magnes.

1040. DAVID BRONN (s)
(432) POMPOSE MONTANARY (s)
 15 April 1814, ratification of civil marriage.
 Groom: aged 30, native of Batan Rus /Baton Rouge/ legitimate son of Julian Bronn and Polée Ellees /Paulette/Polly?/. Bride: 23, native of this post, legitimate daughter of Benito Montanary and Francisca Grappa. Signed: Davidson Bronn (s) /Groom/; Franca. Grappe Montanary (x); Remon Dortolant (s); Pierre Trichel (s); Jean Bte. Besson (s); Cezer Fredieu (s). Priest: Franco. Magnes.

1041. TOUSSAINT PINSOUNEAU
(433) MARIA JOSEFA GAGNER
 15 April 1814. Ratification of civil marriage.
 Groom: aged 31, bachelor, native of Canada, parish of Sn. Tiago /St. James/, legitimate son of Francisco Pinsouneau and Maria Josefa Trouidou. Bride: 23, native of this parish, legitimate daughter of Pedro Gagné and Maria Luis Davion. Signed: Maria Luisa Davion (x); Jose Martin (x); Juan Bautista Davion (x); Manuel Trise (x); Juan Bautista Davion the elder (x). Priest: Franco. Magnes.

1042. JUAN BAPTISTA LARENAUDIERE
(434) MARIA FRANCISCA BODOIN

13 June 1816. Ratification of civil marriage.
Groom: 20, native of this parish, legitimate son
of Pedro Larenaudiere and Juana St. Laveri /La
Berry/. Bride: 20, native of this post, legiti-
mate daughter of Pedro Bodain and Ana Rombem.
Signed: Pedro Bodoin (x); Rozemond Chamard (s);
Aé. Chamard (s); Perau?, fils (s); B. Gisarnat (s).
Priest: Franco. Magnes.

1043. JUAN NEPOMUCENO AROSHO /AROCHA/ (s)
(435) MARIE NORIN PALVADO (x)
28 June 1814. Ratification of civil marriage.
Groom: native of Besar, a bachelor, aged 25, legitimate son of Franco. Arosho and Maria Josefa Nuñez, residents of Besar in the province of Texas.
Bride: native of this post, 16, legitimate daughter of Jn. Francisca Palvado, a native of Nantée
in France, and Leonore Tessier, native of Islas
Negras /Illinois/. Signed: Jn. Francois Palvado
(x); Jn. Cortes (s); A. Sompayrac (s); R. _____ss
(s)*. Priest: Franco. Magnes. *Name illegible.

1044. JOSE (FAUSTINO) DEL RIO (s)
(436) MARIA GETRUDIS SANCHEZ (x)
5 August 1814, ratification of civil marriage after
3 bans. Groom: native of Nacogdoches, aged about
23 years, a bachelor, legitimate son of Jose Del
Rio and Juana _____ no *. Bride: aged 17 years,
single and legitimate daughter of Jose Sanchez and
Maria Josefa Ybarbo, all of the province of Texas.
Signed: Faustino del Rio (s)/groom/; Jose Sanchez
(x); Pierre Metoye /Sr./; Carlos Totem (x); Cazenave (s); Juan Jose Medina (s). Priest: Franco.
Magnes.

*A sliver of the name is torn from the page. The
first illegible letter might be a "v" or "r". The
second appears to be "a" or "e". The name appears
to have only four letters in all.

1045. JOSE LAVIGNE (x)
(437) DOROTEA BUADORE (x)
7 December 1814. Ratification of civil marriage,
after 3 bans. Groom: a free mulatto, natural son
of Maria Juana and a native of this post, aged 23,
and a bachelor. Bride: native of this post, aged
30 years, natural daughter of Francisca, also free
people of color. Agustin Metoyem (x); J. Bte. Metoyer, fils Agtin (s); Florantin Conan (s); Cazenave (s). Priest: Franco. Magnes.

1046. JUAN BTTA. LECOMTE (s)
(438) MARIA ADELE PROUDOMME (s)
22 December 1814, ratification of civil marriage after 3 bans. Groom: native of this post, aged 28 and a widower, legitimate son of Ambrosio Le Comte and Elena Cloutier. Bride: native of this post, aged 15 years, single and legitimate daughter of Manuel Proudhomme and Catalina Lambre. Dispensation from the impediment of affinity in the second degree, occasioned by the marriage of the groom with the elder sister of the bride. Signed: Prudhomme, fils "her brother" (s); Lambre Prudhomme (s); Ambrosio LeComte (x); Prudhomme (s); M. A. Germain (s). Priest: Franco. Magnes.

1047. LOUIS VERCHER (s)
(439) MARIA LUZE BERZOT (x)
2 (or 9?) January 1815, recording of marriage performed 8 December 1812 at Natchitoches by Reverend Father Luis Buhot of Opeloussas. Groom: legitimate son of Louis Vercher and Maria Louise Grillette. Bride: daughter of William Berzot and Cath. Poirrier. 1812 document bears signature of Paillet (s); Bauvard St. Amans (s). Recorded by Franco. Magnes in presence of Joseph Louis Vercher ⟦groom⟧.

1048. HILARIO ALAMILLO
(440) MARIA CONCEPCION ALVARADO
11 January 1815. Ratification of civil marriage. Groom, a Spaniard, legitimate son of Rosalino Alamillo and Maria del Pilar Procela. Bride: legitimate daughter of Francisco Alvarado and Maria Rosa de Leon. All are natives of Province of Texas. Note by Father Maynes: the groom, prior to his embarking at Natchitoches for a trip to New Orleans, indicated to the priest his desire to have his marriage rehabilitated by the Church upon his return from the city. However, he died on the return voyage. Father Maynes now ratifies the marriage for the benefit of the widow.

1049. AMABLE CADIEU (x)
(441) SUSANNE GAGNE (s)
27 February 1815. Ratification of civil marriage after 3 bans. Groom: aged 30 years, native of parish of Sn. Miguel in Canada, legitimate son of Amable Cadieu and Susanne Roulou. Bride: 26, native of this post, legitimate daughter of Pierre Gagne and Marie Louise Davion. Signed: Susanne Davion (x); J. Bte. Peraux (s); Jn. Bte. Davion (x)

Jn. Btte. Dominique (x). Priest: Franco. Magnes.

1050. JOSE SANCHEZ (s)
(442) MARIA JOSEFA VILLEGAR (x)
27 March 1815. Ratification of civil marriage, after publication of 3 bans. Groom: native of Besar, widower in second nuptials of Maria Jetrudis Menchaca. Bride: aged 25, native of Besar, single and legitimate daughter of Jose Antonio Bellegar and Maria de los Dolores. All are Spaniards. Signed: Cresencio Sn. Miguel (s); Juan Soto (x). Priest: Franco. Magnes.

1051. JACQUE SIMON THEODORE DETERVILLE (s)
(443) MARIE ROSE SAUCIERE (s)
/Torn/ 1815. Ratification of civil marriage, after publication of 3 bans. Groom: 28, native of Can /Caën/ in France, a bachelor*, legitimate son of Etien Deterville and Marie Magdalinne Paissant. Bride: Native of New Orleans, aged 22, legitimate daughter of Francois Sousiere and Felicite Dubernée. Signed: Veuve Saucier (s); Aé. Chamard (s); Louis Saucier (s); Fran. Jos.? Saucier (s); Pierre Royere (s); Jose Luis de la Bega (s). J. Pesesbant? (s). Priest: Franco. Magnes.

*Deterville had been previously wed, in a civil ceremony, to Helene Lane, from whom he secured a divorce in 1813. See Microcopy PC.10, 1813, Office of the Clerk of Court, Natchitoches. Since the first marriage was not ratified by the church, it was not recognized as a legitimate marriage; therefore, by church law, he was a bachelor at the time of his Catholic marriage in 1815.

1052. THOMAS CARO (x)
(444) MARIA JETRUDIS TEXEDA (x)
/torn/1815. Ratification of civil marriage after 3 bans. Groom: 24, bachelor, native of Nacogdoches, legitimate son of Pedro Caro and Maria Michaela Equi_. Bride: Widow of Juan Prozela, 28, legitimate daughter of Mariano Texeda and Maria Josefa Flores "all natives of Nacogdoches in province of Texas and presently in this post for 1 year and 8 months." Signed: Jose Tomas Caro (x) /groom/; Pedro Caro (x); Jose Luis de la Bega (s); Bernardo Gisarnat (s); Mariano Mora (x); Jose Toro (x); Manuel Cruz (x). Priest: Franco Magnes.

1053. HILERY LEVESSEUR /LAVESPERE/ (x)
(445) MARIE ODISE RACHAL (x)

26 June 1815. Ratification of civil marriage after 3 bans. Groom: aged /torn/, legitimate son of Francois Levesseur and Marie Louise Dervanne. Bride: aged /torn/, legitimate daughter of Barthelemy Rachal and /torn/, all natives of this post. Signed: Magdaline Grillet (x); Lavespere /the father/ (s); Prudhomme (s); Ls. Derbanne (s); Fcois. Frederic (s); Auguste Langloÿ (s); Hilaire Rachal (s). Priest: Franco. Magnes.

1054. FRANCOIS METOYEM (x)
(446) MARIE ARTHEMISE /MELON/ (x)
27 June 1815. Ratification of civil marriage after 3 bans. Groom, a free mulatto, widower of Margarite, a free mulatress, native of this parish, aged 30. Bride: natural daughter of Victoria Milon and a native of New Orleans. Signed: Victoria Milon (x); Louis Metoyer, m.l. (x); Dominique Metoyem, m.l. (x); Joseph Metoyem, m.l. (x); Jh. Derbanne (s); Anty (s). Priest: Franco. Magnes.

1055. JEANN BTTE. ANDRES VASCOCU (x)
(447) MARIE FAUSTINA CHIRINO (x)
10 August 1815. Ratification of civil marriage. Groom: aged 20, native of this post, legitimate son of Andres Vascocu and Maria Madalena Ramon, all natives of this post. Bride: aged 18, native of Nacogdoches, legitimate daughter of Jose Antonio Chirino and Maria Antonia de los Santos, all Spaniards residing in this post for 2½ years. Signed: Antonio Chirino (x); Bte. Trichel (s); Fois. Grappe (s); Caizere Fontenau (s); Jh. Vasseurs (or F. L. Vasseur?) (s); Jose Luis de la Bega (s). Priest: Franco. Magnes.

1056. PHELIPE FREDERIC (s)
(448) MARIE ROSE LESTAGE (x)
30 August 1815. Ratification of civil marriage after 3 bans. Groom: aged 28, legitimate son of Phelipe Frederic and Maria Barvara /no last name given -- should be Chelette/, already deceased. Bride: 23, legitimate daughter of Guillermo Lestage and Manuela de Riche, all natives of this parish. Signed: Marie Barvare /sic/ Lestage (x); Jn. Btte. Lestage (x); Jean Bte. Rachal (s); Bte. Armant (s); Louis Fort (s); Jans. Fedrique (x). Priest: Franco. Manges.

1057. JOSE IGINIO CASANOVA
(449) MARIA MANUELA SEQUIN
5 September 1815. Ratification of civil marriage

after bans. Groom: native of Bexar, legitimate son of Guillermo Casanova and Gertrudis Montes de Oca. Bride: Natural daughter of Venancia Sta. Cruz, aged 14, native of Nacogdoches. All parties are natives of Texas and the Spanish government. Signed: Juan Jose Seguin (x); Manuel Cadena (x); Juan Sanchez Castro (x); Atan. Bustamente (s); Pedro de la Fuentes (s). Priest: Franco. Magnes.

1058. JEANN BTTE. CHIRINO (x)
(450) MARIE MERZED SANCHEZ (x)
9 October 1815. Ratification of civil marriage after 3 bans. Groom: widower of Trinidad Yldefonsa Garza, aged about 32 years, legitimate son of Bartolo Chirino and Maria Josefa Arriola. Bride: 17, legitimate daughter of Luis Sanchez and Maria Josefa Borsoley. All are from the province of Texas and natives of Los Adayses and Nacogdoches. Signed: Ma. Josefa Bortoley (x); Ponciano Yvarbo (x); B. Gisarnat (s). Priest: Franco. Magnes.

1059. PEDRO FLORES (s)
(451) MARIA MAGDALENA LAFFITTE (x)
12 October, 1815. Ratification of civil marriage after 3 bans. Groom: native of Nachodoches, aged 22, legitimate son of Jose Flores and Ana Maria Guerrero. Bride: native of Natchitoches, 16, legitimate daughter of Pedro Laffitte, Jr. and Ursula Gagne. Signed: Pierre Laffitte (s); Jose Flores (s); Marcel Desoto (s); Man. Bustamente (s); Jose Acosta (s); Marcel Soto, Jr. (s). Priest: Franco. Magnes.

1060. LOUIS JOSEPH TAUZIN (s)
(452) MARIE EUGENIE MURPHY (s)
27 October 1815, ratification of civil marriage. 3 bans. Groom: 23, native of this post, legitimate son of Joseph Tauzin and Marie Chamard. Bride: 14, native of this post, legitimate daughter of deceased Eduard Murphy and Marie Elisabet Buard. Signed: Ve. Murphy (s); Jh. Tauzin (s); Chamard Tauzin (s); A. Sompayrac (s); Bauvard St. Amans (s); Bmn. Dranguet (s); Hri. Ete. Tauzin (s); Thomas M. Linnard (s); Om. Buard (s). Priest: Franco. Magnes.

1061. ALEXY MOREAU (s)
(453) AUSSITE STE. ANDRE (x)
4 December 1815. Ratification of civil marriage. 3 bans. Groom: aged 30, native of St. Luis of Ilinois, legitimate son of Francois Moreau and

Catarina Marichal. Bride: 18, native of this post, legitimate daughter of Andres Ste. Andre and Marie Jacob Rachal. Signed: Alexis Maurau (s) /Groom_7; Aé. Chamard (s); Agustin Lefebvre (x); Felicite Cham/ar_7d (s). Priest: Franco. Magnes.

1062. CELESTIN TOTIN (x)
(454) MARIE MODESTE VASCOCU (x)
22 January 1816. Ratification of civil marriage, after 3 bans. Groom: 23, legitimate son of Remy Totin and Margarita Grillet. Bride: 25, legitimate daughter of Andres Vacocu and Magdelena Remaun. Signed: Margarite Grillet (x); Jn. Btte. Davion, the elder (x); Adelise Pantaleon (s); Bte. Trichel (s); Bernar Pantaleon (s); Andres Gozinles /Gonzales?_7 (s). Priest: Franco. Magnes.

1063. ANTONIO ADLE (x)
(455) MARIE LOUISE GRENEAUX (x)
23 January 1816. Ratification of civil marriage after 3 bans. Groom: 26, legitimate son of deceased Etienne Adle and Genevieve Dubois. Bride: 17, legitimate daughter of Louis Emanuel Grenaux and Victoire Emeranti Bossier. Signed: Veuve Grénaux (s); Btte. Adlé (s); A. Lauve (s); M. Pelagy Adly (s); Eml. Grénaux (s); E. Cr. Murphy (s); Jm. Callaghan (s); D. Bossier (s). Priest: Franco. Magnes.

1064. ALEXANDRE LOUIS DEBLIEUX (s)
(456) EUFRASINE TAUZIN (s)
/Torn_7 1816. Ratification of civil marriage, after 3 bans. Groom: aged 21, legitimate son of Alexandre Deblieux and Terese ___ard, natives of Marsella /Marseilles_7. Bride: 18, native of this parish, legitimate daughter of Joseph Tauzin and Marie Chamard. Signed: Jh. Tauzin (s); O. Buard (s); Bmin. Metoyer (s); Chamard Tauzin (s); Catherin Chamard (s); Hri. Ete. Tauzin (s); A. Sompayrac (s); B. T. Lafon (s); Ls. Tauzin (s); Bauvard de St. Amans (s); Ed. Cr. Murphy (s); B. Dranguet (s). Priest: Franco. Magnes.

> NOTE: This series of marriage records continues with Entry 720. The following baptismal entries for slaves and free children of color is a continuation of the baptismal section that abruptly ends after Entry 2643.

1065. UNKNOWN
(457) 28 _____ 1818. Baptism. Document badly torn.

1066. FRANCOIS
(457) 12 May 1818. Baptism of infant aged _____ /Blank7 years, natural son of Marie, a slave of Joseph Tauzin. Godparents: Joseph Carrier and Me. Jean Messier. Priest: Franco. Magnes.

1067. FRANCOIS VERY
(457) 12 May 1818, baptism of infant aged 3 months, natural son of Francisca, slave of Jn. Bte. Lestages. Godparents: Antoin and Margarite. Priest: Franco. Magnes.

1068. ANTOIN NEVIL
(457) 12 May 1818, baptism of infant aged 18 months, natural son of Alenne, slave of Jn. Bte. Buard. Godparents: Zenon and Francisca, all of color. Priest: Franco. Magnes.

1069. MARIE JEANNE
(457) 12 May 1818. Baptism of an "English Negro" aged 20 years, slave of Philibert Closeau. Godparents: Pier Paul and Marie Jeanne. Priest: Franco. Magnes.

1070. MARIE PELAGIE
(457) 13 May 1818. Baptism of an "English Negro" aged about 30, slave of Mda. Ve. Fontenau. Godparents: Henry Trichel and Mda. Ve. Fonteneau. Priest: Franco. Magnes.

1071. MARIE JEANNE MARCELITE
(457) 13 May 1818, Baptism of an infant aged 10 months, legitimate daughter of Chatarinne, slave of Mda. Ve. Fontaneau. Godparents: Louis and Marie Therese, all of color. Priest: Franco. Magnes.

1072. MARIE CELESTE
(457) 13 May 1818, baptism of an "English Negro" aged 7 years, slave of Bmy. Flemin. Godparents: Zeser Fonteneau and Me. Denis Fonteneau. Priest: Franco. Magnes.

1073. MARIE TECLE
(457) 13 May 1818, baptism of an infant aged 6 months, natural daughter of Magsimino Juannot, a free Negro and Maria Francisca, slave of Bernardo Dortelan. Godparents: Louis Lematte and Me. Jeanne, colored. Priest: Franco. Magnes.

1074. JOSEPH
(457) 6 June 1818, baptism of a "Ginea" Negro aged about 30 years, slave of Dominique Sorel. Godparents: Antonio Fredieu and Felicite Sorel, whites. Priest: Franco. Magnes.

1075. FRANCOIS
(457) 6 June 1818, baptism of infant aged 3 months, natural son of Edé, slave of Hypolite Bordeleau. Godparents: Pier and Marie. Priest: Franco. Magnes.

1076. MARIE
(457) 18 June 1818, baptism of infant aged 2 months, an orphan, slave of Benjamin Metoyer. Godparents: Luvin and B_____. Priest: Franco. Magnes.

1077. UNKNOWN
(458) __ June 1818. Entry is almost completely destroyed.

1078. MARIE LESET
(458) 24 June 1818, baptism of infant of 1 months, natural daughter of Marie Jeanne, slave of Gasparite LaCour. Godparents: Francois Melon and Genoveva, free people of color. Priest: Franco. Magnes.

1079. MARIE LALYE
(458) 24 June 1818, baptism of infant aged 2 years, natural daughter of Rosse, slave of Gasparit LaCour. Godparents: Jean Pier and Marie Jeanne. Priest: Franco. Magnes.

1080. MARIE FEBYE
(458) 24 June 1818, baptism of child of 5 years, natural daughter of Dagues, slave of Gasparite LaCour. Godparents: Gaspar Lecour and Suset LeCour. Priest: Franco. Magnes.

1081. PRUDENCIA
(458) 24 June 1818, baptism of mulatto child of 3 years, natural daughter of Dagues, slave of Gasparite La Cour. Godparents: Michel Dervan and Elenne Anty. Priest: Franco. Magnes.

1082. MARIE NANSY
(458) 24 June 1818, baptism of infant aged 1 year, natural daughter of Dagues, slave of Mr. Gasparite La Cour. Godparents: Jn Bte. Lecour and Marie Emely Lecour. Priest: Franco. Magnes.

1083. JUAN
(458) 24 June 1818, baptism of infant aged 1 year, natu-

ral son of Rosse, slave of Gasparit LeCour. Godparents: Pier and Fanye. Priest: Franco Magnes.

1084. MARIE ADELLE
(458) 27 June 1818, baptism of infant aged 3½, natural daughter of Hortans, slave of Jacob St. Andre. Godparents: Btte. Cheval and Victorie Ste. Andre. Priest: Franco. Magnes.

1085. JOSEPH ESGUAR
(458) 27 June 1818, baptism of child aged 10, slave of Manuel Rachal. Godparents: Antoin Rachal and Marie Eufrosinne Lemoin. Priest: Franco Magnes.

1086. BASTIAN
(458) 27 June 1818, baptism of infant aged 4 months, natural daughter of Marianne, slave of Mda. Ve. Antoine Rachal. Godparents: Louis Solasty Rachal and Eufrasinne Lemoin. Priest: Franco. Magnes.

1087. MARIE CELESTE
(458) 27 June 1818, baptism of English slave aged about 20 years, slave of Narcis Rachal. Godparents: Jacque and Semiry. Priest: Franco. Magnes.

1088. MARIE BELONY
(459) 28 June 1818, baptism of infant aged 10 months, natural daughter of Requinne, slave of Jn. Btte. Gillard. Godparents: Evens and Charlo. Priest: Franco. Magnes.

1089. POLONIO
(459) 28 June 1818, baptism of infant of 4 months, natural son of Pessinne, slave of Leandro Lacour. Godparents: Francois LaCour and Denis Valery. Priest: Franco. Magnes.

1090. MARIE
(459) 28 June 1818, baptism of child of 9 years, natural daughter of Requin, slave of Joseph Gillard. Godparents: Josef and Margarite, both colored. Priest: Franco. Magnes.

1091. MARIE CHARLOT
(459) 28 June 1818, baptism of English Negro about 23 years, slave of Joseph Gillard. Godparents: Desire and Charlot. Priest: Franco. Magnes.

1092. CECILE
(459) 28 June 1818, baptism of infant of 4 months, natural daughter of Olib /Olive/, slave of Mr. Jn.

Marie Lecour. Godparents: Jose Gillard, Jr. and Magdalenne LeCour. Priest: Franco. Magnes.

1093. MARIE ANTOINE
(459) 23 June 1818, baptism of infant of 3 months, natural daughter of Marie, slave of Silvestre Rachal. Godparents: Cayetano Arrañega and Rita Flores.

1094. LOUIS
(459) 23 June 1818, baptism of infant of 1½ years, natural son of Maria, slave of Silvestre Rachal. Godparents: Nicolas Gracia and Lucie Louc. Priest: Franco. Magnes.

1095. MARIE DENISE
(459) 2 August 1818, baptism of the natural daughter of Susanne, slave of Mda. Ve. Morphy. Godparents: Denis Casanova, white, and Magdalenne, colored. Priest: Franco. Magnes.

1096. MARIE ROSSE
(459) 14 August 1818, baptism of infant of 1 year, natural daughter of Bessy, slave of Athanas Poissot. Godparents: Athanas Poisot and Ana Bilo /Baillio7. Priest: Franco. Magnes.

1097. AUGUSTIN
(459) 14 August 1818, baptism of infant of 2 years, natural son of Bessy, slave of Athanas Poisot. Godparents: Luca and Layda, colored slaves of Athanase Poissot. Priest: Franco. Magnes.

1098. FELICITE
(460) 14 August 1818, baptism of infant of 6 months, natural daughter of Marianne, slave of Athanas Poisot. Godparents: Jose Rouquier and Loysse, both colored.

1099. PIER PAUL BASILIO
(460) 16 August 1818, baptism of infant of 2 months, natural son of Maria Louise, slave of Henry Trichel. Godparents: Paul and Marianne, colored. Priest: Franco. Magnes.

1100. MARIE
(460) 23 August 1818, baptism of infant of 5 months, slave of Mda. Ve. Guin. Godparents: Julio Caleghan and Elanna Dille, whites. Priest: Franco. Magnes.

1101. MARIE MATILDE
(460) 30 August 1818, baptism of a "Ginea" negro aged

about 25 years, slave of Jn. Bte. Arman. Godparents: Pier Pa. Ana and Marie Pavi, colored. Priest: Franco. Magnes.

1102. MARIE DELPHINNE
(460) 30 August 1818, baptism of a free infant, born 15 December 1817, natural daughter of Denis who is a slave until the death of her mistress, Madame Berthelmy, widow of deceased Berthelmy, after that time Denis will be free. The child has been registered as free. Godparents: Isac Plesans and Eloys Bron. Priest: Franco. Magnes.

1103. CAROLINE
(460) 20 September 1818, baptism of infant born May 1818, natural child of Guanea?, slave of Ls. Joseph Tauzin, Jr. Godparents: Tauzin and Charlot, colored. Priest: Franco. Magnes.

1104. MARIE POLINERE ARMESY
(460) 28 September 1818, baptism of infant born 18 June 1818, natural daughter of Layde, slave of Francois Levasseur. Godparents: Marcelin and Marie Chatarine, colored. Priest: Franco. Magnes.

1105. FRANCOIS GUILLIOM
(460) 4 October 1818, baptism of slave of Carlos Noryt, natural son of Laty, slave of Mr. Pavi. Godparents: Denis Casanova, white, and Polinne, colored. Priest: Franco. Magnes.

1106. MARIE CELESTE
(461) 12 October 1818, baptism of infant aged 1 year, natural daughter of Cenis, slave of Ceser Laffita. Godparents: Pedro Procela and Maria Jetrudis Procela, whites. Priest: Franco. Magnes.

1107. CARLOS
(461) 13 October 1818, baptism of infant aged 2 months, natural son of Yiné, slave of Mr. Seredem /Sheridan7. Godfather: Jose Maria Mora, white. Priest: Franco. Magnes.

1108. MARIE AGATA
(461) 1 November 1818, baptism of infant of 3½ months, natural daughter of Modeste, slave of Mda. Ve. Btte. Buard. Godparents: Moris and Elisabet, both colored. Priest: Franco. Magnes.

1109. ZENON
(461) November 1818, baptism of a mulatto born 5 August

1818, natural son of Eme, slave of Baptiste Le-
Compte. Godparents: Charles Lamel? and Francoise
Torres, whites. Priest: Franco. Magnes.

1110. MARIE ZELINNE
(461) 1 November 1818, baptism of infant of 6 months,
natural daughter of Catharine, slave of Mda. Ve.
Monet. Godparents: Francois Chan Charme /St. Ger-
maine/ and Margarite Dominique /Marguerite LeComte,
wife of Dominique Metoyer/. Priest: Franco.
Magnes.

1111. MARIE SOPHY
(461) 8 November 1818, baptism of infant born 20 July,
1818, natural daughter of Susanne, slave of Cesar
Morphy. Godparents: Jacob and Marie Louise.
Priest: Franco. Magnes.

1112. LOUIS URSIN
(461) 8 November 1818, baptism of infant of 6 months, natural son of Victoria, slave of Mr. Rouquier, Jr.
Godparents: Jose Rouquier and Marie Louise.
Priest: Franco. Magnes.

1113. MARIE AÑES
(461) 24 November 1818, baptism of infant born 6 September 1818, natural daughter of Charlot, slave of
Dominique Rachal. Godparents: Jacque and Marie
Louise, colored. Priest: Franco. Magnes.

1114. JN. BTTE. BANSEM
(461) 24 November 1818, baptism of infant born 15 February 1818, natural son of Marie, slave of Jn. Btte.
Proudhom. Godparents: Jn. Btte. and Marie Jeanne,
colored. Priest: Franco. Magnes.

1115. MARIE PRUDANS /CHELETTE/*
(461) 24 November 1818, baptism of infant aged 6 months,
natural daughter of July, slave of Pier Slecttre
/Chelettre/ who gives her freedom. Godparents:
Jn. Btte. Slectre and Felicite Pomier.

*This individual used the surname of Chelette of
Schelette throughout her life.

1116. AGUSTIN PREDANES METOYER
(462) 3 November 1818, baptism of infant born 24 April
1818, legitimate son of Juan Baptiste Metoyer and
Suset Metoyer. Godparents: Jn. Bte. Florantin
Cona and Marie Louise Metoyer, all free people of
color. Priest: Franco. Magnes.

1117. JOSEPH ZENES METOYER
(462) 3 November 1818, baptism of infant born 12 August 1818, legitimate son of Joseph Metoyer and Marie Pelagie /LeCourt/. Godparents: Joseph Metoyer, Jr. and Marie Aspasy Metoyer, all free people of color. Priest: Franco. Magnes.

1118. MARIE PRIANA BRIGIDA COLIDAD HERRERA
(462) 13 December 1818, baptism of infant of 2 months, mulatto and legitimate daughter of Pedro Herrera, Spaniard, and Maria Subley Barra, a free Negro. Godparents: Jose La diga and Maria Guadalupe Rodrigues. Priest: Franco. Magnes.

1119. MARIE ROSE
(462) 13 December 1818, baptism of infant of 3 months, natural daughter of Marie Mano (Mario?), slave of Mda. Ve. Gagne. Godparents: Francois Etequan and Marie Rose, colored. Priest: Franco. Magnes.

1120. JOSEPH MARIA
(463) 1 February 1819, baptism of infant of 2 months, natural son of Maria Josefa, slave of Alexy Cloutier. Godparents: Jose Maria Castro and Juana Brom, whites. Priest: Franco. Magnes.

1121. MARIA LOUISA
(463) 1 February 1819, baptism of natural daughter of Felicite, slave of Alexy Cloutier. Godparents: Remy and Marie Louise. Priest: Franco. Magnes.

1122. ANTOIN AGUSTIN
(463) 7 February 1819, baptism of infant of 6 months, natural son of Susanne, slave of Francois Vienne. Godparents: Jn Bte. and Me. Jeanne. Priest: Franco. Magnes.

1123. JN BTTE JULIAN
(463) 7 February 1819, baptism of infant of 1½ months, natural son of Rode, slave of Mr. Yocona. Godparents: Jn Btte. Julian and Fransine, both colored. Priest: Franco. Magnes.

1124. MARIA ESTEFANIA VICTORINA
(463) 7 March 1819, baptism of slave aged 35 years, property of Mr. Vulgar /Villegar?/. Godparents: Joseph and Victorina, both colored. Priest: Franco. Magnes.

1125. PIER
(463) 18 March 1819, baptism of an English mulatto, aged

about 10, slave of Hipolito Bordeleau. Godparents: Joseph Bordeleau and Marie Celeste Bordeleau, whites. Priest: Franco. Magnes.

1126. MARIE ROSE
(463) 18 March 1819, baptism of infant born 2 June 1818, natural daughter of Emelite, slave of Jn. Btte. Besont. Godparents: Jn. Bte. Bessont, Jr. and Me. Felicite Besson, whites. Priest: Franco. Magnes.

1127. MARIA TERESA
(464) 20 March 1819, baptism of English Negro aged about 18 years, slave of Jeann Trechiny. Godparents: Dominique and Marie Therese, both colored. Priest: Franco. Magnes.

1128. FELICITE URSULINE
(464) 20 March 1819, baptism of infant born 4 February 1819, natural daughter of Constance, slave of Mda. Ve. Fonteneau. Godparents: Dominique and Francoise, both colored. Priest: Franco. Magnes.

1129. MARIA
(464) 20 March 1819, baptism of English Negro about 16 years of age, slave of Ramon Dorthelans. Godparents: Jn. Btte. and Marie Ortans, both colored. Priest: Franco. Magnes.

1130. MARIE MANET
(464) 10 April 1819, baptism of infant of 1 year, natural daughter of Loysse, slave of V. Metoyer. Godparents: Julian and Francoise, both colored. Priest: Franco. Magnes.

1131. MARIE DENIS
(464) 10 April 1819, baptism of infant aged 8 months, natural daughter of Marie Jeanne, slave of V. Metoyer. Godparents: Dorsinau Fort and Agat. Priest: Franco. Magnes.

1132. LOUIS
(464) 10 April 1819, baptism of infant of 1 year, natural son of Perin, slave of Vn. Metoyer. Godparents: Jn. Btte. and Francoise, both colored. Priest: Franco. Magnes.

1133. MARIE ROSET
(464) 10 April 1819, baptism of infant of 10 months, natural daughter of Layde, slave of Vn. Metoyer. Godparents: Nicolas and July, both colored. Priest: Franco. Magnes.

1134. MARIE MARGARITE
(465) 10 April 1819, baptism of English Negro aged about 28 years, slave of Noel Bmy. Rachal. Godparents: Andres and Margarita, colored. Priest: F. Magnes.

1135. MARIE CLEOTHILDE
(465) 10 April 1819, baptism of English Negro about 22 years old, slave of Mr. Carr. Godparents: Antoin Demesier and Me. Jeanne Demessier. Priest: F. Magnes.

1136. MARIE ASELY
(465) 10 April 1819, baptism of infant of 7 months, natural daughter of Marie Louise, slave of Jn. Btte. Buard. Godparents: Antoin Lestage and Francois, colored. Priest: F. Magnes.

1137. MAGDALENNE
(465) 10 April 1819, baptism of English Negro of about 29 years, slave of Jeann LaLande. Godparents: Andres and Marie Andres, colored. Priest: F. Magnes.

1138. MARIE THERESSE
(465) 10 April 1819, baptism of infant of 1 year, natural daughter of slave of Jn. Lalande. Godparents: Andres and Marie Andres -- colored. Priest: F. Magnes.

1139. MARIANE
(465) 10 April 1819, baptism of English Negro about 28, slave of Athanas Poissot. Godparents: Jn. Btte. and Francoise, colored. Priest: F. Magnes.

1140. MARIE ADELAYDE
(465) 10 April 1819, baptism of mulato aged 3 months, natural daughter of Eulagie, slave of Placide Bossier. Godparents: Charles Aubauson and Louise Lambre. Priest: F. Magnes.

1141. FRANCOIS
(465) 10 April 1819, baptism of Congo Negro about 22, slave of Athanas Poissot. Priest: Zeno and Sofi, colored. Priest: F. Magnes.

1142. MARIE LOUISE
(465) 10 April 1819, baptism of English Negro, about 31, slave of Athanas Demesier. Godparents: Celestin and Me. Louise. Priest: F. Magnes.

1143. MARIE LISSE
(466) 14 April 1819, baptism of infant of 2½ months, natural daughter of Hortans, slave of Jn. Btte. Dervan. Godparents: "Pier Metoyer, the son, free," and Henriet /his wife/, free. Priest: F. Magnes.

1144. MARIE ADELAYDE
(466) 14 April 1819, baptism of infant of 6 months, natural daughter of Marie Therese, slave of Jacques LaCasse. Godparents: Michel and Rosaly, colored. Priest: F. Magnes.

1145. MARIE JENYE /JEANNE/
(466) 14 April 1819, baptism of English Negro, aged about 18, slave of Jacques LaCasse. Godparents: Francois Dervan and Marie Asely Langois, whites. Priest: F. Magnes.

1146. HENRY
(466) 14 April 1819, baptism of English Negro, about 17, slave of Mda. Ve. Etien Vercher /Verger/. Godparents: Sucier /Cesaire/ Langois and Marie Asely Langois. Priest: F.Magnes.

1147. MARIE CLARISSE
(466) 14 April 1819, baptism of infant of 1 year, natural daughter of Fany, slave of Mda. Ve. Bmy. Rachal. Godparents: Pier and Therese, colored. Priest: F. Magnes.

1148. ADRIAN
(466) 14 April 1819, baptism of mulato of 24 days, natural son of Any, slave of Ciprian Rachal. Godparents: Pier Lemoin and Marie Frousin Lemoin, whites. Priest: F. Magnes.

1149. URSIN
(466) 18 April 1819, baptism of infant of 5½ months, natural son of Marie Louise, slave of Dufrois and Dorselin Galien. Godparents: Zifroyin Dervan and Marie Oresy Anty, whites. Priest: F. Magnes.

1150. MARIE
(466) 18 April 1819, baptism of infant of 2 months, natural daughter of Eleyse, slave of Ambrosio /Le/ Comte. Godparents: Gavriel and Marie Lolite, colored. Priest: F. Magnes.

1151. MARIE ZELINE
(467) 14 April 1819, baptism of infant of 4 months, natural daughter of Marie Sirin, slave of Ambrosio /Le/ Comte. Godparents: Alexy and Marie Francoise, colored. Priest: F. Magnes.

1152. MARIE CONSTANS
(467) 14 April 1819, baptism of infant of 1½ months, natural daughter of Francoise, slave of Mr. /Le/

Comte, the son. Godparents: Antoin and Marianne, colored. Priest: F. Magnes.

1153. RAFAEL
(467) 19 April 1819, baptism of infant aged 2½ months, natural daughter of Charlot, slave of Agustin Metoyer, free man of color. Godparents: Joseph Metoyer, the son, and Zusette Metoyer, both free. Priest: F. Magnes.

1154. JN. BTTE. MIGUEL
(467) 24 May 1819, baptism of mulato, natural son of Maria Catarina, slave of Mr. Pier Ternier. Godparents: Jn. Btte. and Marie Jean Jean /sic7, free people of color. Priest: F. Magnes.

1155. CHARLES
(467) 29 May 1819, baptism of infant of 2 months, natural son of Marie, slave of Jn. Bte. Proudhomme. Godparents: Andres and Layde, colored. Priest: F. Magnes.

1156. DORSELIN
(467) 29 May 1819, baptism of infant born 15 February 1819, natural son of Phany, slave of Jn. Btte. Proudhomme. Godparents: Louis and Marie Louise, both colored.

1157. MARIE ESPRIT
(467) 10 June 1819, baptism of infant born 5 February 1819, natural daughter of Marie Rosaly, slave of Louis Tauzin, the son. Godparents: Pierr and Marie Louis, both colored. Priest: F. Magnes.

1158. MARCELITE
(467) 10 June 1819, baptism of infant born 12 February 1819, natural daughter of Marie Jean, slave of Louis Tauzin, the son. Godparents: Celestin and Adelayde. Priest: F. Magnes.

1159. LOUIS MILON
(468) 1 April 1819, baptism of infant born 9 February 1819, legitimate son of Francisco Milon and Marie Louise Metoyer, free people of color. Godparents: Louis Metoyer and Francoise, both free people of color. Priest: F. Magnes.

1160. MARTIN VER
(468) 18 April 1819, baptism of infant born 15 December 1818, natural son of Maria Agustina, free Negro. Godparents: Francisco Milon and Maria Antoinet. Priest: F. Magnes.

1161. AGUSTIN MAGSIMIN METOYER
(468) 19 April 1819, baptism of infant born 30 January 1819, legitimate son of Magsil Metoyer and Marie Aspasy Metoyer, all free people of color. Godparents: Agustin Metoyer and Agnes, his paternal grandparents, both free. Priest: F. Magnes.

1162. JOSEPH CLERVIL METOYER
(468) 19 April 1819, baptism of infants born 30 January 1819, legitimate son of Francisco Metoyer and Arthemis, all free people of color. Godparents: Francois Metoyer, Jr. and Adelle Metoyer, both free people of color. Priest: F. Magnes.

1163. MARIE CAROLINNE
(469) 14 June 1819, baptism of child of 11 years, English Negro, slave of Louis Tausin, the son. Godparents: Celestin and Ufrasinne, both colored. Priest: F. Magnes.

1164. MARIE ARTHEMIS
(469) 2 July 1819, baptism of infant of 10 months, natural daughter of Melye, slave of Pier Nolasco de Porcuna. Godparents: Gavriel Duvois and Marie Adele Rachal. Priest: F. Magnes.

1165. JEAN FRANCOIS
(469) 5 July 1819, baptism of infant of 1½ years, natural son of Denis, slave of Manuel Proudhom. Godparents: Tousin and Celeste, colored. Priest: F. Magnes.

1166. MARTA
(469) 5 July 1819, baptism of infant of 1 year and 1 month, natural daughter of Therese, slave of Manuel Proudhom. Godparents: Jean Btte. and Marta. Priest: F. Magnes.

1167. MARIE LOYSE
(469) 5 July 1819, baptism of child of 2 years, natural daughter of Louisse, slave of Manuel Proudhom. Godparents: Louis and Loysa. Priest: F. Magnes.

1168. CHARLES
(469) 5 July 1819, baptism of child of 3 years, natural son of Me. Salys, slave of Manuel Prudhomme. Godparents: Louis and Marta. Priest: F. Magnes.

1169. ZENON
(469) 5 July 1819, baptism of child of 13 years, natural son of Me. Salys, slave of Manuel Prudhomme. God-

parents: Louis and Theresse. Priest: F. Magnes.

1170. MARIE SIRINE
(469) 5 July 1819, baptism of natural daughter of Me. Salys, slave of Manuel Prudhomme. Godparents: Jean Btte. and Me. Celeste. Priest: F. Magnes.

1171. PAUL
(470) 5 July 1819, baptism of child of 9 years, natural son of Marie Salys, slave of Manuel Prudhomme. Godparents: Alexy and Nanet. Priest: F. Magnes.

1172. MARIE DE LOS DOLORES
(470) 5 July 1819, baptism of natural child, daughter of Marie Salys, slave of Manuel Prudhomme. Godparents: Jn. Btte. and Marta. Priest: F. Magnes.

1173. JEAN
(470) 5 July 1819, baptism of child of about 12 years, natural son of Me. Salys, slave of Manuel Prudhomme. Godparents: Jean Btte and Marta. Priest: F. Magnes.

1174. JEAN PIER
(470) 5 July 1819, baptism of Negro about 21 years, natural son of Me. Salys, slave of Manuel Prudhomme. Godparents: Tousin and Me. Jeanne. Priest: F. Magnes.

1175. MARIE ARTHEMIS
(470) 5 July 1819, baptism of child of about 2 years, natural daughter of Marie Salyse, slave of Manuel Prudhomme. Godparents: Andres and Me. Jeanne. Priest: F. Magnes.

1176. MARIE SALYS
(470) 5 July 1819, baptism of slave aged about 36, property of Manuel Prudhomme. Godparents: Jean Btte and Marie Louisse. Priest: F. Magnes.

1177. MARIE LEONOR
(470) 5 July 1819, baptism of infant of 8 months, natural daughter of Angelica, slave of Manuel Prudhomme. Godparents: Jean Btte. and Leonor. Priest: F. Magnes.

1178. AGUSTIN
(470) 5 July 1819, baptism of English Negro aged about 45, property of Manuel Prudhomme. Godparents: Louis and Marie Loys. Priest: F. Magnes.

1179. JEAN BTTE
(470) 5 July 1819, baptism of English Negro aged about
49, property of Manuel Prudhomme. Godparents:
Jean Btte. and Me. Catharine. Priest: F. Magnes.

1180. HONORE
(470) 5 July 1819, baptism of infant of 3 months, natural son of Marie Francoise, slave of Manuel Prudhomme. Godparents: Honore and Marie Catarinne.
Priest: F. Magnes.

1181. JULIAN
(471) 6 July 1819, baptism of English Negro, about 25,
slave of Benjamin Metoyer. Godparents: Michel
and Marie Catharine. Priest: F. Magnes.

1182. ALEXANDRE
(471) 6 July 1819, baptism of English Negro about 26,
slave of Benjamin Metoyer. Godparents: Jacque
and Loyse. Priest: F. Magnes.

1183. MARIE PILAR
(471) 6 July 1819, baptism of infant of 1 year, natural
daughter of Marie Catharinne, slave of Benjamin
Metoyer. Godparents: Jacque and Marie Francoise.
Priest: F. Magnes.

1184. MARIE DELPHINE
(471) 5 August 1819, baptism of infant of 2 months, natural daughter of Loc Cilia, slave of Andres Chamard.
Godparents: Thomas Gonzalez and Marie Julian,
negresse. Priest: F. Magnes.

1185. ANTOIN
(471) 4 September 1819, baptism of English Negro aged 12
years, slave of Samuel Davimport. Godparents:
Charles and Juliana, both colored. Priest: F.
Magnes.

1186. JOSEPH TITOS
(471) 4 September 1819, baptism of English Negro about 7
years, slave of Samuel Davimport. Godparents:
Benigne Davimport and Marie Aselye Davimport.
Priest: F. Magnes.

1187. MARIE SARA
(471) 4 September 1819, baptism of infant of 2 years,
natural daughter of Biolet, slave of Samuel Davimport. Godparents: Charles and Marie.

1188. MARIE LOUISE - MARIE JEANNE
(472) 5 September 1819, baptism of twins born 24 August

1819, natural daughters of Marie Jeanne, slave of Mda. Ve. Gagne. Godparents of Marie Louise: Cenon Demesier and Me. Celeste, both free people of color. Godparents of Marie Jeanne: Louis Lamot and Marie Manon, both colored. Priest: F. Magnes.

1189. SANTIAGO
(472) 5 September 1819, baptism of child born 4 July 1813, natural son of Anna, slave of Pier Ternie. Godparents: Jose Victoriano Barbarrus and Marie Aselinne Davion. Priest: F. Magnes.

1190. MARIE LOUISE
(472) 12 September 1819, baptism of infant of 10 months, natural daughter of Clara, slave of Andres Valentin. Godparents: Pier and Marie Louise, both colored.

1191. FRANCISCA
(472) 27 September 1819, baptism of infant of 1 month, natural daughter of Marie, slave of Jean Btte. Duvois. Godparents: Jean Btte. Davois, fils, and Marie Melanye Lemoin, whites. Priest: F. Magnes.

1192. JEAN
(472) 27 September 1819, baptism of infant of 2 months, natural son of Me. Louise, slave of Alexy Cloutier. Godparents: Louis and Margarite, colored. Priest: F. Magnes.

1193. CIRIACO
(472) 27 September 1819, baptism of infant of 2 months, natural son of Rosa, slave of Alexy Cloutier. Godparents: Jose Metoyer, Jr. and Marie Metoyer, both free people of color. Priest: F. Magnes.

1194. ETIEN JACQUE LIBRON /LEBRUN?/
(473) 24 July 1819, baptism of infant born 14 May 1819, natural son of Etion libron of France and Suset Grappe, a free mulata. Godparents: Jacque Grappe and Marie Josephe Grappe, free people of color. Priest: F. Magnes.

1195. PIER EDMON FORT
(473) 14 November 1819, baptism of infant born 18 February 1819, natural son of Louis Dorsineau, French, and Marie Angelique, a free woman of color. Godparents: Andres Fort and Marie Pompose Himel. Priest: F. Magnes.

1196. MARIE LAYS
(474) 27 September 1819, baptism of child of 2 years, natural daughter of Felis, slave of Francois Lattier. Godparents: Francois Lattier, Jr. and Marie Louise Lattier, whites. Priest: F. Magnes.

1197. PIER
(474) 27 September 1819, baptism of infant of 6 months, natural son of Francoise, slave of Antoin Conde. Godparents: Joseph Metoyer and Marie Antoinet Conde, free people of color. Priest: F. Magnes.

1198. MARIE LANIS
(474) 27 September 1819, baptism of a Guinea Negro, aged about 18 years, slave of Antoine Conde. Godparents: Francois and Ursul, colored. Priest: F. Magnes.

1199. HENRY
(474) 27 September 1819, baptism of infant of 4 months, natural son of Me. Francoise, slave of Ambrosio Comt. Godparents: Dominique and Hortans, colored. Priest: F. Magnes.

1200. MARIE ELYSA
(474) 3 October 1819, baptism of infant of 7 months, natural daughter of Suset, slave of "Mr. Rouquier, frere"*. Godparents: Francois Cortes and Marie Louisse Carre. Priest: F. Magnes.

*Entry 1284 identifies Suset (Suzette) as slave of Js. Rouquier.

1201. MARIANNE ANRIETE
(474) 4 October 1819, baptism of infant of 7 months, natural daughter of Euselye, slave of George Scamps. Godmother: Marie Manet Huintar. Priest: F. Magnes.

1202. MAGSIL
(474) 17 October 1819, baptism of infant of 1 month, natural son of Margarite, slave of Theodore Grillet. Godparents: Dominique Grappe, free man of color and Denis, colored. Priest: F. Magnes.

1203. MARIE ASELYE
(474) 28 October 1819, baptism of Guinea Negro, aged about 22 years, slave of Antoine Grillet. Godparents: Jacob and Marie Elenna, colored. Priest: F. Magnes.

1204. ETIENNE
(474)

28 October 1819, baptism of English Negro aged about 23 years, slave of Antoine Grillet. Godparents: Fostin Peraut and Denis Dervan, whites. Priest: F. Magnes.

1205. [Approximately 3 entries are missing at this point.
(475) The page is torn.]

1206. MARIE MAGDALENNE EUPHRASINNE ERSELINNE
(475) 2 January 1820, baptism of infant born 22 November 1819, natural daughter of [blank], slave of Michel Chamard. Godparents: Lemignon Mora and Euphrasine, both colored. Priest: F. Magnes.

1207. MARIA JOSEPHE FELIS?
(475) 2 January 1820, baptism of infant of 3 months, natural daughter of Agat, slave of Antoin Prudhomme. Godparents: Pier, slave, and Marie Josephe Macarty, free. Priest: F. Magnes.

1208. JEAN MANUEL
(475) 2 January 1820, baptism of child of 6 years, natural son of Hette, slave of Mda. Fernand. Godparents: Joseph Manuel and Marie de Jesus, both colored. Priest: F. Magnes.

1209. [Approximately 3 entries are missing at this point.
(476) The page is torn.]

1210. CHARLES NERESTAN ROCQUE
(476) [Date torn] baptism of an infant born 18 December 1819, legitimate son of Charles Nerestan Roque and Marie Pompose Metoyer. Godparents: Agustin Metoyer and Marie Agnes, both free people of color. Priest: F. Magnes.

1211. MARIE CATIS ATHENAIS
(476) 2 April 1820, baptism of woman aged 22 years, a mestiza, natural daughter of Francisca, Indian of the Natchitoches Nation. Godparents: Alexy Bomond and Marie Jeanne Demesier, free people of color. Priest: F. Magnes.

1212. JEAN BTTE. TRICHE
(476) 24 April 1820, baptism of infant born 8 April 1820, natural son of Mr. Athanas Trichel, French, and Marie Josephe Grappe, free mulattress. Godparents: Juan Btte. David and Marie Osinne David. Priest: F. Magnes.

1213. SEVERINNE
(477)

20 March 1820, baptism of infant of 3 months, natural daughter of Delphine, slave of Louis Metoyer. Godparents: Jean Btte. Metoyer and Suset Metoyer. Priest: F. Magnes.

1214. ANGELIQUE
(477) 20 March 1820, baptism of infant born 20 October 1819, natural daughter of Agnes, slave of Susanne Metoyer. Godparents: Jn. Btte. Metoyer and Suset Metoyer, free people of color. Priest: F. Magnes.

1215. FRANCOIS
(477) 20 March 1820, baptism of infant born 10 November 1819, natural son of Pelagie, slave of M. Susanna Metoyer. Godparents: Francois Metoyer, Jr. and Arthemis Deloy, free people of color. Priest: F. Magnes.

1216. BALSIN
(477) 20 March 1820, baptism of infant born December 1819, natural son of Sil /Marie Side/, slave of Francois Metoyer. Godparents: Magsil Metoyer and Carmelite Anty, free people of color. Priest: F. Magnes.

1217. MARCELITE
(477) 20 March 1820, baptism of infant born 10 May 1819, daughter of Jeny, slave of Agustin Metoyer. Godparents: Joseph Lavigne and Dorothee, free people of color. Priest: F. Magnes.

1218. ANGELINE
(477) 28 March 1820, baptism of infant of 8 months, natural daughter of July, slave of Pierr Delous. Godparents: "her master" and Felicite Pomier. Priest: F. Magnes.

1219. MARIE JULY
(478) 28 March 1820, baptism of English Negro aged 25 years. Slave of Pierr Deloux. Godparents: Jacque Lacasse and Marie Phany Masipe. Priest: F. Magnes.

1220. MARIE SUSANNE
(477) 28 March 1820, baptism of child aged 12 years, English Negro, slave of Pierr Deloux. Godparents: Jn. Btte. Dervan and Angelique Langois. Priest: F. Magnes.

1221. PIERRE
(477)

28 March 1820, baptism of child of 3 years, natural son of Marie, slave of Jean Btte. Anty. Godparents: Felis Langois and Me. Leysa Langois. Priest: F. Magnes.

1222. MARIE
(477) 28 March 1820, baptism of English Negro aged 16 years, slave of Francois Ruvio /Roubieu/. Godparents: Oscar Ruvio and Francoise Adelayde Ruvio. Priest: F. Magnes.

1223. LOUIS
(477) 2 April 1820, baptism of child aged 8 years, English Negro, slave of Mr. Arnoc. Godparents: Michel and Me. Josephe, colored. Priest: F. Magnes.

1224. MARIE LORINE
(477) 2 April 1820, baptism of infant of 8 months, natural daughter of Marie, slave of Mr. Dominique Fort. Godparents: Pier and Marie. Priest: F. Magnes.

1225. MARIE GENOVEVA POLINAIR
(477) 2 April 1820, baptism of infant born 7 June 1819, natural daughter of Veronique, slave of Jn. Btte. Peraut. Godparents: Dominique and Felicite.

1226. MARIE URSUL URANY
(478) 2 April 1820, baptism of infant born 21 December 1819, natural daughter of Jeanton, slave of Fansonet Trichel. Godparents: Etien and Marie. Priest: F. Magnes.

1227. MARIE JEANNE
(478) 2 April 1820, baptism of English mulatto, aged about 35 years, slave of Jn. Btte. Buard. Godparents: Pr. Louis and Marie, colored. Priest: F. Magnes.

1228. MARIE JOANY
(478) 2 April 1820, baptism of mulatto infant of 4 months, natural daughter of Geny, slave of Guillon More. Godparents: Francois Ubauson /Aubuchon/ and Marie Rose Demesier. Priest: F. Magnes.

1229. JEAN FRANCOIS
(478) 2 April 1820, baptism of English Negro aged about 16 years, slave of Jean Cortes. Godparents: Pierre and Bove, colored. Priest: F. Magnes.

1230. MARIE CELESTE
(478) 9 April 1820, baptism of infant born 5 April 1819,

natural daughter of Marie Louise, slave of Remy
Peraut. Godparents: Jean Btte. and Marie Jeanne,
colored. Priest: F. Magnes.

1231. MARGARITE
(478) 9 April 1820, baptism of infant born 10 September
1819, natural daughter of Aspasy, slave of Remy
Peraut. Godparents: Jean Pierr and Marie Louise,
colored. Priest: F. Magnes.

1232. MARIE ZELINE
(478) 25 April 1820, baptism of infant born 2 April
1820, natural daughter of Celesinne, slave of Mda.
Ve. Btte. Grappe. Godparents: Remy and Marie Joseph, colored. Priest: F. Magnes.

1233. LOUIS JOSEPH ELOI
(478) 27 April 1820, baptism of infant of 12 days, natural son of Marie, slave of Louis Peraut. Godparents: Louis Joseph, free mulatto, and Maria Guadalupe Mindez. Priest: F. Magnes.

1234. JOSEPH TERANS
(478) 3 May 1820, baptism of infant of 2 months, natural son of Loise, slave of Victorin Metoyer. Godparents: Manuel and Me. Ositte. Priest: F. Magnes.

1235. AGUSTIN
(478) 21 May 1820, baptism of infant of 6 months, natural son of Felicite, slave of Ceser Morphy. Godparents: Moris and Marie Louise, both colored.
Priest: F. Magnes.

1236. JOSEPH
(478) 15 May 1820, baptism of a Guinea Negro, about 30,
slave of Mr. Bel. Godparents: Jn. Btte. Laflor,
free, and Me. Denis, slave of Marcelo Soto.
Priest: F. Magnes.

1237. JEAN BTTE.
(479) 5 May 1820, baptism of child born 25 April 1814,
natural son of a Cado Indian named Nenchas. Godparents: Simeon Trichel, mulato, and Rosalye,
Indian. Priest: F. Magnes.

1238. MARIE ARSIDE
(479) 13 May 1820, baptism of infant born 29 March 1819,
natural daughter of Marie Rosalye, daughter of a
Cado Indian. Godparents: Pier Roubleau and Marie

Suset Roubleau, his daughter. Priest: F. Magnes.

1239. MARIE ZELINA ANDREA RACHAL
(479) 8 June 1820, baptism of infant born 15 November 1819, legitimate daughter of Jean Btte. Rachal and Maria Susanne Metoyer. Godparents: Jean Btte. Dominique Metoyer and Maria Cidalise Rachal, all free people of color. Priest: F. Magnes.

1240. JEANN BTTE. BIENNE METOYER
(479) 9 June 1820, baptism of infant born 10 January 1819, legitimate son of Jean Btte. Dominique Metoyer and Marie Adelayde Rachal. Godparents: Narcis Dominique Metoyer and Marie Ystasile /Astasie/ Rachal, all free people of color. Priest: F. Magnes.

1241. FRANCOIS EUGIEN DORTHELANS
(479) 18 June 1820, baptism of infant born 6 December 1819, natural son of Mr. Ramon Dortelans, French, and Magdelinne Grappe, free woman of color. Godparents: Francois Bart and Marie Adeline Grappe. Priest: F. Magnes.

1242. BTE. LEANDRE BERTIL
(480) 28 May 1820, baptism of a quarteron, natural son of Marta, slave of Arneau Lauve. Godparents: Arnau Louve, fils, and Marie Louise. Priest: F. Magnes.

1243. WELLOM GEORGE
(480) 21 May 1820, baptism of infant born 17 December 1819, natural son of Flor, slave of Louis Tauzin. Godparents: Len____ /torn/ and Me. Louise, both colored. Priest: F. Magnes.

1244. ZELESTIN
(480) 21 May 1820, baptism of English Negro of 7 years, slave of Mda. Ve. Louis Buard. Godparents: Pier and Erise, both colored. Priest: F. Magnes.

1245. URSIN
(480) 21 May 1820, baptism of English Negro of about 10 years, slave of Mda. Ve. Louis Buard. Godparents: Louis and Me. /H/onorine, both colored. Priest: F. Magnes.

1246. MARIE FLORENTINE
(480) 27 May 1820, baptism of *quarterone*, natural daughter of Victoriana, slave of Jean Cortes. Godparents: Benjamin Balcour Cortes and Hermina Emé

Carr, whites. Priest: F. Magnes.

1247. CELESTIN BAL
(480) 27 May 1820, baptism of infant born 1 October 1819, natural son of Mariana, slave of John Carr. Godparents: Celestin Bal and Me. Theresse, both colored. Priest: F. Magnes.

1248. MARIE CLEOTIL
(480) 18 June 1820, baptism of infant born 22 June 1819, "natural daughter of Casimire Peraut, slave of Mr. Casimire Peraut." Godparents: Dominique and Marie Louise. Priest: F. Magnes.

1249. MARIE ASPASY
(480) 24 June 1820, baptism of infant born 17 April 1820, natural daughter of Marie Jeanne, slave of Louis Galien. Godparents: Louis Ceser Lecour and Marie Damasain Galien. Priest: F. Magnes.

1250. PIERR BRISET
(480) 24 June 1820 baptism of child of 3 years, natural son of Maly, slave of Nicolas Gracia. Godparents: Nicolas Gracia and Maria Roven. Priest: F. Magnes.

1251. LOUIS
(480) 24 June 1820, baptism of infant of 1 year, natural son of Maly, slave of Nicolas Gracia. Godparents: Antoin and Me. Theresse. Priest: F. Magnes.

1252. MANUEL SENCIEL
(481) 25 June 1820, baptism of infant of 1 year, natural son of Celeste, slave of Alexy Cloutier. Godparents: Remy and Denis. Priest: F. Magnes.

1253. MARIE LOYSE
(481) 25 June 1820, baptism of infant of 18 months, natural daughter of Dorothee, slave of Dorothee Monet. Godparents: Pier and Proudans. Priest: F. Magnes.

1254. JEAN BAPTISTE ELOIS
(481) 25 June 1820, baptism of infant of $1\frac{1}{2}$ months, natural son of Marie Zelesy, slave of Ambroisee Comt. Godparents: Dominique and Francoise. Priest: F. Magnes.

1255. DORSELIN
(481) 27 June 1820, baptism of infant born 22 March 1820, natural son of Marie, slave of Louis Metoyer. Godparents: Sinsin and Francois, free. Priest: F. Magnes.

1256. MODESTE MARIE
(481) 27 June 1820, baptism of infant born 19 May, 1820, natural daughter of Marianne, slave of Louis Metoyer. Godparents: Jean Btte. and Euphrasinne. Priest: F. Magnes.

1257. MARIE CELESTE
(481) 11 July 1820, baptism of child aged 7 years, natural daughter of Laysa, slave of Pier Dolle. Godparents: Jean Btte. Adlle and Marie Denis Dolle. Priest: F. Magnes.

1258. LOUIS SOUSIN
(481) 11 July 1820, baptism of child of 3 years, natural son of Laysa, slave of Pier Dolle. Godparents: Andres Valentin and Euphrasin Poissot. Priest: F. Magnes.

1259. JOSEPH MANUEL
(481) 11 July 1820, baptism of natural son of Layse, slave of Pier Dolle. Godparents: Joseph Antonio Villegar and Me. Zefaly Dolé. Priest: F. Magnes.

1260. CIRIAC -- ISAC JOSE
(481) 11 July 1820, baptism of twins, natural sons of Laysa, slave of Pier Dolle. Godparents of Ciriac: Pier Dolle, the master, and Marie Denis Dolle. Godparents of Isac Jose: Pier Dolle and Marie Louise Adle. Priest: F. Magnes.

1261. JOSE ANTOINE -- EDUARDO
(481) 11 July 1820, baptism of sons of Laysa, slave of Pier Dolle, the first 7 years old; godparents: Andres Valentin and Maria Loucouvidhe. The second aged 5 years; godparents: Pier Dolle, son and Me. Rosa Dupre, the mistress. Priest: F. Magnes.

1262. MARIE ZELESY -- JEAN -- FRANCOIS NETTE
(482) 12 July 1820, baptism of three slaves of Pier Dolle. The first is aged 7 months, natural daughter of his slave Marie. Godparents: Andres Valentin and Marie Loucouvidhe. The second, an English Negro aged about 20 years; godparents: Andres Valentin and Me. Rosse Dupre. The third, an English Negro of about 28 years; godparents: Jean Batte. Adle and Marie Pompose Proudhomme. Priest: F. Magnes.

1263. MARIA ZELINA -- MARIA JUDET
(482) 12 July 1820, baptism of two slaves of Joseph Valentin. The first, aged about 3 years, natural

daughter of his slave Chatarina; godparents: Jean Bte. Proudhomme and Ma. Eusevia Ybarvo. The second, natural daughter of the same slave. Godparents: Andres Valentin and Maria Locuviche. Priest: F. Magnes.

1264. JACQUES -- LOUIS
(482) 12 July 1820, baptism of two slaves of Jean Andres Valentin. The first, an English Negro of about 26 years. Godparents: Pier Dolle, Sr. and Marie Rose Dupre. The second, an English Negro of about 30 years. Godparents: Jn Btte Adle and Marie Loucouviche. Priest: F. Magnes.

1265. NICOLAS BALIEN -- PAUL
(482) 13 July 1820, baptism of two slaves of Marcelo Soto. The first, aged 1½ years, natural son of Ma. Barbara; godparents: Jose Arocha and Carmelita Palvado. The second, aged 5 years, natural son of Maria Santon. Godparents: Simon Marcelo Soto and Marie Horror /Aurora/ Laffitte. Priest: F. Magnes.

1266. MARIE JOSEPH
(482) 13 July 1820, baptism of infant born 22 November 1819, natural daughter of Zeny, slave of Cezer Laffitte. Godparents: Joseph Flores and Maria Nieves Soto. Priest: F. Magnes.

1267. MARIE CELESTE -- MARIE CHARLOT
(482) 13 July 1820, baptism of two slaves of Francois Prudhomme. The first, aged 11 years, an English Negro. Godparents: Pier Dolle, Sr. and Marie Louise Gagne. The second, Maria Charlot, English Negro aged 30 years. Godparents: Jn Btte. Timotee Adle and Euphrasine Prudhomme.

1268. PAUL (PABLO)
(482) 13 July 1820, baptism of slave of about 60 years, property of Louis Lamalaty. Godparents: Pier and Jeanne. Priest: F. Magnes.

1269. MARIE DENIS
(482) 13 July 1820, baptism of infant of 10 months, natural daughter of Maria Louisse, slave of Henry Trichel. Godparents: Jn Btte Fonteneau and Marie Zenet Fontaneau. Priest: F. Magnes.

1270. JUAN BTTA. SANTOS COY
(483) 20 June 1820, baptism of Indian child, born 8 March 1820, natural son of Toucaye, an Yguanes Indian.

Godparents: Joseph de los Sta. Coy and his wife Maria Concepcion Hopam, who have adopted the child. Priest: F. Magnes.

1271. FRANCOIS
(483) 24 June 1820, baptism of a free infant born 7 August 1819, natural son of Marianne, a free woman of color. Godparents: Dorseline Levasseur and Marie Louise Rachal. Priest: F. Magnes.

1272. FRANCOIS URSIN RACHAL
(483) 25 June 1820, baptism of a free infant born 30 December 1820 /sic/, natural son of Francisco Machal and Marie Louise Adelle, a free woman of color. Godparents: Etien Rachal and Marie Louisse Adeline. Priest: F. Magnes.

1273. AGUSTIN CLOUTIER
(483) 25 June 1820, baptism of a free infant born 6 October 1819, legitimate son of Agustin Cloutier and Theresse Metoyer. Godparents: Luis Metoyer and Theresse Comte. Priest: F. Magnes.

1274. FLORANTIN CONA
(484) 27 June 1820, baptism of a free infant born 21 April 1820, legitimate son of Florantin Cona and Marie Louis Metoyer. Godparents: Jean Btte. Metoyer, son of Agustin, and Marie Suset Metoyer, all free people of color. Priest: F. Magnes.

1275. MARIE ZELINE BADIN
(484) 5 July 1820, baptism of infant born 20 May 1820, natural daughter of Maria Elena Baden, a free woman of color. Godparents: Julio Estrada and Maria Adelisa Ysude /Hissoura/. Priest: F. Magnes.

1276. JOSEPH POLONIO
(484) 11 July 1820, baptism of Indian of 3 years, of the Yocase nation. Godparents: Jn. Btte. Adle and Ma. Manuela Aragon. Priest: F. Magnes.

1277. JUAN BEKAR
(484) 21 October 1820, baptism of a man who says he is 32 years old, native of Virginia, natural son of Juan Bekar, a free man of color and of Nansi, a white. Godparents: Zenon Demesier and Marie Rosse Demesier, both colored. Priest: F. Magnes.

1278. SERAPHIN /ST. ANDRE/*
(484) 22 November 1820, baptism of an infant born 10 September 1819, slave of Onesime Ste. Andre who

declared the child to be free; infant is the natural son of Susanne, slave of the same. Godparents: Felis Ste. Andre and Lois Ste. Andre.

*In 1831, Onesime St. Andre emancipated Susanne and her five children, Seraphin, aged 11; Antoine Chata, aged 8; Marie Zelia, aged 6; Janvier, aged 4; and Claire, aged 1. See *Miscellaneous Book* 20, pp. 413-14, Natchitoches Parish Civil Records.

1279. JOSEPH TOUZIN
(485) 6 August 1820, baptism of infant aged 8 months, natural son of Me_____ /torn/, slave of Bmy. Lecour. Godparents: Isac and /torn/. Priest: F. Magnes.

1280. JEANN BAPTISTE
(485) 6 August 1820, baptism of infant of 1 month, natural son of Ortans, slave of Marcos Sompairat. Godparents: Juan Pier and Genoveva. Priest: F. Magnes.

1281. JEANN BAPTISTE
(485) 13 October 1820, baptism of infant of 1 month, natural son of Maria Juliana, slave of Pier Ferme. Godparents: Jn. Btte. Val____/torn/ and Clara Olfenau. Priest: F. Magnes.

1282. MARIE ANTOINE
(485) 13 October, 1820, baptism of child of 2 years, natural daughter of Criede, slave of Ve. Quin. Godparents: Julian and Luc____/torn/. Priest: F. Magnes.

1283. NICOLAS CELESTIN
(485) 18 October 1820, baptism of infant born 10 September 1820, natural son of Marie Louise, slave of Mlle. Fra____net /Fanchonette/ Trichel. Godparents: Jacque ____ and Marie Nies /page torn/. Priest: F. Magnes.

1284. JEANN BTTE
(485) 18 October 1820, baptism of infant born 3 July 1820, natural son of Suzette, slave of Mie. Js. Rouquier. Godparents: Juan Car, the son, and Marie Celia Poissot, whites. Priest: F. Magnes.

1285. JOSEPH ADOLFO
(485) 24 October 1820, baptism of infant of 6 months, natural son of Genoveva, slave of Francois Ruquier. Godparents: Francois Rouquier, Jr. and Marie Adelyde Cham____ /torn/. Priest: F. Magnes.

1286. MARIE SOPHY
(485) 24 October 1820, baptism of child of 3 years, natural daughter of Rechin, slave of Mr. Ch. Norit. Godparents: Remy Soto and Emé Peraut. Priest: F. Magnes.

1287. MARIE FELICITE
(485) 24 October 1820, baptism of child of 5 years, natural daughter of Rechin, slave of Ch. Norit. Godparents: Athanas Celestin and Chatarin. Priest: F. Magnes.

1288. MARIE LOUISE
(485) 24 October 1820, baptism of child of 7 years, natural daughter of Rechin, slave of Ch. Noyrit. Godparents: Athanas Celestin and Chatarine, both colored. Priest: F. Magnes.

1289. NOEL
(485) 24 October 1820, baptism of child of 7 years, natural son of Gret, slave of Ch. Noyrit. Godparents: Agustin and Marie. Priest: F. Magnes.

1290. MARIE CEFERIORE
(486) 24 October 1820, baptism of child of 5 years, natural daughter of Gret, slave of Ch. Noyrit. Godparents: Paul and Pompose, both colored. Priest: F. Magnes.

1291. MARIE CELESTINE
(486) 19 November 1820, baptism of infant of 1½ months, natural daughter of Marie Louise, slave of Dufroi Dorseline Galien. Godparents: Francois and Theresse, both colored. Priest: F. Magnes.

1292. MARIE PRUDANS
(486) 20 November 1820, baptism of infant of 10 days, natural daughter of Besse, slave of Pier Michel. Godparents: her master and Marie Adelle Rachal. Priest: F. Magnes.

1293. JEAN FRANCOIS
(486) 20 November 1820, baptism of infant born 10 July 1820, natural son of Melye, slave of Pier Nolasco. Godparents: Magximo Guillon /Aguillon/ and Marie Refugia Cortinas. Priest: F. Magnes.

1294. JOSEPH
(486) 22 November 1820, baptism of child of 3 years, natural son of Josephe, slave of Andre Ste. Andre. Godparents: Erven and Me. Joseph Genaive. Priest: F. Magnes.

1295. JACQUE
(486) 22 November 1820, baptism of infant of 3 months, natural son of Josephe, slave of Andre Ste. Andre. Godparents: Manuel Rachal and Louisse Ste. Andre. Priest: F. Magnes.

1296. JEAN BAPTISTE
(486) 22 November 1820, baptism of natural son of Sira, slave of Andres Ste. Andres. Godparents: Jacque Lemigat and Genauva. Priest: F. Magnes.

1297. ANTOIN
(486) 22 November 1820, baptism of an English Negre aged 14 years, slave of Francois Boudin. Godparents: Antoin and Louise.

1298. MARIE CELESTE
(486) 22 November 1820, baptism of an English Negro, slave of Narcis Rachal. Godparents: Antoin Le Moin, Jr. and Me. Louise Lemoin. Priest: F. Magnes.

1299. PIERRE
(486) 22 November 1820, baptism of an English Negro, aged 16, slave of Manuel Rachal. Godparents: Narcis Rachal and Nanet /Manette/ Rachal. Priest: F. Magnes.

1300. MARIE JEANNE
(486) 22 November 1820, baptism of infant of 1 month, natural daughter of Susanne, slave of Jean Louis Deloux. Godparents: "her master and her mistress Me. Louise Dupre." Priest: F. Magnes.

1301. MARIE NENSY
(486) 23 November 1820, baptism of child of 3 years, natural daughter of Ysabel, slave of Mr. Aguste Bailiou. Godparents: Leandre Lacour and Philonye Bailiou. Priest: F. Magnes.

1302. EDWARD LESTAN
(487) 28 May 1821, baptism of an infant aged 18 months, son of Marie Rosse, free woman of color. Godparents: Edward Lestan Roubleau and Me. Celeste Roubleau. Priest: F. Magnes.

1303. MARIE URSINA DIAS
(487) 28 May 1821, baptism of an infant born 17 February 18__ /torn/, natural daughter of Vicenta Dias, *coyota**. Godparents: Julian Fontaneau and Maria Petra Dias. Priest: F. Magnes.

*A term defined by different authorities as a mixture of *mestizo* with mulatto or *mestizo* with white.

1304. MARIE ASELYNE
(487) 17 September 1821, baptism of infant born 3 June 1821, natural daughter of Catarina, free woman of color, and a father unknown. Godparents: Tousaine Metoyer and Dorotea, both free people of color.

1305. FRANCOIS NAVIL
(487) 17 September 1821, baptism of an infant born 25 September 1820, natural son of Maria Celeste, slave of Bn. Metoyer, fils, who has shown me his registration as free. Godparents: Cezer and Marie Celeste, represented by Jose Geronimo and Marie Ositte Metoyer, both colored. Priest: F. Magnes.

1306. MARIA FRANCISCA
(487) 5 October 1821, baptism of infant aged 1 year, natural daughter of Frosine, a Chatas Indian. Godparents: Nasario Hortis and Regina Reyes?. Priest: F. Magnes.

1307. PIER PAUL
(488) 10 January 1821, baptism of infant born 18 December 1820, natural son of Layde, slave of Mde. Ve. Fonteneau. Godparents: Pierre Paul and Margarita, both colored. Priest: F. Magnes.

1308. MANUEL
(488) 10 January 1821, baptism of infant born 20 October 1820, natural son of Phany, slave of Louis Lamalaty. Godparents: Tetus Gomes, Spaniard, and Susanne, colored. Priest: F. Magnes.

1309. MARIE LAYSE
(488) 7 January 1821, baptism of an infant aged 6 months, natural daughter of Adelle, slave of Jean Cortes. Godparents: Jean Francois Cortes, the son, and Mlle. Prudans Ste. Amans. Priest: F. Magnes.

1310. AGUSTIN
(488) 9 January 1821, baptism of infant of 2 months, natural son of Rosse, slave of Manuel Proudhomme. Godparents: Agustin and Felicite. Priest: F. Magnes.

1311. MARIE SUSET
(488) 9 January 1821, baptism of infant of 1 month, natural daughter of Theresse, slave of Manuel Proudhomme. Godparents: Louis and Jeanne. Priest: F. Magnes.

1312. MARIE CHARLOT
(488)

9 January 1821, baptism of infant of 2 months, natural daughter of Elenne, slave of Julien Rachal. Godparents: Jacob and Julye. Priest: F. Magnes.

1313. CELESTIN
(488) 9 January 1821, baptism of child of 2 years, natural son of Elenne, slave of Julien Rachal. Godparents: Louis and Therese. Priest: F. Magnes.

1314. JEAN FRANCOIS
(488) 9 January 1821, baptism of infant of 8 months, natural son of Julye, slave of Pierre Slectre. Godparents: Baré and Laydé. Priest: F. Magnes.

1315. LEON
(488) 9 January 1821, baptism of infant of 6 months, natural son of Emé, slave of Francois Rouvio /Roubieu/. Godparents: Francois Rouvio, the son, and Pupon? Rouvio. Priest: F. Magnes.

1316. JOSEPH PATERNE
(489) 9 January 1821, baptism of child of 2 years, natural son of Daphanet, slave of Sevastian Comper. Godparents: Michel and Rosaly. Priest: F. Magnes.

1317. MARIE EMELY
(489) 9 January 1821, baptism of an English mulattress, aged 22, slave of Sevastien Comper. Godparents: Jacob and Marianne. Priest: F. Magnes.

1318. JEANN SATURIN
(489) 10 January 1821, baptism of infant born 19 August 1820, natural son of Nanet, slave of Mde. Ve. Bmy. Rachal. Godparents: Dorsino and Marie Theresse. Priest: F. Magnes.

1319. SERAPHIN /LACAZE/
(489) 10 January 1821, baptism of infant born 10 October 1820, natural son of Marie Jeanne, slave of Jacques LaCase. Godparents: Faustino Hortis and Caroline Lemoin, whites. Priest: F. Magnes.

1320. FRANCOIS ZENON
(489) 13 January 1821, baptism of infant born 15 February 1820, natural son of Melite, slave of Joseph Tauzin. Godparents: Francois Tauzin and Adelle Nafry. Priest: F. Magnes.

1321. FRANCOIS
(489) 13 January 1821, baptism of infant born 30 February 1820, natural son of Celeste, slave of Joseph

Tauzin. Godparents: Francois Chavus and the slave's mistress, Marie Chamard. Priest: F. Magnes.

1322. MARIE JOSEPHE
(489) 5 March 1821, baptism of English Negro, aged 35 years, slave of Felis Trudeau. Godparents: Antoin and Marie, both colored. Priest: F. Magnes.

1323. MARIE AMIRE
(489) 7 March 1821, baptism of infant born 3 September 1820, natural daughter of Marie Jeanne, slave of Mde. Ve. Jn. Btte. Trichel. Godparents: David Hortelans /Dortelant/ and Marie Emily Trichel. Priest: F. Magnes.

1324. MODESTE
(489) 23 March 1821, baptism of infant aged 1 year, natural daughter of Geneveva, slave of Narcisse Proudhomme. Godparents: Noret and Fourain, colored. Priest: F. Magnes.

1325. ANTOIN GASION
(489) 23 March 1821, baptism of infant aged 1 year, natural son of Flor, slave of Narcis Proudhome. Godparents: Jn. Btte. and Louise, colored. Priest: F. Magnes.

1326. JOSEPH
(489) 23 March 1821, baptism of infant of 3 months, natural son of Perine, slave of Mr. Metayer, the son. Godparents: Francois and Elenne, colored. Priest: F. Magnes.

1327. MANUEL
(490) 23 March 1821, baptism of infant of 4 months, natural son of Therese, slave of Louis Bmy. Rachal. Godparents: Francois and Marie, colored. Priest: F. Magnes.

1328. PIERRE
(490) 23 March 1821, baptism of infant of 1 years, natural son of Therese, slave of J. Lambre. Godparents: Louis and Nanet. Priest: F. Magnes.

1329. JACQUES
(490) 23 March 1821, baptism of child of 6 years, natural son of Phequi /Vicki?/, slave of J. Lambre. Godparents: Dominique and Me. Louise, colored. Priest: F. Magnes.

1330. THERESE
(490) 23 March 1821, baptism of child of 4 years, natural daughter of Phequi /Vicky?/, slave of J. Lambre. Godparents: Joseph and Therese, colored. Priest: F. Magnes.

1331. MARIE
(490) 23 March 1821, baptism of child of 6 years, natural daughter of Phequi /Vicky?/, slave of J. Lambre. Godparents: Avis and Marie. Priest: F. Magnes.

1332. FRANCOIS NEUVIL
(490) 24 March 1821, baptism by Mnsgr. L'Eveque of a mulattress slave of Benjamin Metoyer. Godparents: Mr. Felicin Benjamin and Mlle. Marie Susanne Lambre.

1333. MANUEL
(490) 24 March 1821, baptism by Mnsgr. L'Eveque of a Negro slave of Benjamin Metoyer. Godparents: Jean Btte. and Marianne Nouvelle, colored.

1334. JN BTTE. FELIS
(490) 25 March, 1821, baptism of infant of 8 months, natural son of Marie Saly, slave of Cezer Brosect. Godparents: Joseph Valery /LeCourt/ and Barvara Lecour. Priest: F. Magnes.

1335. JULIEN JEAN PIERRE
(490) 25 March 1821, baptism of infant of 7 months, natural son of Ana, slave of Marcos Sompairact. Godparents: Jean Pierre and Ursulle. Priest: F. Magnes.

1336. MARGARITE
(490) 25 March 1821, baptism of infant of 6 months, daughter of Celeste, slave of Jn. Btte. Adlle. Godparents: Francois and Marie Josephe, colored. Priest: F. Magnes.

1337. TOISSAIN
(490) 25 March 1821, baptism of infant born 25 November 1820, natural son of Marthe, slave of Athanas Le Cour. Godparents: Francois and Genevieve. Priest: F. Magnes.

1338. JN. BTTE
(490) 25 March 1821, baptism of infant of 3 months, natural son of Marie, slave of Jacque Bercher. Godparents: Isac and Horrore /Aurore/, colored. Priest: F. Magnes.

1339. FRANCOISE
(490) 25 March, 1821, baptism of infant of 4 months, daughter of Marie, slave of Alexi Cloutier. Godparents: Despalier and Me. Francoise. Priest: F. Magnes.

1340. FRANCOISE
(491) 25 March 1821, baptism of infant of 6 months, natural daughter of Frouasine, slave of Jn. Btte. Dervan. Godparents: Joseph and Francoisse, both colored. Priest: F. Magnes.

1341. LUCIANE
(491) 25 March 1821, baptism of slave born 9 January 1821. No further information given. Priest: F. Magnes.

1342. MARIE PHANCHAN /FANCHON/
(491) 25 March 1821, baptism of infant of 4 months, daughter of Felicite, slave of Ambroise Comt. Godparents: Narcis and Marie Louise, colored. Priest: F. Magnes.

1343. URSIN
(491) 25 March 1821, baptism of infant of 4 months, son of Susanne, slave of Jean Btte. LeComt. Godparents: Athanas Lecour and Me. Barbara Lecour. Priest: F. Magnes.

1344. MARIE ALYSA
(491) 30 March 1821, baptism of infant born 29 January 1821, natural daughter of Elenne, slave of Joseph Dervan. Godparents: Pierre and Laysa, both colored. Priest: F. Magnes.

1345. JULIEN
(491) 15 April 1821, baptism of infant born 15 August 1820, natural son of Modeste, slave of Francois Vienne. Godparents: Joseph and Margarita, colored. Priest: F. Magnes.

1346. JOSEPH
(491) 22 April 1821, baptism of infant born 18 August 1820, natural son of Eulaly, slave of Mda. Ve. Morphy. Godparents: Antoin and Victoire. Priest: Franco. Magnes.

1347. MANUEL
(491) 22 April 1821, baptism of infant born 17 January 1821, natural son of Ma. Barbara, slave of Antoin Prudhomme. Godparents: Andres Celestin and Me.

Susanne, colored. Priest: F. Magnes.

1348. MARIE MODESTE
(491) 22 April 1821, baptism of infant born 17 August 1820, natural daughter of Layde, slave of Mda. Ve. Francoisse Levasseur. Godparents: Marcelin and Margarite, colored. Priest: F. Magnes.

1349. URSIN
(491) 22 April 1821, baptism of infant born 6 February 1821, natural son of Venory,* slave of Jean Btte. Peraut. Godparents: Pierre and Layde. Priest: F. Magnes.

*Possibly this is same as Veronique, the Peraut slave in Entry 1225.

1350. MARIE DESIRE
(491) 22 April 1821, baptism of infant born 2 August, 1820, natural daughter of Marie, slave of Noel Rachal. Godparents: Agustin and Layde, colored. Priest: F. Magnes.

1351. FRANCOIS LASAR
(492) 22 April 1821, baptism of infant born 21 September 1819, natural son of Layde, slave of Mda. Ve. Dominique Davion. Godparents: Jean Pierre and Me. Rosse, colored. Priest: F. Magnes.

1352. DELPHINE
(492) 22 April 1821, baptism of child of 5 years, daughter of Laly, slave of Jn. Btte. Buard. Godparents: Jacque and Magdaline. Priest: F. Magnes.

1353. MARIE DELINE
(492) 22 April 1821, baptism of infant of 6 months, natural daughter of Eulaly, slave of Placide Bossier. Godparents: Francois Lestage and Marie Pomposse. Priest: F. Magnes.

1354. JEANN BTTE.
(492) 22 April 1821, baptism of infant of 2 years, slave of Placide Bossier, "ditto" /child of Eulaly_7. Godparents: Francois and Felicite. Priest: F. Magnes.

1355. FRANCOIS DORCELIN
(492) 22 April 1821, baptism of infant born 9 October 1820, natural son of Juliane, slave of Charles Norit. Godparents: Louis and Perine. Priest: F. Magnes.

1356. MARIE ASELYE
(492) 22 April 1821, baptism of infant born 26 May 1820, natural daughter of Me. Francois, slave of Jn. Btte. Buard. Godparents: Marceline and Marie Louisse, colored. Priest: F. Magnes.

1357. JOSEPH
(492) 22 April 1821, baptism of infant of 6 months, natural son of Marie, slave of John Carr. Godparents: Joseph and Margarita. Priest: F. Magnes.

1358. JEAN BTTE.
(492) 22 April 1821, baptism of child of 5 years, natural son of Lister, slave of John Sibley. Godparents: Hodman and Marie, colored. Priest: F. Magnes.

1359. URSIN
(492) 28 April 1821, baptism of infant of 2 months, natural son of Rosse, slave of Jn. Btte. Lattier. Godparents: Nevil Galien and Marie Deloyse Lattiere. Priest: F. Magnes.

1360. MARIE NATALY
(492) 2 May 1821, baptism of infant of 6 months, natural daughter of Ene, slave of M. Barvarus /Barberousse/ Sr. Godparents: Joseph Cristi and Meanne. Peraut. Priest: F. Magnes.

1361. JEAN PIERRE CLAIREVIL
(492) 6 May 1821, baptism of infant born 29 January 1821, natural son of Me. Pompose, slave of Jn. Btte. Proudhome. Godparents: Jn. Btte. and Victoire. Priest: F. Magnes.

1362. MARGARITA
(492) 14 May 1821, baptism of infant of 6 months, natural daughter of Melite, slave of Jn. Btte. Bessoin. Godparents: Agustin and Margarita. Priest: F. Magnes.

1363. MARIE LALYE
(493) 23 November 1820, baptism of infant of ____ months /page torn/, natural daughter of Ysabel, slave of Mr. Agu/ste Bail/liou. Godparents: Jean Lacour and Marianne Bailliou. Priest: F. Magnes.

1364. JEANET
(493) 23 November 1820, baptism of infant of 14 months, natural daughter of Margarite, slave of Joseph Gillard. Godparents: Etvans and Sin____ /page torn/. Priest: F. Magnes.

1365. HONORE
(493) 23 November 1820, baptism of infant aged 4 months, natural son of Olde, slave of Leon Lacour. Godparents: Jn Marie Lacour and Mar__ Lacour /page torn/. Priest: F. Magnes.

1366. GUILLON
(493) 23 November 1820, baptism of infant aged ___ and a half, natural son of Polé, slave of Jn Btte. G_____ /Gillard?/. Godparents: Leandre Lacour and Magdalenne Gillard. /page torn/. Priest: F. Magnes.

1367. AGUSTIN
(493) 25 November 1820, baptism of infant aged 3____. Natural son of Celeste, slave of Mr. Bolon L____ /Layssard/. Godparents: Asor and Perine. /Page torn/. Priest: F. Magnes.

1368. SOUQUE /SUKIE?/
(493) 25 November 1820, baptism of child of 11 years, daughter of Bete, slave of P._____. Godparents: George and Felicite. /page torn/. Priest: F. Magnes.

1369. MARIE JANYE
(493) 25 November 1820, baptism of infant aged ____ year, natural daughter of Anrriet, slave of E____ Kerklam. Godparents: Mr. N____ Bilain /Nicolas Villain/ and Emely Lacour. /Page torn/. Priest: F. Magnes.

1370. JOSEPH VUTLIA /BUTLER?/
(493) 25 November 1820, baptism of English mulatto of 35 years, slave of Agustu Bailliou. Godparents: /Sosth/en Bailliou and Emely Lacour. /Page torn/. Priest: F. Magnes.

1371. JOHON
(493) 25 December 1820, baptism of English mulatto aged 20 years, slave of Sostin /Baillio/. Godparents: Eduarde /Kirkland/ and Celeste Bailliou. /Page torn/. Priest: F. Magnes.

1372. MARIE FLOREY
(493) 25 November 1820, baptism of English Negro aged 27 years, slave of A. Bailliou. Godparents: _____ Kerkllam and Celeste Bailliou. /Page torn/. Priest: F. Magnes.

1373. MARIE DESIENT
(493) 25 November 1820, baptism of slave aged ____ year

a slave of _____. Godparents: _____ Bailliou and Mlle. Anrriet Chonse. /Page torn/. Priest: F. Magnes.

1374. HENRY CH___
(493) 25 November 1825, baptism of slave aged ___ year, slave of _____. Godparents: Mr. Ge_____ and Emely LaCour. /Page torn/. Priest: F. Magnes.

1375. A_____
(493) 25 November 1820, baptism of slave of _____. Godparents: Mr. _____ and _____ Rosillon. /Page torn/. Priest: F. Magnes.

1376. MARIE MORAYA /MARIAH?/
(494) 25 November 1820, baptism of slave of Pierr Bailliou in Rapides, English mulatto, aged 21 years. Godparents: Joseph Chatman and Celeste Bailliou. Priest: F. Magnes

1377. MARIE ELSE
(494) 25 November 1820, baptism of English griffe of Pierr Bailliou, aged 20 years. Godparents: Eduard Kerklan and Celeste Bailliou. Priest: F. Magnes.

1378. CHARLES
(494) 25 November 1820, baptism of English Negro of Pierr Bailliou. Godparents: Landry Bailliou and Louis/e/ Rosillon. Priest: F. Magnes.

1379. CLARISSE
(494) 25 November 1820, baptism of infant of 4 months, natural daughter of Nanet, slave of Pier Bailliou. Godparents: Agustin and Francoise. Priest: F. Magnes.

1380. ALBINE
(494) 25 November 1820, baptism of infant of 3 months, natural son of Louseie? /Lucy?/, slave of Pierr Bailliou. Godparents: Jean and Leonor. Priest: F. Magnes.

1381. MAGDALENNE
(494) 25 November 1820, baptism of infant of 2 years, daughter of Magdalenne, slave of Pierr Bailliou. Godparents: Agustin and Felicite. Priest: F. Magnes.

1382. MARTIN
(494) 25 November 1820, baptism of infant of 8 months, natural son of Ana, slave of Pierr Bailliou. God-

parents: Silver Bailliou and Anrriete Chonse.
Priest: F. Magnes.

1383. MARIE EMY
(494) 25 November 1820, baptism of infant of 18 months, natural daughter of Anrriet, slave of Pierr Bailliou. Godparents: James and Christ_____.
Priest: F. Magnes.

1384. LORANS
(494) 25 November 1820, baptism of infant of 15 months, mulatto and natural son of J____hy, slave of Pierr Bailliou. Godparents: Antoine Revoil and Emy La Cour. Priest: F. Magnes.

1385. JOSEPH DANIEL
(494) 25 November 1820, baptism of English Negro of 25 years, slave of Pierr Bailliou. Godparents: Pier Bailliou and Marie Emely LaCour. Priest: F. Magnes.

1386. ME. PLESANS
(494) 25 November 1820, baptism of English Negro aged 16 years, slave of Pierr Bailliou. Godparents: Joseph Chapman and "her mistress, Marie Emely LaCour." Priest: F. Magnes.

1387. MARIE CLO
(494) 27 November 1820, baptism of child of 5 years, natural daughter of Clo, slave of Mda. Ve. Hodman. Godparents: Pier Lafon and Marie Hodman. Priest: F. Magnes.

1388. MANUEL
(494) 27 November 1820, baptism of child of 5 years, natural son of Catarine, slave of Mda. Ve. Mellon. Godparents: Basil and Louisse, colored. Priest: F. Magnes.

1389. CATARINE
(494) 25 December 1820, baptism of infant born 2 October 1820, natural daughter of Cla_____, slave of Honore Fredieu. Godparents: Joseph and Catarine, colored. Priest: F. Magnes.

1390. MARCELINE LESAR /LAYSSARD7
(495) /torn7 1820, baptism of mulatto aged 10 days, natural son of Balentin Lesar and Marie _____, free. Godparents: Zenon and Lisse, both free people of color. Priest: F. Magnes.

1391. CLARA BORD
(495) ⟦no date⟧ 1820. Baptism of quadroon aged 6 years, natural daughter of Mas Bord and Francoise Me____, free. Godparents: Joseph Chapelin and Josephine Horenois. Priest: F. Magnes. ⟦Document torn.⟧

1392. MARIE ADELLE GRAPPE
(495) 13 January 1821, baptism of infant born 15 April, 1820, daughter of Baltasar Grappe and Marianne ____, free. Godparents: M____ Grappe and Marie Pompose Grappe, free people of color. Priest: F. Magnes. ⟦Document torn.⟧

1393. ELISAVET OBOUSAUN ⟦Aubichon⟧
(495) 13 January 1821, baptism of infant born 12 ____, natural daughter of Charles Obousaun and Marie _____, both free people of color. Godparents: Jeanne Baptiste Charlevi____ and Marie Theresse. Priest: F. Magnes.

1394. MARIE ROSALYE
(496) March 1821, baptism of free infant born 23 December 1820, natural daughter of Angelye, a free mulattress. Godparents: Guillom Callagham and Rosalye Grenaux. Priest: F. Magnes.

1395. MARIE FELICITE MELON
(496) 25 March 1821, baptism of infant born 15 January 1821, "fille ____"* of Francois Milon and Marie Louise Metoyer, both free people of color. Godparents: Emil Dupart and Arthemisse De Loya ⟦Dupart⟧. Priest: F. Magnes. ⟦*Left blank on original.⟧

1396. FRANCOIS FLORIBAL METOYER
(496) 29 March 1821, baptism of infant born __ October 1820, legitimate son of Jean Btte. Metoyer and Marie Suset Anty. Godparents: Manuel Lorans and Marie Arsine Anty. Priest: F. Magnes. ⟦torn⟧

1397. ANTOINE LESIERE CONDET
(496) 29 March 1821, baptism of infant born 9 January 1821, natural son of Antoin Condet of the French nation and Rosse Metoyer, free woman of color. Godparents: Nicolas Gracia and Estasie Rachal. Priest: F. Magnes.

1398. MARIE DELPHINE
(497) 27 May 1821, baptism of child born 11 May 1814, natural daughter of Odisse, slave of Silvestre Poissot. Godparents: Marcelo Soto and Marie Damassi Soto. The child's master has declared her to be free. Priest: F. Magnes.

1399. MARIE ROSSE
(497) 27 May 1821, baptism of child born 5 October 1816, natural daughter of Odisse, slave of Mr. Silvestre Poissot. Godparents: Marcelo Soto and Marie Benus /Venus_7. The child's master has declared her to be free. Priest: F. Magnes.

1400. JACQUE
(497) 27 May 1821, baptism of child of 7 years, natural son of Susanne, slave of Pierr Robleau. Godparents: Louis and Marie, both colored. Priest: F. Magnes.

1401. MARIE ROSSE
(497) 27 May 1821, baptism of child of 4 years, natural daughter of Susanne, slave of Pierre Rubleau. Godparents: Athanas and Me. Rose, colored. Priest: F. Magnes.

1402. URSIN
(497) 31 May 1821, baptism of child born 2 August 1812, natural son of Onye, slave of Francois Rambin. Godparents: Christine Hesser and Marie Modeste Proudhomme, whites. Priest: F. Magnes.

1403. MARIE JEANNE
(497) 31 May 1821, baptism of infant of 9 months, natural daughter of Charlot, slave of Francois Proudhomme. Godparents: Francois Rambin and Marie Josephine Hesser, whites. Priest: F. Magnes.

1404. ZELESTIN
(497) 10 June 1821, baptism of infant of 1 year, natural son of Carlen, slave of Jn Btte Buard. Godparents: Francois and Elenne, both colored. Priest: F. Magnes.

1405. MARIE JULYE
(497) 10 June 1821, baptism of infant born 2 April 1821, natural daughter of Marye, slave of Mda. Ve. Morphy. Godparents: Andres Lendor and Louisse, both colored. Priest: F. Magnes.

1406. ENERES
(497) 8 July 1821, baptism of infant born 6 March 1821, natural son of Adelye, slave of Francois Rouquier. Godparents: Charles Simon and Lise Metoyer, both colored. Priest: F. Magnes.

1407. MARIE FRANCOISE
(497) 29 July 1821, baptism of infant born 1 May, natural daughter of Chanet /?Janet_7, slave of Mda.

Ve. Chavus. Godparents: Jacque and Marie Louisse, both colored. Priest: F. Magnes.

1408. JACOB
(498) 30 July 1821, baptism of English Negro aged 20 years, slave of Antoin Proudhomme. Godparents: Nevil Proudhomme and Suset Proudhomme. Priest: F. Magnes.

1409. MARIE PHEVITE /̄PHOEBE?_7
(498) 30 July 1821, baptism of English Negro, aged about 14 years, slave of Antoin Proudhomme. Godparents: Noret and Jeanne, both colored. Priest: F. Magnes.

1410. NANET
(498) 30 July 1821, baptism of English Negro about 14 years, slave of Antoin Proudhomme. Godparents: Richard Hertzog and Henriette Amire Proudhome. Priest: F. Magnes.

1411. MARIE SALÉE
(498) 30 July 1821, baptism of English Negro of 12 years, slave of Antoine Proudhomme. Godparents: Mr. Cayelle and Dme. Horrore Lambre. Priest: F. Magnes.

1412. MARIE NATÉ
(498) 30 July 1821, baptism of English Negro about 13 years, slave of Antoine Proudhome. Godparents: Noret and Hortans, both colored. Priest: F. Magnes.

1413. JOSEPH DANIEL
(498) 30 July 1821, baptism of slave aged 12 years, property of Antoine Proudhomme. Godparents: Francois Hertzog and Desire Proudhome. Priest: F. Magnes.

1414. JACOB BRON
(498) 30 July 1821, baptism of English Negro about 11 years, slave of Antoine Proudhome. Godparents: Henry and Barbare, both colored. Priest: F. Magnes.

1415. MARIE VIRGINE
(498) 30 July 1821, baptism of infant of 3 months, natural daughter of Agat, slave of Antoine Proudhome. Godparents: Henry Hertzog and Antonet Proudhome. Priest: F. Magnes.

1416. MARIE EMELY
(498) 30 July 1821, baptism of infant of 8 months, natural daughter of Marte, slave of Baltasar Brevel. Godparents: Jeann Btte. and Marie, both colored. Priest: F. Magnes.

1417. MARIE JULY
(498) 30 July 1821, baptism of child of 3 years, natural daughter of Me. Emely, slave of Francois Hertzog. Godparents: Charlot and Celestin. Priest: F. Magnes.

1418. JOSEPH BOSEM
(498) 30 July 1821, baptism of English Negro, aged 32, slave of Francois Hertzog. Godparents: Nevil Proudhome and Phany Hertzog. Priest: F. Magnes.

1419. JEANN PIERRE
(498) 7 August 1821, baptism of child of 5 years, natural son of Victoire, slave of Pierre Gagne. Godparents: Alexi Trichel and Pompose Lafitte. Priest: F. Magnes.

1420. ME. EMELY ASTASY
(498) 7 August 1821, baptism of infant of 6 months, natural daughter of Catarine, slave of Ceser Fontaneau. Godparents: Etien and Emely. Priest: F. Magnes.

1421. MARIE SUSET
(499) 2 September 1821, baptism of mulatto infant of 5 months, natural daughter of Marie Louise, slave of Jn Bte Prudhomme. Godparents: Charles Simon and Charlot. Priest: F. Magnes.

1422. MARIE SILBY
(499) 2 September 1821, baptism of infant aged about 4 months, natural daughter of Clarisse, slave of Mr. Hazeton. Godparents: Zenon Demesier and Marie Theresse, both colored. Priest: F. Magnes.

1423. LOUISE
(499) 2 September 1821, baptism of child of 2 years, natural daughter of Matilde, slave of Mr. Hazeton. Godparents: Jn. Btte. Choval, Jr. /Charleville7* and Me. Euphrosine, both colored. Priest: F. Magnes.

*/A free *metive* of St. Louis who also appears in Entry 1393. He is not to be confused with Jean Baptiste Charleville, his French cousin of St. Louis who appeared in the parish in 1825.7

1424. BALSIN MICHEL
(499) 16 September 1821, baptism of infant of 2 months, natural son of Marcelite, slave of Francois Bossier. Godparents: Alexandre Buard and July Buard. Priest: F. Magnes.

1425. HILAIRE -- ME. NANET
(499) 17 September 1821, baptism of twins, born 3 August

1821, natural children of Emeli, slave of Clement Rachal. Godparents of Hilaire: Hilaire and Me. Theresse, both colored. Godparents of Me. Nanet: Cezer and Me. Theresse. Priest: F. Magnes.

1426. MARIE CRIOSTIN
(499) 17 September 1821, baptism of infant of 2 days, natural daughter of Fansonet, slave of Manuel Proudhomme. Godparents: Jean Btte. and Me. Pomposse, both colored. Priest: F. Magnes.

1427. ME. HORTANS
(499) 17 September 1821, baptism of infant of 6 months, natural daughter of Grec, slave of Ciriac Levaseur. Godparents: Jn. Btte. and Me. Louisse, both colored. Priest: F. Magnes.

1428. AGUSTINA
(499) 17 September 1821, baptism of infant of 1 month, natural daughter of Marie, slave of Mda. Ve. Jn. Bte. Trichel. Godparents: Jean Louis and Me. Josephe, both colored. Priest: F. Magnes.

1429. MARIE ASELY
(499) 17 September 1821, baptism of infant born 26 February last, natural daughter of a slave of B. Metoyer. Godparents: Jacque and Marie Louisse Baden, both colored. Priest: F. Magnes.

1430. MARIE ROSALY
(499) 17 September 1821, baptism of English Negro, aged 18 years, slave of Antoin Himel. Godparents: Joseph and Marguerite, both colored. Priest: F. Magnes.

1431. MARIE HENRRIET
(500) 17 September 1821, baptism of infant of 4 months, natural daughter of Fany, slave of Louis Bmy. Rachal, Jr. Godparents: Tousain Metoyer and Doroté /Monet-Cloutier/, free people of color. Priest: F. Magnes.

1432. MARIE THERESSE
(500) 23 September 1821, baptism of infant of 3 months, natural daughter of Constance, slave of Joseph Dervan. Godparents: Felis and Marie Theresse, both colored. Priest: F. Magnes.

1433. JOSEPH DIC
(500) 12 October 1821, baptism of infant of 8 months, natural son of Crede, slave of Mda. Ve. Guin.

Godparents: Ignacio de los Santos Coy and Trinidad Gonsales. Priest: F. Magnes.

1434. JEANN FRANCOIS
(500) 18 November 1821, baptism of natural son of Margarite, slave of Theodore Grillet. Godparents: Joseph and Marie Manon, both colored. Priest: F. Magnes.

1435. JOSEPH
(500) 20 November 1821, baptism of child of 12 years, natural son of Felicite, slave of Mr. Thomas Wales /Wallace/. Godparents: "his master" and Marie Josefa Palvado. Priest: F. Magnes.

1436. MARIE JULYE
(500) 27 November 1821, baptism of infant born 7 September 1821, natural daughter of Marie Jeanne, slave of Francoise Trichel. Godparents: Louis and Celeste, both colored. Priest: F. Magnes.

1437. MARIE MODESTE
(500) 3 November 1821, baptism of infant of 6 months, natural daughter of Delphine, slave of Pierre Metoyer. Godparents: Athanasse Viene Metoyer and Marie Osite Metoyer. Priest: F. Magnes.

1438. MARIE PHANY /Fanny/
(500) 30 November 1821, baptism of English Negro aged about 22 years, slave of Pier Metoyer. Godparents: Tousain Metoyer and Dorothea /Monet-Cloutier/. Priest: F. Magnes.

1439. JN BTTE. ZIPHORINE
(500) 30 November 1821, baptism of infant born 10 September 1821, natural son of Me. Felicite, slave of Susanne Metoyer. Godparents: Denis and Marie Pompose, both colored. Priest: F. Magnes.

1440. CHARLES MERTIL
(500) 30 November 1821, baptism of infant born 3 September 1821, natural son of Charlot, slave of Agustin Metoyer. Godparents: Charles Rocque and Me. Liset Metoyer. Priest: F. Magnes.

1441. MARTIN
(501) 6 December 1821, baptism of infant of 1 month, natural son of Marie, slave of Jean Bte. Duvois. Godparents: Ambrois Lemoin and Barbara Charvonet. Priest: F. Magnes.

1442. MAGDALENE
(501) 6 December 1821, baptism of infant of 3 months,

natural daughter of Requiole, slave of Jn. Btte. Gilard. Godparents: Jean Bte. Gillard, Jr. and Magdalenne Gillard, whites. Priest: F. Magnes.

1443. FRANCOIS FERDINAND
(501) 11 December 1821, baptism of mulatto born 11 August 1821, natural son of Sophy, slave of Mda. Ve. Pierre Nolasco. Godparents: Francois Adlley and Marie Assely Adlley, whites. Priest: F. Magnes.

1444. MARIE FELICITE
(501) 11 December 1821, baptism of infant born 25 July 1821, natural daughter of Dossé, slave of Mda. Ve. Pierre Nolasco. Godparents: Bernarde Rachal and Marie Adelle Rachal, whites. Priest: F. Magnes.

1445. MARIE ZELINE
(501) 18 December 1821, baptism of infant of 6 months, natural daughter of Emely, slave of Mr. Porter. Godparents: Simon Rachal and Me. Adlley. Priest: F. Magnes.

1446. JOSEPH
(501) 16 December 1821, baptism of infant of 1 month, natural son of Marie Jeanne, slave of Jean Btte. Chenal. Godparents: Joseph Boudoin and Margarite de Ravaly [Rabalais]. Priest: F. Magnes.

1447. JOSEPH
(501) 16 December 1821, baptism of infant of 6 months, natural son of Marie, slave of Alexi Cloutier. Godparents: Dominique and Marie Jean, colored. Priest: F. Magnes.

1448. ATHANAS
(501) 16 December 1821, baptism of English Negro aged 22 years, slave of Alexy Cloutier. Godparents: Pier and Marie Ortans, both colored. Priest: F. Magnes.

1449. MARIE PALMIRE
(501) 16 December 1821, baptism of infant of 2 months, natural daughter of Elisavet, slave of Louis Dervan. Godparents: Joseph Metoyer and Adelayde, free people of color. Priest: F. Magnes.

1450. MARIE JEANNE
(501) 16 December 1821, baptism of English slave aged 18 years, belonging to Mr. Magsil Metoyer. Godparents: Francois Metoyer and Me. Louisse, free Negress. Priest: F. Magnes.

1451. JEANN
(501)

16 December 1821, baptism of English slave aged 20 years, property of Magsil Metoyer. Godparents: Francois Metoyer and Me. Louise, free Negress. Priest: F. Magnes.

1452. MARIE EUPHRASIN
(501) 16 December 1821, baptism of English slave of Francois Metoyer, aged 19 years. Godparents: Francois Metoyer, Jr. and Me. Aspasy Anty. Priest: F. Magnes.

1453. YSIDRE
(501) 16 December 1821, baptism of English slave, aged 22 years, property of Francois Metoyer. Godparents: Louis Asty [Solasty] Dervan and Pelagie Lemoin. Priest: F. Magnes.

1454. PAUL
(501) 16 December 1821, baptism of Guinea Negro aged 24 years, slave of Jn. Btte. Metoyer, son of Augustin. Godparents: Louis Metoyer and Marie Suset Metoyer. Priest: F. Magnes.

1455. LENDOR
(502) 17 December 1821, baptism of Guinea Negro aged 26 years, slave of Agustin Metoyer. Godparents: Magsil Metoyer and Me. Aspasy Anty. Priest: F. Magnes.

1456. GAVRIEL
(502) 17 December 1821, baptism of Guinea Negro aged 24 years, slave of Agustin Metoyer. Godparents: Elise Rocque and Me. Susete Metoyer. Priest: F. Magnes.

1457. JEAN BTTE.
(502) 17 December 1821, baptism of Guinea Negro aged 24 years, slave of Agustin Metoyer. Godparents: Louis and Me. Louise, free Negress. Priest: F. Magnes.

1458. ANTOIN FORTUN
(502) 17 December 1821, baptism of Guinea Negro aged 12 years, slave of Agustin Metoyer. Godparents: Francois Metoyer and Me. Arthemise. Priest: F. Magnes.

1459. NICOLAS
(502) 17 December 1821, baptism of Guinea Negro, aged 21 years, slave of Agustin Metoyer. Godparents: Remy and Felicite, free Negroes. Priest: F. Magnes.

1460. CHARLES
(502) 17 December 1821, baptism of Guinea Negro aged 18 years, slave of Agustin Metoyer. Godparents: Francois Gassion Metoyer and Me. Louise Metoyer. Priest: F. Magnes.

1461. ATANAS
(502) 17 December 1821, baptism of a Guinea Negro aged 19 years, slave of Agustin Metoyer. Godparents: Joseph Lavigne and Me. Dorothea. Priest: F. Magnes.

1462. PAUL
(502) 17 December 1821, baptism of Guinea Negro, aged 22, slave of Agustin Metoyer. Godparents: Francois Gassion Metoyer and Me. Aragon. Priest: F. Magnes.

1463. JEANN NED
(502) 17 December 1821, baptism of Guinea Negro aged 18 years, slave of Agustin Metoyer. Godparents: Charles Rocque and Me. Pompose Metoyer. Priest: F. Magnes.

1464. JOSEPH BRON
(502) 17 December 1821, baptism of English Negro aged 15 years, slave of Agustin Metoyer. Godparents: Jn. Btte. Metoyer and Me. Suste. Metoyer. Priest: F. F. Magnes.

1465. HENRY
(502) 17 December 1821, baptism of English Negro aged 23 years, slave of Agustin Metoyer. Godparents: August Metoyer and Me. Suset Metoyer. Priest: F. Magnes.

1466. JEANN PIERRE
(502) 17 December 1821, baptism of English Negro aged 12 years, slave of Agustin Metoyer. Godparents: Elset /Elisée/ Rocque and Me. Suset Metoyer. Priest: F. Magnes.

1467. ANDRES
(502) 17 December 1821, baptism of a Guinea Negro aged 24 years, slave of Agustin Metoyer. Godparents: Jose Lavigne and Dorothee. Priest: F. Magnes.

1468. JEANN
(502) 17 December 1821, baptism of Guinea Negro aged 17 years, slave of Augustin Metoyer. Godparents: Jose Metoyer and Me. Adelle Metoyer. Priest: F. Magnes.

1469. ME. ZALYE /SALLY7
(502) 17 December 1821, baptism of English Negro aged 23 years, slave of Agustin Metoyer. Godparents: Francs. Gasn. Metoyer and Me. Polonia Aragon. Priest: F. Magnes.

1470. ME. ZEPHANY
(502) 17 December 1821, baptism of English Negro aged 25 years, slave of Agustin Metoyer. Godparents: Louis Metoyer and Me. Agnes. Priest: F. Magnes.

1471. MARIE CHARLOT
(502) 17 December 1821, baptism of English Negro, aged 20 years, slave of Agustin Metoyer. Godparents: Elise Rocque and Me. Suset Metoyer. Priest: F. Magnes.

1472. ME. FELICITE
(502) 17 December 1821, baptism of Guinea Negro aged 18 years, slave of Agustin Metoyer. Godparents: Francs. Gasn. Metoyer and Me. Louise Metoyer. Priest: F. Magnes.

1473. MARIE GENYE
(502) 17 December 1821, baptism of slave aged 32 years, property of Agustin Metoyer. Godparents: Louis Metoyer and Me. Theresse. Priest: F. Magnes.

1474. JOSE DAVID
(503) 18 December 1821, baptism of Guinea Negro aged 12, slave of Jn. Btte. Metoyer, son of Agustin Metoyer. Godparents: Auguste Metoyer and Me. Therese Anty. Priest: F. Magnes.

1475. MARIE ROSSE
(503) 18 December 1821, baptism of English slave, aged 16 years, property of Francois Frederic. Godparents: Francois Lavespere and Elenne Lavesper. Priest: F. Magnes.

1476. RAFAEL
(503) 18 December 1821, baptism of English slave aged 12 years, property of Mayil Metoyer. Godparents: Florantin Cona and Me. Carmelite Metoyer. Priest: F. Magnes.

1477. MARIANNE
(503) 18 December 1821, baptism of English slave, aged 13 years, property of Susanne Metoyer. Godparents: Jean Btte. Metoyer and Me. Suset Anty. Priest: F. Magnes.

1478. MARIE NENSE
(503) 18 December 1821, baptism of English slave aged 18 years, property of Gerome Charpi /Sarpy/. Godparents: Auguste Metoyer and Me. Emely Metoyer. Priest: F. Magnes.

1479. JEAN BTTE.
(503) 18 December 1821, baptism of Guinea Negro aged 24 years, slave of Mr. Frans. Metoyer. Godparents: Charles Nerestan /Rocque/ and Me. Agnes, wife of Agustin /Metoyer/. Priest: F. Magnes.

1480. JACQUE
(503) 18 December 1821, baptism of Guinea Negro aged 23 years, slave of Francois Metoyer. Godparents: Jose Lavigne and Dorothee. Priest: F. Magnes.

1481. MARIE
(503) 18 December 1821, baptism of slave aged 19 years, property of Charles Nerestan Rocque. Godparents: Pierre Metoyer and Marie Ahrriete. Priest: F. Magnes.

1482. MARIE
(503) 19 December 1821, baptism of English slave aged 29 years, property of Florantin Cona. Godparents: Charles Rocque and Me. Emely Metoyer. Priest: F. Magnes.

1483. MARIE POLINE
(503) 19 December 1821, baptism of child of 3 years, natural daughter of Marie, slave of Florantin Cona. Godparents: Charles Rocque and Me. Suset Metoyer. Priest: F. Magnes.

1484. CHARLES LEMB
(503) 19 December 1821, baptism of Guinea Negro aged 12 years, slave of Florantin Cona. Godparents: Louis Metoyer and Me. Theresse. Priest: F. Magnes.

1485. MARIE CELESINE
(503) 19 December 1821, baptism of infant of 2 months, natural daughter of Me. July, slave of Pierre Deloux. Godparents: Michel Deloux and Me. Deloye Frederic. Priest: F. Magnes.

1486. MICHEL
(503) 20 December 1821, baptism of infant of 8 months, natural son of Emily, slave of Sevastian Comper. Godparents: Michel and Marie Theresse, both colored. Priest: F. Magnes.

1487. JOSEPH ERRANTE
(503) 20 December 1821, baptism of infant of 8 months, natural son of _____*, slave of Sevastian Comper. Godparents: Joseph Magsimo Comper and Me. Alida Comper. Priest: F. Magnes.

*/Left blank on entry. This is probably a twin of the child baptized in the previous entry._7

1488. JACQUE
(503) 20 December 1821, baptism of child of 3 years, natural son of Richel, slave of Sevastian Comper. Godparents: Jn. Btte. and Emily. Priest: F. Magnes.

1489. FRANCOIS HONORE
(503) 20 December 1821, baptism of child aged 12 years, natural son of Richel, slave of Sevastian Comper. Godparents: Jean Louis and Modeste, colored. Priest: F. Magnes.

1490. JOSEPH PAIN
(503) 20 December 1821, baptism of English Negro aged 29 years, slave of Sevastian Compere. Godparents: Louis and Me. Elenne, both colored. Priest: F. Magnes.

1491. MARIE ELOYSE
(504) 1 January 1822, baptism of infant born 13 May 1821, natural daughter of Susanne, slave of Mde. Ve. Morphy. Godparents: Noel and Marie Theresse, both colored. Priest: F. Magnes.

1492. MARIE VIRGINI
(504) 5 January 1822, baptism of infant born 5 December 1821, natural daughter of Sesten, slave of David Som Bron. Godparents: "her master and her mistress, Me. Pompose Montanery." Priest: F. Magnes.

1493. ZENON
(504) 22 January 1822, baptism of infant of 6 months, natural son of Me. Beké, slave of Francois Rouquier, the brother. Godparents: Zenon and July, both colored slaves. Priest: F. Magnes.

1494. MARIE BEKÉ
(504) 22 January 1822, baptism of English Negro aged 19 years, slave of Francois Rouquier, the brother. Godparents: Andres and Marie Angelique, both colored slaves. Priest: F. Magnes.

1495. JOSEPH
(504) 4 February 1822, baptism of child of 8 years, English Negro slave of Mr. Francois Milon. Godpar-

ents: Guillon Baden, free, and Marie Augustin, both colored. Priest: F. Magnes.

1496. FOSTEN NED
(504) 14 February 1822, baptism of English Negro aged 21 years, slave of Pierre Boudoin. Godparents: Migner Larnodier and Euphrasin Boudoin. Priest: F. Magnes.

1497. MARIE FRANCOISE
(504) 14 February 1822, baptism of slave aged 36 years, property of Pierre Boudoin. Godparents: Jean Btte. Larnodier and Aspasy Larnodier. Priest: F. Magnes.

1498. MARIE MANUELA
(504) 24 February 1822, baptism of infant of 2 months, natural daughter of Marie Francoisse, slave of Mda. Ve. Dominique Davion. Godparents: Jean Louis and Me. Magdalene Vaden /Baden/, free. Priest: F. Magnes.

1499. MARIE LASTASY
(504) 6 March 1822, baptism of infant of 3½ months, natural daughter of Marie Theresse, slave of Hipolite Bordelon. Godparents: Jose Rouquier, free, and Roset, slave. Priest: F. Magnes.

1500. MARCELIN
(504) 8 March 1822, baptism of infant of 1 year, natural son of Maraya /?Mariah/, slave of Fs. Ruvio /Roubieu/. Godparents: Jacob and Modeste, both colored. Priest: F. Magnes.

1501. MARIE TILDE
(504) 8 March 1822, baptism of the natural daughter of Richel, slave of Fs. Ruvio /Roubieu/. Godparents: Jn Btte and Emé, both colored. Priest: F. Magnes.

1502. MARIE CELESTE
(504) 8 March 1822, baptism of child of 4 years, natural daughter of Richel, slave of Fs. Ruvio /Roubieu/. Godparents: Andreson and Maraya /Mariah?/, both colored. Priest: F. Magnes.

1503. JEAN BTTE.
(504) 9 March 1822, baptism of infant of 1 year, natural son of Anne, slave of Cypriane Rachal. Godparents: Nicolas and Phanye, both colored. Priest: F. Magnes.

1504. ANTOIN
(504) 13 March 1822, baptism of infant of 1 year, natu-

ral son of <u>Ohut?</u>, slave of Dominique Metoyer. Godparents: Jn. Btte. Metoyer and Me. Silby Metoyer. Priest: F. Magnes.

1505. JOSEPH GEORGE
(505) 19 March 1822, baptism of English Negro aged about 22 years, former property of Father Magnes who has freed him. Godparents: Ramon Lefalla and Maria Louisa, represented by Maria Ignacio Ramos. Priest: F. Magnes.

1506. JOSEP FRANCOIS
(505) 19 March 1822, baptism of English Negro aged 15 years, purchased for and charged to Father Magnes by a friend in Mexico. Godparents: Rafael Ramos Arispe, his master, represented by Apolinario Marmela, and Maria Luisa, represented by Manuela Garcia. Priest: F. Magnes.

1507. JOSEPH VICTORIANO
(505) 21 March 1822, baptism of infant born 3 January 1822, natural son of Me. Elenne, slave of Antoin Grillet. Godparents: Joseph Feliciano la Cerda, represented by Father Magnes, and Maria Procela. Priest: F. Magnes.

1508. MATILDE
(505) 21 March 1822, baptism of child of 7 years, natural daughter of Loucie, slave of Isac Fredieu. Godparents: Jn Btte. Fontaneau, Jr. and Me. Denis Fontaneau. Priest: F. Magnes.

1509. JN. BTTE.
(505) 21 March 1822, baptism of child of 4 years, natural son of Loucie, slave of Isac Fredieu. Godparents: Cezer Fontaneau, Jr. and Marie Celeste Lafitte. Priest: F. Magnes.

1510. ME. JEANNE
(505) 23 March 1822, baptism of infant born 4 May 1821, natural daughter of Celeste, slave of Jn. Btte. Fontaneau. Godparents: Alexy Trichel and Me. Pompose Lafitte. Priest: F. Magnes.

1511. ME. ANRRIET
(505) 23 March 1822, baptism of infant born 18 September 1821, daughter of Francoisse, slave of Casimire Peraut. Godparents: Agustin and Layde, both colored. Priest: F. Magnes.

1512. VALERY
(505) 7 April 1822, baptism of infant born 12 November

1821, natural son of Marie Jeanne, slave of Louis Tauzin. Godparents: Pierre and Frosine. Priest: F. Magnes

1513. JEAN FLORANTIN
(505) 7 April 1822, baptism of infant born 23 October 1821, natural son of Me. Francois, slave of Mda. Ve. Francois Levaseur. Godparents: Alexandre and Chatarine, free. Priest: F. Magnes.

1514. JEAN LOUIS
(505) 7 April 1821, baptism of infant born September 1821, natural son of Marie, slave of Jn. Btte. Proudhomme. Godparents: Jn. Francois and Marie Adelayde. Priest: F. Magnes.

1515. MARIE DELPHINE
(505) 7 April 1822, baptism of infant born 4 August 1821, natural daughter of Me. Theresse, slave of Mde. Ve. Morphil. Godparents: Valery, f.m.c., and Marta. Priest: F. Magnes.

1516. ROSALYE
(505) 7 April 1822, baptism of infant of 3 months, natural daughter of Marianne, slave of Athanas Poisot. Godparents: Lamot and Marie Enos. Priest: F. Magnes.

1517. MANUEL
(506) 7 April 1822, baptism of infant born 8 May?, 1821, natural son of Fany, slave of Jn. Btte. Proudhomme. Godparents: Manuel and Me. Pompose. Priest: F. Magnes.

1518. LOUIS LAMOT
(506) 7 April 1822, baptism of infant born 13 January 1822, natural son of Me. Layde, slave of Francois Peraut. Godparents: Louis Lamot and Marie Mae?. Priest: F. Magnes.

1519. TOUSAIN
(506) 7 April 1822, baptism of infant of two months, natural son of Marie Louisse, slave of Jn. Btte. Buard. Godparents: Pierre and Marie, colored. Priest: F. Magnes.

1520. JN. PIERRE
(506) 7 April 1822, baptism of infant of 6 months, natural son of Chene /Jenny?/, slave of Jn. Bte. Buard. Godparents: Jeann Pierre and Susanne, colored. Priest: F. Magnes.

1521. MARIE CALAHIN

(506) 7 April 1822, baptism of infant of 6 months, natural daughter of Choqui, slave of Mr. Pavi and Norit. Godparents: Jose and Marie Francoisse, colored. Priest: F. Magnes.

1522. ETIENNE
(506) 7 April 1822, baptism of child of 4 years, natural daughter of Chené /Jenny?/, slave of Jn. Btte. Buard. Godparents: Jacob and Elenne, colored. Priest: F. Magnes.

1523. MARIE ADELINE
(506) 7 April 1822, baptism of infant of 11 months, natural daughter of Eugenie, slave of Mr. Sibley, the son. Godparents: Jeann Btte. Landreau and Felicite. Priest: F. Magnes.

1524. MARIE ROSILIA
(506) 20 May 1822, baptism of infant born 5 April 1822, natural daughter of Celeste, slave of Joseph Tausin. Godparents: Jeann Lupart and Marcelite Josephine Arman. Priest: F. Magnes.

1525. MARIE ROSET
(506) 27 May 1822, baptism of child of 3 years, natural daughter of Merye, slave of M. Lenard. Godparents: Francois Ervin and Me. Rosse, both colored. Priest: F. Magnes.

1526. FRANCOIS GREGOIRE
(506) 30 May 1822, baptism of infant of 6 months, natural son of Marie Chenye /Jenny?/, slave of Mr. Ceser Lafitte. Godparents: Ygnacio Ybarbo and Me. Laffitte. Priest: F. Magnes.

1527. JOSE CELESTIN
(506) 31 May 1822, baptism of infant of 6 months, natural son of Susanne, slave of Pierre Roubleau. Godparents: Enrry and Me. Denis, both colored. Priest: F. Magnes.

1528. MARIE ROSALIE
(506) 31 May 1822, baptism of English slave aged 43, property of Mde. Ve. Laffitte. Godparents: Pierre Laffitte and Marie Antonia Flores. Priest: F. Magnes.

1529. JUAN PIERRE
(506) 21 May 1822, baptism of infant of 3 months, natural son of Marie, slave of Pierre Dollet. Godparents: Jose Ybarvo and Me. Louis, slave of Jn.

Btte. Adlle. Priest: F. Magnes.

1530. REMY
(506) 21 May 1822, baptism of infant of 3 months, natural son of Phany and slave of Pierre Dollet. Godparents: Jn. Btte. Proudhome and Me. Eusevia Ybarbo. Priest: F. Magnes.

1531. MARCELINA
(506) 21 May 1822, baptism of infant of 1½ months, natural daughter of Laysa /slave of Mr. Dolet_7. Godparents: Felix? Flores and Me. Eusevia Ybarbo. Priest: F. Magnes.

1532. ATHANAS
(507) 6 June 1822, baptism of infant of 6 months, natural son of Jean, slave of Francois Vienne. Godparents: Louis Francois Maxil? Vienne and Marie Eliset. Tauzin. Priest: F. Magnes.

1533. JEAN BTTE. URSIN
(507) 9 June 1822, baptism of infant of 1 month, natural son of Geneveva, slave of Manuel Levasseur. Godparents: Lesin Oseme Levaseur and Genoveva Levasseur. Priest: F. Magnes.

1534. MAGDALENNE
(507) 30 June 1822, baptism of infant of 6 months, natural daughter of Julie, slave of Ambrois Sompairact. Godparents: Jean Btte. Landreau and Polerie. Priest: F. Magnes.

1535. GRUILLON
(507) 6 July 1822, baptism of English Negro aged 12, slave of Benjamin Metoyer. Godparents: Charles and Victoire. Priest: F. Magnes.

1536. MARIE FANY
(507) 6 July 1822, baptism of an English Negro aged 22 years, property of Benjamin Metoyer. Godparents: Charles and Victoire. Priest: F. Magnes.

1537. MARIE LAYDE
(507) 6 July 1822, baptism of infant of 2½ months, natural daughter of Su_____ /?Sa___ or ?Sil___7, slave of Benjamin Metoyer. Godparents: Michel and Modeste. Priest: F. Magnes.

1538. LOUIS
(507) 6 July 1822, baptism of English Negro of 3? years, slave of Benjamin Metoyer. Godparents: Michel and Victoire. Priest: F. Magnes.

1539. JEAN BTTE.
(507) 6 July 1822, baptism of English Negro aged 14,
slave of Benjamin Metoyer. Godparents: Jn. Btte.
and Marie Jeanne. Priest: F. Magnes.

1540. AGUSTIN
(507) 6 July 1822, baptism of slave aged 10 years, property of Benjamin Metoyer. Godparents: Btte. and
Nanete. Priest: F. Magnes.

1541. MARIE DORALIE?
(507) 6 July 1822, baptism of English Negro, aged 9,
slave of Benjamin Metoyer. Godparents: Jn. Btte.
and Dolores. Priest: F. Magnes.

1542. ANA
(507) 6 July 1822, baptism of infant of 2 months, natural daughter of Nanse, slave of Benjamin Metoyer.
Godparents: Benjamin Metoyer, Jr. and Me. Susett
Lambre. Priest: F. Magnes.

1543. MARIE NANCI
(507) 6 July 1822, baptism of an English Negro aged 30
years. Godparents: Valsin Lambre and Maria Lorror /Aurora/ Lambre. Priest: F. Magnes.

1544. ETIENNE
(507) 6 July 1822, baptism of infant of 8 months, natural son of Manete, slave of Antoine Proudhomme.
Godparents: Philip and Marie, colored. Priest:
F. Magnes.

1545. JUSEPH
(507) 6 July 1822, baptism of infant of 3½ months, natural son of Marie, slave of Jn Btte. Lattier, Sr.
Godparents: Joseph Lavigne and Marie Dorathee,
free. Priest: F. Magnes.

1546. JOSEPH
(507) 6 July 1822, baptism of infant aged 6 months,
son of Marianne, slave of Louis Metoyer. Godparents: Lansir and Rosalie, both colored. Priest:
F. Magnes.

1547. ROMAIN
(507) 6 July 1822, baptism of son of Marie, slave of
Louis Metoyer. Godparents: Vienne Metoyer and
Ositte Metoyer. Priest: F. Magnes.

1548. MANUEL
(507) 6 July 1822, baptism of infant of 7 months, son

of Saly, slave of Agustin Metoyer. Godparents: Gasion Metoyer and Susete Metoyer. Priest: F. Magnes.

1549. ME. MAGDALENNE
(508) 8 August 1822, baptism of infant of 2 months, natural daughter of Susanne, slave of Jn. Bpte. Comte. Godparents: Victor Charvonier and Elenne Cloutier. Priest: F. Magnes.

1550. ALPHONSINE /LE COMTE/*
(508) 8 August 1822, baptism of infant of 2 months, natural daughter of Margarite, slave of Ambrois Comte. Godparents: Alphonso Matihore and Celest Cloutier.

*/This slave was later manumitted and became the wife of Antoine Nerestan Rachal. Throughout her life she used the surname LeComte./

1551. MARIE FLOR
(508) 8 August 1822, baptism of infant of 18 months, natural daughter of Me. Jeanne, slave of Jn. Bte. Comte. Godparents: Tranquiline Comte and Juana Cicil /Jeanne Cecile/. Priest: F. Magnes.

1552. FLORANTIN
(508) 8 August 1822, baptism of infant of 10 months, natural daughter of Eme, slave of Jn. Btte. Comte. Godparents: Edmond and Marie Denis, both colored. Priest: F. Magnes.

1553. ALEXANDRE
(508) 9 August 1822, baptism of infant of 8 months, natural son of Betze, slave of Athanas Broset. Godparents: Athanas Denis and Catarina Bodioin. Priest: F. Magnes.

1554. MARIA MELISA
(508) 9 August 1822, baptism of infant of 4 months, natural daughter of Celeste, slave of Bmy. Lecour. Godparents: Jac/que/ Brosset and Adeline Query. Priest: F. Magnes.

1555. MARIE
(508) 9 August 1822, baptism of infant of 4 months, natural daughter of Me. Velony, slave of Marco Sompairait. Godparents: Louis and Susanne, both colored. Priest: F. Magnes.

1556. TAUZIN
(508) 10 August 1822, baptism of infant of 3 months, natural son of Maria Phani, slave of Paul Cheletre.

Godparents: Jose Ursin and Me. Therese. Priest: F. Magnes.

1557. JACQUE
(508) 10 August 1822, baptism of English Negro aged 20, slave of Francois Latier. Godparents: Elise Rocqe. and Me. Agnes. Priest: F. Magnes.

1558. MARIA
(509) 10 August 1822, baptism of English Negro, aged 20, slave of Elisee Rocque. Godparents: "her master" and Maria Louisse Metoyer. Priest: F. Magnes.

1559. MARIA LOUISA
(509) 10 August 1822, baptism of English Negro aged 3 years, property of Elisee Rocque. Godparents: Charles Rocque and Me. Louisse Metoyer. Priest: F. Magnes.

1560. MARIE ANNETE
(509) 10 August 1822, baptism of natural daughter of Maria, slave of Elise Rocque. Godparents: Gerome Charpi /Sarpy/ and Suset Metoyer. Priest: F. Magnes.

1561. ATHENAS
(509) 10 August 1822, baptism of English Negro of 20 years, slave of Dominige Metoyer. Godparents: Jose Lavigne and Dorothee. Priest: F. Magnes.

1562. MARIE MODESTE
(509) 10 August 1822, baptism of infant of 7 months, natural daughter of Me., slave of Susanne Metoyer. Godparents: Gerome Charpi /Sarpy/ and Clara Bery. Priest: F. Magnes.

1563. FELIS
(509) 10 August 1822, baptism of English Negro of 15 years, slave of Narcis Proudhome. Godparents: Dominique and Marie Rine. Priest: F. Magnes.

1564. MARIE ANRIETTE
(509) 10 August 1822, baptism of English Negro, aged 25, slave of Narcis Proudhome. Godparents: Francois and Elayde, both colored.

1565. JN. BTTE. VIL /?BILL/
(509) 10 August 1822, baptism of English slave of Jn. Btte. Proudhomme. Godparents: Grand Btte. and Neni, both colored. Priest: F. Magnes.

1566. ME. CHARLOT
(509) 10 August 1822, baptism of infant of 1 month, nat-

ural daughter of Mely, slave of Pierre Nolasco.
Godparents: Bernard Rachal and Me. Denis de Denis.
Priest: F. Magnes.

1567. MARIE JUDIT
(509) 10 August 1822, baptism of infant of 6 months,
natural daughter of Maria, slave of Alexy Cloutier.
Godparents: Etienn and Meliana. Priest: F. Magnes.

1568. ME. TRANQUILINA
(509) 10 August 1822, baptism of infant of 6 months,
natural daughter of Sidalisse, slave of Alexy
Cloutier. Godparents: Nicolas Boudoin and Louisse
Clemanin? (Clernanier?) /La Renaudier?/. Priest:
F. Magnes.

1569. VICTOR TRICHEL
(510) 18 August 1822, baptism of infant born 21 July
1822, natural son of Mr. Athanas Trichel, French,
and of Maria Josefa Grappe, a free woman of color.
Godparents: Alexy Trichel and Felicese Trichel.
Priest: F. Magnes.

1570. MARIE CECILIA
(510) 18 August 1822, baptism of infant aged 2 months,
natural daughter of Maria Louisa, slave of Mlle.
Francoisse Trichel. Godparents: Jn. Btte.
Grappe and Maria Asseni Pasano. Priest: F. Magnes.

1571. MARIA CLARA
(510) 18 August 1822, baptism of mulatto infant aged 6
days, natural daughter of Maria, slave of Davidson
Bron. Godparents: Simeyon and Serena, both
colored. Priest: F. Magnes.

1572. MARIA ADELAYDE
(510) 25 August 1822, baptism of mulatto infant of 1
month, natural daughter of Bade /Betty?/, slave of
Juan Cortes. Godparents: Jean Francois and Me.
Adelle, both colored. Priest: F. Magnes.

1573. JN. BTTE
(510) 1 September 1822, baptism of infant of 2 months,
natural son of Maria, slave of Mda. Ve. Remy Peraut. Godparents: Jn. Btte. and Marie. Priest:
F. Magnes.

1574. FRANCISCO
(510) 1 September 1822, baptism of English Negro of 12
years, slave of Jean Lalande. Godparents: Bta.
and Rose, both colored. Priest: F. Magnes.

1575. MARIA MAGDALENA
(510) 2 September 1822, baptism of Cado Indian aged 5 years, natural daughter of Maria, a Cado Indian, and a father unknown. Godparents: Athanas and Maria Celesi, both colored. Priest: F. Magnes.

1576. MARIA ADELLE
(511) 8 September 1822, baptism of infant born 27 September 1822, natural daughter of Maria Marta, a slave of Arnau Lauve. Godparents: Silvestre Poisot and Sodelle. Priest: F. Magnes.

1577. FRANCOIS MOSES
(511) 2 October 1825, baptism of infant of 2 months, son of Marie Marthe, slave of Mr. Lave /Lauve7. Godparents: Joseph Lazare, free, and Marie Thérèse. Priest: Bishop Louis Dubourg.

1578. MARIE MELFROINENE
(511) 2 October 1825, baptism of infant born 10 July 1824, child of Marie Marthe, slave of Mr. Lowe /Lauve7. Godparents: Louis Lamate and Marie Trenier. Priest: Bishop Louis Dubourg.

1579. MARIE ELIZA
(511) 2 October 1825, baptism of infant born 28 July 1825, daughter of Marie Angelique, a free woman. Godparents: Alexandre Buart and Althalie Buart. Priest: Bishop Louis Dubourg.

1580. LOUIS ONEZIME
(511) 2 October 1825, baptism of child born November 1823, son of Marie Angelique, a free woman. Godparents: Manuel Prout and Marie Carmelite Prout. Priest: Bishop Louis Dubourg.

1581. HYPPOLITE
(511) 2 October 1825, baptism of child born 13 August 1823, son of Perrine, slave of Mr. Bertrand. Godparents: Pierre and Marie Joseph. Priest: Bishop Louis Dubourg.

1582. MARIE NISA MEZIERES
(511) 2 October 1825, baptism of infant of 4 months, daughter of Rosette Mezieres, a free woman. Godparents: Marie Antoine Mezieres and Marie Jeanne Mezieres. Priest: Bishop Louis Dubourg.

1583. ACHILLE
(511) 2 October 1825, baptism of infant born April 1825, son of Perine, slave of Mr. Bertrand. Godparents:

Charles and Carmelite. Priest: Biship Louis Dubourg.

1584. JOSEPH
(511) 2 October 1825, baptism of child of 3 years, son of Marie Felicité, slave of Mr. Brossé. Godparents: Gregoire Augustin and Perrine. Priest: Bishop Louis Dubourg.

1585. JN. CHRISTOPHE
(511) 2 October 1825, baptism of infant of 1 year and 10 months, son of Helene, a free Negress. Godparents: Victor, free, and Catherinne, free Negress. Priest: Bishop Louis Dubourg.

1586. ALEXANDER
(511) 2 October 1825, baptism of infant born 1 April 1824, son of Genevieve, slave of Manuel Vasseur. Godparents: Theodore Chabaut and Helen Vaqari?. Priest: Bishop Louis Dubourg.

1587. THEODORE
(511) 2 October 1825, baptism of infant born 11 January 1824, son of Marie Martha, slave of Celestin Elie. Godparents: Pierre Elie and Marie Darbone. Priest: Bishop Louis Dubourg.

1588. SILVAIN
(511) 8 October 1825, baptism of infant born 14 March 1824, son of Jeanne, slave of Jn. Darbone. Godparents: Antoine and Marie Claire. Priest: Bishop Louis Dubourg.

1589. BARTHELEMI
(512) 8 October 1825, baptism of infant born 23 August 1825, son of Clarisse, slave of Jn. Darbone. Godparents: Dominique and Julie. Priest: Bishop Louis Dubourg.

1590. MARIE
(512) 8 October 1825, baptism of infant born 29 January 1823, daughter of Helene, slave of Jn. Darbane. Godparents: Pierre and Marie Constance. Priest: Bishop Louis Dubourg.

1591. MARIE ADÉLE
(512) 28 October 1825, baptism of infant born 15 August 1825, daughter of Carline, slave of Jn. F. Hertzog. Godparents: Bernard Theophile Hertzog and Marie Hertzog. Priest: Bishop Louis Dubourg.

1592. MARIE FLORENCE
(512) 28 October 1825, baptism of infant born 24 March

1822, daughter of Magdelinne, slave of Jn. Bapt. Rachal. Godparents: Pierre Masippe and Marie Pierre Schelette. Priest: Bishop Louis Dubourg.

1593. MARIE CONSTANCE
(512) 28 October 1825, baptism of infant born 26 April 1825, daughter of Magdelinne, slave of Jn. Bapt. Rachal. Godparents: Luger Rachal and Marie Louise Rachal. Priest: Bishop Louis Dubourg.

1594. MARIE CATHERINE
(512) 28 October 1825, baptism of infant born 6 November 1825, daughter of Julia, slave of Pierre Schelette. Godparents: Francois Lattier, Jr. and Lte. Shelette, represented by M. Lattier. Priest: Bishop Louis Dubourg.

1595. NARCISSE
(512) 28 October 1825, baptism of child of 3 years, son of Marie Julie, slave of Pre. Sclette. Godparents: Severe Lattier and Emilie Rachal. Priest: Bishop Louis Dubourg.

1596. JN BAPTISTE
(512) 28 October 1825, baptism of infant of 19 months, son of Marie Jeanne, slave of Michel Cesa [Casanova? LaCaze?]. Godparents: Pierre and Marie Jeanne. Priest: Bishop Louis Dubourg.

1597. JN BAPTISTE
(512) 28 October 1825, baptism of infant born 4 July 1824, son of Marguerita, slave of Mr. Pierre. Godparents: Hilaire and Marie Therese. Priest: Bishop Louis Dubourg.

1598. RAIMOND
(512) 28 October 1825, baptism of child of 5 years, son of Milia, slave of Mr. Hertzoc. Godfather: Alexis. Priest: Bishop Louis Dubourg.

1599. BAPTISTE
(512) 28 October 1825, baptism of infant born 21 February, 1825, son of Marie Therese, slave of Mde. Vve. Morphy. Godparents: Jn Bapt. and Marie Louise. Priest: Bishop Louis Dubourg.

1600. BENJAMIN
(512) 28 October 1825, baptism of infant born 6 August 1824, son of Marie Caroline, slave of Ls. Tozin. Godparents: Philippe and Marie Jeanne. Priest: Bishop Louis Dubourg.

1601. ANDRE
(512) 28 October 1825, baptism of infant born 15 April 1825, son of Eulalie, slave of Ls. Touzin. Godparents: Alexandre and Adelaide. Priest: Bishop Louis Dubourg.

1602. MARIE AGNES
(512) 28 October 1825, baptism of infant born 21 September, daughter of Marie, slave of Mde. Veuve Bte. Triche. Godparents: Jn Pierre and M. Louise. Priest: Bishop Louis Dubourg.

1603. MARIE ANTOINETTE
(512) 28 October 1825, baptism of infant born 28 October 1823, daughter of Jeanne, slave of Ve. B. Triche. Godparents: Cyprien and M. Antoinette. Priest: Bishop Louis Dubourg.

1604. JN PIERRE
(513) 28 October 1825, baptism of infant of 1 year, son of Catherinne, slave of Mr. Batoche Buard. Godparents: Jn Pierre and Marie. Priest: Bishop Louis Dubourg.

1605. ELIZA
(513) 28 October 1825, baptism of child of 3 years, the daughter of Jenny, slave of Mr. Barberousse. Godparents: Zenon and Pelagie. Priest: Bishop Louis Dubourg.

1606. MARIE JEANNE
(513) 28 October 1825, baptism of infant of 1 year, daughter of Jenny, slave of Mr. Batoche Buart. Godparents: Zenon and Marie. Priest: Bishop Louis Dubourg.

1607. CELESTE
(513) 28 October 1825, baptism of infant born February 1825, daughter of Charlotte, slave of B. Buart. Godparents: Joseph and Mie Celeste. Priest: Bishop Louis Dubourg.

1608. PHILIPPE
(513) 28 October 1825, baptism of infant of 1½ years, son of Elise, slave of Mr. Rouquier. Godparents: Jacquitte and Pompose. Priest: Bishop Louis Dubourg.

1609. MARIE LOUISE
(513) 28 October 1825, baptism of infant born 9 September 1825, daughter of Marie, slave of Rhemi Pe-

rault. Godparents: Bapt. and Marie. Priest: Bishop Louis Dubourg.

1610. CARMELITE
(513) 28 October 1825, baptism of infant of 2 months, daughter of Therese, slave of B. Buard. Godparents: Jn. Bapt. and Pompose, free. Priest: Bishop Louis Dubourg.

1611. ELIZABETH
(513) 28 October 1825, baptism of infant born 10 November 1822, daughter of Esther, slave of Aldre. Dublieux. Godparents: Jean Pierre and Zoe. Priest: Bishop Louis Dubourg.

1612. BENJAMIN
(513) 28 October 1825, baptism of child born 11 November 1823, son of Betzi, slave of Amb. Sompeyrat. Godparents: Claude Ant. Chaupin and Mde. Pavie. Priest: Bishop Louis Dubourg.

1613. JULIENNE
(513) 28 October 1825, baptism of infant born 10 September 1825, daughter of Esther, slave of Mr. Dublieux. Godparents: Ls Alexdre. and Julienne. Priest: Bishop Louis Dubourg.

1614. VALSIN
(513) 28 October 1825, baptism of infant aged 2 years, son of Clarisse, slave of Mr. Hazelton. Godparents: Pierre and Clarisse. Priest: Bishop Louis Dubourg.

1615. MARIE
(513) 28 October 1825, baptism of infant born October 1823, daughter of Marie, slave of [left blank on document -- possibly Mr. Hazelton]. Godparents: Martin Bastien. Priest: Bishop Louis Dubourg.

1616. LOUIS
(513) 28 October 1825, baptism of infant born 26 October 1824, son of Clarisse, slave of Mr. Hazelton. Godparents: Ls. Aldre. and Eupheme. Priest: Louis Dubourg.

1617. ANNA
(513) 28 October 1825, baptism of child born 20 October 1817, daughter of Clarisse, slave of Mr. Hazelton. Godparents: Miguel Angelin and Marie Therese. Priest: Louis Dubourg.

1618. SUZANNE
(513) 28 October 1825, baptism of infant of 1 year, daughter of Louise, slave of Mr. Richard Erttoc /Hertzog/. Godparents: Jn. Pierre and Charlotte. Priest: Bishop Louis Dubourg.

1619. JOHN
(513) 28 October 1825, baptism of child born 20 October 1819, son of Clarisse, slave of Mr. Hazelton. Godparents: Jose de Jesus and Marie Louisa Catherine. Priest: Bishop Louis Dubourg.

1620. CATHERINE
(514) 28 October 1825, baptism of child born 12 July 1818, daughter of Clarisse, slave of Mr. Hazelton. Godparents: Pierre and Marie Mathilda. Priest: Bishop Louis Dubourg.

1621. EUPHROSINE SARPY
(514) 25 October 1825, Baptism* of child born 15 April 1823, of legitimate marriage of Jerome Sarpy and Marie Jeanne Metoyer. Godparents: Charles Nerestan Roques and Artemise des Laudes /Dupart/. Priest: Bishop Louis Dubourg.

1622. MARGUERITE ROQUES
(514) 25 October 1825, baptism* of infant born 20 July 1824, of legitimate marriage of Charles Nerestan Roques and Marie Pompose, daughter of Augustin Metoyer. Godparents: Jerome Sarpygs and Marie Jeanne Metoyer. Priest: Bishop Louis Dubourg.

1623. MARIE ARSENE LLORENS
(514) 25 October 1825, baptism* of infant born 9 April 1824, of legitimate marriage of Manuel Llorens and Marie Arsene Anty. Godparents: Florentin Conan and Suzette Metoyer. Priest: Bishop Louis Dubourg.

1624. MARIE CLAIRE ROQUES
(514) 25 October 1825, baptism* of infant born 30 December 1822 of legitimate marriage of Mr. Charles Nerestan Roques and Marie Pompose Metoyer. Godparents: Florentin Conant and Marie Therese Carmelite Anty. Priest: Bishop Louis Dubourg.

1625. MARIE ELINA ROQUES
(514) 25 October 1825, baptism* of infant born 18 June 1823 of legitimate marriage of Elisée Roques and Marie Suzette Metoyer. Godparents: Augustin

*These baptisms are prefaced by the note that they were performed at the home of Mr. Augustin Metoyer on Isle Brevelle.

Metoyer and Marie Agnes Metoyer. Priest: Bishop
Louis Dubourg.

1626. MARIE ANAIS METOYER
(514) 25 October 1825, baptism* of child born 2 September 1823, of legitimate marriage of Maxile Metoyer
and Marie Aspasie Anty. Godparents: Jean Baptiste
Metoyer and Suzette Metoyer. Priest: Bishop
Louis Dubourg.

1627. AUGUSTE DORESTAN METOYER
(514) 25 October 1825, baptism* of child born 24 May
1823, of legitimate marriage of Pierre Metoyer and
Marie Henriette Cloutier. Godparents: Augste. Metoyer and Marie Carmelitte Anty. Priest: Bishop
Louis Dubourg.

1628. MARIE ILETTE [LILETTE] SARPY
(514) 25 October 1825, baptism* of infant born 20 March
1825, daughter of the legitimate marriage of Jerome
Sarpigs and Mrie. Jeanne Metoyer. Godparents: Joseph Lavigne and Marie Dorothée. Priest: Bishop
Louis Dubourg.

1629. VICTORIN
(514) 25 October 1825, baptism* of child born 19 January
1822 of Euphrosine, slave of Francois Metoyer.
Godparents: Francois Metoyer and Marie Suzette.
Priest: Bishop Louis Dubourg.

1630. CESAIRE
(514- 25 October 1825, baptism* of child born 7 May 1823,
515) of Delphine, slave of Pierre Metoyer. Godparents:
Hilaire and Delphine. Priest: Bishop Louis Dubourg.

1631. MARIE SEVERINE
(515) 25 October 1825, baptism* of child born 15 July
1825, of Marie Perine, slave of Jean Baptiste Lemoine. Godparents: Henri Denis and Olympie Boisdore. Priest: Bishop Louis Dubourg.

1632. CHARLES DARCOURT CONAN
(515) 27 May 1826, baptism* of infant born 27 September+
1825, of legitimate marriage of Florentin Conan
and Marie Louise Metoyer. Godparents: Charles
Nerestan Roques and Marie Metoyer. Priest: Bishop
Louis Dubourg. [See note accompanying next entry.]

*These baptisms are prefaced by the note that they
were preformed at the home of Mr. Augustin Metoyer
on Isle Brevelle.

1633. AUGUSTIN ARNOLD CONAN
(515) 27 May 1826, baptism* of infant born 7 January 1826,+ legitimate son of Florent Conan and Marie Louise Metoyer. Godparents: Manuel Laurence /Llorens7 and Arsene Anti. Priest: Bishop Louis Dubourg.

+The birthdates of this child and that of his brother in the preceding entry are very legibly written. Yet it is obvious that one is in error.

1634. MARIE JULIA METOYER
(515) 27 May 1826, baptism* of infant born 18 January 1826, legitimate daughter of Jean Baptiste Metoyer and Suzette Anti. Godparents: Louis Metoyer and Marie Agnes. Priest: Bishop Louis Dubourg.

1635. PIERRE
(515) 27 May 1826, baptism* of infant born 5 April 1826, son of Marie Laisa, slave of Louis Metoyer. Godparents: Zenon and Marie, slaves of Louis Metoyer. Priest: Bishop Louis Dubourg.

1636. MARIE LOLITTE
(515) 27 May 1826, baptism* of child born 16 July 1824, daughter of Marie Laiza, slave of Louis Metoyer. Godparents: Francois and Marie Side, slaves of Francois Metoyer. Priest: Bishop Louis Dubourg.

1637. CHARLES
(515) 27 May 1826, baptism* of child born 5 August 1823, son of Marie, slave of Louis Metoyer. Godparents: Toussaint and Brigitte, slaves of Ls. Metoyer. Priest: Bishop Louis Dubourg.

1638. ANTOINE
(515) 27 May 1826, baptism* of infant born 6 January 1825, son of Marianne, slave of Louis Metoyer. Godparents: Gabriel, slave of Augustin Metoyer and Marie, slave of L. Metoyer. Priest: Bishop Louis Dubourg.

1639. GILLES
(515) 27 May 1826, baptism* of infant born 31 May 1825 /no mother named7, slave of Louis Metoyer. Godparents: Toussaint and Marie, slave of Florentin Conant.

1640. J. B. LUDGEAIRE
(515) 27 May 1826, baptism of child born 26 May 1825,

*These baptisms are prefaced by the note that they were performed at the home of Mr. Augustin Metoyer.

son of Marie, slave of Louis Metoyer. Godparents: Louis and Felicite. Priest: Bishop Louis Dubourg.

1641. CAROLINE
(515- 27 May 1826, baptism* of child of 5 years, daughter
516) of Rose, slave of L. Metoyer. Godparents: Aug. Metoyer and Marie Louise. Priest: Bishop L. Dubourg.

1642. MERRY
(516) 27 May 1826, baptism* of child of 4 years, daughter of Phebie, slave of Aug. Metoyer. Godparents: Gabriel, slave of Augustin Metoyer, and Zenny, the slave of Aug. Metoyer. Priest: Bishop L. Dubourg.

1643. DESIRE DEZILIE /DERZILIE/
(516) 27 May 1826, baptism* of child born 15 December 1826 /sic/ of Phebie, slave of Aug. Metoyer. Godparents: Bron and Zenny, slaves of A. Metoyer. Priest: Bishop Louis Dubourg.

1644. CHARLOTTE
(516) 27 May 1826, baptism* of infant born 24 December 1826 /sic/, a slave of Fcs. Metoyer. Godparents: Jasmin and Brigitte, slave of L. Metoyer. Priest: Louis Dubourg.

1645. MARIE AGATHE
(516) 27 May 1826, baptism of daughter of Phebie, slave of A. Metoyer. Godparents: Michel and Marie, slaves of Aug. Metoyer. Priest: Bishop Louis Dubourg.

1646. J. B. FAUSTIN
(516) 27 May 1826, baptism* of son of Marie Louise, a slave of Florentin Conan. Godparents: J. B. and Agnes, slaves of Suzanne Metoyer. Priest: Bishop Louis Dubourg.

1647. MARIE GILLES
(516) 27 May 1826, baptism* of infant born 2 January 1825, daughter of Marie Louise, slave of Florentin Conan. Godparents: Joseph /LaVigne/ and Marie Dorothee /Boisdore/. Priest: Bishop Louis Dubourg.

1648. LEANDRE
(516) 27 May 1826, baptism* of child born 10 October 1825, "infant of color belonging to Pierre Metoyer." Godparents: Louis Mollet /Monette/ and M. Ant. Coton-Maï. Priest: Bishop Louis Dubourg.

*These baptisms are prefaced by the note that they were performed at the home of Mr. Augustin Metoyer.

1649. MARIE CLEMENCE
(516) 28? May 1826, baptism of infant born 19 October 1825, daughter of Marie Marthe, slave of Mr. A. Love. Godparents: Em. Grenex and Julie Buard. Priest: Bishop Louis Dubourg.

1650. MARIE CLAIRE
(516) 28 May 1826, baptism of infant born 3 October 1825, daughter of Henriette, slave of Eugene Michaut. Godparents: Hilaire and Marie Genevieve. Priest: Bishop Louis Dubourg.

1651. MARIE PAULINE
(516) 29 July 1826, baptism of infant born 28 December 1826 /sic/, slave of Honnore Freideau. Godparents: Pierre, slave of Mr. Derbanne, and P__y, slave of Bertrand Plaisance. Priest: Bishop Louis Dubourg.

1652. NORENS BELISER LLORENS
(517) 30 November 1821, baptism of a free infant born 31 January 1820, legitimate son of Seraphin Llorens and Maria Aspasy Metoyer. Godparents: Manuel Llorens and Maria Arsine Anty. Priest: F. Magnes.

1653. MARIE ELINA METOYER
(517) 1 December 1821, baptism of free infant born 15 November 1821, legitimate daughter of Joseph Metoyer and Marie Pelagie Lecour. Godparents: Valery Lecour and Marie Denis Metoyer, all free people of color. Priest: F. Magnes.

1654. MARIE ZEPHALY /CEPHALIDE/ METOYER
(517) 1 December 1821, baptism of infant born 1 January 1821, legitimate daughter of Dominique Metoyer and Margarita. Godparents: Nereste Rocque and Maria Pomposse Metoyer, all free people of color. Priest: F. Magnes.

1655. MARIE GLAEE METOYER
(517) 1 December 1821, baptism of infant born 17 February, 1821, of Juan Bta. Dominique Metoyer and Maria Layde Rachal. Godparents: Antonio Rachal and Marie Perine Metoyer, all free people of color. Priest: F. Magnes.

1656. JACQUE RUBIN /MARIOTTE/
(517) 2 December 1821, baptism of free infant aged 3 months, natural son of Maria Layde /Mariotte/, a free woman of color, and a father unknown. Godparents: Ambrois LeComte and Me. Louis LeComote. Priest: F. Magnes.

1657. SERAPHIN LLORANS
(518) 13 March 1822, baptism of free infant born 14 December 1821, legitimate son of Seraphin Llorens and Marie Aspasy Metoyer. Godparents: Jose Metoyer, Jr. and Marie Denis Metoyer, all free people of color. Priest: F. Magnes.

1658. MARIE RIN PLERYS DE MESSIER
(518) 7 April 1822, baptism of free infant born 6 January 1822, natural daughter of Marie Rosse de Messier, a free woman of color. Godparents: Maria Fortuna and Marie, the infant's grandmother. Priest: F. Magnes.

1659. MARIE LOUISSE
(518) 18 May 1822, baptism of Indian aged 6 months, natural daughter of Louis and Amiyaese of the Chata nation. Godparents: Francois Peraut and his wife Manot Fontaneau. Priest: F. Magnes.

1660. FRANCOIS VALSIN
(518) 6 May 1822, baptism of a free infant born 3 March 1822, natural son of Suset, a free mulatto. Godparents: Juan Bta. and Angela, colored. Priest: F. Magnes.

1661. MARIA JULIA BECAR /BAKER/
(518) 7 July 1822, baptism of a free mulatto aged 1 year, purchased by Juan Becar, a free mulatto, from Mr. More for the purpose of freeing her, since he recognizes her as his daughter. Godparents: Maria Sosthene and Maria Phelavi, colored. Priest: F. Magnes.

1662. MARIE LODOYSA LLORANS
(519) 6 August 1822, baptism of infant born 14 July 1822, legitimate daughter of Manuel Llorans and Maria Arsene Anty. Godparents: Joseph Geronimo Charpi /Jerome Sarpy/ and Susanne Metoyer, all free people of color. Priest: F. Magnes.

1663. MARIA LUISA CLOUTIER
(519) 8 August 1822, baptism of infant born 15 February 1822, legitimate daughter of Agustin Cloutier and Teresa Metoyer. Godparents: Louis Baltasar and Maria Rosa Baltasar, all free people of color. Priest: F. Magnes.

1664. MARIA DENIS
(519) 8 August 1822, baptism of free infant born 2 March 1822, natural daughter of Susete, free Negro. God-

parents: Jn. Btte. Dominique Metoyer and Maria Perine Metoyer. Priest: F. Magnes.

1665. LUIS URSIN
(519) 8 August 1822, baptism of free infant born 2 March, natural son of Maria Agustin, a free woman of color. Godparents: Jose Metoyer and Ma. Luisa. Priest: F. Magnes.

1666. JN. BTTA. BOLIVAR RACHAL
(519) 8 August 1822, baptism of infant born 1 June 1822, legitimate son of Jn. Btte. Rachal and Susanne Metoyer. Godparents: Valery Lecour and Marie Sofoi Metoyer. Priest: F. Magnes.

1667. BALSIN /VALSAIN/
(520) 30 November 1821, baptism of infant of 4 months, natural son of Ruchel, slave of Franc. Vienne. Godparents: Zenon and Denis, both colored. Priest: F. Magnes.

1668. MARIE ROSSE (ROSET)
(520) 30 November 1821, baptism of infant of 1 year, natural daughter of Me. Jeanne, slave of Mde. Ve. Bmy. Rachal. Godparents: Augustin and Margarita, both colored. Priest: F. Magnes.

1669. ZELESTIN
(520) 30 November 1821, baptism of infant of 4 months, natural son of Nano, slave of Mda. Ve. Bmy. Rachal. Godparents: Zelestin and Bave, both colored. Priest: F. Magnes.

1670. JACQUE
(520) 1 December 1821, baptism of English slave aged 17? years, property of Joseph Metoyer. Godparents: Valeri Lecor and Me. Barbare Lecour. Priest: F. Magnes

1671. MARIE LOUISSE
(520) 2 December 1821, baptism of infant aged 7 months, natural daughter of Me. Alé, salve of Michel Dervan. Godparents: Manl. Marcelo Couty and Marie Pilar Rachal, whites. Priest: F. Magnes.

1672. GUILLON
(520) 2 December 1821, baptism of infant of 3 months, natural son of Marie, slave of Nicolas Gracia. Godparents: Agustin Cloutier and Me. Rose Baltazar. Priest: F. Magnes.

1673. JOSEPH
(520) 2 December 1821, baptism of infant of 6 months,

natural son of Me. Francoisse, slave of Marie Rose
Metoyer. Godparents: Antoin Neres Rachal and Marie Rosse Baltasar, colored. Priest: F. Magnes.

1674. MARGARITE
(520) 4 December 1821, baptism of infant of 6 months,
natural daughter of July, slave of Andres Ste. Andres. Godparents: Francs. Ste. Charne /Germaine7
and Marie Louise Ste. Andres, whites. Priest: F.
Magnes.

1675. MARIE PHELONISSE /FELONISE7
(520) 4 December 1821, baptism of infant of 11 months,
natural daughter of Sira, slave of Andres Ste. Andres. Godparents: Felis Ste. Andres and Me. Celine. Priest: F. Magnes.

1676. LOUISE
(520) 4 December 1821, baptism of English slave aged 26
years, property of Andres Ste. Andres. Godparents:
Francois and Marie, both colored. Priest: F.
Magnes.

1677. JOSEPH WASINTON
(520) 4 December 1821, baptism of English slave, aged 5
years, property of Onesim Ste. Andres. Godparents:
Antoin and Susanne, both of color. Priest: F.
Magnes.

1678. LOUIS PHANEAU /ST. ANDRE7 *
(520) 4 December 1821, baptism of mulatto aged 4 months,
natural son of Susanne, slave of Onesim Ste. Andres.
Godparents: Louis Rachal and Marie Celina Ste. Andres. Priest: F. Magnes.

*/See note accompanying Entry 12378.7

1679. MARIE ZELESINE
(520) 4 December 1821, baptism of infant of 4 months,
natural daughter of Chanet /Janet7, slave of Franc.
St. Charme /Germaine7. Godparents: Remy and July.
Priest: F. Magnes.

1680. MARIE ASELY
(521) 30 November 1821, baptism of infant born 22 April
1821, natural daughter of Marie, slave of Louis
Metoyer. Godparents: Luca and Marie, both colored. Priest: F. Magnes.

1681. MARIE LOYSE
(521) 30 November 1821, baptism of infant born 25 August

1821, natural daughter of Delphine, slave of Louis Metoyer. Godparents: Nevil and Denisse, both colored. Priest: F. Magnes.

1682. HENRY
(521) 17 December 1821, baptism of English Negro aged about 28, slave of Louis Metoyer. Godparents: Jn. Btte. Metoyer, the son, and Me. Susete Anty. Priest: F. Magnes.

1683. CHARLES
(521) 17 December 1821, baptism of English Negro aged about 26, slave of Louis Metoyer. Godparents: Etien and Marianne, both colored. Priest: F. Magnes.

1684. FRANCOISE
(521) 17 December 1821, baptism of /?English/ slave aged about 28 years, property of Louis Metoyer. Godparents: Pierre Metoyer, Jr. and Marie Henrriete /Cloutier/. Priest: F. Magnes.

1685. ZENON
(521) 17 December 1821, baptism of English Negro, aged 25 years, slave of Louis Metoyer. Godparents: Remy and Felicite. Priest: F. Magnes.

1686. MANUEL CHASMÉ (?CHARMÉ) /GERMAINE?/*
(521) 17 December 1821, baptism of Guinea Negro aged 17 years, slave of Louis Metoyer. Godparents: Etien and Marton, colored. Priest: F. Magnes.

*/It is not clear whether the fourth letter in this name is "s" or "r." Father Magnes occasionally used "Charmé" as a phoenetic misspelling of "Germaine"./

1687. ATHANAS
(521) 17 December 1821, baptism of Guinea Negro aged 18 years, slave of Louis Metoyer. Godparents: Dupalier Vidol and Dorothee. Priest: F. Magnes.

1688. PHILIPE
(521) 17 December 1821, baptism of Guinea Negro aged 17, slave of Louis Metoyer. Godparents: Luca and Jeanne, colored. Priest: F. Magnes.

1689. JACQUE
(521) 17 December 1821, baptism of Guinea Negro aged 19, slave of Louis Metoyer. Godparents: Toussaint Metoyer and Agnes. Priest: F. Magnes.

1690. CEZAR
(521) 17 December 1821, baptism of English slave aged 12, property of Louis Metoyer. Godparents: "his master and his mistress." Priest: F. Magnes.

1691. MARIE
(521) 17 December 1821, baptism of Guinea Negro aged 22 years, slave of Louis Metoyer. Godparents: Francois Milon and Catisse Metoyer. Priest: F. Magnes.

1692. ROSALY
(521) 17 December 1821, baptism of Guinea Negro aged 24, slave of Louis Metoyer. Godparents: Joseph Metoyer and Me. Therese Metoyer. Priest: F. Magnes.

1693. DELPHINE
(521) 17 December 1821, baptism of English slave aged 20, property of Louis Metoyer. Godparents: Joseph Metoyer and Me. Suset Metoyer. Priest: F. Magnes.

1694. MARIANE
(521) 17 December 1821, baptism of Guinea Negro aged 34, (or 36?), property of Louis Metoyer. Godparents: Jn Baptiste and Margarite, colored. Priest: F. Magnes.

1695. MARIE LAYSA
(521) 17 December 1821, baptism of English Negro aged 16 years, slave of Louis Metoyer. Godparents: Denis and Genevieve, colored. Priest: F. Magnes.

1696. JEAN BTTE. DELORES METOYER
(522) 30 November 1821, baptism of infant born the "2nd of ____ last," /entry is torn/ legitimate son of Pierre Metoyer and Marie Anrriete /Cloutier/. Godparents: Jn. Btte. Metoyer, son of Louis, and Marie Susete Metoyer, all free people of color. Priest: F. Magnes.

1697. JOSEPH BALCOUR /VALCOUR/ METOYER
(522) 30 November 1821, baptism of infant born 28 October 1820, legitimate son of Magsil Metoyer and Marie Aspasy Metoyer. Godparents: Auguste Metoyer and Maria Therese Carmelita Anty, all free people of color. Priest: F. Magnes.

1698. GERONIMO CHARPI /JEROME SARPY/
(522) 30 November 1821, baptism of infant born 27 June 1821, legitimate son of Geronimo Charpy and Maria Juana Metoyer. Godparents: Francois Metoyer, his grandfather, and Agnes his aunt, all free people of

color. Priest: F. Magnes.

1699. MARIE ELYSA ROCQUE
(522) 30 November 1821, baptism of infant born 28 May 1821, legitimate daughter of Charles Nerest Rocque and Marie Pompose Metoyer. Godparents: Elise Rocques and Eliset Glapion, all free people of color. Priest: F. Magnes.

1700. MARIE ELISEE ROCQUE
(522) 30 November 1821, baptism of infant born 9 September 1821, legitimate daughter of Elise Rocque and Marie Susete Metoyer. Godparents: Luis Metoyer and Theresa, the uncle and aunt of the child, all free people of color. Priest: F. Magnes.

1701. CLOUTIER-SALVAN-PRUDHOMME-LAMBRE
(523) An undated note inserted in register at this point reads:

Jean Pierre Cloutier and Marie Salvan, their children:
   Marie Marguerite Cloutier, b. in 1799
   Jean Baptiste Cloutier, b. in 1804;
   Marie Cloutier, b. in 1804   twins
   Pierre Cloutier, b. in 1808

                J. B. Prudhomme. Jacques Lambre.
Jacques Lambre. J. B. Prudhomme, Ant. Prudh.
Mie. Lambre. Remi
Remi-Suz. Desirée Prudhomme
Valsin   Clarisse
Delphin

        J. B.   J. L.
Jean B. Jacques L. Emanuel, Catherine, Mie.
                                  Th. Buard
Antoine, Marie _____

/Remainder of bottom and side of sheet is torn._/7

1702. BLANK PAGE
(524)
§§
"Enterrements de Negres et Mulatres Esclaves, 1802"

1703. JEAN BAPTISTE
(525) 10 April 1802, burial of a Congo slave of Me. Veuve Triche who died the preceding day without receiving the sacraments. Aged about 70 years. Priest: P. Pavie.

1704. FRANCOIS
(525) 27 June 1802, burial in cemetery of this parish of a Negro slave of Mr. Metoyer, a native of the Guinea coast, aged about 50 years, who died the preceding day without receiving the sacraments since the priest was not told of his illness. Priest: P. Pavie.

1705. JOSEPH
(525) 14 August 1802, burial in cemetery of this parish of a slave who died the preceding day at age of 30 years, son of Sophie, Negress slave of Mr. Morphil, habitant at this post. Priest: P. Pavie.

1706. LOUIS
(525) 19 August 1802, burial in cemetery of this parish of a Negro of Guinée, who died the preceding day at the age of 45 years, slave of Mr. Demesiere. Louis died without the sacraments since the priest was not called during the illness of the slave. Priest: P. Pavie.

1707. MARIE FLORE
(526) 23 August 1802, burial in cemetery of this parish of a Negro infant who died the preceding day at the age of 5 weeks, daughter of the Negress, Magdaleine, slave of Mr. Badin. Priest: P. Pavie.

1708. MARIE MANUEL
(526) 6 October 1802, burial in cemetery of this parish of an infant who died the preceding day at age of 15 months, daughter of Pauline, mulatresse slave Mr. Capuran. Priest: P. Pavie.

1709. MARIE FRANCOISE
(526) 9 November 1802, burial in cemetery of this parish of a native of this post, aged 35 years, who died the preceding day. Deceased was slave of Louis Buart and died without the sacraments because the priest was not called. Priest: P. Pavie.

1710. MARIE ANNE
(526) 24 July 1803, recording by Father Pavie of a burial in the parish cemetery which occurred while he was "en ville" /In the city of New Orleans7. Deceased was a Negress, aged 70, slave of Mr. Maes. Priest: P. Pavie.

1711. ROQUE
(526) 28 July 1803, recording by Father Pavie of a burial in the parish cemetery which occurred while

he was on a voyage to *"la Ville."* The deceased was a free Negro of 45 years, to whom the priest had administered the sacraments before his departure. Priest: P. Pavie.

1712. JEAN BAPTISTE
(527) 16 November 1803, burial in cemetery of this parish of a Negro of 80 years, native of Guinée, slave of Mr. Badin, who died after receiving the sacraments. Priest: P. Pavie.

1713. JEANNE
(527) 21 November 1803, burial in cemetery of this parish of a Negress slave of Dominique Davion, aged 20 years, who died without receiving the sacraments since the priest was not called. Priest: P. Pavie.

1714. MARIE
(527) 24 December 1803, burial in cemetery of this parish of a mulatress of 19 years, slave of Mr. Rambin, who died without receiving the sacraments because it was not thought that her illness was serious. Priest: P. Pavie.

1715. PELAGIE
(527) 30 January 1804, burial in cemetery of this parish of a slave aged 27 years, property of Mr. Hilaret. She died after receiving the sacrament of extreme unction, but did not make her confession because she lost consciousness almost immediately after falling sick. Priest: P. Pavie.

1716. JEAN BAPTISTE
(527) 1 June 1804, burial in cemetery of this parish or a child of 3 years, son of Louison, slave of Joseph Pavie. Priest: P. Pavie.

1717. UNNAMED
(528) 29 August 1804, burial in cemetery of this parish of a little Negro boy who died after being privately baptized in expectation of death. He was son of Magdelein, negro slave of Louis Buart. Priest: P. Pavie.

1718. UNNAMED
(528) 3 March 1805, burial in cemetery of this parish of a little Negro boy who died after being privately baptized at the time of his birth. He was son of Marie Louise, Negro slave of Jacques Bastien Prudhomme. Priest: P. Pavie.

1719. JULIE
(528) 21 March 1805, burial in cemetery of this parish of a Guinée Negro, aged 45 years, slave of Mr. Rambin. She died suddenly the preceding day without receiving the sacraments. Priest: P. Pavie.

1720. JACQUES
(528) 2 June 1805, burial in cemetery of this parish of a Guinée Negro, slave of Me. Veuve Lestase. He died the preceding day at aged 60 or about, without receiving the sacraments since the priest was not called during his illness. Priest: P. Pavie.

1721. MARGUERITTE SOPHIE
(529) 13 June 1805, burial in cemetery of this parish of a Guinée Negro who died the preceding day at aged 60 years, after receiving the sacrament of penitence. Deceased was slave of Mr. Morphil. Priest: P. Pavie.

1722. UNNAMED
(529) 15 June 1805, burial in cemetery of this parish of a little Negro boy who died the day of his birth after being baptized privately. Deceased was son of Marie Anne, Negro slave of Mr. Maes, and of a father unknown. Priest: P. Pavie.

1723. UNNAMED
(529) 23 November 1805, burial in cemetery of this parish of a little Negro boy who died at the time of his birth. He was baptized privately, and was the son of Constance, slave of Me. Veuve Pantaleon. Priest: P. Pavie.

1724. UNNAMED
(529) 4 December 1805, burial in cemetery of this parish of a little Negro boy who died the preceding day after having been privately baptized. He was son of Susanne, mulatress slave of Mr. Metoier. Priest: P. Pavie.

1725. PIERRE
(530) 20 January 1806, burial in cemetery of this parish of a Negro slave of deceased Mr. Badin. He was a native of Guinea, aged 40, and was accidentally drowned. Priest: P. Pavie.

1726. MARIE ANNE
(530) 26 February 1806, burial in cemetery of this parish of a free Negress, native of Guinée, who died the preceding day without knowledge of her illness.

Deceased was 70 hears old or about, had been married to the Negro Pierre Joseph Prince, by the Rev. Father Louis, Capucin, when he was pastor of this post. Priest: P. Pavie.

/See Entry 1021 of Mills, *Natchitoches 1729-1803*. This couple were slaves of Capt. Louis Borme at the time of their marriage./

1727. MARIE
(530) 25 May 1806, burial in cemetery of this parish of a Negress of 9 months, a slave of Mr. Paillet. Priest: P. Pavie.

1728. ETIENNE
(530) 29 May 1806, burial in cemetery of this parish, a slave of Mr. Paillet. He died the preceding day at the age of 4 months or about. Priest: P. Pavie.

1729. UNNAMED
(530) 24 July 1806, burial in cemetery of this parish of an infant Negro who died the preceding day after being privately baptized. He was son of Marie, Negro slave of Mr. Rouquié. Priest: P. Pavie.

1730. UNNAMED
(531) 29 August 1806, baptism in cemetery of this parish of a male mulatto who died the preceding day at the age of 4 days after being privately baptized. He was the son of Genevieve, mulatress slave of Mr. Morphil. Priest: P. Pavie.

1731. VALENTIN
(531) 9 September 1806, burial in cemetery of this parish of a Guinée Negro, slave of Mr. Baptiste Triche. Deceased was 50 years old or about and was found drowned in the river. Priest: P. Pavie.

1732. UNNAMED
(531) 13 September 1806, burial in cemetery of this parish of an infant who died the day of his birth, after being privately baptized, son of Felicite, a free mulatto. Priest: P. Pavie.

1733. ALEXANDRO
(531) 12 June 1813, burial of a free Negro aged 60 years, servant of Luis Buard. Deceased was a bachelor and died of fever. Priest: F. Magnes.

1734. MARIA LUISA CONDE
(531) 12 July 1813, burial in cemetery of this parish of a free *"morena"* aged 55 years, an unmarried

woman, who died of the fever. Priest: F. Magnes.

1735. TERESA
(532) 22 August 1813, burial in cemetery of this parish of a slave of Mad. St. Anne. Deceased was 25 and died of dropsy. Priest: F. Magnes.

1736. PEDRO
(532) 22 August 1813, burial in cemetery of this parish of a Negro aged about 60 years, slave of Mr. Cortes, who died of fever. Priest: F. Magnes.

1737. LUIS
(532) 29 October 1813, burial of a child of 1½ years, slave of Mr. Rambin. Priest: F. Magnes.

1738. ELENA
(532) 4 December 1813, burial of a small child of 1 year, natural daughter of *Fambi?*, slave of "Madaimoasel Marceli Puesau" /Poissot/. Priest: F. Magnes.

1739. DOMINGO BADEN
(532) 19 December 1813, burial of a free Negro child of 7 days, natural son of Elena Badem, a free mulatto. Priest: F. Magnes.

1740. GENOVEVA
(533) 20 December 1813, burial of a Negro aged 30 years, slave of "Madaimoasel Puesau" /see Entry 1738/. Priest: F. Magnes.

1741. FRANCISCO
(533) 22 December 1813, burial of Negro aged 28 years, who died of *imallo?*. Deceased was slave of Benjamin Metoyer. Priest: F. Magnes.

1742. UNNAMED
(533) 22 December 1813, burial in cemetery of this parish of a 3 or 4 year old child named /blank/, slave of Madame Lavious. Priest: F. Magnes.

1743. YSABEL
(533) 1 January 1814, burial in cemetery of this parish of a mulatto aged 40 years, slave of Felis Trudeau, who died of asthma after receiving the sacraments. Priest: F. Magnes.

1744. GENOVEVA
(533) 11 January 1814, burial in cemetery of this parish of a slave aged 45, property of Mr. Jose Bram,

death from asthma. Priest: F. Magnes.

1745. BALSEM /VALSAIN/ METOYER
(534) 2 September 1814, burial of a natural son of Susana Metoyer who died of fever at the age of eight. Priest: F. Magnes.

1746. ROSA
(534) 9 September 1814, burial of the natural daughter of Felicite, slave of Mda. Monsineau. Deceased died of fever at age of 14 days. Priest: F. Magnes.

1747. DENIS
(534) 18 September 1814, burial of a 7 month old natural son of Maria, slave of Mnr. Bta. Buard. The child died of fever. Priest: F. Magnes.

1748. MARIA LEON
(534) 26 September 1814, burial in the cemetery of this parish of a child of 6 years, slave of Mnr. Mesierre, natural daughter of the slave Maria Juana. The child died of fever. Priest: F. Magnes.

1749. AGUSTINA
(535) 3 October 1814, burial in the cemetery of this parish of a child of 4 years, natural daughter of Arsene, a slave of Mnr. Sompayract. The child died of intestinal worms. Priest: F. Magnes.

1750. ANORE /HONORE/
(535) 17 October 1814, burial in cemetery of this parish of a boy of 15 years, natural son of Magdalena, slave of Mnr. Grenoble. Death caused by "the accidental falling of a stick." Priest: F. Magnes.

1751. ATANASIO
(535) 14 May 1815, burial in cemetery of this parish of the natural son of Susanne, slave of Mda. Ve. Jn. Btte. Buard. Death caused by epilepsy. Priest: F. Magnes.

1752. MARIE OSIT
(535) 29 May 1815, burial of a slave about 14 years, property of Mda. Ve. Jn. Btte. Buard. Death caused by fever. Priest: F. Magnes.

1753. MARIE NANET PIERNAS
(536) 9 August 1815, burial in cemetery of this parish of a 4-year old child, legitimate daughter of Agustin Piernas and Delayde Troudeau, free mulattoes. Priest: F. Magnes.

1754. MARIE PERIN METOYER
(536) Note by Father Magnes: "The Entry for Marie Perin, wife of Pier Metoyer, a free mulatto, is recorded in Book 12, folio 37."

/The book and folio cited has since been bound with other small registers into what is the present Book 5. The burial of Marie Perine LeComte Metoyer may be found under Entry 940./

1755. JUAN BTTE. BADEN
(536) 10 January 1816, burial in cemetery of this parish of a free Negro, aged 38 years, natural son of Cecil, a free Negro. Death caused by fever. Priest: F. Magnes.

1756. ALEXANDRO
(536) 23 March 1816, baptism of a slave of Jn. Btte. Trichel. Death caused by pain. Priest: F. Magnes.

1757. MARIE LOUISE
(537) 13 April 1816, burial of a free Negro aged about 72 years, who left 1 son and 1 daughter, slaves of Louis Buard. Death caused by a pain. Priest: F. Magnes.

1758. JOSEPH METOYER
(537) 13 May 1816, burial in cemetery at Riviere aux Cannes of the legitimate son of Dominique Metoyer, a free mulatto, and Margarite LeComt. Death caused by a pain. Priest: F. Magnes.

1759. NICOLAS DOCLA
(537) 8 July 1816, burial of Nicolas Docla, a free Negro who died of fever, leaving a widow named /torn/ who also is a free Negro. Deceased left no children. Priest: F. Magnes.

1760. UNNAMED
(537) 28 August 1816, burial of /blank/, a slave of Mr. Rouquier, the brother. Death caused by fever. Priest: F. Magnes.

1761. ARSEN
(537) 29 November 1816, burial of a Negro slave of Mr. Sompayract. Priest: F. Magnes.

1762. GAVRIEL
(537) 11 May 1817, burial of a slave of about 30 years, property of Felis Trudeau, who died of pain. Priest: F. Magnes.

1763. JN BTTE.
(538) 18 May 1817, burial of a slave, aged about 16, who died of fever, property of Ve. Morphy. Priest: F. Magnes.

1764. MARIE
(538) 31 August 1817, burial of child of 6 years, natural daughter of Agata, slave of Jn. Btte. Buard. Death caused by fever. Priest: F. Magnes.

1765. ARICE? /CLARISSE?7
(538) 23 September 1817, burial of a mulatto slave of Jn. Btte. Buard, aged about 20 years. Death by fever. Priest: F. Magnes.

1766. MARIA JUANA
(538) 28 November 1817, burial of a slave who died of fever, property of Bte. Buard. Priest: F. Magnes.

1767. MARIA JUANA
(538) 21 January 1818, burial of a slave of Mde. Ve. Morphy, who died of fever. Priest: F. Magnes.

1768. UNNAMED
(538) 21 March 1818, burial of a slave of Joseph Tauzin who died of a lung disease. Priest: F. Magnes.

1769. AOVIDON
(539) 16 April 1818, burial in cemetery of this parish of a 53-year old slave of Placido Bossier who died of pain. Priest: F. Magnes.

1770. CYPRIAN
(539) 9 May 1818, burial of an 18-year old slave of Mda. Ve. Bmy. Rachal. Death caused by fever. Priest: F. Magnes.

1771. MARIANNA
(539) 13 June 1818, burial of slave of Athanas Demessier, who died of fever. Priest: F. Magnes.

1772. CELESTE
(539) 26 May 1818, burial of a slave aged about 18 years, property of Mda. Ve. Rouquiere. Deceased "died of a sudden death." Priest: F. Magnes.

1773. SOCO
(539) 16 September 1818, burial of a slave of about /blank7 years, slave of Fs. Bienne. Death by fever. Priest: F. Magnes.

1774. MARIE
(539) 5 October 1818, burial of a Comanche Indian who died of fever. Priest: F. Magnes.

1775. MARIE CECILIA BADEN
(539) 22 November 1818, burial of a free woman of 72 years who died leaving 3 free daughters. Priest: F. Magnes.

1776. PACALE
(539) 18 December 1818, burial of a free Negro "known as Pacale"*, aged about 80 years, who died of fever. Priest: F. Magnes.

*/The baptismal name of the deceased was Yves; he was a former slave of the Derbanne family./

1777. FRANCISCA NIVET
(540) 20 March 1819, burial of a free mulatto, aged about 60 years and a native of New Orleans. She died of asthma, leaving 3 sons and 1 daughter, after receiving the sacraments.

1778. MAGDALENA
(540) 18 March 1819, burial of a slave aged about 58 years, property of Pier Ternier. Death by fever. Priest: F. Magnes.

1779. MARIE /Adelayde/
(540) 31 October 1819, burial of a child of 8 months, natural daughter of Ulalye, slave of Placide Bossier. Priest: F. Magnes.

1780. MARIE SENEGAL
(540) 10 January 1820, burial of a free Negro about 60 years of age, who died of fever. Priest: F. Magnes.

1781. MARIE PHANI
(540) 31 September 1820, burial of a Negro of about 40, slave of Mr. Detervil. Death by fever. Priest: F. Magnes.

1782. ZENON
(540) 29 November 1820, burial in cemetery of this parish of a free man of color of about 28 years, native of /blank/. Death caused by gunshot. Priest: F. Magnes.

1783. FRANCOIS ALEXY BADEN
(541) 6 January 1821, burial of a child of 8 years, natural son of Elena Baden, a free woman of color.

1784. PIERÓ [PIERROT]
(541) 2 February 1821, burial in cemetery of this parish of a slave of about 80 years, property of Mr. Bladuhort [Bludworth]. Death by fever. Priest: F. Magnes.

1785. BALTASAR
(541) 5 March 1821, burial of a slave of 10 years, property of Francois Vienne. Death by fever. Priest: F. Magnes.

1786. JUAN PIERRE
(541) 1 April 1821, burial of a free Negro of about 80 years; death by fever. Priest: F. Magnes.

1787. FRANCISCA
(541) 9 May 1821, burial of a slave of Joseph Tauzin. Death by dropsy. Priest: F. Magnes.

1788. ZENON
(541) 8 July 1821, burial of a child of 2 years, slave of Joseph Tausin. Death by fever. Priest: F. Magnes.

1789. JACQUE
(541) 15 July 1821, burial of a slave of Placido Bossier who died of fever. Priest: F. Magnes.

1790. MARIE MODESTE
(542) 22 July 1821, burial of a slave of Francois Vienne who died of fever. Priest: F. Magnes.

1791. MARIE JEANNE
(542) 3 September 1821, burial of a slave of about 24 years, property of Mda. Ve. Bmy. Rachal. Death by fever. Priest: F. Magnes.

1792. VICTOIRE
(542) 9 September 1821, burial of a slave of 24 years property of Arnau Lauve. Death caused by tetanus. Priest: F. Magnes.

1793. LAYSA
(542) 18 September 1825, burial of a child of 1 year, daughter of Marie Lise, a free woman of color. Death caused by fever. Priest: F. Magnes.

1794. YSAVEL
(542) 22 September 1821, burial of a slave of about 35 years, property of Francisco Landrau. Death by fever. Priest: F. Magnes.

1795. ROSALY
(542) 13 October 1821, burial of a mulato of about 8 years, slave of Mde. Ve. Bmy. Rachal. Death by fever. Priest: F. Magnes.

1796. JOSEPH
(542) 8 November 1821, burial of a slave of about 25 years, property of Jacque Lambre. Death by fever. Priest: F. Magnes.

1797. BALTASAR
(542) 11 February 1822, burial of a slave of Francois Bossier, aged 38 years, who died of fever. Priest: F. Magnes.

1798. SATURIN
(543) 5 March 1822, burial of a slave, 15 years old, property of Hipolito Bordeleau, who died of injuries sustained in falling off a horse. Sacrament of extreme unction was administered. Priest: F. Magnes.

1799. MARIE
(543) 6 March 1822, burial of a slave of Mde. Ve. Morphil, aged about 20 years, who died of fever. Priest: F. Magnes.

1800. JACQUE
(543) 7 August 1822, burial of a slave of about 50 years, property of Jn. Btte. Buard. Death by fever. Priest: F. Magnes.

1801. MARIE BADIN
(543) 24 August 1822, burial of Maria Vadin, free Negro* aged 36 years, natural daughter of Catarina. Death by fever. Priest: F. Magnes.

*/This entire entry was recorded twice, then the first entry was scratched through. This original entry identified deceased as "free Negro, daughter of Catarina." The revised version identifed the deceased as "a free woman of color" rather than "free Negro" and omitted parental information./

1802. BLANK PAGE
(544)

1803. BLANK PAGE
(545)

1804. MARIE _____ ANS
(546) /torn/December 1821, baptism of an Indian child of

1 year, natural daughter of Jacque and Tonton, Indians. Godparents: Louis and Conomichel?, "both of the nation." /See entry below./ Priest: F. Magnes.

1805. JACOB
(546) 8 December 1821, baptism of Indian child of 3 (13?) years, son of Jacque and Tonton. Godparents: Jacob and /torn/, "both of the Apalache nation." Priest: F. Magnes.

1806. MARIE FELISERE
(546) 8 December 1821, baptism of Indian child of 1 year, natural daughter of Joseph Touasa and Victoria Crisostome. Godparents: Francois Lattier and Thereseta Enes. Priest: F. Magnes.

1807. MARIE LOUISE
(546) 8 December 1821, baptism of Indian child of 6 months, natural daughter of Crisostom and Margarite. Godparents: Athanas and Felicite, all of the Apalache Nation. Priest: F. Magnes.

1808. JUAN MARIA
(546) 8 December 1821, baptism of Indian child of 6 months, natural son of Joseph Foloquier and Maria Luisa. Godparents: Jacques Valery and Marie Elenne Valery. Priest: F. Magnes.

1809. VALERIEN
(547) 10 January 1802, baptism of a Negro boy born 15 December 1801 in this post, son of Magdeleine, a Negro slave of Mlle. Marie Joseph Triche. Godparents: Romual, slave of Mlle. Triche, and Adelaide, slave of Me. Widow Triche. Priest: P. Pavie.

1810. JEAN BAPTISTE
(547) 12 January 1802, baptism of a Negro boy born 16 March 1801, son of Marie, slave of Pierre Jarri, living in this post, and of a father unknown. Godparents: Antonio Laineir /LeNoir/ and Marie Dupre. Priest: P. Pavie.

1811. FELIX /FELICITE/ AIMÉ LEVASSEUR   WHITE
(547) 31 January 1802, baptism of a white infant born 19 May 1800. Grandparents: Louis Levasseur and Marie Bourdon; Marin Grille and Marie Brevel. The child is the legitimate daughter of Jacques Levasseur and Marie Therese Grillé. Godparents: Andre Chamart and Euphrosine Rambin. Priest: P. Pavie.

1812. JOSEPH DANIEL
(548)

14 March 1802, baptism of a Negro born 7 February 1802, son of Marie Joseph, slave of Me. Veuve Grillé, and of a father unknown. Godparents: Jacques and Francoise, slave of Veuve Grillé. Priest: P. Pavie.

1813. LOUIS AUGUSTIN
(548) 28 March 1802, baptism of a Negro boy born 26 January 1802 in this post, son of Marie Jeanne, slave of Marie Louise Davion, Veuve Gagne, and of a father unknown. Godparents: Louis Gagne and Mari Gagne. Priest: P. Pavie.

1814. MARIE
(548) 28 March 1802, baptism of a mulatto born 4 February 1802 in this post, daughter of Catherinne, Negro slave of Marie Louise Davion, Veuve Gagne, and of a father unknown. Godparents: Rosaimon Chamart and Marie Cilesie Triche. Priest: P. Pavie.

1815. MARIE MODESTE
(548- 4 April 1802, baptism of a Negro girl of 2½ years,
549) born in this post, daughter of Celeste, a slave of Louis Gallien, and of a father unknown. Godparents: Pierre Toussaint /Metoyer/, a free mulatto, and Marie Ursule, a free quadroon. Priest: P. Pavie.

1816. JOSEPH LUCAS
(549) 18 April 1802, baptism of a Negro boy of 6 months, son of Jeanne, Negro slave of Susanne /Metoyer/, also a Negro, and of a father unknown. Godparents: Bernard, slave of Me. Gaspart, and Eulalie, Negro slave of Me. Monginot. Priest: P. Pavie.

1817. ANTOINE
(549) 18 April 1802, baptism of a Congo Negro aged 20 years, slave of Augustin /Metoyer/, a free Negro living at this post. Father and mother are unknown. Godparents: "a slave of Me. Veuve Lecomte" and Magdeleine, mulatto slave of Widow Lecomte.

1818. MARIE
(549) 16 May 1802, baptism of a Negro girl born 24 March 1802, daughter of Julienne, Negro slave of Me. Veuve Triche, living in this post. Godparents: Basil Gagné and Susanne Gagné. Priest: P. Pavie.

1819. MICHEL
(549) 6 June 1802, baptism of a Negro boy of 1 year, son of Elisabeth, Negro slave of Pierre Derbanne. Father unknown. Godparents: Michel, slave of

Rhemi Lambre, and Marie Therese, slave of Anty. All live in this post. Priest: P. Pavie.

1820. MARIE JOSEPH
(550) 11 July 1802, baptism of a Negro girl born 11 February 1802, daughter of Francoise, slave of Madame Veuve Fonteneau. The infant belongs to Marie Therese Fonteneau. Godparents: Jean Baptiste Fonteneau and Marie Joseph Henriette Rouquié. Priest: P. Pavie.

1821. JEAN PIERRE
(550) 11 July 1802, baptism of a Negro boy born 15 June 1802, son of Marie Jeanne, slave of Dame Widow Grillé, living in this post. Father unknown. Godparents: Pierre, slave of Francois Levasseur, and Marie, mulatto slave of Mr. Badin. Priest: P. Pavie.

1822. MARIE FLORE
(550) 8 August 1802, baptism of a Negro girl born 15 of last month in this post, daughter of Magdeline, Negro slave of Mr. Badin. Father unknown. Godparents: Louis Alexandre, slave of Mr. Buart, and Catherine, slave of Francois Levasseur. Priest: P. Pavie.

1823. PIERRE
(550- 19 September 1802, baptism of a Negro boy born 16
551) July 1801 in this post, son of Salie, Negro slave of Mr. Metoie, resident of this post. Father unknown. Godparents: Francois Rambin and Marie Therese Elisabeth Metoyer. Priest: P. Pavie.

1824. MARIE JEANNE
(551) 19 September 1802, baptism of a Negro girl born 3 March 1802, daughter of Elisabeth, Negro slave of Mr. Metoie. Father unknown. Godparents: Jean Baptiste, slave of Mr. Aillot, and Genevieve, slave of Louis Buart. Priest: P. Pavie.

1825. LOUIS LECLERC /GRAPPE7
(551) 17 October 1802, baptism of a quadroon born 29 October 1801, son of Magdaleine /Grappe7, slave of Francois Grape, living at this post. Father unknown. Godparents: Dominique, mulatto slave of Francois Grape, and Marie Joseph, slave of the same master. Priest: P. Pavie.

1826. JOSEPH
(551) 15 November 1802, baptism of a mulatto, already privately baptized at home while in danger of death, son of Genevieve, mulatto slave of Mr. Morphil.

Godparents: Edouard Morphil and Marie Louise Gagnon. Priest: P. Pavie.

1827. MARIE LOUISE
(552) 15 November 1802, baptism of a Negro boy /sic/ born 28 July 1802, son of Margueritte, Negro slave of Mr. Morphil, a resident of this post. Godparents: Claude Mars, free Negro, and Marie Louise, Negro slave of Mr. Badin. Priest: P. Pavie.

1828. ROSE
(552) 20 February 1803, baptism of a mulatto born 25 January 1803, daughter of Laide /Marie Helene Adelayde/, Negro slave of deceased Madame St. Denis. Godparents: Jean Baptiste Buart and Marie Rouquie. Priest: P. Pavie.

1829. GENEVIEVE
(552) 3 April 1803, baptism of mulatto born 27 August 1802, daughter of Constance, Negro slave of Joseph Derbane. Father unknown. Godparents: Maurice, slave of Me. Veuve Denis Buart, and Francois, mulatto slave of Manuel Prudhomme. Priest: P. Pavie.

1830. DOMINIQUE
(552- 9 April 1803, baptism of Negro born 5 December
553) 1802, in this post, son of Esther, Negro slave of Mr. Metoier. Father unknown. Godparents: Joseph, slave of Mr. Badin, and Margueritte, Negro slave of Mr. Metoier. Priest: P. Pavie.

1831. MICHEL HONORE
(553) 9 April 1803, baptism of a Negro boy born 6 November 1802, in this post, son of Charlote, Negro slave of Mr. Aillot de St. Anne. Father unknown. Godparents: Michel Chamart and Marie Therese Victoire called St. Anne. Priest: P. Pavie.

1832. MARTHA
(553) 9 April 1803, baptism of a mulatto born 15 July 1802, daughter of Cilisie, mulatto slave of Mr. Metoyer, resident of this post. Father unknown. Godparents: Joseph, Negro slave of Mr. Badin, and Francoise, mulatto slave of Manuel Prudhomme. Priest: P. Pavie.

1833. JOSEPH
(553) 10 April 1803, baptism of a mulatto born 6 June 1802, daughter /sic/ of Jeanne, Negro slave of Mr. Jean Baptiste Benoist, native of this post. Father unknown. Godparents: Jean David and Marie Silvie Dubardeau. Priest: P. Pavie.

1834. LOUIS
(554) 10 April 1803, baptism of Negro boy born 5 August 1802, son of Marie, slave of Me. Veuve Denis Buart, a native of this post. Godparents: Maurice, a slave of Widow Denis Buart, and Marguerite, a slave of Baptiste Buart. Priest: P. Pavie

1835. VICTORINE
(554) 10 April 1803, baptism of Negro born 10 July 1802, daughter of Marie Anne, slave of Mr. Metoier, resident of this parish. Father unknown. Godparents: Francois Roubiau and Elisabeth Rachal. Priest: P. Pavie.

1836. AUGUSTIN
(554) 10 April 1803, baptism of Negro boy, native of this parish, son of Marie, slave of Mr. Metoier, born 15 May 1802 of an unknown father. Godparents: Florentin /Conant/, a free mulatto, and Marie Modeste, slave of Mr. Metoyer. Priest: P. Pavie.

1837. MARIE JOSEPH
(554) 10 April 1803, baptism of a mulato girl born 26 September in this parish, daughter of Marie, Negress of Me. Veuve Monginot, a resident of this post. Father unknown. Godparents: Louis Alexandre, slave of Louis Buart, and Brigite, mulatto slave of Mr. Morphil. Priest: P. Pavie.

1838. LOUIS /MONET/*
(555) 10 April 1803, baptism of mulatto born 25 December in this parish, son of Marie Louise /LeComte/, mulatto slave of Louis Monet. Father unknown. Godparents: Louis Monet and Francoise Lecomte. Priest: P. Pavie.

*/This infant was eventually freed by Monet's widow through a special act of the legislature in 1825. See Gary B. Mills, *The Forgotten People* (LSU Press, 1977), 90./

1839. SUSANNE
(555) 10 April 1803, baptism of Negro born 2 March 1802, daughter of Marie Jeanne, slave of Joseph Dupre, a native of this post. Father unknown. Godparents: Pierre Toussaint /Metoyer/, a free mulatto, and Susanne, mulatto slave of Mr. LeComte. Priest: Pavie.

1840. MARIE LOUISE
(555) 10 April 1803, baptism of a Negro born 4 December 1802 in this post, daughter of Susanne, Negro

slave of Mr. Morphil. Godparents: Joseph Fouente
and Marie Louise, slave of Mr. Metoyer. Priest:
P. Pavie.

1841. MARTHE
(555) 18 April 1803, baptism of a mulatto born 3 October 1802, in this post, daughter of Marie Jeanne, Negro slave of Me. Veuve Rachal. Godparents: Jean Baptiste Adelet and Marie Joseph Melanie Rachal. Priest: P. Pavie.

1842. CELESTIN /LACAZE7
(556) 18 April 1803, baptism of a mulatto born 18 July 1798, son of Rosalie, slave of Jacques Lacase. Father unknown. Godparents: Etienne, slave of Varangue, and Marie Perine, a freed slave. Priest: P. Pavie.

1843. MICHEL /LACAZE7
(556) 18 April 1803, baptism of a mulatto born 12 April 1801, son of Rosalie, slave of Jacques Lacase, living at this post. Father unknown. Godparents: Jean Baptiste David and Catherinne Bastien. Priest: P. Pavie.

1844. AUGUSTIN
(556) 1 May 1803, baptism of a Negro born 16 May 1802, in this post, son of Magdeleine, slave of Athanase Demesiere. Father unknown. Godparents: Joseph, slave of Mr. Gaspard, and Francoise, slave of Mr. Rouquier. Priest: P. Pavie.

1845. AUGUSTINE
(556) 16 May 1803, baptism of Negro born at this post, 6 May 1803, daughter of Marie Louise, slave of Madame Widow St. Denis, deceased. Father unknown. Godparents: Francois Robin and Marie Silvie Hubardo. Priest: P. Pavie

1846. MARIE ADELAIDE
(557) 22 May 1803, baptism of a mulatto, aged two months, daughter of Genevieve, mulatto slave of Louis Buart. Father unknown. Godparents: Guillaume, a slave of Mr. Badin, and Marie, mulatto slave of Mr. Badin. Priest: P. Pavie.

1847. JEAN BAPTISTE HILAIRE
(557) 29 May 1803, baptism of a Negro born 15 September 1802, son of Margueritte, slave of Marie Therese, a free Negress. Father unknown. All are residents of this post. Godparents: Antoine Joseph

/Metoyer/, slave /son/ of Marie Therese, and Pelagie /LaCourt/, free Negro. Priest: P. Pavie.

1848. CECILE
(557) 29 May 1803, baptism of a Negro aged 14 months, daughter of Francoise, slave of Joseph Dupre. Father unknown. All are residents of this post. Godparents: Charles, slave of Remi Lambre, and Ursule, slave of Mr. St. Anne. Priest: P. Pavie.

1849. MARIE
(557) 29 May 1803, baptism of a Negro aged 3 months, daughter of Francoise, native of this post, slave of Mr. Joseph Dupre. Father unknown. Godparents: Manuel, slave of Mr. Antoine Prudhomme, and Marie Therese, slave of Mr. Anti. Priest: P. Pavie.

1850. FRANCOIS
(558) 29 May 1803, baptism of a Negro born 5 March 1803, son of Rosete, slave of Mr. Rouquier, living in this post. Father unknown. Godparents: Francois Olivier and Marie Rouquié. Priest: P. Pavie.

1851. FRANCOIS
(558) 5 June 1803, baptism of a Congo Negro aged 20 years, father and mother unknown. Godparents: Francois Rouquié and Marie Victoire Poissot, widow of Denis Buart, owner of the slave. Priest: P. Pavie.

1852. ETIENNE
(558) 5 June 1803, baptism of a Negro born 27 July 1802, in this post, child of Celeste, Negro slave of Mr. Tite Perau. Father unknown. Godparents: André Chamart and Marie Catherine Perau. Priest: P. Pavie.

1853. HILAIRE
(558) 15 August 1803, baptism of Negro born 20 July 1803, in this post, son of Marie Anne, slave of Monsieur Trudeau, commandant of this post. Father unknown. Godparents: Augustin, brother of the infant, and Marie Joseph, slave of Monsieur Trudeau. Priest: P. Pavie.

1854. LEON
(559) 23 August 1803, baptism of a mulatto born 8 October 1801 in this post, son of Marie Jeanne, mulatto slave of Monsieur Demesiere. Father unknown. Godparents: Manuel Triche and Francoise Grappe. Priest: P. Pavie.

1855. ETIENNE
(559) 23 August 1803, baptism of a Negro born 2 August

1803, in this post, son of Catherinne, Negro slave of Marie Louise Davion, widow of Pierre Gagné. Father unknown. Godparents: Jean Baptiste, Negro slave of Manuel Triche, and Jeanne, mulatress slave of Manuel Trichel. Priest: P. Pavie.

1856. LOUIS ALEXANDRE
(559) 4 September 1803, baptism of a Negro born 28 May 1803, in this post, son of Louison, slave of Joseph Pavie. Father unknown. Godparents: Louis Alexander, slave of Louis Buart, and Catherine, slave of Francois Levasseur. Priest: P. Pavie.

1857. HENRIETTE
(559- 4 September 1803, baptism of a Negro aged 10 months
560) or about, native of this post, daughter of Felicite, slave of Madame Fonteneau. Godparents: Simeon, mulatto slave of Henri Triche, and Jeanne, slave of Henry Triche. Priest: P. Pavie.

1858. GERASIME
(560) 18 September 1803, baptism of a Negro born 26 November 1802, in this post, son of Louise, slave of Louis Derbanne. Father unknown. Godparents: Barthelemi Rachal and Marie Arthemise Rachal. Priest: P. Pavie.

1859. LOUIS
(560) 18 September 1803, baptism of Negro born 25 August 1803, son of Margueritte, slave of Francois Levasseur. Father unknown. Godparents: Louis Levasseur and Marie Aspasie Murphy. Priest: P. Pavie.

1860. HENRI
(560) 18 September 1803, baptism of Negro born 8 August 1803, son of Marie, slave of Guillaume Chevert. Godparents: Cesair Murphil and Susanne Plaisance. Priest: P. Pavie.

1861. MARIE LOUISE
(561) 25 September 1803, baptism of Negro born 24 April 1803 in this post, daughter of Marie Jeanne, slave of Jean Baptiste Buart. Father unknown. Godparents: Maurice and Susanne, slaves of Widow Buart. Priest: P. Pavie.

1862. MARIE JOSEPH
(561) 20 November 1803, baptism of a Negro born 23 March 1802, daughter of Susanne, slave of Simeon Rachal. Godparents: Simeon Rachal and Elisabet Rachal. Priest: P. Pavie.

1863. CATHERINE
(561) 23 November 1803, baptism of mulatto born 29 October in this post, daughter of Magdeleine, Negress slave of Mr. Badin. Father unknown. Godparents: Jose Escoval, corporal of the 7th company of the 2nd Battalion of the La. Regiment, and Laide, Negro slave of Mr. Badin. Priest: P. Pavie.

1864. ETIENNE FRANCOIS
(561) 25 December 1803, baptism of Negro born 6 June 1803, son of Francoise, Negro slave of Mr. Metoier. Father unknown. Godparents: Pierre Victorin Metoier and Marie Therese Elisabeth Metoier. Priest: P. Pavie.

1865. MARIE
(562) 12 February 1804, baptism of a Negro born 7 August 1803 in this post, daughter of Marie Louise, slave of Mr. Palliet. Father unknown. Godparents: Celestin, slave of Jean Baptiste Buart and Marie, slave of Mr. Palliet. Priest: P. Pavie.

1866. JEAN BAPTISTE AUGUSTIN
(562) 19 February 1804, baptism of a Negro born 26 July 1803 in this post, son of Francoise, Negress slave of Francois Rouquié, *syndic*. Father unknown. Godparents: Jean Baptiste and Therese, Negro slaves of Mr. Aillot de St. Anne. Priest: P. Pavie.

1867. FRANCOIS
(562) 25 March 1804, baptism of mulatto born 15 December 1803, son of Marie, Negro slave of Francois Roquier, living at this post. Godparents: Rosaimon Chamart and Henriette Rouquié. Priest: P. Pavie.

1868. IGNACE
(562) 31 March 1804, baptism of a Negro born 15 November 1803 in this post, son of Marie Louise, mulatto slave of Mr. Metoié. Father unknown. Godparents: Dominique, slave of Francois Grape, and Genevieve, slave of Me. Gaspart. Priest: P. Pavie.

1869. CHARLES HONORÉ
(563) 31 March 1804, baptism of a quadroon born 4 November 1803 in this post, son of Marie Cilesia, slave of Mr. Metoier. Father unknown. Godparents: Francois, slave of Mr. Rouquier, *syndic*, and Marie Celeste, slave of Mr. Metoié

1870. MODESTE
(563) 31 March 1804, baptism of a Negro aged one year,

born in this post, daughter of Margueritte, slave of Jacob Lambre. Father unknown. Godparents: Joseph, slave of Mr. Badin, and Charlotte, slave of Mr. Ste. Anne. Priest: P. Pavie.

1871. MANUEL JOSEPH ANATHALIE
(563) [MARIE MANUEL JOSEPHE NATALIE DE MEZIERES]
1 April 1804, baptism of a mulatto born 22 November 1803, in this post, daughter of Marie Jeanne, mulatto slave of Mr. Athanase Demesiere. Father unknown. Godparents: Manuel Soto and Marie Victoire Brevel. Priest: P. Pavie.

1872. MARIE JEANNE
(563) 1 April 1804, baptism of a Negro born 25 June 1803 in this post, daughter of Elisabeth, slave of Pierre Derbanne. Father unknown. Godparents: Antoine, slave of [Illegible] Derbane and Marie Jeane, slave of Pommie. Priest: P. Pavie.

1873. THERESE
(564) 20 May 1804, baptism of a Negro aged 1 year, daughter of Therese, slave of Me. Veuve Jacques Fort. Godparents: Jean Baptiste, slave of Mr. Metoier and Dorothee, a free mulattresse. Priest: P. Pavie.

1874. MARIE
(564) 20 May 1804, baptism of a mulatto aged 2 months, daughter of Marie Jeanne, mulatto slave of Mr. Fonteneau. Godparents: Antoine, slave of Manuel Prudhomme, and Pelagie, slave of Me. Monginot.
Priest: P. Pavie.

1875. MARIE BRIGITE
(564) 20 May 1804, baptism of a Negro born 9 April 1804 daughter of Claris, slave of Mr. Metoier. Father unknown. Godparents: Jean Louis, Negro slave of Mr. Bidol [Vidal], and Marie Brigite, slave of Mr. Morphil. Priest: P. Pavie.

1876. JEAN PIERRE
(564) 20 May 1804, baptism of a Negro born 29 March 1804, son of Elisabeth, Negro slave of Mr. Metoier. Father unknown. Godparents: Francois, free mulatto, and Eulalie, mulatress. Priest: P. Pavie.

1877. AUGUSTIN
(565) 20 May 1804, baptism of a Negro born 8 March 1804, son of Margueritte, Negro slave of Mr. Metoier. Father unknown. Godparents: Michel Chamart and Marie Therese Metoier. Priest: P. Pavie.

1878. MARIE
(565) 27 May 1804, baptism of Negro born 4 May 1804, daughter of Adelaide, Senegal Negro slave of Mr. Lauve the younger, resident of this post. Father unknown. Godparents: Mr. Trudeau and Marie Francoise. Priest: P. Pavie.

1879. MARIE MAGDELEINE
(565) 24 June 1804, baptism of a quadroon born 20 January 1804 in this post, daughter of Genevieve, mulatto slave of Mr. Morphil. Godparents: Andre Chamart and Marie Francoise Buart, widow Monginot. Priest: P. Pavie.

1880. MARIE DENEGE
(566) 24 June 1804, baptism of a Negro born 15 April 1804, daughter of Francoise, slave of Mr. Fonteneau. Father unknown. Godparents: Louis, slave of Me. Fonteneau, and M____ [Illegible], slave of Mr. Badin. Priest: P. Pavie.

1881. ALEXANDRE
(566) 19 August 1804, baptism of a Negro born 10 April 1804, son of Magdeleine, Negro slave of Mademoiselle Lolet Demesiere, living in this post. Father unknown. Godparents: Louis Alexandre, slave of Louis Buart, and Marie Anne, sister of the infant, also a Negro slave of Mlle. Demesiere. Priest: P. Pavie.

1882. PIERRE PAUL
(566) 12 September 1804, baptism of a Negro born 2 July 1804, son of Marie, Negro slave of Henri Trichel, resident of this post. Father unknown. Godparents: Antoine, free mulatto, and Marie Ortance, free mulatto. Priest: P. Pavie.

1883. JEAN BAPTISTE
(566) 13 September 1804, baptism of Negro born 19 August 1804, son of Julienne, Negro slave of Manuel Baptiste Triche, resident of this post. Father unknown. Godparents: Louis Clausau and Margueritte, a free Negro. Priest: P. Pavie.

1884. MARIE CELESTE
(567) 13 September 1804, baptism of a Negro born 3 September 1804, daughter of Marie Anne, slave of Me. Veuve Fonteneau, resident of this post. Father unknown. Godparents: Hypolite Bordelon and Marie Celeste Bordelon. Priest: P. Pavie.

1885. MARIE ROSE
(567) 23 September 1804, baptism of a Negro born 6 June 1804, daughter of Marie Anne, Negress of Mr. Metoier. Father unknown. Godparents: Joseph and Elisabeth, Negro slaves of Mr. Rouquier. Priest: P. Pavie.

1886. LOUIS ALEXANDER
(567) 23 September 1804, baptism of a Negro born in the month of August 1804, son of Marie Anne, slave of Widow Gagne. Father unknown. Godparents: Louis Alexander, slave of Louis Buart, and Catherinne, slave of LeVasseur. Priest: P. Pavie.

1887. MARIE ARCENE /ANTY/
(567) 7 October 1804, baptism of a quadroon born in this post 24 July 1803, daughter of Susanne /Metoyer/ mulattress slave of Mr. Metoier. Father unknown. Godparents: Joseph /Metoyer/, free mulatto and uncle of the infant, and Pelagie /LeCourt/, free mulattress. Priest: P. Pavie.

1888. MARIE LOUISE
(568) 7 October 1804, baptism of a Negro born 18 July 1804 in this post, daughter of Marguerite, slave of Marie Therese Coincoin. Father unknown. Godparents: Jean Baptiste, free mulatto, and Henriette /Marie Henriette Dorothee Cloutier/, mulatto slave of Mr. Monet. Priest: P. Pavie.

1889. NICOLAS
(568) 13 November 1804, baptism in house of Mr. /Pierre/ Metoyer of a mulatto, born 25 April 1804, son of Marie Deneige, mulatto slave of Mr. Alliot de St. Anne. Godparents: Pierre /Metoyer/, a free mulatto, and Marie Anne Docras /Doclas/, a free mulatto. Priest: P. Pavie.

1890. JUDITH
(568) 14 November 1804, baptism of a Guinee Negro aged 15 years. Father and mother unknown. Slave of Manuel Prudhomme. Godparents: Guillaume and Margueritte, slave of Mr. Proudhomme. Priest: P. Pavie.

1891. ANTOINETTE
(568) 14 November 1804, baptism in house of Manuel Prudhomme, of a Guinee Negro, aged 12 years, slave of Manuel Prudhomme. Father and mother unknown. Godparents: Jacques and Marianne, slaves of Manuel Prudhomme. Priest: P. Pavie.

1892. LOUISE
(569) 14 November 1804, baptism in home of Manuel Prudhomme of a Guinea Negress, aged 12 years, property of Manuel Prudhomme. Father and mother unknown. Godparents: Charles and Francoise, slaves of Mr. Prudhomme. Priest: P. Pavie.

1893. CELESTIN
(569) 14 November 1804, baptism in home of Manuel Prudhome of a Guinea Negro aged 13 years, father and mother unknown. Property of Manuel Prudhomme. Godparents: Antoine and Maria Anne, slaves of Mr. Prudhomme. Priest: P. Pavie.

1894. MARTIN
(569) 14 November 1804, baptism in home of Manuel Prudhome of a Guinea Negro aged 17. Father and mother unknown. Property of Manuel Prudhomme. Godparents: Dominique and Clemence, slaves of Mr. Prudhomme. Priest: P. Pavie.

1895. BRUNO ATHANASE
(569) 14 November 1804, baptism in home of Manuel Prudhome of a Guinea Negro aged 15 years. Father and mother unknown. Godparents: Guillaume and Clemence. Priest: P. Pavie.

1896. LOUISE
(570) 14 November 1804, baptism in home of Manuel Prudhomme of a Guinea Negro aged 12 years. Father and mother unknown. Property of Manuel Prudhomme. Godparents: Antoine and Marie Louise, slaves of Manuel Prudhomme. Priest: P. Pavie.

1897. JACQUES
(570) 14 November 1804, baptism in home of Manuel Prudhomme of a Guinea Negro aged 14. Father and mother unknown. Property of Manuel Prudhomme. Godparents: Jacques and Marie, slaves of Mr. Prudhomme. Priest: P. Pavie.

1898. JACQUES CHARLES*
(570) 14 November 1804, baptism in home of Manuel Prudhomme of a Guinea Negro aged 14. Mother and father unknown, property of Manuel Prudhomme. Godparents: Charles and Pouponne. Priest: P. Pavie.

*/In margin slave's name is given as Jacque, but it appears as Charles in the text._7

1899. MARTHE
(570) 14 November 1804, baptism in home of Manuel Prud-

homme, of a Guinea Negro aged 15. Father and mother unknown, slave of Manuel Prudhomme. Godparents: Jean Louis and Manon. Priest: P. Pavie.

1900. FRANCOISE
(571) 14 November 1804, baptism in home of Manuel Prudhomme of a *Negrite* aged 2 years, native of this post, daughter of Marie called Manon, slave of Manuel Prudhomme. Father unknown. Godparents: Guillaume and Clemence, slaves of Mr. Prudhomme. Priest: P. Pavie.

1901. PIERRE
(571) 14 November 1804, baptism in home of Manuel Prudhomme of a Negro of 2 years, native of this post, slave of Manuel Prudhomme and son of Susanne. Godparents: Jacques and Marie. Priest: P. Pavie.

1902. MICHEL
(571) 14 November 1804, baptism in home of Manuel Prudhomme of a Negro aged 4 years, native of this post, son of Susanne, slave of Manuel Prudhomme. Godparents: Jean Baptiste and Annette. Priest: P. Pavie.

1903. LOUISE
(571) 14 November 1804, baptism in home of Manuel Prudhomme of a Negro aged 1 year, native of this post, daughter of Barbe, slave of Antoine Prudhomme. Godparents: Guillaume and Felicite, slaves of Manuel Prudhomme. Priest: P. Pavie.

1904. MARIE JEANNE
(572) 14 November 1804, baptism in home of Manuel Prudhomme of a Negro aged 2 years, native of this post, daughter of Francoise, slave of Antoine Prudhomme. Father unknown. Godparents: Guillaume and Clemence. Priest: P. Pavie.

1905. JEAN BAPTISTE
(572) 14 November 1804, baptism in home of Manuel Prudhomme of a Negro aged 4 years, native of this post, son of Marie Joseph and a father unknown, slaves of Antoine Prudhomme. Godparents: Jean Baptiste and Poupone, slave of Manuel Prudhomme. Priest: P. Pavie.

1906. MARIE CLAIRE
(572) 15 November 1804, baptism at home of Pierre Jarri on Isle a Brevel, of a Negro born in this post, aged 3 months, daughter of Constance, Negro slave

Joseph Derbane. Godparents: Jean Baptiste Derbane and Silvie Brosset. Priest: P. Pavie.

1907. ATHANASE
(573) 15 November 1804, at home of Ambroise LeComte at Riviere aux Cannes, baptism of a Guinea Negro aged 12 years. Father and mother unknown, slave of Ambroise LeComte. Godparents: Francois Davion and Marguerite Cloutier. Priest: P. Pavie.

1908. NARCIS
(573) 15 November 1804, at Riviere aux Cannes home of Ambroise LeComte, baptism of a Guinea Negro aged 10, slave of LeComte. Father and mother unknown. Godparents: Cesair Cloutie and Marie Esther Davion. Priest: P. Pavie.

1909. LOUIS
(573) 15 November 1804, at Riviere aux Cannes home of Ambroise LeComte, baptism of a Guinea Negro aged 9 years, slave of LeComte. Godparents: Athanase Lecour and Marie Robin. Priest: P. Pavie.

1910. FRANCOISE
(574) 16 November 1804, at Riviere aux Cannes home of Ambroise LeComte, baptism of a Guinea Negro aged 10 years, slave of LeComte. Father and mother unknown. Godparents: Paul Couti and Jeanne Le Roi /Juana de los Reyes7. Priest: P. Pavie.

1911. JEANNE
(574) 16 November 1804, at Riviere aux Cannes home of Ambroise LeComte, baptism of a Guinea Negro aged 12 years. Godparents: Jean Baptiste Couti and Marie Antoinette Corretor /Corretant Torres7. Priest: P. Pavie.

1912. JEANNE
(574) 16 November 1804, at Riviere aux Cannes home of Ambroise LeComte, baptism of his English Negro, a native of Natchez, aged 5 years, daughter of Herée the English Negro slave of LeComte. Father unknown. Godparents: Pierre Lecour and Marie Therese Brevel. Priest: P. Pavie.

1913. SUSANNE
(575) 16 November 1804, at Riviere aux Cannes home of Ambroise LeComte, baptism of his Negro slave, a native of Natchée, aged 4 years, daughter of Heré, English Negro slave of LeComte. Father unknown. Godparents: Silvestre Anti and Celeste Anti. Priest: P. Pavie.

1914. LOUISE
(575) 16 November 1804 at Riviere aux Cannes home of Ambroise LeComte, baptism of a Negro aged 1 year, native of this post, daughter of Marie des douleurs a slave of LeComte. Father unknown. Godparents: Jean Baptiste, free mulatto, and Genevieve, a free Negress. Priest: P. Pavie.

1915. ARCENE
(575) 16 November 1804, at Riviere aux Cannes home of Ambroise LeComte, baptism of a Negro of 15 days, native of this post, daughter of Marie des douleurs, slave of Ambroise LeComte. Father unknown. Godparents: Dominique and Clemence, slaves of LeComte. Priest: P. Pavie.

1916. MARIE
(576) 16 November 1804, at Riviere aux Cannes home of Ambroise LeComte, baptism of a mulatto, aged 2 years, native of this post, daughter of Magdeleine, mulatto slave of LeComte. Father unknown. Godparents: Augustin [Cloutier] slave of Alexis Cloutié, and Susanne, mulatto slave of LeComte. Priest: P. Pavie.

1917. MARIE
(576) 16 November 1804, at Riviere aux Cannes home of Ambroise LeComte, baptism of a mulatto aged 15 months, native of this post, daughter of Francoise, Negro slave of Alexis Cloutier. Father unknown. Godparents: Augustin [Cloutier], mulatto, and Marie Jeanne, mulatto, both slaves of Alexis Cloutier. Priest: P. Pavie.

1918. JEAN BAPTISTE OLIER
(576) 16 November 1804, baptism at Riviere aux Cannes home of Ambroise LeComte of a Negro aged 1 year, native of this post, son of Celeste, a Negro slave of Nicolas Gallien. Father unknown. Godparents: Jean Baptiste, free mulatto, and Genevieve, slave of Francois Davion. Priest: P. Pavie.

1919. MARIE
(577) 16 November 1804, baptism at Riviere aux Cannes home of Ambroise LeComte of a Negro aged 2 years, native of this post, daughter of Celeste, Negro slave of Nicolas Gallien. Father unknown. Godparents: Silvestre Anty and Marie Celeste Anty. Priest: P. Pavie.

1920. ROSE
(577)

16 November 1804, baptism at Riviere aux Cannes home of Ambroise LeComte of a Negro aged 1 year, native of this post, daughter of Marie Jeanne, Negress slave of Joseph Dupré. Father unknown. Godparents: Cesair, a Canneci Indian, and Francoise, mulatto slave of Jean Baptiste Rachal. Priest: P. Pavie.

1921. PIERRE /MISSION RACHAL/
(577) 16 November 1804, baptism at Riviere aux Cannes home of Ambroise LeComte of a mulatto, native of this post, aged 3 years, son of Francoise, mulatto slave of Jean Baptiste Rachal. Father unknown. Godparents: Athanase, free Negro, and Genevieve, free Negro. Priest: P. Pavie.

1922. MARIE ASPASIE /RACHAL/
(578) 16 November 1804, baptism at Riviere aux Cannes home of Ambroise LeComte of a mulatto aged two months, daughter of Francoise, mulatto slave of Jean Baptiste Rachal. Father unknown. Godparents: Cesair Cloutier* and Marie Athanase Davion. Priest: P. Pavie.

*/This Cesair Cloutier, or "Cesair, a Canneci" who appears in Entries 1908, 1920 and 1922 above, is probably the same individual as the Luis Ceserio who was baptized on March 11, 1788 and described at that time as *pardo* slave of Widow LeComte (mother-in-law of Alexis Cloutier). See Mills, *Natchitoches, 1729-1803*, Entry 2565./

1923. JEAN BAPTISTE /MARIOTTE/
(578) 16 November 1804, baptism at Riviere aux Cannes home of Ambroise LeComte of a free quadroon, native of this post, aged 3 years, son of Adelaide /Mariotte/, a mulattress. Father unknown. Godparents: Jean Baptiste Lecunt and Marie Francoise Leonte /LeComte/. Priest: P. Pavie.

1924. LOUIS ST. CIR
(578) 18 November 1804, at Ecords home of Widow Monet, baptism of a Negro aged 4 years, native of this post, slave of Widow Monet and son of Anne. Godparents: Charles, slave of Widow Monet, and Susanne, slave of Widow Rachal. Priest: P. Pavie.

1925. STEPHANIE
(579) 18 November 1804, at Ecords home of Widow Monet, baptism of a Negro aged 2 years, native of this post and daughter of Anne, Negro slave of Widow

Monet. Father unknown. Godparents: Colas, slave of Widow Monet, and Marie, slave of Widow Rachal. Priest: P. Pavie.

1926. CYPRIEN
(579) 18 November 1804, baptism at Ecords home of Widow Monet, of a Negro aged 2 years, son of Marie Joseph, Negro slave of Widow Monet. Father unknown. Godparents: Charles and Celeste, slaves of Widow Monet. Priest: P. Pavie.

1927. MARIE TÊTE
(579) 18 November 1804, baptism at Ecords home of Widow Monet of a Negro aged 3 years, native of this post and daughter of Marie Joseph, slave of Widow Monet. Godparents: Francois and Susanne, slaves of Widow Monet. Priest: P. Pavie.

1928. ROSE
(580) 18 November 1804, baptism at Ecords home of Widow Monet of a Negro of 3 years, native of this post, daughter of Francoise, Negro slave of Me. Monet. Godparents: Baltasar /Monet7, free mulatto, and Hortance, mulatto slave of Widow Monet. Priest: P. Pavie.

1929. PIERRE
(580) 18 November 1804, baptism at Ecords home of Widow Monet of a Negro aged 8 years, native of this post, son of Francoise, slave of Widow Monet. Godparents: Francois, slave of Widow Monet, and Marie, a free Negro. Priest: P. Pavie.

1930. MARIE LOUISE /MARIE LOUISE PERINE VARANGUE7*
(580) 18 November 1804, baptism at Ecords home of Widow Monet of a mulatto aged 4 months, native of this post, daughter of Celeste, Negro slave of Widow Monet. Father unknown. Godparents: Jean Baptiste, mulatto slave of Widow Monet, and Marie Louise /Mariotte7, free Negro. Priest: P. Pavie.

*/The manumission of this infant identifies her as the daughter of Mons. Jean Varangue. See Doc. 3127, dated 10 May 1804, in Natchitoches Parish Courthouse.7

1931. AMBROISE CECILE
(581) 18 November 1804, baptism at Ecords home of Widow Monet of a free mulatto born 15 August 1804, son of Cecile, a free mulatto. Father unknown. Godparents: Joseph Dupre and Marie Louise LeComte. Priest: P. Pavie.

1932. MARIE
(581) 19 November 1804, baptism at Ecords home of Jean Baptiste Cloutier, of a Negro aged 12 years, native of this post, daughter of Zair, slave of Louis Lambre. Godparents: Louis Lambre and Marie Anne Dupre. Priest: P. Pavie.

1933. ATHANASE
(581) 19 November 1804, baptism at Ecords home of Jean Baptiste Cloutier, of a mulatto aged <u>nine?</u> years, son of deceased Cecile, slave of Cloutier. Godparents: Pierre, slave of Jean Baptiste Cloutier, and Zaire, slave of Mr. St.Andre. Priest: P. Pavie.

1934. HONORÉ
(582) 19 November 1804, baptism at Ecords home of Jean Baptiste Cloutier, of a Negro aged 1 year, native of this post, son of Angelique, slave of Jean Baptiste Cloutié. Godparents: Bernard Rachal and Marie Zeline Cloutié. Priest: P. Pavie.

1935. FRANCOIS
(582) 19 November 1804, baptism at Ecords home of Jean Baptiste Cloutier, of a Negro of 6 years, native of this post, son of Angelique, slave of Jean Baptiste Cloutié. Father unknown. Godparents: Jean Louis Ocop /Hoppock/ and Adelaide Bricou. Priest: P. Pavie.

1936. SUSANNE
(582) 19 November 1804, baptism at Ecords home of Jean Baptiste Cloutier of a Negro aged 8 years, daughter of Angelique, Negro slave of Cloutier. Father unknown. Godparents: Jeannot, an Apelussas Indian, and Felicité, a Canneci Indian. Priest: P. Pavie.

1937. MAGDELEINE ZAIRE
(583) 19 November 1804, baptism at Ecords home of Jean Baptiste Cloutier of a Guinea Negro aged 25 years, slave of Louis Lambre. Mother and father unknown. Godparents: Jean Pierre Cloutié and Marie Louise Lambre. Priest: P. Pavie.

1938. ANTOINE
(583) 20 November 1804, at Ecords home of Mr. Gillard, baptism of a mulatto born 11 June 1804 in this post, son of Judith, mulatto slave of Mr. Gillard. Father unknown. Godparents: Rosaimon Chamart and Marie Louise Gillart. Priest: P. Pavie.

1939. MARIE LOUISE
(583) 22 November 1804, baptism at Isle a Brevelle home
of Jean de Cado, of a mulatto, native of this
post, aged 4 years, slave of Augustin Langlois
and daughter of Marie Jeanne, slave of Gaspart La
Cour. Godparents: Pierre, free mulatto, and Therese, Negro slave of Jean Baptiste Anti. Priest:
P. Pavie.

1940. JEAN BAPTISTE
(584) 22 November 1804, baptism at Isle a Brevelle home
of Jean de cado of a mulatto aged 7 years, native
of this post, slave of Augustin Langlois, son of
Marie Jeanne, slave of Gaspart LaCour. Godparents: Jean Baptiste Larenaudiere and Felicité
Lavespere. Priest: P. Pavie.

1941. PIERRE
(584) 22 November 1804, baptism at Isle a Brevelle home
of Jean de Cado of a Guinea Negro aged 10 years,
slave of Jean Baptiste Anti. Father and mother
unknown. Godparents: Pierre, free mulatto, and
Marie Therese, Negro slave of Jean Baptiste Anti.
Priest: P. Pavie.

1942. PIERRE
(584) 23 November 1804, baptism at Isle a Brevelle home
of Remi Lambre of a Negro aged 1 year, son of Angelique, slave of Lambre. Father unknown. Godparents: Michel and Therese, slaves of Remi Lambre. Priest: P. Pavie.

1943. PIERRE
(585) 23 November 1804, baptism at Isle a Brevelle home
of Remi Lambre of a Negro aged 3 years, native of
this post, son of deceased Marie Therese, slave
of Lambre. Father unknown. Godparents: Pierre
and Marie Victoire, slaves of Remi Lambre.
Priest: P. Pavie.

1944. CHARLES
(585) 23 November 1804, baptism at Isle a Brevelle home
of Remi Lambre of a Negro aged 3 years, native of
this post, son of Marie Borne, slave of Lambre.
Father unknown. Godparents: Pierre and Francoise,
slaves of Lambre. Priest: P. Pavie.

1945. MAXIMIN
(585) 23 November 1804, baptism at Isle a Brevelle home
of Remi Lambre of a Negro aged 5 years, native of
this post, son of Magdeleine, slave of Lambre.

Godparents: Pierre and Francoise Genevieve.
Priest: P. Pavie.

1946. AUGUSTE
(585) 23 November 1804, baptism at Isle a Brevelle home of Remy Lambre of a Negro of 1 month, son of Marthe, slave of Lambre. Godparents: Louis and Francoise Genevieve. Priest: P. Pavie.

1947. MARIE CLAIRE
(586) 23 November 1804, baptism at Isle a Brevelle home of Remy Lambre of a Negro of 2 years, native of this post, daughter of Magdeleine, slave of Lambre. Father unknown. Godparents: Pierre and Francoise Genevieve, slaves of Lambre. Priest: P. Pavie.

1948. JEANNE
(586) 23 November 1804, baptism at Isle a Brevelle home of Remy Lambre of a Negro aged 3 years, native of this post, daughter of Cecile, slave of Lambre. Father unknown. Godparents: Gabriel and Marie Anne. Priest: P. Pavie.

1949. MARIE
(586) 23 November 1804, baptism at Isle a Brevelle home of Remy Lambre of a Negro of 5 months, native of this post, daughter of Marie, Negro slave of Remy Lambre. Father unknown. Godparents: Michel and Marie, slaves of Lambre. Priest: P. Pavie.

1950. ROSE
(586) 23 November 1804, baptism at Isle a Brevelle home of Remy Lambre, of a Negro aged 3 years, native of this post, daughter of Cecile, Negro slave of Lambre. Godparents: Daniel, mulatto slave of Mr. Lavespere, and Marie Joseph, slave of Remi Lambre. Priest: P. Pavie.

1951. MARTHE
(587) 17 February 1805, baptism of Negro born 3 September 1804, daughter of Catherine, slave of Baptiste Triche, resident of this post. Father unknown. Godparents: Pierre, Negro slave of deceased Guillaume Chevert, and Marie, Negro slave of Mlle. Francoise Triche. Priest: P. Pavie.

1952. MARIE FRANCOISE
(587) 10 March 1805, baptism of Negro born 29 September 1804 in this post, daughter of Celeste, Negro slave of Francois Perau. Father unknown. Godparents: Francois, slave of Mr. Rouquier, the younger and Francoise, slave of Mr. Colin. Priest: P. Pavie.

1953. MARIE FORTUNAT
(587) 31 March 1805, baptism of a mulatto born 7 November 1804 in this post, son of Marie Rose, mulatto slave of Mademoiselle Demesiere. Father unknown. Godparents: Rosaimond Chamart and Mlle. Marie Felicite Demesiere. Priest: P. Pavie.

1954. HONORÉ
(588) 14 April 1805, baptism of mulatto born 10 March 1805, son of Marie Louise, mulatto slave of Mr. Metoier. Godparents: Pierre, Negro slave of Mr. Morphil, and Marie Louise, free mulattress. Priest: P. Pavie.

1955. MARIE LOUISE
(588) 14 April 1805, baptism of a Negro, native of this post, born 14 March 1805, daughter of Ester, mulatto slave of Mr. Metoier. Godparents: Maurice, slave of Mr. Paillet and Cilesie, mulatto of Mr. Metoier. Priest: P. Pavie.

1956. HONORE
(588) 14 April 1805, baptism of a Negro aged 1 year, son of Marguerite, Negro slave of Mr. Rouquier. Father unknown. Godparents: Joseph, free Negro, and Marie Anne, slave of Mr. Levasseur. Priest: P. Pavie.

1957. NOEL
(588) 14 April 1805, baptism of a Negro born 25 December 1804, son of Margueritte, Negro of Jacob Lambre. Godparents: Jean Baptiste, slave of Mr. St. Anne, and Marie, slave of Manuel Prudhomme. Priest: P. Pavie.

1958. JOSEPH RAPHAEL
(589) 15 April 1805, baptism of a Negro born 17 February 1805, son of Salis, Negro slave of Mr. Metoier. Father unknown. Godparents: Francois Benjamin Metoyer and Marie Therese Victoire Aillot de St. Anne. Priest: P. Pavie.

1959. ROSALIE
(589) 2 June 1805, baptism of a Negro aged 6 weeks, native of this post, daughter of Anne, Negro slave of Mr. Metoier. Father unknown. Godparents: Toussaint [Metoyer], free mulatto, and Anne, Negro slave of Mr. Metoier. Priest: P. Pavie.

1960. MARIE
(589) 2 June 1805, baptism of Negro aged 4 months, native of this post, daughter of Marie Jeanne, Negro

slave of Gaspart Lacour. Father unknown. Godparents: Baltasar, free Negro /J. B. Baltasar Monet_7, and Marie Jeanne, free Negro. Priest: P. Pavie.

1961. ALEXANDRE
(589) 16 June 1805, baptism of a Negro born 28 March 1805, son of Susanne, Negro slave of Mr. Morphil, native of this post. Godparents: , Alexandre, a slave of Louis Buart, and Catherinne, Negro slave of Francois Levasseur. Priest: P. Pavie.

1962. JOSEPH FLORENTIN
(590) 23 June 1805, baptism of a Negro aged 8 months, born in this post, son of Genevieve, Negro slave of Mr. Paillet. Father unknown. Godparents: Joseph, Negro slave of Mr. Rouquié, and Modeste, Negro slave of Jean Baptiste Gabriel /Buard_7. Priest: P. Pavie.

1963. SATURNIN
(590) 29 July 1805, baptism of a Negro born 9 February 1805 in this post, child of Didée, Negro slave of Louis Lamalatie. Father unknown. Godparents: Silvestre, Negro slave of Louis Lamalatie, and Marie Heleine, Negro slave of Me. Fonteneau. Priest: P. Pavie.

1964. MARIE GLORIA (CLARIS?)
(590) 22 September 1805, baptism of a mulatto aged 1 month, native of this post, daughter of Marie Euphrosine, mulatto slave of Mr. de Mesiere. Godparents: Marie Zenon /De Mezieres_7, mulatto slave of Mr. Demesiere, and Marie, slave of Mr. Demesiere. Priest: P. Pavie.

1965. JEAN LOUIS
(590) 29 September 1805, baptism of a Negro born 1 January 1805 in this post, son of Marie Anne, Negro slave of Me. Veuve Fonteneau. Father unknown. Godparents: Jean Louis, slave of Mr. Badin, and Heleine, slave of Me. Veuve Fontenau. Priest: P. Pavie.

1966. JOSEPH
(591) 29 September 1805, baptism of a Negro born 5 March 1805 in this post, son of Felicité, Negro slave of Me. Fonteneau. Father unknown. Godparents: Alexandre and Susanne, Negro slaves of Me. Fonteneau. Priest: P. Pavie.

1967. SILVESTRE
(591)

29 September 1805, baptism of a Negro born 20 June 1805 in this post, son of Adelaide, Negro slave of Me. Fonteneau. Father unknown. Godparents: Alexandre, slave of Louis Buart, and Magdeleine, slave of Mr. Badin. Priest: P. Pavie.

1968. MARIE
(591) 13 October 1805, baptism at Riviere aux Cannes home of Ambroise Leconte, of a Negro aged 12 years, native of Guinea. Father and mother unknown, slave of Jacques, called LeComte. Godparents: Athanase, free Negro, and Marie Ursule, free quadroon. Priest: P. Pavie.

1969. LOUIS
(591) 13 October 1805, baptism at Riviere aux Cannes home of Ambroise Leconte of a Negro slave of Jacques, called LeComte, native of Marlande [Maryland] in America, aged 8 years. Father and mother unknown. Godparents: Jean Baptiste, slave of Ambroise Lecomte, and Louison, Canneci Indian. Priest: P. Pavie.

1970. JEAN LOUISE
(592) 13 October 1805, baptism at Riviere aux Cannes home of Ambroise Leconte of a Guinea Negro slave of Jacques, called Lecomte, aged 15, father and mother unknown. Godparents: Pierre Capitaine, Canneci Indian, and Marie Louise, free Negro. Priest: P. Pavie.

1971. JEANNE
(592) 13 October 1805, baptism at Riviere aux Cannes home of Ambroise Leconte of a Guinea Negro aged 18 years, a slave of Jacques called Lecomte, father and mother unknown. Godparents: Jean, slave of Alexis Cloutié, and Marie Jeanne, slave of A. Cloutié. Priest: P. Pavie.

1972. MARIE
(592) 13 October 1805, baptism at Riviere aux Cannes home of Ambroise Leconte of a mulatto born 24 June 1805 in this post, daughter of Magdeleine, mulatto slave of Ambroise Lecomte. Godparents: Jean Batiste Cloutier and Marguerite Cloutier. Priest: P. Pavie.

1973. MICHEL
(592) 13 October 1805, baptism at Riviere aux Canens home of Ambroise Leconte of a Guinea Negro of Alexis Cloutier, aged 18, father and mother unknown.

Godparents: Cesair [Cloutier], a Canneci Indian, and Magdeleine, mulatto slave of LeComte. Priest: P. Pavie.

1974. ANTOINE
(593) 13 October 1805, baptism at Riviere aux Cannes home of Ambroise Leconte of a Guinea Negro aged 20 years and slave of Joseph Dupre. Mother and father unknown. Godparents: Louis, slave of Alexis Cloutier, and Francoise, mulatto slave of Jean Baptiste Rachal. Priest: P. Pavie.

1975. PIERRE
(593) 13 October 1805, baptism at Riviere aux Cannes home of Ambroise Leconte of a Guinea Negro aged 18. slave of Alexis Cloutier. Father and mother unknown. Godparents: Etienne, mulatto slave of Ambroise Lecomte, and Marie Deneige, slave of Cesair Cloutier. Priest: P. Pavie.

1976. MARIE ANNE
(593) 13 October 1805, baptism at Riviere aux Cannes home of Ambroise Leconte of a Guinea Negro aged 14 years, slave of Alexis Cloutié. Father and mother unknown. Godparents: Joseph, slave of Alexis Cloutier, and Marie Therese, slave of Athanase Le Cour. Priest: P. Pavie.

1977. VICTOIRE
(593) 13 October 1805, baptism at Riviere aux Cannes home of Ambroise Leconte of a Guinea Negro aged 14 years, slave of Alexis Cloutier. Godparents: Jean, slave of Alexis Cloutier, and Marie Jeanne, slave of Joseph Dupre. Priest: P. Pavie.

1978. MARIE DAMACINE
(594) 16 October 1805, baptism at Ecords home of Antoine Rachal of a Negro aged 6 days, daughter of Marie Anne, Negro slave of Rachal. Father unknown. Godparents: Rachal and Marie Zeline Cloutier. Priest: P. Pavie.

1979. MARIE
(594) 16 October 1805, baptism at Ecords home of Antoine Rachal of a Guinea Negro aged 14 years. Father and mother unknown, slave of Rachal. Godparents: Joseph Marie Torre and Susanne, his wife. Priest: P. Pavie.

1980. ATHANASE
(594) 16 October 1805, baptism at Ecords home of Antoine

Rachal, of a Guinea Negro aged 18 years, slave of
Rachal. Father and mother unknown. Godparents:
Narcise Rachal and Andrienne de St. André.
Priest: P. Pavie.

1981. JEAN BAPTISTE
(594) 17 October 1805, baptism at home of Widow Monet of
a Negro born 6 April 1805, son of Susanne, Negro
slave of Widow Martinau*. Father unknown. Godparents: Jean Baptiste Baltasar /Monet/, free mulatto, and Marie, free Negro. Priest: P. Pavie.

*/This name was originally written "Monet," then
Martinau was superimposed in Father Pavie's hand./

1982. JEAN
(595) 19 October 1805, at Isle a Brevelle home of Pierre
Jarri, baptism of a Negro born 29 June 1805 in
this post, son of Marie, Negro slave of Pierre Jarri. Father unknown. Godparents: Jean Delacroix
and Silvie Brosset. Priest: P. Pavie.

1983. MARIE
(595) 19 October 1805, at Isle a Brevelle home of Pierre
Jarri, baptism of a Guinea Negro aged 14 years,
slave of Jean Baptiste Latié. Father and mother
unknown. Godparents: Jean Baptiste Latié and
Marie Adelaide Latié. Priest: P. Pavie.

1984. PIERRE
(595) 19 October 1805, baptism at Isle a Brevelle home
of Pierre Jarri, of a Guinea Negro of 14 years,
slave of Jean Baptiste Latié. Father and mother
unknown. Godparents: Francois Latié and Marie
Euphrosine Frederik. Priest: P. Pavie.

1985. JEAN PIERRE
(596) 19 October 1805, baptism at Isle a Brevelle home
of Pierre Jarri, of a Negro born 29 June 1805 in
this post, son of Francoise, Negro slave of Augustin /Metoyer/, a free mulatto. Father unknown.
Godparents: Louis /Metoyer/, free mulatto, and
Marie Rose /Metoyer/, free mulatto. Priest: P. Pavie.

1986. LEGER (LEGÉ)
(596) 20 October 1805, baptism of a Negro born 1 October
1805 in this post, son of Marie, Negro slave of
deceased Guillaume Chevert. Godparents: Jacques
Plaisance and Jeanne Pero. Priest: P. Pavie.

1987. FRANCOISE
(596) 5 November 1805, baptism of a mulatto born 3 Octo-

ber 1805, daughter of Marie Anne, slave of Mr. Trudeau, captain of the La. Regiment. Father unknown. Godparents: Henry and Hortance, slaves of Mr. Trudeau. Priest: P. Pavie.

1988. MARIE JOSEPH
(596) 24 November 1805, baptism of a mulatto born 1 October 1805, daughter of Heleine, mulatto slave of Mr. Badin. Godparents: Francois and Marie, mulatto slaves of Mr. Badin. Priest: P. Pavie.

1989. MARIE GENEVIEVE
(597) 1 December 1805, baptism of a Negro born 27 October 1805, daughter of Margueritte, Negro slave of Francois Levasseur. Father unknown. Godparents: Pierre, Negro, and Marie Perine, slaves of Francois Levasseur. Priest: P. Pavie.

1990. PIERRE
(597) 10 April 1806, baptism of a Negro aged 6 months, son of Susanne, Negro slave of Mr. Aillaud St. Anne. Godparents: Pierre, Negro slave and Brigitte, also a slave. Priest: P. Pavie.

1991. TOUSSAINT
(597) 6 April 1806, baptism of a Negro aged 15 months, born in this post, son of Sophie, Negro slave of Jean Baptiste Prudhomme. Father unknown. Godparents: Francois and Marie Anne Sali, Negro slaves of Mr. Metoyer. Priest: P. Pavie.

1992. SUSANNE
(597) 6 April 1806, baptism of a Negro aged 2 months, native of this post, daughter of Marie Desneiges, Negro slave of J. B. Prudhomme. Godparents: Toussaint and Marie Anne Susanne. Priest: P. Pavie.

1993. FRANCOIS
(598) 6 April 1806, baptism of a Negro born 21 April 1805 in this post, son of Marie Jeanne, slave of Jean Baptiste Buart. Godparents: Celestin, Negro of Jean Baptiste Buart, and Ursule, slave of Mr. Aillaud St. Anne. Priest: P. Pavie.

1994. MARIE NOLET
(598) 6 May 1806, baptism of a mulatto born 27 September 1805 in this post, daughter of Marie Louise, slave of Metoyer. Godparents: Augustin, mulatto slave of Bertran Mailloche, and Marie Cilesie, a free mulatto. Priest: P. Pavie.

1995. JOSEPH NOEL ⟦DE MEZIERES⟧
(598) 6 April 1806, baptism of a quadroon born 24 December 1805, in this post, son of Marie Jeanne, mulatto slave of Mr. Demesiere. Godparents: Joseph Antoine and Marie Rose, mulatto slaves of Mr. De Mesiere. Priest: P. Pavie.

1996. MARIE
(598) 6 May 1806, baptism of a Negro aged 8 months, native of this post, daughter of Marie, Negro slave of Bertran Mailloche. Godparents: Gaspart, Negro of Louis Buart and Marie, Negro slave of Widow Lestase. Priest: P. Pavie.

1997. MARIE GRILLAU
(599) 4 May 1806, baptism of a Negro born 3 August 1805 in this post, daughter of Marie, Negro slave of Mr. Paillet. Father unknown. Godparents: Antoine Adelet and Marie Ris. Priest: P. Pavie.

1998. LOUIS
(599) 25 May 1806, baptism of a Negro of 5 months, native of this post, son of Elisabeth, slave of Pierre Derbanne. Godparents: Julien Rachal and Celeste, slave of Paul Poissot. Priest: P. Pavie.

1999. ETIENNE
(599) 25 May 1806, baptism of Negro born 2 February 1806, son of Susanne, slave of Mr. Paillet. Father unknown. Godparents: Mongineau ⟦Badin⟧, a free mulatto, and Marie Louise, slave of Mr. Rouquié. Priest: P. Pavie.

2000. FRANCOIS
(599) 25 May 1806, baptism of a Negro born last March, son of Marie Anne, slave of Henri Triche. Godparents: Francois, slave of Francoise Triche, and Francoise, a free quadroon. Priest: P. Pavie.

2001. PIERRE NOEL
(600) 1 June 1806, baptism of a Negro born 24 December 1805, son of Margueritte, slave of Marie Therese, free Negro. Godparents: Athanase, free Negro, and Dorothee, free mulatto. Priest: P. Pavie.

2002. MARIE CELESTE
(600) 27 July 1806, baptism of a mulatto aged 4 months, daughter of Marie Heleonore, Negro slave of Manuel Prudhomme. Father unknown. Godparents: Dominique, mulatto slave of Manuel Prudhomme, and Marie, Negro slave of Widow Monginot. Priest: P. Pavie.

2003. NARCISE
(600) 27 July 1806, baptism of a Negro born 26 March 1806, son of Marie, Negro slave of Louis Buart. Godparents: Eugene, slave of Julien Rachal, and Heleine, Negro slave of Louis Buart. Priest: P. Pavie.

2004. CELESTIN (CASTIN)
(600) 27 July 1806, baptism of Negro aged about 5 years, native of the post of Rapides, son of Marianne, Negro slave of Baptiste Buart. Father unknown. Godparents: Celestin, slave of Baptiste Grape, and Marie, Negro slave of Louis Buart. Priest: P. Pavie.

2005. CATHERINE
(601) 27 July 1806, baptism of a Negro aged about 2 years who was born at Couteil, daughter of Marie Anne, Negro slave of Baptiste Buart. Father unknown. Godparents: Louis Alexandre, slave of Louis Buart, and Heleine, Negro slave of Louis Buart. Priest: P. Pavie.

2006. LOUISE DESNEIGE
(601) 10 August 1806, baptism of a Negro born 13 July in this post, daughter of Marie Heleine, Negro slave of Marie Margueritte Prudhomme. Father unknown. Godparents: Antoine, free Negro, and Marie Louise, free Negresse. Priest: P. Pavie.

2007. BARTHELEMI CIFROI
(601) 24 August 1806, baptism of a Negro born at Rapides but now living in this post, son of Marie Anne, slave of Jean Louis Buart. Father unknown. Aged 7 years. Godparents: Marie Zenon, slave of Athanase Demesiere, and Felicite, Negro slave of Mr. Rouquié. Priest: P. Pavie.

2008. LOUIS
(601) 24 August 1806, baptism of Negro aged 5 years, born at Couteil, now living in this post, son of Marie Ann, slave of Jean Louis Buart. Father unknown. Godparents: Jean Louis, Negro slave of Jean Louis Buart, and Marie Louise Hiacinthe, slave of Mr. Rambin. Priest: P. Pavie.

2009. MARIE
(602) 24 August, 1806, baptism of a Negro born in this post, aged 8 months, daughter of Marie, Negro slave of Jean Louis Buart. Father unknown. Godparents: Julien, Negro of Mme. Widow Monginot, and Marie Louise, Negro of Louis Buart. Priest: P. Pavie

2010. SOPHIE
(602) 20 September 1806, baptism of a quadroon born 11 July 1806, daughter of Marie Cilesie, mulatto slave of Mr. Metoyer. Father unknown. Godparents: Francois and Marie Therese Metoié. Priest: P. Pavie.

2011. MARIE JUDITH
(602) 20 September 1806, baptism of a Negro born 5 June 1806, daughter of Francoise, Negro slave of Mr. Metoié. Father unknown. Godparents: Jean Francois and Catharinne, Negro slaves of Mr. Metoier. Priest: P. Pavie.

2012. MARIE DES DOULEURS
(602) 20 September 1806, baptism of a Negro born in August 1806 in this post, daughter of Claurice, Negro slave of Mr. Metoié. Father unknown. Godparents: Francois, mulatto of Me. Monginot, and Margueritte, Negro slave of Widow Cadet Mounion. Priest: P. Pavie.

2013. MARIE
(603) 20 September 1806, baptism of Negro born at this post in August 1806, daughter of Esther, Negro slave of Mr. Metoié. Father unknown. Godparents: Francois, mulatto of Me. Widow Monginot, and Adelaide, mulatto slave of Mr. Metoié. Priest: P. Pavie.

2014. MARIE AUGUSTIN
(603) 21 September 1806, baptism of Negro aged 3 months, son of Margueritte, slave of Mr. Rouquié. Godparents: Augustin Joseph, Negro slave of Mr. Trudeau, and Marie Jeanne, slave of Mr. Demesiere. Priest: P. Pavie.

2015. MARIE MARGUERITE
(603) 9 August 1807, baptism of a Negro aged 1 month, daughter of Marie Madeleine, slave of Mr. de Meziere. Godparents: Antoine, free mulatto, and Marguerite, a Negro. Priest: L. Buhot of Opelousas.

2016. JOSEPH LAZARE
(604) 9 August 1807, baptism of Negro aged 1 year, son of Rosalie, slave of Louis Closeau. Godparents: Joseph, mulatto, and Marie Rose, mulattress. Priest: L. Buhot of Opelousas.

2017. MARIE DES NEIGES
(604) 9 August 1807, baptism of a free mulatto, born 11 April 1807, daughter of Marianne, free mulatto. Father unknown. Godparents: Antoine and Marie, Negroes. Priest: L. Buhot of Opelousas.

2018. MARIE MODESTE
(604) 9 August 1807, baptism of Negro aged 9 months, daughter of Nanette, slave of Mr. Metoyer. Godparents: Antoine and Marie, Negroes. Priest: L. Buhot of Opelousas.

2019. MARIE
(605) 9 August 1807, baptism of a child born 7 January 1807, daughter of Isabel, slave of Mr. Metoyer. Godparents: Jean Bte. and Marie Frozine, Negroes. Priest: L. Buhot of Opelousas.

2020. FULGENCE
(605) 9 August 1807, baptism of child born 27 January 1807, slave of Mad. Pantaleon and daughter of Constance, a slave of the same. Godparents: Fois. Peraut and Marie Luecile Plaisance. Priest: L. Buhot of Opelousas.

2021. MARIE ANGELIQUE
(606) 9 August 1807, baptism of child born 9 December 1806, slave of Fois. Perault. Godparents: Jean Bte. and Francoise, Negroes. Priest: L. Buhot of Opelousas.

2022. JOSEPH
(607) 10 August 1807, baptism of child born 2 January, son of Lucie, slave of Hypolite Bordelon. Godparents: Jacques, free mulatto, and Emilie, free mulattress. Priest: L. Buhot of Opelousas.

2023. ETIENNE
(607) 10 August 1807, baptism of child born 10 January 1807, slave of Mad. Fontenot and son of Susanne, slave of the same. Godparents: Baptiste and Emelie, free mulattoes. Priest: L. Buhot of Opelousas.

2024. SUSANNE
(607) 10 August 1807, baptism of child born 4 June 1807, slave of Henry Trischel, and daughter of Eugenie, slave of the same. Godparents: Jacques and Marie Josephe, free mulattoes. Priest: L. Buhot of Opelousas.

2025. MARIE
(608) 10 August 1807, baptism of child born 8 March 1807, daughter of Jeane, slave of Mde. Fontenot. Godparents: Remond Ortolon and Marie Jeanne, free mulattoes. Priest: L. Buhot of Opelousas.

2026. MARIE AGSÉ
(608)

10 August 1807, baptism of child aged 15 days, daughter of Marie Anne, slave of Mad. Fontenot. Godparents: Baltazar /Grappe7 and Celeste /Grappe7 Free mulattoes. Priest: L. Buhot of Opelousas.

2027. CATHERINE
(608) 10 August 1807, baptism of child born 6 December 1806, slave of Mad. Fontenot and daughter of Marie, slave of the same. Godparents: Joseph, free mulatto, and Marie Jeane, free Negro. Priest: L. Buhot of Opelousas.

2028. FRANCOIS /METOYER7
(609) 16 August 1807, baptism of free mulatto born 15 January 1807, legitimate son of Francois /Metoyer7 and Margueritte /La Fantasy7, free mulattoes. Godparents: Jean Bte. and Susette Metoyer, also free mulattoes. Priest: L. Buhot of Opelousas.

2029. PIERRE METOYER
(609) 16 August 1807, baptism of a free mulatto, son of Pierre Metoyer and Perine /LeComte7, free mulattoes, aged 10 months. Godparents: Fois. Milon and Marie Louise, free mulattoes. Priest: L. Buhot of Opelousas.

2030. MARIE ANNE
(609) 16 August 1807, baptism of child aged 3 months, Negro daughter of Madeleine, slave of Fois. Bossier. Godparents: Baltasar and Marie Louise, free mulattoes. Priest: L. Buhot of Opelousas.

2031. FRANCOIS
(610) FRANCOIS
ADELAIDE
JEAN
16 August 1807, baptism of "four brute Negroes," all adult slaves of Nicolas Lauve. Francois, aged 30, whose godparents are Michel and Francoise; Francois, aged 20, whose godparents are Francois and Marie; Adelaide, aged 25, whose godparents are Joseph and Marie; Jean, aged 30, whose godparents are Alexander and Marie Anne. Priest: L. Buhot of Opelousas.

2032. SUSANNE METOYER
(610) 23 August 1807, baptism of a free mulatto born 6 February 1806, legitimate daughter of Augustin Metoyer and Agnes /Poissot7, free mulattoes. Godparents: Jn. Bte. and Marie Louise, free mulattoes. Priest: L. Buhot of Opelousas.

2033. MARIE PERINE
(611) 23 August 1807, baptism of child born 1 July 1806, daughter of Gennevieve, slave of Bte. Lemoine. Godparents: Augustin Metoyer and Agnes, free mulattoes. Priest: L. Buhot of Opelousas.

2034. AUGUSTIN
(611) JOSEF
23 August 1807, baptism of "two adult brute slaves" of Mad. Ve. Fontenot: Augustin, aged 30 years, whose godparents are Augustin and Marie, Negroes; and Josef, aged 40, whose godparents are Pierre, a free mulatto, and Pelagie Grappe, also a free mulatto. Priest: L. Buhot of Opelousas.

2035. PIERRE
(611) JACQUES
CATHERINE
23 August 1807, baptism of "three adult brute Negro slaves" of Fois. Grappe: Pierre, aged 30, whose godparents of Jacques [Grappe] and Agnes Closeau; Jacques, aged 40, whose godparents are Augustin and Celeste Grappe; and Catherine, aged 30, whose godparents are Augustin and Madeleine [Grappe], free mulattoes. Priest: L. Buhot of Opelousas.

2036. PIERRE
(612) 23 August 1807, baptism of a 30 year old slave of Jn. Bte. Buard. Godparents: Jacques Grappe and Francoise, a Negro. Priest: L. Buhot of Opelousas.

2037. TRANQUILINA SUSANA PAILLETTE
(612- 11 September 1808, baptism at Natchitoches of a
 613) [white] child born 6 July 1808 at 3 p.m., legitimate daughter of Juan Santiago Paillette, leading justice of this region and Captain and Commandant of the Artillery of the French Emperor, son of Susana Le Roy and Pedro Jorge Paillette. Mother of the child is Victoire Poisot, daughter of Luisa Cavet and Remy Poissot. Godparents: Edwardo Cesair Murphy, merchant, and Mercelite Poisot. Witnesses: Baptiste Buard, Jn. Bapte. Armand, and Joseph Tauzin. Priest: Dn. D. Vizte. Simon Gonzales de Cossio of the Holy Cathedral in the City of Mexico, Kingdom of New Spain, in absence of a parish priest.

2038. JOSE MARCELINA ARMANT [white]
(613- 11 September 1808, baptism of a child born 30 July
 614) 1808, legitimate daughter of Juan Bautista Armant,

son of Joseph Armant and Therese LeGros. Mother of
the child is Catherine Frederic, daughter of Catherine Sauvage and Philippe Frederic. Godparents:
J. J. Paillette, Justice of the Peace, and Aimee
Chelettre. Witnesses: J. Paillette and J. B.
Buard. Priest: Simon Gonzales de Cossio, Durango.

2039. MARIE MATIL
(615) 20 September 1808, baptism of a *muchachacha* /sic/.
Godparents: Andres Andele and Pelage Andele.
Priest: Simon Gonzales de Cossio of Durango.

2040. MARIA LEON
(615) 17 September 1808, baptism of child born 17 May
1808, daughter of Maria Juana, mulatto slave of Mr.
Mesier. Priest: Simon Gonzales de Cossio, Durango.

2041. JOSE GRAPPE
(616) 17 September 1808, baptism of a little boy born
3 January 1808, son of Pelagie Grap, free mulatto.
Godparents: Alexi Trich and Feliciana Triche, both
whites. Priest: Simon Gonzales de Cossio, Durango.

2042. PEDRO GRAPPE
(616) 18 September 1808, baptism of a little boy born
10 April 1808, son of Maria Joseph Tulin /Grappe/,
free mulatto. Godparents: Tulin Grap and Emelita
Tulin Grap, free mulattoes. Priest: Simon Gonzales de Cossio, Durango.

2043. MARIA POMPOSA
(617) 18 September 1808, baptism of a child born 29 March
1808, daughter of Susanna, Negro slave of Ma. Morphy. Godparents: Luis Alexandro Espinen, and Felicite Labre, a free mulatto. Priest: Simon Gonzales de Cossio, Durango.

2044. ATANACIO
(617) 18 September 1808, baptism of a child born 13 January 1808, son of Maria Pallette. Godparents:
Julian Moreno (Maximo?) and Elena Vivan, all Negro
slaves. Priest: Simon Gonzales de Cossio, Durango.

2045. JOSE
(618) 18 September 1808, baptism of child born 13 January
1808, son of Lait /Layde/, slave of David Cess
/Case/. Priest: Simon Gonzales de Cossio, Durango.
Godparents: Moximo (Moreno?) and Catarina Baden,
free mulattoes.

2046. JUAN BAPTISTA
(618)

18 September 1808, baptism of a child born 15 February 1808, son of Brigida, Negro slave of David Cese. Godparents: Jose Maria and Ysabel Cess [Case], whites. Priest: Simon Gonzales de Cossio of Durango.

2047. LOUIS JOSEPH
(619) 3 December 1809, baptism of a mulatto slave of the Murphy Succession. Godparents: Louis Josef and Louis Marie, free Negroes. Priest: L. Buhot of Opelousas.

2048. AUGUSTE   DENIS
(619) CESAIRE   DOMINIQUE
MARIE JEANNE   JOSEPH
MARIE THERESE
7 December 1809, baptism of seven slaves of Antoine Prudhomme: Auguste, whose godparents are Noel and Helene; Cesaire, whose godparents are Louis and Sophie; Marie Jeane, whose godparents are Manuel and Francoise; Marie Therese, whose godparents are Gustin and Adelaide; Denis, aged 2, whose godparents are Jean Louis and Fcoise; Dominique, aged 1, whose godparents are Henry and Catherine; Joseph, aged 2, whose godparents of Josef Bisonette and Adeline Prudhomme. Priest: L. Buhot of Opelousas.

2049. 7 December 1809, baptism of 22 slaves of Manuel
(620) Prudhomme, whose godparents are as follows:

ZENON, 20	Dominique and Marie Anne
ALEXIS	Dominique and Marie Anne
FRANCOIS	Charles and Francoise
GEORGE	Jean Louis and Marie Anne
PIERRE	Charles and Marie Anne
AUGUSTIN	Jean Na. and Marie Anne
THIBAUTH	Jean Bte. and Constance
JOSEPH	Dominique and Francoise
RIGOBERT	Jacques and Celeste
NICOLAS	Charles and Francoise
CLAIRE	Jacque and Marie Anne
ANGELIQUE	Jacques and Jeane
AGNES	Jacques and Susanne
CHARLES	Francois and Felicite
ALEXIS	Jacques and Marie Anne
HILAIRE	Jean and Manon
ROSE	Jean Bte. and Pouponne
JOSEF	Jean Louis and Marie Anne
PIERRE	Jean Louis and Marie Anne
BARBE	Jacques and Marie Louise
NICOLAS	Nicolas and Louison
ANTOINE	Antoine and Constance

2050. 8 December 1809, baptism of twelve slaves of Jean
(621) Bte. Prudhomme, whose godparents are as follows:

VALERI	Jacques and Susanne
CELESTIN	Jean Louis and Marie
ROBERT	Francois and Urusle
JAMES	Dominique and Helene
FROSINE	Baptiste and Charlotte
SARAH	Jean Bte. and Marie Jeane
ISABELE	Jean Bte. and Babet
JACQUES	Louis and Reine
FRANCOISE	Jean Bte. Prudhomme and wife
ROSE	Mr. Ste. Anne & M. Louise Buart
JEAN	Bte. and Therese
PIERRE	Athanase and Eulalie

Priest: L. Buhot of Opelousas.

2051. AUGUSTIN
(621) PHILIPPE
8 December 1809, baptism of two slaves of Aillaud Ste. Anne: Augustin, whose godparents were Baptiste and Perine, a free mulatto; and Philippe, whose godparents were Francois and Marie Jeanne. Priest: L. Buhot of Opelousas.

2052. GUILLEAUME
(622) 8 December 1809, baptism of an adult Negro of Louis Buard. Godparents: Josef and Therese. Priest: L. Buhot of Opelousas.

2053. FROSINE
(622) 8 December 1809, baptism of a mulatto slave born 15 August 1807, property of Therese KuenKuen. Godparents: Florentin /Conant/ and Susanne /Metoyer/, free mulattoes. Priest: L. Buhot, Opelousas.

2054. AUGUSTIN
(622) BAPTISTE
MARIE
8 December 1809, baptism of three slaves belonging to Doclas, a free Negro: Augustin, whose godparents are Dominique and Marie; Baptiste, whose godparents are Zenon and Reine; and Marie, whose godparents are Mago and Susanne, all slaves of Doclas. Priest: L. Buhot of Opelousas.

2055. MARIE ANTOINETTE
(623) 12 December 1809, baptism of a free mulatto. Godparents: Josef and Marie, free Negroes. Priest: L. Buhot of Opelousas.

2056. 19 December 1809, baptism of slaves belonging to
(623) Mr. Metoyer whose godparents are as follows:

    JOSEPH   Christophe and Francoise
    CESAIRE   Toussaint and Marie Louise
    JACQUES   Athanase and Jeane
    EULALIE   Alexis and Francoise
    SILVIE   Jn Louis and Francoise
    PELAGIE   Hilaire and Susanne
    PERINE   Dorsino Fort and Imelle
    OSITTE   Pierre, f.m. and Aspasie
    MARIE DESIREE   Francois and Marie Arsene
    MARIE IRENE   Pierre and Adelaide
    SUSANNE   Jean Bte. and Susanne
    PHILIPPE   Pierre and Marie Perine
    GEORGES   Florentin and Susanne
    JAMES   Colas and Louison
    ISAAC   Jn. Louis and Susanne
    BENJAMIN   Fois. and Marinette

2057. 20 December 1809, baptism at Rapides of slaves
(624) belonging to Mr. Paillet, whose godparents are as
       follows:

    GERMAIN   Jn. Jacques Lattier & Victoire Poisso
    FRANCOIS   Barthelemi and Victoire
    FLORENTIN   Joseph Tauzin & Denis Buart
    SOPHIE   Jn. Jq. Paillet & his wife
    JULIEN (JULIA?)   Charles Grenau & Adelaide Buart
    MARIE   Josef Bonnet (Bonner?) & Marie Anne
    BAZILE   Fois. Gonin & Foise Greneau
    SEBASTIEN   Bmy. Lestages & Louise Grenau
    MARIE LOUISE   Alexandre and Eleonor
    FRANCOISE   Ben Metoyer and Marie Anne Grenau
    LOUIS   Jean and Marie
    Priest: L. Buhot of Opelousas.

2058. MARIE THERESE   CARMELITE /ANTY/
(624) 21 December 1809, baptism of a free mulatto aged
       2 years, daughter of Marie /Susanne Metoyer/. God-
       parents: Toussaint /Metoyer/ and Therese, a free
       mulatto. Priest: L. Buhot of Opelousas.

2059. ANTOINE
(625) 20 December 1809, baptism of an adult Negro slave
       of Bertrand Mayoche. Godparents: Jn. Bte. Flor-
       entin /Conant/ and Marie Louise. Priest: L.
       Buhot of Opelousas.

2060. LOUIS
(625) MARGUERITE
       20 December 1809, baptism of two slaves of Marie

Therese, a free Negro. Godparents of Louis: Andre and Francoise; godparents of Margueritte: Jn. Bte. Florent[ine Conant] and Aspasie [Anty]. Priest: L. Buhot of Opelousas.

2061. JACQUES MANUEL
(625) ALEXANDER MARGUERITTE
20 December 1809, baptism of four slaves of the free mulatto, Pierre Metoyer. Godparents of Jacques: Antoine and Victoire; godparents of Alexandre: Nicolas and Marie Perine; godparents of Manuel: Manuel and Marie Francoise; godparents of Margueritte: Jn. Bte. and Aspasie. Priest: L. Buhot of Opelousas.

2062. JULIE
(626) 10 December 1809, baptism of Negro born 3 October 1809, slave of Me. Ve. Grenau. Godparents: Silvestre Buart and Marie Anne Grenau. Priest: L. Buhot of Opelousas.

2063. AUGUSTIN
(626) 10 December 1809, baptism of slave of Hippolite Bordelon. Godparents: Louis and Marie Hortense, Negroes. Priest: L. Buhot of Opelousas.

2064. MARIE EUPHEMIE
(626) 10 December 1809, baptism of slave of Me. Ve. Mongino. Godparents: Victorin Metoyer and Marie Eugenie Murphi. Priest: L. Buhot of Opelousas.

2065. MARIE CELESTE
(626) JEAN LOUIS
MARIE THERESE
10 December 1809, baptism of three slaves of Fois. Rouquier. Godparents of Marie C.: Etienne and Foise. Godparents of Jean L.: Francois and Marie des Neiges. Godparents of Marie T.: Josef Rouqui and Marie Anne Rouquier. Priest: L. Buhot of Opelousas.

2066. CHARLOTTE
(627) GILLES
[no date] 1809, baptism of two slaves of Pre. Shlater: a girl of three months, whose godparents are Francois and Anne; and a male whose godparents are Pierre amd Marinette. Priest: L. Buhot of Opelousas.

2067. JN. BTE. HONORÉ
(627) 10 December 1809, baptism of a slave of Jean Cortes. Godparents: Valentin and Pelagie Adle.

Priest: L. Buhot of Opelousas.

2068. GASPART
(627) 10 December 1809, baptism of a slave of Mr. Lestage. Godparents: Baptiste Lestage and Marie Barbe Frederic. Priest: L. Buhot of Opelousas.

2069. ADELAIDE
(627) LUCILLE
24 December 1809, baptism of two slaves of Joseph Tauzin: Adelaide, aged 8 months, whose godparents are Jn. Pre. Marie Dubois and Adelaide Tauzin; and Lucille, whose godparents are Franco. Laurent and Euphrosine Tauzin. Priest: L. Buhot of Opelousas.

2070. CHARLES
(628) JACQUES
24 December 1809, baptism of two slaves of Louis Rachal. Godparents of both are Jn. Louis and Victorine. Priest: L. Buhot of Opelousas.

2071. HENRIETTE
(628) 24 December 1809, baptism of slave of Barthelemy Rachal. Godparents: Jn. Louis and Jeanne. Priest: L. Buhot of Opelousas.

2072. 24 December 1809, baptism of six Negroes of Bte.
(628) Buart whose godparents are as follows:

JACQUES	Fcois and Marie
LOUIS	Tom and Madeleine
MARIE	Pierre and Jeane
SARAH	Jacques and Jeanne
HORTENSE	Jean Louis and Hortense
LOUISE	Gustin and Marie

Priest: L. Buhot of Opelousas.

2073. JEAN BTE.
(628) BENJAMIN
24 December 1809, baptism of 2 Negroes of Cesair Murphy. Godparents of J.B.: Celestin and Marie Francoise; godparents of Benjamin: Cesair Fontenot and Eugenie Murphy. Priest: L. Buhot of Opelousas.

2074. CELESTE
(629) MONTANARI
24 December 1809, baptism of two Negroes of Mde. Ve. Murphy. Godparents of Celeste: Cesair Fontenot and Pompose /Montenary?/; Godparents of Montanari: Marie Louis Peraut and Constance Fontenot. Priest: L. Buhot of Opelousas.

2075. HONORE
(629) 24 December 1809, baptism of a Negro slave of Me.
Ve. Fontenot. Godparents: Fois. and Marie des
Neiges, Negroes. Priest: L. Buhot of Opelousas.

2076. MATHILDE
(629) LOUISE
26 December 1809, baptism of small slaves of Mr.
Tauzin. Godparents of Mathilde: Mr. and Mde. Tauzin. Godparents of Louise: Evariste Tauzin and
Mad. Newman. Priest: L. Buhot of Opelousas.

2077. 28 December 1809, baptism of Negro slaves of Remi
(630) Lambre whose godparents are as follows:

RAIMOND	Michel and Eleonor
MARCELLIN	Paul and Denise
MARIE ANNE	Gme. and Eleonor
JEANNE	Gabriel and Marie Foise.
GUSTIN	Louis and Celeste
MARIE	Magsille and Marie Marthe
HENRY	Pierre and Francoise
DOMINIQUE	Gme. and Rosalie
ANTOINE	Gabriel and Pelagie
MAGLOIRE	Maninga and Foise.
GREGOIRE	Basile and Eleonore
MINDA	Pierre and Eleonore
CELESTIN	Fois. and Marie Louise
JN PRE	Michel and Cecile
CHARLES	Tom and Celeste
LIVONI	Mel. and Venus
MELITE	Gme. and Rosalie
JACQUES	Lindor and Venus
JEAN	Maninga and Rosalie
CHARLES	Jn. Louis and Angelique

Priest: L. Buhot of Opelousas.

2078. MARIE
(631) 28 December 1809, baptism of a slave of Louis Rachal. Godparents: Michel and Angelique, Negroes.
Priest: L. Buhot of Opelousas.

2079. JOSEPH METOYER
(631) 29 December 1809, baptism of a free mulatto born
22 November 1807, legitimate son of Joseph Metoyer
and Marie Pelagie Le Coute, free mulattoes. Godparents: *Louis Cesair /LeCourt7 and Marie Louise,
free mulattoes. Priest: L. Buhot of Opelousas.

2080. JACQUES ELOY LECOURT
(631) 29 December 1809, baptism of a free mulatto* aged
3 years, son of Barth. LeCourt and Marie Ursulle,

*See next page

a free mulatto*. Godparents: Louis Cesair /Le Court7 and Marie Louise /LeCourt7.

*/The identification of Jacques Eloy LeCourt, Louis Cesair LeCourt and their mother Marie Ursulle as a mulatto is in error. See note accompanying entry 85.7   Priest: L. Buhot, Opelousas.

2081. JEANNE
(632) 29 December 1809, baptism of a free mulatto aged 3 years, daughter of Marie Louise, free mulatto. Godparents: Josef Taure and Marie Jeane Le Roy /Maria Juan de los Reyes, wife of Joseph Torres7. Priest: L. Buhot of Opelousas.

2082. VALSIN /PHILIPPE VALSAIN DUPRE7*
(632) 29 December 1809, baptism of a free mulatto aged 4 years, natural son of Adelaide /Mariotte7. Father unknown*. Godparents: Severe Cloutier and Marie Celeste Anti. Priest: L. Buhot of Opelousas.

*/See note accompanying following entry.7

2083. MARIE D. /MARIE DORALISE DUPRE7*
(632) 29 December 1809, baptism of a free mulatto, aged 2 years, daughter of Adelaide /Mariotte7, free mulatto. Godparents: Josef Valery /LeCourt7 and Marie Louise /Mariotte?7. Priest: L. Buhot of Opelousas.

*/In 1810, Sieur Joseph Dupre, III, made a legal acknowledgement of these children as his offspring and they used his surname throughout their lives. See Philippe Valsain *vs* Cloutier, District Court Record Book 3, pp. 118-26, Natchitoches Parish Courthouse, and Gary B. Mills, *The Forgotten People* (LSU Press, 1977), 91-94.7

2084. MARIE SIDALISE /RACHAL7
(633) 29 December 1809, baptism of free mulatto aged 3 years, daughter of Marie Francoise. Godparents: Fois. Mulon and Marie Rose /Metoyer7, free mulatto. Priest: L. Buhot of Opelousas.

2085. MARIE LOUISE CLARISSE /RACHAL7
(633) 19 December 1809, baptism of a free mulatto born 5 March 1809, daughter of Marie Francoise, a free mulatto. Godparents: Jean Bte. Despallieres /Rachal7 and Marie Francoise. Priest: L. Buhot of Opelousas.

2086. MARIE SILVIE METOYER
(633) 19 December 1809, baptism of a free mulatto, legit-

imate daughter of Dominique Metoyer and Margtte. [LeComte], free mulattoes. Godparents: Jean Pre. M. Dubois and Silvie Brossé. Priest: L. Buhot of Opelousas.

2087. JEAN BTE [DOMINIQUE] METOYER
(634) 29 December 1809, baptism of a free mulatto aged 13 months, legitimate son of Dominique Metoyer and Margtte. [Le Comte], free mulattoes. Godparents: Jean Louis Rachal and Marie Robin. Priest: L. Buhot of Opelousas.

2088. MARIE ANNE
(634) 4 August 1811, baptism of a mulatto born 6 January 1810, slave of Felicite Trische. Godparents: Alexis Trische and Felicite Trische. Priest: L. Buhot of Opelousas.

2089. MARIE ARSENE
(634) 4 August 1811, baptism of a free mulatto born 6 September 1810, daughter of Madeleine, free mulatto. Godparents: Cesair and Marie Hortense, Negroes. Priest: L. Buhot of Opelousas.

2090. MARIA ELISABETE DEL SANCITISIMO ROSARIO*
(635) 15 September 1811, baptism of a mulatto slave of Mr. Sibli?, aged 17, born in "Esixsis in Berginja". Godparents: Josef Ruquier, a free *morena*, and Maria Rosa Bave, a *morena* slave of Sr. Ruqe.

2091. MARIA ANTONIA*
(635) 15 September 1811, baptism of a griffe of Mr. Cortes, aged 17, born in Baltimore. Godparents: Serafin Loren, free quadroon, and Maria Ruquier, slave of the same.

2092. MARIA TENSA*
(635) 15 September 1811, baptism of a Negro aged [Illegible], born in Baltimore. Godparents: Juan Bautista, mulatto of Mr. Ruq^e, and Maria Teresa, a dark mulatto slave of Mr. Pabi [Pavie].

2093. BLANK
(636)

*[These three slave baptisms were recorded on a scrap of paper tucked into the register. They were not recorded in the same form as that used by the other identified priests and bear no name of the priest who administered the sacrament. The handwriting is totally unlike any other in the register.]

2094. MARIE
(637) 11 August 1811, baptism of a free mulatto born 15 October 1810. Godparents: Honore Trische and Genevieve Ries. Priest: L. Buhot of Opelousas.

2095. JOSEF NOEL /JOSEPH EMANUEL DUPRE/*
(637) 13 August 1811, baptism of a free quadroon, son of Marie Adelaide /Mariotte/, a free woman of color. Godparents: Ambroise Lecomt and Eloise Dupre. Priest: L. Buhot of Opelousas.

*/See note accompanying Entries 2082-2083./

2096. MARIE LOUISE /GRAPPE/
(637) 10 December 1812, baptism of a free mulatto, aged 1 year, natural daughter of Emeline /Grappe/, free mulatto. Godparents: Cesair Grappe and Marie Jos. Grappe. Priest: L. Buhot of Opelousas.

2097. JULIEN TRISCHE
(638) 6 December 1812, baptism of free mulatto born 9 April 1812, son of Madeleine /Grappe/. Godparents: Henry Trische and Margte, a free mulatto. Priest: L. Buhot of Opelousas.

2098. VALERIN LEANDRE /METOYER or ANTY/
(638) 6 December 1812, baptism of a free mulatto born 8 March 1811, son of Susanne, free mulatto. Godparents: Jean Bte. Florentin /Conant/ and Marie Louise Metoyer. Priest: L. Buhot of Opelousas.

2099. MARIE ROSE /BALTASAR/*
(638) 6 December 1812, baptism of a free mulatto aged 15 months, daughter of Baltazar Monette and Marie Rose /Metoyer/. Godparents: Jean des pallieres /Rachal/ and Marie Louise Coinde. Priest: Louis Buhot of Opelousas.

*/Although the father of this child used Monette as his surname, Marie Rose and her brother Louis, upon reaching adulthood, used their father's given name as their surname./

2100. SUSETTE
(639) 6 December 1812, baptism of a free mulatto born 25 September 1811, daughter of Catiche, a free mulatto. Godparents: Francois Grappe and Susette Grappe. Priest: F. Magnes.

2101. MARGARITA
(639) 9 February 1813, baptism of a slave, natural child of /blank/. Godparents: /blank/. Priest: F. Magnes.

2102. LUISA
(639) 9 February 1813, baptism of slave of Samuel Davenport, natural daughter of Nansy. Godparents: Juan and Mlle. Asely Davemport. Priest: F. Magnes.

2103. MARIA SILVA
(639) 9 February 1813, baptism of a slave of Samuel Davemport, aged 8, natural daughter of Marie. Godparents: Saml. Davemport and Elaysa Keizer. Priest: F. Magnes.

2104. FRANCISCA
(640) 9 February 1813, baptism of a slave of Samuel Davemport, natural daughter of Roda, aged 6 years. Godparents: Benigno Davemport and Juliana. Priest: F. Magnes.

2105. SUSANA
(640) 9 February 1813, baptism of slave of Samuel Davemport, aged 8 years, natural daughter of Espuesta. Godparents: Gavriel and Rachel. Priest: F. Magnes.

2106. MARIA ELEYSA
(640) 9 February 1813, baptism of slave of Samuel Davemport, aged 6 years, natural daughter of Heré. Godparents: Juan and Elysa Davemport. Priest: F. Magnes.

2107. MATILDE
(640) 9 February 1813, baptism of slave of Samuel Davemport, aged 10 months, natural daughter of Emé. Godparents: Miguel Arsenega? and Sara Cayser [Keiser]. Priest: F. Magnes.

2108. MARIA ANTONIA
(641) 9 February 1813, baptism of slave of Samuel Davemport, aged 15, natural daughter of Nansy. Godparents: Nicolas and Charite. Priest: F. Magnes.

2109. JOSE ALEXANDRE
(641) 6 April 1813, baptism of slave of Marcelo Soto, aged 1 year and 1 month. Godparents: Martin Cruz and Rita Peralta. Priest: F. Magnes.

2110. LUIS ATANASIO
(641) 6 April 1813, baptism of slave of Pedro Dolet, aged [torn], nine and ½ months, natural son of [torn]. Godparents: Andres Valentin and Maria Teresa Proudhomme. Priest: F. Magnes.

2111. JOSE LESINI
(641) 6 April 1813, baptism of a Negro aged 12 days,

natural son of Laysa, slave of Pedro Dollet. Godparents: Jose Valentin and his wife. Priest: F. Magnes.

2112. MARIA TERESA
(642) 30 May 1813, baptism of child of two months, natural daughter of Laset, Negro slave of Atanasio Poissot. Godparents: Andres Bosie and Maria Franca., slaves. Priest: F. Magnes.

2113. BALTASAR
(642) 6 June 1813, baptism of the natural son of Mariean? Negro slave of Mda. Baptista Buard. Godparents: Andres Bossie and Franca. Ruquier. Priest: F. Magnes.

2114. MARIA MARGARITA
9642) /Torn/ 1813, baptism of child born 12 November 1812, natural daughter of Maria, slave of Mr. Polit Bordelon. Godparents: Agustin Beson and Maria Angela Cade. Priest: F. Magnes.

2115. LUIS
(642) 14 July 1813, baptism of slave of 15 years, property of Baptista Anti. Godparents: Jose Dervan and Maria Dervam. Priest: F. Magnes.

2116. MARIA ADOLIN GRAP
(643) 18 July 1813, baptism of child born 24 December 1812, natural daughter of Pelese Grapp, free woman. Godparents: Franco. Grapp and Maria Ortans. Priest: F. Magnes.

2117. MARIA SOLIMON GRAPP
(643) 18 July 1813, baptism of child of 3 months and 12 days, natural daughter of Maria Josefa Grap, free woman. Godparents: Franco. Grapp and Francisca Luri. Priest: F. Magnes.

2118. MARIA
(643) 18 July 1813, baptism of a slave of Atanasio Poissot, natural daughter of /torn/ _en. Godparents: Frasem and Maria Mesier. Priest: F. Magnes.

2119. MARIANA
(643) 15 August 1813, baptism of a slave of 8 months, natural daughter of Mariana, slave of Baptista Plesans. Godparents: Pedro and Maria. Priest: F. Magnes.

2120. LUIS
(643)

29 August 1813, baptism of a slave, aged 3, natural son of ___ona, slave of Manuel Proudhomme. Godparents: Franco. Mori and Maria Mori. Priest: F. Magnes.

2121. CELESTINO
(644) 19 September 1813, baptism of "a child of color," 10 months old, natural son of Juliana, Negro. Godparents: Marcelo and Agustina, colored. Priest: F. Magnes.

2122. URSULA
(644) 26 September 1813, baptism of a child of 11 months, daughter of Maria, slave of Domingo Rachal. Godparents: Cardeno and Ortans, both colored. Priest: F. Magnes.

2123. MARIA DEL ROSARIO
(644) 21 September 1813, baptism of infant aged 7 months, natural daughter of ___ria /torn/, slave of Domingo Rachal. Godparents: Jose Ruquier and Maria. Priest: F. Magnes.

2124. MARIA ROSA
(644) 2 October 1813, baptism of slave of Mr. Pavie, aged 15, "natural daughter of Rosa: *en __harlegra*". Godparents: Jose Ruquier and Emery Trudeau. Priest: F. Magnes.

2125. MARIA LUISA
(645) 3 October 1813, baptism of a slave aged ___ and a half months, natural daughter of Constancs, slave of Joseph Derban. Godparents: _____nio la Nuor /Antoine Le Noir/ and Francisca. /Entry torn/. Priest: F. Magnes.

2126. FRANCISCO
(645) 24 October 1813, baptism of a slave aged 5 months, natural son of Dolores, slave of Jn. Baptista Peraut. Godparents: Miguel Casanova and Maria Grapp. Priest: F. Magnes.

2127. JOSEFA AGUSTINA PIERNAS
(645) 5 December 1813, baptism of a child of 2 months /torn/ 6 days, legitimate daughter of Agustin Piernas and Maria Adelayda, free mulattos. Godparents: Jose Maria Carrier and Md. Margarita Verson /Robertson/. Priest: F. Magnes.

2128. ATANASIO BIEN /VIENNE/ METOYEM
(645) 13 January 1814, baptism of a child born 7 July

1813, legitimate son of Pedro Metoyem and Maria Perin /Le Comte/, free mulattoes. Godparents: Jn Btta. Florentin Metoyer /Conant/ and Laict /Layde or Adelayde/ Rachal. Priest: F. Magnes.

2129. MARIA JOSEF TEODUS
(646) /Torn/ February 1814, baptism of slave aged 9 months, natural daughter of Maria Frosin, slave of Atanasio Messier. Godparents: Jose Antoine Mesier and Maria Rosa. Priest: F. Magnes.

2130. PEDRO JOSE
(646) 27 February 1814, baptism of a slave aged 1 month, natural son of Angelica, slave of Pierre Brossie. Godparents: Pierre Loucourt and Franca. Prudard. Priest: F. Magnes.

2131. JUAN BAUTISTA
(646) 12 March 1814, baptism of a slave aged 9 months, natural son of Charlota, slave of Jose Perault. Godparents: Juan Btta. Anty and Maria Luisa Brom. Priest: F. Magnes.

2132. JUAN BAUTISTA
(646) 13 March 1814, baptism of slave, natural son of Sali, slave of Btta. Buard. Godparents: Bautista and Pelagia. Priest: F. Magnes.

2133. MARIA
(647) 13 March 1814, baptism of slave aged 1 year, natural daughter of Saly, slave of Btta. Buard. Godparents: Andres and Maria. Priest: F. Magnes.

2134. MARIA CECILIA
(646) 13 March 1814, baptism of slave aged 6 months, natural daughter of Layde, Negro slave of Francois Levasseur. Godparents: Franco. Baden and Magdalena Baden. Priest: F. Magnes.

2135. CRISTINA
(647) 13 March 1814, baptism of slave /age torn away/, natural daughter of Ete, slave of /torn/. Godparents: Nuel and Pelagia. Priest: F. Magnes.

2136. MARIA CATARINA
(647) 22 March 1814, baptism of a slave, natural daughter of Juky (Suky?), Negro slave of Ceser Fredieu. Godparents: Benjamin Dranguet and Eufrosin Tauzin. Priest: F. Magnes.

2137. JOSEFINA
(647)

22 March 1814, baptism of slave of 14 months, natural daughter of Franca., Negro slave of Joseph Tauzin. Godparents: Pierre Comper and Celeste Tauzin. Priest: F. Magnes.

2138. JOSE
(648) /torn/ April 1814, baptism of a child aged 25 months natural son of Eufrosint, a free Negro. Godparents: Jose and Dorotea. Priest: F. Magnes.

2139. JOSE MANUEL
(648) 10 April 1814, baptism of child of 2 months, legitimate son of Magsimiliano and Janot, slaves of Mr. Dorthelom. Godparents: Rafael and Maria Luisa Badem. Priest: F. Magnes.

2140. ANGELA (ANGELICA)
(648) /torn/ 1814, baptism of slave aged 14 months, natural daughter of Angelica, slave of Benjamin Metoyer. Godparents: Jose Buard and Mariana Celezi. Priest: F. Magnes.

2141. SILVESTO
(648) 10 April 1814, baptism of child of 3 months, natural son of Fanchon, slave of Mr. Metoyer, the son. Godparents: Jose and Maria, slaves. Priest: F. Magnes.

2142. IGNACIO HERRERA
(649) 12 April 1814, baptism of a free mulatto, natural son of Pedro Herrera, Spaniard, and Silva Barr, a free Negro. Godparents: Ignacio Santuche and Juana Siverino. Priest: F. Magnes.

2143. MARIA ADELAYDA
(649) 17 April 1814, baptism of a child of 5 months and 11 days, natural daughter of Frosin, slave of Cesar Morphy. Godparents: Atanasio and Maria Juana. Priest: F. Magnes.

2144. JOSE
(649) 29 May 1814, baptism of child of 5 months, natural son of Maria Juana, slave of Jn. Btta. Buard. Godparents: Moris and Susana. Priest: F. Magnes.

2145. JUAN BTTA
(649) 19 June 1814, baptism of slave born 25 April 1814, natural son of Maria Luisa, slave of Enrique Trisselle. Godparents: Juan Crux and Guadalupe Soso. Priest: F. Magnes.

2146. MARIE DAMACENA
(650) 29 June 1814, baptism of child of 7 months, natural daughter of Maria Teresa Grappa, free woman of color. Godparents: Antonio and Maria Teresa Grapp, free. Priest: F. Magnes.

2147. JUAN BTTA.
(650) 18 July 1814, baptism of child of 3 months, natural son of Elena, slave of Antonio Grillet. Godparents: Faustino del Rio and Maria Getrudis Sanchez, Spaniards. Priest: F. Magnes.

2148. JUAN BTTA.
(650) 26 July 1814, baptism of child of 3 years, natural son of Pelagia, slave of Narciso Proudhomme. Godparents: Celestino and Maria Toni?. Priest: F. Magnes.

2149. PEDRO
(650) 26 July 1814, baptism of child of 1 year, natural son of Pelagia, slave of Narciso Prudhomme. Godparents: Luis and Maria Juana. Priest: F. Magnes.

2150. FRANCOIS
(651) 26 July 1814, baptism of slave aged 3 years, natural son of Estere, slave of Narciso Proudhomme. Godparents: Pedro and /torn/. Priest: F. Magnes.

2151. RAFAEL
(651) 26 July 1814, baptism of slave aged 1 year, natural son of Estere, slave of Narciso Proudhomme. Godparents: Celestino and Maria Luisa. Priest: F. Magnes.

2152. MARIA
(651) 26 July 1814, baptism of child of 4 years, natural daughter of Sophine, slave of Narciso Proudhomme. Godparents: Luis and Maria Celeste. Priest: F. Magnes.

2153. AGUSTINA
(651) 26 July 1814, baptism of child of 8 months, natural daughter of Hise, slave of Narciso Proudhomme. Godparents: Juan Btta. and Mannet. Priest: F. Magnes.

2154. ELENA
(652) 26 July 1814, baptism of child of 7 months, natural daughter of /torn/ slave of Pierre Paillet. Godparents: Juan Btta. and Celeste. Priest: F. Magnes.

2155. MARIA LUCIA
(652) 31 July 1814, baptism of a child of 3 months, daughter of Magdalena, slave of Atanasio Poissot. Godparents: Franco. and Anes /Agnes? Ines?7. Priest: F. Magnes.

2156. FRANCISCA
(652) 31 July 1814, baptism of child of 1 year, natural daughter of Maria Ynes, slave of Mr. Bossie. Godparents: Franco. Onore and Maria Luisa. Priest: F. Magnes.

2157. DOMINGO
(652) 7 August 1814, baptism of child of 1 year, natural son of Maria, slave of Remy Lambre. Godparents: Jose Ruquier, and Margarita Buard. Priest: F. Magnes.

2158. URSIN ANDRES /DORTOLANT/
(653) 14 August 1814, baptism of a free child aged 1 month, natural son of Ramon Ortelano, white, and Magdalena Grapp, free mulatto. Godparents: Crisostomo Peraut and Pompos Montaneri Brom. Priest: F. Magnes.

2159. ATANASIO
(653) 4 September 1814, baptism of child aged 25 months, natural son of Juliana, Negro slave of Jn. Btta. Buard. Godparents: Luis Baden and Manuela Maria. Priest: F. Magnes.

2160. MARIA VICTORIA
(653) 25 September 1814, baptism of child of 1½ years natural daughter of Maria Luisa, slave of Jn. Btte. Bertelmy Rachal. Godparents: Julian and Isavel. Priest: F. Magnes.

2161. LUIS ALEXANDRO
(653) 25 September 1814, baptism of child of 5 months, natural son of Teresa, Negro slave of Joseph Luis Buard. Godparents: Nuel and Carrin. Priest: F. Magnes.

2162. PELAGIA
(654) 27 October 1814, baptism of a mulata of 2 years, natural daughter of Francisca, slave of Antonio Proudhomme. Godparents: Manuel and Cantri (Coutri?). Priest: F. Magnes.

2163. LUIS
(654) 27 October 1814, baptism of mulatto of 1 year, nat-

ural son of Elena, slave of Antonio Proudhomme. Godparents: Mr. Arsoc /Hertzog/ and his wife. Priest: F. Magnes.

2164. PEDRO
(654) 27 October 1814, baptism of a Guinea Negro aged 30 years, slave of Antonio Proudhomme. Godparents: Juan Santiago Proudhomme and his sister Maria Anrriet. Priest: F. Magnes.

2165. ANDRES
(654) 27 October 1814, baptism of a slave aged about 20 years, property of Antonio Proudhomme. Godparents: Luis and Felicite. Priest: F. Magnes.

2166. MIGUEL
(655) 27 October 1814, baptism of a Negro of about 30 years, slave of Antoine Proudhomme. Godparents: Andres and Claire. Priest: F. Magnes.

2167. JOSE
(655) 27 October 1814, baptism of a Negro of about 20 years, slave of Antonio Proudhomme. Godparents: Francisco and Maria Juana. Priest: F. Magnes.

2168. MARIA LUISA
(655) 27 October, baptism of a Negro of about 25 years, slave of Antonio Proudhomme. Godparents: Andres and Susana. Priest: F. Magnes.

2169. MARIA CHARLOTA
(655) 27 October 1814, baptism of a Negro of 30 years, slave of Antonio Proudhomme. Godparents: Francisco and Maria Teresa. Priest: F. Magnes.

2170. JOSE
(655) 27 October 1814, baptism of Negro of about 30 years, slave of Antonio Proudhomme. Godparents: Enrique and Maria Barbara. Priest: F. Magnes.

2171. JUAN BTTA.
(656) 27 October 1814, baptism of a Negro slave of Antonio Proudhomme, aged about 22. Godparents: Pierre and Sofi. Priest: F. Magnes.

2172. JUAN PEDRO
(656) 27 October 1814, baptism of a Negro slave of Antonio Proudhomme of about 30 years. Godparents: Juan Btta. and Sofi. Priest: F. Magnes.

2173. SANTIAGO
(656)

27 October 1841, baptism of a Negro of about 20 years, slave of Antonio Proudhomme. Godparents: Pierre and Maria Josefa. Priest: F. Magnes.

2174. MANUEL
(656) 27 October 1814, baptism of a Negro aged about 18 years, slave of Antonio Proudhomme. Godparents: Manuel and Agata. Priest: F. Magnes.

2175. FELIPE
(656) 27 October 1814, baptism of a Negro aged about 20 years, slave of Antonio Proudhomme. Godparents: Agustin and Teresa. Priest: F. Magnes.

2176. CELESTE
(657) 27 October 1814, baptism of a Negro of about 15 years, slave of Antonio Proudhomme. Godparents: Enrique and Susana. Priest: F. Magnes.

2177. AGUSTIN FORTUNÉE
(657) 20 November 1814, baptism of a mulatto born 15 September 1814, natural son of Popona, Negro slave of Miguel Chamard. Godparents: Andres Chamard and Artemisse Chamard. Priest: F. Magnes.

2178. FRANCISCO ORRINO
(657) 4 December 1814, baptism of mulatto aged 3 months, natural son of Adelay, slave of Domingo Davion. Godparents: Franco. Badem and Catalina Levaseur. Priest: F. Magnes.

2179. SANTIAGO
(657) 21 December 1814, baptism of a Negro aged 12 years, slave of Manuel Proudhomme. Godparents: Agustin and Maria. Priest: F. Magnes.

2180. GREGORIO
(657) 21 December 1814, baptism of Negro of 18 years, slave of Manuel Proudhomme. Godparents: Btta. and Maria. Priest: F. Magnes.

2181. ALEXANDRO
(658) 21 December 1814, baptism of slave of Manuel Proudhomme, aged 10 years. Godparents: Btta. and Nanette. Priest: F. Magnes.

2182. FELIPE
(658) 21 December 1814, baptism of Negro aged 3 years, slave of Manuel Proudhomme, natural son of Barvara, slave of the same. Godparents: Santiago and Francisca. Priest: F. Magnes.

2183. PABLO
(658) 21 December 1814, baptism of slave aged 12 years, property of Manuel Proudhomme. Godparents: Francisco and Sophy. Priest: F. Magnes.

2184. ANDRES
(658) 21 December 1814, baptism of a Negro of 11 years, slave of Manuel Prudhomme. Godparents; Franco. and Maria Juana. Priest: F. Magnes.

2185. MARIA FANNII
(658) 21 December 1814, baptism of slave of 2 years, natural daughter of Rosa, slave of Manuel Proudhomme. Godparents: Luis and Maria. Priest: F. Magnes.

2186. MARIA JUANA
(659) 21 December 1814, baptism of slave aged 1 year, natural daughter of Anis /Agnes/, slave of Manuel Proudhomme. Godparents: Agustin and Maria. Priest: F. Magnes.

2187. ROSA
(659) 21 December 1814, baptism of slave aged 2 years, natural daughter of Maria Luisa, slave of Manuel Proudhomme. Godparents: Miguel and Nanet. Priest: F. Magnes.

2188. MARIA ONET /ANNETTE?/
(659) 21 December 1814, baptism of slave aged 8 months, natural daughter of Maria Luisa, slave of Manuel Proudhomme. Godparents: Agustin and Constans. Priest: F. Magnes.

2189. MARIA ASELI
(659) 31 December 1814, baptism of slave born 18 May 1814, natural daughter of Maria Teresa Morphy /sic -- Maria Teresa, slave of Mr. Morphy?/. Godparents: Evariste Lauve and Victoria Selesta Tauzen. Priest: F. Magnes.

2190. ATANACIO
(660) 1 January 1815, baptism of child of 7 months, natural son of Jana, slave of Madama Morphy. Godparents: Peoro /Veoro?/ and Maria. Priest: F. Magnes.

2191. LUIS PHELIPE
(660) 8 January 1815, baptism of child of 4 months, natural son of Genoveve, slave of Francisco Rouquierre the son. Godparents: Atanasio and Pompose. Priest: F. Magnes.

2192. AGATA
(660) 27 January 1815, baptism of 8 month old child, natural daughter of Sophy, Negro slave of Jn. Btta. Proudhomme. Godparents: Famme and Rosalia, both Negroes. Priest: F. Magnes.

2193. AGUSTIN
(660) 27 January 1815, baptism of a child of 1 year, natural son of the Negro Froisein, slave of Jn. Btta. Proudhomme. Godparents: Jn. Btta. and Maria Juana, both colored. Priest: F. Magnes.

2194. DOMINGO
(660) 27 January 1815, baptism of a Negro of 6 months, natural son of Laide, Negro slave of Jn. Btta. Ailhaud Ste. Anne. Godparents: Domingo and Rosalia, both colored. Priest: F. Magnes.

2195. CESSERRE
(660) 27 January 1815, baptism of a Negro of 7 months, natural son of Susana, Negro slave of Jn. Btta. Ailhaud Ste. Anne. Godparents: Jn. Btte. and Maria, both colored. Priest: F. Magnes.

2196. MARIA
(660) 27 January 1815, baptism of a Negro of 11 months, natural daughter of Francisca, slave of Teresa Coincoin, a free Negro. Godparents: Francois and Ma. Arsin. Priest: F. Magnes.

2197. JOSE IGNACIO
(661) 30 January 1815,*baptism of a mulatto child of 9 months, natural son of Maria Teresa, Negro slave of Luis Bartelmil Rachal. Godparents: Jose Ignacio Turret and Dlle. Artamil. Priest: F. Magnes.

2198. JOSE
(661) 30 January 1815, *baptism of a Negro of 6 months, natural son of Angelica, slave of Luis Bartelmil Rachal. Godparents: Carlos and Marie, both colored. Priest: F. Magnes.

2199. FRANCISCO
(661) 30 January 1815, *baptism of Negro of 4 years, natural son of Charlot, slave of Domingo Rachal. Godparents: Santiago and Maria Luisa, both colored. Priest: F. Magnes.

*This series of baptisms is prefaced by the note that they were performed at the Rivière aux Cannes home of Alexis Cloutier.

2200. CYPRIANO
(662) 30 January 1815, *baptism of Negro of 3 months, natural son of Bresit [Brigitte?], slave of Domingo Rachal. Godparents: Jn. Btte. and Mariana, both colored. Priest: F. Magnes.

2201. CIRIACO
(661) 30 January 1815, *baptism of Negro of 3 years, natural son of Breset [Brigitte?], slave of Domingo Rachal. Godparents: Luis and Leonor, both colored. Priest: F. Magnes.

2202. LUIS FERMIN
(661) 30 January 1815, *baptism of a Negro aged 3½ years, natural son of Celeste, slave of Bertelmil [Le] Court. Godparents: Pierre Brosai and Luise [Le] Court. Priest: F. Magnes.

2203. MARIE MELIAC BARBARA
(661) 30 January 1815, *baptism of a Negro aged 2 years, natural daughter of Celeste, slave of Bertelmil [Le] Court. Godparents: Dufra Dupré and Maria Barvara [Le] Court. Priest: F. Magnes.

2204. MARIA FRANCISCA
(662) 1 February 1815, *baptism of a Negro of 1 month, natural daughter of Nanet, slave of Pierre Dervan, Jr. Godparents: Francisco and Susana, both colored. Priest: F. Magnes.

2205. MARCELITA
(662) 1 February 1815, *baptism of a Negro of 3 years, natural daughter of Nanet, slave of Pierre Dervan, Jr. Godparents: Valery Anty and Francisco Vrevel [Brevel]. Priest: F. Magnes.

2206. FRANCISCO
(662) 1 February 1815, *baptism of a Negro of 15 years, slave of Pierre Dervan, Jr. Godparents: Francisco and Denis. Priest: F. Magnes.

2207. JUAN
(662) 1 February 1815, *baptism of a Negro of 18 years, slave of Narcisco Proudhomme. Godparents: Btta. and Susana, colored. Priest: F. Magnes.

*This series of baptisms is prefaced by the note that they were performed at the Rivière aux Cannes home of Alexis Clouiter.

2208. MARIA SOPHY
(662) 1 February 1815, *baptism of a Negro aged 16 years, slave of Narcisco Proudhomme. Godparents: Franco and Clemencia. Priest: F. Magnes.

2209. JOSE SIORS
(662) 1 February 1815, *baptism of a Negro aged 17 years, slave of Narcisco Proudhomme. Godparents: Agustin and Juana Vici___. Priest: F. Magnes.

2210. JUAN POMPER /POMPEY?/
(662) 1 February 1815, *baptism of a Negro aged 22, a slave of Narciso Proudhomme. Godparents: Alexi Cloutierre and Margarita Cloutierre. Priest: F. Magnes.

2211. ENRIQUE
(662) 1 February 1815, *baptism of a Negro aged 14 years, slave of Narcisco Proudhomme. Godparents: Pierre Dervanne and Maria Francisca Vrevel /Brevel/. Priest: F. Magnes.

2212. MANUEL
(662) 1 February 1815, *baptism of a Negro aged 21 years, slave of Narcisco Proudhomme. Godparents: Jose Guisarnac and Maria Rovin. Priest: F. Magnes.

2213. SANTIAGO
(662) 1 February 1815, *baptism of Negro aged 24, slave of Francisco Davion. Godparents: Bautista and Susana, both colored. Priest: F. Magnes.

2214. MARIA DIVIN
(662) 1 February 1815, *baptism of a Negro aged 4, natural daughter of Maria Luisa, slave of Jn. Btte. Anty. Godparents: Meles Anty and Melin Rachal. Priest: F. Magnes.

2215. BASILIO
(662) 1 February 1815, *baptism of a child of 10 months, natural son of Maria, Negro slave of Jn. Btta. Anty. Godparents: Cenon and Maria Anes, colored. Priest: F. Magnes.

2216. AGUSTIN
(662) 1 February 1815, *baptism of a child of 10 months, natural son of Maria Luisa, slave of Jn. Btte. Anty. Godparents: Michel Rachal and Victoria

*This series of baptisms is prefaced by the note that they were performed at the Rivière aux Cannes home of Alexis Cloutier.

2217. MARIE DORALISE
(663) 3 February 1815, *baptism of a child of 3 months, natural daughter of Sirene, Negro slave of Ambrosio Le Compt. Godparents: Domingo and Me. Jeanne, both colored. Priest: F. Magnes.

2218. MARIA ROSA
(663) 3 February 1815, *baptism of child of 2 years, natural daughter of Maria Dolores, slave of Ambrosio LeCompt. Godparents: Luis V. and Me. Popon, both colored. Priest: F. Magnes.

2219. MARIE MAUSIL /MARCEL?/
(663) 3 February 1815, *baptism of child of 1 year, natural daughter of Ma. Dolores, slave of Ambrosio LeCompt. Godparents: Francisco and Agustina, both colored. Priest: F. Magnes.

2220. MARIA JUDIC
(663) 3 February 1815, *baptism of a child of 1 month, natural daughter of Marie Orosil, slave of Ambrosio LeCompt. Godparents: Jn Btte Cloutierre and Me. Adelle Proudhomme, whites. Priest: F. Magnes.

2221. MARIE ASENT
(663) 3 February 1815, *baptism of child of 1 year, natural daughter of Marie Jeanne, Negro slave of Ambrosio LeCompt. Godparents: Agustin and Me. Laie. Priest: F. Magnes.

2222. MARIE BEQUE /BECKY/
(663) 3 February 1815, *baptism of child of 4 years, natural daughter of Dayna /Dianh?/, slave of Ambrosio LeCompt. Godparents: Dorsino and Pompon, colored. Priest: F. Magnes.

2223. FRANCISCO
(663) 3 February 1815, *baptism of child of 2 years, natural son of Dayna, slave of Ambrosio LeCompt. Godparents: Alexi and Jeanne, colored. Priest: F. Magnes.

2224. ATANASIO
(663) 3 February 1815, *baptism of child of 2 months, natural son of Daynaa, slave of Ambrosio LeCompt. Godparents: Atanasio and Me. Jenebelle. Priest: F. Magnes.

*This series of baptisms is prefaced by the note that they were performed at the Riviere aux Cannes home of Alexis Cloutier.

2225. ENRIQUE
(663) 3 February 1815, *baptism of Negro aged 18 years, slave of Ambrosio LeCompt. Godparents: Josef and Crée. Priest: F. Magnes.

2226. MARIE SALY
(663) 3 February 1815, *baptism of Negro aged 21 years, natural daughter of Rosa, Negro slave of Ambrosio LeCompt. Godparents: Balsem and Me. Eluas. /Eloise?/. Priest: F. Magnes.

2227. ME. DAYNA /DINAH?/
(663) 3 February 1815, *baptism of Negro aged 22 years, slave of Ambrosio LeCompt. Godparents: Jeann and Etienne. Priest: F. Magnes.

2228. JN. BTTE
(663) 3 February 1815, *baptism of English Negro aged 15 years, slave of Jn Btte. LeCompt. Godparents: Agustin and Adelaye, both colored. Priest: F. Magnes.

2229. MARIE NANET
(663) 3 February 1815, *baptism of child of 5 years, natural daughter of Jeanne, Negro slave of Jn. Btte. LeCompt. Godparents: Guasinton /Washington/ and Dolores. Priest: F. Magnes.

2230. MARIE ORTANS
(663) 3 February 1815, baptism of child of 3 years, natural daughter of Janne, Negro slave of Jn Btte. LeCompt. Godparents: Joseph and Marie Bor. Priest: F. Magnes.

2231. MARIE CATARINA
(664) 3 February 1815, *baptism of child of 5 years, natural daughter of Herée, Negro slave of Jn Bte. LeCompte. Godparents: Pierre and Jeanne. Priest: F. Magnes.

2232. JN BTTE. CLEMAN
(664) 3 February 1815, *baptism of a mulatto aged 6, natural son of Jeanne, slave of Jn Btte LeCompt. Godparents: Jn Btte. Cloutierre and Me. Oresin Gallien, whites. Priest: F. Magnes.

2233. MAGDALENA
(664) 3 February 1815, *baptism of a child of 2 years,

*This series of baptisms is prefaced by the note that they were performed at the Rivière aux Cannes home of Alexis Cloutier.

natural daughter of Marta, Negro slave of Alexi Cloutierre. Godparents: Michel Dervan and Me. Estasie Davion, whites. Priest: F. Magnes.

2234. MARIE EMILIANA
(664) 3 February 1815, *baptism of a child of 3 years, natural daughter of Susana, Negro slave of Alexi Cloutier. Godparents: Manuel and Francisca, both colored. Priest: F. Magnes.

2235. JOSE ECHEN /ETIENNE7
(664) 3 February 1815, *baptism of child of 1 year, natural son of Susana, Negro slave of Alexi Cloutier. Godparents: Luis and Clemencia, both colored. Priest: F. Magnes.

2236. FRANCISCO
(664) 3 February 1815, *baptism of a child of 1 year, natural son of Jeanne, Negro slave of Alexi Cloutier. Godparents: Andres and Francisca, colored. Priest: F. Magnes.

2237. LUIS
(664) 3 February 1815, *baptism of a child of 7 months, natural son of Jeanne, Negro slave of Alexi Cloutierre. Godparents: Atanasio and Me. Luisa, both colored. Priest: F. Magnes.

2238. FRANCISCO
(664) 3 February 1815, *baptism of a child of 7 years, natural son of Rechil, Negro slave of Alexi Cloutierre. Godparents: Antonio and Celeste, both colored. Priest: F. Magnes.

2239. MARIE CONSTANCE
(664) 3 February 1815, *baptism of a child of 10 months, natural daughter of Nanse, Negro slave of Alexi Cloutierre. Godparents: Pierre and Me. Teresa, both colored. Priest: F. Magnes.

2240. JOSE LUISET
(664) 3 February 1815, *baptism of child of 3 years, Negro slave of Rechil, Negro slave of Alexi Cloutierre. Godparents: Jn. Btte. and Ma. Rosa, both colored. Priest: F. Magnes.

2241. SANTIAGO
(664) 3 February 1815, *baptism of a Negro of 23 years,

*This series of baptisms is prefaced by the note that they were performed at the Rivière aux Cannes home of Alexis Cloutier.

slave of Alexis Cloutier. Godparents: Manuel and Francisca, both colored. Priest: F. Magnes.

2242. MARIA MARIANA
(664) 3 February 1815, *baptism of a Negro of 35 years, slave of Alexi Cloutier. Godparents: Valery Anty and Ma. Aspasi [Anty?], whites. Priest: F. Magnes.

2243. MARIA FANAI
(665) 4 February 1815, baptism at Isle Brevelle of a child of 4 years, natural daughter of Banée, slave of Mda. Magdalena, widow of Bertelmil Rachal. Godparents: Jn Btte. Ignacio [Anty?] and Mlle. Frausin [Rachal?], whites. Priest: F. Magnes.

2244. MARIA URSIN
(665) 4 February 1815, baptism at Isle Brevelle of child of 7 years, natural daughter of Banée, Negro slave of Mda. Magdalena, widow of Bertelmil Rachal. Godparents: Domingo and Suasin. Priest: F. Magnes.

2245. NICOLAS
(665) 4 February 1815, baptism at Isle Brevelle of child of 3 years, natural son of Banée, slave of Mda. Magdalena, widow of Bertelmil Rachal. Godparents: Ursen Rachal and Me. Odis Rachal. Priest: F. Magnes.

2246. AGUSTIN
(665) 4 February 1815, baptism at Isle Brevelle of child of 2 months, natural son of Bané, slave of Mda. Magdalena, widow of Bertelmil Rachal. Godparents: Luis and Me. Nies. Priest: F. Magnes.

2247. MARIE TRANQUILIN
(665) 4 February 1815, baptism at Isle Brevelle of child of 2 years, natural daughter of Ortans, slave of Santiago LaCas. Godparents: Pierre Lemoin and Me. Delfine Dervan, whites. Priest: F. Magnes.

2248. JN BTTE
(665) 4 February 1815, baptism at Isle Brevelle of child of 3 years, natural son of Ortans, slave of Santiago Lacas. Godparents: Franco. Ferans [Llorens?] and Marcelita Dupree, whites. Priest: F. Magnes.

2249. LEANDRO
(665) 4 February 1815, baptism at Isle Brevelle of child

*This series of baptisms is prefaced by the note that they were performed at the Rivière aux Cannes home of Alexis Cloutier.

of 5 years, natural son of Mariana, slave of Santiago LaCas. Godparents: Ignacio Anty and Victoria, whites. Priest: F. Magnes.

2250. ALEXANDRO
(665) 4 February 1815,*baptism of child of 3 years, natural son of Mariano, slave of Santiago LaCas. Godparents: Veles /Melice/ Anty and Emely Rachal, whites. Priest: F. Magnes.   *At Isle Brevelle.

2251. FAVIAN
(665) 4 February 1815,*baptism of child of 2 years, natural son of Maria, slave of Jn. Btte. Lattierre. Godparents: Lestan and Me. Aselin Langois, whites. Priest: F. Magnes.   *At Isle Brevelle.

2252. MARIA ANRRIET
(665) 4 February 1815, baptism at Isle Brevelle of a mulatto of 2 years, natural daughter of Me. Surron, Negro slave of Jn. Btte. Lattierre. Godparents: Agustin Metoyer, free man of color, and Me. Jean, colored. Priest: F. Magnes.

2253. JOSE DORSINO
(665) 4 February 1815, baptism at Isle Brevelle of child of 1 month, Negro son of Maria, slave of Jn Btte. Lattierre. Godparents: Jn Btte. Metoyer and Me. Luisa, free people of color. Priest: F. Magnes.

2254. MARIA FANY
(665) 4 February 1815, baptism at Isle Brevelle of child of 10 years, natural daughter of Francisca, Negro slave of Agustin Langois. Godparents: Jose Lattierre, Jr. and Me. Carmelita Langois, whites. Priest: F. Magnes.

2255. MANUEL
(666) 4 February 1815, baptism at Isle Brevelle of mulatto of 6 years, natural son of Magdalena, Negro slave of Francisco Lavespere. Godparents: Jn Btte. Lattierre and Ma. Odis Rachal. Priest: F. Magnes.

2256. JN BTTE
(666) 4 February 1815, baptism at Isle Brevelle of child of 6 years, natural son of Jeane Bierre, Negro slave of Agustin Langois. Godparents: Sufiere /Severe/ Langois and Me. Asely, whites. Priest: F. Magnes.

2257. MARIA ROSA
(666)

4 February 1815, baptism at Isle Brevelle of child
of 1 month, natural daughter of Maria July, Negro
slave of Francisco Lattierre. Godparents: Jose
Medina and Josefa Adlee. Priest: F. Magnes.

2258. FRANCISCO BASIEM
(666) 4 February 1815, baptism at Isle Brevelle of child
of 1½ months, Negro son of Victoria, slave of Benjamin Metoyer. Godparents: Jn Btte. and Nanet.
Priest: F. Magnes.

2259. MARIA LUISA
(666) 4 February 1815, baptism at Isle Brevelle of child
of 2 months, mulatto daughter of Maria Celesi, Negro slave of Victorem Metoyer, fils. Godparents:
Michel and Me. Louise, colored. Priest: F. Magnes.

2260. MARIA ARTEMIS
(666) 4 February 1815, baptism at Isle Brevelle of mulatto of 6 months, natural daughter of Felicitée,
slave of Mr. Metoyer, Sr. Godparents: Francisco
and Maria, both colored. Priest: F. Magnes.

2261. MARIE MAGDALENE
(666) 12 February 1815, baptism of English Negro aged
about 40 years, after examining her in principles
of the Catholic faith. Godparents: Francisco Tousin and Me. Luisa, both colored, and all slaves
of Francois Rouquier. Priest: F. Magnes.

2262. FRANCOIS MONSINEAU
(666) 12 February 1815, baptism of child of 1 year, natural son of Agata, slave of Jn Btte. Buard. Godparents: "Francois and Marcelita, mulatto, both
colored." Priest: F. Magnes.

2263. MARIA SEDALIS
(666) 12 February 1815, baptism of a child of 1 month
and 8 days, natural daughter of Francisca, slave
of Dominique Davion. Godparents: Celestino Bernard and Marie Teresa Davion. Priest: F. Magnes.

2264. MARIE LOUISE
(667) 27 February 1815, baptism of a mulatto born 25
March 1814, and said to be free by her master.
Infant is natural daughter of Maria Juana, a slave
of Francisco Tris. Godparents: Miguel and Mariana, both colored. Priest: F. Magnes.

2265. VICTOR BADEN
(667) 12 March 1815, baptism of a free mulatto, natural

son of Elena Baden, free. Godparents: Pedro and Catalina Baden, both col. Priest: F. Magnes.

2266. FRANCOIS
(667) 26 March 1815, baptism of Negro slave of Mr. Rouquie. Godparents: Francois and Marie Louise, both colored. Priest: F. Magnes.

2267. MARIE JEANNE
(667) 26 March 1815, baptism of a slave aged 4 months, natural daughter of Maneau, slave of Francois Grappe. Godparents: Valerin and Celeste, both free people of color. Priest: F. Magnes.

2268. VALSEM
(667) 13 April 1815, baptism of child of 1 year, natural son of Susanne, slave of Mda. Fonteneau. Godparents: Jn Btte. Tris and Marie Terese Fonteneau, whites. Priest: F. Magnes.

2269. ASPASI
(668) 14 April 1815, baptism of child born 25 January 1815, natural daughter of Laied, slave of Mda. Fonteneau. Godparents: Jn Btte. Agustan and Elena, free people of color. Priest: F. Magnes.

2270. FRANCISCO
(668) 14 April 1815, baptism of child born 17 September 1814, natural son of Isabel, slave of Dlle. Marcelite Poisot. Godparents: Jose LaVigne and Marie Louise, free people of color. Priest: F. Magnes.

2271. FRANCOIS
(668) 14 April 1815, baptism of child born 8 September 1814, natural son of Nana, slave of Bertelmil Rachal. Godparents: Pierre and Marie Margarite, colored. Priest: F. Magnes.

2272. PIERRE
(668) 14 April 1815, baptism of child born 18 September 1814, natural son of Marie Ros, slave of Mr. Pallett. Godparents: Pedro and Luisa, both colored. Priest: F. Magnes.

2273. MARIE LOUISE
(668) 14 April 1815, baptism of a child aged 1½ years, natural son of July, slave of Pierre Slecttre. Godparents: Agustin and Marie Louise, both col. Priest: F. Magnes.

2274. MARIE LOUISE
(668)

19 April 1815, baptism of child born 28 September 1814, natural daughter of Pelagie, slave of Francois Levaseur. Godparents: Bertelmy and Perin, both colored. Priest: F. Magnes.

2275. TERESE
(668) 23 April 1815, baptism of child of 3 years, natural daughter of Alesy, Negro slave of Agustin Piernas. Godparents: Agustin and Terese, both colored. Priest: F. Magnes.

2276. CARMELITA
(668) 23 April 1815, baptism of child of 5 years, natural daughter of Alesy, Negro slave of Agustin Piernas. Godparents: Santiago and Carmelita, both colored. Priest: F. Magnes.

2277. JN BTTE.
(668) 23 April 1815, baptism of child aged 5 years, natural son of Charlot, slave of Francois Llorens. Godparents: Melansont and July, both colored. Priest: F. Magnes.

2278. URSULA
(668) 23 April 1815, baptism of child of 4 years, natural daughter of Charlot, slave of Francois Llorens. Godparents: Jose Laflore and Ursula. Priest: F. Magnes.

2279. MARIA MAGDALENA
(669) 13 May 1815, baptism of child of 10 months, natural daughter of Fany, slave of Louis Lamalaty. Godparents: Simeon and Mariana, both colored. Priest: F. Magnes.

2280. BALTASAR
(669) 23 April 1815, baptism of child of 4 years, natural son of Celesy, slave of Widow Jn Btta. Grappe. Godparents: Francois Grappe and Vely. Priest: F. Magnes.

2281. LOUIS FANO
(669) 21 May 1815, baptism of child of 4 months, natural son of Marie Louise, slave of Jeann Louis Buard. Godparents: Louis and Marie Magdalenne, both colored. Priest: F. Magnes.

2282. JN BTTE
(669) 28 May 1815, baptism of child of 2 months, natural son of Marianne, slave of Mr. Rouquiere, Sr. Godparents: Jn. Btte. and Susanne, both colored. Priest: F. Magnes.

2283. SANSON /SAMPSON?/
(669) 6 June 1815, baptism of a child of 2 months, natural son of Emé, slave of Samuel Davemport. Godparents: Isac and Maria, both colored. Priest: F. Magnes.

2284. BENJAMIN
(669) 6 June 1815, baptism of child of 2 months, natural son of Luisa, slave of Samuel Davemport. Godparents: George and Rachel, both colored. Priest: F. Magnes.

2285. THOMAS
(669) 6 June 1815, baptism of child of 3 months, natural son of Heré, slave of Samuel Davemport. Godparents: Estevan and Eme, both colored. Priest: F. Magnes.

2286. JOSE
(669) 6 June 1815, baptism of child of 2½ years, natural son of Maria, slave of Samuel Davemport. Godparents: Carlos and Charlota, both colored. Priest: F. Magnes.

2287. LIDIA
(669) 6 June 1815, baptism of child of 2 years, natural daughter of Judée, slave of Samuel Davemport. Godparents: Isac and Charite, both colored. Priest: F. Magnes.

2288. MARIA CASIA
(670) 6 June 1815, baptism of slave of 12 years, natural daughter of Judée, slave of Samuel Davemport. Godparents: Carlos and Maria Antonia, all colored. Priest: F. Magnes.

2289. MARIE MINERVA
(670) 6 June 1815, baptism of child of 6 years, natural daughter of Judée, slave of Samuel Davemport. Godparents: Benigno Davemport and Pelagie Keiser. Priest: F. Magnes.

2290. GUILLERMO
(670) 6 June 1815, baptism of child of 8 years, natural son of Judée, slave of Samuel Davemport. Godparents: Roverto and Judée, all colored. Priest: F. Magnes.

2291. MARIA BAYNE
(670) 6 June 1815, baptism of child of 10 years, slave of Samuel Davemport. Godparents: Juan Dost and

Maria Sara Keiser, whites. Priest: F. Magnes.

2292. FRANCISCA
(670) 8 June 1815, baptism of child born 10 March 1807, natural daughter of Mariana, slave of Louis Metoyer, free mulatto. Godparents: Magsil /Metoyer/ and Aspasie /Anty/, free mulattoes. Priest: F. Magnes.

2293. MARIE FELICITE
(670) 8 June 1815, baptism of child born 22 March 1808, natural daughter of Maria, slave of Louis Metoyer, free mulatto. Godparents: Jn Btte. Florantin Co-/Conant/, free mulatto, and Susana, free mulatto. Godparents: F. Magnes.

2294. ONORE
(670) 8 June 1815, baptism of child born 10 August 1809 natural son of Maria, slave of Louis /Metoyer/, free mulatto. Godparents: Jn. Btte. Florantin /Conant/ and Susanne, free mulattoes. Priest: F. Magnes.

2295. MICHEL
(670) 8 June 1815, baptism of child born 20 January 1810, natural son of Mariana, slave of Dominique Metoyer, free mulatto. Godparents: Jn. Btte. and Pompose, free mulattoes. Priest: F. Magnes.

2296. JOSE HILARIO
(671) 8 June 1815, baptism of child born 15 February 1813, natural son of Maria, slave of Dominique Metoyer, free mulatto. Godparents: Francois and Marie Loise, free mulattoes. Priest: F. Magnes.

2297. JOSE SENSIR /St. Cyr?/
(671) 8 June 1815, baptism of child born 26 May 1813, natural son of Rosaly, slave of Louis Metoyem. Godparents: Agustin and Dorotea, free mulattoes. Priest: F. Magnes.

2298. BERNARD
(671) 8 June 1815, baptism of child born 25 August 1813, natural son of Mariane, slave of Louis Metoyem, free mulatto. Godparents: Joseph and Susanne, free mulattoes. Priest: F. Magnes.

2299. ANDRES
(671) 8 June 1815, baptism of child born 25 August 1815 /sic/, natural son of Marie, slave of Dominique Metoyem, free mulatto. Godparents: Joseph and Perin, free mulattoes. Priest: F. Magnes.

2300. MARIE CELESTE
(671) 8 June 1815, baptism of child born 1 January 1813, natural son of Liuc, slave of Dominique Metoyer, free mulatto. Godparents: Agustin and Perine, free mulattoes. Priest: F. Magnes.

2301. CASIMIR
(671) 8 June 1815, baptism of child born 6 March 1815, natural son of Liuc, slave of Dominique Metoyer, free mulatto. Godparents: Dominique and Layde, free mulattoes. Priest: F. Magnes.

2302. CELESTIN
(671) 8 June 1815, baptism of child born 6 March 1814, natural son of Maria, slave of Dominique Metoyer, free mulatto. Godparents: Joseph and Maria Silby, free mulattoes. Priest: F. Magnes.

2303. MARIE DORALIS
(671) 8 June 1815, baptism of child born 10 October 1810, natural daughter of Roset, slave of Joseph Metoyem, a free mulatto. Godparents: Joseph and Marie Aspasy, free mulattoes. Priest: F. Magnes.

2304. JEAN RAFAEL
(671) 8 June 1815, baptism of child born 6 January 1813, natural son of Roset, slave of Joseph Metoyem, a free mulatto. Godparents: Valery and Denis, free mulattoes. Priest: F. Magnes.

2305. MARIE PELAGIE
(672) 8 June 1815, baptism of child of 8 years, natural daughter of Jeny, slave of Agustin Metoyer, free mulatto. Godparents: Joseph and Arcene, free mulattoes. Priest: F. Magnes.

2306. JACQUE
(672) 8 June 1815, baptism of child of 5 years, natural son of Jeny, slave of Agustin Metoyen, free mulatto. Godparents: Joseph and Ponpose, free mulattoes. Priest: F. Magnes.

2307. MARIE CELESTE
(672) 8 June 1815, baptism of child of 3 years, natural daughter of Jeny, slave of Agustin Metoyer, free mulatto. Godparents: Joseph and Me. Adelle, free mulattoes. Priest: F. Magnes.

2308. ROSE
(672) 8 June 1815, baptism of child of $2\frac{1}{2}$ years, natural daughter of Marie Fany, slave of Agustin Metoyer,

Metoyer, free mulatto. Godparents: Agustin and Susanne, free mulattoes. Priest: F. Magnes.

2309. ATANASIO
(672) 10 June 1815, baptism of child of 6 years, natural son of Me. Anna, slave of Gasparite LaCour. Godparents: Pierre LaCour and Me. Emely LaCour, whites. Priest: F. Magnes.

2310. CELESTIN
(672) 10 June 1815, baptism of child of 2 years, natural son of Mariana, slave of Gasparite LaCour. Godparents: Firme LaCour and Me. Elys Lecour, whites.

2311. JUSTIN
(672) 10 June 1815, baptism of child of 6 months, natural son of Marie Anne, slave of Gasparite Lacour. Godparents: Michel Dervam and Elenne Dervanne, whites. Priest: F. Magnes.

2312. FRANCOISE
(672) 10 June 1815, baptism of child of 6 years, natural daughter of Francoise, slave of Gaspar LaCour. Godparents: Jn. Btte. Lacour and Me. Odis Rachal, whites. Priest: F. Magnes.

2313. MARIE OLYS [ALICE?]
(672) 10 June 1815, baptism of child of 3 years, natural daughter of Francoise, slave of Gasparite LaCour. Godparents: Louis Dervanne and Juana e Brom [Le Brun], whites. Priest: F. Magnes.

2314. MARIE FANY
(672) 10 June 1815, baptism of English Negro of 19 years, slave of Charles Lemoin. Godparents: Geranimo? and Louise, both colored. Priest: F. Magnes.

2315. MANUEL
(672) 10 June 1815, baptism of child of 1½ years, natural son of Marie Fany, slave of Charles Lemoin. Godparents: Louis Dervan and Pelagie Lemoin, whites. Priest: F. Magnes.

2316. MARIE SELIN METOYER
(673) 8 June 1815, baptism of child born 4 June 1813, legitimate daughter of Dominique Metoyem, free mulatto, and Margarite LeCompt, free mulatto. Godparents: Francois Metoyem and Marie Louise Metoyem, all free people of color. Priest: F. Magnes.

2317. JOSE OSEM METOYER
(673)

8 June 1815, baptism of child born 6 May 1815, legitimate son of Dominique Metoyem and Marguerite LeCompt, free mulattoes. Godparents: Jose Metoyer and Marie Pelagie Lecour, both free people of color. Priest: F. Magnes.

2318. ANTONIO
(673) 8 June 1815, baptism of mulatto child born 6 December 1814, son of Maria, slave of Louis Metoyer, free mulatto, who gave liberty to the child before his baptism. Godparents: Jose LaVigne and Dorotee, free mulattoes. Priest: F. Magnes.

2319. MARIE VELEM
(674) 11 June 1815, baptism of child of 3 years, natural daughter of Marie, slave of Jacque Vercher. Godparents: Manuel Bercher /Vercher/ and Arsene Le Cour, whites. Priest: F. Magnes.

2320. MARIE
(674) 11 June 1815, baptism of Negro of 14 years, slave of Jacque Vercher. Godparents: Cesere Brosset and Marie Barbare LeCour, whites. Priest: F. Magnes.

2321. MARIE JOULY
(674) 11 June 1815, baptism of slave aged 13, property of Jacque Vercher. Godparents: Ceser LeCour and Marie Louise Lecour, whites. Priest: F. Magnes.

2322. FRANCOIS VALENTIN
(674) 11 June 1814, baptism of child of 8 months, slave of Velony Vercher, natural son of Marie. Godparents: Jn Btte. Pompe and Celeste, both colored. Priest: F. Magnes.

2323. MICHEL
(674) 11 June 1814, baptism of child of 4 months, natural son of Celeste, slave of Bertelmil Lecour. Godparents: Jacque Lecour and Tranquilin Lecour, whites. Priest: F. Magnes.

2324. JOSEPH
(674) 11 June 1815, baptism of mulatto aged 6 years, natural son of Sofy, slave of Felipe Brosset. Godparents: Antonio Brosset and Maria Celesi Gallien, whites. Priest: F. Magnes.

2325. JN. BTTE.
(674) 11 June 1815, baptism of mulatto of 1 year, natural son of Sofy, slave of Felipe Brosset. Godpar-

ents: Jn Btte. Savayau and Me. Francoise, both colored. Priest: F. Magnes.

2326. MARIE SALY
(674) 11 June 1815, baptism of Negro of 10 years, slave of Alexi Cloutiere. Godparents: Santiago and Maria, both colored. Priest: F. Magnes.

2327. PIERRE
(674) 11 June 1815, baptism of child of 3 months, natural son of Francoise, slave of Jn. Btte. LeCompt. Godparents: Janvier and Celeste, both colored. Priest: F. Magnes.

2328. GENOVEVA
(674) 11 June 1815, baptism of Negro aged 16, slave of Antonio Condé. Godparents: Michel Dupre and Marie Horrer /Aurora/ Dupre, whites. Priest: F. Magnes.

2329. JACQUES
(675) 12 June 1815, baptism of child of 1 year and 3 months, natural son of Marie Rose, slave of Pierre Michel Zary /Zoriche/. Godparents: Pierre Fredieu and Marie Oresyl, whites. Priest: F. Magnes.

2330. MARIE BELONY
(675) 12 June 1815, baptism of child of 3 years, natural daughter of Marie Rosa, slave of Pierre Michel Zary /Zoriche/. Godparents: Julien Delouche and Marie Rose Michel Zary, whites. Priest: F. Magnes.

2331. AGUSTIN
(675) 13 June 1815, baptism of a mulatto of 6 months, natural son of Marie Jeanne, slave of Mda. Ve. Monet. Godparents: Pierre and Marie, both colored. Priest: F. Magnes.

2332. MARIE DESIRAI
(675) 13 June 1815, baptism of child of 9 months, natural daughter of Marie Louisse, slave of Mda. Ve. Me. Louise LeCompte Monet. Godparents: Louis and Francoisse, both colored. Priest: F. Magnes.

2333. JEANN. BTTE.
(675) 3 June 1815, baptism of child of 9 days, natural son of Francoise, slave of Mda. Ve. Me. Louisse LeCompt Monet. Godparents: Tousaint Metoyem, free mulatto and Arriete /Henriette Monet Cloutier/. Priest: F. Magnes.

2334. FRANCOIS
(675)

13 June 1815, baptism of child of 2 years, natural son of Ortanse, slave of Mda. Ve. Me. Louisse Le Compt Monet. Godparents: Jn Btte. Dupouey and Maria Refugia Cortinas, whites. Priest: F. Magnes.

2335. TRANQUILIN
(675) 13 June 1815, baptism of child of 2 months, natural son of Ortans, slave of Mda. Ve. Me. Louisse LeCompt Monet. Godparents: Antonio and Marie Jeanne, both colored. Priest: F. Magnes.

2336. BALSEM [VALSAIN]
(675) 13 June 1815, baptism of child of 11 months, natural son of Celeste, slave of Mda. Ve. Me. Louisse Le Compt Monet. Godparents: Jose Maria Cortinas and Me. Louisse LeComte, whites. Priest: F. Magnes.

2337. MARIA LORETA
(675) 13 June 1815, baptism of child of 14 months, natural daughter of Nanet, slave of Mda. Ve. Me. Louisse Lecompt Monet. Godparents: Jn Btte. Dupouey and Marie Oresyl, whites. Priest: F. Magnes.

2338. MARIE JULIE
(676) 29 June 1815, baptism of Guinea Negro of 14 years, slave of Andres Ste. Andres. Godparents: Jacobo Ste. Andres and Osit Ste. Andres, whites. Priest: F. Magnes.

2339. MARIE DORALY
(676) 29 July 1815, baptism of child of 2 years, natural daughter of Sudie (Judie?), slave of Andres St. Andres. Godparents: Celestin and Sofy, both colored. Priest: F. Magnes.

2340. CATALINA
(676) 29 June 1815, baptism of child of 6 years, natural daughter of Sudie (Judie?), slave of Andre St. Andres. Godparents: Francois Boudry and Victoire Ste. Andres. Priest: F. Magnes.

2341. MARIE SUSANNE
(676) 29 June 1815, baptism of child of 5 years, natural daughter of Marianne, slave of Andres Ste. Andres. Godparents: Adrienne Ste. Andres and Silvestre Rachal. Priest: F. Magnes.

2342. ROSALY
(676) 29 June 1815, baptism of child of 2 years, natural daughter of Marianne, slave of Andres Ste. Andres. Godparents: Atanas and Marianne, both colored. Priest: F. Magnes.

2343. MARIE CONSTANS
(676) 29 June 1815, baptism of child of 8 months, natural daughter of Marian, slave of Andres Ste. Andres. Godparents: Guillom and Marie, both colored. Priest: F. Magnes.

2344. MARIANNE
(676) 29 June 1815, baptism of Guinea Negro slave of Andres Ste. Andres. Godparents: Francois and Nanet, both colored. Priest: F. Magnes.

2345. CARLOS
(676) 29 June 1815, baptism of child of 4 years, natural son of Marie, slave of Andres Ste. Andres. Godparents: Jose Louis Cortes and Mariana Dupre, whites. Priest: F. Magnes.

2346. MARIE LOUISE
(676) 29 June 1815, baptism of child of 1 year, natural daughter of Marie, slave of Andre Ste. Andres. Godparents: Louis Simeon Rachal and Osit Ste. Andres, whites. Priest: F. Magnes.

2347. JOSE
(676) 29 June 1815, baptism of Guinea Negro, slave of Andres Ste. Andres. Godparents: Francois St. Charmant /Germaine/ and Marianne Dupre, whites.

2348. ANTONIO
(676) 29 June 1815, baptism of Guinea Negro, slave of Andre Ste. Andre. Godparents: Francois Budry and Marie Louise Ste. Andres, whites. Priest: F. Magnes.

2349. LOUIS DROSIN
(677) 11 July 1815, baptism of a free child born 15 September 1814, natural son of Layde /Mariotte?/, a free quadroon. Godparents: Louis Hopok and Mde. Ve. Ruvio /Roubieu/, née Marie Judec Levaseur. Priest: F. Magnes.

2350. CECILIE CHATARINE
(677) 11 July 1815, baptism of a free child of 3 years, natural daughter of Cecilia, a free mulatto. Godparents: Louis Tensá and Felicité. Priest: F. Magnes.

2351. JEAN BTTE
(677) 11 July 1815, baptism of a free child of 9 months, natural son of Felicité, free mulatto. Godparents: Jeann Btte. Cecil and Celeste Cecil. Priest: F. Magnes.

2352. JEAN JOSEP BALANGE
(677) 15 December 1815, baptism of a free mulatto child of 7 months, natural son of Joseph Balange and Marie Susette, a free Negro. Godparents: Francois Metoyer and Margarite, free people of color. Priest: F. Magnes.

2353. CONSTANS
(678) 29 June 1815, baptism of a Guinea Negro aged 12* years, slave of Jacobo Ste. Andres. Godparents: Francois Budry and Menent /Manette/ Rachal, whites. Priest: F. Magnes.

*/This age was first written as *tres*, then "12" was superimposed. However, even this age appears questionable in view of the 2 entries following./

2354. FRANCOIS
(678) 29 June 1815, baptism of a child aged 5 years, natural son of Constans, slave of Jacobo Ste. Andres. Godparents: Etienne Rachal and Me. Osite Ste. Andres, whites. Priest: F. Magnes.

2355. MARIE LOUISE
(678) 29 June 1815, baptism of a child of 3 years, natural daughter of Constans, slave of Jacob Ste. Andres. Godparents: Narcis Rachal and Marie Louisse Ste. Andres. Priest: F. Magnes.

2356. AGUSTIN
(678) 29 June 1815, baptism of a Guinea Negro of 13 years, slave of Antonio Rachal. Godparents: Silvestre /Rachal/ and Me. Rose Michel, whites. Priest: F. Magnes.

2357. REMY
(678) 29 June 1815, baptism of a Guinea Negro of 16, slave of Antonio Rachal. Godparents: Antonio Rachal, Jr. and Osiet Ste. Andre, whites. Priest: F. Magnes.

2358. MAGDALENA
(678) 29 June 1815, baptism of a Guinea Negro of 16, slave of Antonio Rachal. Godparents: Pierre /Rachal/, free mulatto, and Marie, colored. Priest: F. Magnes.

2359. THOMAS
(678) 29 June 1815, baptism of a Guinea Negro of 14, slave of Antonio Rachal. Godparents: Manuel Rachal and Celim Dupre, whites. Priest: F. Magnes.

2360. JOSE SEGUNDE
(678) 29 June 1815, baptism of child of 2 years, natural son of Marianne, slave of Antonio Rachal. Godparents: Narciso Rachal and Me. Manet Rachal. Priest: F. Magnes.

2361. MARIE LOUISSE
(678) 29 June 1815, baptism of child of 2 years, natural daughter of Rosaly, slave of Joseph Gillard, Jr. Godparents: Joseph and Sidony, both colored. Priest: F. Magnes.

2362. JUANA
(678) 29 June 1815, baptism of a Guinea Negro aged 16, slave of Francois Boudry. Godparents: Maria Luise Lemoin and Antonio Rachal. Priest: F. Magnes.

2363. MARIE ESTERRE
(679) 1 July 1815, baptism of a child of 2 years, natural daughter of Rical /Raquel/, Negro slave of Joseph Gillard, Sr. Godparents: Jn Btte, slave of Gillard, and Petronille LeCourd, white. Priest: F. Magnes.

2364. ME. ELISSA
(679) 1 July 1815, baptism of child of 1 year, natural daughter of Rical, slave of Joseph Gillard, Sr. Godparents: Joseph Gillard and Margerite LeCourd, whites. Priest: F. Magnes.

2365. PIERRE
(679) 1 July 1815, baptism of child of 2 months, natural son of Manet, Negro slave of Bret Le Cour. Godparents: Miliano and Margarite, both colored. Priest: F. Magnes.

2366. MARIE ARRIETE
(679) 1 July 1815, baptism of child of 2 years, natural daughter of Manet, Negro slave of Bret Le Cour. Godparents: Miliano and Margarita, both colored. Priest: F. Magnes.

2367. MARIE FANY
(679) 1 July 1815, baptism of child of 11 months, natural daughter of Quete /Kitty?/, slave of Thomas Boold. Godparents: Nete /Ned?/ and Chiny /Jenny/, colored. Priest: F. Magnes.

2368. MARIE NETE
(679) 1 July 1815, baptism of child of 2 years, natural

daughter of Guiny /Jenny? Queenie?/, slave of Agustin Baliau. Godparents: Jose Lattiere and Marie Josephe Lattiere, whites. Priest: F. Magnes.

2369. MARIE TEMPLY
(679) 1 July 1815, baptism of child of 3 years, natural daughter of Dys /Dicey?/, slave of Thomas Bold. Godparents: Francois Lattiere and Felonis Bornée, whites. Priest: F. Magnes.

2370. JOSEPH
(679) 1 July 1815, baptism of child of 1 month and 8 days, natural daughter of Marie, slave of "Me. Magdalem Grillet and Rachal". Godparents: Jn Btte. Anty and Me. Emely Rachal. Priest: F. Magnes.

2371. FRANCOIS
(679) 1 July 1815, baptism of child born 17 February 1815 natural son of Ortans, slave of Jacques LaCase. Godparents: Jn Btte. Dervan, Jr. and Me. Carmelite Langois, whites. Priest: F. Magnes.

2372. MARIANNE
(679) 1 July 1815, baptism of Negro aged 25 years, slave of Jacques LaCase. Godparents: Jn Btte Frederic and Me. Asely Langois, whites. Priest: F. Magnes.

2373. MARGARITA
(680) 5 July 1815, baptism of child of $2\frac{1}{2}$ years, natural daughter of Ana, slave of Pierre Bailio. Godparents: Landry Bailio and Emely Bailio, whites. Priest: F. Magnes.

2374. LOUIS
(680) 5 July 1815, baptism of child of 15 months, natural son of Nanet, slave of Pierre Bailio. Godparents: Silvestre Bailio and Emely LaCour, whites. Priest: F. Magnes.

2375. JOSE ASIC /ISAAC?/
(680) 5 July 1815, baptism of child of 3 years, natural son of Cris, slave of Pierre Bailio. Godparents: Landry /Baillio?/ and Delsy Lesar /Layssard/, whites. Priest: F. Magnes.

2376. MARIE SALIE
(680) 5 July 1815, baptism of child of 10 months, natural daughter of Cris, slave of Pierre Bailio. Godparents: Silvestre Bailio and Amely Bailio, whites. Priest: F. Magnes.

2377. VALERY
(680) 5 July 1815, baptism of child of 2 years, natural son of Marie, mulatto slave of Balentin Lesar /Layssard/. Godparents: Furzy and Delayde, free people of color. Priest: F. Magnes.

2378. ANTONIO BLESTE
(680) 5 July 1815, baptism of a slave of 18 years, propperty of Mda. Celeste Bailio et Vaillem. Godparents: Sostin Bailio and Amely Bailio, whites. Priest: F. Magnes.

2379. CATARINA
(680) 5 July 1815, baptism of a slave of 16 years, property of Mda. Celeste Bailio et Vaillim. Godparents: Carlo and Bave. Priest: F. Magnes.

2380. SANTIAGO
(680) 5 July 1815, baptism of a slave of 12 years, property of Mda. Celeste Bailio et Vaillim. Godparents: Polinario Bailio and Artemis Andresom, wh. Priest: F. Magnes.

2381. JUAN
(680) 5 July 1815, baptism of child of 9 months, natural son of Bonaparte, female slave of Mda. Ve. Hodman. Godparents: Juan Tausin and Juny Pouarret /Poirier/. Priest: F. Magnes.

2382. MARIE
(680) 5 July 1815, baptism of slave of Michel Laprery. Godparents: Jn Btte. Vergar and Marie Jeanne Castel. Priest: F. Magnes.

2383. ALEXANDRO
(680) 6 July 1815, baptism of child of 4 years, natural son of Marianne, slave of Jeann Archinard. Godparents: Felipe and Chatarina, all of color. Priest: F. Magnes.

2384. MARIE ANRRIET
(681) 6 July 1815, baptism of child of 3 years, natural daughter of Marianne, slave of Jeann Archinard. Godparents: Louis and Benus, colored. Priest: F. Magnes.

2385. JUAN CLOVIN
(681) 6 July 1815, baptism of child of 3 months, natural son of Marianne, slave of Jeann Archinard. Godparents: Tomas and Venus, both colored. Priest: F. Magnes.

2386. ANTONIO HARRY
(681) 6 July 1815, baptism of child of 3 years, natural son of Benus /Venus_7, slave of Jeann Archinard. Godparents: Lucas and Carlota, both colored. Priest: F. Magnes

2387. JEAN ELSY (Ersy? Essy?)
(681) 6 July 1815, baptism of child of 7 years, natural son of Nansy, slave of Jeann Archinard. Godparents: Carlos and Benus. Priest: F. Magnes.

2388. NANSY MARIE
(681) 6 July 1815, baptism of child of 5 years, natural daughter of Nansy, slave of Jeann Archinard. Godparents: Silvestre and Marianne. Priest: F. Magnes.

2389. SUSANNE
(681) 6 July 1815, baptism of child of 1½ years, natural daughter of Nansy, slave of Jean Archinard. Godparents: Felipe and Elenne. Priest: F. Magnes.

2390. JEANN BTTE.
(681) 6 July 1815, baptism of child of 5 years, natural son of Marianne, slave of Jean Archinard. Godparents: Silvestre and Victoria. Priest: F. Magnes.

2391. CELESTIN
(681) 6 July 1815, baptism of child of 15 months, natural son of Marianne, slave of Jean Archinard. Godparents: Carlos and Marianne. Priest: F. Magnes.

2392. SANTIAGO
(681) 6 July 1815, baptism of child of 10 years, natural son of Marianne, slave of Jean Archinard. Godparents: Thomas and Susy. Priest: F. Magnes.

2393. JUANN BTTE.
(681) 31 September 1815, baptism of child of 3 months, natural son of Agata, slave of Antonio Proudhomme. Godparents: Manuel, free man of color, and Maria Teresse. Priest: F. Magnes.

2394. JOSE ADAM
(682) 11 July 1815, baptism of child of 10 years natural son of Dosée, slave of Pierre Nolasco de Porcuna and Marie Magdalene Lavery. Godparents: Nicolas Capitan, Indian, and Me. Louise Bodain. Priest: F. Magnes.

2395. MARIE LIDE
(682) 11 July 1815, baptism of child of 8 years, natural

daughter of Dosé, slave of Pierre Nolasco de Porcuna and Me. Magdalene Lavery. Godparents: Jose Rachal and Nanet Deny. Priest: F. Magnes.

2396. SANTIAGO
(682) 11 July 1815, baptism of child of 6 years, natural son of Dosé, slave of Pierre Nolasco de Porcuna and Marie Magdalene Lavery. Godparents: Simeon Rachal and Magdalena Larnodierre. Priest: F. Magnes.

2397. BALSEM /VALSAIN/
(682) 11 July 1815, baptism of a child of 1 year and 1 month, natural son of Dosé, slave of Pier Nolasco de Portuna and Marie Magdalena Lavery. Godparents: Eugenio and Victoria, a free Negro. Priest: F. Magnes.

2398. FRANCOISE FANY
(682) 11 July 1815, baptism of a child of 6 years, natural daughter of Emely, slave of Pierre Nolasco de Porcuna and Marie Magdalene Lavery. Godparents: Ettiem, a free Negro, and Francoisse, slave. Priest: F. Magnes.

2399. MARIE LUCIA
(682) 11 July 1815, baptism of child born 7 November 1813, natural daughter of Emely, Negro slave of Pier Nolasco and Me. Louisse Magdalena Lavery. Godparents: Joseph Rachal and Anne Deny. Priest: F. Magnes.

2400. MARIE ROSE
(682) 11 July 1815, baptism of child of 6 months and 6 days, natural daughter of Emely, slave of Pierre Nolasco de Porcuna and Me. Magdalene Lavery. Godparents: Simeon Rachal and Marie Agate de Porcunne. Priest: F. Magnes.

2401. JOSE FRANCISCO
(682) 11 July 1815, baptism of a mulatto of 11 years, natural son of a Negro in Virginia, slave of Pierre Nolasco de Porcuna and Me. Magdalene Lavery. Godparents: Jose Magsimo Aguillon and Ma. Guadalupe de Rios, whites. Priest: F. Magnes.

2402. ANNE
(683) 11 July 1815, baptism of Negro of 14 years, slave of Pierre Nolasco de Porcuna and Marie Magdalene Lavery. Natural daughter of Marie. Godparents: Etiem, a free Negro, and Marie, also a free Negro. Priest: F. Magnes.

2403. MARIE MAGDALENNE AGUSTINNE
(683) 4 October 1815, baptism of a Negro of 2 months and 6 days, natural daughter of Marie Terese, slave of Henry Trichel. Godparents: Jose Fonteneau and Magdalenne Baden, free. Priest: F. Magnes.

2404. ALEXY CARLE
(683) 29 October 1815, baptism of a free child of $2\frac{1}{2}$ months, natural son of Etiemm Carlé and Catys, a free mulatto. Godparents: Jn Btte. Carlé and Jeanne Henry. Priest: F. Magnes.

2405. MELONY
(683) 28 January 1816, baptism of child of $1\frac{1}{2}$ years, natural daughter of Mellitt, slave of Joseph Tauzin. Godparents: Antonio Marcarty and Charlot, both colored. Priest: F. Magnes.

2406. MARIE ANTOINNE CONDÉ
(683) 11 February 1816, baptism of a free child born 30 August 1815, natural daughter of Antonio Condé and Me. Rosse Metoyer, a free mulatto. Godparents: Michel Dupre and Me. Layde Rachal. Priest: F. Magnes.

2407. MARIE ZELINE
(684) 11 February 1816, baptism of a child of 1 month, natural daughter of Me. Jeanne, slave of Nicolas Gallien. Godparents: Jeann Louis Vercher and Me. Adelin Gallien, whites. Priest: F. Magnes.

2408. JOSEPH SOLOMON
(684) 11 February 1816, baptism of a child of 4 months, natural son of Me. Jeanne, slave of Ambrosio Le Comte. Godparents: Ambrosio, LeComte, Jr. and Me. Zeline Cloutier, whites. Priest: F. Magnes.

2409. MARIE
(684) 11 February 1816, baptism of child of $1\frac{1}{2}$ months, natural daughter of Marie Nette, slave of Ambrosio Le Comte. Godparents: Alexy and Theresse, colored. Priest: F. Magnes.

2410. MARIE HANRIETT
(684) 11 February 1816, baptism of a child of 1 month, natural daughter of Emé, slave of Jn. Btte. Le Comte. Godparents: Agustin Duran and Me. Luz Cloutier. Priest: F. Magnes.

2411. MARIE JEANNE
(684) MARIE LASYR
11 February 1816, baptism of twins aged 3 days,

natural daughters of Jouly, slave of Pierre Schelectre. Godparents: Manuel and Marie Jeanne; Joseph Lattier and Me. Carmelitte /Anty?/. Priest: F. Magnes.

2412. ELENNE
(684) 11 Feb. 1816, baptism of child of 15 days, natural daughter of Florencea, slave of Joseph Dervan. Godparents: Dominique Metoyer, free mulatto, and Victoriana, free mulatto. Priest: F. Magnes.

2413. L. SILBEN /SILVAIN/
(684) 11 Feb. 1816, baptism of child of 10 months, natural son of Charlot, slave of Agustin Metoyer. Godparents: Joseph Metoyer and Carmelitte /Anty?/ free mulattoes. Priest: F. Magnes.

2414. MARIE VICTOIRE
(684) 11 Feb. 1816, baptism of child of 1 year and 6 months, natural daughter of Magdalene, slave of Btte. Berthelmil Rachal. Godparents: Btte. Berthelmil Rachal, Jr. and Marie Lemoin. Priest: F. Magnes.

2415. GUILLERMO
(685) 12 February 1816, baptism of child of 1½ years, natural son of Mely, slave of Mr. Harsioc /Hertzog/. Godparents: Btte. and Marie Jeanne, colored. Priest: F. Magnes.

2416. MARIE ROSE
(685) 12 February 1816, baptism of child of 2 years, natural daughter of Mely, slave of Mr. Haresioc /Hertzog/. Godparents: Btta. and Angelica, colored. Priest: F. Magnes.

2417. MODESTE
(685) 12 February 1816, baptism of child of 8 years, natural daughter of Louisse Lucie, slave of Mr. Compere. Godparents: Alexy and Me. Teresse, colored. Priest: F. Magnes.

2418. ETIEN
(685) 12 February 1816, baptism of child of 5 years, natural son of Louisse Lucie, slave of Mr. Compere. Godparents: Alexy and Me. Josephine, colored. Priest: F. Magnes.

2419. MARIE LOUISSE LUCIE
(685) 12 February 1816, baptism of a woman of 25 years, slave of Mr. Comperre. Godparents: Remy Massip

and Rosalye Masip, whites. Priest: F. Magnes.

2420. JN BTTE.
(685) 12 February 1816, baptism of child of 4 years, natural son of Mely, slave of Mr. Harcsioc /Hertzog7. Godparents: Jn Btte. and Angelica, colored.

2421. TOSIN
(685) 12 February 1816, baptism of a child of 6 months, natural son of Emery, slave of Mr. Jn. Louis Hopoc. Godparents: Me. Josephe and Alexy, colored. Priest: F. Magnes.

2422. PIERRE ANDRESON
(685) 12 February 1816, baptism of a boy of 13 years, natural son of Me. Emy, slave of Francois Ruvio /Roubieu7. Godparents: Pierre Masip and Andresse Rachal. Priest: F. Magnes.

2423. JN LOUIS
(685) 12 February 1816, baptism of a boy of 11 years, natural son of Me. Emy, slave of Francois Ruvio. Godparents: Jn Louis Hopoc and Mda. Ruvio, whites. Priest: F. Magnes.

2424. MARIE EMÉE
(685) 12 February 1816, baptism of a woman of 26 years, slave of Francois Ruvio. Godparents: Jn Louis Hopoc and Mda. Jn. Btte. Barthelmis /Rachal7, whites. Priest: F. Magnes.

2425. MARIE FANSON
(685) 12 February 1816, baptism of a woman of 20 years, property of Francois Rubio. Godparents: Pierre Rachal and Ositte Rachal, whites. Priest: F. Magnes.

2426. MATHEO FAMP
(686) 13 February 1816, baptism of a man of 20 years, slave of Benjamin Metoyer. Godparents: Joseph and Marie, colored. Priest: F. Magnes.

2427. SUSANE
(686) 13 February 1816, baptism of a child of 6 months, natural daughter of Felicite, slave of Jn Btte Proudhomme. Godparents: Athanasio and Saly, colored. Priest: F. Magnes.

2428. ME. MODESTE
(686) 13 February 1816, baptism of child of 1 year, natural daughter of Sara, slave of Jn Btte Proud-

homme. Godparents: Rovim and Me. Rim /Reine/, colored. Priest: F. Magnes.

2429. ME. ARSENE
(686) 13 February 1816, baptism of child of 1 year, natural daughter of Lu Saly, slave of Mr. Aliot Ste. Anne. Godparents: Francois and Liset, colored. Priest: F. Magnes.

2430. MARIE DESPASY /ASPASY/
(686) 13 February 1816, baptism of child of 8 months, natural daughter of Marta, slave of Benjamin Metoyer. Godparents: Balentin and Jeanne, colored. Priest: F. Magnes.

2431. JN BTTE
(686) 13 February 1816, baptism of child of 8 months, natural son of Perin, slave of Victorim Metoyer. Godparents: Francois and Me. Jeanne, colored. Priest: F. Magnes.

2432. BALSIM /VALSAIN/
(686) 13 February 1816, baptism of child of 6 months, natural son of Louisse, slave of Victorim Metoyer. Godparents: Jn Btte and Margarite, colored. Priest: F. Magnes.

2433. FRANCOISE
(686) 13 February 1816, baptism of child of 6 months, natural daughter of Charlot, slave of Dominique Rachal. Godparents: Jacque and Marie, colored. Priest: F. Magnes.

2434. MARIE CELESTE ADLIN
(686) 13 February 1816, baptism of child of 3 months, natural daughter of Layde, slave of Francois Levasseur. Godparents: Marcelino and Chatarine, colored. Priest: F. Magnes.

2435. AGUSTIN JULIAN
(686) AOUGUST LUCIEN
13 February 1816, baptism of twins aged 2 months and 6 days, natural sons of Janet, slave of Ve. Manett Malegs Chavus. Godparents: Benjamin Dranguer and Euprasin Tauzin Dublieu; Arnaude Lauve and Pelagie Adle. Priest: F. Magnes.

2436. MARIE ROSALY
(687) 10 March 1816, baptism of child /age is town away/ natural daughter of Me. Jeanne, slave of Mda. Ve. Berthelmy Rachal. Godparents: Senon and Denis. Priest: F. Magnes.

2437. JN BTTE.
(687) 12 April 1816, baptism of natural son of Emery, slave of Mr. Corte. Godparents: Pierre and Vade, both colored. Priest: F. Magnes.

2438. MARIE VICTORINE
(687) 13 April 1816, baptism of natural daughter of Me. Jeanne, slave of Md. Ve. Gagne. Godparents: Joseph La Flor and Chatarine. Priest: F. Magnes.

2439. MARIE IRENE
(687) 14 April 1816, baptism of natural daughter of Charlot, slave of Mde. Ve. Grenaux. Godparents: Atanas and Me. Marta. Priest: F. Magnes.

2440. MARIE CELESTE
(687) 14 April 1816, baptism of child of 2 months, natural daughter of Sophy, slave of Athanasio Poissot. Godparents: Louis and Carmelita. Priest: F. Magnes.

2441. MARIE
(687) 16 April 1816, baptism of child of 10 years, Guinea Negro, slave of Mda. Ve. Arman. Godparents: Pierre and Arriet. Priest: F. Magnes.

2442. LOUIS
(687) 14 April 1816, baptism of child of 6 months, natural son of Me. Francoise, slave of Joseph Tauzin. Godparents: Joseph and Margarite. Priest: F. Magnes.

2443. CELESTINE
(687) 28 April 1816, baptism of child of 1 month and 14 days, natural daughter of Me. Pompos. Celese Cayacac, slave of Louis Tauzin. Godparents: Gavriel and Me., both colored. Priest: F. Magnes.

2444. MARIE POLONINE
(687) 30 April 1816, baptism of child of 5 years, natural daughter of Victorora, slave of Pierre Gagne. Godparents: Antonio and Catarina, colored. Priest: F. Magnes.

2445. FRANCOIS
(687) 30 April 1816, baptism of child of 3 years, natural son of Victoria, slave of Pierre Gagne. Godparents: Francois and Marie, col. Priest: F. Magnes.

2446. ETIEN
(687) 30 April 1816, baptism of child of 4 years, son of Dony, slave of Jn LaLande. Godparents: Remy Gagne and Marcelite Peraut, whites. Priest: F. Magnes.

2447. ONORE [HONORE]
(687) 30 April 1816, baptism of child of 1 year, natural child of Luisset, slave of Mr. Jn LaLande. Godparents: Alexy Grillet and Celina Grillet, whites. Priest: F. Magnes.

2448. JN PIERRE
(688) 1 May 1816, baptism of child of 10 months, natural son of Asely, slave of Mr. Antonio Grillet. Godparents: Jn Pierre and Victoria, colored. Priest: F. Magnes.

2449. MARIE LOUISE
(688) 1 May 1816, baptism of child of 13 days, natural daughter of Mariane Fany, slave of Louis Lamalaty. Godparents: Antonio, free Negro, and Veroni. Priest: F. Magnes.

2450. GEORGE
(688) 14 May 1816, baptism of child of 10 years, English Negro slave of Dominique Rachal. Godparents: Pierre and Marie Josephe, colored. Priest: F. Magnes.

2451. JACQUE FIRME
(688) 14 May 1816, baptism of child of 6 months, natural son of Me. Francoisse, slave of Mda. Ve. Lestage. Godparents: Joseph and Marie Margarite, colored. Priest: F. Magnes.

2452. MAGDALENA
(688) 13 June 1816, baptism of child of "months and a half," natural daughter of Margarite, slave of Victorin Metoyer. Godparents: Lendor and Me. Louisse, colored. Priest: F. Magnes.

2453. MARIE SADONIS
(688) 19 June 1816, baptism of child of 2 months, natural daughter of Me. Adelayde, slave of Victorin Metoyer. Godparents: Louis Fort and Me. Louisse. Priest: F. Magnes.

2454. MANUELL
(688) 21 June 1816, baptism of child of 1 year, natural son of Estere, slave of Narcis Proudhomme. Godparents: Athanas and Margarite. Priest: F. Magnes.

2455. VICTORIA
(688) 21 June 1816, baptism of child of 1 year, natural daughter of Fany, slave of Narcis Proudhomme. Godparents: Valentin and Genoveva. Priest: F. Magnes.

2456. MARIE
(688) 21 June 1816, baptism of child of 1 year, natural
daughter of Pelage, slave of Narcis Proudhomme.
Godparents: Phanor Proudhomme and Eloiza Proudhomme, whites. Priest: F. Magnes.

2457. LOUIS
(688) 21 June 1816, baptism of a Guinea Negro of 22,
slave of Narcis Proudhomme. Godparents: Prince
and Louise, colored. Priest: F. Magnes.

2458. MARIE ESTER
(688) 21 June 1816, baptism of a Guinea Negro aged 18,
slave of Narcis Proudhomme. Godparents: Cristofero and Margarita, colored. Priest: F. Magnes.

2459. FRANCOIS VERTHIL TRICHEL
(689) /date torn/, baptism of a free child born 5th of
/torn and illegible/, natural son of Athanasio
Trichel and Me. Josephe Grappe. Godparents: Jacque Grappe and Arsis Grappe. Priest: F. Magnes.

2460. MARIE LOUISE DORTHILAN
(689) 2 May 1816, baptism of free child aged 10 (16? 18?)
days, natural daughter of Ramon Dorthelan and Magdalena Grappe, a free mulatto. Godparents: Pierre Trichel and Marie Louise Grappe. Priest: F.
Magnes.

2461. MARIE SUSET COTON-MAIS
(689) 14 May 1816, baptism of a free child of 6 months,
natural daughter of Antonio Coton-Mais and Agata
Peper, free mulattoes. Godparents: Tousin Metoyer and Marie Suset Metoyer, both free. Priest:
F. Magnes.

2462. MARIE FELONY LEVASSEUR
(689) 27 June 1816, baptism of child of 1 month and 10*
days, natural daughter of Victoriano Levaseur and
Marie Adelayde /Mariotte/, a free mulato. Godparents: Ambrosio Conte and Elenne Cloutier.
Priest: F. Magnes.

   */Compare this age with the following entry./

2463. MARIE EMY /LEVASSEUR/
(689) 27 June 1816, baptism of child of 1 month and 2*
days, natural daughter of Adelayde /Mariotte/ a
free mulatto. Godparents: Pier Me. Dubois and Me.
Celeste Boudoin. Priest: F. Magnes.

   */Compare this age with the above entry./

2464. MARIE LOUISSE
(690) 26 June 1816, baptism of slave born /torn/ of January 1815, natural daughter of Marie, slave of Louis Metoyer, free mulatto. Godparents: Louis Baltasar and Carmalite /Anty/, both free. Priest: F. Magnes.

2465. JULIAN
(690) 26 June 1816, baptism of child of 1 year, natural child of Jeanne, Negro slave of Florantin Cona, free Negro. Godparents: Joseph Metoyer, free mulatto, and Marie, slave. Priest: F. Magnes.

2466. MARIE FANY
(690) 26 June 1816, baptism of child of 4 years, natural daughter of Fany, slave of Jean Btte. Metoyer, free mulatto. Godparents: Agustin Metoyer, free mulatto and Carmelite Metoyer /Anty/, free mulatto. Priest: F. Magnes.

2467. MARIE SIDONY
(690) 27 June 1816, baptism of slave of 3 months, natural daughter of Fany, slave of Charles Lemoin. Godparents: Jose LaVigne and Marie Louis, colored. Priest: F. Magnes.

2468. AMBROSIO
(690) 28 June 1816, baptism of child of 4 months, natural son of Susanne, slave of Jn Btte. LeComt. Godparents: Ambrosio Lecomt, *fils* and Marie Adeline Prudhomme. Priest: F. Magnes.

2469. MARIN
(690) 28 June 1816, baptism of child of 1 month, natural son of Jeanne, slave of Jn Btte. Lecomt. Godparents: Louis and Loleet, slaves. Priest: F. Magnes.

2470. FELICITE
(690) 29 June, baptism of an English Negro of 7 years, slave of Antonio Rachal. Godparents: Louis Solasty Rachal and Me. Louis Rachal, whites. Priest: F. Magnes.

2471. MARGARITE
(690) 29 June 1816, baptism of an English Negro aged 5 years, slave of Antonoin Rachal. Godparents: Manuel Rachal and Adelle Rachal, whites. Priest: F. Magnes.

2472. JOSEPH
(690) 29 June 1816, baptism of child of 3 months, natu-

ral son of Marie, slave of Antonoin Rachal. Godparents: Thomas and Marianne. Priest: F. Magnes.

2473. JEANN
(690) 2 July 1816, baptism of Congo Negro of 16 years, slave of Joseph Chilard, Jr. [Gillard]. Godparents: Agustin and Margarita. Priest: F. Magnes.

2474. ANTONION
(690) 2 July 1816, baptism of Congo Negro of 20 years, slave of Leandre LeCourd. Godparents: Leandre Lecourd, Jr. and Margarite Lecour, whites. Priest: F. Magnes.

2475. NARCIS
(690) 2 July 1816, baptism of Congo Negro of 20 years, slave of Jn Btte Chilart [Gillard]. Godparents: Ciprian Lovaser and Me. Catarin Lovaser. Priest: F. Magnes.

2476. PIERRE DIGNE
(691) 3 July 1816, baptism of child of 2 months, natural son of Jeannet, slave of Auguste Balloud. Godparents: Jn Btte Valeri, Jr. and Rosa Tanson [Thompson?], whites. Priest: F. Magnes.

2477. MARIE LOUISSE
(691) 3 July 1816, baptism of child of 2 months, natural daughter of Pacians [Patience], slave of Jn Btte Balery [Vallery]. Godparents: Joseph Procela and Marie Padillo, whites. Priest: F. Magnes.

2478. MARIE CHARLOT
(691) 5 July 1816, baptism of child of 18 days, natural daughter of Sidony, slave of Joseph Chilard [Gillard]. Godparents: Jeannon Marie Lecour and Petronilla Lecour, whites. Priest: F. Magnes.

2479. MARIA REFUGIA
(691) 5 July 1816, baptism of child of 6 months, natural daughter of Catarina, slave of Mda. Maria Louis Lecomte. Godparents: Jacinto Mora and Ma. Refugia Cortinas. Priest: F. Magnes.

2480. MARIE JOSEPH
(691) 5 July 1816, baptism of child of 4 months, natural daughter of Maria, slave of Mda. Marie Louis Le Comte. Godparents: Louis [Monet?] and Marie Louis Delin [Marie Louise Adeline Monet-Rachal?]. Priest: F. Magnes.

2481. CECILIA
(691) 5 July 1816, baptism of child of 9 days, natural daughter of Felicite, slave of Mda. Marie Louisse LeComt. Godparents: Etien Lacas and Me. Louis LeComte, whites. Priest: F. Magnes.

2482. MARIE LOUISSE
(691) 6 July 1816, baptism of child of 5 months, natural daughter of Ana, slave of Pier Nolasco de Porcuna. Godparents: Btte. Wallte and Ma. Louisse Boudain. Priest: F. Magnes.

2483. MARIA FORENTINA
(691) 6 July 1816, baptism of child of 1 month, natural daughter of Dosé, slave of Pierr Nolasco de Porcuna. Godparents: Joseph Francs Martineau and Ma. Florentina de Porcuna, whites. Priest: F. Magnes.

2484. MARIE EMELY
(691) 8 July 1816, baptism of Guina Negro, aged 25, slave of Jn. F. Hertzog. Godparents: Bte. Brevelle and Susette Prudhomme. Priest: F. Magnes.

2485. JOSEPH
(691) 21 July 1816, baptism of Guinea Negro of 20 years, slave of Beltran Plesans. Godparents: Manuel Levasseur and Elenne Vascocu, whites. Priest: F. Magnes.

2486. PIERRE ELY
(691) 28 July 1816, baptism of natural son of Clara, slave of Andres Valentin. Godparents: Lestan Rambin and Frouasin Malloud. Priest: F. Magnes.

2487. MARIE LOUISSE
(692) 26 August 1816, baptism of child of 11 days, natural daughter of Marie Louisse, slave of Henry Trichel. Godparents: Tragnia Gonzales and Jeanole. Priest: F. Magnes.

2488. JOSEPH MARIA LUCIANO
(692) 19 September 1816, baptism of child born 5 January 1812, natural son of Marie Frosy, slave of Mlle. Joseph Demesier. Godparents: Athanas Demessier and Felicite Demesier. Priest: F. Magnes.

2489. MARIE JEANNE
(692) 22 September 1816, baptism of child of 1 month, natural daughter of Teresa, slave of Louis Buard. Godparents: Louis Alexandre and Marie Francois. Priest: F. Magnes.

2490. MARGARITE
(692) 24 September 1816, baptism of slave aged 26 years, property of Honory Bergard. Godparents: Jn Btte. David and Margarrite Grappe. Priest: F. Magnes.

2491. MARIE ROSSE
(692) 26 September 1816, baptism of slave aged 17 years, property of Mr. Bluduar /Bludworth7. Godparents: Manuel, free Negro, and Bave, slave. Priest: F. Magnes.

2492. MARIE ELAYA /EULALAH?7
(692) 13 October 1816, baptism of child of 4 months, natural daughter of Clara, slave of Mr. Quin. Godparents: Jn. Dosst and Me. Elayá Dill. Priest: F. Magnes.

2493. MARIE ELENNE
(692) 20 October 1816, baptism of child of 4 months, natural daughter of Marie Modeste, slave of Frans. Bienne. Godparents: Seraphin and Marie Celesy, both colored. Priest: F. Magnes.

2494. MARIE JEANNE
(692) 27 October 1816, baptism of child of 4 months, natural daughter of Marie Jeanne, slave of Fs. Bienne. Godparents: Lender and Suset. Priest: F. Magnes.

2495. ROSELENE
(692) 3 November 1816, baptism of child of 6 months, natural daughter of Marie Francoisse, slave of Louis Buard. Godparents: Diego la Cruz and Marie Marta. Priest: F. Magnes.

2496. MARIE PALMIER
(692) 8 November 1816, baptism of child of 4½ months, natural daughter of Suly /Enselye7, slave of George Scemps. Godparents: Louis Adley and Marie Egepsiace Rogé. Priest: F. Magnes.

2497. MARIE LIESTRE
(692) 9 November 1816, baptism of child of 8 months, "natural daughter of Jn Btte Gaspar Lemoin"*. Godparents: Antonio Berthelmy and Maria Celesty?, whites. Priest: F. Magnes.

*/No name of mother is given. It is probable that the priest intended to write "natural daughter of _____, slave of J. B. G. Lemoine."7

2498. MARIE FELICITE
(693) 10 November 1816, baptism of child of 3 months, natural daughter of Marie Marte, slave of Alexy

Cloutier. Godparents: Btte and Marie, colored. Priest: F. Magnes.

2499. MARIE ZELIN
(693) 10 November 1816, baptism of child of eight days, natural daughter of Denis, slave of Alexy Cloutier. Godparents: Narciso and Francoise, colored. Priest: F. Magnes.

2500. URSIN
(693) 10 November 1816, baptism of child of 2 months, natural son of Marie Jeanne, slave of Alexy Cloutier. Godparents: Jn Btte and Susanne, colored. Priest: F. Magnes.

2501. OZEINNE
(693) 10 November 1816, baptism of child of 2 months, natural daughter of Marie Jeanne, slave of Alexi Cloutier. Godparents: Pierr and Me. Louisse, colored. Priest: F. Magnes.

2502. LOUIS OLIBERTE
(693) 10 November 1816, baptism of child of two months, natural son of Nansy, slave of Antonio Condé. Godparents: Jacque and Me. Louisse. Priest: F. Magnes.

2503. MARIE NATALY
(693) 10 November 1816, baptism of child of 4 months, natural daughter of Dolores, slave of Ambrosio Le Comte. Godparents: Guillon and Me. Agustine, colored. Priest: F. Magnes.

2504. PIERRE
(693) 10 November 1816, baptism of child of 4 months, natural child of Susanne, slave of Dorotee Monet, a free mulatto. Godparents: Athanas and Pelagie, colored. Priest: F. Magnes.

2505. FRANCOISSE
(693) 18 January 1817, baptism of child of 6 months, natural daughter of Anrriette, slave of Pierr Bailio. Godparents: Agustin and Babe. Priest: F. Magnes.

2506. JOSEPH
(693) 18 January 1817, baptism of child of 6 months, natural son of Lucie, slave of Pierr Bailio. Godparents: Bles and Lucie. Priest: F. Magnes.

2507. ANTONIO BILL
(693) 18 January 1817, baptism of child of 4 years, natural son of Lucia, slave of Pierr Bailio. Godpar-

ents: Asor and Cherinne. Priest: F. Magnes.

2508. MARIA BELSE
(693) 18 January 1817, baptism of child of 2½ years, slave of Pierr Bailio. Godparents: Landry and Emely Bailio, whites. Priest: F. Magnes.

2509. JEANN BTTE. LEANDRE METOYERE
(694) /torn/ November 1816, baptism of child born 25 August 1816, legitimate son of Jeann Btte. Metoyer and Marie Suset Metoyer, free mulattoes. Godparents: Agustin Metoyer and Susanne Metoyer. Priest: F. Magnes.

2510. JOSEPH AGAPITE MESIER
(694) 6 January 1817, baptism of child born 18 August 1816, natural son of Marie Eufrosinne Messier, free mulatto. Godparents: Joseph Carrier and Maria Josepha Natali /de Mezieres/. Priest: F. Magnes.

2511. ANTONIO NERES RACHAL
(694) 23 January 1817, baptism of child born 16 November 1816, natural son of Jn Btte. Rachal, white, and Marie Francoisse, free mulatto. Godparents: Jean Btte. Metoyer and Susanne Dominique /Metoyer/, free mulattoes. Priest: F. Magnes.

2512. MARIE SUSETE METOYER
(694) 21 April 1817, baptism of child born 10 December 1816, legitimate daughter of Francisco Metoyer and Margarite Melon /Dupart/. Godparents: Francois Metoyer, Jr. and Marie Arsene Metoyer /Anty/, all free people of color. Priest: F. Magnes.

2513. MANUEL HABRAHAM
(695) 18 January 1817, baptism of child of 1 year, natural son of Ana, slave of Pierre Bailio. Godparents: Agustin and Catarina. Priest: F. Magnes.

2514. PHILIPE
(695) 18 January 1817, baptism of Guinea Negro aged about 15 years, slave of Pierr Bailio. Godparents: Charles and Nanet. Priest: F. Magnes.

2515. JN BTTE. QUIETO /CATO?/
(695) 18 January 1817, baptism of an American mulatto aged 17 years, slave of Pierr Bailio. Godparents: Louis Buard and Chatarinne. Priest: F. Magnes.

2516. JACOVO DEMBA
(695) 18 January 1817, baptism of Guinea Negro aged 21

slave of Pierr Bailio. Godparents: Arson and Perine. Priest: F. Magnes.

2517. LUCIA
(695) 18 January 1817, baptism of Guinea Negro aged 27 years, slave of Pierre Bailio. Godparents: Valentin Lisard and Emely Bailio, whites. Priest: F. Magnes.

2518. BASILIO
(695) 18 January 1817, baptism of child of 1½ years, natural son of Celeste, slave of Mr. Bolon /Layssard/ Godparents: Charles and Margarite. Priest: F. Magnes.

2519. ME. LOUISSE
(695) 21 January 1817, baptism of child of 6 months, natural daughter of Palie, slave of Jn Btte Dubois. Godparents: Valentin Dubois and Me. Slecttre, whites. Priest: F. Magnes.

2520. JOSEPH
(695) 23 January 1817, baptism of child of 1 year, natural son of Ortans, slave of Jacob Ste. Andres. Godparents: Francois and Maria. Priest: F. Magnes.

2521. ME. JEANNE BERNADIET
(695) 28 January 1817, baptism of child born 26 December 1816, natural daughter of Marianne, slave of Louis Metoyer. Godparents: Jn Btte and Marie Jeanne. Priest: F. Magnes.

2522. DORSELIN
(695) 28 January 1817, baptism of child of 6 months, natural son of Jeny, slave of Agustin Metoyer, free mulatto. Godparents: Magsil and Espasy /Anty/. Priest: F. Magnes.

2523. ME. PERIN
(695) 28 January 1817, baptism of child of 1 year, natural daughter of Lucil, slave of Jn Btte. Metoyer, free mulatto. Godparents: Agusto and Adelle Metoyer. Priest: F. Magnes.

2524. JN LOUIS
(695) 28 January 1817, baptism of Guinea Negro of 25 years, slave of Susanne Metoyer, free mulatto. Godparents: Agusto Metoyer, free mulatto, and Me. Louisse /Metoyer/, free mulatto. Priest: F. Magnes.

2525. MARIE SUSET
(696)

30 March 1817, baptism of child born 12 February 1817, natural daughter of Theresse, slave of Mde. Ve. Morphy. Godparents: Fortuna and Agustin, both colored. Priest: F. Magnes.

2526. MARIE ELOYS
(696) 30 March 1817, baptism of child of 4 months, natural daughter of Marcelite, slave of Mr. Bossier, Sr. Godparents: Mons and Marie Margarite, both colored. Priest: F. Magnes.

2527. TERESA
(696) 6 April 1817, baptism of child /āge illegible_7, natural daughter of Francoisse, slave of Athanase Poisot. Godparents: Pier and Genoveva. Priest: F. Magnes.

2528. JUAN
(696) 6 April 1817, baptism of natural son of Magdalenne, slave of Athanas Poissot. Godparents: Pier and Juana. Priest: F. Magnes.

2529. MARIE LOUISSE
(696) 6 April 1817, baptism of natural daughter of Marie, slave of Narciso Proudhomme. Godparents: Pierre and Marie Louisse. Priest: F. Magnes.

2530. JUAN
(696) 6 April 1817, baptism of natural son of Luissa, slave of Atanas Poisot. Godparents: Jonó and Marie Cler. Priest: F. Magnes.

2531. JOSEPH
(696) 6 April 1817, baptism of natural son of Jeanne, slave of Mr. Bienne. Godparents: Jonó and Marie Louisse. Priest: F. Magnes.

2532. URSIN
(696) 7 April 1817, baptism of child of 4 months, natural son of Charlot, slave of _____ Grenau. Godparents: Baile and /Illegible_7. Priest: F. Magnes.

2533. BENSAN OVIL
(696) 7 April 1817, baptism of a mulato, natural son of Ulaly, slave of Placido Bossier. Godparents: Joseph and Elenne, both colored. Priest: F. Magnes.

2534. MARIE CAROLINE
(696) 13 April 1817, baptism of child of 1½ months, natural daughter of Marie Frosin, slave of Ambrois LeComt. Godparents: Despalier /J.B. Espallier_7

Rachal and Margarite LeComt. Priest: F. Magnes.

2535. MARIE CELEZI (ZELI)*
(697) 13 April 1817, baptism of child of 3 /months or years -- entry is torn/, natural daughter of Rosse, slave of Mad. Monet. Godparents: Francois and Theotise. Priest: F. Magnes.

*/Name appears as "Marie Zeli" in margin and "Marie Celezi" in text/.

2536. MARIE ROSSE
(697) 21 April 1817, baptism of English Negro of 12 years, slave of Jn Btte. Lattier. Godparents: Severe Lattier and Me. Felonie Lattier. Priest: F. Magnes.

2537. MARIE ADELLE
(697) 21 April 1817, baptism of child of 2 months, natural daughter of Marie, slave of Jn Btte. Lattier. Godparents: Francois Lattier, Jr. and Me. Louisse Lattier. Priest: F. Magnes.

2538. ROSSE
(697) 21 April 1817, baptism of child born 25 December 1816, natural daughter of Sidra, slave of Francois Metoyer, free mulatto. Godparents: Francois Metoyer, Jr. and Me. Adele Metoyer. Priest: F. Magnes.

2539. MARIE
(697) 22 April 1817, baptism of Guinea Negro aged 15, slave of Jn Btte. Anty. Godparents: Leston Langois and Me. Emely Langois. Priest: F. Magnes.

2540. MARIE LOUISSE
(697) 20 October 1817, baptism of Guinea Negro aged 10, slave of Jn Btte. Anty. Godparents: Jn Btte. Anty and Marie Asely Langois. Priest: F. Magnes.

2541. JOSEPH ISAC
(697) 22 April 1817, baptism of child born 2 March 1817, natural son of Me. Jeanne, slave of Jacques La Casse. Godparents: Jacques Pomie and Felicite Pomie. Priest: F. Magnes.

2542. CHARLES
(697) 22 April 1817, baptism of Guinea Negro aged 22, slave of Francois Slecttre. Godparents: Jacque Pomie and Me. Rose /Illegible/. Priest: F. Magnes.

2543. JOSEPH SOFY
(697) 23 April 1817, baptism of child of 4½ months, nat-

ural son of Marie Theresse, slave of Pier Sevastien Comper. Godparents: Basil and Charlot. Priest: F. Magnes.

2544. CELESTIN
(697) 23 April 1817, baptism of child of 6 months, natural son of Marie Nasely, slave of Jn Btte. Adley. Godparents: Etien Dervan and Marie Assi___? Adley. Priest: F. Magnes.

2545. MARIE ODISSE
(697) 25 April 1817, baptism of child of 3 months, natural daughter of Me. Celeste, slave of Jn Btte. Adley. Godparents: Francs. Adley, and Rosaly Larnodier. Priest: F. Magnes.

2546. JEAN BAPTISTE
(698) 23 April 1817, baptism of child born 10 October 1816, natural son of Me. Theresse, slave of Louis Bmy. Rachal. Godparents: Noel and Marie, both colored. Priest: F. Magnes.

2547. JUAN FRANCOIS
(698) 23 April 1817, baptism of child born 16 October 1816, natural son of Francisca, slave of Louis Bmy. Rachal. Godparents: Theodoro Cleman Rachal and Me. Louisse Vergau. Priest: F. Magnes.

2548. ME. TERESSE
(698) 23 April 1817, baptism of child of 5 months, natural daughter of Sofy, slave of Jn Btte. Proudhomme. Godparents: Franco. Onore and Elenne. Priest: F. Magnes.

2549. ME. CAROLINNE
(698) 23 April 1817, baptism of child of 3 months, natural daughter of Fany, slave of Jn Bte. Proudhomme. Godparents: Nicolas and Marie. Priest: F. Magnes.

2550. MARIE SUSETTE
(698) 23 April 1817, baptism of mulata of 5 months, natural daughter of Rosalia, slave of Jn Btte. Prudhomme. Godparents: Agustin and Marie Jeanne.

2551. MARIE PERINNE
(698) 23 April 1817, baptism of child of 2 months, natural daughter of Marie, slave of Jean Baptiste Proudhomme. Godparents: Louis and Layde. Priest: Magnes.

2552. JN BTTE.
(698) 23 April 1817, baptism of child of 3 months, natu-

ral son of Layde, slave of Mda. Ve. Haliot Sta.
Ana. Godparents: Nicolas and Isavel. Priest: Magnes.

2553. JULIEN MARIE NARCIS
(698) 13 May 1817, baptism of mulatto born 13 February
1817, natural son of Josephinne, slave of P. C. La
Fontaine. Godparents: Manuel Llorens, free, and
Me. Leonore Demesier. Priest: F. Magnes.

2554. GEORGE
(698) 17 June 1817, baptism of English Negro aged 12,
slave of Mr. Wells. Godparents: Estivin and Catarinne, both colored. Priest: F. Magnes.

2555. MARIE EMÉE
(698) 19 June 1817, baptism of natural daughter of Anrriet, slave of Eduard Kerclem /Kirkland/. Godparents: Juedo? and Felicite. Priest: F. Magnes.

2556. JOSEPH BOB
(698) 19 June 1817, baptism of child of 6 months, natural son of Anrriet, slave of Eduard Kerclen /Kirkland/. Godparents: Agustin and Catarinne.
Priest: F. Magnes.

2557. MARGARITE METOYER
(699) 25 June 1817, baptism of child born 24 January
1817, legitimate daughter of Dominique Metoyer and
Margarite LeComte, free people of color. Godparents: Francois Milon and Jeanne Laffitte. Priest:
F. Magnes.

2558. MARIE MELIA METOYER
(699) 25 June 1817, baptism of child born 14 April 1817,
legitimate daughter of Jn Btte. Dominique Metoyer
and Layde Rachal, free people of color. Godparents: Jn Btte. Rachal and Elenne Cloutier. Priest:
F. Magnes.

2559. MARIE TRANQUILINNE FORT
(699) 10 August 1817, baptism of child born 18 April
1817, natural daughter of Louis Dorsinau Fort,
French, and Marie Angelinne Metoyer, a free quadroon. Godparents: Jacque Paillette and Dlle.
Denis Buard. Priest: F. Magnes.

2560. LOUIS TOUSAINT LECOUR
(699) 29 December 1817, baptism of child born 1 November
1817, natural son of Bmy. Lecour and Me. Delayde
/Mariotte/, a free mulatto. Godparents: Louis
Ceser Lecour and Me. Barbart. Lecour. Priest: F.
Magnes.

2561. _____ EM
(700) 2 June 1817, baptism of the natural son of Marie
Louisse, slave of Mda. Monet. Godparents: Jn.
Btte. Dupouey and Francoisse. Priest: F. Magnes.
[Document torn]

2562. ETIEN
(700) 2 June 1817, baptism of child of 1 month, natural
son of Celeste, slave of Mda. Ve. Monet. Godparents: Etien Rachal and the slave's mistress, Me.
Louisse LeComt. Priest: F. Magnes.

2563. MARIE DESIRE
(700) 24 June 1817, baptism of child of two months, the
natural daughter of Meisoly [Marie Sallie], slave
of Pier Brosse. Godparents: Btte. Atanas and Me.
Arsene. Priest: F. Magnes.

2564. MARIE ANGLANTIN
(700) 24 June 1817, baptism of child of 2½ months, natu-
natural daughter of Marie, slave of Dominique
Metoyer. Godparents: Jn Btte. Rachal and Susanne
Metoyer. Priest: F. Magnes.

2565. RAFAEL
(700) 25 June 1817, baptism of child born 22 April 1817,
natural son of Susanne, slave of Dominique Metoyer.
Godparents: Narcis Metoyer and Perin Metoyer.
Priest: F. Magnes.

2566. PEDRO
(700) 26 June 1817, baptism of Guinea Negro of 18 years,
slave of Etien Vercher [Verger]. Godparents: Btte
Lattier and Marie Louise Carmelitte Langois.
Priest: F. Magnes.

2567. HILARIO
(700) 26 June 1817, baptism of Guinea Negro about _2?
years, slave of Louis Agustin Langois. Godparents:
Jacques Lestan and Me. Adelayde Langois. Priest:
F. Magnes.

2568. PIER PAUL
(700) 2 July 1817, baptism of child of 1 month, natural
son of Marie Jean, slave of Mda. Ve. Gagne. Godparents: Amable Cayeu and Laly Bacour, whites.
Priest: F. Magnes.

2569. CELESTIN
(700) 20 July 1817, baptism of child of 4 months, natural
son of Layde, slave of Pelagia Gagne. Godparents:

Celestin and Agnes. Priest: F. Magnes.

2570. ME. ELENE
(700) 20 July 1817, baptism of child of 15 days, natural daughter of Rosse, slave of Pelagie Gagne. Godparents: Valery and Elenne. Priest: F. Magnes.

2571. ME. BRESINE
(700) 20 July 1817, baptism of child of 4 months, natural daughter of Francisca, slave of Pelagie Gagne. Godparents: Valery and Rose. Priest: F. Magnes.

2572. MARIE MELEGIE
(701) /20 July 1817/, baptism of a slave of Francoise Trichel. Godparents: ___lery, free mulatto, and Felicite, colored. Priest: F. Magnes. /Entry is badly torn./

2573. MARGARITE
(701) 20 July 1817, baptism of English slave aged 18 years, property of Louis Clos____. Godparents: Pier and Agnes, colored. Priest: F. Magnes.

2574. MARIE VICTORIA
(701) 20 July 1817, baptism of child of 9 months, natural daughter of Marie, slave of Pier Ternier. Godparents: Louis and Marie Louise Melani, both colored. Priest: F. Magnes.

2575. CESER CHARMIN
(701) 20 July 1817, baptism of child of *8 months, natural son of Espasy, slave of Remy Peraut. Godparents: /Illegible except for the words "of color."/ Priest: F. Magnes.

2576. FRANCOIS CHESON
(701) 20 July 1817, baptism of child of *7 months, natural son of Espasy, slave of Remy Peraut. Godparents: Louis Geoffrois and Me. Selesy Davion, whites. Priest: F. Magnes.

*/These two figures are distinctly written in the original entries, yet one is obviously in error./

2577. MARGARITA
(701) 21 July 1817, baptism of child of 3 days, natural daughter of Bernice, slave of Jn Btte. Peraut. Godparents: Paul and M. Jeanne. Priest: F. Magnes.

2578. MARIE
(701) 22 July 1817, baptism of Guinea Negro aged about

20 years, slave of Hypolite Bordeleau. Godparents: Jn Btte. Besson and Dasette Dervan, whites. Priest: F. Magnes.

2579. EMELY
(701) 22 July 1817, baptism of English Negro aged 15, slave of Jn Btte. Besson. Godparents: the master and Genoveva Ris. Priest: F. Magnes.

2580. JOSE DAVID
(701) 9 August 1817, baptism of English Negro aged 16, slave of Benjamin Metoyer. Godparents: Rafael and Modeste, colored. Priest: F. Magnes.

2581. JACQUE
(701) 9 August 1817, baptism of English Negro aged 12, slave of Benjamin Metoyer. Godparents: Michel and Marta, colored. Priest: F. Magnes.

2582. MARIE ARTEMIS
(701) 9 August 1817, baptism of child of 6 months, natural daughter of Anrriette, slave of Benjamin Metoyer. Godparents: Michel and Angelique, colored. Priest: F. Magnes.

2583. UNKNOWN
(702) __ August 1817, baptism of natural child of Rosse, slave of /Ma/nuel Pr/udhomme/. Priest: F. Magnes. /Entry is badly torn./

2584. AGUSTIN BILL
(702) 9 August 1817, baptism of Guinea Negro about 15, slave of Manuel Prudhomme. Godparents: Aguste and Francoise, colored. Priest: F. Magnes.

2585. BALZIN /VALSAIN/
(702) 10 August 1817, baptism of child of 6 months, natural son of Marie, slave of Louis Fort. Godparents: Ceser Morphy and his wife. Priest: F. Magnes.

2586. MARIE ANTONOINA
(702) 2 August 1817, baptism of child of __ months, natural daughter of Marie Perinne, slave of Francois Levaseur. Godparents: Alexy Borman and Me. Theresse Emely. Priest: F. Magnes.

2587. JUAN FRANCO.
(702) 5 October 1817, baptism of child of 6 months, natural son of Felicite, slave of Mr. Car. Godparents: Pedro and Victorine, both colored. Priest: F. Magnes.

2588. JOSE FRANCO
(702) 12 October 1817, baptism of child of 2 months, natural son of Maria Juliana, slave of Ignacio Pie___ me /Piedferme?/. Godparents: Pablo Samuel and Ma. Lina Padillo, whites. Priest: F. Magnes.

2589. MARIE JENY
(702) 17 October 1817, baptism of child of 4 years, natural daughter of Jeny, slave of Ceser Laffitte. Godparents: Pedro Flores and Jetrudis Chirino, whites. Priest: F. Magnes.

2590. JOSE DE LOS SANTOS
(702) __ October 1817, baptism of child of 11 months, natural son of Marie, slave of Marcelo Soto. Godparents: Pedro Flores and Trinidad Gonzales, whites. Priest: F. Magnes.

2591. MARIE SUSET
(702) 26 October 1817, baptism of child of 2 months, natural daughter of Maria Antonia, slave of Samuel Davenport. Godparents: /torn/ and Marie Magdalenne, colored. Priest: F. Magnes.

2592. MARIE BAVE
(702) 26 October 1817, baptism of child of 7 months, natural daughter of /blank/, slave of Mr. Bluduare. Godparents: Pier and Me. Bave, both colored. Priest: F. Magnes.

2593. SERAPHIM
(703) 11 December 1817, baptism of slave of ___ Bailloud. /Remainder of entry is destroyed./ Priest: F. Magnes.

2594. JOSEPH STE. CLOU
(703) 11 December 1817, baptism of natural son of Nanes, slave of ___ /Nanet, slave of Pierre Bailliou?/. Godparents: Estivan and Marie. /Remainder of entry is destroyed./. Priest: F. Magnes.

2595. JACQUE
(703) 11 December 1817, baptism of slave of Pier Bailloud. Godparents: Pier Bailloud and the slave's mistress. /Most of entry is destroyed./ Priest: F. Magnes.

2596. JOSEPH VIET
(703) 8 January 1818, baptism of child of 6 months, natural son of Felicite, slave of _____ Metoyer. Godparents: Joseph /Illegible and torn/, free. Priest: F. Magnes.

2597. JN BTTE. SENVIL [ST. VILLE]
(703) 8 January 1818, baptism of child of 4 months, natural son of Anries, slave of Susana Metoyer. Godparents: Manuel and Marie Jeane Bade. Priest: F. Magnes.

2598. JUAN BTTA
(703) 8 January 1818, baptism of child born 8 October 1817, natural son of Marie Rosa, slave of Jose Metoyer. Godparents: Michel Voltaris and Marie Perinne Metoyer. Priest: F. Magnes.

2599. SINVIL [ST. VILLE]
(703) 8 January 1818, baptism of child born 8 October 1817, natural son of Marie Rosse, slave of Joseph Metoyer. Godparents: Jn Btte. Leand. Metoyer and Marie Tranquilinne LeCour. Priest: F. Magnes.

2600. MARIE ROSE
(703) 8 January 1818, baptism of Negro of 26 years, slave of Joseph Metoyer. Godparents: Dominique Metoyer and Marguerite. Priest: F. Magnes.

2601. EDUARD
(703) 1 February 1818, baptism of child of 1 year, natural son of Genoveva, slave of Mr. Rouquier, Jr. Godparents: Louis and Marie Adelayde, both colored. Priest: F. Magnes.

2602. JOSEPH FORTUNA
(703) 17 February 1818, baptism of child of 1½ months, natural son of Maria, slave of Mr. Carr. Godparents: Manuel Llorens and Marie Rosse Messier. Priest: F. Magnes.

2603. FLORANTIN
(704) [torn], baptism of child of 2 months, son of Juana, slave of Louis Gallien. Godparents: Michel Dervan and Me. Elenne Anty. Priest: F. Magnes.

2604. MARIE CELINE
(704) [torn], baptism of natural child of Elena, slave of Joseph [torn -- may be Derbanne]. Godparents: Jn Btte. Metoyer and Pant_____ [Derbanne?]. Priest: F. Magnes.

2605. LEONORE PERINA
(704) [torn] 1818, baptism of natural child of Agata, slave of Mr. Antoin [Prudhom]me. Godparents: Jacques Lambres and M_____ [torn]. Priest: F. Magnes.

2606. LOUIS
(704) 1 /torn/ 1818, baptism of child born 19 December /torn/, natural son of Charlot, slave of Joseph Crisostome Peraut. Godparents: Alexy Trichel and Mlle. Emely. Priest: F. Magnes.

2607. MARCELITA
(704) 13 March 1818, baptism of child born 30 January 1818, natural daughter of Marie, slave of Louis Peraut. Godparents: Pedro Sosa and Elenne Grappe. Priest: F. Magnes.

2608. MARIE EMERANT
(704) 22 May 1818, baptism of child of 2 months, natural daughter of Pelagie, slave of Michel Chamard. Godparents: Dominique and Frouassine. Priest: F. Magnes.

2609. MARIE JEANNE
(704) 22 March 1818, baptism of child of 1 year, natural daughter of Elenne, slave of Jn Francs. Hertzog. Godparents: Henry Hertzog and Aime Proudhomme. Priest: F. Magnes.

2610. JOSEPH MARIA
(704) 22 March 1818, baptism of a child of 8 months, natural son of Recha, slave of Fs. Vienne. Godparents: Dominique and Jeanne. Priest: F. Magnes.

2611. MARIE CELESTE
(704) 22 March 1818, baptism of a child of 10 years, natural daughter of Bezsse, slave of Jn Btte. Buard. Godparents: Antoin and Celeste. Priest: F. Magnes.

2612. MARIE LOUISIE
(704) 22 March 1818, baptism of child of 8 years, natural daughter of Bezsse, slave of Jn Btte. Buard. Godparents: Joseph and Marie. Priest: F. Magnes.

2613. HENRY
(704) 22 March 1818, baptism of a child of 3 years, natural son of Charlot, slave of Ant. Pannelle. Godparents: Moris and Susette. Priest: F. Magnes.

2614. */MARIE OZITTE/ METOYER
(705) 8 January 1818, baptism of child born 14 /approximately the month of January/ 1816, legitimate daughter of Pier Metoyer and /Henriette Cloutier/, all free people of color. Godparents: Ciriac and Dorotee, both colored. Priest: F. Magnes.

*/̲B̲racketed information in preceding entry, which is badly damaged, has been taken from the Metoyer-Cloutier marriage contract dated December 31, 1817 and filed in *Book 2 & 3, Marr. & Misc.*, Natchitoches Courthouse./̲

2615. PIERRE NEREST METOYER
(705) 8 January 1818, baptism of child born 1 April 1817, legitimate son of Pier Metoyer and Anrriette /̲Cloutier/̲, free people of color. Godparents: Tausain Metoyer and Arsenne Metoyer, both free people of color. Priest: F. Magnes.

2616. MARIE ESELY RACHAL
(705) 6 March 1818, baptism of child born 15 January 1818, legitimate daughter of Juan Btta. Rachal and Maria Susana Metoyer, both free people of color. Godparents: Pier Rachal and Maria Perina Metoyer. Priest: F. Magnes.

2617. ETIEN ALEXY LEBRUM
(705) 13 March 1818, baptism of a free child born 28 September 1817, natural son of Paul Etien Lebrum and Susette Grappe, free woman of color. Godparents: Alexy Trichel and Marie Louis Grappe. Priest: F. Magnes.

2618. MARIA ODISSE GRAPPE
(705) 13 March 1818, baptism of free child born 17 January 1818, natural daughter of Marie Josephe Grappe. Godparents: Baltasar Grappe and Margarita Grappe. Priest: F. Magnes.

2619. MARIE DORALISSE COINDET
(706) /̲date torn/̲ 1818, baptism of a free child born "in January of the current year," daughter of Antoin Coindet, habitant of Riviere aux Cannes, and of Rose Metoyer, a free mulatto. Godparents: Athanas LeCompte and Genoveva Lecompt, both free people of color. Priest: F. Magnes.

2620. JEAN URSEL DORTELAN
(706) 25 May 1818, baptism of a free child born 7 March 1818, natural son of Ramon Dortelan and Maria Magdalena Grappe. Godparents: Alexy Trichel and Celeste Grappe. Priest: F. Magnes.

2621. MARIE ESPASIT TOCOUR /̲LECOUR/̲
(706) 24 June 1818, baptism of free child of 3 months, natural daughter of Felicite Tocour. Godparents: Louis Metoyer and Theresse, all free people of color. Priest: F. Magnes.

2622. JACQUE CLAVER TOCOUR /LECOUR/
(706) 24 June 1818, baptism of free child of 3 months,
natural son of Celeste Tocour, free woman of color.
Godparents: Etien Rachal and Marie Louisse Bodin.
Priest: F. Magnes.

2623. MARIE JULIANA
(706) 22 March 1818, baptism of child of 1 year, natural
daughter of Charlot, slave of Ant. Pannelle. Godparents: Joseph Rouquier and Marie Orsula.
Priest: F. Magnes.

2624. MARIE LOUISE ASPASY
(706) 22 March 1818, baptism of child born 6 October 1817,
natural daughter of Marie Josephe, slave of Joseph
Tauzi/n/. Godparents: Francois and Me. Louise.
Priest: F. Magnes.

2625. ME. LOUISE ASPASY
(707) /All of entry is torn away with exception of marginal note identifying the slave that is being
baptized. It is possible that this is a fragment
or a continuation of the above entry./

2626. MARIE SALY
(707 22 March 1818, baptism of English Negro aged about
/torn/. Godparents: Genere Bon____. Priest:
F. Magnes. /Remainder of entry is torn./

2627. PRUDANS
(707) 26 March 1818, baptism of child born 19 December
/year is torn/, child of ___rie, slave of Mda. Ve.
Bmy. Rachal. Godparents: Basil and Therese, both
colored. /Entry is badly torn/. Priest: F. Magnes.

2628. URSEN
(707) 26 March 1818, baptism of a natural child of Celeste, slave of Mr. B/arthelemy Lecourt/. Godparents: Cezer LeCour and Marie _____. Priest: F.
Magnes. /Entry is badly torn./

2629. JOSEPH TOUSAINT
(707) 29 March 1818, baptism of natural child of Felicite, slave of Amb/roise Le/ Compte. Godparents:
Btte. S__voye and Marie Doralisse, both colored.
Priest: F. Magnes. /Entry is badly torn./

2630. MARIE THERESSE
(707) 29 March 1818, baptism of child of 3 months, natural daughter of Dolores, slave of Ambrois Compte.
Godparents: Antonie and Me. Theresse. Priest: F.
Magnes.

2631. JOSEPH DANIEL
(707) 29 March 1818, baptism of child of 1 year, natural son of Dayna /Dinah?/, slave of Ambrois Compte. Godparents: Antoin and Me. Francoise. Priest: Magnes.

2632. CECILIA
(707) 29 March 1818, baptism of child of 6 months, natural daughter of Marie Jeanne, slave of Jn Btte. LeCompte. Godparents: Athanas and Susanne, both colored. Priest: F. Magnes.

2633. MARIE POMPOSE
(707) 29 March 1818, baptism of child of 4 months, natural daughter of Marie Jeanne, slave of Mda. Ve. Monet. Godparents: Jn Btte. and Elenne, both colored. Priest: F. Magnes.

2634. MAR/IE/
(707) 5 April 1818, baptism of a female slave aged about 31 years, property of Mr. Josep_____ /Tauzin?/. Godparents: Landor and ____. Priest: F. Magnes. /Remainder of entry is destroyed./

2635. JOSEPH DANIEL
(707) 5 April 1818, baptism of English slave, aged about 18 years, property of Mr. Jo___ Tauzin. Godparents: Theophil Tauzin and Felicite Sausier. Priest: F. Magnes.

2636. UNKNOWN
(708) /Entry has been completely destroyed./

2637. GEORGE
(708) /date torn/, baptism of slave aged about 20 years, property of Mr. Joseph Tau /zin/. Godparents: Landor and Benus. Priest: F. Magnes.

2638. JN BTTE.
(708) April 1818, baptism of slave of Joseph Tauzin. Godparents: Monsineau Baden and Charlot. /Entry is badly torn./ Priest: F. Magnes.

2639. HENRY
(708) April 1818, baptism of slave of Joseph Tau /zin/. Godparents: Monsineau Badin and Cha/rlot?/. Priest: F. Magnes.

2640. VICENTE CIRIACO
(708) 5 April 1818, baptism of a child born 29 May 1817,

natural son of Me. Jeanne, slave of Mda. Ve. Bmy. Rachal. Godparents: Joseph and Marie Louisse, colored. Priest: F. Magnes.

2641. MARIE VELONY
(708) 5 April 1818, baptism of English mulatto aged 15, slave of /Mar7cos Sompayract. Godparents: Evariste Tauzin and Margarite Roverson. Priest: F. Magnes.

2642. AGATA
(708) 12 April 1818, baptism of child born 5 February 1818, natural daughter of Chatarinne, slave of Jn Btte. Trichel. Godparents: Joseph Rouquier and Cecil Baden. Priest: F. Magnes.

2643. JOSEPH
(708) 12 April 1818, baptism of natural son of Marie, slave of Joseph Tauzin. Godparents: Joseph Carrier and Marie Rosse Messier. Priest: F. Magnes.

NOTE: This series of baptisms continues with Entry 1065.

§§§

NOTE: The following series of burials is a continuation of the series that ended with entry 420.

2644. FRANCO. GOMES
(709) 21 July 1818, burial in cemetery of this parish of a native of Adayses, aged 78 years, who left a widow Dolores, as well as one son and one daughter. He received the sacraments before dying of fever. burial at public expense. Priest: F. Magnes.

2645. AGUSTIN PHILIBER
(709) 23 July 1818, burial of child of 4 years, legitimate son of Gaspar Philibert and Marie Felicite Lemettre. Death was sudden. Priest: F. Magnes.

2646. JOSEPH MALEGS
(709) 24 August 1818, burial in cemetery of this parish of a native of "Saldeore" in France, aged 69 years, who left a widow, Mariana Bardon, with three daughters and one son. Death caused by dropsy. Priest: F. Magnes.

2647. MARIA MARTINEZ
(709) 3 August 1818, burial of child of 10 days, daughter of Esmeregildo Marti[nez] and Maria. Burial at public expense. Priest: F. Magnes.

2648. FRANCO. DAVIER GONIE
(709) 4 September 1818, burial of a child aged about 5 months, legitimate son of Francois Gonie and Marie Federic, who died of fever. Priest: F. Magnes.

2649. JOSEPH GAGNE
(710) 24 September 1818, burial in cemetery of this parish of a bachelor aged 46 years, legitimate son of Pier Gagne and Marie Louisse Davion, who died of fever. Priest: F. Magnes.

2650. SUSANNE GAGNE
(710) 25 September 1818, burial in cemetery of this parish of the widow of Amabale Cayeu. Deceased was 30 years of age. Death caused by fever. Priest: F. Magnes.

2651. EUPHROSINNE RACHAL
(710) 4 October 1818, baptism in cemetery of this parish of a native of this post, widow of Jn Btte. Slecttre, who died in confinement leaving 2 sons and 2 daughters. Priest: F. Magnes.

2652. ELISABET MARIE FELICITE NEPOMUCINE MARG[ARITA?]
(710)   MESSIER
       [date torn] October 1818, burial in cemetery of this parish of a single lady, aged [torn], native of this parish. Death by fever. Priest: F. Magnes.

2653. GASPAR PHILIVERT
(711) 18 December 1818, burial in cemetery of this parish of a native of Marsella [Marseilles] France, aged 52, who left a pregnant widow, Felicite Lemettre, and a daughter Caroline. Death by fever. Priest: F. Magnes.

2654. JOSEF MARIA AMADOR
(711) 18 January 1819, burial of a child of 2 months, who died of fever. Priest: F. Magnes.

2655. MARIA GOMES
(711) 19 January 1819, burial of a legitimate child of Francisco Gomes and Dolores, who died of a pain. Burial at public expense. Priest: F. Magnes.

2656. TRINIDAD MARTINEZ
(711)

20 February 1819, burial of a child of 5 years, legitimate daughter of Josef Dolores Martines and Manuella Gomes, who died of burns. Priest: F. Magnes.

2657. LESTAGE
(711) 28 February 1819, burial of a child of 8 days "who received the water," legitimate son of Jn Btte. Lestage and Leocadia Bossier. Death caused by epilepsy. Priest: F. Magnes.

2658. JOSEPH LESTAGE
(712) 12 March 1819, burial of a child of 9 days "who received the water," legitimate son of Bmy. Lestage and Marie Pelagie Federic; death caused by epilepsy. Priest: F. Magnes.

2659. MARIE EUPHRASIN RACHAL
(712) 1 April 1819, burial at the chapel at Riviere aux Cannes of the 22 year old wife of Michel Dervan, who died leaving a daughter aged 2 months. Priest: F. Magnes.

2660. JUAN MASIP
(712) 30 January 1819, burial at Riviere aux Cannes. Priest: F. Magnes.

*/name of widow and numbers of surviving sons and daughters were left blank in the entry.7

2661. MARIA ESTRADA
(712) 3 April 1819, burial of a child of 1 month, legitimate daughter of Felis Estrada and of /blank7 Casanova. Death by epilepsy. Priest: F. Magnes.

2662. JACQUES LANDREAUX
(712) 14 April 1819, burial of a bachelor of 2 /sic7 years, legitimate son of Franco. Landreaux and Marie Constance Meilleur. Death by *aogado*.* Priest: F. Magnes.

*/Note: This word is quite distinctly written, although no Spanish word exists with that precise spelling. The closest approximation is *aojado*, which translates as "witchcraft." This cause of death appears in only one other entry recorded by Father Magnes, Entry 2702.7

2663. JOSE ANTONIO CARDENAS
(713) 15 May 1819, burial of a child of 7 days, legitimate son of Franco Cardenas and Martina Prado. Death by epilepsy. Burial at public expense. Priest: F. Magnes.

2664. MARIA GREGORIA CARDENAS
(713) 10 July 1819, burial of a child of 1 year, legitimate daughter of Franco. Cardenas and Martina Prado. Death by fever, burial at public expense. Priest: F. Magnes.

2665. BENTURA BOCA
(713) 13 July 1819, burial of a Negro child of 11 months, legitimate son of Nepomuceno Boca Negro and Ma. Paula Adams. Death by fever. Priest: F. Magnes.

2666. ANDRES CHAMARD
(713) 17 July 1819, burial of a child of /blank/ days, legitimate son of Andres Chamard and /blank/, death by fever. Priest: F. Magnes.

2667. ROUBEAU
(713) 1 August 1819, burial of a legitimate daughter of Francois Ruvio and /blank/. Death by fever. Priest: F. Magnes.

2668. MARIE LAUVE BAURD
(713) 2 August 1819, burial of the legitimate daughter of deceased Louis Buard and Maria Ulalye Bossier. Death by fever. Priest: F. Magnes.

2669. LOUIS RAMON
(714) 25 July 1819, burial of a native of "Armana". Marital state and parents of the deceased are not known. Death by fever, burial at public expense. Priest: F. Magnes.

2670. JUANA _____
(714) 9 August 1819, burial of a forty year old woman, widow of /blank/, death by cancer, burial at public expense. Priest: F. Magnes.

2671. FRANCOIS LEVASSEUR
(714) 15 August 1819, burial of a native of this parish, aged 82 years, widower in first numptials of Maria Juana Mader, by whom he left 3 sons, and in second nuptials of Maria Juana Grillet, by whom he had no children. Death by fever. Priest: F. Magnes.

2672. JUAN JOSE GOMES
(714) 19 August 1819, burial of a man "said to be a native of Havadia," aged 64, a widower who left no children. Burial at public expense. Priest: F. Magnes.

2673. ALEXANDRE PONTIEU
(714)

23 August 1819, burial of the legitimate son of Alexandre Pontieu and Margarite Johanson. Priest: F. Magnes.

2674. JULIANA JOSEPHA SLOCUM
(715) 27 August 1819, burial in cemetery of this parish of the wife of Firmin Poissot, who died of miscarriage leaving no children. Priest: F. Magnes.

2675. JAMES HEATING
(715) 11 September 1819, burial of an Irishman, aged 45, native of the town of Anniscorthay in the state of Wesford, who had been married in the same city with Marie Goodall, by whom he left four children. Heating died of fever only "about 17 months after leaving his country." Last rites administered. Priest: F. Magnes.

2676. MARIE SOMPAYRACT
(715) 12 September 1819, burial of a child of about 8 months, legitimate daughter of Ambrosio Sompayract. death by fever. Priest: F. Magnes.

2677. JEAN PIER BTTE. BACOCU
(715) 13 September 1819, burial of the legitimate son of Jean Btte. Andres Bacocu and Maria Faustina Chirino. Death by fever. Priest: F. Magnes.

2678. PELAGIA
(715) 16 September 1819, burial of a Spaniard, who died of fever. Father Magnes was not apprised of her birthplace or parentage. Burial at public expense.

2679. JOSEPH FRED FORSAET
(716) 24 September 1819, burial of a child of 3 months, legitimate son of Santiago Forsaet and Ma. Luis Larnodier. Death by fever. Priest: F. Magnes.

2680. MARIE NIEVES CERVERA
(716) 26 September 1819, burial of a two month old child, natural daughter of Enrique Cervera and Maria Basilia Guetierrez. Death by fever. Burial at public expense. Priest: F. Magnes.

2681. PIER BERNARDO GUISARNAC
(716) 6 October 1819, burial of a native of this post, legitimate son of deceased Bernardo Guisarnac and Marie Luisa Larnodier, who died of a sudden blow. Priest: F. Magnes.

2682. ANTOIN BARRAS
(716)

9 October 1819, baptism of a twenty year old bachelor, a native of Castres, France, whose father and mother were not known to Father Magnes. Death was sudden.

2683. CHARLES TOTIN
(716) 24 October 1819, burial of a native of this post, a widower who left one daughter and received the sacraments before dying. Priest: F. Magnes.

2684. MARIA DOLORES TRAVIESO
(717) 6 November 1819, burial of an Indian of the Apache nation, aged about 40, widow of Sulas Gomes by whom she left a son named Damasio Nepomuceno. Deceased received the sacraments before dying of fever. Burial at public expense. Priest: F. Magnes.

2685. JOSEPH ANTONIO LA GARZA
(717) 7 November 1819, burial of "a native of Camargo, in the colony of Nuevo Sn. Tander," legitimate son of Marcelino La Garza. Death by fever. No sacraments administered since death was sudden. Priest: F. Magnes.

2686. MARIE DETERVIL
(717) 19 December 1819, burial of a child of 6 months, legitimate daughter of "Mr. Detervil and of /blank7 Sorier /Saucier7. Death by fever. Priest: F. Magnes.

2687. IGNACIO HORNOS
(717) 5 January 1820, burial of a "native of /blank7, aged about /blank7 years, who left a widow, Ignacia Casanova, with one daughter." He received the sacraments before dying of a pain in the side. Burial at public expense. Priest: F. Magnes.

2688. JOSEPH FRANCISCO SALINES
(718) 6 January 1820, burial of a child of 8 months, legitimate son of Jose Leno Salines and Petro Inofosa. Death by fever. Priest: F. Magnes.

2689. MARIE ANTOINE GARZA
(718) 22 January 1820, burial of a child of 17 days, natural daughter of Casimira La Garza. Death by fever. Burial at public expense. Priest: F. Magnes.

2690. JOSEPH LAVEGA
(718) 13 January 1820, burial of a native of Mexico, aged 70 years, widower of Maria Aroy Peralta by

whom he left no children, then widower of Guadalupe
Pru. Deceased received the sacraments, and died of
dropsy. Priest: F. Magnes.

2691. JEAN BTTE. DAVION
(718) 31 January 1820, burial of a man of 55 years, native of this jurisdiction, who left a widow, Marie
Lalye Bascocu, and no children. He received all
the sacraments and died of lung disease.

2692. JOHON SIBLEY
(719) /torn/ February 1820, burial of a child of 8 days,
legitimate son of Johon Sibly and of /blank/ Malgs.
Death was by fever. Priest: F. Magnes.

2693. JUAN
(719) 8 February 1820, burial of a Spaniard, last name
and marital state unknown, but said to be from Havana. Death by fever. Burial at public expense.
Priest: F. Magnes.

2694. LOUIS LEVASEUR
(719) 22 /torn/ 1820, burial in cemetery of this parish
of a native of this jurisdiction, aged 42 years, a
bachelor and son of Francois Levaseur by Marie
Jean Mader, both already deceased. Death was sudden. Priest: F. Magnes.

2695. JEAN FRANCOIS VASEUR
(719) 30 March 1820, burial in cemetery of this parish of
a native of this parish, aged 49 years, who left a
widow, Maria Francisca Trichel, 2 sons and 1 daughter. He received the sacraments before dying of a
pain. Priest: F. Magnes.

2696. MARIE FRANCOISE GRAPPE
(719) 3 April 1820, burial in cemetery of this parish of
the widow of Antoin Benoist Montanery, who left 1
married daughter. She received all the sacraments
before dying of a pain. Priest: F. Magnes.

2697. JOSEPH FELIS ESTRADA
(719) 5 April 1820, burial of a child of 1 month and 7
days, baptized by necessity, legitimate son of Felis Estrada and Manet Casanova. Death caused by
pain. Priest: F. Magnes.

2698. JOSEF SANDOVAL
(719) 5 April 1820, burial of a bachelor, a native of
Createro, aged 45 years, death from pain. Burial
at public expense. Priest: F. Magnes.

2699. MARIE TOMASA VIMONEZ
(719) 29 April 1820, burial of the widow of Fernando Menchaca, by whom she left 2 sons and 1 daughter. Deceased was 49, and received the sacraments before dying of a pain in the side. Priest: F. Magnes.

2700. IGNACIO DE LOS STOS. COY
(720) /torn/ 1820, burial of a native of Besar, aged 27 years, legitimate son of Ignacio de los Stos. Coy and Manuela Garcia Falcon. Deceased received the sacraments before dying of lung disease. Burial at public expense. Priest: F. Magnes.

2701. JUANA PEREZ
(720) 16 June 1820, burial of a child of 1 year, natural daughter of Francisco Perez and Maria, an Indian. Death by fever. Burial at public expense. Priest: F. Magnes.

2702. JEAN BTTE. MINORON
(720) 5 July 1820, burial of a Canadian aged 65, who died of *aogado**. Priest: F. Magnes.

*/See note accompanying Entry 2662./

2703. FRANCOISE HIMEL
(720) 15 July 1820, burial of the legitimate daughter of Antonio Himel and Margarita Slecttre, who died of fever at the age of 40 years, leaving one daughter. Priest: F. Magnes.

2704. RAFAEL HERMOSILLO
(720) 18 July 1820, burial of a native of Aguas Calientes, a bachelor aged 48 years who received the sacraments before dying of lung disease. Burial at public expense. Priest: F. Magnes.

2705. EVARISTE TAUZIN
(720) 30 July 1820, burial of a bachelor, aged 20 years, legitimate son of Joseph Tauzin and Marie Chamard, who died of lung disease. Priest: F. Magnes.

2706. FRANCISCO ALAMILLO
(721) 16 August /1820/, burial of a child of 2 years, natural son of Maria Paula de Alamillo. Death by fever. Burial at public expense. Priest: F. Magnes.

2707. JOSEPH VEMENEZ
(721) 16 August 1820, burial of a child of 8 years, legitimate son of Francisco Vimenez and Maria Albina /blank/. Killed by a horse. Priest: F. Magnes.

2708. ONESIME BUARD
(721) 16 September 1820, burial in cemetery of this parish of a man aged 30, who left a widow, Rosalia Grenaux, by which marriage he left no children. Death by fever. Priest: F. Magnes.

2709. MARIA DEL PILAR EQUIS
(721) 19 September 1820, burial of a Spaniard, the widow of Mariano Garza who left 2 living sons and one living daughter. Death by fever. Priest: F. Magnes.

2710. MARGARITA SLLECTRE
(721) 19 September 1820, burial of the widow of Antonio Himel, who died leaving one daughter and one son. Death by fever. Priest: F. Magnes.

2711. MARIA LARNODIER
(721) 17 October 1820, burial of a child of 1 year, daughter of Asely Larnodier. Death by fever. Priest: F. Magnes.

2712. JOSEPH NAZARIO GUERRA
(722) [torn] 1820, burial of a child of 8 years, legitimate son of Jose Guerra and Basilia Gutierrez, who died of fever and was buried at public expense. Priest: F. Magnes.

2713. MARIA SIMONA CHIRINO LUNA
(722) 12 December 1820, burial of "Maria Simona Chirino or Luna," [sic], aged 40 years, wife of Sacramiento Basquez, from which marriage she left no children. Deceased received sacraments before dying of fever. Priest: F. Magnes.

2714. MARIE ADELAYDE VERGER [VERCHER]
(722) 5 January 1821, burial of the wife of Jean LaLande, aged 40, who left no children. The sacrament of Extreme Unction was administered before deceased succumbed to fever. Priest: F. Magnes.

2715. MARIE FRANCOISE GRILLET
(722) 16 January 1821, burial in cemetery of this parish of a native of this post, wife of Louis Bmy. Rachal, by which marriage she left 3 sons and 4 daughters. Death by dropsy. Priest: F. Magnes.

2716. FRANCISCO TORRES
(722) 31 January 1821, burial in cemetery of this parish of a Spanish soldier of the Alamo, aged about 45 years, who left a widow named Matilde and 1 son. Death from sudden pain, burial at public expense. Priest: F. Magnes.

2717. JUAN BTTE. TRICHEL
(723) /Torn/, 1821, burial in cemetery of this parish of a man aged 48 who left a widow, Marie /blank/ Fontaneau, by whom he also left 3 sons and 1 daughter. Death by fever. Priest: F. Magnes.

2718. MARIA RICHAL
(723) 17 February 1821, burial in cemetery of this parish of a child of 1 month, natural daughter of Maria Louisa Richal, who died of fever. Burial at public expense. Priest: F. Magnes.

2719. MARIA MARTINA NAVARRO
(723) 20 February 1821, burial of a 20 year old native of Sn. Antonio de Besar, unmarried. Deceased received the sacraments before dying of fever. Priest: F. Magnes.

2720. JUAN BORGAS
(723) 1 April 1821, burial of a Spaniard of about 50 years, said to be a bachelor and a native of Sta. Rosa. Death from a sudden pain. Burial at public expense. Priest: F. Magnes.

2721. JETRUDIS GUERRA
(723) 23 October 1821, burial of a native of Sn Antonio de Besar, aged about 35 years, wife of Louis Brisiño, who left 2 daughters and 1 son. She received the sacraments before dying of a pain. Priest: F. Magnes.

2722. URSIN GRILLET
(723) /torn/, burial of a child of "6 or 7 years," legitimate son of Theodore Grillet and /blank/ Peraut, already deceased. Death was from pain. Priest: F. Magnes.

2723. JOSEPH FRANCO. ESTRADA
(724) 10 May 1821, burial of a child of 6 months, legitimate son of Felis Estrada and Me. Nanet Casanova. Death by fever. Priest: F. Magnes.

2724. JEAN BTTE. VIENNE
(724) 16? June, 1821, burial of a child of 2 years, legitimate son of Francois Vienne and Marianne Buard. Died of fever. Priest: F. Magnes.

2725. ESQUIBEL
(724) 2 July 1821, burial of /blank/ Esquibel, aged 24 years, native of Candela and married there. Death by fever. Burial at public expense. Priest: F. Magnes.

2726. MANUEL FLORES
(724) 18 July 1821, burial of an unmarried Spaniard, aged 18, legitimate son of Hea___ Flores and Maria Antonia Benster, death by fever, burial at public expense. Priest: F. Magnes.

2727. JUAN MANUEL CANTAM
(724) 22 July 1821, burial of a native of Besar, who left as his widow Maria Antonia Losoya, as well as one child. Sacraments were administered before he died of fever. Priest: F. Magnes.

2728. BOCA
(725) /torn/, burial of a child of 2 years, legitimate daughter of Nepomuceno Boca Negro and /torn/. Died of fever. Burial at public expense. Priest: F. Magnes.

2729. ME. ASELY
(725) /torn/ July 1821, burial of a child of 17 days, legitimate daughter of Carlos ____ie and Asely Lambre. Death by epilepsy. Priest: F. Magnes.

2730. SIMON LOPEZ
(725) /torn/ August 1821, burial of a Spaniard, aged 34?, burial at public expense. Priest: F. Magnes. /Remainder of entry is illegible./

2731. ALEXY MORIN
(725) 18 August 1825, burial of a bachelor, native of Sn Louis Ysinua /St. Louis of the Illinois jurisdiction/, aged 27 years, who died of fever. Priest: F. Magnes.

2732. JEANN LOUIS MORIER
(725) 20 August 1821, burial of a native of France, aged about 35 years, who died of fever. Priest: F. Magnes.

2733. PIERRE BROSSET
(725) 9 October 1821, burial of Pierre Brosset, aged /torn/, who left a widow Maria Josefa Grillet, and 6 sons and 2 daughters. Death by fever, after administration of the sacraments. Priest: F. Magnes.

2734. JULIO ESTRADA
(725) 23 October 1821, burial of a Spaniard aged about 32 years, who left a widow named /blank/ by whom he had no children. Death by convulsions, after receipt of the sacraments. Priest: F. Magnes.

2735. JOSE MARIA CHAPA
(726) /Torn/ burial of a native of Besar, aged 28 years, legitimate son of /blank/ Chapa and /blank/. Death from fever, after receipt of the sacraments. Burial at public expense. Priest: F. Magnes.

2736. ALE PINDRO?
(726) 24 October 1821, burial of a native of France, about whom nothing else is known. Burial at public expense. Priest: F. Magnes. /Entry is badly torn./

2737. MARIE DENIS SHAILER /CHALER/
(726) 2_ October 1821, burial in the cemetery of this parish of a native of this jurisdiction, who died in childbirth leaving a widower, Eugenio Mechamps, by whom she had no children. Priest: F. Magnes. /Entry is badly torn./

2738. MARIE ROSSE SOPHONNY GRAPPE
(726) 26 November 1821, burial in the cemetery at Campte. Deceased left a widower, Placido Dervan, by whom she had no children. Death by fever. Priest: F. Magnes. Priest: F. Magnes.

2739. MARIE JEANNE MANET MALEGS
(726) /Torn/ burial in cemetery of this parish of the widow of Francisco Chavus. Death by fever. Sacraments were administered. Priest: F. Magnes.

2740. GUILLON BARBARUS
(727) /Torn/ 1822, burial of a native of Marsella /Marseilles/, France, aged 64 years, who left a widow Marie Chanet /Janet/ Chaneau and one married son. Sacraments were administered before he died of fever. Priest: F. Magnes.

2741. FELIS TROUDEAU
(727) 10 February 1822, burial in the cemetery of this parish of a 60 year old man who left a widow by whom he had no children. Priest: F. Magnes.

2742. ALEXANDRA SN. MIGUEL
(727) 10 February 1822, burial of a native of Besar, aged about 24 years, who left as her widow Miguel Leal, by whom she also left 2 daughters. Death was quite sudden, no sacraments were administered. Priest: F. Magnes.

2743. JOSE PROCELA
(727) 25 March 1822, burial of child of 8 days, legiti-

ate son of "L Cuate". Burial at public expence. Priest: F. Magnes.

2744. ALEXANDRE DETERVIL
(727) 13 April 1822, burial of a child of 8 days, "who received the waters," legitimate son of Mr. Detervil and Me. /blank/ Saucier. Priest: F. Magnes.

2745. GENOVEVA DUVOIS
(727) 22 April 1822, burial in cemetery of this parish of a 67 year old woman who left as her widower Juan Etien Adlle, as well as one daughter and seven sons. Death by fever. Priest: F. Magnes.

2746. MARIA LOUISA BREVEL
(727) 27 April 1822, burial of the 85 year old widow of Marin Grillet, by whom she left 8 sons and 2 daughters. Death by fever. Priest: F. Magnes.

2747. MARIA LOUISA PLESANS
(728) /torn/, burial of a 17 year old who died of childbirth fever, leaving as her widower Germain? (Gervais?) Trichel. Priest: F. Magnes.

2748. JETRUDIS FLORES
(728) 14 May 1822, burial of a native of Sn Antonio who died of dropsy after receiving the sacraments. Burial at public expense. Priest: F. Magnes.

2749. RICHARD PLESANS
(728) 2_ May 1822, burial of a child of Jn Btte. Plesans and Me. _____ esa _____ . Priest: F. Magnes. /Entry is badly torn./

2750. JOSE ANTONIO ESTRADA
(728) 4 June 1822, burial of a Spaniard aged about 60 years, who died of fever. Burial at public expense. Priest: F. Magnes.

2751. MARIA ATHANAS DE G_____ER ISARD /HISSOURA/
(728) 5 June 1822, burial of the legitimate daughter of Barnardo Isard, who died of fever. Priest: F. Magnes.

2752. JOSE FLORES
(728) 15 July 1822, burial of a man of about 60 years, husband of Maria Ignacio Procela, by whom he left one daughter. Burial at public expense. Priest: F. Magnes.

2753. MARIA CONCEPCION FORSAET
(728) 12 July 1822, burial of a child of 6 months and
10 days, legitimate daughter of Santiago Forsaet,
already deceased, and of Maria Luisa Larnodier.
Death by fever. Priest: F. Magnes.

2754. MIGUEL VILLEGAR
(728) 20 July 1822, burial of a Spaniard aged 45 years,
who left a widow, Ignacia Flores, and 2 daughters
and 1 son. Priest: F. Magnes.

2755. ALFRED BUARD
(729) 5 August 1822, burial of a child of 13 years, legitimate son of Jeann Btte. Buard and Aspasie Bossier. Death by fever. Priest: F. Magnes.

2756. BENJAMIN DRANGUET
(729) 6 August 1822, burial of a child of 11 months,
legitimate son of Benjamin Dranguet and /blank/
Tauzin. Death by fever. Priest: F. Magnes.

2757. MARIE TAUZIN
(729) 28 August 1822, burial of a child of 8 months,
legitimate daughter of Louis Tausin and Ma. /blank/
Murphy. Death by fever. Priest: F. Magnes.

APPENDIX

Extracts from Register 19, "Index to Baptisms," 1800-1816

NOTE: On scattered pages of Register 19 of the Parish of Immaculate Conception a mid-nineteenth century priest compiled an "Index to Baptisms" performed in the old Parish of St. François between 1724 and 1850. This index, in which each year's baptisms are listed separately in alphabetical order, is far more informative than the name "Index" suggests. However, it is *not* a duplicate copy, or a complete transcription, as is sometimes assumed.

The single-line entries of this "Index" provides names of child, parents, godparents, and dates of baptism and birth, and they contain certain inherent shortcomings: 1) space limitations required abbreviations of many given names; 2) the compiler "translated" all names into French, even those of Spanish and English residents; 3) compiler occasionally misread the less common family names; and 4) all additional data in the original entries (i.e. grandparents, places of birth or residence, occupation of parents, legitimacy of child, etc.) was omitted. This Index has, for a number of years, been microfilmed and made available in the larger libraries of Louisiana. However, researchers are advised to consult the original entries to which this Index refers, for more complete data. In most cases, these originals are still extant.

Register 5, which has been abstracted, translated, and published in this volume, is the exception. A portion of the baptismal entries for 1800-01, 1810, 1814-16 have been either destroyed or extensively damaged. On the following pages appear the Index entries for the missing or severely damaged baptismal entries in Register 5. Page numbers refer to Index entries in Volume 19.

2758. MARIE ARMAND
(516) 20 April 1800, baptism of infant born 17 March 1800,
v19 daughter of J. Baptiste Armand and Mie. Cat. Frederic. Godparents: J. M. Armand and M.C. Sauvage. Priest: P. Pavie.

2759. CLEMENT BOUET [LA FITTE]
(517) 7 December 1801, baptism of infant born 23 November 1801, son of Clement Bouet and Ursul Grappe
v19 [Gagne?]. Godparents: Louis Gagne and Fois. Grape. Priest: P. Pavie.

2760. JOSEPH DUBOIS
(517) 13 September 1801, baptism of infant born 14 January 1801, son of Antoine Dubois and Mie. Jh. Malige. Godparents: Jos. Tessier and Rose Dupre. Priest: P. Pavie.

2761. MARIE FREDERIC [GONIN?]
(517) 7 June 1801, baptism of child born 6 May 1801,
v19 daughter of Francois Frederic and Mie. Bbe. Gonin. Godparents: Ph. Frederic and Gen. Gonin. Priest: P. Pavie. *[? Child of Franc. Gonin and M. Barbe Frederic?]

2762. J. BAPTISTE SALVADOS [PALVADOS]
(517) 13 September 1801, baptism of child born 15 April
v19 1800, son of Jean Salvados and Eleonore Tessier. Godparents: J. B. Plaisance and Mie. Daragon. Priest: P. Pavie.   [See Entry 1]

2763. ETIENNE WALLES
(517) 7 December 1801, baptism of child born 12 October
v19 1801, son of E. Jacques Walles and*Catherine Gagne. Godparents: P. Ternier and Anne Gagne. Priest: P. Pavie. [See Entry 4]   *[Hyacinthe]

2764. MARIE ANNE FRANCOISE LEFEVRE
(524) 21 December 1810, baptism of child born 3 October
v19 1810, daughter of Jn Bte. LeFevre and M. L. V. Charrio. Godparents: Jean Cortes and Mie. A. Rouquie. Priest: L. Buhot. [See Entry 3237]

2765. JN FRANCOIS ADLEY
(527) 24 May 1814, baptism of child born 28 March 1814,
v19 son of Thimothe Adley and Mie. De. Prudhomme. Godparents: Fois. Bienne and M. P. Adle. Priest: F. Magnes.

2766. FRANCOIS ARMAND
(527) 16 May 1814, baptism of child born 27 October 1813,
v19 son of Jean Armand and Mie Anas^{ie} Mayou. Godpar-

ents: J. F. Magnes and M. A. Peraut. Priest: F. Magnes.

2767. IGNACE ARMAND
(527) 18 October 1814, baptism of child born 27 October
v19 1813, son of Jean Armand and Mie. Anasie. Mayou. Godparents: A. M. Rambin and Mie. Fis. Peraut. Priest: F. Magnes. /See Entry 49<u>1</u>7/

2768. JN. FELIX BOZELA (PROCELLA)*
(527) 2 April 1814, baptism of child of 15 days, son of
v19 J. Baptiste Procella and Marzelina de la Zerda. Godparents: Louis Buard and Jeanne Laveda. Priest: F. Magnes. /See Entry 46<u>8</u>7/

*Name is written both ways in the Index Entry. Procella is correct.

2769. MIE. NATALIE BUART
(527) 28 May 1814, baptism of child born 7 February 1814,
v19 daughter of Jn. Baptiste Buart and Mie. Aspie. Bossie. Godparents: Pl. Bossier and Mie. T. Buard. Priest: F. Magnes.

2770. FAUSTIN CHAVANA
(528) 3 April 1814, baptism of a child of 32 days, son
v19 of Raymond Chavana and Mie. Jh. Sanchez. Godparents: J. B. Belange and J. J. Ruiz. Priest: F. Magnes.

2771. MARTIN CHAVANA
(528) 4 February 1814, baptism of child of 7 days, son
v19 of Lin. Chavana and Barb. Chaver. Godparents: Rosmd. Chamard and Gd. Alamillo. Priest: F. Magnes. /See Entry 45<u>9</u>7/

2772. JN. VENANCIO CORTINAS
(528) 26 May 1814, baptism of infant born 1 April 1814,
v19 child of Jh. Marie Cortinas and Mie. Gde. Procella. Godparents: J. M. Carriere and Laysa Bille. Priest: F. Magnes.

2773. J. F. ROMUALD CUELLAR
(528) 12 April 1814, baptism of child of 3 days, infant
v19 of Jh. Marie Cuellar and Mie. Victana. Falcon. Godparents: Jh. Vict. <u>Foldomo?</u> and L. Casman. Priest: F. Magnes.

2774. HENRI CUERCA /QUIRK/
(528) 20 November 1814, baptism of child of 47 days, son
v19 of Guillaume Cuerca and Juliena Nover /Norris/.

Godparents: Ap. Marmela and Mie. Robinson. Priest: F. Magnes. /See Entry 500/

2775. PABLO DELGADO
(528) 12 March 1814, baptism of child of 10 days, son of
v19 Jean Delgado and Concepon. Zebeda. Godparents: Fois. Pearia and Aug. Marmello. Priest: F. Magnes.

2776. JEAN BAPTISTE THEODULE DERBANNE
(528) 27 April 1814, baptism of child born 9 March 1814,
v19 son of Jn. Baptiste Derbanne and Mie. L. Plaisance. Godparents: Brd. Plaisance and Mie. B. Grillet. Priest: F. Magnes.

2777. ETIENNE BREVIL ESLECT /CHELETTE/
(528) 20 July 1814, baptism of child of 7 months, son of
v19 Jn. Baptiste Eslect and Mie. Phos. Rachal. Godparents: J. P. Eslect and Mie. Laur. Rachal. Priest: F. Magnes. /See Entry 485/

2778. POLICARPE FLORES
(528) 21 June 1814, baptism of child born 26 January
v19 1814, son of Vital Flores and Gertde. Mora. Godparents: Ls. Procela and Mie. Soto. Priest: F. Magnes. /See Entry 476/

2779. M. PAMEDA FOSTON /JOHNSON/
(528) 28 June 1814, baptism of child born 25 January
v19 1814, daughter of Jean Foston and Fcois. Grenoble. Godparents: Et. Brown and Mie. Grenoble /Greneaux/ Priest: F. Magnes. /See Entry 482/

2780. MIE. HENRIETTE FREDERICK
(528) 8 May 1814, baptism of child born 16 January 1813,
v19 daughter of Francois Frederick and Mie. Fis. Lavespere. Godparents: J. B. Armand and Ma. Lavespere. Priest: F. Magnes.

2781. MIE. MICHEL FREDERIK
(528) 11 April 1814, baptism of child of 11 months, in-
v19 fant of Michel Frederik and Mie. Luz. Bossie. Godparents: F. Peraut and Mie. Leodie. Bossie. Priest: F. Magnes.

2782. ISIDORE CESAR FREDIEU
(528) 26 June 1814, baptism of child born 15 May 1814,
v19 son of Césair Fredieu and Rosa Derbanne. Godparents: J. Fredieu and Jne. Perault. Priest: F. Magnes. /See Entry 480/

2783. MIE. PAUL GALLARDO
(528)
v19

7 March 1814, baptism of child of 5 days, infant of Jh. Louis Gallardo and Mie. Albina Martinez. Godparents: J. M. Sanchez and Mie. Roberson. Priest: F. Magnes.

2784. MELIZERE GALLIEN
(528) 10 April 1814, baptism of child of 1 year, child
v19 of Louis Gallien and Mie. Cte. Anty. Godparents: Jac. Vercher and Mie. Jne. Gallien. Priest: F. Magnes.

2785. JH. MARIE HORTIZ
(528) 15 September 1814, baptism of child born 12 Octo-
v19 ber 1813, child of Faustin Hortiz and Mie. Aragon. Godparents: Hilario Carrasco and Mia. Servantes. Priest: F. Magnes. [See Entry 494]

2786. MIE. THOMAS IBARBO
(528) 29 January 1814, baptism of child of 1 month, daugh-
v19 ter of J. Domingo Ibarbo and Mie. Sanchez. Godparents: Jn. Isid. Acosta and M. G. Sanchez. Priest: F. Magnes. [See Entry 458]

2787. MARIE U. LESTAGE
(528) 2 June 1814, baptism of child born 7 November 1813,
v19 daughter of Jn. Baptiste Lestage and Mie. Jne. Sheletre. Godparents: Fcois. Lestage and Mie. Frederick. Priest: F. Magnes. [See Entry 470]

2788. MIE JOS. MARTINEZ
(529) 21 February 1814, baptism of child born 19 Febru-
v19 ary 1814, daughter of Ermenegilde Martinez and Marie D. Castro. Godparents: Rond. Chamard and Mie. T. Guerra. Priest: F. Magnes. [See Entry 462]

2789. JACQUES MECHEON
(528) 30 April 1814, baptism of child of 3½ months, son
v19 of Eleysa Mechon. Godparents: Bn. Guisarnat and Lo. Larnaudiere. Priest: F. Magnes.

2790. MARIE DEL CARMEN MORA
(528) 8 June 1814, baptism of child born 13 October 1813,
v19 daughter of Etienne Mora and Mie. Get. Zerda.*
Godparents: Jac. Lacase and Mie. Lie. Dupre. Priest: F. Magnes. [See Entries 465 and 472, abstracted from separated fragments of the same entry.]

*Pencilled above this name appears the corrected name "Cerda."

2791. J. BTA. DA. MORANTI
(528) 8 May 1814, baptism of child born 5 April 1814,
v19 son of Jn. Baptiste Moranti and Mie. Phrs.
Frederick. Godparents: J. B. Armand and Mie. Fie.
Lavespere. Priest: F. Magnes.

2792. DAMAS B. PERAUT
(528) 10 April 1814, baptism of child born 12 December
v19 1813, son of Jn Fostin Peraut and Mie. Cte. Bordelon. Godparents: Jn. Ls. Peraut and Mie. Cel.
Triche. Priest: F. Magnes.

2793. FRANCOIS PERAUT
(528) 19 June 1814, baptism of child of 12½ months, son
v19 of Louis Peraut and Mie. Mie. Trichel. Godparents: H. Trichel and M. A. Labery. Priest: F.
Magnes. /See Entry 4757/

2794. JH. M. ANDRE RACHAL
(528) 9 July 1814, baptism of child born 30 November
v19 1813, son of Etienne Rachal and G. Ramon. Godparents: P. G. Billet and Mie. Lse. Rachal. Priest:
F. Magnes. /See Entry 4837/

2795. J. MANUEL RODRIGUEZ
(528) 18 June 1814, baptism of child of 3 days, son of
v19 C. Augustin Rodriguez and Maria Dias. Godparents:
Sil. Poissot and F. Th. Lamath. Priest: F.
Magnes. /See Entry 4747/

2796. MARIE THERESE SANCHEZ
(529) 3 March 1814, baptism of child of 6 months, daughter of Jh. Leonard Sanchez and Mie. Casimire Garza. Godparents: Jn. Ant. Gonzales and Josh.
Paloma. Priest: F. Magnes. /See Entry 4637/

2797. JH. FACUNDIN SANTOS
(529) 23 July 1814, baptism of a child of 16 days, son
v19 of Francois Santos and Mie. Jha. Rios. Godparents: Fcis. Robain and Jne. Mamillo. Priest: F.
Magnes. /See Entry 4867/

2798. MIE ARSINE TRICLE
(529) 16 May 1814, baptism of child born 30 December
v19 1813, daughter of Manuel Triche and Ls. Ph. Prudhomme. Godparents: Ls. Clauso and Mie. P. Prudhomme. Priest: F. Magnes.

2799. MIE. LAŸSA VERCHER
(529) 10 April 1814, baptism of child of 16 months,
v19 daughter of Jacques Vercher and Mie. Jne. Gallien.

Godparents: N. Gallien and Mie. Adlle. Gallien.
Priest: F. Magnes.

2800. MIE. CELINE VERCHER
(529) 10 April 1814, baptism of child of 10 months,
v19 daughter of Beloni Vercher and Mie. Ozel. Gallien.
Godparents: Louis Gallien and Mie. F. Grillet.
Priest: F. Magnes.

2801 FOIS. LS. ARMAND AUGUESSE
(529) 13 July 1815, baptism of child born 7 October 1814,
v19 son of Jn. Armand Aguesse and Mie. Lse. Massipe.
Godparents: Fois. Lattier and Mie. P. Chelette.
Priest: F. Magnes.

2802. MIE. CELESTE BT. LAFITTE
(529) 11 September 1815, baptism of child of 4 years,
v19 daughter of Paul Bt. Lafitte and Mariana Soto.
Godparents: Ces. Fonteneau and Mie. Lafitte.
Priest: F. Magnes.

2803. PELAGIE BUARD
(529) 22 October 1815, baptism of child born 6 October
v19 1814, daughter of Jn. Louis Buard and Eulalie Bossie. Godparents: Onez. Buard and Au. Bossie.
Priest: F. Magnes.   [See Entry 6847]

2804. JN. JH. PHIL. BUSTAMENTE
(529) 16 October 1815, baptism of child of 1 month, son
v19 of Manuel Bustamente and Mie. Lse. Sanchez. Godparents: Jn. Bte. Chirino and Mie. Gde. Chirino.
Priest: F. Magnes.

2805. MIE. CLEMINE CHELETRE
(529) 13 September 1815, baptism of child born 24 July
v19 1814, daughter of Pierre Cheletre and Eulalie Bossier. Godparents: Ces. Bossie and M.P. Chelete.
Priest: F. Magnes.

2806. JH. MAXIMIN COMPERE
(530) 28 November 1815, baptism of child born 29 May
v19 1815, son of P. Sebastian Compere and Mie. Lolette Rachal. Godparents: Y.B.D. [sic] Armant and Jne. Briant. Priest: F. Magnes. [See Entry 6877]

2807. MARIE ANTOINETTE CRUZ
(530) 12 October 1815, baptism of child of 8 days, daugh-
v19 ter of Jn. Antoine Cruz and Mie. Simona Ruiz.
Godparents: Ponz. Ibarbo and Mie. P. Padilla.
Priest: F. Magnes.

2808. ANT. URSIN DERBANNE
(530)
v19

13 July 1815, baptism of child born 27 July 1814, son of Jn. Bte. Derbanne and Mie. Dupre. Godparents: A. B. Rachal and Asp. Derbanne. Priest: F. Magnes.

2809. ANT. HONORE FLORES
(530) 12 October 1815, baptism of child of 2 years, son
v19 of Joseph Flores and ?. Equis. Godparents: B. Bustamente and Lina Padilla. Priest: F. Magnes.

2810. JULIEN GRADNER
(530) 5 July 1815, baptism of child born 7 April 1814,
v19 son of Jacques Gradner and Art. Andreson. Godparents: Geo. Andreson and Delsir Lesar. Priest: F. Magnes. [See Entry 6087]

2811. MIE. EMILY HERNANDEZ
(530) 11 July 1815, baptism of child born 15 November
v19 1811, daughter of Jerome Hernandez and Isabelle Rachal. Godparents: Fois. Rachal and Jeanne Rachal. Priest: F. Magnes.

2812. J. B. OB. HERNANDEZ
(530) 14 July 1815, baptism of child born 1815, son of
v19 Jerome Hernandez and Isabelle Rachal. Godparents: Jn. B. Lecomte and Fois. Rachal. Priest: F. Magnes.

2813. MIE. J. CELESTINE HESER
(530) 10 September 1815, baptism of child born 14 May
v19 1815, daughter of Christian Hesser and Mie. F. A. Rambin. Godparents: M. Chamard and Mie. D. Soto. Priest: F. Magnes.

2814. MARIE FELICITE LEMOINE
(531) 13 July 1815, baptism of child born 27 July 1814,
v19 daughter of Jn. Baptiste Lemoine and Fel. Lacase. Godparents: J. B. Lemoine and Fel. Pomier. Priest: F. Magnes.

2815. JOSEPH LETON
(531) 12 October 1815, baptism of child of 6 years, son
v19 of Jean Leton and Suz. Andrez. Godparents: Jh. Flores and Trin. Procela. Priest: F. Magnes.

2816. M. JACQUES LETON
(531) 12 October 1815, baptism of child of 2 years, son
v19 of Jean Leton and Suz. Andrez. Godparents: Mar. Soto and Trin. Procela. Priest: F. Magnes.

2817. FRANCOIS MORIN
(531) 12 October 1815, baptism of child of 6 months, son
v19

of Etienne Morin and Thel. de la Cerda. Godparents: J. O. Chirino and An. Santos. Priest: F. Magnes.

2818. CATHERINE MIETA /NIETA?/
(531) 12 October 1815, baptism of child of 9 months, son
v19 of Jean Mieta and Denise Christian /Christy?/. Godparents: Fois Santos and M. Christin. Priest: F. Magnes.

2819. LAURENT POIRRIER /CURANY? LAURENT POIRRIER?/
(531) 1 February 1815, baptism of child born 22 December
v19 ber 1813, son of Francois Poirrier and Th.*Lestage. Godparents: Jh. Thomassy and M.F. Thomassy. Priest: F. Magnes. /See Entry 517/ */Thomassie/

2820. JH. VICTOR PERAUT
(531) 22 December 1815, baptism of child born 22 November
v19 ber 1815, child of Jh. Crysosto Peraut and Mie. Ol. Fredieu. Godparents: Hon. Fredieu and M. M. Peraut. Priest: F. Magnes. /See Entry 690/

2821. MIE. MAURICIA SANCHEZ
(532) 12 October 1815, baptism of child born 22 September
v19 ber 1815, daughter of Ludgard Sanchez and C. La Garza. Godparents: P. Acosta and Mie. F. Griar__. Priest: F. Magnes.

2822. JN. FRANCOIS TOVAL
(532) 23 December 1815, baptism of child of 1 month, son
v19 of Jean Toval and Mie. Th. Rodriguez. Godparents: Jh. Carrier and Gert. Procela. Priest: F. Magnes. /See Entry 688/

2823. JH. ANTOINE YDALGO /HIDALGO/
(532) 13 October 1815, baptism of child of 28 days, son
v19 of Marie Idalgo. Godparents: J. B. Procela and Mie. M. Cerda. Priest: F. Magnes.

2824. ALEXIS ANTY
(532) 1 November 1816, baptism of child born 17 July
v19 1816, son of Silvestre Anty and Mie. C. Baudouin. Godparents: Louis Baudouin and Phro. Baudoin. Priest: F. Magnes.

2825. MARIE AGLAE ANTY
(532) 13 February 1816, baptism of child born 20 November
v19 ber 1815, daughter of Valery Anty and Mie. Asp. Derbanne. Godparents: Al. Cloutier and Mie. ?. Davion. Priest: F. Magnes. /See Entries 696 and 708, abstracted from separated fragments of the same original entry./

2826. MARIE LOUISE ARCE
(532) 23 July 1816, baptism of child aged 5 months, daugh-
v19 ter of J. Baptiste Arce and Mie. Chinny.* Godparents: Vin. Esparza and Mie. Jh. Ceda. Priest:
F. Magnes. */Sims/

2827. MIE. FELONY AREVALO
(532) 6 July 1816, baptism of infant of 2 years, child
v19 of Jacques Arevalo and Mie. Ant. Torres. Godparents: Michel Teal and Osite André. Priest: F.
Magnes.

2828. JEANE MIE. ARRANOGA
(532) 6 July 1816, baptism of infant of 1 year, child of
v19 Cayeton Arranoga and Mie. Risa Conisa. Godparents:
Mie. Peraut and Mie. Orezil. Priest: F. Magnes.

2829. MIE. AIMEE BAUDOUIN
(532) 27 June 1816, baptism of child of 1 month, daugh-
v19 ter of Pierre Baudouin and Anne Robert /Robin/.
Godparents: Ath. Denis and Mie. ?. Baudouin.
Priest: F. Magnes.

2830. EDOUARD BAULIEU
(532) 22 October 1816, baptism of infant of 8 years, child
v19 of Pierre Baulieu and There_____ /sic - should be
Marie Therese Beaudouin/. Godparents: D. Sorel
and Gen. Henry. Priest: F. Magnes.

2831. JULIEN BESSOM
(532) 14 March 1816, baptism of infant born 16 July 1815,
v19 child of Jn. Baptiste Bessom and Mie. Jeane. Pievert. Godparents: Hyp. Bordelon and Rosa Derbanne.
Priest: F. Magnes.

2832. MIE. ELYSSA BOSSIER
(532) 13 January 1816, baptism of child born 14 March
v19 1815, daughter of Soulange Bossier and Eleonore
Imble. Godparents: N. Bossier and Sol. Bossier.
Priest: F. Magnes. /See Entries 692 and 711, abstracted from separated fragments of the same original entry./

2833. MARIE BT. LAFITTE
(532) 11 October 1816, baptism of infant born /blank/,
v19 child of Cesar Lafitte and Mie. Isab. Leton. Godparents: _____ Lafitte and Mie. J. Laberry.
Priest: F. Magnes.

2834. JH. FLUGEAU BTE. LAFITTE
(532) 11 October 1816, baptism of infant born 16 January
v19

        1814, child of Cesar Lafitte and Mie. Isab. Leton. Godparents: Phil. Flores and Mie. A. Flores. Priest: F. Magnes.

2835. RAND. RUB. BULLET
(532) 1 September 1816, baptism of child born 13 __
v19 1816 /sic/, child of Benjamin Bullet and Mie. Furgerson. Godparents: Reuben Ross and Mat. Blère?. Priest: F. Magnes.

2836. MIE. BASILIO CARO
(532) 1 October 1816, baptism of infant born 11 June 1816,
v19 child of Thomas Caro and Mie. Gert. Texeda. Godparents: Phil. Flores and Tamid. Flores. Priest: F. Magnes.

2837. MIE. CLETA CARO
(532) 27 December 1816, baptism of infant born 14 July
v19 1816, child of Joseph Caro and Michel. Equis. Godparents: Jn. Mora and Jacinta Procella. Priest: F. Magnes.

2838. JOSEPH V. CASENAVE
(532) 18 October 1816, baptism of infant born 6 March,
v19 child of Suz. Casenave. Godparents: Jh. Brom and Lse. Brom. Priest: F. Magnes.

2839. JH. CRISANTO CASENAVE
(532) 20 December 1816, baptism of infant of 55 days, son
v19 of Joseph Casenave and Mie. Mel. Seguin. Godparents: J. M. Delgado and M. A. Rodriguez. Priest: F. Magnes.

2840. JN. MARIE CASTRO
(532) 1 March 1816, baptism of child of 1 day, infant of
v19 Mie. Gert. Castro. Godparents: J. J. M. Acosta and Mie. Tri. Sanchez. Priest: F. Magnes. /See Entry 70_37_/

2841. M. E. E. CHAMARD
(532) 30 January 1816, baptism of child of 30 days, in-
v19 fant of Andre Chamard and Fel. Saucier. Godparents: M. Chamard and H. Soucier. Priest: F. Magnes.

2842. J. GUILL. CHAVANE
(532) 1 March 1816, baptism of child of 17 (19?) days,
v19 son of Raymond Chavana and Jhine. Sanchez. Godparents: J. A. Sepalveda and N. B. Sta. Cruz. Priest: F. Magnes. /See Entries 702 and 714, abstracted from separated fragments of the same original entry./

2843. JEAN RAYM. CHENOWETH
(533) 23 July 1816, baptism of child born 13 March 1816,
v19 son of Thomas Chenoweth and Anne Marie Querca.
Godparents: Et. Mora and Mie. Gde. de la Cerda.
Priest: F. Magnes.

2844. MARIE THEM. CHIRINO
(533) 26 May 1816, baptism of infant born 26 November
v19 1815, daughter of Jh. Lucas Chirino and Mie. Anastasie Sanchez. Godparents: B. Y. Pantaleon and
Mie. A. Pantaleon. Priest: F. Magnes.

2845. JN. JOSEPH CLARC
(533) 11 October 1816, baptism of infant born 29 September
v19 ber 1816, child of Joseph Clarc and Ther. Sidrec.
Godparents: Jh. Cand. Miguel and M. J. I. Chanac.
Priest: F. Magnes.

2846. DUFROIT CRET-ANTY
(532) 11 November 1816, baptism of infant born 9 January
v19 1816, son of Mie. Jne. Cret-Anty. Godparents: Ls.
Galien and Mie. C. Anty. Priest: F. Magnes.

2847. DERZILIN CRET-ANTY
(532) 11 November 1816, baptism of child born 9 July
v19 1808, son of Mie. Jne. Cret-Anty. Godparents: Alexis Cloutier and Mie. L. Rachal. Priest: F.
Magnes.

2848. MANUEL DERBANNE
(533) 6 July 1816, baptism of child of 1 month, infant
v19 of Manuel Derbanne and Margte. Denis. Godparents:
Pierre Michel and Mne. Baudouin. Priest: F. Magnes.

2849. MIE. MARGTE. DERBANNE
(533) 10 November 1816, baptism of child born 2 October
v19 1816, infant of Pierre Derbanne and Mie. Asp. David
[Davion]. Godparents: Louis Derbanne and Mie. Hn.
Cloutier. Priest: F. Magnes.

2850. JOSEPH EL. DESPALLIER
(533) 14 April 1816, baptism of child born 1 December
v19 1815, infant of B. Marin Despallier and Mie. Ct.
Grande. Godparents: Charles Norys and Gen. Dubois.
Priest: F. Magnes.

2851. EDOUARD ELY
(533) 14 April 1816, baptism of child born 3 November
v19 1815, son of Pierre Ely and Marie Derbanne. Godparents: Pla. Derbanne and Suz. Derbanne. Priest:
F. Magnes.

2852. MIE. TELESPHORE FLORES
(533) 3 July 181 , baptism of child of 6 months, daugh-
v19 ter of Joseph Flores and Stephanie Ekeris?. God-
     parents: Pierre Chirino and Mie. Sanchez. Priest:
     F. Magnes.

2853. MIE. BARBE FREDERIC
(533) 6 May 1816, baptism of child born 6 February 1815,
v19 daughter of André Frederic and Suz. Soul. Bossier.
     Godparents: Cesair Bossier and Margte. Frederic.
     Priest: F. Magnes.

2854. MIE. EMELIE FREDERIC
(533) 15 October 1816, baptism of child born 30 June
v19 1816, daughter of Philippe Frederic and Rosalie
     Lestage. Godparents: Andres Frederic and Margte.
     Frederic. Priest: F. Magnes.

2855. MIE. LOLET FREDERIC
(533) 3 November 1816, baptism of child born 3 August
v19 1816, daughter of Francois Frederic and Felicite
     Lavespere. Godparents: God. Lavespere and Azelie
     Langlois. Priest: F. Magnes.

2856. JN. BAPTISTE GAGNIE
(533) 1 May 1816, baptism of child born 9 July 1816, son
v19 of Pierre Gagnie and Jeanne Lalande. Godparents:
     Pierre Rasaly and Layde Gagnie. Priest: F. Magnes.

2857. MIE. EULALIE GALLIEN
(533) 16 November 1816, baptism of child born 23 Septem-
v19 ber 1816, daughter of Manuel Gallien and Mie.
     Eloise Lattier. Godparents: Al. Cloutier and
     Mie. P. Frederic. Priest: F. Magnes.

2858. LOUIS GALLIEN
(533) 10 November 1816, baptism of child born 20 August
v19 1816, son of Louis Gallien and Mie Cel. Anty.
     Godparents: Ml. Derbanne and Mie. Ad. Gallien.
     Priest: F. Magnes.

2859. JEANNE GARZA
(533) 18 October 1816, baptism of child of 2 years,
v19 daughter of Pierre Garza and Incarnation Soto.
     Godparents: J. A. Chirino and Mie. A. Los Sanctos.
     Priest: F. Magnes.

2860. MARIE LOUISE PETRA GARZA
(533) 11 October 1816, baptism of child born 29 ___ 1816
v19 /sic/, daughter of Pierre Garza and Incarnation
     Soto. Godparents: Ml. Lafitte and Mie. In. Soto
     Priest: F. Magnes.

2861. JOSEPH GILARD
(533) 2 July 1816, baptism of child born 5 May 1816, son
v19 of Jn. Baptiste Gilard and Cecile LaCour. Godparents: Jh. Gillard and Lse. Gillard. Priest: F. Magnes.

2862. LOUIS WALLET
(533) 2 May 1816, baptism of child born 15 June 1814,
v19 son of Louis Wallet and Angela Gagnie. Godparents: Louis Gagnie and Celesie Davion. Priest: F. Magnes.

2863. MARIE ELENNE WALLET /WALLACE/
(533) 28 May 1816, baptism of child born 14 May 1814,
v19 daughter of Thomas Wallet and *Constance Bertrand. Godparents: Al. Dublieu and Mie. Chamard. Priest: F. Magnes.   */Hortense/

2864. THOMAS WALLET /WALLACE/
(533) 28 May 1816, baptism of child born 14 May 1815,
v19 son of Thomas Wallet and *Constance Bertrand. Godparents: Beno. Bertrand and Adel. Tauzin. Priest: F. Magnes.   */Hortense/

2865. FOIS. BARTHELEMY GONIN
(533) 7 April 1816, baptism of child born 27 September
v19 1815, son of Francois Gonin and Mie. Bbe. Frederic. Godparents: Bmy. Lestage and Mod. Gonin. Priest: F. Magnes.

2866. JH. MARTIN GONZALEZ
(533) 1 March 1816, baptism of child of 15 days, son of
v19 Ignace Gonzalez and Marie Rosalis. Godparents: Jh. Ybarbo and Jhine. Arriola. Priest: F. Magnes.

2867. MIE. TIMOTHE GONZALEZ
(533) 27 August, 1816, baptism of child of 4 days, child
v19 of Jacques Gonzalez and Mie. Foise. Gonzalez. Godparents: Henry Trichel and Genev. Ris. Priest: F. Magnes.

2868. CHARLES HARRIS
(533) 28 May 1816, baptism of child born 9 August 1814,
v19 infant of William Harris and Marie Patton. Godparents: Joseph Tauzin and Mie. Chamard. Priest: F. Magnes.

2869. MIE. HENRIETTE HARRIS
(533) 28 May 1816, baptism of infant born 14 March 1814,
v19 child of William Harris and Marie Patton. Godparents: Charles Pavie and Mariana Rouquier. Priest: F. Magnes.

2870. MIE. ANTOI. HERNANDEZ
(533) 1 March 1816, baptism of child of 43 days, daugh-
v19 ter of Mie. Tel/esfora/ Hernandez. Godparents:
     Jn. Bte. Chirino and Gert. Chirino. Priest: F.
     Magnes. /See Entries 704 and 719, abstracted
     from separated fragments of the same original
     entry./

2871. ANTOINE HORTIS
(533) 14 May 1816, baptism of child of 6 months, son of
v19 Faustin Hortis and Marie Aragona. Godparents:
     Jacques Lacase and Mie. Langlois. Priest: F. Magnes.

2872. NICOLAS LACOUR
(533) 2 July 1816, baptism of child born 25 January 1816,
v19 son of Jean Marie LaCour and Jhine. Gillard. God-
     parents: Jh. Gillard and Cec. Lacour. Priest:
     F. Magnes.

2873. MIE. SUZETTE LACOUR
(533) 10 November 1816, baptism of child born 27 April
v19 1816, daughter of Gaspar LaCour and Felicite Bre-
     vel. Godparents: Pierre Derbanne and Asp. David
     /Davion/. Priest: F. Magnes.

2874. MARIE LAPLACE
(533) 15 May 1816, baptism of child born 28 October 1816
v19 /sic/, daughter of Jean Laplace and Eli. Mejall*
     Godparents: Guillaume C. Shumas /Thomas?/ and
     Ann Holt. Priest: F. Magnes.   */McFall/

2875. M. L. O. LARENAUDIERE
(533) 8 September 1816, baptism of child born 27 July
v19 1816, daughter of Jh. Baptiste Larenaudiere and
     Marie F. Baudouin. Godparents: B. Guisarnac and
     Mie. L. Larenaudiere. Priest: F. Magnes.

2876. MARIE ZELINE LATTIER
(533) 12 November 1816, baptism of child born 13 October
v19 1816, daughter of Francois Lattier and Pelagie
     Sheletre. Godparents: Jh. Lattier and Mie. Lse.
     Lattier. Priest: F. Magnes.

2877. MIE. JH. ZEPH. LENOIR
(533) 2 May 1816, baptism of child of 2½ months, infant
v19 of Antoine Lenoir and Desneiges Derbanne. Godpar-
     ents: Pl. Derbanne and Mie. R. Derbanne. Priest:
     F. Magnes.

2878. JN. BAPTISTE LESTAGE
(533) 18 May 1816, baptism of child born 24 November
v19

1815, infant of Jn. Baptiste Lestage and Mie. Jn. Sheletre. Godparents: Bmy. Lestage and Mie. M. Laforet. Priest: F. Magnes.

2879. MARIE LOM
(533) 18 October 1816, baptism of infant born 27 March
v19 1815, daughter of Jean Lom and *_____ Cheredem [sic]. Godparents: Ed. Morphy and Elis. Cheredem [Sheridan]. Priest: F. Magnes. *[Rebecca]

2880. JH. IGNACE LOSA [SOSA]
(533) 13 December 1816, baptism of child of 8 months,
v19 son of Jean-Andre Losa and Mie. A. Casenave. Godparents: Sil. Estrada and Mie. T. Guerra. Priest: F. Magnes.

2881. JNE. FRANCOISE LOSOYA
(533) 20 December 1816, baptism of child born 4 October
v19 1816, infant of Ventura Losoya and Mie. C. Estrada. Godparents: Jh. Mie. Delgado and M. A. Rodriguez. Priest: F. Magnes.

2882. MIE. ANTETTE. MEGNY
(533) 10 September 1816, baptism of child born 15 April
v19 1815, daughter of Jean Megny and Saly Borchez. Godparents: Jh. Dos and Mie. Dill. Priest: F. Magnes.

2883. MARIE MARTINEZ
(533) 16 December 1816, baptism of infant of 5 days,
v19 child of Dolores Martinez and Man. Gomez. Godparents: J. A. Rodriguez and Mie. Lopez. Priest: F. Magnes.

2884. MIE. CASILDA MATA
(533) 26 June 1816, baptism of child of 2 months, infant
v19 of Jn. Joseph Mata and Mie. Josine. Obday (Olday). Godparents: Jn. Bte. Lattier and M. P. Frederic. Priest: F. Magnes.

2885. MIE. LOUIS MATHER [MCTYRE]
(533) 8 March 1816, baptism of child born 17 December
v19 1815, daughter of George Mather and Louis Malloux. Godparents: Laurent Malloux and Barb. Roc. Priest: F. Magnes.

2886. JH. DAVID MECLELUM
(533) 1 April 1816, baptism of child born 28 February
v19 1816, son of David Meclelum and Mie. Lse. Richard. Godparents: Ma. Richard and Ma^{ne} Lemaitre. Priest: F. Magnes.

2887. MARIE MENCHECO
(533) 23 July 1816, baptism of child of 6 months, infant
v19 of Manuel Mencheco and Mie. A. Procella. Godparents: Jn. Bte. Arce and Marie Chinny [Sims].
Priest: F. Magnes.

2888. MIE. LOUISE MORA
(533) 13 July 1816, baptism of infant of 6 months, child
v19 of Etienne Mora and Gert. Cerda. Godparents: Jn. Procella and Mie. Mne. Cerda. Priest: F. Magnes.

2889. MIE. CLOTILDE MORANTINE
(533) 10 August 1816, baptism of child born 6 April 1816,
v19 daughter of Jean Morantine and Euphrosine Frederic. Godparents: Nic. Gracia and Mie. P. Tiery.
Priest: F. Magnes.

2890. MIE. SARA MOREL
(533) 27 October 1816, baptism of child born 10 August
v19 1810, daughter of Jerome Morel and Marie Martin. Godparents: Jn. Cockram and Mie. R. Saydec.
Priest: F. Magnes.

2891. MIE. FELICITE PLAISANCE
(533) 13 September 1816, baptism of child born 14 July
v19 1816, daughter of Bertrand Plaisance and Barbara Grillet. Godparents: Em. Rachal and Suz. Plaisance. Priest: F. Magnes.

2892. AUGUSTIN PADILLA
(534) 2 July 1816, baptism of child of 3 months, son of
v19 Jh. Antoine Padilla and Jne. Procella. Godparents: J. Bte. Vallery and Jul. Torres. Priest: F. Magnes.

2893. MARIE MELANIE PERAUT
(534) 5 June 1816, baptism of child born 7 February 1816,
v19 daughter of Ls. Derzelin Peraut and Melany Trichel. Godparents: Pierre Trichel and Jne. <u>Elisin?</u> Peraut. Priest: F. Magnes.

2894. MARIE CELINE PERAUT
(534) 27 April 1816, baptism of child born 10 June 1816,
v19 daughter of Fostin Peraut and Celeste Bordelon. Godparents: Jh. Bordelon and Mie. Mte. Peraut.
Priest: F. Magnes.

2895. MIE. CL. PHILIBERT
(534) 11 August 1816, baptism of child born 6 July 1816,
v19 daughter of Gaspard Philibert and Felicite Lemaitre. Godparents: Reuben Ross and Amelie Garro.
Priest: F. Magnes.

2896. JACQ. VICTOR POISSOT
(534) 13 June 1816, baptism of child born 18 December
v19 1814, son of Paul Poissot and Marie Lse. Anty.
Godparents: Fois. Vienne and Mie. Buard. Priest:
F. Magnes.

2897. EDOUARD PONTHIEU
(534) 16 February 1816, baptism of child born 16 January
v19 1815, son of Alexandre Ponthieu and Marg. Johnson.
Godparents: Jn. J. Lambre and Mie. A. Lambre.
Priest: F. Magnes. /See Entries 700 and 716, abstracted from separated fragments of the same original entry.7

2898. MIE. PETRA PROCELLA
(534) 2 July 1816, baptism of child born 1 October 1815,
v19 infant of Joseph Procella and Mie. Padilla. Godparents: Jh. Gillard and Pet. Lacour. Priest: F.
Magnes.

2899. JH. POLYCARPE PROCELLA
(534) 23 July 1816, baptism of child of 17 months, son of
v19 Jh. Marie Procella and Mnla. de la Cerda. Godparents: Jh. Mie. Mora and Mie. A. Cordova. Priest:
F. Magnes.

2900. MIE. EMELIE PRUDHOMME
(534) 18 June 1816, baptism of child born 27 December
v19 1815, daughter of Jn. Baptiste Prudhomme and Mie.
B. Malege. Godparents: And. Valentine and M. J.
Maligs. Priest: F. Magnes.

2901. MIE. THERESE PRUDHOMME
(534) 3 November 1816, baptism of daughter of Narcisse
v19 Prudhomme and Mie. Th. Metoyer. Godparents: F. B.
Metoyer and Mie. Ls. David. Priest: F. Magnes.

2902. JH. MANUEL QUESADA
(534) 8 September 1816, baptism of child of 1 month, son
v19 of Jh. Cayetan Quesada and Mie. R. de la Cerda.
Godparents: Bert. Plaisance and Jne. Fcoise Texedo. Priest: F. Magnes.

2903. CH. ANTOINE QUIN
(534) 24 July 1816, baptism of child born 25 December
v19 1815, son of Michel Quin and L. Cheredem Godparents: Th. Sepalvedo and A. M. Cheredem. Priest:
F. Magnes.

2904. HIL. VALIER RACHAL
(534) 16 February 1816, baptism of child born 7 Septem-
v19

ber 1815, son of J. B. Barthelemy Rachal and Mie. Lemoine. Godparents: Hil. Rachal and Mte. Frederic. Priest: F. Magnes. /See Entries 699 and 715, abstracted from separated fragments of the same original entry./

2905. MARIE ELIPSIN? RACHAL
(534) 16 February 1816, baptism of child born 27 December 1815, daughter of Julien Rachal and Melanie Lavesper. Godparents: Silv. Rachal and Mie. Frederic. /See Entry 698./ Priest: F. Magnes.
v19

2906. VICTOR RACHAL
(534) 16 February 1816, baptism of child born 14 March, 1814, son of Julien Rachal and Mel. Lavespere. Godparents: Pierre G. Lavespere and El. Lavespere. Priest: F. Magnes. /See Entry 697./
v19

2907. JN. BAPTISTE RACHAL
(534) 12 May 1816, baptism of child born 13 March 1815, son of /J.B./ Julien Rachal and Rosalie Derbanne. Godparents: Ml. Derbanne and M. Ai. Levasseur. Priest: F. Magnes.
v19

2908. JEAN BILL. RACHAL
(534) 13 March 1816, baptism of child born 2 March 1816, son of Louis Rachal and Mie. Lse. Cheletre. Godparents: Narcisse Rachal and Eup. Rachal. Priest: F. Magnes.
v19

2909. LS. RAYMOND RACHAL
(534) 29 June 1816, baptism of child of 1 year, son of Ls. Julien Rachal and Mie. Ren. Thomassy. Godparents: Nar. Rachal and Man. Rachal. Priest: F. Magnes.
v19

2910. LS. GACION RACHAL
(534) 13 May 1816, baptism of child born 16 March 1816, son of Silvestre Rachal and Marie Rose Michel. Godparents: Ant. Rachal and Cec. Dupre. Priest: F. Magnes.
v19

2911. A. JN. BTE. RAMBIN
(534) 4 March 1816, baptism of child born 15 March 1815, son of Francois Rambin and Mie. Dam. Soto. Godparents: And. Rambin and Eup. Rambin. Priest: F. Magnes.
v19

2912. MARIE OSITE RAMBIN
(534) 18 August 1816, baptism of child of 1½ years, daughter of Michel Rambin and Ther. Maillou. Godpar-
v19

ents: And. Rambin and Art. Chamard. Priest: F. Magnes.

2913. MIE. LOUISE RENDON
(534) 6 February 1816, baptism of child of 5 months,
v19 daughter of Jh. Manuel Rendon and J. Getrude Gomez. Godparents: An. Rambin and A. Jhine. Flores. Priest: F. Magnes. ⟦See Entry 694.⟧

2914. JNE. FOISE. RODRIGUEZ
(534) 16 June 1816, baptism of child born 12 May 1816,
v19 daughter of Cyprien Rodriguez and Marianne Dias. Godparents: Jh. Laflor and Jne. Foise. Flores. Priest: F. Magnes.

2915. MIE. CATHERINE RIO
(534) 4 November 1816, baptism of child born 25 October
v19 1815, daughter of Victor Rio and Getrude Morin. Godparents: Al. Cloutier and Anast. Davion. Priest: F. Magnes.

2916. FOISE. ADELDE. ROUBIEU
(534) 14 April 1816, baptism of child born 23 September
v19 1815, daughter of Francois Roubieu and Osite Rachal. Godparents: Jn. F. Segound and Hon. Lauve. Priest: F. Magnes.

2917. MARIE LUZ ROUBIEU
(534) 10 November 1816, baptism of child of $1\frac{1}{2}$ months,
v19 daughter of Francois Roubieu and Mie. Osite Rachal. Godparents: Pierre Dubois and Mie. Luz Rachal. Priest: F. Magnes.

2918. MIE. ANTETTE. BOUIZ ⟦RUIZ⟧
(532) 1 March 1816, baptism of child born 7 November 1815,
v19 daughter of Jacquez Bouiz and Jene. Rosa Gonzales. Godparents: Man. Gonzales and M. P. Padilla. Priest: F. Magnes. ⟦See Entry 701.⟧

2919. MIE. NETTE SIBLEY
(534) 28 April 1816, baptism of child born 23 July 1815,
v19 daughter of John Sibley and Eulalie Maligs. Godparents: Robert Sibley and Mie. Chavas. Priest: F. Magnes.

2920. HENRY HOP. SIBLEY
(534) 26 August 1816, baptism of child born 27 May 1816,
v19 son of Sam. Hopkins Sibley and Margte. Lamis ⟦sic⟧. Godparents: Henry Sibley and Anne Keizer. Priest; F. Magnes.

2921. PIERRE TEAL
(534) 27 October 1816, baptism of child born 1812, son
v19 of Jacques Teal and Mie. Rose Saydec. Godparents:
Guil. Ettredge and Mie. Brown. Priest: F. Magnes.

2922. MARIE SOPHIE THOMSON
(534) 2 July 1816, baptism of child born 3 November 1814,
v19 daughter of Joseph Thomson and Mie. Jhine. Sheletre. Godparents: Jn. Mie. LeCourt [LaCour]
and Jhine. Gillard. Priest: F. Magnes.

2923. MIE. EMELINE THOMSON
(534) 2 July 1816, baptism of child born 27 February
v19 1814, daughter of Thomas Thomson and Anne B. Dubois. Godparents: Fois. Lattier and Elenore Baillio. Priest: F. Magnes.

2924. MANUEL TESSIER
(534) 11 October 1816, baptism of child born 27 February
v19 1815, son of Pierre Tessier and Marianne Sidrec.
Godparents: Guilleri Babé and Clar. B. Heinoy? .
Priest: F. Magnes.

2925. SEVERIN TRICHE
(534) 14 April 1816, baptism of child born 27 February
v19 1816, son of Jn. Baptiste Triche and Mie. Mte. Fonteneau. Godparents: Ces. Fonteneau and El. P.
_____ nny [sic]. Priest: F. Magnes.

2926. MIE. CELEDINA TRICHEL
(534) 15 June 1816, baptism of child born 9 January 1816,
v19 daughter of Manuel Trichel and Lse. Eup. Prudhomme.
Godparents: Bte. Trichel and Mie. E. Prudhomme.
Priest: F. Magnes.

2927. MIE. LOUISE VALENTIN
(534) 14 June 1816, baptism of child born 27 September
v19 1814, daughter of Joseph Valentin and Mie. The.
Prudhomme. Godparents: Mic. Rambin and Carm.
Chav_____ [Illegible]. Priest: F. Magnes.

2928. MIE. LOUISE VASCOCU
(534) 2 May 1816, baptism of child born 23 October 1815,
v19 daughter of Louis Vascocu and Celeste Ris. Godparents: Vital Vascocu and Foise. Vascocu.
Priest: F. Magnes.

2929. JN. BAPTISTE VERCHER
(534) 11 February 1816, baptism of child of 3½ months,
v19 son of Bellony Vercher and Mie. Orezil Gallien.
Godparents: Jac. Vercher and Mie. Luz Rachal.
Priest: F. Magnes.

2930. MIE. BRIGITTE VILLAREAL
(534) 20 October 1816, baptism of child born 8 October
1816, son of Lucianne Villareal. Godparents: Jul.
Estrada and Mie. F. Texeda. Priest: F. Magnes.

2931. ANTOINE UTREDGE /ETTRIDGE7
(534) 27 October 1816, baptism of child born 2 November
1815, son of Guillaum Utredge and Marie Brown.
Godparents: Jn.*Cortram and Mie. Rosa Saydre.
Priest: F. Magnes. /*Cockram7

2932. JH. ANTOINE YBARBO
(534) 31 March 1816, baptism of child born 6 September
1815, son of Jh. Polonio Ybarbo and Mie. Luciane
Ybarbo. Godparents: Jh. A. Caro and Mie. G.
Texeda. Priest: F. Magnes.

2933. MIE. EL. RIO-YBARBO
(534) 31 March 1816, baptism of child born 13 January
1816, child of Francois Ybarbo /?Rio7 and Mie.
Gert. Ybarbo. Godparents: Jac. Grappe and El.
Grappe. Priest: F. Magnes.

2934. JH. MANUEL YBARBO
(534) 11 October 1816, baptism of child born 12 June
1815, son of Pierre Ybarbo and Jeanne de la Garza.
Godparents: Jh. Ybarbo and M. A. Padilla.
Priest: F. Magnes.

2935. MIE. CELESTE YSTOR
(534) 29 June 1816, baptism of child of $3\frac{1}{2}$ years, daughter of Harrison Ystor and Marie Naget. Godparents:
An. Rachal and Mie. Lse. St. Andre. Priest: F.
Magnes.

2936. MARIE YSTOR
(534) 29 June 1816, baptism of child of 1 year, daughter
of Harrison Ystor and Marie Naget. Godparents:
Guil. Dupre and Mie. Dupre. Priest: F. Magnes.

INDEX

NOTE: When searching for females under a known given name (i.e.: Celeste or Victoire), if the individual is not found, look also under Marie (i.e.: Marie Celeste or Marie Victoire). Most Catholic girls were given the first name Marie at their baptism or at confirmation, although many of them never used that name otherwise. Also, some priests automatically included that name when recording entries involving females who did not use the name.

__edride, Santiago, 480

Abraham, slave. *See Manuel Abraham.*
Abransa?, Maria (Dna. Guillermo Ris), 351
Achille, slave, 1583
Acosta,
  J. Ŝ. M., 2840
  José, 444, 748-749, 757, 1059
  Juan Isidore, 458, 2786
  Luis Ramon, 444
  Maria Antonia Encarnacion (Dna. Ma. Borrego), 876
  Maria del Pilar (Dna. Joseph Cleto? Torres), 758
  Mariana, 703
  P., 2821
Acoye, Appalache Indian. *See Louis Acoye, Marie Jeanne Acoye, Lorenzo Acoye, Tamonet? Acoye.*
Adam, slave. *See Joseph Adam.*
Adame, Maria Paula (Dna. Nepomuceno Bocanegro), 2665
Adelaide (var. Adelayde, Delayde, Elayde, Laide, Layde), slave, 1097, 1104, 1155, 1158, 1307, 1314, 1348-1351, 1511, 1564, 1601, 1809, 1863, 1878, 1967, 2013, 2031, 2048, 2056, 2069, 2134, 2178, 2194, 2228, 2269, 2377, 2434, 2551-2552, 2569
Adeline, slave. *See Marie Celeste Adeline.*
Adelle, slave, 1309
Adlé (vars. Adley, Adelet, Adles, Adelette, Adlley)
  _____, Sieur, 783
  Andres, 747, 1028
  Antoine, 799, 1063, 1997
  Baptiste. *See Jean Baptiste.*

Adlé (continued)
  Etienne (Etin), 1021
  François, 228, 965, 1037, 1443, 2545
  Jean Baptiste, *fils* J.B. (husband of Marie Victoire Brevel), 30, 186, 228, 461, 774, 961, 966, 1000, 1021-1022, 1029, 1841
  Jean Baptiste, *fils* J.B. (husband of Marie Denise Dolle), 1021, 1263-1264, 1257, 1276, 1336, 2544-2545
  Jean Baptiste Etienne, 186, 240, 242, 961, 966, 981, 984, 1021-1022, 1063, 2745
  Jean Baptiste Timothe (Timoteo), 1022, 1267, 2765
  Jean François, *fils* J.B. II, 228
  Jean François, *fils* J.B. Timothe, 2765
  Louis, 2496
  Marie, 966, 1446?
  Marie Assely, 1443, 2544?
  Marie Egilde, 186
  Marie Josephe, 2257
  Marie Louise, 1260
  Marie Pholoe, 461
  Pelagie Marie Deneige (Mme. François Roger), 182, 218, 273, 343, 461, 984, 1063, 2067, 2435, 2765?
  Valentine, I, 186, 461, 966, 981, 1028, 2067
  Valentine, II, 261
Adolph, slave. *See Joseph Adolph.*
Adrian, slave, 1148
Agathe (vars. Agat, Agata), 1131, 1207, 1415, 1764, 2174, 2192, 2262, 2393, 2605, 2642
Agent. *See Aragon.*
Agnes (vars. Anes, Anis), 1214, 1646, 2049, 2155, 2186, 2569, 2573

Aguesse (var. Augesse)
 Jacques, 365
 Jean Armand Renaud, 300, 2801
 Jean Renaud I, 364-365, 994
 Jean René, 364
 Marie, 364
 Marie Zeline, 300
Aguillon, José Maximo (Magsimo), 764, 1293, 2401
Agustin. *See Augustin.*
Agustina. *See Augustine.*
Ailhaud Ste. Anne (vars. Aillot, Aillotte, Aylhaud, Haliot, Sta. Ana)
 _____, Madame, 1735, 2552
 Jean Baptiste, 255, 962, 1824, 1831, 1848, 1866, 1870, 1889, 1957, 1993, 2050-2051, 2194-2195, 2429
 Marie Thérèse Victoire (Mme. J.B. Prudhomme), 87, 134, 191, 254-255, 360, 962, 1831, 1958
Aimée, slave. *See Emé.*
A____llo (Alamillo?), Agustina (Dna. Julian Rosales?), 466
Alamillo,
 Francisco, 2706
 Hilario, 1048
 José Francisco I, 902
 José Francisco II *(hijo* Juan José), 524, 923
 Juan José, 525, 923
 Maria Jetrudis, 459, 532, 2771
 Maria Paula (de), 2706
 Rosalino, 1048
Albine, slave, 1380
Albre, Remigio (Remy), 449
Alenne, slave. *See Hélène.*
Alexandré (var. Alexandro), slave. 643, 665, 1182, 1513, 1553, 1586, 1601, 1733, 1756, 1881, 1961, 1967, 2031, 2057, 2061, 2181, 2250, 2383
Alexandré, slave. *See also Joseph Alexandré, Louis Alexandré.*
Alexi, Appalache Indian, 670
Alexi, slave (vars. Alexis, Alexy), 1151, 1171, 1598, 2049, 2056, 2223, 2275-2276, 2409, 2417-2418, 2421
Alice, slave. *See Marie Olys.*
Allais, Marie Anne (Mme. Charles Antoine Dranguet), 728
Allday. *See Olday.*
Alvarado,
 Francisco, 1048
 Maria Antonia, 609
 Maria Concepcion (Dna. Hilario Alamillo), 1048

Alvarado (continued),
 Mateo, 609
Amador,
 José Maria, 2654
 Juana Maria (Dna. Pedro Cruz), 559
Ambrosio, slave, 2468
Amien (Brianne), Marie (Mme. Michel Jarri I), 7, 111, 213
Amiyaese, Choctaw Indian, 1659
Amy, slave. *See Emé.*
Anathalie, slave. *See Manuel Joseph Anathalie.*
Andele (Adlé?)
 Andres, 2039
 Pelagie, 2039
Andre (var. Andres), slave. 1134, 1137-1138, 1155, 1175, 1467, 1494, 1601, 2060, 2133, 2165-2166, 2168, 2184, 2236, 2299
Andres Bossie, slave, 2112-2113
Andres Celestin, slave, 1347
Andres Lendor, slave, 1405. *See also Lendor.*
Andre, Teresa, 425
Andres, Juan, 600
Andre-Andres. *See also Andrez, St. André.*
Andreson, slave. *See Pierre Andreson.*
Andreson,
 Artemise (Mme. Jacques Gradner), 608, 2380, 2809
 George, 608, 2809
Andrez, Suz. (Mrs. John Litton). 2815-2816
Angelique (vars. Angelye, Angelica, Angelina, Angeline)
 Canneci Indian, 834
 Free Mulattress, 1394
 Slave, 1177, 1214, 1218, 1934-1936, 1942, 2049, 2077-2078, 2130, 2140, 2416, 2420, 2582
Aniniya (Arsiniga?) Miguel, 2107
Anis, slave. *See Agnes.*
Anne (vars. Ana, Anna, Annie, Any, Nanet)
 slave, 1148, 1189, 1335, 1382, 1503, 1617, 1924-1925, 1959, 2066, 2336, 2373, 2402
Antoine (vars. Antoin, Antonio, Antonion),
 Natchitoches Indian, 138
 Free Mulatto, 1882, 2015
 Free Negro, 2006, 2449
 Slave, 1067, 1152, 1185, 1251, 1297, 1322, 1346, 1504, 1588, 1638, 1677, 1817, 1872, 1874, 1893, 1896, 1938, 1974, 2017-2018, 2049, 2059, 2061, 2077, 2146, 2335, 2338, 2348, 2444, 2474, 2611

Antoine Augustin, slave, 1122
Antoin(e) Gasion, slave, 1325
Antoine Nevil, slave, 1068
Antonio Baptiste, Appalache Indian, 663-664
Antonio Bill, slave, 2507
Antonio Bleste (Blaise?), slave, 2378
Antonio Charle(s), Appalache Indian, 653-654, 674
Antonio Fonteneau, Appalache Indian, 659
Antonio Fortune, slave, 1458
Antonio Harry, slave, 2386
Anton___ Celestin, Appalache Indian, 679
Antoinette, slave, 1891
Anty,
   Alexis, 2824
   Celeste. *See Marie Jeanne Celeste.*
   Euphrosine, 823
   Jean Baptiste I, 17, 36, 137, 187, 243, 823
   Jean Baptiste Ignace II, 17, 137, 560, 948, 2243?, 2249
   Jean Baptiste III, 17
   Jean Baptiste (I or II?), 362, 515, 720-721, 785, 950, 970, 1054, 1221, 1819, 1849, 1939, 1941, 2131, 2214-2217, 2370, 2539-2540
   Jean Baptiste, *fils* Valery, 509
   Ignace, 35
   Louis, 35, 997
   Marie Aglantine, 708, 2825
   Marie Arsene (Mme. Manuel Llorens), 1396, 1623, 1633, 1652, 1662, 1887, 2305, 2512
   Marie Aspasie (Mme. Maxille Metoyer), 773, 1161, 1452, 1455, 1626, 1697, 2060, 2242?, 2292, 2303, 2522
   Marie Auresile (Oresy), 35, 1149
   Marie Aurora, 565
   Marie Clemire (Mme. Michel Derbanne), 775
   Marie Heleine (Elenne), 376, 1081, 2603
   Marie Jeanne Celeste (Mme. Louis Gallien), 117, 137, 314, 320, 376, 565, 997, 1913, 1919, 2082 2784, 2846
   Marie Louise (Mme. Paul Poissot), 36, 243, 304, 367, 836, 2896
   Marie Susanne "Susette" (Mme. J. B. Augustin Metoyer), 720, 1116, 1396, 1477, 1626, 1634, 1682, 2509

Anty (continued),
   Marie Thérèse Carmelite (Mme. Auguste Metoyer). 1216, 1474, 1476, 1624, 1627, 1697, 2058, 2411?, 2413?, 2464?, 2460
   Melece (Veles), 137, 2214, 2250
   Michel, 514
   Silvestre, 35, 117, 514, 759, 1913, 1917, 2824
   Valery I, 362. 509, 696, 708, 2205, 2242, 2825
   Valery II, 362
Any, slave. *See Anne ("Annie").*
Aovidon, slave, 1769
Apache Indian, 2684
Appalache Indians & Appalache Village, 598-601, 643-681
Apalas, an Appalache Indian. *See Nicolas Apalas.*
Appart, Marie Madeleine Giraud (Mme. Jean Joseph Bauvard St. Amand, 369, 460
Aguillon. *See Aguillon.*
Aragon (vars. Argin, Agent, D'Aragon),
   Jean Baptiste, 84, 164
   Jean Baptiste Sévère, 164
   Maria, 1, 2762
   Maria, *hija* Santo, 130
   Maria Apolonia (Dna. Francisco Gonsalez), 807
   Maria Manuela, 1276
   Maria Polonia, 1469
   Maria Santos (Dna. Faustin Ortis), 494, 1462, 2785, 2871
   Merante, 84
   Michel, 84
   Santo, 130
Arbau, Vital, 562
Arce. *See Arze.*
Archinard,
   Cesard, 639
   Evariste, 639
   François, 640
   Jean, 639-641, 2383-2392
   Marie Desirée, 641
   Rosemond, 641
   Samuel, 640
Arevalo, Marie Felony, 2827
   Marie Felony, 2827
   Santiago (Jacques), 2827
Arice?, slave. *See Clarisse.*
Ariole. *See Arriola.*
Arispe, Rafael Ramos, 1506
Armand (Armant),
   Baptiste. *See Jean Baptiste.*
   Cecile, 278

Armand (continued)
  François, 2766
  Françoise, 387
  Henriette, 340
  Ignace, 497, 2767
  Jean Baptiste I, 9, 87, 233-234, 340, 505, 760, 805, 909, 957, 964, 1056, 1101, 2758, 2780, 2791
  Jean Baptiste, II (the elder), 805, 2038
  Jean Baptiste, II (the younger), 87, 340
  Jean Baptiste (I?), 278, 497, 873, 2766, 2767
  Joseph Marie, 87, 234, 934, 947, 952, 2038, 2758
  Joseph, Widow, 2441
  Josephe Marceline (Marcelite), 234, 1524, 2038
  Magdeleine (Mme. Nicolas LaCour), 579-580, 583
  Marie, *fille* J.B. I, 2758
  Marie Adelaide, 505
  Marie Fani, 909
  Y? B.D., 2806
Armesy, slave. *See Marie Polinere Armesy.*
Arnaudiere. *See La Renaudeire*
Arnmega, Miguel, 405
Arnoc, Mr., 1223
Arocha,
  Damian, 441
  Francisco, 1043
  José (Josef), 796, 1265
  José Nepomanceno, 473
  Juan Nepomuceno, 1043
Arrañoga (var. Arreñago)
  Cayetano, 764, 1093, 2828
  Juana Maria (Jeane Mie.), 2828
Arriola (var. Ariole),
  Eduardo, 521
  Francisco (François) Xavier de Jesus, 521
  Maria Josefa (Dna. Bartolome Chirino), 821, 1058, 2866?
Arsene (Arcene, Arsen), slave, 1749, 1761, 1915, 2516
Arsiniga, Miguel, 2107. *See also Arnmega.*
Arta?, Fer. Juan Isidro, 741
Arthemis Deloy. *See Arthemise Dupart.*
Arze (var. Arce),
  Jean Baptiste, 734, 2826, 2887
  Marie Louise, 2826

Aselie-Azelie, slave. *See Ensely.*
Asenor, Appalache Indian. *See José Asenor, Asor.*
Aslau, Françoise (Mme. Pierre Royer), 539
Asor, slave, 1367, 2507
Aspasie (var. Aspasi), slave. 1231, 2056, 2061, 2269, 2575-2576. *See also Marie Louise Aspasie.*
Astasie. *See Marie Emely Astasie.*
Athanase (vars. Athanas, Athanace, Atanasio, Atanacio, Athenais),
  Appalache Indian, 1807. *See also Marie Catis Athenais.*
  Free man of color. *See Athanas LeComte.*
  Slave, 1401, 1448, 1461, 1532, 1561, 1687, 1751, 1907, 1933, 1980, 2044, 2050, 2056, 2143, 2159, 2190-2191, 2224, 2237, 2309, 2342, 2427, 2439, 2454, 2504, 2632?. *See also Bruno Athanase, Louis Athanase.*
Atanasio Guany, Appalache Indian, 666-667
Atanasio Palier, Appalache Indian, 666
Athanase Celestin, 1287-1288
Aubichon (var. Aubauson),
  Charles, 1140, 1393
  Elisabeth, 1393
  François, 1228
Augeraut, Magdeleine (Mme. Jean Lavespere), 46
Auguste, slave, 1945, 2048, 2584
Auguste (Aougust) Lucien, slave, 2435
Augustin (vars. Agustin, Gustin), slave, 1097, 1178, 1236, 1289, 1310, 1350, 1362, 1367, 1379, 1381, 1511, 1540, 1668, 1836, 1844, 1853, 1877, 2034-2035, 2048-2049, 2051, 2054, 2063, 2072, 2077, 2175, 2179, 2186, 2188, 2193, 2209, 2216, 2221, 2228, 2246, 2273, 2275, 2331, 2356, 2473, 2505, 2513, 2550, 2556. *See also Antoine Augustin, Jean Baptiste Augustin, Gregoire Augustin, Louis Augustin, Marie Augustin.*
Augustin (Agustin) Fortunee, mulatto, 2177
Augustin Bill, slave, 2584
Augustin Julian, slave, 2435
Augustine (vars. Augustina, Agustina), slave, 1428, 1749, 1845, 2121, 2153, 2219, 2525. *See also Marie Magdalene Augustine.*
Aurore (Horrore), slave, 1338
Avis, slave, 1331

Babet (Babé, Bave), slave, 1669,
  2050, 2379, 2491, 2505. *See also
  Bove, Marie Jeanne Bade.*
Babé, Guilleri (Guillaume?), 2924
Bacour, Laly, 2568
Bade (Betty?), slave, 1572
Badin (vars. Baden, Vadin),
  Antoine, 867
  Catharine, 1801, 2045, 2265
  Dominique (Domingo), 1739
  François, 2134, 2178
  François Alexy, 1783
  Guillaume, 1495, 1846
  Jean Baptiste, 1755
  Louis, 2159
  Magdalena, 2134
  Manuel, 2597?
  Marie, 1801, 1846
  Marie Cecile (Cecilia), 1755,
    1775, 2642
  Marie Hélène (Elena), 1275, 1739,
    1783, 1988, 2265
  Marie Jeanne?, 2597
  Marie Louise, 1429, 1827, 2139
  Marie Zeline, 1275
  Monsineau, 1999, 2638-2639
  Pierre (Pedro), 2265
  Pierre, Mr., 846, 1707, 1712, 1725,
    1821-1822, 1830, 1832, 1846,
    1863, 1870, 1880, 1967
  Victor, 2265
Bailes. *See Bayles.*
Bailey. *See Beille.*
Baillio (Vars. Bailio, Bailloud, Baiou)
  _____, Mr., 1373
  Amelie (Mrs. J. Compton), 610,
    618, 623, 767
  Anne, 1096
  Apolinario, 635, 2380
  Augustin, 585, 589, 597, 602, 650,
    1301, 1363, 1370-1372, 2368, 2476
  Celeste (Mme. Nicolas Villain; Mrs.
    Edward Kirkland), 613, 754, 1371-
    1372, 1376-1377, 2378-2380
  Elenne, 592, 597, 601, 603-604, 2923
  Emely, 2373, 2376, 2378, 2508, 2517
  Jean Louis, 592, 597, 603, 607, 610,
    612, 620, 649, 655, 659, 676-677,
    968-969
  Landry, 1378, 2373, 2375?, 2508
  Marie (Mme. Marcel de Soto), 1020
  Marie Anne (Marianne), 597, 1363
  Marie Adelle, 610
  Philonye, 1301

Baillio (continued),
  Pierre II, 613-614, 754, 767, 781,
    1376-1386, 2373-2376, 2505-2508,
    2513-2517, 2593, 2594?, 2595
  Sosthene (Sauzthaine) A., 754, 781,
    1370-1371, 2378
  Sylvestre (Silvere), 609, 1382, 2374,
    2376
Baker (var. Becar),
  John (Juan) H., 1277, 1661
  Marie Julia, 1661
Belanger (var. Belangé),
  Jean Joseph, 2352
  Joseph, 2352
Balbo, Clara Maria (Dna. Santo Aragon),
  130
Balcour, slave. *See Valcour.*
Balien, slave. *See Nicolas Balien.*
Balsem (Valsain?), slave, 2226
Bals_en, Linée (Mrs. J. Wallace), 1030
Baltasar, free, 2030. *See also J.B.
  Baltasar Monet, Baltasar Grappe.*
Baltasar, slave, 1785, 1797, 2280
Balthasar,
  Louis (Monet), 1663, 2099n, 2464
  Marie Rose (Monet), 1663, 1672-1673,
    2099
Banée, slave, 2243-2245
Baptiste (vars. Bautista, Btta. Btte.)
  Appalache Indian. *See Antonio Baptiste,
    Margarite Baptiste, Jean Baptiste.*
  Free Mulatto, 2023. *See also Jean
    Baptiste.*
  Slave, 1574, 1599, 2050, 2054, 2132,
    2207, 2213, 2180-2181, 2415-2416,
    2498. *See also Grand Baptiste, Jean
    Baptiste.*
Baptiste Leandre Bertil, slave, 1242
Bar__, Mariana, 927
Barberousse (vars. Barbarous, Barbarrus),
  Guillaume I, 240, 985, 1360, 2740
  Guillaume II. *See Michel Guillaume.*
  Joseph Victorin, 274, 1189
  Marie Ernestine, 240
  Michel Guillaume Jean, 240, 274, 963,
    985 - 986
Barbe (vars. Barbare, Barvara), slave,
  1414, 2049, 2182
Barcas, Jean Baptiste, 827
Bardon (vars. Bardo, Bardeau),
  Marie Anne (Mme. Joseph Malige), 40,
    78, 86, 730, 951, 1019, 2646
  Marie Catherinne (Mme. Louis Charles
    Chamart), 38, 53, 86, 106, 142-143,
    439, 712, 967

409

Baré (var. Barre), Rosalie Charlotte (Mme. Fr. Bossier I), 54, 77, 110, 203
Baré. See also Barrette.
Baré, slave, 1314
Bargas, Maria Paula (Dna. José Ignacio Rios), 522
Bargas. See also Borgas.
Barra (Barr), Maria Silva (Subley), 1118, 2142
Barras, Antoin, 2682
Barre, Guillaume, 954
Barrera. See Varrera.
Barrette (var. Baré), Elisabeth (Mme. Saucier), 712, 726
Bart, François, 1241
Bartheau, Jeanne (Mme. Girard Tausin), 38, 106
Barthelemi (Bertelmy), slave, 1589, 2057, 2274
Barthelemi Cifroi, slave, 2007
Basquez, Sacramiento, 2713
Basiem, slave. See François Basiem.
Basile (vars. Basilio, Basil), slave, 1388, 2057, 2077, 2215, 2518, 2532, 2543. See also Pier Paul Basil, François Basiem.
Basinure (vars. Bassinure, Bassignau), Susana (Mme. Ambroise Sompayrac I), 452, 685, 990
Bastian, slave, 1086. See also Martin Sebastien, Sebastien.
Bastien, Catherinne, 1843
Baudouin (vars. Beaudouin, Boudoin, Bodioin, Boudoin),
  _____, 759
  Antoine Denis, 168
  Catarina, 1553
  Euphrosine, 28, 1496, 2824
  Elisabeth (Bontems), 163
  François, 28, 117, 167-169, 212
  Jean Baptiste Benjamin, 561
  Jean Louis, 117
  Jean Pierre, 28, 117, 162, 212, 276, 507, 513, 743, 746, 1042, 1496-1497, 2829
  Joseph, 169, 1446
  Louis, 2824
  Marie, fille Jean Pierre, 276
  Marie (Mme. Silvestre Anty), 514, 2824
  Marie (identity uncertain), 561
  Marie Aimée, 2829
  Marie Celeste (Mme. Athanas Brosset), 64, 512, 743, 2463
  Marie (Marianne) Felonise, 507, 2848?
  Marie Françoise (Mme. J.B. La Renaudiere), 167, 513, 1042, 2875

Baudouin (continued)
  Marie Joseph Adelaide, 212
  Marie Louise, 319, 587, 2394, 2482, 2622?
  Marie Modeste (Mme. Athanase Denis), 746, 2829?
  Marie Thecle, 212
  Marie Thérèse (Mme. Pierre Beaulieu), 220-221, 2830
  Marie Zemire, 168, 174, 316
  Nicolas, 167-169, 310, 561, 759, 772, 1568
  Philippe, 310
  Pierre, 759, 772. See also Jean Pierre.
Baudouin. See also Bodin.
Baudry (var. Beaudry),
  François, 573-574, 763, 1297, 2340, 2348, 2353, 2362
  François II, 573
  Marie Cephalide (Zephaly), 574
Bauvard St. Amand. See St. Amand.
Bave, slave. See Babet.
Bavé,
  Felicité Elisabeth, 539
  Richard, 539
Bayles,
  Benjamin I, 557
  Benjamin II, 557
Bazile, slave. See Basil.
Beaudouin. See Baudouin.
Beaulieu (var. Baulieu),
  Edouard, 2830
  Marie Fanny, 220
  Marie Pelagie, 221
  Pierre, 220-221, 2830
Beaumond. See Bomond.
Beauregard. See Bouregart.
Bebé (vars. Beve, Bebee, Bebis),
  Eduardo, 456
  Ludi (Mme. Remy Christy), 535
  Maria Francisca (Mme. Jean Pierre Bodin), 723
Bebé. See Babé also.
Becker. See Baker.
Becky, slave. See Vici, Rebecca.
Beille, _____ (female), 483
Bekar. See Baker.
Bel, Mr., 1235
Belange, J.B., 2770. See also Belanger.
Bell, John (Juan Bautista), 455.
Bell. See also Beille.
Bellegarde (vars. Bergard, Belgar, Bellegar, Velgar, Velgardo, Villegar),
  Dorothée (Mrs. August O'Neal), 633

Bellegarde (continued)
  Genevieve Xambiez (Mme. Jean Antoine LeMoine), 107, 173, 308, 577-578
  Honoré, 2490
  Jean Baptiste, 107, 173, 624
  Jean Baptiste II, 630, 632, 766?
  José Antonio, 1050, 1124?, 1259
  Maria de los Dolores (Mda. José Antonio Bellegarde), 1050
  Maria Dolores (Mme. Jacques Paul), 633, 675, 766
  Maria Josefa (Mda. José Sanchez), 1050
  Miguel, 2754
  Thomas, 632
Beloz?,
  José Francisco, 1814
  Juan Diego, 910
Beltran. *See Bertrand.*
Benge, Appalache Indian, 672. *See also Pierre Nolasco Benge.*
Beniol, Pierre, 781
Benjamin, slave, 1600, 1612, 2056, 2073, 2284
Benson Ovil, slave, 2533
Benson (var. Bensan),
  José Miguel, 407
  Miguel, 407
Benster, Maria Antonia (Dna. H. Flores), 2726
Beque (vars. Bequer, Bequete), Françoise (Mme. Antoine Querry), 9, 71, 157
Bergard. *See Bellegarde.*
Bergeron (var. Bergeon),
  Antoine, 168
Bernadette, slave. *See Marie Jeanne Bernadiet*
Bernard, slave, 1816, 2298
Bernard (var. Bernardo),
  André, 547
  Anne (Mme. J.B. Pavie), 975
  Charles Grados, 449
  Guillaume, 300, 449
Bernard *dit* Elie,
  Celestin, 368, 547, 722, 1010, 1587, 2263
  Celestin Agapito, 547
  Edouard, 2851
  Elie, 963, 1010
  Jean Baptiste, 270
  Jean Pierre, 223, 270, 383, 963, 1587, 2851
  Joseph, 223

Bernard *dit* Elie (continued)
  Marie Desirée, 383
  Pierre, *fils* Elie, 963
  Pierre, *fils* Jean Pierre, 223
  Jeanne (Mme. F. Palvados), 56
  Marguerite, 368
Bernice, slave, 2577
Bertil. *See Baptiste Leandre Bertil.*
Bertrand,
  ____, Mr., 1581, 1583
  Benoist, 2864
  Denée, Mrs. J. Wallace, Sr.), 4
  Louis, 1030
  Marie Hortense (Mrs. Thomas Wallace), 412, 422, 1030, 2863-2864
  Marie Louise (Mme. Etienne Gagné), 4, 19, 102, 135, 240, 795, 986
Bery, Clara, 1562
Berzot (vars. Verger, Vergau, Berziou),
  Marie Luce (Luz), Mme. Joseph Louis Vercher, 272, 506, 682, 1047
  William, 1047
Bessie (vars. Bessy, Bezsse), slave, 1096-1097, 1292, 2611-2612
Besson (vars. Beson, Berentt),
  Antoine, 1002
  Jean Baptiste I, 285, 435, 955, 1002, 1040, 1126, 1362, 2578-2579, 2831
  Jean Baptiste II, 8, 435, 1126
  Julien, 848, 955
  Julien, *fils* J.B., 2831
  Julien François, 13, 180, 493, 1002
  Marie Aurore, 285
  Marie Felicité, 1126
  Pierre Emile, 493
Betsy (Betze), slave, 1553
Betty (Bete), slave, 1368. *See also Bade.*
Bienne. *See Vienne.*
Bierre, female slave. *See Jeanne Bierre*
Bill, slave. *See Jean Baptiste Vil, Antonio Bill, Augustin Bill.*
Bille (Billet?), Laysa, 2772
Billet, P.G., 2794
Bimenez. *See Vimenez.*
Bisonette, Josef, 2048
Blaise (Bles), slave, 2506. *See also Antoine Blest.*
Blans. *See Meson Blans.*
Blere?, Mat. (female), 2835
Bleste, slave. *See Antonio Bleste.*
Blondé,
  François, 634
  Guillom, 634

Bludworth (vars. Bludword, Bladuhart, Bluduare),
  Amilia, 397
  Anne (Ana), 398
  Anne Julie (Ana Juliana), 398
  Franklin T., 399
  James (Santiago), 397-399, 857, 1784, 2491, 2592
  Marianne Eliza, 399
Boc____, Josef, 896
Bocanegro,
  ____ (infant), 2728
  Bentura, 2665
  Nepomuceno, 2665, 2728
Bodin (vars. Baudin, Boudoin),
  Gaspar, 31, 342, 723, 946-947
  Jean, 723
  Jean Laurent I, 31, 43
  Jean Laurent II, 43, 942, 947
  Jean Nicolas, 43
  Jean Pierre, 723
  Laurent. See Jean Laurent.
  Michel Gaspart, 31
  Nicolas. See Jean Nicolas.
Bodo, Marie Louise, 557-558
Boisdore (var. Buadoré),
  Dorothée (Mme. Joseph LaVigne), 1045, 1217, 1461, 1467, 1480, 1545, 1561, 1628, 1647, 2318
  Olympie, 1631
Boisselier (var. Bossalié, Bauchellié),
  Marie Rose (Mme. Pierre Sorel), 6, 22, 99, 125, 959
Boissier. See Bossier.
Bold, Thomas. See Boold.
Boman. See Borman.
Bon____, Genere?, 2626
Boniol. See Beniol.
Bonnet (var. Bonnee, Bonete, Bonne),
  Athanase, 512
  Belony, 676
  Catarina (Dna. Pedro Gonsalez), 41, 177, 248, 840
  Jean Baptiste I, 319
  Jean Baptiste II, 319, 511
  José (Joseph), 248, 319, 2057
  Juan, 41, 177, 248
  Luce (Mme. J. B. Leonard), 242
  Margarita (Dna. Luis Surigni), 473
Bontems, Elisabeth (Mme. J. B. Denis)
  Elisabeth (Mme. J. B. Denis), 954
  Marie Anne Louise (Mme. François? Beaudouin), 16, 28, 64, 117, 163, 167-169, 212

Bontems (continued)
  Marie Anne Joseph (Mme. Joseph Rabalais II), 16, 64, 163, 309, 562
Boold, Thomas, 2367, 2369
Bor?____, ____rcelo, 917
Borchez, Sally (Mme. Jean Megny), 2882
Bord, Clara, 1391
Bord, Mas, 1391
Bordelon (var. Bordeleau),
  Alexis, 222
  Hilaire. See Manuel Hilaire.
  Hypolite, 44, 99, 144, 222, 267, 371, 1012, 1075, 1125, 1499, 1798, 1884, 2022, 2063, 2114, 2578, 2831?
  Hypolite II, 686
  Joseph, 1125, 2893
  Manuel Hilaire, 44
  Marie Celeste (Mme. Jean Celestin Faustin Pereau), 371, 547, 1012, 1125, 1884, 2792, 2894
  Marie Louise, 266
  Nicolas, 44, 144, 266
  Pierre Geofroi, 144
  Polite. See Hypolite I.
Borgas, Juan, 2720. See also Bargas.
Borman (Bomond), Alexy, 1211, 2586
Borman?, Marie Thérèse Emely, 2586
Bormé, Louis Caesar, 832, 1726
Borné(e),
  Felonis, 602, 2369
  Françoise, 673
  Juan, 602-603
  Marie, 603
  See also Bonnet.
Borrego,
  José Estevan, 876
  Ma____, 876
Bortoley (Borsoley), Maria Josefa (Dna. Luis Sanchez), 1058
Bosem, slave. See Joseph Bosem.
Bossie, slave. See Andres Bossie
Bossier (var. Bossie, Boissie, Baussier, Bossierre),
  ____, Mlle, 700.
  ____, Sieur, 1026, 2156
  Alexandre. See Louis Alexandre.
  Alexandre Hildebert, 227, 389, 401, 429
  Aurore. See Marianne Rosalie Aurora.
  Bernard. See Philipe Bernard.
  Cesaire, 338, 760, 984, 2805, 2853
  D., 799, 1063
  Emerante. See Marianne Victoire Emeranciane.
  Eulalie (Mme. Jn. Pierre Chelette), 229, 429, 906?, 2805

Bossier (continued),
  Evariste, 760
  François, I, 54, 77, 110, 203
  François, II, 54, 227, 239, 244, 403, 1424, 1797, 2030, 2526
  Hildebert. *See Alexandre Hildebert*
  Jean Baptiste (*fils* Soulange), 77
  Jules Victor, 227
  Marianne Rosalie Aurore, 406, 2803
  Marianne Victoire Emerante (Mme. Emanuel Greneaux), 203, 403, 799, 1063
  Marie (*fille* Soulange), 338
  Marie Aspasie (Mme. J. B. Buard) 54, 244, 275, 401, 2755, 2769
  Marie Clista?, 692
  Marie Elisa, 711, 2832
  Marie Eulalie (Mme. Jn. Louis Buard), 244, 275, 279, 389, 906? 2668, 2803
  Marie Leocady (Mme. J. B. Lestage) 760, 2657, 2781
  Marie Lolitte, 229
  Marie Luz (Mme. Michel Frederick) 2781
  Marie Suzanne Soulange (Mme. André Frederic), 338, 2853
  P.N., 760, 2832
  Philipe Bernard, 110
  Pierre, 243
  Placide, 16, 45, 226, 239, 244, 284, 1140, 1353-1354, 1769, 1779, 1789, 2533, 2769
  Rosalie, 54
  Soulange, 77, 110, 229, 338, 692, 760, 2832
  Victoire. *See Marianne Victoire Emerante Bossier.*
Bossier *dit* Le Brun. *See LeBrun.*
Botien *dit* St. André. *See St. André.*
Boucher,
  Bernard, 1011
  Jean, 370, 1011
  Marie Caroline, 370
Boudry. *See Baudry.*
Bourdon, Marie (Mme. Louis LeVasseur) 1811
Bouregart, Hypolite, 992
Boulet,
  Marie Louise (Mme. Michel Robin), 28, 212
  Marie Ursulle (Mme. Jean Baptiste Delouche), 789
Boull. *See Bull.*
Bourdeleau. *See Bordelon.*

Bove (Bave?), female slave, 1229. *See also Babet.*
Boyd? *See Boid.*
Boyd, Margarette Catherine Rowen (Mrs. Theophile Carr), 989
Boyer, _____, 735, 753
Brandt, Josef, 366
Bram. *See Brown.*
Brevel (vars. Vrevel)
  Balthazar, 226, 774-775, 783, 1416
  Jean Baptiste, II, 37, 55, 66, 80-81, 109, 136, 146, 186, 198, 209, 847, 961, 966
  Jean Baptiste, III, 109, 146, 2484
  Marie Cidre, 109
  Marie Felicité (Mme. Gaspard LaCour, I), 81, 209, 271, 564, 2873
  Marie Françoise (Mme. Pierre Derbanne II) 17, 66, 137, 307, 519, 979, 2205, 2211
  Marie Heleine (Mme. J. B. Derbanne *fils* Gaspard), 80, 136, 280, 995
  Marie Louise (Mme. Marin Grillet), 5, 20, 25, 59, 79, 93-94, 152, 193, 202, 237, 950, 971, 1009, 1811, 2746
  Marie Louise (Mme. Julien Rachal, I), 37, 786, 938, 983, 1001, 1017, 1023, 1025
  Marie Pelagie (Mme. J. B. Barthelemy Rachal), 26, 55, 198, 253, 386, 1037
  Marie Pelagie, 146, 842
  Marie Thérèse (Mme. Philippe Brosset), 511, 560, 1912
  Marie Victoire (Mme. J. B. Adlé, II), 37, 82, 186, 228, 961, 966, 1871
  Placide, 226
Briand (var. Briant),
  François, 452, 685, 990
  Josephine (Mme. Ambroise Sompayrac), 369, 452, 685, 687, 990, 2806
Brianne, Marie. *See Amien, Marie (Mme. Michel Jarri, I).*
Bricou, Adelaïde (Mme. Jacques St. André, II), 311, 1935
Brigitte (var. Brisit), slave, 1637, 1644, 1990, 2200-2201
Brisiño, Luis, 2721
Brisit, slave. *See Brigitte and Pierr Briset.*
Brom. *See Brown, Was Brom.*
Brosset (vars. Brosay, Brosse, Broseay),
  _____, Mr., 1584
  _____, (Mme. Joseph Derbanne), 948
  Antoine, 25, 2324
  Athanase, 511, 743, 1553
  Athanase Alfred, 511
  Catherine, 7, 46, 276, 559

Brosset (continued),
  Cesaire I. *See Pierre Cesaire*
  Cesair Ablin, 563
  Cilesie. *See Marie Silesie.*
  Jacques, 1554
  Jean, 25
  Jean Baptiste, 507
  Marie Silesie (Mme. Valentin Adlé I), 261, 563, 981
  Marie Silvie (Mme. Jacques Le Comte), 110, 322, 336, 998, 1982, 2086
  Marie Sophy, 560
  Philippe, 32, 110, 560, 2324-2325
  Pierre I, 25, 261, 317, 948, 981, 1034, 2130, 2733
  Pierre Cesaire (Pierre II), 440, 563, 743, 1034, 1334, 2202, 2320, 2563
Brown, slave. *Jacob Bron; Joseph Bron.*
Brown (vars. Brom, Bram, Bronn),
  Davidson, 1040, 1492, 1571
  Jeanne (Juana), 1120
  John, 607, 754-755
  Joseph, 1744, 2838
  Julian, 1040
  Marie Adeline, 607
  Lucy? *See Lucia Ebrom.*
  Maria Luisa (Eloyse), 524, 1102, 2131, 2838
  Mary Nancy. *See Mary Nancy Teal.*
  Stephen (Etienne), 482, 2779
Brown. *See also Ebrom.*
Brunet,
  Euphrosine Celeste (Mme. Evariste Lauve I), 283, 523, 869
  François, 242
  Marie Bienvenu, Sieur, 523
Bruno Athanase, slave, 1895
Buard (vars. Buart, Buhart),
  _____, 760
  Alexandre Monvil, 401, 1424, 1579
  Alfrede, 275, 2755
  Aselie. *See Marie Francoise Aselie.*
  Athalie. *See Natalie.*
  Baptiste. *See Jean Baptiste.*
  Denis. *See Jean Denis.*
  Denize (Mme. Germaine Paillette), 304, 780, 2057, 2559
  Eugenie. *See Marie Therese Eugenie.*
  Gabriel, 8, 188
  Jean Baptiste Gabriel, 34, 71, 77, 187-188, 233-234, 244, 727, 953, 962, 974, 1865, 1962, 1993, 2038
  Jean Baptiste Gabriel, I, Widow, 744, 1108, 1751-1752

Buard (continued),
  Jean Baptiste II "Batoche", 275, 347, 401, 970, 1068, 1136, 1227, 1352, 1356, 1404, 1519-1520, 1604, 1606-1607, 1610, 1764-1766, 1800, 1802, 1834, 1861, 2004-2005, 2072, 2132-2133, 2144, 2159, 2262, 2611-2612, 2755, 2769
  Jean Denis, 8, 504, 780, 806, 812, 953, 1016
  Jean Denis, Widow, 1829, 1834, 1851, 1861
  Jean Louis, 244, 275, 279, 389, 450, 614, 744, 928, 984, 2007-2009, 2281, 2668, 2803
  Jose, 2140
  Joseph Louis (called "Louis"), 2161, 2489, 2495, 2515
  Julie, 279, 1424, 1649
  Louis, 2768
  Louis Alexandre, 389
  Louis Gabriel, 188, 244, 400, 744, 861, 953, 1005, 1709, 1717, 1733, 1757, 1822, 1824, 1837, 1846, 1881, 1967, 2003-2004, 2009
  Louis Gabriel, Widow, 1244-1245
  Louise, 254
  Marguerite, 2157
  Marie Adelaïde (Mme. Edouard Cesaire Murphy), 327, 504, 1016, 2057, 2585
  Marie Anne (Mme. François Vienne), 243, 346, 727, 2724, 2896
  Marie Catherine (Mme. André Antoine Rambin), 34, 53, 142, 151, 893, 1020
  Marie Elisabeth (Mme. Jean Marie F. Rouquier), 324, 389, 400, 1005
  Marie Elisabeth Josephe (Mme. Edouard Murphy), 96, 227, 503-504, 978, 1060, 1095
  Marie Eugenie (Mme. Louis Joseph Tauzin), 260, 279, 284, 334, 1060
  Marie Françoise (Mme. F. M. Monginot II) 1879
  Marie Françoise Aselie, 8, 812
  Marie Lauve, 2668
  Marie Locodie, 347
  Marie Louise (Mme. J. B. Ailhaud de Ste. Anne), 962, 2050
  Natalie (vars. Nathalie, Athalie), 1579, 2769
  Marie Thérèse, 1701, 2769
  Marie Thérèse Eugenie (Mme. Etienne Pavie; Mme. C. T. P. Metoyer), 13, 61, 77, 134, 361, 401, 415, 531, 860, 974
  Onesime, 684, 744, 791, 799, 1060, 1064, 2708, 2803

Buard (continued)
　Pelasy, 684
　Placide, 244, 928
　Silvestre, 861, 2062
　Susanne, 188
Bucley,
　Constant Freeman, 281
　James, 281
Buhart. *See Buart.*
Bull (Boull), Catherinne (Mrs. Frederick Hesser), 34, 151
Bullett,
　Benjamin, 544-545, 2835
　Marcelite Louciana, 545
　Marie Elaysa, 544, 2772?
　Randolph Reuben, 2835
Bustamente (vars. Busta, Bustante)
　Atanasio, 1054
　B., 2809
　Juan Joseph Philipe, 2804
　Manuel, 741, 765, 1059, 2804
Butler, slave. *See Joseph Vutlia?.*

Caddo Indians, 407-408, 1237-1238, 1575
Cade, Maria Angela, 2114
Cadena, Manual, 501, 1054
Cadieu,
　Amable I, 1049
　Amable II, 1049, 2568, 2650
Cailleau. *See La Fontaine.*
Callaghan (vars. Calegham, Callahan),
　＿＿＿, 760, 795
　J.M., 1063
　Julio, 1100
　William (Guillom), 1394
Callahan. *See also Marie Calahin, slave.*
Calvit,
　Betsy (Mrs. Oliviet Wells), 618
　Joseph, 618
Canneci Indians, 43, 69-70, 82-83, 159, 171, 827, 834, 1969-1970, 1973
Cannon, John M., 755
Cantam, Juan Manuel, 2727
Cantri, slave, 2162
Capitan (Capitaine), Indian. *See Nicolas Capitan and Pierre Capitaine.*
Capite, Françoise (Mme. Antoine Peré), 952
Capuran, Joseph, 837, 1708
Cardena (Cardenas),
　Francisco, 751, 2663-2664
　Jose Antonio, 2663
　Maria Gregoria, 2664
Cardena. *See also de Cardenes.*

Cardeno, slave, 2122
Carlen, slave. *See Charlotte.*
Carles (Carle),
　Alexy, 2404
　Etienne, 2404
　Jean Baptiste, 2404
Carlos, Apalache Indian, 648, 661. *See also Charlo.*
Carlos. *See also Charles.*
Carlos Michel, Apalache Indian, 648
Carlos, Nicolas, Apalache Indian, 661
Carmelite (Carmelita), slave, 1583, 1610, 2276, 2440. *See also Melite.*
Carmona, Maria Jetrudis (Dna. Antonio Del Rio), 532, 887
Caro,
　Joseph. *See Pierre Joseph.*
　Joseph Antonio, 752, 2932
　José Tomas, 1052, 2836
　Maria Antonia Clemencia, 467
　Maria Basilio, 2836
　Maria Cleta, 2837
　Maria R＿＿＿a (Dna. Francisco Maria? Estrada?), 768
　Pierre Jose (Joseph, Sote), 467, 768, 1052, 2837
　Tomas. *See José Tomas.*
Caro. *See also Garro.*
Caroline (Carlen), slave, 1103, 1404, 1591, 1641
Carr,
　Hermina Emé, 1246
　John C., 373, 796, 988, 989, 1135, 1247, 1357, 2587, 2602
　John II, 1284
　Marie Hermina, 375
　Marie Louise, 1200
　Marie Josephe Henriette, 374
　Theophile, 989
Carrasco (Cirrasco),
　Geraldo, 792, 1039
　Hilario, 494, 1792, 1039, 2785
　Mario, 443
Carrier (vars. Charrié, Charier, Charrio),
　Joseph Marie, 551, 688, 748, 1011, 1066, 2127, 2510, 2643, 2772, 2822
　Marie Louise Victoire (Mme. J. B. Le Fevre), 323, 345, 363, 2764
Carrin, slave, 2161
Carson?, slave. *See Arson.*
Case (vars. Cess, Gues),
　David, 295, 379, 945, 2045-2046
　Elisabeth (Ysabel) 2046
　Eusebe, 295
　George Washington, 945
　James Edward, 379

Case (continued),
  Joseph Marie, 2046
Casenave (vars. Casanova, Cassenave, Cazanave),
  _____, Mlle. (Mme. Joseph _____, 753
  Bernard, 131
  Denis. *See Michel Denis Aimé.*
  Denis Etienne, 184-185, 753
  Guillermo, 931, 1054
  Ignacio (Dna. Ignacio Hornos), 2687
  Jean Baptiste, 794
  Joseph Crisanto, 2839
  Jose Eginio, 1054, 2839
  Joseph V., 2838
  Justa Rusina, 437
  Marie A. (Dna. Juan Andre Sosa), 2880
  Marie Manet (Nanet) (Dna. Felis Estrada), 2661, 2697, 2723
  Michel Denis Aimé, 131, 247, 391, 743, 745, 976, 978, 1011, 1014, 1018, 1023-1024, 1027-1031, 1034-1036, 1044-1045, 1095, 1105, 1596?, 2126
  Marie Aimeé, 131, 753
  Paul, 740, 749
  Suzanne, 2838
Casimir, slave, 2301
Casman, L. (female) 2773
Cassau, Marie Clarar. *See Marie Claverie Dassou.*
Castel,
  Marie Jeanne, 2382
  Ursule (Mme. Jacques Rachal), 51, 121-122
Castañeda,
  Juan Antonio, 478
  Maria Josefa, 478
Castrier, José, 488
Castro,
  José Maria, 736, 1120
  Juan Maria, 2840
  Juan Sanchez, 1054
  Juana Maria, 718
  Juana Maria Ruderinda, 703
  Maria Daria (Dna. Esmeregilde Martinez), 462, 2788
  Maria Jacinta, 448
  Maria Jetrudis, 703, 2840
Catalina. *See Catharine.*
Catalina, Apalache Indian, 645
Catherine, f.w.c. *See Catherine Badin.*

Catherine (vars. Catherinne, Catarina, Catalina, Catarina, Chatarine), slave, 1071, 1110, 1263, 1287-1288, 1304, 1388-1389, 1420, 1513, 1585, 1620, 1814, 1822, 1855-1856, 1863, 1951, 1961, 2005, 2011, 2027, 2048, 2340, 2379, 2383, 2434, 2438, 2444, 2479, 2513, 2515, 2554, 2556, 2642
Catherine (Catarine) Jouafa, Apalache Indian, 681
Catherine (Chatarine) Thomas, Apalache Indian, Wife of Joseph, 658-659
Catiche, Indian. *See Marie Catis Athenais.*
Cauranson, _____, 1015
Cavé (Cabet),
  Marie "Manon" (Mme. Robert Dupré), 7, 111, 213
  Marie Louise (Mme. Remy Poissot, II), 8, 36, 97, 187-188, 233, 243, 487, 858, 953, 2037
Cazanova. *See Casenave.*
Cayacac, slave. *See Pompose Celeste Cayacac.*
Cayelle, _____, Mr., 1411
Cayeu. *See Cadieu.*
Cecile, free Negro, 1755, 2350. *See also Marie Cecile Baden.*
Cecile (Cecilia, Cecille), slave. 1092, 1848, 1933, 1948, 1950, 2077, 2481, 2632
Cecile (Cecilie),
  Ambroise, 118, 1931
  Celeste, 50, 2351
  Chatarine, 2350
  Jacques, 49
  Jean Baptiste, 2351
  Jeanne, 1559
Cedars (Ceda), Marie Josephe, 2826.
Cedars. *See also Sidrec.*
Celesie, slave. *See Marianne Celezi.*
Celesinne (Celesy), slave, 1232, 2280.
Celeste, f.w.c., 2267
Celeste (Celestine), slave, 1252, 1321, 1336, 1436, 1510, 1524, 1554, 1772, 1815, 1852, 1910, 1930, 1952, 1998, 2049, 2074, 2077, 2154, 2176, 2202-2203, 2238, 2322-2323, 2327, 2336, 2443, 2562, 2611, 2628. *See also Pompose Celeste Cayacac.*
Celestin, Apalache Indian. *See Andres Celestin, Athanase Celestin, Anton__ Celestin, Touton Celestin, Nicolas Celestin, Joseph Celestin.*
Celestin (Celestine, Castin, Zelestin), slave, 1142, 1158, 1163, 1244, 1313,

Celestin, slave (continued)
  1404, 1417, 1669, 1842, 1865, 1893,
  1993, 2004, 2050, 2073, 2077, 2121,
  2148, 2151, 2302, 2310, 2339, 2391,
  2544, 2569
Celestin, Bal, slave, 1247
Cenis, slave. *See Marie Jenny.*
Cenon. *See Zenon.*
Cervantes. *See Servantes.*
Cervera,
  Enrique, 2680
  Maria Nieves, 2680
Cesaire (Cesserre, Cezer), slave,
  1305, 1425, 1630, 1690, 2048, 2056,
  2089, 2195
Ceser Charmen, 2575
Cevallos, Juan Nepomano, 939
Chabaut (Chabot), Theodore, 1586
Chabus,
  Widow, 1407, 2435
  Barbara (Dna. Lino Chavana), 459
  Barthelemis, 38
  François, 40, 86, 231, 730, 1321,
    2739
  Françoise. *See Marie Carmelite Françoise.*
  Jean François, 40, 86
  Joseph François, 86
  Ma/ria/, 730
  Marie Carmelite Francoise, 40,
    730, 2927?
Chaconil, Marie, 631
Chagneau (Chanot, Chagnaux),
  Eleonore (Mme. Elie Bernard), 963,
    1010
  Felicité, 624
  Jean Baptiste, 633
  Marie Jeanne "Jeanette" (Mme.
    Guillaume Barberousse), 240,
    986, 2740
  Marie Jeanne (Mme. Jean-Ris; Mme.
    François Frederic *dit* Pievert),
    30, 98, 131, 181, 210, 955
  Michel, 955
Chagneau. *See also Chaquet.*
Chaimbre, Marie (Mrs. Israel Fosom),
  183
Chaisson, slave. *See Francois Cheson.*
Chaler (Chale, Shelere, Shailer, Sha-
  lere),
  François, 790
  Marie Denis (Mme. Jean Eugene Mi-
    champs), 788, 2737
  Lemant. *See Pierre Clement Dupre.*

Chaler (Continued),
  Pierre, 788
  Terence. *See Francois Terence Dupre.*
Cham___, Marie Adelyde, 1285
Chamard (Chamart),
  _____ly, 112
  André, 73, 693?, 712, 726, 730, 747, 779,
    967, 1042, 1051, 1061, 1184, 1811,
    1852, 1879, 2177, 2666, 2841
  André II, 2666
  Catherine, 231, 726, 728, 1064
  Edmon, 439
  Felicité, 1061
  Louis Charles, 38, 53, 106, 142-143, 693,
    948, 951, 959-960, 967
  M. E. E., 2841
  Marie, 2863
  Marie (Mme. Joseph Tauzin I), 38, 241,
    295, 380, 728, 750, 1003, 1060, 1064,
    1321, 2705, 2868
  Marie(*fille* Michel), 142
  Marie Arthemise, 53, 2177, 2912
  Marie Emely, 693
  Michel, 31, 53, 142, 224, 335, 726, 728,
    949, 977, 1031, 1206, 1831, 1877,
    2608, 2813, 2841
  Rosaimond, 10, 21, 200, 241, 459, 462,
    1042, 1814, 1867, 1938, 1953, 2771,
    2788
Chambers. *See Chaimbre.*
Chanac, M. J. I, (female), 2845
Chanet, slave. *See Janet.*
Chanot. *See Chagneau.*
Chapa, Jose Maria, 2735
Chapelin, Joseph, 1390
Chapman, Joseph, 1376, 1386, 1390?
Chapman. *See also Chazman.*
Chaquet,
  Manuel Samuel, 635
  Robin I, 635-636
  Robin II, 636
Charbonneau (Charbonnet, Sarvounau, Char-
  vaneau, Charvonet, Charvonier),
  Barbara, 1441
  Joseph Louis I, 593-594, 688
  Joseph Louis II, 594
  Joseph Michel, 594
  Marie Rose, 593
  Victor, 1549
Charité, slave, 2108, 2287
Charlé, Antonio. *See Antonio Charlé.*
Charlene. *See Carlen.*
Charles (Carlo, Carlos), 1107, 1168, 1185,
  1187, 1378, 1460, 1535, 1583 (continued)

Charles (continued),
    1637, 1683, 1892, 1898, 1944, 2049,
    2070, 2077, 2198, 2286, 2288, 2345,
    2379, 2387, 2391, 2514, 2518, 2542
Charles. *See also Jacques Charles.*
Charles Honoré, slave, 1869
Charles Lemb, slave, 1484
Charles Mertil, slave, 1440
Charles Simon, f.m.c., 1406, 1421
Charleville,
    Jean Baptiste *(fils* Baptiste),
        1393, 1423
    Jean Baptiste *(fils* Joseph), 1393
Charlo, Apalache Indian, 665-668
Charlotte, Canneci Indian, 827
Charlot, Pierre, 95
Charlotte (Carlota, Charlot, Charlota, Charlo), slave, 1088, 1091,
    1103, 1113, 1153, 1404, 1417, 1421,
    1440, 1618, 1644, 1831, 1870, 2050,
    2066, 2131, 2199, 2277-2278, 2286,
    2386, 2405, 2433, 2439, 2532, 2543,
    2606, 2613, 2623, 2638-2639
Charmin, slave. *See Ceser Charmen.*
Charnac, Apalache Indian. *See François Charnac.*
Charnau,
    Pierre I, 1004
    Pierre II, 720, 772, 788, 1004
Charnau. *See also Chenal.*
Charpenel (Charpanée), Marie Anne (Mme. Jean François Chabus), 40, 86
Charrio. *See Carrier.*
Chatman. *See Chapman, Chazman*
Chavana,
    Faustin, 2770
    Jose Guillaume, 714, 2842
    Lino, 459, 2771
    Maria Guadalupe (Dna. J. Antonio Sepulveda), 765.
    Martin, 459, 2771
    Ramon, 765, 2770, 2842, 714?
Chavinda,
    Luis Tiohua, Indian, 491
    Maria Paula, 491
Chazman,
    Maria Candelaria, 395
    Nancy (Nansi), 395
Chelette (Cheletre, Chelectre, Sllectre, Slecttre, Eslect, Chalaitre, Chelte, Chellettre, Esletre, Eslecctre, Shlette, Shleter, Sheletre, Schelette, Sclette, Slyder),
    Anne Barbe (Mme. Philippe Frederick II), 27, 101, 815, 964, 1056
    Anne Marguerite (Mme. Antoine Hymel), 77, 110, 204, 2703, 2710
    Barnabé, 45, 195, 589
    Denis, 589
    Etienne Brevel, 485, 2777
    Euphrosine Manuelle, 402
    François, 789, 790, 2542
    Françoise (Mme. Joseph Lattier II), 195, 204
    Françoise (Mrs. Moris McGlothin), 590-591
    Jean Baptiste, 357-378, 402, 485, 1006, 1115, 2651, 2777
    Jean Baptiste Pierre, 429
    Jean Pierre, 229, 257-258, 429, 485, 2777, 2805
    Joseph, 195, 590
    Lte. (Lolette?), 1594
    Marguerite. *See Anne Marguerite.*
    Marie, 2519
    Marianne Jeanne (Mme. J. B. Lestage), 45, 257, 418, 470, 944, 2787, 2878
    Marie Arcene, 595
    Marie Clara, 595
    Marie Clementine, 2805
    Marie Elene (Mrs. Denis Quinnelty), 589, 590, 592-593
    Marie Emanuel (Mme. Jacques Quinnelty), 450
    Marie Emelie? (Mme. Jn. Pierre Vercher), 330, 357, 530, 912, 999
    Marie Josephine (Mrs. Joseph Thompson), 92, 2922
    Marie Louise (Mrs. Louis Rachal *fils* Louis Barthelemy), 330, 353, 508, 1008, 2908
    M.P., 2805
    Marie Pelagie (Mme. François Frederic), 73, 90, 217, 353
    Marie Pelagie (Mme. François Lattier I), 257-258, 358, 498, 972, 2801, 2876
    Marie Pierre, 1592
    Marie Prudence, f.w.c., 1115
    Marie Rosse (Bonne?), 45, 2542?
    Michel, 45, 153, 195, 204
    Paul, 1556
    Pierre, 41, 87, 277, 402, 790, 957-958, 972, 1006, 1008, 1115, 1594-1595, 2066, 2273, 2411
    Rose (Mme. Valentin J. B. Dubois), 153, 648, 793
    Ursulle (Mme. Françoise Pierre Clavis Saidek *dit* LeConte), 154
Chenal, J. B. *See J. B. Cheval.*
Chenoweth,
    Jean Raymond, 2843
    Thomas, 2843

Cheredem (Sheridan?),
  A.M., (female), 2903
  Celeste L. (Mrs. Michel Guin), 496, 2903
  Elisabeth, 2879
  Rebecca (Mrs. Jean Lom), 2879
Cherinne, slave, 2507
Cheval (Chenal), Jean Baptiste, 772, 1084, 1446
Chevalier, Therese (Mme. Charles Durand de St. Romes), 1011
Chever (Chaver, Chevert),
  Guillaume, 839, 1860, 1951, 1986
  Marie Jeanne (Mme. Bastien Prudhomme), 78, 951
Chifilef (Shilé), Charity (Mrs. Frederick Walker), 542-543, 575
Chirino (Chirine, Guiriné),
  Bartolome, 821, 1058
  Jetrudis, 2870
  José Antonio, 1055, 2817?, 2859
  José Encarnacion, 552, 768
  Joseph Lucas, 2844
  Juan Bautista, 395, 704, 1058, 2804, 2870
  Juan Joseph, 821
  Maria Faustina (Mme. J. B. Andres Vascocu), 1055, 2677
  Maria Guadalupe Lucia (Dna. Manuel Santos), 552
  Maria Jetrudis, 444, 719, 2589, 2804
  Maria Simona (Luna) (Dna. Sacramiento Basquez), 2713
  Marie Them., 2844
  Pedro (Pierre), 2852
Chloe. *See Clo and Marie Clo.*
Choctaw Indians, 306, 1659
Chonse, Henriette (Anriette), Mlle. 1373, 1382
Choppin (Chaupin), Claude Antoine, 1612
Choy? (Chamard?), Rozamond, 1031
Chris, slave. *See Cris.*
Christ____, slave, 1383
Christophe, f.m.c. *See Jn. Christophe.*
Christophe, slave, 2056
Christy (Christi, Christian, Christin, Christii, Sn. Cristin),
  Denize (Mme. Julien François Besson), 287, 1002
  Denise (Dna. Juan Mieta), 2818
  Jacques, 960, 1002, 1031
  Jose, 535, 1360
  M. (female), 2818

Christy (continued),
  Marie Deneige. *See Marie Deneige Tihoua.*
  Marie Felicité, 535
  Marie Magdeleine (Mme. Louis Tihoua) 12, 491, 492, 960
  Marie Marguerite. *See Marie Marguerite Tihoua.*
  Remy, 535, 960, 1002, 1031
Christine (Cristina), slave, 2135
Christopher (Cristofero), slave, 2458
Cidalise, slave. *See Sidalise.*
Cidonie, slave. *See Sidonie.*
Cid-Cidre Family. *See Cedars.*
Cidre, slave. *See Ysidre.*
Cifroi, slave. *See Barthelemi Cifroi.*
Cigouielle (Aciguirie), Thereze (Dna. Michel Aragon), 164
Ciriac (Ciriaco), slave, 1193, 1260, 2201, 2614. *See also Vincent Ciriac.*
Claire, Angelique (Mme. Frediéu), 6, 126.
Claire (Clara, Clarisse, Arice, Claris, Claurice), slave, 1190, 1379, 1422, 1589, 1614, 1616-1617, 1619-1620, 1765, 1875, 2012, 2049, 2166, 2486.
  See also Clavis, Crisse.
Claire. *See also LeClerc.*
Clairevil, slave. *See Jn. Pierre Clairevil.*
Clairmont (Clairemont),
  Marie Françoise (Mme. André Rambin), 194.
  Marie Josephe (Mme. J. B. F. Dubois, I), 30, 153, 181-182, 210
Clark (Clarc),
  Jean Joseph, 2845
  Joseph, 2845
Claude Mars, Free Negro, 1827
Clauseau. *See Closeau.*
Clemanin, Louise. *See Clernanin.*
Clemence (Clemencia), 1894-1895, 1900, 1904, 1915, 2208, 2235
Clement, slave. *See Jean Baptiste Cleman.*
Clement, Marie Louise, 70
Clernanin, Louise, 1568
Clo (Chloe? Clothilde?), slave, 1387
Closeau (Clauseau),
  Agnes, 2035
  Gilbert, 47, 131, 205, 329
  Louis, 57, 102, 158-159, 286, 288, 537, 1883, 2016, 2573, 2798
  Philibert, 1069

Cloutier (Cloutierre),
　———, 696
　Alexis I, 123-124, 996
　Alexis II, 123, 320, 487, 508,
　　777, 996, 1001, 1120-1121, 1192-
　　1193, 1252, 1339, 1567-1568,
　　1916-1917, 1971, 1974-1977, n2197-
　　n2242, 2210, 2233-2242, 2326,
　　2498-2502, 2825, 2847, 2857, 2915
　Arselina (Zeline?), 509
　Augustin, I, 1273, 1663, 1672,
　　1916-1917
　Augustin, II, 1273
　Celeste, 490, 1550
　Cesair, Canneci Indian, 1908,
　　1922, 1973, 1975
　Hélèine (Elenne) (Mrs. Ambroise
　　LeComte), 123, 322, 970, 1046,
　　1549, 2462, 2558
　J. B., 1933-1936, 1972
　Jean Baptiste *fils* Jean Pierre,
　　124, 574, 1701, 2220, 2232
　Jean Baptiste Sévère, 164, 306,
　　2082
　Jean Pierre I, 121, 123-124, 306,
　　1701, 1937
　Jean Pierre II, 306, 1701
　Marie Aurore, 123
　Marie Denis, 564
　Marie Helene, 2849
　Marie Henriette (Anrriete) Doro-
　　thée Monet (Mme. Pierre Metoyer
　　II), 784, 1143, 1304, 1431,
　　1438, 1481, 1627, 1684, 1696,
　　1888, 2297?, 2333, 2614-2615
　Marie Louise, 1663
　Marie Luce, 124, 1701
　Marie Marguerite (Mme. François
　　Davion), 115, 165, 209, 979,
　　1701, 1907, 1972, 2210
　Marie Zeline (Mme. Marc Sompayrac),
　　490?, 509?, 777, 1934, 1978,
　　2408
Cobb (Cobbs),
　Eggleston. *See Theophile Eggleston.*
　John C., 242
　Marie Elisabeth, 335
　Samuel, 242, 335
　Rachel, 242
　Theophile Eggleston, 242
Cockram (Cortram), John, 2890, 2931
Coincoin (KuenKuen), Marie Thérèse,
　23, 305, 946, 956, 1888, 2001,
　2053, 2058, 2060, 2196

Coindet (Condet, Condé),
　Antoine, 762, 1197, 1397, 2328, 2406,
　　2502, 2619
　Antoine Lesiere, 1397
　Jean Baptiste, 490
　Marie Antoinet, 1197, 2406
　Marie Doralisse, 2619
　Marie Louise, 1734, 2099
Col, Jacobo, 631
Colantin, Marie Henriette Josephe (Mme.
　J. B. Prudhomme I), 62-63, 108, 128-
　129, 191, 211
Colas, slave, 1925, 2056. *See also
　Nicolas.*
Colau (Coleau)
　Lazare I, 219
　Lazare II, 219
Colin, ———, Mr. 1952
Commanche Indians, 1774
Compere,
　Joseph Maximin, 687, 1487, 2806
　Marie Alida, 1487
　Pierre Sebastien, 265, 354, 687, 736,
　　774, 777, 786, 980, 1017, 1023,
　　1032, 1316-1317, 1486, 1490, 2137,
　　2543, 2806
　Robert, 1023
Compton, John, 767
Conant (Cona, Conan),
　Augustin Arnold, 1633
　Charles Darcourt, 1632
　Florentin I. *See Jean Baptiste Floren-
　　tin.*
　Florentin II, 1274
　Jean Baptiste Florentin Metoyer, 14,
　　720-721, 773, 784-785, 1045, 1116,
　　1274, 1476, 1482-1484, 1623-1624,
　　1632-1633, 1646, 1836, 2052, 2059-
　　2060, 2098, 2128, 2293, 2294, 2465
Condé. *See Coindet.*
Conelty (Quinnelty, Coneltin),
　Denis. 592
　Jacques, 450
　Jean Louis, 450
　Marie Nancy, 592
Conisa, Maria Risa (Dna. Cayetano Arre-
　ñago), 1816, 2828
Conomichel, Apalache Indian, 1804
Constance (Constans), 1432, 1723, 1829,
　1 906, 2020, 2049, 2188, 2353-2355
Corde, Barbe Pierre (Mme. Joseph Rosse),
　5, 76, 185

Cordova,
  Guadalupe (Dna. José Dionisio Lopez) 534
  Joseph, 768
  Maria A., 2899
Corinne, slave. *See Carrin.*
Corona, Maria Isabel (Dna. Jose Francisco Gonzales Hidalgo), 443, 571
Cortes,
  Benjamin Valcour, 451, 1246
  Jean Baptiste, 782
  Jean (d'Artheits), 289, 345, 367, 373, 379, 394, 404, 451, 729, 753, 988, 1019, 1043, 1229, 1246, 1309, 1572, 2067, 2091, 2437, 2764
  Jean François, 373, 1200, 1309
  José Louis, 2345
  Marie Louise Marcelitte, 289, 545
  Pierre (d'Artheits), 451, 988
Cortinas,
  ?Jean Baptiste, 782
  Jean Venancio, 2772
  José Maria, 2772
  Maria Eudona (Dna. José Maria Medrano), 546
  Maria Refugia (Dna. Maximo Aguillon), 764, 1293, 2334, 2336, 2479.
Coté (Couti?), Joseph, 969.
Coton-Mais,
  Antoine, 2461
  Marie Antoinette, 1648
  Marie Suset, 2461
Couart,
  Adouen, 184
  Marie (Mrs. Laigne Paret) 184
Couia,
  Gracia, 75
  Marie Anne (Mme. François Giron), 75
Courteri, Marie Louise (Dna. Gracia Couia), 75
Coutret (Couterette), Catherine (Mme. Nicolas Lauve), 503, 978
Coutri, slave, 2162
Couti (Couty, Coté),
  Jean, 115, 165
  Jean Baptiste, 1901
  Jean Paul, 115, 165, 566-568, 1910
  Joseph, 969?
  Joseph Marcel, 566
  Manuel Marcel, 115, 1671
  Marie Damascene, 567
  Marie Joseph, 165
  Marie Seosy, 568

Cowart. *See Couart.*
Cox, Margaret (Mrs. Constant Freeman), 281-282, 295
Coyota, Indian?, 1303
Crede. *See Cuede.*
Crée, slave, 2225
Crete (Checte, Crete-Anty),
  Marie Jeanne (Mme. Louis Anty), 35, 320, 997, 2846-2847
  Pierre, 35
  Derzilin, 2847
  Dufroit, 2846
Cris, slave, 2375-2376
Crisostomé (Crisostomo), Apalache Indian, 647, 660, 663, 1807.
Crisostomo, Apalache Indian. *See also Victoria Crisostomo.*
Cristofero. *See Christopher.*
Cruz (Croux, Chuz),
  Celeste, 630
  Estevan, 629
  Feliciana (Dna. Ficente del Rio), 871
  Felipe, 631
  Juan Antonio, 2807
  Juan Bautista, 675, 2145
  José, 1020-1021
  Joseph, 629-631
  Manuel, 782, 1052
  Marie Antoinette, 2807
  Marie Celeste, 630
  Maria Concepcion (Dna. José Pablo Montoya), 886
  Maria Encarnation, 559
  Maria Magdalenne (Mrs. Louis Guet), 619-623
  Martin, 1020-1022, 2109
  Pedro, 559
Cruz. *See also Sta. Cruz and de la Cruz.*
Cuede (Crede), slave, 1282, 1433
Cuellar,
  J. F. Romuald, 2773
  Joseph Maria, 2773
Cuerca. *See Quirk.*
Cuny, Cesar, 626
  Cesar, 626
  Edith (Mrs. Stephen Cuny?), 616
  R. C., 615
  Samuel, 627
  Steven (Estevan), 616, 628
  Tabitha (Mrs. R. C. Cuny), 615
Cyprien (Cypriano), 1603, 1770, 1926, 2200

Dagobert. *Dit* of P.E. LeBrun, 736
Dalbarcq, Marie. *See Holbarcq, Marie*.
Dagues, slave, 1080
Danalle, Sara (Mme. Morico Richal), 914
Daniel, slave, 1950. *See also Joseph Daniel*.
Daphanet, slave, 1316
D'Aragon. *See Aragon*.
Darst. *See Dost*.
D'Artheits. *See Cortes*
Dassou, Marie Claverie (Mme. Pierre Cortes), 451, 988
Daublin (Doblin), Marie Anne (Mme. J. B. Triche I), 47, 158, 238, 810, 987
Daugherty. *See Douty*.
Davenport (Davimport, Davemport),
  Benjamin (Benigno), 1186, 2104, 2289
  Eliza, 2106
  John (Juan), 2102?, 2106
  Louis, 1024
  Margaret (Mrs. Jacob Keiser), 403-406
  Marie Azelie, 235, 1186, 2102
  Samuel, 235, 406, 1027, 1185-1187, 2102-2108, 2283-2291, 2591
  William, 235
David, slave. *See Jose David*.
David,
  Elisabeth, 24, 363, 366
  Eloise. *See Marie Pelagie Eloise*.
  Jean Baptiste, 1212, 1833, 1843, 2490
  Louis Mathurin, 230, 959
  Marie (Mme. Louis Prevot), 799
  Marie Euphrosine Mathurine (Mme. Dominique Sorel), 230, 787, 959
  Marie Louise, 2901
  Marie Osinne, 1212
  Marie Pelagie Eloise, 24
  Mathurin, 959
Davidson, Ann (Mrs. William Davenport) 235
Davion,
  _____, 722
  Avis Jean, 102
  Celesie, 2862
  Dominique. *See Jean Baptiste Dominique Davion*.
  Estase. *See Marie Anastasie*.
  Elisabeth (Mme. Louis Bertrand), 1030
  Etienne, 19
  François, 115, 209, 307, 979, 1907, 1918, 2213

Davion (continued)
  Jean Baptiste (identity uncertain), 19, 102, 1049
  Jean Baptiste (husband of M. Hiacinthe Triche), 19, 891, 1041
  Jean Baptiste (Louis) Davion, 2691
  Jean Baptiste Dominique, 19, 102, 1041, 1049, 1062, 1713, 2178, 2263
  Jean Baptiste Dominique, Widow, 1351, 1498, 2569, 2571
  Geoffrois, 2576?
  Marie, 164, 2825
  Marie Anastasie (Estasy) (Mme. Pierre Derbanne, III), 307, 490, 708, 2233, 2849, 2873, 2915
  Marie Aselinne, 1189
  Marie Athanase, 1922
  Marie Esther, 1908
  Marie Louise (Mme. Pierre Gagne, I), 42, 178, 1041, 1049, 2649
  Marie Selesy, 2576
  Marie Susanne, 1049
  Marie Thérèse (Mme. Louis Geoffrois), 527, 733, 2263
De Alamillo. *See Alamillo*.
Deblieux,
  Alexandre, 1064, 2863
  Alexandre Louis, 750, 769, 776, 797, 1064, 1611, 1613
de Cado, Jean, 1939-1941
de Cardenes, Maria Francisca (Dna. Juan Diego Beloz), 910
de Cardenes. *See also Cardena*.
Dejones, Rebecca (Mrs. Edward Teal), 154
de la Baume, _____ Sieur, 787
de la Bega, Jose Luis, 723, 736, 743, 748, 752, 765, 1039, 1051-1052, 1055, 2690
de la Cerda (Laserda, De la Zerda),
  Joseph Felician, 1507
  Manuel, 764
  Manuela (Dna. Joseph Maria Procella), 2899
  Maria Marzelina (Dna. J. B. Procella), 2768, 2823, 2888
  Maria Rosa (Dna. José Cayetano Quesada), 484, 2902
  Maria Jetrudis (Dna. Estevan Mora), 465, 2790, 2843, 2888
  Marie Telesfora (Dna. Estevan Morin), 2817
De la Croix,
  Jean, 1982
  Marie Gregoir (Mme. François Langlois) 801
De la Cruz, Maria (Dna. Luis Ramon Acos-

ta, 444
De la Cruz. *See also Sta. Cruz, Cruz.*
De la Fuentes (de la Fuertes), Pedro, 471, 1054.
De la Fuentes. *See also Fouente.*
De la Garza (Garza)
  C. (Dna. Ludgard Sanchez), 2821
  Cayetano?, 1036
  Cypriano, 522
  Joseph Antonio, 2685
  Juana (Jeanne) (Dna. Pedro y Barbo), 2934
  Juana (Jeanne) (*hija* Pedro), 2859
  Junian, 591
  Marcelino, 2685
  Maria Antonia, 2689
  Maria Casimire (Dna. Jose Leonardo Sanchez), 463, 2689, 2796
  Maria Josefa (Dna. Francisco Trevino), 864
  Maria Luisa Petra, 2860
  Mariano, 2709
  Pedro (Pierre), 2859-2860
  Trinidad Yldefonsa (Dna. Juan Bautista Chirino), 1058
De Landa, Maria Josefa, 443, 571
De Landa. *See also La Lande.*
De la Peña. *See Peña.*
De la Rivière (Delerio, Del Rio), Jeanne (Mme. Charles La Renaudiere), 88
De la Vega. *See de la Bega.*
De la Vigne. *See La Vigne.*
Delayde. *See Adelayde.*
De Leon, Maria Rosa (Dna. Francisco Alvaredo), 1048
De Leon. *See also Lion.*
Delgado,
  Gavino, 1033
  Jose Maria, 2839, 2881
  Juan (Jean), 2775
  Maria Candida, 525, 552
  Maria Josefa, 535
  Miguel, 525, 768
  Pablo, 2775
Delores. *See Dolores.*
De los Reyes, Maria Juana (also called Marie Jeanne/Anne De Roi. Dna. Joseph Courretant Torres I), 72-73, 84, 90-92, 115, 164-165, 170, 207-208, 969, 1910, 2081
De los Santos. *See also Santos.*
De los Santos Coy (vars. de los Santa, Sta. Coy),

De los Santos Coy (continued),
  Ignacio, I, 2700
  Ignacio, II, 444, 1433, 2700
  Joseph, 1270
  Juan Bautista (Yguaneo Indian), 1270
  Maria (Dna. Juan Nepomano Cevallos), 939
  Maria Antonia (Dna. Jose Antonio Chirino), 1055, 2817, 2859
Delouche (Deslouche, Destouches, Deloux, de Louex),
  Félicité, 258, 596, 660?
  Jean Baptiste, 789
  Jean Louis, 1300
  Julien, 596, 743, 761-762, 2300
  Marie Françoise, 606
  Michel, 1485
  Nanet, 596, 676
  Pierre, 737, 789, 1218-1220, 1485
  Ursulle, 596
De Loya (des Laudes), Marie Arthemisa, 1395, 1621 (Possibly same as Marie Arthemise Mulon or Dupart)
Delphine, slave, 1213, 1352, 1437, 1630, 1681, 1693
Del Rio,
  Antonio, 532
  Facunda, 871
  Faustino. *See José Faustino Del Rio.*
  Ficente, 871
  Juana. *See Jeanne de la Rivière.*
  José, 1044
  José Faustino, 1044, 2147
  Maria de los Dolores, 532
Del Rio. *See also de la Riviere, de Rios.*
De Luna. *See Luna.*
Demba, slave. *See Jacob Demba.*
De Mezières (Demesier, Demesiere, Messier, Mezieres),
  Antoine I, 915
  Antoine II. *See Marie Joseph Antoine.*
  Athanas, 1142, 1706, 1748, 1771, 1844, 1854, 1871, 1964, 1995, 2007, 2014-2015, 2040, 2129, 2488
  Elisabeth Marie Félicité Nepomucine Margarita, 1953, 2488, 2652
  Joseph Agapite, 2510
  Joseph Antoine. *See Marie Joseph Antoine.*
  Joseph Noel, 1995
  Lolet, 1881, 1953
  Marie Eufrosinne, 2510
  Maria Fortunat, 1658, 1953
  Marie Jeanne, 1066, 1135, 1211, 1582, 1748, 1854, 1871, 1995, 2014, 2040

De Meziérès (continued),
  Marie Joseph Antoine, 1135, 1582, 1995, 2129
  Marie Josephe, Mlle. 2488
  Marie Manuel Josephe Anathalie, 1871, 2510
  Marie Leonore, 2553
  Marie Nicolas Zosime, 155
  Marie Nisa, 1582
  Marie Reine Plerys, 1658
  Marie Rose "Rosette", 1228, 1277, 1582, 1658, 1995, 2129, 2602, 2643
  Marie Zenon (Cenon), 1188, 1277, 1422, 1964, 2007
De Meziérès, f.w.c. *See also Marie Mesier.*
De Mora. *See Mora.*
Denain,
  Eugenie, 292
  Jean Baptiste, 292
Denain. *See also Denis.*
Denay. *See Denis.*
Denes. *See Denis.*
Denis, male slave, 1439, 1695, 1747
Denise (Denis, Denisse), female slave, 1102, 1165, 1202, 1252, 1667, 1681, 2048, 2077, 2206, 2436, 2499. *See also DeNeige, Des Neiges.*
Denis (Denes, Deny),
  Anne "Nanette"- Mrs. Simon Guey), 317-318, 520, 2395, 2399
  Athanase, 512, 746, 1553, 2829
  Euphrosine. *See Lucide Euphrosine.*
  Henri, 1631
  Jean Baptiste (husband of Elisabeth Bontems), 28, 162, 174, 745, 954
  Jean Baptiste (husband of Elisabeth Dumont), 832
  Jean Baptiste *(fils* Lucide), 174
  Lucide Euphrosine (Mme. J. B. Bonnet), 28, 174, 319, 512
  Marguerite (Mme. Manuel Derbanne), 16, 162, 169, 318, 519, 2848
  Marie, 162
  Marie Denis, 1566
  Marie Elisabeth (Mme. Louis Ceaser Bormé), 832
Denis. *See also Denain.*
De Oca, Gertrude Montes (Dna. Guilluermo Casanova), 1054
De Porcuna. *See Porcuna.*
Derbanne (Dervan, Dervam, Darbone), _____, 1872
  Antoine Ursin, 2808

Derbanne (continued),
  Etien, 2544
  François Sumovil?, 432, 1145
  Gaspard I, 57, 80, 136
  Gaspard II, 57, 854, 963, 1024, 1026
  Helene (Elenne), 2311
  Jacques, 136
  Jean Baptiste, *fils* Gaspard I, 80-81, 136, 280, 995
  Jean Baptiste, *fils* Gaspard II, 683, 1024, 2776
  Jean Baptiste, *fils* Jean Baptiste, 2371
  Jean Baptiste, *fils* Pierre I, 109, 146
  Jean Baptiste, *fils* Pierre II, 490
  Jean Baptiste, husband of Marie Marcelite Dupre, 297, 432, 2808
  Jean Baptiste, identity uncertain, 383, 555, 994, 1038, 1143, 1220, 1340, 1588-1590, 1906
  Jean Baptiste Theodule, 2776
  Joseph, *fils* Pierre I, 17, 276, 775, 788, 948, 1344, 1432, 1829, 2412
  Joseph, *fils* Pierre II, 66
  Joseph, *fils* Manuel, 316
  Joseph, identity uncertain, 316, 1054, 2115
  Lasette, 2578
  Louis, *fils* Pierre, 59, 80, 109, 761, 786, 958, 970, 995, 1004, 1015, 1037, 1053, 1449, 1858, 2313, 2315, 2849?
  Louis Gaspard, 80
  Louis Sepherin (Simphorien, Zifroyin) 307, 1149
  Louis Solasty, 1453
  Louise Marguerite (Mme. Louis Juchereau de St. Denis), 814
  Manuel I, *fils* Pierre I, 162-163, 316, 318, 519, 954, 2848, 2857?, 2907
  Manuel II, 2848
  Manuel, *fils* Gaspard II, 57
  Marcelitte, 57
  Marie (Mme. Jn. Pierre Elie Bernard), 223, 270, 383, 963, 1587, 2851
  Marie (identity uncertain), 270-271, 383, 2115
  Marie Arsene, 519
  Marie Aspasie (Mme. Valery Anty I), 146, 362, 509, 696, 708, 2825
  Marie Astasie (Aspaz) (Mme. Antoine B. Rachal), 995, 2808
  Marie Cypriene (Mme. J. B. Ignace Anty II), 17, 137, 560

Derbanne (continued),
  Marie de l'Incarnacion (Mme. Joseph Dupre I, Mme. Jean Varangue dit Marchand), 2, 119-120, 141
  Marie Delphine, 297, 2248
  Marie DeNeige (Denis) (Mme. Antoine LeNoir II), 555, 1204, 2877
  Marie Irene, 280
  Marie Louise (Mme. F. Lavespere), 46, 206, 958, 983, 1053
  Marie Marguerite, 2849
  Marie Rose (Mme. Augustin Cesaire Fredieu), 480, 1026, 2782, 2831, 2877
  Marie Victoire (Mme. Pierre Chaler) 788
  Melanie (Mme. J. B. Brevel, III), 109, 146
  Michel, 509, 564, 775, 1081, 1671, 2233, 2311, 2603
  Pierre I, 40, 66, 162, 954
  Pierre II, 17, 66, 137, 979, 1819, 1872, 1998, 2204, 2211, 2873
  Pierre III, 307, 490, 979, 2849
  Pierre, fils Manuel, 162
  Placide, 2738, 2851, 2877
  Placide Mertil, 683
  Rosalie (Mme. Jean Baptiste Julien Rachal), 303, 2907
  Suzanne, 2851
  Ursin. See Antoine Ursin Derbanne.
  Zepherin. See Louis Sepherin.
Derbanne Family, 1776
De Rios, Maria Guadalupe, 2401. See also Del Rio; de la Riviere.
De Roi, Marie Jeanne. See Maria Juana de los Reyes.
Derzelie, slave. See Desire Derzelie.
Derzelin, slave. See Francois Dorcelin.
De St. Denis. See St. Denis.
De St. Romes. See Durand de St. Romes.
Desbordes, Margueritte, 283
Desire, male slave, 1091
Desire Derzilie (Dezilie), slave, 1643
Des Laudes (De Loya), Marie Arthemise 1395, 1621 (possibly same as Marie Arthemise Mulon or Dupart)
DesNeige. See Denise, Louise DesNeiges.
De Sose. See Sose.
De Soto (Soto),
  Antoine Manuel Bermudez y, 156
  Joseph Michel Benson, 407
  Manuel, 1871
  Marcel I, 407-408, 521, 1020, 1059, 1265, 1398-1399, 2109, 2590, 2816?

De Soto (continued),
  Marcel II, 1059
  Marcel. See also Simon Marcel.
  Marie (Mme. Athanase Poissot), 13, 134
  Marie, 409
  Marie Anne Elisabeth (Ysabel) (Mme. Paul Boüet Lafitte), 156, 976, 1036, 2802
  Marie Antoinette Morvant, 408
  Marie D., 2813
  Marie Demascene (Mme. François Augustin Rambin), 438, 1020, 1398, 2911
  Marie des Nieves, 1266
  Maria Jetrudis (Mme. Jose Prad   439
  Remy, 1286
  Simon Marcel, 1265
De Soto. See also Soto.
Despalier, slave, 1339. See also Rachal, J. B. Despallier.
Despallier (Despallion, Despulier),
  Bernardo Martin (Marin?), 392, 761, 922, 2850
  Joseph El., 2850
  Victorio Madison, 392
Destouches. See De Louche.
Detchou, Bernarde (Mme. J an Hissoura), 93-94.
Deterville (Detervil),
  Alexandre, 2744
  Etienne, 1051
  Jacques Simon Theodore, 726, 1051, 1781, 2686, 2744
  Marie, 2686
De Torres. See Torres.
Detuil,
  Catherinne, 155
  Marguerite, 155
  Marie Ulalie, 155
DeVille (Devil, De Vil),
  Margarite (Mme. Valentin Duvil), 624
  Marie (Mme. J. B. Bellegarde), 632
DeVille. See also Duvil.
De Vimenez. See Vimenez.
Dias,
  Maria Matiana (Dna. Cypriano Agustino Rodriguez), 474, 2795, 2914
  Maria Petra, 1303
  Maria Ursina, 1303
  Vicente, 1303
Dicey, slave. See Dys.
Dick, slave. See Joseph Dic.
Didee, slave, 1963.
Digne, slave. See Pierre Digne.
Dill (Dille),
  Elenna, 1100
  Francisco, 496

Dill (continued),
  Marie, 2882
  Marie Eulalah (Elaya, Layla), 496, 2492
Doblin. *See Daublin.*
Docla (Doclas, Docras),
  Nicolas, 150, 1759
  Marie Anne (Mme. Nicolas), 1889
Dolet (Dollé, Dolé),
  Jean Pierre, 750, 1261
  Marie Deneige (Denise) (Mme. J.B. Adley), 133, 1021, 1257, 1260
  Marie Zefaly (Cephalide), 1259
  Pierre, 74, 202, 737, 747, 1021, 1257-1262, 1264, 1267, 1529-1531, 2110-2111
  Pierre. *See also Jean Pierre.*
Dolores, slave, 1541, 2126
Dominguez, José Ipolito, 448
  Maria del Rosario, 526
  Maria Rosalia, 448
Dominique (Domingo), slave, 1127-1128, 1199, 1225, 1248, 1329, 1447, 1563, 1589, 1830, 1894, 1915, 2002, 2048-2050, 2054, 2077, 2157, 2194, 2245, 2608, 2610
Dony, slave, 2446
Dorothée, f.w.c., 1873, 2001, 2138. *See also Marie Dorothé, Dorothée Monet, Dorothée Boisdore, Marie Henriette Dorothée Cloutier.*
Dorothée, slave, 1253, 1687
Dorsino, Apalache Indian. *See Francois Dorsino.*
Dorsilin (Dorcino, Dorcelin, Dorsino), slave, 1156, 1255, 1318, 2222, 2522
Dortolant (Dorthelom, d'Ortolan, Hortelans, Dorthelan, Dorthelans, Dorthelan, Ortelano, Ortolan)
  _____, Mr., 2139
  Bernard, 1079
  Charles, 740
  David, 1323
  François Eugien, 1241
  Jean Ursel, 2620
  Marie Louise, 2460
  Remond, 1040, 1241, 2025, 2158, 2460, 2620
  Ursin Andres, 2158
Dossé (Dosée, Dosé), slave, 1444, 2394-2397, 2483
Dost, Juan, 2291, 2492
Douty, Robert, 328

Dranguet (Dranguer),
  Benjamin, 728, 769, 798, 1060, 1064, 2136, 2435, 2756
  Benjamin II, 2756
  Charles Antoine, 728
Dubardeau. *See Hubardeau.*
Dubernée, Felicité (Mme. François Saucier), 1051
DuBois (Dubois, Diu Bua),
  Alexis, 359
  Antoine, 182, 424, 2760
  Aurelie Aurore, 182
  Edouard, 153, 593
  François I. *See Jean Baptiste Francois.*
  François II, 210
  Gabriel, 1164
  Jean Baptiste I, 30, 153, 181-182, 210
  Jean Baptiste II. *See Valentin J. B.*
  Jean Baptiste III?, 1191
  Jean Baptiste François, 30, 181, 210, 963, 1010
  Jean Pierre Marie, 325, 775, 788, 990, 993, 995-998, 1032, 2069, 2086, 2463, 2917
  Joseph, 2760
  Marie Aspasie, 181
  Marie Baltide (Balty, Balsy) (Mme. Joseph Louis Charbonneau), 593-594, 688
  Marie Delphine, 30
  Marie Genevieve (Mme. J. B. Etienne Adlé I), 153, 186, 261, 343, 961, 966, 984, 1021-1022, 1063, 2745, 2850.
  Marie Joseph, 424
  Marie Oror (Aurore), 594
  Marie Suzanne, 181
  Pierre. *See Jean Pierre Marie.*
  Valentin J. B., 153, 181, 671, 793, 1441, 2519
Dufroi, slave. *See Barthelemi Cifroi.*
Dufy, Michel, 828
Duguillen, Magdeleine (Mme. Robert Compere), 1073
Dumas, François Bellabre, 970, 978
Dumont, Elisabeth (Mme. J. B. Denis), 832
Dupalier Vidol, slave, 1687
Duparig, Jn. The. Lemonnser, 991
Dupart,
  Arthemise (Marguerite) Mulon Deloy (Mme. François Metoyer), 1215, 2512
  Emil, 1395
Duplessis, Marie Ines (Mme. Michel Goutierrez), 97

Dupouey (Dupre?), J. Baptiste, 2334, 2337, 2561
Dupré (Duprez, Duiprae),
  Adolf, 576
  Aselie, 120
  Athanase I, 119-120, 122, 575-576, 793
  Athanase II, 119, 574, 793
  Cecile Celeste (Mme. Pierre Michel dit Zoriche/Jarri), 7, 111, 213, 1032, 2910
  Celine, 513, 574, 2359
  Clement. *See Pierre Clement Dupre.*
  Dufroi (Dufra), 2203
  Elisabeth (Mme. Charles François LeMoine), 10, 26, 32, 107, 160-161, 173
  Eloise, 2095
  François Terence (Chaler), 127
  Geufrois. *See Louis Geufrois Dupre.*
  Gradas, 520
  Guil., 2936
  Joseph I, 2, 119-120, 141, 166
  Joseph II, 118, 141, 169, 207, 1839, 1848-1849, 1920, 1931, 1974, 1977,
  Joseph, III, 2083n
  Joseph, *fils* Pierre, 141
  Joseph Emanuel, 2095
  Louis Geufrois, 2, 519
  Manuel Prevost, 762, 772, 777, 789, 994
  Marie, 1810, 2936
  Marie, 126-127
  Marie Anne, 120, 543, 575, 653, 1932, 2345, 2347
  Marie Aurore (Horrer), 166, 2328
  Marie Catherine (Mme. F. Pereau; Mme. Jean LaLande), 42, 52, 57, 105, 178, 180, 205
  Marie Doralise, 2083
  Marie Françoise (Mme. Etienne Verger), 33, 133
  Marie Louise (Mme. Jacques LaCaze) 136, 198, 543, 790, 2790
  Marie Louise (Mme. Jean Louis De Louche), 1300
  Marie Marcelitte (Mme. J. B. Derbanne), 126-127, 166, 297, 433, 2248, 2808
  Marie Ozite (Mme. Julien DeLouche), 308, 761
  Marie Robert (Mme. Jean Pommier) 789
  Marie Rose (Mme. Pierre Dolet), 1021, 1261-1262, 1264, 2760

Dupre (continued)
  Michel, 2328, 2406
  Philippe Valsain, 2082
  Pierre, 2, 33, 141, 166
  Pierre Clement (Lemant Chaler), 126
  Prevost. *See M. Prevost Dupre.*
  Robert, 7, 111, 213
  Terence. *See François Terence.*
Dupuis. *See Dupouey.*
Dur___, Jos. Luis, 920
Duran,
  Augustin, 2410
  Jose Luis, 879
Durand de St. Romes,
  Charles, Chevalier, 1011
  Marie Anne (Mme. Jean Boucher), 370, 1011
Duret?, Joseph, 741
Durie, François, 266
Durey, _____, 982
Durranton, Pierre, 868
Duroque,
  Marguerite, 185
  Marie Celeste, 5
  Nicolas, 5, 76, 185
  Nicolas Damien, 76
  Pierre, 5, 76, 185
Du Rosé, Marie (Mme. Louis Saucier I), 550
Durst (Dos), Joseph, 2882.
Durst. *See also Dost.*
Duval, Ambroise, 981
  Julie, 219
  Marie Margueritte (Mme. Laurent Mayou), 121, 377, 551
Duverné, Felicité (Mme. Richard Bavé), 539. *See also Felicité Dubernée.*
Duvil,
  Marie Felicité, 624
  Valentin, 624
Dys (Dicey?), slave, 2369

Ebrom, Lucia (Mme. Juan Borné), 602-603
Ecasse? Indians, 89
Edé, slave, 1075
Edmond, slave, 1552
Edouard (Eduardo), slave, 1261 2601
Edward Lestan, f.m.c, 1302
Elde, Maria Josef (Dna. Juan José Mata Medina), 441
Elena Vivian, slave, 2044
Elene (Elenne, Elena), slave. *See Hélène.*
Eleonor (Leonor), slave, 1177, 1380, 2057, 2077, 2201.
Eleonore Perina, slave, 2605
Eleyse, slave, 1150. *See also Lise.*

Elie. *See Bernard dit Elie.*
Elisabeth (Elisabet, Isabel, Isabela, Isavel, Ysabel, Ysavel), slave, 1108, 1301, 1363, 1611, 1743, 1794, 1819, 1824, 1872, 1876, 1885, 1998, 2019, 2050, 2160, 2270, 2552
Elise, slave, 1608. *See also Eleyse, Lise, Liset, Eliza.*
Eliza, slave, 1605 *See also Elyse, Laysa.*
Ellees, Polée (Paulette Ellis?) (Mrs. Julian Brown), 1040
Ellen, slave. *See Hélène.*
Eloi, slave. *See Louis Joseph Eloi, Jean Baptiste Elois.*
Eloise. *See Loysse, Loysa, Marie Loyse, Eleyse, Elise.*
Elsey (Ersy? L.C.?), male slave. *See Jean Elsy.*
Ely, slave. *See Pierre Ely.*
Ely. *See Bernard dit Elie.*
Emanuel, slave. *See Manuel, Noel*
Emé, 1109, 1552, 2107, 2283, 2285, 2410
Emelie, f.w.c., 2022-2023
Emery, slave, 2421, 2437
Emery, William N., 1019
Emma, slave. *See Emé, Marie Emé.*
Eneres, slave, 1406
Enery, Alexandro, 604
Enes, Thereseta, 1806
Enrique, slave. *See Henry.*
Enselye (Euselye?), slave, 1201, 2496
Equis,
  Stephanie (Dna. Joseph Flores), 2809, 2852
  Maria del Pilar (Dna. Mariano Garza), 2709
  Maria Micaella (Dna. Pedro Jose?/Sote? Caro), 467, 751, 1052, 2837
Erise (Clarisse?), slave, 1244
Errié. *See Herrié, Terrié.*
Errante, slave. *See Joseph Errante.*
Erselinne, slave. *See Marie Magdalenne Euphrasinne Erselinne.*
Erven, G. P., 1294
Ervin, slave. *See François Ervin.*
Escoffie (Escofie, Escophiee),
  Jean François, 604
  Julien I, 61
  Julien, *fils* Jean François, 604
Escoval, Jose, Corp. 1863
Esguar (Esquire?). *See Joseph Esguar.*
Eslect. *See Chelette.*
Esparza, Vin, 2826

Espinen, Luis Alexandro, 2043
Esprink, Marie Louise (Mrs. Christopher Lee), 556, 558
Espuesta, slave, 205
Esquibel, ____, 2725
Esquire. *See Joseph Esguar.*
Estele, Ermete, 234
Estevan. *See Etienne.*
Esther (Ester), 1611, 1613, 1830, 1955, 2013. *See also Lister.*
Estrada,
  Asencio, 526, 753
  Enrique, 796
  Felis, 752-753, 2661, 2697, 2723
  Francisco Maria?, 768
  José Antonio, 2750
  José Franco., 2723
  Joseph Felis, 2697
  Julio, 796, 1275, 2734, 2930
  Maria, 2661
  Maria C. (Dna. Ventura Losoya), 2881
  Silvest, 2880
Eté (Hetty?), slave, 2135.
Etienne (Estevan, Etien, Ettiem, Estivin), Apalache Indian, 643-646, 662, 669
  Slave, 1204, 1226, 1420, 1522, 1544, 1567, 1683, 1686, 1728, 1842, 1852, 1855, 1999, 2023, 2065, 2227, 2285, 2398, 2402, 2418, 2446, 2554, 2594
  See also Joseph Etienne, Estevan Toró.
Etienne François, slave, 1864
Estevan Toró, Apalache Indian, 673
Ettredge (Ettridge),
  Anthony (Antoine), 2931
  William I, 457, 2931
  William II, 457
Eugene (Eugenio), 2003, 2397
Eugenie, slave, 1523, 2024
Eulalie (Eulagie, Eulaly, Ulalye), slave, 1140, 1346, 1353-1354, 1601, 1779, 1816, 1876, 2050, 2056, 2533
Euly. *See Uuily.*
Euphemie, slave, 1616
Euphrosine (Eufrosint, Euphrasinne, Frosine, Ufrasinne),
  Free Negro, 2138
  Slave, 1163, 1206, 1256, 1512, 1629, 2050. *See also Frosine, Marie Magdalenne Euphrasinne Erselinne.*
Evens (Etvans), slave, 1088, 1364
Fabian (Favian), slave, 2251
Fabro, François, 776
Falcon, Manuela Garcia (Dna. Coy), 2700
  Maria Victoriana (Dna. Cuellar), 2773
Fambi, slave, 1738
Fammme, slave, 2192
Famp, slave. *See Mathew Famp.*

Fanny (Fany, Fanye, Phany, Fannie),
  slave, 1083, 1147, 1156, 1431, 1503,
  1517, 1530, 2455, 2460, 2549. *See
  also Françoise, Marie Fanny, Marie
  Françoise, Marianne Fanny.*
Fano (Faro?), slave. *See Louis Fano.*
Faustin (Fosten) Ned, slave, 1496
Faustin. *See Jean Baptiste Faustin.*
Felice (Felis), slave, 1196, 1207.
  See also Marie Josephe Felis.
Felicité,
  Apalache Indian, 1807
  Cannèci Indian, 1936
  Free Mulatto, 1732, 2350-2351
    See also Felicité Grappe.
  Free Negro, 1459
  Free Negro of New Orleans, 973
  Slave, 1098, 1121, 1225, 1236, 1310,
    1342, 1354, 1368, 1381, 1435,
    1523, 1640, 1685, 1746, 1857,
    1903, 1966, 2007, 2165, 2427,
    2470, 2481, 2555, 2572, 2587,
    2596, 2629
Felicité Guary, Apalache Indian (wife
  of Louis Acoye), 651-652, 680
Felicité Ursuline, slave, 1128
Felix (Felis), slave, 1432, 1563.
  See also Jean Baptiste Felis.
Ferans, Francisco, 2248
Ferdinand, slave, 1443. *See François
  Ferdinand.*
Ferguson, Marie (Mrs. Benjamin Bullett)
  544-545, 2835
Ferme, Pierre (Piedferme?), 1281
Fernand, Mda., 1208
Fernandez, Antonio, 599, 654
Fiol?, Gaspard, 1844
Fiol?, Gaspart, Madame, 1816
Firmin, slave. *See Jacques Firme,
  Louis Fermin.*
Fleming, Barthele
  Barthelemy, 540-541, 740, 1072
  Emily Laiesa, 541
  François, 540
Flibot. *See Philipot.*
Flor, slave, 1243, 1325
Florantin, slave, 1552, 2056-2057,
  2603. *See also Joseph Florentin.*
Florencea, slave, 2412
Flores (Florens, La Fleur, Laflore),
  A. Josephine, 2913
  Antonio Honore, 2809
  Cleta (Dna. Jose Ignacio y Barbo)
    477
  Encarnacion (Dna. Eligio Flores) 437, 570
  Felipe de Jesus, 734, 798

Flores (continued),
  Hea____, 2726
  Ignacia (Dna. Miguel Villegar), 2754
  Jetrudis, 2748
  Jose, 776, 2278, 2438, 2752, 2815?
  Jose (Joseph), 734, 765, 798, 1059,
    1266
  Jose Miguel, 1033
  Jose Policarpio, 476
  Joseph, 2809, 2852
  Juana Francesca, 2914
  Lelis, 1531
  Manuel, 2726
  Maria A., 2834
  Maria Angela, 437
  Maria Antonia (Mme. Charles Wallett),
    441, 569
  Maria Antonia (Mme. Louis Lafitte),
    734, 1528
  Maria Josefa (Dna. Mariano Texada), 1052
  Maria Telesfora, 2852
  Matilda (Gonzalez), (Dna. Geraldo Car-
    rasco), 792, 1039
  P____ ____ologo, 734
  Pedro, 1059, 2589 - 2590
  Philipe, 2834, 2836
  Policarpe, 2778
  Rita, 1093
  Trinidad, 477, 2836?
  Vital, 476, 2778
Flotroiz, Felix, 1002
Foldomo?, Joseph Victor, 2773
Folocque, Apalache Indian. *See Joseph
  Folocque.*
Folsom (Fulson),
  Adelaïde, 288
  Israel, 183
  Marie Paule, 183
  Moise, 183, 288
Fonteneau, Apalache Indian. *See Antonio
  Fonteneau.*
Fonteneau (Fontenot, Fontenaux),
  Cesaire I, 97, 390, 447, 538, 1036,
    1055, 1072, 1420, 2073-2074, 2802,
    2925
  Cesaire II, 447, 1509
  Ciriaque (Ciriaco), 538
  Constance, 2074
  François Jean Baptiste, 294
  François Louis, 238
  Jean Baptiste, 294, 390, 446-447, 541,
    976, 1269, 1510, 1820
  Jean Baptiste, II, 1508
  Julien, 1303
  Louis I, 47, 158, 192, 238 *(continued)*

Fonteneau (continued)
  Louis I (continued), 803, 976, 982, 1036
  Louis I, Widow, 1070-1071, 1128, 1307, 1820, 1857, 1874, 1880, 1884, 1963, 1965-1967, 2023, 2025-2027, 2075, 2268-2269. See also Marie Pelagie Grappe.
  Louis II, 982
  Manot (Mme. François Pereau), 1659
  Marie des Neiges (Denis), 390, 1072, 1508
  Marie Modeste (Mme. J. B. Triche II) 47, 158, 238, 326, 355, 446, 541, 845, 2717, 2925
  Maria Thereza Constansa (Mrs. Barthelemy Fleming), 238, 540-541, 1820, 2268
  Marie Zenet, 1269
Forg, Marie Rose, 562
Forsythe (Forsaet),
  Joseph Fred, 2679
  Maria Concepcion, 2753
  Santiago (James), 2679, 2753
Fort,
  Andres, 1195
  Dominique, 1224
  Jacques, 22
  Jacques, Widow, 1873
  Louis Dorsineau, 743, 1056, 1131, 1195, 2056, 2453, 2559, 2585
  Marie Marthe (Mme. Dominique Pierre Sorel dit Marly), 22, 822, 830
  Marie Tranquilinne, 2559
  Pier Edmon, 1195
Fortchuse, James, 754-755
Fortune, Apalache Indian. See François Fortune.
Fortune (Fortuna), slave, 2525
  See also Antoine Fortune, Augustin Fortunée, Joseph Fortuna, Maria Fortuna
Foston. See Johnson
Fouente, Joseph, 1840
Fouente. See also de la Fuentes.
Fourain, 1324
Fraidieu. See Fredieu.
Francesca, slave. See Francoise
Francklin,
  Lesky, 328
  Mary Anne, 328
François (Francisco),
  Apalache Indian, 644, 668
  Mobile (Ansa) Indians, 838
  Free Negro, 1271

François (continued),
  Slave, 1066, 1075, 1141, 1198, 1215, 1291, 1321, 1326-1327, 1336-1337, 1354, 1404, 1564, 1574, 1636, 1676, 1704, 1741, 1850-1851, 1867, 1869, 1927, 1929, 1935, 1952, 1988, 1991, 1993, 2000, 2010, 2012-2013, 2031, 2049-2051, 2056-2057, 2065-2066, 2072, 2075, 2077, 2126, 2150, 2155, 2167, 2169, 2183-2184, 2196, 2199, 2204, 2206, 2208, 2219, 2223, 2236, 2238, 2260, 2262, 2266, 2270-2271, 2234, 2344, 2354, 2371, 2429, 2431, 2445, 2520, 2535, 2624
François. See also Etienne François; Jean François; Joseph François.
François (Francisco) --
  -- Basiem, slave, 2258
  -- Charnac, Apalache Indian, 677
  -- Cheson, slave, 2576
  -- Dorcelin, slave, 1355
  -- Dorsino, Apalache Indian, 678
  -- Erven, 1525
  -- Etequan, slave, 1119
  -- Ferdinand, slave, 1443
  -- Fortune, Apalache Indian, 643
  -- Gregoire, slave, 1526
  -- Guilliom, slave, 1105
  -- Honore, slave, 1489, 2548, 2156
  -- Lasar, slave, 1351
  -- Monsineau, slave, 2262
  -- Moses, slave, 1577
  -- Nette (Ned?), slave, 1262
  -- Neuville (Navil), free, 1305
  -- Neuville, slave, 1332
  -- Orrino, slave, 2178
  -- Pancho, Apalache Indian, 656
  -- Tousin (Toussaint), slave, 2261
  -- Valentin, slave, 2322
  -- Valsin, free, 1660
  -- Very, slave, 1067
  -- Zenon, slave, 1320, 1788
Françoise (Francesca),
  Apalache Indian (wife of Joseph Jouafa) 647-650
  Apalache Indian (wife of Nicolas La Palaches), 678
  Natchitoches Indian, 1211
  Free Woman of color, 190, 1045, 1255, 2000
  Slave, 946, 956, 1067-1068, 1128, 1130, 1132, 1136, 1139, 1152, 1191, 1197, 1254, 1339-1340, 1379, 1684, 1812, 1844, 1848-1849, 1864, 1866, 1880, 1900, 1904, 1910, 1917, 1928-1929,

Franoise (Francesca). *See also Fany, Marie Francoise.*
Françoise (Francesca) --
-- Matheo, Apalache Indian (wife of Estevan Toró), 673
-- Nicolas, Apalache Indian, 666-667
-- Magdalenne, Apalache Indian, (Wife of Jean Baptiste), 674
-- Me_____, f.w.c., 1391
Frank, slave. *See Francois.*
Franklin,
  Lisky, 328
  Mary Anne, 328
Frasem, slave male, 2118
Frayar, Robert, 611
Frederic (Frederick, Frederik, Frederique),
  _____, Dlle. 717
  André, 101, 221, 331, 797, 799, 957, 964, 2853-2854
  Edouard, 387
  François *dit* Pievert, 955
  François, 2761
  François. *See also Jean François.*
  François Hubert, 298
  Jans?, 1056
  Jean Baptiste, 206, 2372
  Jean Baptiste Narcisse, 206
  Jean François, 206, 277, 298, 387, 788, 958, 972, 1053, 1475, 2780, 2855
  Jerome, 946
  Marie, 2787, 2905
  Marie, *fille* François, 2761
  Marie, *fille* Philippe, 331
  Marie Barbe (Mme. François Gonin), 27, 101, 214, 334, 382, 427, 797, 2068, 2648, 2761? 2865
  Marie Barbe, *fille* André, 2853
  Marie Catherine (Mme. J. B. Armant I),9, 87, 234, 340, 805, 909, 2038, 2758
  Marie Deloye, 1485
  Marie Emelie, 2854
  Marie Euphrosine. *See Marie Madeleine Euphrosine Frederic.*
  Marie Henriette, 2780
  Marie Jeanne *dit* Pievert (Mme. J.B. Besson), 285, 955, 2831
  Marie Josephe Rosalie (Mme. Pierre Quierry), 9, 71, 157
  Marie Lolet, 2855
  Marie Louise, 277
  Marie Magdeleine Euphrosine (Mme.

Frederic (continued),
  Jean Baptiste Morantine, 71, 213, 301, 993, 1984, 2791, 2889
  Marie Marguerite (Mme. F. Adley; Mme. J. B. Bmy Rachal I), 699, 1037, 2853?, 2854?, 2904
  Marie Marguerite Reine (Mme. Pierre Chelette), 41, 217, 277, 340, 429, 470, 699, 932, 972, 1006, 1008
  Marie Michel, 2781
  Marie Pelagie (Mme. Barthelemy Lestage), 27, 221, 256, 331, 382, 414, 505, 964, 2658, 2857
  Michel, 2781
  Philippe I, 9, 71, 86, 101, 157, 206, 234, 958, 993, 2038
  Philippe II, 26, 334, 778, 797, 815, 964, 1056, 2761?
  Philippe III, 1056, 2854
Fredieu (Fraidieu, Freideau),
  Antoine, 1074
  Augustin I, 6, 125
  Augustin II, 6, 125, 1026, 1029
  Augustin Cesaire, 480-481, 1026, 1040, 2136, 2782
  Cesair. *See also Isidore Cesair.*
  Honoré, 6, 1389, 1651, 2820
  Isaac, 1508-1509
  Isidore Cesair, 480, 2782
  J., 2782
  Marie Olimpe (Polonia) (Mme. Joseph Crisostome Peraut), 481, 690, 1029, 2820
  Pierre Edouard, 125, 2329
Freeman, Constant, Colonel, 281-282, 295
Frosine (Frouasine, Frosin, Froisein),
  Chatas (Choctaw?) Indian, 306
  Slave, 1340, 2053, 2143, 2193
  See also Euphrosine, Marie Magdalenne Euphrasinne Erselinne.
Fuentes. *See Fouente, de la Fuentes.*
Fulerton (Gutertan?), Jeanne (Mrs. John McTyre), 189, 239
Fulgence, slave, 2020
Fulson. *See Folsom.*
Furzy, f.m.c., 2377
Futch? *See Rutch?*

Gabriel (Gavriel), slave, 1150, 1456, 1638, 1642, 1762, 1948, 2077, 2105, 2443
Gagné (Gagner, Gagnié, Ganier, Ganié, Gagnon, Gagone)
  Anne, 4, 19, 2763

Gagné (Continued),
  Basil, 1818
  Etienne, 4, 19, 102, 135, 240, 795, 986
  Hiacinthe (Mme. Etienne Maximien Wallace, Sr.), 4, 2763
  Jean Baptiste, *fils* Etienne, 442, 795
  Jean Baptiste, *fils* Pierre, 2856
  Jean Pierre Rosalie, 42
  Joseph, 291, 527, 2649
  Julien, 528
  Louis, 1813, 2759, 2862
  Manette. *See Nanette.*
  Marie, 1813
  Marie Adelaïde, 291, 2856
  Marie Angelique (Mme. Louis Wallett), 528, 2862
  Marie Françoise Rosalie "Rose), (Mme. Pierre Ternier), 232, 442
  Marie Josephe (Mme. Toussaint Pinsouneau), 105, 178, 527-528, 1041
  Marie Louise (Mrs. Samuel Davenport) 202, 235, 1267, 1826
  Marie Susanne (Mme. Amable Cadieu II), 42, 1049, 1818, 2650
  Nanette (Manette), (Mme. Michel Guillaume Barberousse), 240, 274, 986
  Pelagie (Mme. J. B. Dominique Davion), 19, 102, 135, 274, 385, 727, 733, 2569
  Pierre I, 42, 178, 1041, 1049, 2649
  Pierre I, Widow, 1119, 1188, 1813-1814, 1855, 2438, 2568. *See also Marie Louise Davion.*
  Pierre II, 42, 178, 291, 1419, 2444-2445, 2856
  Pierre III. *See Jean Pierre Rosalie.*
  Pierre (husband of M. T. Valentin), 235, 732, 783
  Remi, 178, 2446
  Ursulle (Mme. Pierre Boüet Lafitte) 135, 384, 1059, 2759?
Gallardo,
  Joseph Louis, 2783
  Marie Paul, 2783
Gallien,
  Catherine (Mme. J. B. Anty I), 17, 36, 137, 187, 243
  Dufrois Derzelin, 1149
  Euphrosine, 315
  Heleine, 36
  Louis I, 147, 320, 376, 565, 997, 1249, 1815, 2603, 2784, 2800, 2846, 2858

Gallien (Continued),
  Louis II, 2858
  Louis Emanuel, 565
  Louis Neuville, 315, 376, 1015, 1359 2857
  Marie (Mme. Belony Vercher), 698
  Marie Adeline, 2407, 2799, 2858
  Marie Celeste, 2324
  Marie Cephaline, 376
  Marie Damascenne, 565, 1249
  Marie Eulalie, 2857
  Marie Jeanne (Jacob) Euphrosine (Mme. Jacques Therin Vercher), 60, 116, 147, 314-315, 510, 2784, 2799
  Marie Lise, 320
  Marie Oresille (Mme. J. B. Beloni Vercher), 698, 1007, 2232, 2800, 2828? 2929
  Marie Rosalie, 116
  Melizere, 2784
  Neuville. *See Louis Neuville.*
  Nicolas I, 60, 116, 147, 514, 997, 1001, 1007, 1015, 1918-1919, 2407, 2799
  Noel I, 116
  Noel II. *See Louis Emanuel.*
Ganier. *See Gagné.*
Garcia,
  Antonia Reimund, 41, 177, 248
  Manuela Falcon (Dna. Ignacio de los Stos. Coy I), 1506, 2690
Garro, Garo,
  Amelie, 2895
  Maria Magdalena, 499, 549
Garro. *See also Caro.*
Gaspart, slave, 1996, 2068
Gassion. *See Antoine Gassion.*
Gastille, Antoinette. *See Antonia Reimund Garcia.*
Gausé,
  Jean *dit* Jourdin, 820
  Jean Charles, 820
Gauvain, M.A., 729
Genevieve (Genoveva, Genauva),
  Free. *See Genoveve LeComte.*
  Slave, 1280, 1285, 1296, 1324, 1337, 1533, 1695, 1730, 1740, 1744, 1824, 1826, 1829, 1846, 1868, 1879, 1918, 1962, 2033, 2191, 2328, 2455, 2527, 2601. *See also Françoise Genevieve.*
Geny, slave, 1228. *See also Jeanne.*
Geoffrois, Louis, 722, 733.
Geoffrois, slave. *See Barthelemi Cifroi.*
George, Free Negro. *See Joseph George.*
George, slave. *See William George.*

George, slave, 1368, 2049, 2056, 2284, 2450, 2554, 2637
Gerasime, slave, 1858, 2314
Germain, slave, 2057. *See also Manuel Charmé.*
Germaine,
   ———, 753
   M. A., 1046
Germeuil, ———, 796
Gillard (Chilart, Chilard, Gillart),
   Jean Baptiste I, 581-582, 584, 598, 1088, 1366, 1442, 2475, 2861
   Jean Baptiste II, 582, 1442
   Joseph I, 579, 580, 583, 1090-1091, 1938, 2363, 2478
   Joseph II, 579-581, 1092, 1364, 2361, 2473, 2861, 2872?, 2898
   Joseph, 2861
   Josephine (Mme. Jean Marie La Cour), 582, 2872, 2922
   Magdalenne, 581, 1442 *(Fille J.B.)*
   Magdeleine, 579, 1366 *(Fille Joseph)*
   Marguerite, 581
   Marie Louise (Mme. Leandre La Cour), 583-586, 1938, 2861
Gillis, slave, 1639, 2066
Gimlech. *See Guymley.*
Giraud, Marie Magdeleine (Appart), (Mme. Jean Joseph Bauvard de St. Amans), 369, 460
Girou,
   François, 75
   Louis, 75
   Marie, 75
Gisarnat. *See Guisarnat.*
Glapion, Eliset, 1699
Glover (Globert), Elisabeth (Mrs. Sabert Hoy), 192, 985
Gnanea, slave, 1103
Gobin, Catherinne (Mme. Pierre Marcollay), 833
Gomes (Gomez),
   Damasio Nepomuceno, 2684
   Dolores (Dna. Franco Gomes), 2644, 2655
   Franco., 2644, 2655
   Gertrudis (Dna. Jose Manuel Rendon), 694, 2913
   Juan, 464
   Juan Jose, 2672
   Manuela (Dna. Joseph Dolores Martinez), 501, 2656, 2883

Gomes (continued),
   Maria, 2655
   Remigio Jose, 464
   Sulas, 2685
   Tetus, 1308
Gonet, François (Laferet), 419
Gonin (Gonne, Gonet),
   François I, 27, 101, 214, 334, 382, 427, 797, 964-965, 2057, 2648, 2865
   François Abraham, 101
   François Barthelemy, 2865
   François Davier, 427, 2648
   Genevieve (Mme. Antoine Vascocu I, Mme. Manuel Le Vasseur), 218, 348, 841, 2761
   Jean Baptiste, 27, 45, 101, 195, 965
   Marie Aurore, 334
   Marie Barbe? (?Mme. F. Frederic?), 2761
   Marie Jeanne Josephe (Mme. Bernabé Chelette), 45, 195, 589, 591
   Marie Manuel (Mrs. J. B. Robinson), 797
   Marie Modeste, 27, 2865
   Sophie, 214
Gonsalez (Gonzales, Gonsaque, Gozinles),
   Andres, 1062?
   Antonia Blasa, 248
   Bernard, 41, 177, 248. *See also Manuel Bernard Pierre.*
   Diego, 723
   Francisco, 807
   Ignace, 2866
   José Antonio, 463, 2796
   José Francisco Hidalgo. *See José Francisco Gonsalez Hidalgo.*
   Joseph Martin, 2866
   Juan Francisco Antonio (Jean Francois Antoine), 807
   Juana Rosa (Dna. Santiago Jacques Ruiz) 701, 2918
   Manuel, 701, 2918
   Manuel Bernard Pierre, 41, 248
   Marie Doe, 177
   Maria Francisca (Dna. Santiago Gonzalez), 2867
   Maria Isabel de Jesus. *See Maria Isabel de Jesus Gonsalez Hidalgo.*
   Maria M. (Dna. Francisco ———), 749
   Maria Timothe, 2867
   Matilda Flores (Dna. Geraldo Carrasco) 792, 1039
   Pedro (Pierre). *See Manuel Bernard Pierre.*
   Pedro (Pierre), 41, 177, 248, 840
   Santiago (Jacques), 2867

Gonsalez (continued),
  Thomas, 1184
  Tragnia, 2487
  Trinidad, 1433, 2590
Goodall, Marie (Mrs. James Heating) 2675
Goutierrez (Gutierrez, Guetierrez),
  Bernardo, 536
  José Alexos Antonio de los Dolores, 536
  Maria Basilia (Dna. José Guerra), 2680, 2713
  Michel, 97
  Silvie (Mme. Antoine Poissot), 97
Gra____, Maria, 705
Gracia, Nicolas, 794, 1094, 1250-1251, 1397, 1672, 2889
Gradner,
  James (Santiago, Jacques) 608, 2810
  Julien, 608, 2810
Graham,
  Joseph, Apalache Indian, 653
  Thomas, 653, 670, 792-793
Grande, Maria Candida, (Dna. Bernardo Marin Despallion), 392, 922, 2850
Grand Baptiste, slave, 1565
Grappe (Grap, Grapp, Grappa),
  Alexis, 99
  Antoine, 2146
  Augustin, 2035
  Baltasar, 1392, 2026, 2618
  Celeste, 2026, 2035, 2620
  Cesaire, 2096
  Dominique, 1202, 1825, 1868
  Emeline (Emelita) Touline, 2042, 2096
  Felicité, 11, 149, 190, 740
  François *dit* Touline, 24, 135, 176, 182, 294, 536, 540, 739-740, 952, 955, 961, 971, 984, 1055, 1825, 2035, 2099, 2116-2117, 2267, 2280
  Hélène (Elenne), 2607, 2933
  Jacques, 1194, 2035-2036, 2459, 2933
  Jean Baptiste, 99, 819, 889, 2004
  Jean Baptiste II, 889
  Jean Baptiste (identity uncertain 1570
  Jean Baptiste, Widow, 1232, 2280
  Jean Pierre, 739-740
  Joseph, 2041
  Louis LeClerc, 1825
  Magdeleine (Mme. Paul Boüet Lafitte) 135
  Magdeleine, f.w.c., 1241, 1825, 2035, 2097, 2460, 2620

Grappe (continued),
  Margueritte, 2097, 2490, 2618
  Marie, 2126
  Marie Adelise (Adolis, Adeline), 1241, 2116
  Marie Adelle, 1392
  Marie Arzile (Arcese, Arsis, Archis), (Dna. Juan Jose Nasario Guillermo), 11, 740, 2459
  Marie Damacena, 2146
  Marie Françoise (Mme. Antoine Benoit Montanary), 1040, 1854, 2696, 2759
  Marie Josephe Touline, 1194, 1212, 1569, 1825, 2042, 2096, 2117, 2459, 2618
  Marie Louise I, 149, 2460
  Marie Louise II, 2096
  Marie Louise (Mme. Manuel Triche), 44, 144, 804, 810, 1010, 2617
  Marie Louise Theodore, 190
  Marie Odisse, 2618
  Marie Pelagie (Mme. Louis Fonteneau), 11, 24, 47, 158, 238, 294, 447, 536, 539, 803, 976, 982, 1036, 1070
  Marie Rose Sophronie (Mme. Placide Derbanne), 99, 230, 2738
  Maria Solimon, 2117
  Marie Therese, 2146
  Pelagie, 2034, 2041, 2116.
  Pelagie. *See also Marie Pelagie.*
  Pierre, 2042
  Sophronie. *See Marie Rose Sophronie.*
  Suset, 1194, 2098?, 2100, 2617
  Touline, 2042
  Ursulle (Gagne?) (Mme. Clement Boüet Lafitte), 2759
Gregoire (Gregorio, Gregorie), 2077, 2180. *See also François Gregoire.*
Gregoire Augustin, slave, 1584
Greneaux *dit* Grenoble (Greneau, Grenau),
  Charles Emanuel, 203, 433, 799, 1063, 1649, 2057
  Emeranciane, 203
  Françoise (Mrs. John Johnson), 482, 2057, 2779, 433
  Louis Emanuel, 203, 799, 1063
  Louis Emanuel, Widow, 2062, 2439, 2532. *See also Victoire Emerante Bossier.*
  Marianne, 482
  Marie Louise (Mme. Antoine Adlé), 1063, 2057
  Rosalie (Mme. Onesime Buard), 2708
  Rosalie Marianne (Mme. Jean Prevot), 405, 433, 799, 1394, 2057, 2062
  Simon, 203

Grenoble. *Dit* of Greneaux and Ternier.
Gret, slave, 1290
Griar__, Marie F., 2821
Grillet (Griet, Grillé),
  Alexy, 2447
  Antoine, 76, 105, 132, 216, 290, 372, 686, 796, 950, 961, 977, 1203-1204, 1507, 2147, 2448
  Celine, 2447
  E., 784, 796
  Jean Baptiste Théodore (Theodule), 5, 79, 199, 216, 236-237, 478, 484, 795, 954, 971, 1009, 1037, 1202, 1434, 2722
  Jean Baptiste Valsin, 237
  Luce Margueritte, 372
  Marguerite (Mme. Remy Totin, I; Mme. Bernard Hissoura *dit* Pantaleon), 93-94, 756, 795-796, 977, 1062
  Marie Adelin, 686
  Marie Azeline, 216
  Marie Barbe (Mme. Bertrand Plaisance), 20, 79, 202, 236, 436, 1024, 2776, 2891
  Marie Françoise (Mme. Louis B. Rachal *fils* Bmy.), 132, 193, 402, 1006, 1008, 2715, 2800
  Marie Jeanne (Mme. Charles F. Le Vasseur), 802, 2671
  Marie Josephe (Mme. Pierre Brosset I), 25, 212, 948, 981, 1034
  Marie Louise (Mme. Louis Vercher), 60, 65, 147, 199, 236, 929, 1007, 1047
  Marie Magdeleine (Mme. Bmy. Rachal II), 59, 152, 786, 911, 1053
  Marie Thérèze (Mme. Jacques Le Vasseur), 774, 1811
  Marin I, 5, 20, 25, 59, 79, 93-94, 132, 152, 193, 202, 237, 950, 971, 1009, 1811, 2746
  Marin I, Widow, 1812, 1821. *See also Marie Louise Brevel.*
  Marin II, 290
  Théodore. *See Jean Baptiste Théodore.*
  Ursin, *fils* Antoine, 132
  Ursin, *fils* J. B. Théodore, 434, 2722
Guallet. *See Wallett.*
Gualtheman, Me., 723
Guany (Guary?), Apalache Indian. *See Atanasio Guany; Felicité Guary.*

Guedon, Jeanne (Mme. J.
  Jeanne (Mme. J. B. LaBerry), 39, 67-68, 88, 967
  Marie Anne (Mme. J. B. LeDuc *dit* Ville Franche), 31, 947
  Marie Louise (Mme. Alexis Grappe), 99
Gueraco, Franco., 734
Guerbois, Louis Alexandre, 829
Guerin, Catherine (Mme. Ignace Anty), 35
Guerra,
  Jetrudis (Dna. Luis Brisiño), 2721
  José, 2712
  Joseph Nazario, 2712
  Maria T., 2788, 2880
Guerrero, Ana Maria (Dna. José Flores), 798, 1059
Guey (Goy, Guet),
  Apolonia, 623
  Clara, 619
  François, 623
  Joseph Evariste, 318
  Louis I, 619-623
  Louis II, 620
  Louis Balsem, 520
  Margarita, 622
  Marie, 617
  Marie Denis, 621
  Marie Françoise, 318
  Rosalie (Mme. Cypriano Luc), 425
  Simon, 318-319, 520
Guillaume (Guillermo, Guillom, William),
  Free Negro, 305
  Slave, 1366, 1535, 1672, 1890, 1895, 1900, 1903-1904, 2052, 2077, 2343, 2415, 2503.
  See also Francois Guilliom; and Gullym, Francisco.
Guillerie,
  Louis, 312
  Marie Susanne, 312
Guillermo, Jean Joseph Nasario, 740
Guilscem (Wilson?),
  John (Juan) I, 611
  John (Juan) II, 611
Guin. *See Quin.*
Guiny (Jenny? Queeny?), slave, 2368
Guirine. *See Chirino.*
Guisarnat (Gisarnat, Guisarnac),
  A. Bernard, I, 39, 68, 145, 556, 743, 748-749, 751, 818, 967, 1042, 1052, 2681, 2789
  A. Bernard II, 743, 745, 749, 751, 1039, 1058, 2681, 2875
  François, 516
  Jean, 145

Guisarnat (continued),
  Joseph, 516, 2212
  Josephe Honore, 516
  Philipe Valerin, 145
Gullym, Francisco, 888
Gustin. See Augustin.
Gutierrez. See Goutierrez.
Guymley, Charlotte (Mrs. George Lair), 183

Halein, Marie (Mme. Henri Provot II), 89
Harman (Harmon)
  Louise Cloden (Mme. Antoine Ruelle), 791
  Mary Elisabeth, 489
  Worner, 489
Harriet. See Henriette, Heré, Heré.
Harris,
  Charles, 2868
  Marie Henriette, 2869
  William, 2868-2869
Harry, slave. See Antoine Harry.
Hays (Hayes),
  Peter (Pedro) Nolasco, 393
  William (Guillermo), 393
Hazelton, _____, Mr., 1422-1423, 1614, 1617
Heating, James, 2675
Hecer. See Hesser.
Heinoy. Clar. B.. 2924
Helbeuf (Le Boeuf), Jeanne (Mrs. Leonard Webb, 196-197
Hélène (Elenne, Heleine, Elena),
  Apalache Indian, 671
  F.W.C., 1585, 2269. See also Marie Hélène Baden.
  Slave, 1068, 1312-1313, 1326, 1344, 1404, 1522, 1590, 1738, 2003, 2005, 2048, 2050, 2154, 2389, 2412, 2533, 2548, 2570, 2604, 2609, 2633, 2163
Helie. See Bernard dit Elie.
Henriette. See also Marianne Henriette, Marie Henriette Dorothée Cloutier.
Henriette (Anrriette, Anriette, Arriet), slave, 1369, 1383, 1857, 2071, 2441, 2505, 2555-2556, 2582. 2597.
Henry (Henri, Enrique), slave,1146, 1199, 1414, 1465, 1527, 1682, 1860, 1987, 2048, 2077, 2170, 2176, 2211, 2225, 2613, 2639

Henry Ch____, slave, 1374
Henry,
  Gen., 2830
  Jeanne, 2404
Heré, (Harriet?), slave, 2106, 2285
Herée (Harriet?), slave, 1912, 1913, 2231
Herkham,
  Elisabeth (Isabel), (Mrs. James Herkham) 471
  James (Santiago), 471
  John Washington, 471
Hermosillo, Rafael, 2704
Hernandez,
  _____, Senorita, 719
  Isidoro, 890
  J. B. Ob., 2811
  Jerome, 2811
  Maria Antonia, 719, 2870
  Marie Emily, 2811
  Marie Telesfora, 2870
Herrera,
  Ignacio, 2142
  Marie Priana Brigida Colidad, 1118
  Pedro, 1118, 2142
Herrié,
  François. See Jean Baptiste Marie François.
  Jacques I, 18, 74, 831, 856, 873, 949
  Jacques, II, 18, 74
  Jean Baptiste Marie François, 18
  Pierre, 74
  See also Terrié.
Hertzog (Arsoc, Erttoc, Harcsioc, Harsioc),
  Bernard Theophile Henry, 548, 1591
  Henry, 1415, 2609
  Henry Matthew, 598, 980
  Jean François, 250, 337, 354, 548, 729, 736, 786, 789, 791, 980, 990, 1413, 1417-1418, 1591, 1595, 2163, 2415-2416, 2420, 2609
  Marie, 1591
  Marie Françoise "Fanny", 337, 1418
  Marie Jeanne, 354
  Matthew. See Henry Matthew.
  Richard, 1410, 1618
Hesser (Hecer),
  André Isaac, 34
  Christian, 34, 151, 1402, 2813
  Frederic, 34, 151
  Frederik Felix, 151
  Marie J. Celestine, 2813
  Marie Josephine, 1403
Hester. See Ystor.

Hetty, slave. *See Eté*.
Hibarbo. *See y Barbo*.
Hidalgo (Idalgo, Ydalgo),
  José Francisco Gonsalez, I, 443, 571
  José Francisco Gonsalez II, 571
  Joseph Antoine, 2823
  Marie, 2823
  Maria Isabel de Jesus Gonsalez, 443
Hilaire (Hilario), slave, 1425, 1597, 1630, 1650, 1853, 2049, 2056, 2567
Hilaret, ____, Mr., 1715
Himmel. *See Hymel*.
Hipolite. *See Hypolite*.
Hise, slave, 2153
Hissoura *dit* Pantaleon (Issoura, Ysurd, Isard, Isurd),
  Adonis Isidore, 94
  Bernard, 93-94, 796, 948, 2751, 2844?
  Bernard II, 796
  Bernard, Widow, 1723, 2020
  Eusebe (Isebe), 93, 372
  Jean, 93-94
  Marie Adeline, 372
  Marie Athanase de G__er, 2751
  Marie Adelise Bernard (Dna. Julio Estrada), 796, 1062, 1275, 2844
Hodman, 1358
Hodman, ____
  Barbary, 611
  Elisabeth (Mrs. Guillom Blondé), 634
  Louis, 632
  Marie, 634, 1387
  Nanet (Mrs. John Guilscem/ ?Wilson), 611
  ____, Widow, 1387, 2381
Hoffman,
  Esther or Hester (Mrs. Ben Richey, Mrs. Henry O'Connor), 553
  Manuel, 738
  See also Huffman.
Holbarcq (Dalbarcq),
  Marie (Mme. Pierre Duroque), 5, 76, 185
Hollier (Holié, Olié, Haulié), Sophie 30, 158, 194, 214
Holt, Ann, 2874
Honoré (Anore, Onore), slave, 1180, 1365, 1750, 1934, 1954, 2075, 2294, 2447. *See also Charles Honoré, Francois Honoré, Jean Baptiste Honoré, Michel Honoré*.
Hooper,
  Elizabeth, 612
  Thomas, 612

Hoppock (Hopoc),
  Jean Louis, 1935, 2349, 2421, 2423-2424
Hopam, Maria Concepcion (Dna. Joseph de los Sta. Coy) 1270
Horenois, Josephine, 1391
Hornos, Ignacio, 2687
Hortense (Ortans, Hortans, Hortance), slave, 1084, 1143, 1199, 1280, 1412, 1928, 1987, 2072, 2122, 2247-2248, 2334-2335, 2371, 2520
Hortiz (Hortis). *See Ortis*.
Hossop, Marie (Mrs. Adouen Couart), 184.
Hoy (Hoye),
  Dorset David, 192, 246, 342, 453, 691, 936, 985
  Eugene Manuel, 691
  François Joseph Elisée, 453
  Guillaume, 192
  Marie Anne Arthemise, 342
  Prudent, 246
  Sabert, 192, 985
Hubardeau (Dubardeau, Hubardo), Marie Silvie, 1833, 1845
Huffman, Adam, 766
Huffman, *see also Hoffman*.
Hunter (Huintar), Marie Manet, 1201
Hyistimin?, Juan, 351
Hymel (Himel, Imble, Ymblée),
  Antoine, 77, 91, 110, 347, 1430, 2703, 2710
  Eleonore (Mme. Soulange Bossier), 77, 110, 229, 338, 347, 692, 2832
  Marie Françoise, 91, 347, 2703
  Marie Pompose, 1195
  Paul, 957
Hypolite, slave, 1581

Ibarbo. *See y Barbo*.
Idalgo. *See Hidalgo*.
Ignace, slave, 1868. *See also Joseph Ignace*.
Imble. *See Hymel*.
Imelle, slave, 2056
Indians, 140, 305, 312, 491, 1936, 2701. *See also: Apelussas, Ansa, Apalache, Caddo, Canneci, Choctaw, Commanche, Ecasse, Marcisogne, Mobile, Natchitoches, Yguanes, Yocase Indians*.
Inez (Anes), slave, 2155. *See also Yiné*.
Inofoso, Petra (Dna. José Leno Salinas), 2668.
Isaac (Isac), slave, 1279, 1338, 2283, 2287.
Isac Jose, slave, 1260. *See also Joseph Isaac*.

Isabel (Ysabel, Isavel). *See Elisabeth*.
Isurd. *See Hissoura*.
Isidre. *See Ysidre*.
Issoura. *See Hissoura*.

J____hy, slave, 1384
Jacob, Apalache Indian, 1805
Jacob, slave, 1111, 1203, 1312, 1317, 1408, 1500, 1522
Jacob Bron, slave, 1414
Jacob (Jacovo) Demba, slave, 2516
Jacques (Jacque, Santiago),
  Apalache Indian, 1804-1805
  Free Mulatto, 190, 2022, 2024. *See also Jacques Grappe*.
  Slave, 1087, 1113, 1182-1183, 1189, 1264, 1283, 1295, 1352, 1400, 1407, 1484, 1557, 1670, 1689, 1720, 1789, 1800, 1812, 1891, 1897, 1901, 2035, 2049-2050, 2056, 2061, 2070, 2072, 2077, 2173, 2179, 2182, 2199, 2213, 2241, 2276, 2306, 2326, 2329, 2380, 2392, 2396, 2433, 2502, 2581, 2585
Jacques Charles, slave, 1898
Jacque Firme, slave, 2451
Jacques Lemigat, slave, 1296
Jacquitte, slave, 1608
James, 1383, 2050, 2056. *See also Jacques*.
Jana, slave, 2190
Janet (Chanet), 1407, 1679, 2435
  See also Jana, Janot, Jeanette, Jenny, Jeanne, Geny.
Janot, slave, 2139
Janvier, slave, 2327
Jarri. *Variant spelling of the dit Zoriche*.
Jasmin, male slave, 1644
Jean (Juan, John, Jeann), slave, 1083, 1173, 1192, 1262, 1380, 1451, 1468, 1971, 1977, 1982, 2031, 2049-2050, 2057, 2077, 2102, 2207, 2381, 2473, 2528, 2530. *See also Jeanot, Jonó, Julien Jean Pierre*.
Jean Baptiste (Juan Bautista),
  Apalache Indian, *fils* Joseph Jouafa, 649
  Apalache Indian (husb of Fran. Magd.), 674

Jean Baptiste (continued),
  Caddo Indian, 1237
  F.M.C., 85, 179, 773, 1154, 1888, 1914, 2032, 2351. *See also Baptiste*.
  Slave, 149, 1114, 1123, 1129, 1166, 1132, 1170, 1172-1173, 1176-1177, 1179, 1139, 1230, 1256, 1280-1281, 1284, 1296, 1325, 1333, 1338, 1354, 1358, 1361 1416, 1426-1427, 1457, 1479, 1488, 1501, 1503, 1509, 1539-1541, 1573, 1596-1597, 1599, 1610, 1646, 1694, 1703, 1712, 1716, 1763, 1810, 1824, 1866, 1873, 1883, 1902, 1905, 1930, 1940, 1957, 1981, 2019, 2021, 2046, 2049-2050, 2056, 2061, 2073, 2092, 2131-2132, 2145, 2147-2148, 2153-2154, 2171-2172, 2193-2195, 2201, 2228, 2248, 2256, 2258, 2277, 2282, 2325, 2363, 2390, 2393, 2420, 2431-2432, 2437, 2500, 2521, 2546, 2552, 2598, 2633, 2638. *See also Grand Baptiste*.
Jean Baptiste --
  -- Augustin, f.m.c., 2269
  -- Augustin, slave, 1866
  -- Bansem, slave, 1114
  -- Bill. *See Jean Baptiste Vil*.
  -- Cleman, slave, 2232
  -- Elois, slave, 1254
  -- Faustin, slave, 1646
  -- Felis, slave, 1334
  -- Hilaire, f.m.c., 1847
  -- Honoré, slave, 2067
  -- Ludgeaire, slave, 1640
  -- Miguel (Michel), slave, 1154
  -- Olier, slave, 1918
  -- Pompé, slave, 2322
  -- Quieto, slave, 2515
  -- St. Ville, slave, 2597
  -- Savoyau, slave, 2325, 2629
  -- Ursin, slave, 1533
  -- Vil (Bill?), slave, 1565
  -- Zephorine, slave, 1439
Jean Christophe, free, 1585
Jean (Juan) Clovin, slave, 2385
Jeann Elsy (Ersy? L.C.?), slave, 2387
Jean Florantin, slave, 1513
Jean François (Juan Francisco), slave, 1165, 1229, 1293, 1314, 1434, 1514, 1572, 2011, 2547, 2587
Jean Louis, free, 1498
Jean Louis, slave, 1428, 1489, 1514, 1875, 1899, 1965, 1970, 2048-2050, 2056, 2065, 2070, 2072, 2077, 2423, 2524

Jean Manuel, slave, 1207
Jean Marie (Juan Maria), Apalache Indian, 1808
Jean Na., slave, 2049
Jean Nicolas, Canneci Indian?, 43
Jean Noel, slave, 1463
Jean Pierre (Jeann Pier, Juan Pedro),
  Apalache Indian, 650
  Free Negro, 1786
  Slave, 1079, 1174, 1231, 1280, 1335, 1351, 1419, 1466, 1520, 1529, 1602, 1604, 1611, 1618, 1820, 1876, 1985, 2077, 2172, 2448
Jean Pierre Clairevil, slave, 1361
Jean Pompey (Juan Pomper), slave, 2210
Jean Saturin, 1318
Jeanet, slave, 1364. *See also Janet, Jeanne.*
Jeanne (Juana),
  F.W.C., 2081
  Slave, 1268, 1311, 1409, 1588, 1688, 1713, 1816, 1833, 1857, 1912, 1948, 1971, 2049, 2056, 2072, 2077, 2223, 2227, 2231, 2236-2237, 2362, 2430, 2528, 2577, 2610. *See also Marie Jeane, Jeny, Geny, Janet, Jeanet, Jeanote.*
Jeanne Bierri, slave, 2256
Jeanne (Juana) Vici, 2209
Jeannet, slave, 2476
Jeanot, Apelussas Indian, 1936
Jeannot. *See Maximin Juannot, Jonó, Jean.*
Jeanote, slave, 2487
Jean-Ris. *See Ris.*
Jeanton, slave. *See Marie Jeanne.*
Jenny (Chiny), slave, 2367
Jennie. *See Jeanne, Guiny, Jeny, Geny, Marie Jeanne, Janet, Jeannet Jeanote.*
Jennie Belle (Jenebelle), slave, 2224
Jerome (Geronimo). *See Gerasime.*
Joacen, Remigio, 425
John, slave, 1371, 1619. *See also Jean.*
Johnson (Johanson, Foston),
  John, 433, 482, 2779
  Margaret (Mme. Alexandre Ponthieu), 716, 2673, 2897
  Mary Pamela, 482, 2779

Johnson (continued),
  Victoriana Amedi, 433
Johnson. *See also Chonse.*
Johnston, Josiah J., 392
Jonah, slave, *see Jonó.*
Jones,
  John, 849
  Rebecca D.?. *See Rebecca Dejones.*
Jonó, slave, 2530-2531. *See also Jeanot.*
José. *See Isac José, Joseph.*
Joseph (José, Josef),
  Apalache Indian, 658-659
  F.M.C., 201, 2027, 2138. *See also Joseph Metoyer, Joseph LaVigne.*
  Free Negro, 2138
  Slave, 1074, 1090, 1124, 1235, 1294, 1326, 1330, 1340, 1345-1346, 1357, 1389, 1430, 1434-1435, 1446-1447, 1495, 1521, 1545-1546, 1584, 1607, 1673, 1705, 1796, 1826, 1830, 1832-1833, 1844, 1870, 1885, 1962, 1966, 1976, 2016, 2027, 2031, 2034, 2045, 2048-2049, 2052, 2056, 2141, 2144, 2167, 2170, 2198, 2225, 2230, 2286, 2324, 2347, 2361, 2370, 2426, 2442, 2451, 2472, 2485, 2506, 2520, 2531, 2533, 2612, 2640, 2643
  See also Isaac Jose, Louis Joseph Eloi, Manuel Joseph Anathalie, Pierre Joseph, Pierre Joseph Prince.
Joseph (Jose) --
--Adam, slave, 2393
--Adolph (Adolfo), slave, 1285
--Alexander, slave, 2109
--Antonio, ?Indian, 654
--Antoine, slave, 1261
--Asenor, Apalache Indian, 646
--Bob, slave, 2556
--Bosem, slave, 1418
--Bron, slave, 1464, 1643
--Daniel, 1385, 1413, 1812, 2631, 2636
--David, 1474
--Celestin, 1527
--Etienne (Jose Echen), slave, 2234
--Folocque (Foloquier), Apalache Indian, 665, 1808
--Florentin, slave, 1962
--Fortunat, slave, 2602
--Francisco (Françoise), 1506, 2401, 2588
--George, free Negro, 1505
--Hilario, 2296, slave
--Ignacio, slave, 2197
--Isaac (Isac, Asic), slave, 2375, 2541

Joseph (Jose) -- (continued)
-- Jouafa (Joufa), Apalache Indian, 647-650
--Lazare, f.m.c., 1577
--Lazare, slave, 2016
--Lesine, slave, 2111
--Luiset, slave, 2240
--Lucas, slave, 1816
--Manuel, slave, 1208, 1259, 2139
--Marie (Maria), slave, 1120, 2610
--Maria Luciano, slave, 2488
--Noel, slave, 1995
--Pain, slave, 1490
--Paterne, slave, 1316
--Polonio, Yocase Indian, 1276
--Raphael, slave, 1958
--Resit, Apalache Indian, 673
--Ste. Clou, slave, 2594
--Segunda, slave, 2360
--Sensir (St. Cyr? Cesar?), slave, 2297
--Siors, slave, 2209
--Sofy, slave, 2543
--Solomon, slave, 2408
--Tensa, Apalache Indian, 678
--Terans, slave, 1234
--Thomas, Apalache Indian, 658
--Titos, slave, 1186
--Touasa, Apalache Indian, 1806
--Touazin (Toussaint?), Apalache Indian, 676
--Touzin (Toussaint?), slave, 1279, 2629
--Ursin, slave, 1556
--Viet, slave, 2596
--Victoriano, slave, 1507
--Vutlia (Butler?), slave, 1370
--Wasinton, slave, 1677
Josephe, slave, 1294-1295
Josephine (Josefina), slave, 2137
Jouafa (Joufa), Apalache Indian.
 See Joseph Joufa, Catarine Jouafa.
Jourdin. *Dit of Jean Gausé.*
Joval, Juan, 466. *See also Juan Tovar.*
Juannot, Maximin, Free Negro, 1073
Juchereau de St. Denis. *See St. Denis.*
Judy (Judée), slave, 2287-2290
Juky, slave, 2136
Judith, slave, 1890, 1938
Juedó, male slave, 2555
Julie (Julia, Juliane, Juliana, July, Julye), slave, 984, 1133, 1185, 1281, 1312, 1355, 1493, 1534, 1589, 1613, 1719, 1818, 1883, 2057, 2062, 2104, 2121, 2277

Julien (Julian), 1130, 1181, 1282, 1345, 2009, 2160, 2465. *See also Augustin Julian.*
Julien Marie Narcis, slave, 2553
Julien Moreno (Moximo? Maximin?), slave, 2044-2045
Julien Jean Pierre, slave, 1335
Juny Pouarret, 2381
Justin, slave, 2311

Keiser (Keizer, Keisem, Cayser),
 Anne, 554, 2920
 Eliza (Elaysa) Victorina, 403, 2103
 Jacob, 403-406
 Manuel Samuel, 405
 Mary Margaret, 406
 Mary Sara, 2107, 2291
 Pelagia Procela, 404, 2289
Kerkly, John (Jean), 622
Kerry. *See Querry.*
Kirk. *See Cuerca.*
Kirkham. *See Herkham.*
Kirkland (Kerklam, Kerclem), Edward, 754, 767, 1369, 1371-1372?, 1377, 2555-2556
Kitty, slave. *See Quete.*
Kob. *See Cobb.*

L. Silvain (Silben), slave, 2413
La _____, François, 1089
La_____n, Michel, 798
La Berry (La Beri, La Bairie, Lavery, St. Laveri),
 Agathe. *See Marie Louise Agathe.*
 Françoise (Mme. Louis Bmy. Rachal *fils* Louis), 68
 Jean Baptiste, 39, 67-68, 88, 967
 Jeanne (Mme. Pierre La Renaudiere), 88, 145, 825, 1042
 M. A. (Female), 2793
 Marie J., 2833
 Marie Jeanne, 777
 Marie Josephe (Mme. Louis Rachal II), 39, 51, 813, 835
 Marie Louise Agathe (Mme. François Pereau II), 139, 183, 219, 224, 237, 388, 396, 469, 941, 971, 1014
 Marie Magdeleine (Mme. Simeon Rachal I; Mme. Pierre Nolasco de Porcuna), 67, 388, 568-569, 967, 2394-2402
LaBoeuf (LaBauf), Françoise (Mme. Guillaume Bernard), 449. *See also Helbeuf*
Labre, Felicité, 2043

LaCaze (Lacase, La Casse),
  Celestin, 1842
  Charles I, 5, 48, 160-161
  Charles *fils* Etienne I, 3
  Etienne I, 3, 48, 2481
  Félicité (Mme. Jean Baptiste Le
    Moine), 10, 160-161, 225, 299,
    449, 2814
  François, Dr., 851
  Jacques (Santiago), 2, 33, 48,
    126-127, 136, 198, 297, 365,
    465, 542-543, 790, 994, 1144-
    1145, 1219, 1319, 1842, 1843,
    2247-2250, 2371-2372, 2541,
    2790, 2871
  Michel, 1596, 1843
  Modeste, 48
La Cerda. *See De la Cerda.*
La Cour (Le Cour, Le Courd),
  See also Le Court.
  Athanase, 772
  Bret, 2365-2366
  Cecile (Mme. J. B. Gillard), 581,
    583, 598, 2861, 2872
  Firmin, 271, 2310
  Gaspard I, 81, 209, 271, 564,
    1078-1083, 1939-1940, 1960,
    2309-2313, 2873
  Gaspard II, 564
  Jean Baptiste, 81, 1082, 2312
  Jean Marie I, 582-583, 586, 1092,
    1363, 2478, 2872, 2922
  Jean Marie II, 586
  Jean Marie *fils* Leandre, 583, 1365
  Leandre, *fils* Jean Marie, 586, 1301
  Leandre (Leon), *fils* Nicolas,
    583-586, 1089, 1365-1366, 2474
  Leandre II, 2474
  Magdalenne, 1092
  Marguerite, 585, 2364, 2474
  Marie Claire, 619, 639
  Marie Elys, 2310
  Marie Emely, *fille* Gaspard, 1083,
    2309
  Marie Emily (Mme. Pierre Baillio)
    609, 613, 754, 767, 1369-1370,
    1374, 1384-1385, 2374, 2595
  Marie Louise, *fille* Gaspard, 209
  Marie Louise, *fille* Leandre, 584
  Marie Suzette, 2873
  Nicolas, II, 579-580
  Nicolas, *fils* Jean Marie, 2872
  Petronille (Mme. Joseph Gillard II),
    579-581, 584, 2364, 2478, 2898
  Pierre I, 81, 209, 972

La Cour (continued),
  Pierre II, 146, 1912, 2130, 2309
  Susette, 1080
LaCroix, Marie Rosalie. *See Sta. Cruz.*
La Cruz, Diego, 2495
La Cruz. *See also Cruz, Sta. Cruz.*
Ladega, Jose, 1118
Lady, slave. *See Laty.*
La Fantasy, Marguerite (Mme. François
  Metoyer I), 956, 1054, 2028, 2352
Laferet?, François Gonet, 419
La Ferne, Marianne (Mme. Gaspard Roubieu)
  431, 1025
La Fitte (Lafita),
  _____, Widow, 1528
  Cesaire. *See Joseph Cesaire.*
  Clement Boüet I, 2759
  Clement Boüet II, 2759
  Denis, 734
  François Boüet, 156
  Jeanne, 2558
  Joseph Antoine, 410
  Joseph Cesaire (Severe?), 410-412,
    1106, 1266, 1526, 2589, 2833-2834
  Joseph Flugeau Boüet, 2834
  Joseph Marie Boüet, 135
  Jose Olivie, 409
  Louis, 734
  Manuel, 2860
  Marianne, 412
  Marie, 1526
  Marie Aurore (Horror) Boüet, 156, 1265
  Marie Boüet, 2833
  Marie Celeste, 1509, 2802
  Marie Des Neiges (Denis), 390, 747
  Marie Felicité Boüet (Mme. Cesaire
    Fonteneau), 446-447, 538, 1036, 2802
  Marie Madeleine (Dna. Pedro Flores),
    1059
  Marie Pompose (Mme. J. B. Fontenot),
    294, 390, 538, 976, 1419, 1510
  Paul Boüet, 135, 156, 976, 1036, 2802
  Pierre, 1528
  Pierre Boüet (Clement?), 135, 384,
    408, 410, 740, 1059, 2759?
  Remy, 411
  Sévère, 384
LaFlor?, Jean Baptiste, 1235
Laflore, Joseph, 2914
LaFlore (LaFleur). *See also Flores.*
Lafon (Lafont),
  Bernard Théophile, 548, 685, 729, 780,
    791, 1034-1035, 1064, 1387
  Jeanne (Mme. Pierre Massip), 26
LaFontaine, Pierre David Cailleau, 553,
  738, 745, 753, 779, 1026, 2553

Laforet, Marie M., 2878
LaGarza. *See de la Garza.*
Lair,
  George, 183
  Mary Magdeleine, 183, 288
Lajbache, Maria, 351
La Lande (La Landa),
  Jean I, 20, 42, 65, 178, 435, 787
  Jean Pierre, 42, 971, 1137-1138, 1574, 2446-2447, 2714
  Marie Anne (Jeanne), (Mme. Pierre Gagne II), 42, 178, 291, 2856
  Maria Sora, 350
Lallemand (Lalemand),
  Marie (Mme. Luc Peré), 952
  Pierre, 952
Laly, slave, 1352. *See also Eulalie.*
La Malathy (Lamalaty, Lamalatie),
  Louis, 235, 237-238, 955, 1268, 1308, 1963, 2279, 2449
  Marie Anne (Mme. Mathurin David), 959
  Marie Françoise (Mme. Bmy. Rachal I) 55, 59, 65, 152, 193, 198-199, 236, 995
Lamate. *See Lamot.*
Lambre,
  _____, Sieur, 774, 1032
  Adelphe (Adelphine?), 333
  Asely (Mme. Charles/Carlos ____ie), 2729
  Aurore (Horrore), 1411
  Delphine. *See Eloise Delphine.*
  Dominique, 956
  Eloise Delphine, 260
  Emerante, 232
  J., 1328-1331
  Jacques, 1701
  Jacques Jacob, 62, 63, 108, 128-129, 191, 211, 1870, 1957
  Jean Baptiste, 54
  Jean Jacques, 62, 252, 2605, 2897
  Joseph, 195, 260, 333
  Josephine, 333
  Louis, 119, 1932
  Louise, 1140
  Marianne Cephalide (Mme. J. B. Le Comte), 48, 104, 264, 970
  Marie, 128, 1701
  Marie Anne Stephalie (Cephalide?) 211
  Marie Aurore (Horror, Orror), (Mme. François Benjamin Metoyer), 252, 531, 791, 1027, 1543, 2897?
  Marie Catherine (Mme. Antoine Prudhomme), 62, 108, 130, 191, 250, 337, 548

Lambre (continued)
  Marie Catherine (Mme. Emanuel Prudhomme), 251, 254, 824, 962, 974, 1046
  Marie Catherine Pelagie (Mme. F. Bossier II), 10, 54, 227, 244, 249, 404
  Marie Delphine, 63
  Marie Elise (Lise) (Mme. François Ruelle), 454, 791
  Marie Henriette, 211
  Marie Louise (Mme. Jean Salvant), 105, 123-124, 180, 1937
  Marie Rose (Mme. Louis Buard), 244, 861, 1005
  Marie Susanne "Suset", 1332, 1542
  Pelagie. *See Catherine Pelagie.*
  Remi, 10, 63, 128-130, 211, 252, 454, 531, 791, 935, 948, 951, 962, 970, 974, 980, 1027, 1819, 1848, 1942-1950, 2077, 2157
  Valsin, 1543
Lamel, Charles, 1109
Lamot, f.m.c., 1516
Lamot (Lamate, Lomate),
  Belony, 626
  Caroline, 625
  Jacques (Santiago), 625
  Louis, 1188, 1516, 1518, 1578, 1073
  Marie Dagues, 628
  Marie Françoise (Mme. Jean F. Escofie), 604
  Policarp, 625-628
  Samuel, 627
  Sophar, 528
Lamot. *See also Louis Lamot, slave.*
Lamougne, Catherinee (Dna. Bernard Gonsalez), 41, 177, 248
Landor, slave. *See Lendor.*
Landreaux,
  François, 413, 2662
  François II, 744, 1794
  Jacques, 744, 780, 1796, 2662
  Jean Baptiste, 722, 744, 1523, 1534
Lane, Mary (Mrs. James Bucley), 281
Langevin,
  Louis, 366
  Marie, 366
  Sarah (Mme. Louis Langevin), 366
Langlois (Langloi, Langois),
  Angelique, 1220
  Auguste, 786, 1053
  Augustin (husband of M. Celeste Bringel), 391
  Augustin (husband of M. L. Riche), 33, 133

Langlois (continued),
  Augustin Louis, 33, 133, 301, 2254, 2256
  Cesaire, 1146
  Felicité (Mme. Charles LaCaze, I), 3, 48, 160-161
  Felix, 391, 1221
  François, 801
  Jacques Lestan, 301, 2251, 2539, 2567
  Louis I, 33
  Louis II, 33
  Louis Augustin, 2567
  Manuel Ulger (Ludger?), 133
  Marie, 33, 2871?
  Marie Adelaÿde, 2567
  Marie Anne (Mme. Simon Greneaux), 203
  Marie Azelie, 587, 1145-1146, 2251, 2256, 2372, 2540, 2855
  Marie Divine, 301
  Marie Emely, 2539
  Marie Lise (Leysa, Laysa), 587, 1221
  Marie Louise Carmelitte, 344, 2254, 2371, 2566
  Marie Nite (Rite?), 200
  Marie Thérèse, 200, 952
  Sévère Langlois, 2256
Lansir, slave, 1546
Lansom. *See Sanson.*
LaPlace,
  Jean, 2874
  Marie, 2874
  François, 800
La Prairie (La Prery, La Berry),
  Louise, 632
  Margarita, 606
  Marie (Dna. Joseph Cruz), 629-631
  Marie Felesy, 606
  Marie Jeanne, 638
  Michel, 638
  Rosalie, 614
La Renaudiere (Larnodierre, Larnodier, Arnaudiere),
  Aspasy, 1497
  Asely, 2711
  August, 636
  Charles, 88
  Jean Baptiste, 513, 777, 1042, 1497, 1940, 2875
  Jean Pierre, 513
  M. L. O., female, 2875
  Magdeleine (Mme. F. Guisarnac), 516, 2396
  Marie, 636

La Renaudiere (continued),
  Maria *fille* Asely, 2711
  Marie Louise (Mme. Bernard Guisarnat, Mrs. James Forsythe), 145, 516, 818, 2679, 2681, 2753, 2789, 2875
  Marie Rosalie, 83, 145, 515, 2545
  Maximilien, 88
  Migner, Sieur, 1496
  Philippe, 88, 145, 310, 515, 825, 1042
  Pierre, 88, 145, 825, 1042
  Roselin Olis, 515
Lartigue, Marie Jeanne (Mme. Henry Matthew Hertzog), 354, 548, 980
Latham. *See Litton.*
Lattier (Lattie, Lattiere)
  Catherine (Mme. Luis Thomassino), 95, 359, 957
  François I, 204, 217, 257-258, 358, 498, 737, 761, 968-969, 972, 1196, 1806, 1984, 2257, 2369, 2801, 2876, 2923
  François II, 257, 1196, 1544, 2537
  François Sévère, 353, 1595, 2536
  Jean Baptiste I, 217, 298, 353, 505, 559, 1545, 1983, 2251-2253, 2255, 2536, 2537
  Jean Baptiste II, 783, 789
  Jean Baptiste (I or II?), 1359, 2566
  Jean Jacques, 2057
  Joseph I, 95, 204, 766, 972
  Joseph II, 90, 204, 587, 601, 606, 645, 743, 2254, 2368, 2411, 2876
  M. (female), 1594
  Marie Adelaÿde, 1983
  Marie Eloise (Deloyse), (Mme. Neuville Gallien), 298, 1015, 1359, 2857
  Marie Felonise, 258, 2536
  Marie Joachine, 358
  Marie Josephe, 2368
  Marie Louise, 217, 1196, 2537, 2876
  Marie Zeline, 2876
  Michel, 204
  Pierre Naysa, 497
  Sévère. *See François Sévère.*
Laty, slave, 1105. *See also Laly, Eulalie.*
Laurance (Laurence),
  Alexandré, 196-197
  Eugenie, 196
  Jean, 196-197
  See also Lorans, Llorens.
Laurent, Franco., 2069
Lauve (Love, Lowe, Louve),
  _____, Mr., the younger, 1878
  Apolinario, 869
  Arnauld, 58, 235, 237, 243-244 (cont'd.)

Lauve (continued),
  Arnauld (cont'd), 324, 503, 904,
    961, 976, 978, 981, 983-984,
    1063, 1242, 1576-1578, 1649,
    1792, 2435
  Arnaud II, 503, 948, 1242
  Evariste I, 238, 240, 242, 244,
    283, 523, 869, 975-976, 981-
    982, 987, 998, 2189
  Evariste II, 283, 997
  Hon., (female), 2916
  J., 791
  Marie Aspasy, 324
  Marie Marcelite Celeste, 523
  Nicolas, 153, 283, 324, 503, 971,
    975, 978
  Nicolas II, 954
  Renaud, 971
Laveda, Jeanne, 2768
La Vega. *See de la Bega.*
Laveri. *See La Berry*
Lavespere (Lavespair),
  _____, 697
  Elenne, 1475, 2906
  François I, 46, 206, 958, 983,
    1053, 1475, 2255
  François II, 46
  Hilaire, 302, 387, 1053
  Jean, 46
  Maria, 2780
  Marie Aimée, 302
  Marie Felicité (Mme. Jean F.
    Frederic), 206, 277, 298, 387,
    958, 1940, 2780, 2791, 2855
  Marie Melanie (Mme. Julien Rachal
    II), 206, 265, 302, 697-698,
    983, 2905-2906
  Pierre Godfroy, 2855, 2906
Lavigne, Joseph, 721, 1045, 1217,
  1461, 1467, 1480, 1545, 1561,
  1628, 1647, 2270, 2318, 2467
Lavius, _____, Mme. 1742
Lawrence. *See Lorans, Laurance.*
Laÿde. *See Adelaÿde; Marie Adelaÿde
  Marriotte.*
Layly, Heleine (Mme. Jacques Uuily),
  96
Laysa,
  f.w.c., 1793
  slave, 1257-1261, 1344, 1531, 2111
  See also Elisa.
Layseme, slave. *See Onesime.*
Layssard (Lesar, Lesard, Lisard,
  Lexar),
  _____, Sieur, 754-755
  Adelinne (Mrs. John M. Cannon), 755

Layssard (continued),
  Andres Marafrete, 657, 755
  Bolon, 1367, 2518
  Celeste (Mrs. Thomas Hooper), 612
  Clere (Mrs. John Brown), 607
  Deline, 607
  Delsir "Delsy" Bolon, 608, 2375, 2810
  Felonise (Mme. Augustin Baillio),
    585, 597, 599-600, 602
  Joseph, 657
  Louise, 612
  Maraffret. *See Andres Marafret.*
  Marcelin, 1390
  Marie Constance (Mme. Jean Louis Bail-
    lio), 610
  Valentin, 767, 1390, 2377, 2517
Lazare, Joseph, f.m.c. *See Joseph Lazare.*
Leal,
  Franco., 1033
  José Miguel, 1033, 2742
  Miguel, 757
Leandre (Leandro), slave, 1648, 2249.
  See also Baptiste Leandre Bertil.
Le Boeuf. *See Helbeuf, La Boeuf.*
Le Brun (Lebrum, Libron, Levron, El
  Brom),
  Etienne Alexy, 2617
  Etienne Jacques, 1194
  Guillaume Bossier *dit* LeBrun, 32
  Jeanne "Janette" Bossier (Mme. Charles
    Le Moine II), 32, 212, 225, 498, 511,
    2313
  Paul Etienne *dit* Dagobert, 735, 740,
    1194, 2617
LeClerc (Claire)
  Marie (Mme. Pierre Lefevre), 176, 949
  Marie Louise "Manon" (Mme. Pierre Der-
    banne I), 46, 66, 162, 948, 954
LeComte,
  _____, 946
  Alphonsine, 1550
  Ambroise I, 104, 124, 165-169, 172,
    264, 322, 970, 998, 1046, 1150-1152,
    1254, 1342, 1656, 1839, 1907-1923,
    1968-1977, 2095, 2217-2227, 2408-
    2409, 2462, 2503, 2534, 2629-2631
  Ambroise II, 264, 2408, 2468
  Athanase, 34, 201, 1575, 1921, 1968,
    2001, 2619
  Genevieve, 1078, 1914, 1921, 2619
  Jacques, 171, 322, 336, 998, 1968-1971
  Jacques Tranquillen, 336, 1559
  Jacques Valcour, 322
  Jean Baptiste I, Widow, 1817
  Jean Baptiste II, 50, 114, 124, 165,
    208, 211, 264, 761, 775, 788 (cont'd)

LeComte (continued)
  Jean Baptiste II (continued),
    789, 791, 970, 998, 1032, 1046,
    1109, 1343, 1549, 1551-1552,
    1923, 2228, 2232, 2410, 2468,
    2469, 2632, 2812
  Marie Marguerite Louise (Mme. Dominique Metoyer), 23, 112-113,
    175, 762, 1110, 1654, 1758, 2086-2087, 2316-2317, 2534, 2557,
    2600
  Marie Françoise (Mme. Joseph Dupré II, Mme. Alexis Cloutier II),
    114, 124, 163, 761, 1838, 1923
  Marie Louise (Mme. J. B. Dupré, Mme. Louis Monet, Mrs. Jacques Porter), 69, 118, 124, 171-173,
    1656, 1931
  Marie Louise, f.w.c. 1838
  Marie Perine (Mme. Pierre Metoyer II), 112-113, 784, 940, 946,
    1754, 1842, 2029, 2051, 2128,
    2299-2300
  Marie Thérèse (Mme. Louis Metoyer),
    175, 1273, 1473, 1484, 1690,
    1692, 1700, 2621
  Tranquillen. *See Jacques Tranquillen.*
LeCourt de Prelle (LaCour),
  Athanase, 309, 737, 1337, 1343,
    1909, 1976
  Barthelemy, 14n, 85, 120, 440,
    1034, 1279, 1554, 2202-2203,
    2628
  Cecile (Mme. Athanase Dupré), 119,
    576, 793
  Françoise "Fanchonette" (Mme. Pierre Dupré), 2, 119, 440, 737?
  Jacques Eloy, 2080, 2323
  Jean Baptiste Neuville, 14
  Joseph Valery, 1334, 1653, 1666,
    1670
  Louis Mathias, Sieur de Prelle,
    2, 116, 119-120, 141, 166
  Louis Cesaire, 29, 1249, 2079-2080, 2320, 2560, 2628
  Louis Toussaint, 2560
  Marie, 2
  Marie Antoinée (Mme. Nicolas Gallien
    I) 60, 116, 147, 997, 1015
  Marie Arsene, 85, 2319
  Marie Barbe, 1334, 1343, 1670,
    2203, 2320, 2560
  Marie Françoise (Mme. Pierre Dupré),
    2, 33, 141, 166, 297. *See also Françoise "Fanchonette".*

LeCourt (continued)
  Marie Louise (Mme. Pierre Cesaire Brosset), 85, 563, 1034, 2202, 2321
  Marie Pelagie (Mme. Joseph Antoine Metoyer), 14, 29, 104, 816, 1116, 1653,
    1847, 1887, 2079, 2317
  Marie Tranquelline, 440, 2323, 2599
  Mathias. *See Louis Mathias.*
LeCourt. *See also LaCour.*
LeDoux,
  Emely (Emery), 626, 638
  Félicité, 651, 657, 660?
  Lolete, 641
  Melizet, 640
  Marie Françoise, 625
LeDuc, *dit* Ville Franche,
  Jean Baptiste Joseph, 31, 947
  Marie Louise (Mme. F. LeMaitre; Mme. Gaspar Bodin), 31, 176, 192, 947, 949,
    985
Lee (Ly),
  Alex, 556
  Anne Marie, 557
  Christopher, 556, 558
  Mary, 558
Lefalla, Ramon, 1505
LeFevre (Lefevre, LeFebre, Lefebvre),
  _____, 892
  Adelaïde, 359
  Augustin Louis, 176, 247, 293, 359, 455,
    499, 949, 1061
  Constance Benoite, 176
  François Aquilain, 455
  François Leopold, 499
  Hilaire, 363
  Jean Baptiste, 345, 363, 2764
  Louis. *See Augustin Louis.*
  Marcelitte, 293
  Marguerite, 428
  Marie Anne Françoise, 323, 345, 2764
  Marie Louise, *fille* Augustin, 247
  Marie Louise (Mme. Louis Mercier), 15,
    61, 817
  Pierre, 176, 949
Leger (Legé), slave, 1986
Leger family. *See Piedferme.*
LeGrand, Marie Barbe Josephe. *See Marie Barbe Josephe Varangue.*
LeGros, Marie Thérèse (Mme. Joseph Marie Armand), 87, 234, 934, 2038
LeMaitre (LeMetre, LeMettre, LeMarttu),
  François, 176, 192, 947, 949, 985
  Marianna (Mme. Matheo Richard), 738,
    2886
  Marie Anne Artemise (Antoinette),
    (Mme. Dorset David Hoy), 192, (cont.)

LeMaitre (continued),
  Marie Anne Artemise (cont.), 246, 259, 342, 378, 453, 691, 936, 985
  Marie Félicité Théophile (Mme. Gaspard Philibert), 246, 378, 460, 474, 991, 2645, 2653, 2795, 2895
  Marie Louise, 325
  Victoire Constance (Mme. Augustin Louis LeFevre), 176, 184, 247, 293, 359, 455, 499
LeMatte, Louis. See Louis Lamot.
Lemb, slave. See Charles Lemb.
LeMoine (Lemoin),
  Ambroise, 1441
  Antoine I. See Jean Antoine.
  Antoine II, 578, 1298
  Caroline, 299, 1319
  Charles II, 32, 212, 498, 2314-2315, 2467
  Charles François, 10, 26, 32, 107, 160-161, 173
  Charles, fils J.B., 225
  François. See Charles Francois.
  Jean Antoine, 107, 173, 308, 577-578
  Jean Baptiste I, 10, 107, 160-161, 213, 225, 299, 794, 1000, 1631, 2033, 2814
  Jean Baptiste, fils Antoine, 308, 2814?
  Jean Baptiste Gaspard, 2497
  Joseph, 853
  Judith, 173
  Marie (Mme. J. B. ___, 715
  Marie, fille J. B.), 161, 2414
  Marie Aimée, 578
  Marie Denise (Mme. J. B. Bmy. Rachal II), 160-161, 1000, 2904
  Marie Euphrosine, 160, 1085-1086, 1148
  Marie Félicité, 3814
  Marie Louise (Mme. Antoine Rachal), 6, 572, 577, 794, 1017, 1032, 1086, 1298, 2362, 2470?
  Marie Louise (Mme. Jean B. Massip), 3, 26, 48, 790, 994
  Marie Melanie, 107, 1191
  Michel, 299
  Pelagie, 32, 1453, 2315
  Pierre, 1148, 2247
  Sylvestre, 577
  Valeri, 10

Lemoine. See also Lamougne.
Len___, slave, 1243
Lendor (Landor, Lindor), slave, 1455, 2077, 2452, 2494, 2635, 2637. See also Andres Lendor
Lennard. See Linnard
LeNoir (Lainoir, Le Nouart, Laineir),
  Antoine I, 7, 189, 197
  Antoine II, 555, 2125, 2877
  Antoine (I or II), 1810
  Jean Baptiste Desir, 555
  Marie Josephe Zepherine, 2877
Leon, 1315, 1854
Leon Family. See Lion.
Leonard (Leonardo),
  Jean Baptiste, 242
  Margaret (Mrs. Samuel Cobb), 242, 335
  See also Linnard.
Leonor. See Eleonore.
LeRoy (LeRoi),
  Jeanne (Mme. Louis Mathias LeCourt de Prelle), 2, 116, 119-120, 141, 166
  Jeanne. See also Susanne Jeanne Le Roy; Jeanne de los Reyes
  Marie Louise (Mme. Louis Rachal I), 37, 39, 67-68
  Susanne Jeanne (Mme. Marie Pierre Jorge Paillette), 233, 953, 2037
LeRoy. See also Roy.
Lesine, slave. See Joseph Lesine.
Lestage (Lestase, L'estage, Lestages, Lestas),
  ___, 2657
  ___, Widow, 1996, 2451, 1720
  Antoin, 1136
  Barthelemy, 214, 256, 331, 382, 414, 797, 964, 2057, 2068, 2658, 2865, 2878
  François, 27, 1353, 2787
  Guillaume I, 256, 1056
  Guillaume II, 256
  Jean Baptiste I, 256, 418, 470, 760, 797, 799, 944, 964-965, 1056, 1067, 2068, 2657, 2787, 2878
  Jean Baptiste II, 2878
  Joseph, 2658
  Marie Aimée, 331
  Marie Euphrosine, 382
  Marie Feliciane, 944
  Marie Rosalie "Rose" Barbe (Mme. Philippe Frederic III), 101, 256, 450, 1056, 2854
  Sephalin, 414
  Marie U., 470, 2787

446

Lestan, f.m.c. *See Edward Lestan.*
Leton. *See Litton.*
LeVasseur (Levaseur, Lovaser, Levassau, La Veseur),
   _____, Mr., 1956
   Aimée. *See Marie Louise Aimée.*
   Catherine (Catalina), 2178
LeVasseur, Charles François, 15, 61, 802, 965, 987, 1104?, 2671, 2694
   Ciriac, 1426
   Cyprian, 2475
   Dorseline, 1271
   F.?, 1055
   Felicite Aimeé, 1811
   François I. *See Charles François.*
   François II. *See Jean François.*
   Françoise (Mme. J. B. Anty), 823
   Gennevieve Amelie, 218, 1533
   Jacques, 1811
   Jacques, Mda., 769
   Jean, 61
   Jean François I, 329, 355, 537, 954, 987, 1104?, 1821-1822, 1856, 1859, 1961, 1989, 2134, 2274, 2434, 2586, 2695
   Jean François, Widow, 1348, 1513
   See also Marie Françoise Trichel.
   Jean François II, 329
   Joseph?, 1055?
   Louis (bachelor), 15, 965, 2694, 1859
   Louis (husband of Marie Bourdon), 1811
   Ludger Lessein, 61, 1533
   Manuel Simeon, 15, 61, 210, 218, 348, 355, 464, 808, 826, 965, 1533, 1586, 2485
   Marie Aimée, 2907
   Marie Constance, 355
   Marie Catherine, 2475
   Marie Emy, 2463
   Marie Felony, 2462
   Marie Françoise Selima, 537
   Marie Genevieve, 15, 808
   Marie Jeanne (Mme. J. B. Lambre), 54
   Marie Judith (Mme. Auguste Roubieu; Mme. Athanase Rachal), 119, 768, 2349
   Marie Louise Aimée (Mme. Hilaire Rachal), 774
   Marie Modeste, 348
   Simeon. *See Manuel Simeon.*
   Victorin, 2462-2463
Lexar. *See Layssard.*

Libron. *See Le Brun.*
Lidia, slave, 2287
Lily, Charity. *See Shile, Charity.*
Lindor, slave. *See Lendor*
Linnard (Lennard),
   Henry Joseph Biays, 533
   Susanna (Mrs. William Linnard) 1003
   Thomas M., 380-381, 533, 728, 1003, 1019, 1060, 1525
   William, 1003
   William James, 380
   See also Leonard.
Lion (Leon),
   Jean, 341
   Marie Louise, 341
   See also de Leon
Liset (Lisée),
   f.w.c., 1390
   slave, 2429
   See also Elise, Laysa.
Lister, female slave, 1358. *See also Esther.*
Litton (Leton, Lethon),
   Isavel (Elisabeth), 779
   John (Jean), 2815-2816
   Joseph, 2815
   M. James (Jacques), 2815
   Mary Elisabeth "Bessie" (Mme. Joseph Cesaire Lafitte), 410-412, 2833-2834
Liuc, slave, 2300-2301. *See also Luc.*
Livoni, slave, 2077
Liza. *See Laysa, Elise, Liset, Eliza, Lise.*
Llorens (Lorans, Loren),
   François Montuco, 241, 388, 785, 2277-2278
   Manuel, 785, 1396, 1623, 1633, 1652, 1662, 2553, 2602
   Marie Arsene, 1623
   Marie Lodoiska (Lodoysa), 1662
   Norens Beliser, 1652
   Seraphin I, 1652, 1657, 2091
   Seraphin II, 1657
   See also Laurance.
Locuvichi. *See Lucovichi.*
Loc Cilia, slave, 1184. *See also Lucille.*
Loise. *See Loysse.*
Loleet, slave, 2469
Lom, Jean, 2879
   Marie, 2879
Longert?, Pier, 1033
Lopez (Lopes),
   José Dioniso, 534
   José Pedro Dolores, 534
   Marie, 2883
   Simon I, 2730
   Simon II, 897

Lorans, slave, 1384.
Lorans. *See also Laurence, Lorans.*
Lorenzo Acoye, Apalache Indian, 652
Los Fuertes. *See de los Fuentes.*
Losoya,
  Juana Francisca (Jeanne Françoise), 2881
  Maria Antonia (Dna. Juan Manuel Cantam), 2727
  Ventura, 2881
Louc, Lucie, 1094. *See also Lucie.*
Louis (Luis),
  Apalache Indian, 668, 1804
  Choctaw Indian, 1659
  Free Negro, 1457
  Slave, 1071, 1094, 1132, 1156, 1167-1169, 1178, 1192, 1223, 1245, 1251, 1264, 1311, 1313, 1355, 1400, 1436, 1490, 1616, 1640, 1706, 1737, 1834, 1859, 1909, 1946, 1969, 1998, 2008, 2048, 2050, 2057, 2060, 2063, 2072, 2077, 2115, 2120, 2149, 2163, 2165, 2185, 2200, 2218, 2235, 2237, 2246, 2281, 2374, 2384, 2440, 2442, 2457, 2469, 2551, 2574, 2601, 2606 *See also Jean Louis.*
Louis (Luis) --
  -- Alexandre, 1613, 1616, 1822, 1837, 1856, 1881, 1886, 2007, 2161, 2489
  -- Athanase (Atanasio), 2110
  -- Augustin, 1813
  -- Fano, 2281
  -- Fermin, 2202
  -- Joseph, f.m.c., 1233
  -- Joseph, free Negro, 2047
  -- Joseph, slave, 2047
  -- Joseph Eloi, 1233
  -- Lamot, 1518. *See also Louis Lamot.*
  -- Oliberte, 2502
  -- Onezime, f.m.c., 1580
  -- Phaneau, 1678
  -- Philipe, 2191
  -- Tensa, 2350
  -- St. Cir, 1924
  -- Sousin, 1258
  -- Ursin, 1112
  -- Ursin, f.m.c., 1665
Louise (Luisa, Loysse, Loise, Luissa), F.W.C., 149
  Slave, 1167, 1234, 1297, 1325, 1388, 1405, 1423, 1618, 1676, 1858, 1892, 1896, 1903, 1914, 2072, 2076, 2102, 2272, 2284, 2314, 2432, 2457, 2530 *See also Loyse, Luiset, Marie Louise, Louison.*

Louise --
  -- Clemanin (Clernanin? Clemence?) 1568
  -- Desneige, 2006
  -- Marie, free Negro, 2047
  -- Toro, Apalache Indian, 663-664
Louison,
  Canneci Indian, 1969
  Slave, 1716, 1855, 2049, 2057
Lou Sally (Lu Saly), slave, 2429, 2427?
Louve. *See Lauve.*
Loyse (Loysse), 1098, 1130, 1182. *See also Eleyse, Lise, Louise.*
Luc _____, female slave, 1282. *See also Louc, Lucie, Lucille.*
Luc (Luca, Lucas), slave, 1097, 1680, 1688, 2386. *See also Joseph Lucas, Lucien.*
Luc,
  Cypriano, 425
  Jose Cypriano, 425
Luc, Luce. *See also Louc, Luic.*
Lucie (Lucy, Louseie, Luciane, Loucie), 1341, 1380, 1508, 1509, 2022, 2506, 2508, 2517. *See also Louc, Lucie; Luc___; Liuc, Loc Cilia, Lucille.*
Lucien (Luciano), *See August Lucien, Joseph Maria Luciano.*
Lucille, slave, 2069, 2523. *See also Loc Cilia, Luc____, and Lucie Louc.*
Lucovichi (Loucouviche, Loucouvidhe, Locuvichi), 1261-1264.
Lucy. *See Lucie, Marie Louise Lucie, Lucille, Luc____, Lucie Louc.*
Ludger, slave. *See Jean Baptiste Ludgeaire.*
Lugue,
  Jean, 968
  Marie Constance, 968
Luiset, male slave. *See Joseph Luiset.*
Luisset, female slave, 2447. *See also Louise, Marie Louise, Louison.*
Luna (de Luna),
  Mariana (Dna. Nepomuceno Sn. Miguel), 1033
  Maria Simona Chirino (Dna. Sacramiento Basquez), 2713
Lupart, Jean, 1524
Luri, Francisca, 2117
Luvin, slave, 1076

Macarty, Marie Josephe, 1207
Mactaer. *See McTyre.*
Mader (Matere), Marie Jeanne (Mme. F. LeVasseur I), 15, 61, 965, 987, 2671, 2694.

Maës,
    ____, fils, 988-989
    Josephine, 177
    Marie Genevieve Agathe, 69
    N., 251
    Pierre Joseph, 69, 1710, 1722
Madeleine (Magdalenne, Magdeleine, Magdalena),
    Indian, 305. See also Marie Madeleine, Canneci.
    Apalache Indian. See Françoise Magdalenne
    F.W.C., 100, 179, 2089. See also Madeleine Grappe.
    Slave, 104, 1095, 1137, 1352, 1381, 1442, 1534, 1592-1593, 1707, 1717, 1750, 1778, 1817, 1442, 1534, 1592-1593, 1707, 1717, 1750, 1778, 1817, 1822, 1863, 1881, 1916, 1944, 1947, 1967, 1972-1973, 2030, 2072, 2233, 2255, 2358, 2452, 2528, 2591. See also Marie Magdalenne Euphrasinne Erselinne.
Magdeleine Sarah (Zaire), 1937
Magloire, slave, 2077
Mago, slave, 2054
Magnes, Reverend Francisco, 1505-1507
Mailloux (Mailloche, Mayoche, Mayou, Mayoux, Maiou, Malloud, Maillou, Mailliud, Maulliou),
    Aspasie. See Marie Anastasie.
    Bertrand, 212, 972, 1994, 2059
    Ignace, 12, 18, 74, 189, 194, 239, 278, 341, 356, 493, 933
    Euphrosine, "Frouasin," 2486
    Laurent, 377, 551, 850, 2885
    Marie Anastasie (Mme. Jacques Herrie; Mme. Jean Armand), 18, 74, 278, 497, 831, 856, 873, 2766-2767
    Marie Cecile, 12, 74, 377
    Marie Louise (Mrs. George McTyre), 189, 356, 2885
    N., 859
    Pierre, 236, 238, 933, 999, 1002
    Thérèse (Mme. Michel Rambin), 194, 423, 2912
    Victorine, 377
Maitter, Susanne (Mme. Pierre Charnau I), 1004
Maly, slave, 1250-1251
Malbert (Malbere),
    Jean Baptiste, 167-169
    Marie DeNeige (Mme. Nicolas Baudouin), 167-169, 310, 561

Marie Françoise (Mme. Jacques Fort) 8 22, 95, 883
Malbourg, José, 741
Malige (Malgs, Malegs, Malis),
    ____, 730, 1029
    Angeline, 56
    Eulalie (Mrs. John Sibley), 96, 394, 495, 1019, 2692, 2919
    Joseph, 40, 78, 86, 96, 951, 1019, 2646
    Joseph II, 182
    Marie Jeanne "Manet" (Mme. F. Chabus), 40, 86, 2739
    Marie Josepne (Mme. Antoine Dubois), 182, 424, 2760, 2900
    Marie Rosalie "Rose" Josephe (Mme. J. B. Prudhomme fils Bastien), 31, 38, 78, 231, 951, 426, 2900
    Noel, 426, 1029
Malloud. See Mailloux.
Maltête, Margueritte (Mme. Bernard Boucher), 1011
Mamillo,
    Juana (Jeanne), 2797
    Maria Fina (Dna. Pedro San Carquier), 1814
Manet, slave, 2365-2366
Mannet, slave, 2153
Maninga, slave, 2077
Manon (Maneau), slave, 2267. See also Marie.
Manuel,
    Apalache Indian, 658
    Canneci Indian, 82
    F.M.C., 2393, 2491
    Slave, 1234, 1308, 1327, 1333, 1347, 1388, 1517, 1548, 2048, 2061, 2162, 2174, 2212, 2234, 2241, 2255, 2315, 2411, 2454. See also Joseph Manuel.
Manuel Habraham, 2513
Manuel Charmé (Germaine?), 1686
Manuel Senciel, 1252
Manuela Maria, 2159
Maraya, slave. See Mariah.
Marcarty, slave?, 2405
Marcel (Marcelin, Marcellin), 1104, 1348, 1356, 1500, 2077, 2121, 2434
Marcelite (Marceline, Marcelina, Marcelita), 1158, 1217, 1424, 1531, 2205, 2262, 2526, 2607. See also Marie Jeanne Marcelite.
Marcisogne?, Indian tribe, 89
Marcollay (Marcolet),
    Paul, 833, 947, 950
    Pierre, 833

449

Marguerite (Margarita, Margarite, Margaret, Margueritte),
Free Negro, 1883
Slave, 1067, 1090, 1134, 1192, 1202, 1231, 1307, 1336, 1345, 1348, 1357, 1362, 1364, 1430, 1434, 1550, 1597, 1668, 1674, 1694, 1827, 1830, 1834, 1859, 1870, 1877, 1888, 1890, 1952, 1957, 1989, 2001, 2012, 2014, 2015, 2060-2061, 2101, 2365-2366, 2373, 2432, 2442, 2452, 2454, 2458, 2472-2473, 2490, 2518, 2573, 2577
Margarite Baptiste, Apalache Indian, 660, 663, 1807
Margaret Nicolase, Apalache Indian, 653-654, 668
Margueritte Sophie, slave, 1705, 1721
Mariah (Maraya), slave, 1500, 1502
Marianne. *See Marie Anne.*
Marichal, Catherine (Mme. F. Moreau), 1061
Marie (Maria),
Apalache Indian, wife of Louis Nicolas, 656
Apalache Indian, wife of Michael Tensá, 669-671, 679
Apalache Indian, wife of Pierre Tensá, 676-677
Caddo Indian, 1575
Commanche Indian, 1774
F.W.C., 1658, 1929, 1981, 2094
Slave, 23, 172, 1066, 1075-1076, 1090, 1093, 1094, 1100, 1114, 1129, 1150, 1155, 1187, 1191, 1221-1222, 1224, 1226-1227, 1233, 1255, 1262, 1279, 1289, 1322, 1327, 1331, 1338-1339, 1357-1358, 1390, 1400, 1405, 1416, 1441, 1447, 1481-1484, 1514, 1519, 1544-1545, 1555, 1558-1560, 1562, 1567, 1573, 1590, 1604, 1606, 1609, 1615, 1635, 1637-1640, 1645, 1676, 1680, 1691, 1714, 1727, 1747, 1764, 1799, 1814, 1818, 1822, 1834, 1836-1837, 1849, 1860, 1865-1867, 1874, 1882, 1897, 1901, 1916, 1925, 1951, 1957, 1968, 1972, 1979, 1996-1997, 2002-2004, 2009, 2013, 2017-2019, 2025, 2027, 2031, 2034, 2050, 2057, 2072, 2077-2078,

Marie (Continued),
Slave (Continued), 2103, 2114, 2118-2119, 2133, 2141, 2152, 2157?, 2179-2180, 2185-2186, 2190, 2195-2196, 2198, 2215, 2251, 2253, 2260, 2284, 2286, 2293-2294, 2296, 2299, 2302, 2319-2320, 2326, 2331, 2343-2346, 2358, 2370, 2383, 2402, 2409, 2426, 2433, 2441, 2443, 2445, 2456, 2465, 2472, 2480, 2498, 2520, 2529, 2537, 2539, 2546, 2549, 2551, 2564, 2578, 2594, 2602, 2607, 2612, 2627? 2635, 2643
Marie _____ans, Apalache Indian, 1804
Marie Adélaïde (Adelayde, Layde, etc.),
Free, 2127
Slave, 1133, 1140, 1144, 1514, 1572, 1779, 1846, 2143, 2453, 2601
Marie Adele (Maria Adelle), 1084, 1572 1576, 1591, 2537
Marie Agathe (Agata), 1108, 1645
Marie Aglae, 58
Marie Aglantine (Anglantin), 2564
Marie Agnes (Añes), 1113, 1602, 2215
Marie Agsé, 2026
Marie Alé, 1671
Marie Alice. *See Marie Olys.*
Marie Alysa, 1344
Marie Amire, 1323
Marie Andres, 1137-1138
Marie Angelique,
Free, 1195, 1579-1580. *See also Marie Angelique Metoyer.*
Slave, 1494, 2021
Marie Anne (Marianne, Mariana, Marianna),
Apalache Indian, 643-646
F.W.C., 1271, 2017
Slave, 1086, 1098-1099, 1152, 1139, 1247, 1256, 1317, 1477, 1516, 1546, 1638, 1683, 1694, 1710, 1722, 1726, 1771, 1835, 1853, 1881, 1884-1886, 1891, 1893, 1948, 1956, 1965, 1976, 1978, 1987, 2000, 2004-2005, 2007-2008, 2026, 2030-2031, 2049-2077, 2088, 2119, 2200, 2249-2250, 2264, 2292, 2295, 2298, 2309-2311, 2341-2343, 2372, 2383, 2385, 2388, 2390, 2392, 2472, 2521. *See also Marie Marianne.*
Mariana Celezi, 2140
Marianne Fanny (Phany, Fany), 1308, 2279, 2449
Marianne Henriette (Anrriete), 1201
Marianne Nauvelle, 1333
Marie Anne Salie (Salis, Sali), 1823, 1958, 1991

Marie Anne Susanne, 1992
Marie Annete, 1560. *See also Marie Onet.*
Marie Antoinette (Maria Antoine, Antonia, Antonoina),
  Free, 160
  Slave, 1093, 1282, 1603, 2091, 2108, 2288, 2586
Marie Archange, Canneci Indian, 171
Marie Arside, Indian, 1238
Marie Arsene (Arsin, Arcine),
  Free, 2089
  Slave, 2056, 2196, 2429, 2563
Marie Arthemise (Artemis), 1164, 1175, 2260, 2582
Marie Aselie (Aselye, Asely, Aseli, Aselyne),
  Free, 1304
  Slave, 1136, 1203, 1356, 1429, 1680, 2189
Marie Asint, 2221
Marie Aspasy, 1249
Marie Aspasie (Despasy), 2430
Marie Augustine (Augustin),
  Free, 1160, 1665
  Slave, 1495, 2014, 2503
Marie Auresite. *See Marie Orosil.*
Marie Barbe (Maria Barbara), 1265, 1347, 1904, 2170
Marie Bavé, 2592
Marie Bayne, 2291
Marie Becky (Beke, Beque), 1494, 2222
Marie Belony (Velony), 1088, 1555, 2330, 2641
Maria Belse, 2508
Marie Boc, 2230
Marie Borne, 1944
Marie Bresine, 2571
Marie Brigite, 1837, 1875
Marie Calahin, 1521
Marie Carmelitte, 2411
Marie Caroline (Carolinne), 1163, 2534, 2549
Marie Casia, 2288
Marie Catherine (Maria Catarina, Chatarine, Catarinne), 1104, 1154, 1180, 1181, 1183, 1594, 2136, 2231
Marie Catis Athenais, 1211
Marie Cecile (Maria Cecilia), 1570, 2134
Marie Ceferiore, 1290
Marie Celesi, 1575
Marie Celesine, 1485
Marie Celeste, Apalache Indian, 655

Marie Celeste (Maria Celestia),
  Apalache Indian, 655
  Free, 1188
  Slave, 1072, 1087, 1106, 1165, 1170, 1230, 1257, 1267, 1298, 1305, 1502, 1607, 1869, 1884, 2002, 2065, 2152, 2300, 2307, 2440, 2611
Marie Celeste Adeline, 2434
Marie Celestine, 1291. *See also Marie Zelesine. Marie Celesi, Marie Celesine.*
Marie Celezi "Zeli", 2535.
Marie Celine (Celina), 1675, 2604
Marie Cephalide. *See Marie Sephaly.*
Marie Charlotte (Maria Charlot, Charlota), 1091, 1267, 1312, 1403, 1471, 1566, 2169, 2478
Marie Cidalise. *See Sedalis.*
Marie Cidre. *See Marie Sidre*
Marie Cilesie (Cilesy, Cilisie, Zelesy),
  Free, 1994
  Slave, 1262, 1832, 1869, 2010, 2493
  See also Marie Celesi, Marie Celesine, Marie Celeste, Marie Celezi, Marie Celine.
Marie Claire (Clara, Cler), 1571, 1588, 1650, 1906, 1946, 2530
Marie Claris? (Gloria?), 1964
Marie Clarisse, 1147
Marie Clemence, 1649
Marie Clo, 1387
Marie Cleothilde (Cleotil), 1135, 1248
Maria Concepcion, Apalache Indian, 661-662
Marie Constance (Constans), 1152, 1593, 2239, 2343
Marie Criostin, 1426
Marie Damacine, 1978
Marie de Jesus, 1208
Marie Deline, 1353.
Marie de los Dolores. *See Marie Dolores.*
Marie Delphine (Delphinne),
  free, 1102, 1398
  slave, 1184, 1515
Maria del Rosario, 2123
Marie des Douleurs. *See Marie Dolores.*
Marie Desient, 1373
Marie Desirée (Desire, Desirai), 1350, 2056, 2332, 2563
Marie des Neiges (Deneige, Denege, Denis, Denise),
  free, 100, 201, 1664, 2017
  slave, 172, 1095, 1131, 1235, 1269, 1527, 1552, 1880, 1889, 1975, 2065, 2075
Marie Dinah (Dayna, Daynaa), 2222-2224, 2631

Maria Divin, 2214
Marie Dolores (Maria Dolores, Marie des Douleurs, Marie de los Dolores), 1172, 1914-1915, 2012, 2218-2219, 2230, 2503, 2630
Marie Doralise (Doralie, Doraly), 1541, 2217, 2303, 2339, 2629
Marie Dorothée, f.w.c. *See Marie Dorothée Boisdore, Marie Dorothée Monet.*
Marie Elenne, Elena. *See Marie Hélène.*
Marie Eleonore (Heleonore, Leonor), 1177, 2002
Marie Elisabeth del Sanctissimo Rosario, 2090
Marie Elise (Eleysa, Elissa, Elysa, Eliza), 1200, 1579, 2106, 2364. *See also Marie Laisa, Marie Loyse.*
Marie Eloise (Eloyse, Eluas, Eloys), 1491, 2226, 2526. *See also Marie Loyse.*
Marie Else, 1377
Marie Emé (Emée, Emy), 1315, 1501, 2422-2424, 1383, 2555
Marie Emerant, 2608
Marie Emeliana, 2234
Marie Emelie (Emely, Emelia, Melia, Mely), 1317, 1416-1417, 1595, 2415-2416, 2420, 2484
Marie Emely Astasie, 1420
Marie Enos, 1516
Marie Esprit, 1157
Marie Esther (Ester, Estere, Esterre), 2150-2151, 2363, 2454, 2458
Marie Eulalah (Elaya), 2492
Marie Euphemie, 2064
Marie Euphrosine (Euphrasine, Frosine, Frozine),
  Free, 1423
  Slave, 1452, 1964, 2019, 2129, 2534
Marie Eveline (Aveline), 1523
Marie Fanchon (Fanson, Phanchan), 1342, 2425. *See also Marie Françoise.*
Marie Fannie (Fanny, Phani, Fany, Fanii, Fanai), 1438, 1556, 1781, 2185, 2243, 2254, 2314-2315, 2367, 2460, 2467. *See also Marie Françoise.*
Marie Febye. *See Marie Phoebe.*
Marie Felicité, 1287, 1439, 1444, 1472 1584, 2293, 2498, 2596

Marie Felisere, Apalache, 1806
Marie Felonise (P elonisse), 1675
Marie Flore (Flore, Florey), 1372, 1559, 1707, 1822
Marie Florence, 1592
Marie Florentine (Maria Florentina), 1246, 2483
Marie Fortunat (Fortune), 1953, 1658
Marie Françoise (Maria Francisca),
  Indian (Mme. Pierre Raimond), 140
  Chatas Indian, 306
  F.W.C., 762, 973, 1159, 1921-1922, 1974, 2084-2085, 2511
  Slave, 1073, 1151, 1180, 1183, 1199 1339, 1407, 1497-1498, 1513, 1521, 1673, 1709, 1787, 1829-1832, 1878, 1892, 1952, 1985, 2061, 2073, 2077, 2085, 2112, 2137, 2204, 2308, 2325, 2442, 2451, 2489, 2495, 2581, 2631
Marie Frosine. *See Marie Euphrosine.*
Marie Genevieve, 1650, 1989
Marie Genevieve Polinair, 1225
Marie Genye. *See Marie Jeanne.*
Marie Gilles, 1647
Marie Gloria? Claris? 1964
Marie Grillau, 1997
Marie Hélène (Elenne, Elena, Heleine),
  Ecasse Indian, 89
  Slave, 1203, 1490, 1507, 1828, 1963, 1965, 2006, 2045, 2147, 2493, 2570
Marie Helenore. *See Marie Eleonore.*
Marie Henriette (Maria Anrriet, Arriete, Hanriett), 1431, 1511, 1564, 2252, 2384, 2410, 2365
Marie Honorine, 1245
Marie Hortense (Ortance, Hortance, Ortans),
  Free, 179, 1882, 2089, 2116
  Slave, 1129, 1427, 1448, 2063, 2230
Marie Inez (Maria Ynes), 2156
Marie Irene, 2056, 2439
Marie Janye, 1369
Marie Jean Jean, f.w.c., 1154
Marie Jeanne (Maria Juana, Marie Jenny, Chené, Jenye, Chenye, Cenis, Zeny, Zenny, Genye, Jennie),
  Apalache Indian, 651
  Canneci Indian, 159
  Natchitoches Indian, 138-139
  F.W.C., 150, 1960, 2025, 2027, 29
  Slave, 1045, 1069, 1073, 1078-1079, 1106, 1114, 1122, 1131, 1145, 1158, 1174-1175, 1188, 1217, 1226-1227, 1230, 1249, 1266, 1300, 1319, 1323,

Marie Jeanne, slave (continued),
 1403, 1436, 1447, 1450, 1473, 1510,
 1512, 1520, 1522, 1526, 1532, 1539,
 1559, 1596, 1600, 1603, 1606, 1642-
 1643, 1668, 1766-1767, 1791, 1813,
 1824, 1839, 1841, 1874, 1901, 1904,
 1917, 1920, 1936-1940, 1960, 1971,
 1977, 1993, 2025, 2048, 2050-2051,
 2143-2144, 2149, 2167, 2184, 2186,
 2193, 2221, 2229-2230, 2232, 2252,
 2305-2307, 2331, 2335, 2407-2408,
 2411, 2415, 2431, 2436, 2438, 2469,
 2489, 2494, 2500-2501, 2521-2522,
 2531, 2541, 2550, 2568, 2589, 2603,
 2609, 2632. *See also Marie Jeanne
 Baden, Marie Jeanne DeMézières.*
Marie Jeanne Bade, 2597
Marie Jeanne Bernadiet, 2521
Marie Jeanne Marcelite, 1071
Marie Jennie. *See Marie Jeanne.*
Marie Joany, 1228
Marie Josephe (Joseph, Maria Josefa),
 free, 2024
 slave, 1120, 1223, 1232, 1266, 1322,
  1336, 1428, 1581, 1820, 1837,
  1853, 1862, 1905, 1926-1927, 1950,
  1988, 2173, 2421, 2450, 2480,
  2624
Marie Josephe Felis?, 1207
Marie Joseph Genaive, 1294
Marie Josephe Theodus, 2129
Marie Josephin, 2418
Marie Judith (Judit, Judic, Judet),
 1263, 1567, 2011, 2220
Marie Julie (Julian, July, Julia,
 Julye, Jouly, Juliana), 1115, 1184,
 1218-1219, 1314, 1405, 1417, 1436,
 1485, 1594-1595, 1674, 1679, 2273,
 2321, 2338, 2411, 2623
Marie Laisa (Laiza, Layse, Lays),
 1196, 1309, 1635-1636, 1695
 *See also Marie Eloise, Marie Loyse,
 Marie Lise.*
Marie Lalye, 1363
Marie Lalye (Salye?), 1079
Marie Lanis, 1198
Marie Lastasy, 1449
Marie Lasyr, 2411
Marie Layde (Laie, Lide, Laide), 15,
 18, 1537, 2221, 2395. *See also
 Marie Adelaide.*
Marie Leon, 1748, 1854, 2040
Marie Leonor. *See Marie Eleonore.*
Marie Leset, 1078
Marie Liestre, 2497
Marie Lise, f.w.c., 1793

Marie Lisse, 1143
Marie Lise/Lisse. *See also Marie Eloise,
 Marie Laisa, Marie Louise.*
Marie Lolete, 1150, 1636
Maria Loreta, 2337
Marie Lorine, 1224
Marie Louise (Luisse, Maria Luisa),
 Apalache Indian, wife of Nicolas, 675
 Apalache Indian *fille* Chrisostom, 1807
 Canneci Indian, 82-83
 Choctaw Indian, 1659
 Natchitoches Indian, 139
 F.W.C., 1457, 1757, 1861, 1930, 1970,
  2006, 2009, 2030, 2032, 2079, 2081
  2264, 2270
 Slave, 1099, 1111-1113, 1121, 1123,
  1136, 1142, 1149, 1156-1157, 1176,
  1188, 1190, 1231, 1242-1243, 1248,
  1269, 1283, 1288, 1329, 1356, 1407,
  1421, 1427, 1505-1506, 1529, 1559,
  1570, 1599, 1602, 1609, 1646-1647,
  1671, 1718, 1827, 1840, 1845, 1865,
  1888, 1896, 1939, 1954-1955, 1994,
  1999, 2049, 2056-2057, 2059, 2077,
  2125, 2145, 2156, 2168, 2187-2188,
  2214, 2216, 2237, 2259, 2261, 2266,
  2273-2274, 2332, 2346, 2355, 2361,
  2449, 2452-2453, 2464, 2467, 2477,
  2482-2487, 2501-2502, 2519, 2529,
  2531, 2540, 2561, 2624, 2640. *See
  also Louise Marie, Marie Lise, Marie
  Eloise, Marie Loyse*
Marie Louise Adelayde, f.w.c. *See Marie
 Louise Adelaide Mariotte.*
Marie Louise Adeline/Adelle, f.w.c. *See
 Marie Louise Adeline/Adelle Monet.*
Marie Louise Aspasy, 2634
Marie Louise Catherine, 1619
Marie Louise Hyacinthe, 2008
Marie Louise Melanie, 2574
Marie Louise Lucie, 2417-2419
Marie Louise Nicolas, Apalache Indian
 (wife of Joseph Folocque, Indian),
 655, 1808
Marie Loyse (Loys, Loysa), 1167, 1178,
 1253, 1681. *See also Marie Louise,
 Marie Elise, Marie Laisa, Marie Lise.*
Marie Luce (Lucia, Lucy), 2155, 2399
Marie Mae?, 1518
Marie Magdeleine (Maria Magdalena, Mag-
 dalenne, Madeleine),
 Caddo Indian, 1575
 Canneci Indian, wife of Pierre, 43
 Negro, 1549, 1844, 1879, 2261, 2279,
  2281
Marie Magdalenne Agustinne, 2403

Marie Magdalenne Euphrasinne Erselinne, 1206, 2608
Marie Manet, 1130
Marie Manon, 1119, 1188, 1434, 1899-1900, 2049
Marie Manuelle (Manuel, Manuela), 1498, 1708
Marie Marcel. *See Marie Mausil.*
Marie Marguerite (Margarite, Maria Margarita), 1134, 2015, 2114, 2271, 2451, 2526
Maria Mariana, 2242
Marie Marthe (Marta), 1242, 1576-1578, 1587, 1649, 2077, 2439, 2495
Marie Matilde (Matil, Mathilda, Tilde), 1101, 1501, 1620, 2039
Marie Mausil (Marcel?), 2219
Marie Melegie, 2572
Marie Melfroinene, 1578
Marie Meliac Barbara, 2203
Marie Melite (Maria Melisa), 1554
Marie Mesier, 2118
Marie Minerva, 2289
Marie Modeste,
  Canneci Indian (Mme. Jean Laurent Bodin), 43
  Negro, 1345, 1348, 1437, 1562, 1790, 1815, 1836, 2019, 2428
Marie Moraya (Moriah?), 1376
Marie Nancy (Nanci, Nance, Nensy, Nansy), 1082, 1301, 1478, 1542-1543. *See also Nancy, Nansy Marie.*
Marie Nanet, 1425, 2229
Marie Natalie (Nasalie, Nataly), 1360, 2503, 2544. *See also Marie Asalie.*
Marie Naté (Netty?), 1412
Marie Nette, 2409
Marie Nies, 2246
Marie Nolet, 1994
Marie Odisse, 2545
Marie Olys (Alice?), 2313
Marie Orosil (Auresite?), 2220
Maria Onet (Annette?), 2188
Marie Ortans. *See Marie Hortense.*
Marie Ositte (Osit), 1234, 1572
Marie Palmier, 2496
Marie Palmire, 1449
Marie Pauline (Pallette, Paulett), 1483, 1651, 2044
Marie Pavi, 1101
Marie Pelagie,
  Free, 148
  Slave, 1070, 2305
Marie Perine (Perinne), 1631, 1989, 2033, 2056, 2274, 2523, 2551, 2556, 2586

Marie Phani/Phany. *See Marie Fanny.*
Maria Phelavi. 1661
Marie Phoebe (Phevite), 1080, 1409
Marie Pilar, 1183
Marie Plesans, 1386
Marie Polinere Armesy, 1104
Marie Polonine, 2444
Marie Pompose, 1353, 1361, 1426, 1439, 1517, 2043, 2633
Marie Poupone, 2218
Marie Prudence (Chelette), f.w.c., 1115
Marie Prudence, slave, 1292
Maria Refugia, 2479
Marie Reine (Rine), 1573
Marie Rim (Reine), 2428
Marie Rosalie (Maria Rosaly, Rosalye, Rosely, Rosilia),
  Caddo Indian, 1238
  Free, 1394
  Slave, 1157, 1430, 1524, 1528, 2436
Marie Rose (Maria Rosa, Rosse, Roset),
  Apalache Indian, 664
  Free, 1302
  Slave, 1096, 1119, 1126, 1133, 1399, 1401, 1475, 1525, 1668, 1885, 1953, 2016, 2124, 2218, 2257, 2303-2304, 2329-2330, 2400, 2416, 2491, 2536, 2598-2600
Marie Rose Bave, 2090
Marie Ruquier, 2091
Marie Sallie (Sally, Saly, Salée, Zalye, Salys, Moi. soly), 1168-1176, 1334, 1411, 1469, 2226, 2326, 2376, 2563, 2626
Marie Santon, 1265
Marie Sara, 1187
Marie Sedalis, 2263
Marie Senegar, free Negro, 1780
Marie Sephaly, Apalache Indian, 667
Marie Sidonise (Sadonis, Sidony), 2453, 2467
Marie Severine, 1631
Marie Sidre (Side, Sil), 1216, 1636, 2538
Marie Silvie (Silby, Maria Silva), 1423, 2103
Marie Sirine, 1151, 1170
Marie Sophy, 1111, 1286, 2208
Marie Sosthene, 1661
Marie Souque (Sukie?), 1368
Marie Stephalie, f.m.c., 179
Marie Stephanie (Zephany), slave, 1470
Marie Stephanie Victoire, 1124
Maria Subley Barra, Free Negro. *See Barra, Maria Subley.*
Marie Sukie. *See Marie Souque.*
Marie Surron, 2252

Marie Susanne (Maria Susana, Suset, Susette),
  Apalache Indian, 674
  F.W.C., 2352. *See also Marie Susanne Metoyer.*
  Slave, 1220, 1311, 1347, 1421, 2341, 2525, 2550, 2591. *See also Marie Leset.*
Marie Tecle, 1079
Marie Temply, 2369
Maria Tensa, 2092
Marie Tête, 1927
Marie Thérèse (Maria Teresa, Teresse, Theresse),
  Indian, 305
  F.W.C., 201, 1393, 1422, 1847, *see also Marie Thérèse Coincoin; Marie Thérèse LeComte; Marie Thérèse Metoyer.*
  Slave, 1127, 1138, 1144, 1247, 1251, 1319, 1327, 1425, 1432, 1486, 1491, 1499, 1515, 1556, 1577, 1597, 1599, 1819, 1849, 1939, 1941, 1943, 1976, 2048, 2065, 2092, 2112, 2169, 2175, 2189, 2197, 2240, 2393, 2403, 2417, 2525, 2543, 2548, 2630
Marie Thomas, Apalache Indian, 659
Marie Tilde. *See Marie Mathilde.*
Maria Toni?, 2148
Marie Tranquilline (Tranqueline, Tranquilina, Tranquelin), 1568, 2247
Marie Trenier, 1578
Marie Ursin, 2244
Marie Ursulle, Caddo Indian, 14, 43, 85, 201, 440, 1034, 1815, 1968, 2080
Marie Ursulle (Orsula), slave, 2623
Marie Ursul Urany, 1226
Marie Velem, 2319
Marie Velony. *See Marie Belony.*
Marie Venus, 1399
Marie Victoire (Victoria, Victorine), 1943, 2160, 2414, 2438, 2574
Marie Virginie (Virgine), 1415, 1492
Marie Zelesine (Celestine?), 1679
Marie Zeli. *See Marie Celezi.*
Marie Zeline (Zelin, Zelinne, Zelina), Canneci Indian, 83
  Slave, 1110, 1151, 1232, 1263, 1445, 2407, 2499
Marin, 2469
Marinette, 2056, 2066
Mariotte (Mariott),
  Jacques Rubin, 1656
  Jean Baptiste, 114, 1923

Mariotte (continued),
  Louis Drosin, 2349
  Marie Adelaide "Layde", 114, 1449, 1656, 1923, 2082-2083, 2095, 2301, 2349, 2462-2463, 2560
  Marie Louise, 23, 49, 1450-1451, 1930, 2083?
Marmello (Marmela, Marmelo),
  Apolinario, 393, 489, 500, 1506, 2774
  Aug(ustina?), 2775
  Juan, 742
Marquis. *See Murquiz.*
Mars, free Negro. *See Claude Mars.*
Marte, Apalache Indian, 661-662
Marthe (Marta), 1166, 1168, 1172-1173, 1416, 1515, 1832, 1841, 1899, 1946, 1951, 2233, 2581
Martin, 1382, 1441, 1894
Martin,
  John, 754-755
  José, 1041
  Marie (Dna. Jerome Morel), 2890
  Marie (Mrs. Litch Page Robinson), 797
  Nicolas, 70
Martin (Se)bastien, 1615
Martin Ver, f.m.c., 1160
Martinau, Widow (probably Widow Monet), 1981
Martineau, Joseph François, 2483
Martinez (Marinez, Marttnes),
  Ermenegilde (Esmeregild?), 462, 2647, 2788
  Joseph Dolores, 501, 2656, 2883
  Juana Bautista (Dna. Marcelo Servantes), 874, 1039
  Maria, *hija* Ermenegilde, 2647
  Maria, *hija* Joseph Dolores, 2883
  Maria Albina (Dna. Joseph Luis Gallardo), 2783
  Maria Gavina Josefa Artemisa, 462, 2788
  Maria Trinidad, 501, 2656
Marton, slave, 1686
Mary, slave, 1525
Mary (Merry), slave, 1642
Mary. *See also Marie.*
Massipe (Massip, Massippe, Masippi, Masippe, Masip),
  Dorothée (Mme. Etienne LaCaze) 3, 48
  François, 364
  Jean, 736
  Jean Baptiste, 3, 26, 48, 790, 994, 2660
  Marie Louise (Mme. Jean Renaud Aguesse), 125, 226, 300, 994, 2801
  Marie Louise (Dna. José Maria Castro?) 736

Massipe (Continued),
 Marie Phonisse (Phany), (Mme.
  Jacques LaCaze, 790, 1219
 Marie Rosalie "Rosette," 26, 365
 Pierre I, 26
 Pierre II, 225, 300, 736, 1592,
  2422
 Remy, 2419
 Rosalye, 2419
Mata,
 Juan Joseph, 2884
 Maria Casilda, 2884
 See also Medina.
Matheo, Apalache Indian. See Francisco Matheo.
Matheo Famp, 2426
Matilde, 1423, 1508, 2076, 2107
Matihore, Alphonso, 1550
Maurant, 993. See also Moranti.
Maurice (Moris), 1108, 1236, 1829, 1834, 1861, 1955, 2144
Maxille (Magsil, Magsille), 1202, 2077
Maximin, 1945. See also Julien Moximo (Moreno?).
Maximin (Magsimino) Juannot, 1073
May,
 Juana Baptista, 549
 Maria Magdalena Alexandra, 549
McCarty. See Marcarty, Macarty.
McClellan (Meclelum),
 Dr., 544
 David, 2886
 Joseph David, 2886
 Margaret (Mrs. Samuel Hopkins Sibley), 381, 2920
McFall, E. (Mme. Jean Laplace), 2874
McGlothen. See Negligen.
McGuire. See Magloire.
McKafe, Mahela (Mrs. John Spade), 282
McMichel,
 James, 259
 Sarah, 259
McTyre (Mactier),
 Eugenie, 356
 George, 189, 239, 356, 2885
 Jean (John), 189, 239
 Jean Baptiste, 239
 Marie Louise, 2885
Me____, Françoise, f.w.c., 1391
Mecheon (Mechon),
 Eleysa, 2789
 Jacques (James?), 2789
Meclelum. See McClellan.
Medina,
 José Mario del Pilar Mata, 441

Medina (continued),
 Juan José Mata, 441, 721, 731, 745, 773, 1044, 2257
 Maria Jetrudis (Dna. José Ipolito Dominguez), 448
 See also Mata.
Medrano,
 José Maria, 546
 Maria Genobeva Celeste, 546
Megny,
 Jean, 2882
 Marie Antoinette, 2882
Meilleur, Marie Constance (Mme. F. Landreaux), 413, 2662
Mekam, Famy, 553
Mel, slave, 2077
Melanie (Melony), 2405
Melansont, slave, 2277
Meliana, slave, 1567
Melite, slave, 1320, 2077, 2405. See also Carmelite, Emelite.
Melon. See Mulon.
Mellon, ____, Widow, 1388
Melye, slave. See Emely.
Menchaca,
 Fernando, 870, 2699
 Francisco, 437, 1033
 Manuel, 2887
 Marie, 2887
 Maria Jetrudis (Dna. José Sanchez), 1050
 Maria Josefa (Dna. Juan José Vela), 865
Mendez. See Mindez.
Meneust, Henri, 960
Merchiol,
 Anne (Mme. Pierre Beniol), 781
 François, 781
Mercier (Mercié),
 Charlotte (Mme. Joseph Capuran), 837
 Felicité Adelaïde, 15
 Louis, 15, 61, 817
 Marie Josephe Eulalie (Mme. Manuel Simeon LeVasseur), 15, 61, 808, 826, 965
 See also Messier.
Mere____n, Michel Carlos, 772
Mertil, slave. See Charles Mertil.
Meson Blans, Apalache Indian?, 681
Messier, Maria (Dna. Juan Gomez), 464
Messier. See also De Mézières.
Metoyer (Metoyé, Metoyem, Metoièr, Metoié),
 ____, Sr., 742, 2596
 Adelle, 1162, 2523
 Antoine, 2318

Metoyer (continued),
  Antoine, 2318
  Antoine Joseph, 28, 100, 104, 720-
    721, 816, 956, 973, 1054, 1116,
    1449, 1468, 1653, 1665, 1692-
    1693, 1847, 1887, 2079, 2298,
    2299, 2302-2307, 2317, 2413, 2464
  Arsene, 2615
  Athanase Vienne, 1437, 1547, 2128
  Auguste, *fils* Augustin, 720, 731,
    784-785, 1465, 1474, 1478, 1627,
    2523, 2524
  Auguste Dorestan, 1627, 1697
  Augustin. *See Nicolas Augustin.*
  Augustin Maximin, 1161
  Augustin Predanes, 1116
  Benjamin. *See Francois Benjamin.*
  Catiche (Catisse, Catys), 1691,
    2100, 2404
  Claude Thomas Pierre, 249, 415, 531,
    860, 962, 974, 1027, 1724, 1823-
    1824, 1830, 1832, 1835-1836, 1840,
    1864, 1868-1869, 1873, 1875-1877,
    1885, 1954-1955, 1958-1959, 1991,
    1994, 2010-2013, 2018-2019, 2056,
    2260
  Dominique, 33, 113, 175, 721, 762,
    946, 973, 1054, 1504, 1561, 1654,
    1758, 2086-2087, 2295-2296, 2299-
    2302, 2316-2317, 2412, 2557, 2564-
    2565, 2600
  Dorestan. *See Auguste Dorestan.*
  Felix (Felicien) Benjamin, 530, 1332,
    1542
  François I, 721, 956, 1054, 1162,
    1216, 1450-1453, 1458, 1479-1480,
    1629, 1636, 1644, 1698, 1876, 2028,
    2296, 2316, 2352, 2538
  François II, 1162, 1215, 1452, 2028,
    2512, 2538
  François Benjamin, 531, 729, 777, 788,
    791, 1027, 1038, 1064, 1076, 1181-
    1183, 1305, 1332-1333,1428, 1535-
    1543, 1741, 1958, 2057, 2140-2141,
    2258, 2426, 2430, 2580-2582, 2901
  François Florival, 1396
  François Gassion, 1460, 1462, 1469,
    1472, 1548
  J.B., 2604
  Jean Baptiste Augustin, 720-721, 731,
    773, 784-785, 1045, 1116, 1274,
    1396, 1454, 1464, 1477, 1626,
    1634, 1682, 2028, 2253, 2460, 2509,
    2523
  Jean Baptiste Delores, 1696

Metoyer (continued),
  Jean Baptiste Dominique, 731, 784-785,
    1239-1240, 1504, 1655, 1664, 2087,
    2295, 2511, 2558
  Jean Baptiste Leandre, 2509, 2599
  Jean Baptiste Louis, 731, 785, 1213-
    1214, 1696
  Jean Baptiste Vienne, 1240
  Joseph I. *See Antoine Joseph.*
  Joseph II, 1117, 1153, 1193, 1197,
    1657, 2079
  Joseph Clervil, 1162
  Joseph, 1758
  Joseph Oseme, 2317
  Joseph Valcour, 1697
  Joseph Zenes, 1117
  Lise, 1406
  Louis, 175, 720-721, 956, 1054, 1159,
    1213, 1255-1256, 1273, 1470, 1473,
    1484, 1546-1547, 1634-1641, 1680-
    1681, 1684-1695, 1700, 1985, 2292-
    2294, 2297-2298, 2318, 2464, 2521,
    2596?, 2621
  Margarite, 2557
  Marie, 1193, 1632
  Marie Adelle, 1468, 2307, 2538
  Marie Anaïs, 1626
  Marie Anasthasie, 104
  Marie Aspasie, 1116, 1652, 1657
  Marie Cephalide (Zephaly), 1654
  Marie Celine (Selin), 2316
  Marie Denis, 1653, 1657, 2304
  Marie Elina, 1653
  Marie Elisabeth, 13
  Marie Emely, 1478, 1482
  Marie Glaëe, 1655
  Marie Jeanne (Mme. Jerome Sarpy),
    1621-1622, 1628, 1698
  Marie Julia, 1634
  Marie Liset, 1440
  Marie Louise (Mme. J.B. Florentin
    Conant I), 721, 1116, 1274, 1460,
    1472, 1558-1559, 1632-1633, 2098,
    2253, 2296, 2316, 2524?
  Marie Ozitte, 1305, 1437, 1547, 2614
  Marie Melia, 2558
  Marie Perine, 113, 1655, 1664, 2598,
    2616
  Marie Pompose, (Mme. Charles Nere-
    stan Rocque), 103, 1210, 1463, 1622,
    1624, 1654, 1699, 2295, 2306
  Marie Rose, 1397, 1673, 1985, 2084,
    2099, 2406, 2619
  Marie Silvie (Silby), 1504, 2085, 2302
  Marie Sophie (Sofoi), 1666

Metoyer (continued),
  Marie Susanne, *fille* Antoine Joseph, 29, 816
  Marie Susanne "Susette" C.T.P., 100, 103, 720-721, 773, 785, 1214-1215, 1439, 1477, 1562, 1724, 1745, 1816, 1887, 2028, 2053, 2058, 2293-2294, 2308, 2509, 2524, 2596?, 2597
  Marie Susanne, *fille* Dominique (Mme. J. B. E. Rachal), 23, 762, 1239, 1666, 2298, 2511, 2564, 2616
  Marie Susanne, *fille* Pierre II, 112
  Marie Susanne "Suset", *fille* Augustin (Mme. Elisée Rocques), 1153, 1213-1214, 1274, 1454, 1456, 1464-1466, 1471, 1483, 1548, 1560, 1623, 1625, 1693, 1696, 1700, 2032, 2461
  Marie Susete, *fille* François, 2512
  Marie Thérèse Elisabeth (Mme. Louis Narcisse Prudhomme), 157, 249, 360-361, 502, 974, 1823, 1864, 1877, 2010, 2901
  Maxile (Magsil), 721, 731, 773, 784-785, 1161, 1216, 1450-1451, 1455, 1476, 1626, 1697, 2292, 2522
  Narcisse Dominique, 175, 1240, 2565
  Nicolas Augustin, 23, 103-104, 112, 720-721, 773, 785, 946, 956, 1045, 1153, 1161, 1210, 1217, 1440, 1455-1474, 1548, 1621n, 1622, 1625, 1638, 1641-1643, 1645, 1817, 2032-2033, 2252, 2297, 2300, 2305-2308, 2413, 2460, 2509
  Perip, 2565
  Pierre I. *See Claude Thomas Pierre.*
  Pierre II, 49, 112-113, 731, 784-785, 940, 946, 1044, 1143, 1437, 1481, 1627, 1630, 1648, 1684, 1696, 1754, 1889, 2029, 2061, 2128, 2614-2615
  Pierre III, 2029
  Pierre Neres, 2615
  Pierre Toussaint, 1304, 1431, 1438, 1689, 1304, 1815, 1839, 1959, 2058, 2333, 2461, 2615
  Pierre Victorin, 157, 360, 791, 1130-1133, 1234, 1326, 1864, 2064, 2259, 2431-2432, 2452-2453
  Predanes. *See Augustin Predanes.*
  Susanne, 1662. *See Marie Susanne.*
  Susette, *fille* Catiche, 2100
  Thérèse (Mme. Augustin Cloutier), 1273, 1663

Metoyer (continued),
  Toussaint. *See Pierre Toussaint.*
  Valsain (Balsem), 1745
  Victorin. *See Pierre Victorin.*
Meullion, Ursula (Mrs. William Miller), 637
Mezieres. *See de Mézières.*
Mechamps,
  Eugene, 788
  Jean Eugene, 732, 757, 788, 1650, 2737
Michel (Miguel),
  Apalache Indian. *See Carlos Michel, Susanne Michel.*
  Slave, 1144, 1181, 1223, 1316, 1486, 1645, 1819, 1843, 1902, 1942, 1949, 2031, 2077-2078, 2166, 2187, 2259, 2264, 2295, 2323, 2581-2582. *See J. B. Michel, Valsin Michel, Miguel.*
Michel Angel (Miguel Angeline), 1617
Michel Honoré, 1831
Michel Tensá, Apalache Indian, 669-671, 679
Michel-Zoriche (Zarichi, Zary, Jarri),
  Antoine, 7
  Catherine, 111
  Marie Euphrosine, 213
  Marie Rose (Mme. Sylvestre Rachal), 321, 567, 578, 1032, 2330, 2356, 2910
  Pierre I, 7, 111, 213
  Pierre II, 7, 111, 125, 213, 321, 567, 568, 1032, 1810, 1982, 2329-2330, 2848
  Pierre III, 783, 786, 1292
Mieta,
  Catherine, 2818
  Juan (Jean), 2818
Miguel Angeline, 1617
Miguel, Joseph Cand., 2845
Miliano, 2365-2366
Miller (Millar),
  Emmanuel, 637
  James I, 339, 790
  James John, 339
  Louise, 637
  Marie Dilia, 637
  William (Guillermo), 637
Millie. *See Melye.*
Millikin, _____, 749
Milon. *See Mulon.*
Minda, 2077
Mindez, Maria Guadalupe, 1233
Minoron, Jean Baptiste, 2702
Mobile Indian, 838
Modeste, 1108, 1324, 1489, 1500, 1870, 1962, 2417, 2580

Modeste Marie, 1256
Monet (Monette),
  Jean Baptiste Baltasar, 973, 1928,
    1960, 1981, 2099
  Dorothée, 69-70, 171, 311, 784,
    1253, 2504, 2614?
  Louis, I, 69, 1838
  Louis, I, Widow, 1110, 1924-
    1930, 1981, 2331-2337, 2479-
    2481, 2535, 2561-2562, 2633.
    See also Marie Louise LeComte.
  Louis, *fils* Dorothée, 70, 2332?
  Louis II, 1648, 1838, 2480?
  Marie Louise Adelle (Rachal?),
    69, 1272
  Marie Louise Adeline (Rachal?),
    69, 312, 1272, 2480
  Marie Thérèse Rosalie, 171
Monginot (Mongino, Monsineau),
  _____, Widow, 1746, 1837, 2002,
    2009, 2062
Mons, slave, 2526
Monsineau, slave. *See François
  Monsineau.*
Monsineau, f.m.c. *See Monsineau
  Baden.*
Montalvo, José Simon, 792
Montenary (Montanari),
  Antoin Benoit, 1040, 2696
  Marie Heleine Pompose (Mrs. Da-
    vidson Brown), 97, 148, 262,
    342, 1040, 1492, 2074?, 2158
Montanari, slave, 2074
Montes, Jetrudis (de Oca), (Dna.
  Guillermo Casanova; Dna. Por-
  tuges _____), 931, 1054
Montoya, Jose Pablo, 886
Montpierre, Magdeleine (Mme. J.B.
  Belgarde), 107
Moore, William. *See Moré, Guillom.*
Mora (Morin, Mori, de Mora),
  Estevan, 465, 2790, 2817, 2843,
    2888
  Felipe, 747, 880
  Francisco, 2120
  François, 2817
  Jacinto, 2479
  Jetrudis (Dna. Vitor Rio), 2915
  Jetrudis (Dna. Vital Flores),
    476, 492, 2778
  José Maria, 1107, 2899
  Juan de, 448, 750, 752, 2837
  Lemignon, 1206
  Marie, 2120
  Marie del Carmen, 465, 2790

Mora (continued),
  Maria Josefa (Dna. Santiago Samuel),
    525
  Marie Louise, 2888
  Mariano, 1052
Mora. *See also Moré.*
Morales,
  Alberto, 877
  Juan, 877
  Maria Luisa, 943
Morantine (Moranti, Mauranti),
  Jean Baptiste I, 993
  Jean Baptiste II, 993, 2791, 2889
  Juan Bautista Da., 2791
  Marie Clotilde, 2889
Moré (More),
  _____, Mr., 1661
  Guillon (William?), 1228
Moreau (Maurau), *See also Morin, Mora.*
  Alexis, 1061.
  François, 1061
  Marie Vangile (Mme. Jean Baptiste
    Morantine I), 993
Morel,
  Jerome, 2890
  Marie Sara, 2890
Moriah. *See Marie Moraya.*
Morier, Jeann Louis, 2732
Morin,
  Alexy, 2731.
  Baptiste, 321
  Jean Baptiste, 968
  Jean Marie, 968
  Mal., 791
  Marie Zeline, 321
  See also Mora, Moreau.
Moris, slave, 2613. *See also Maurice.*
Morphil. *See Murphy.*
Morvant (Morban),
  François, 408
  Marie Antoinette, 408
  Marie Euphrosine, 185
Moses, slave. *See François Moses.*
Mounneron, Jean, 89.
Mounion. *See Mourion.*
Mourion (Mounion?), Widow, 2012
Mozar (Mauzard), Marie Elisabeth (Mme.
  François Briand), 452, 685
Mulon (Melon, Mellon, Milon),
  François Maurice, 973, 1078, 1159-
    1160, 1495, 1691, 2029, 2085, 2557
  Louis, 1159
  Marie Arthemise (Mme. François Me-
    toyer), 1054, 1162, 1395?, 1458,
    1621?

Mulon (continued),
  Marie Felicité, 1395
  Victoire, 1054, 1388
Muños, Antoinette (Dna. Juan Manuel de Porcuna), 967
Murphy (Morphil, Morphy, Murphil),
  Edouard, 96, 504, 954, 978, 1016, 1705, 1721, 1730, 1826-1827, 1840, 1875, 1879, 1954, 1961, 2879
  Edouard, Widow, 1095, 1346, 1405, 1491, 1515, 1599, 1763, 1767, 1799, 2043, 2074, ?2189, 2190, 2525. *See also Marie Elisabeth Josephe Buard.*
  Edouard Cesaire, 154, 233, 235, 333, 503-504, 506, 727-728, 742, 744, 780, 983, 1016, 1063-1064, 1111, 1236, 1705, 1721, 1860, 2037, 2073, 2143, 2189?, 2585
  Marie Aspasie, 1859
  Marie Elisabeth Aspasie (Mme. Arnaud Lauve), 154, 324, 503, 904, 978
  Marie Françoise Eugenie (Mme. Louis Joseph Tauzin), 235, 2064, 2073, 2757
  Marie Teresa, 2189
Murquiz, Juaquim, 882
Murray,
  _____, 767
  Francis William, 346, 460
Musgrove, Lidy (Mrs. Samuel Reed), 96

Nachus, Caddo Indian, 408
Nafry. *See Noffre.*
Naget, Marie (Mrs. Harrison Ystor), 2935-2936
Naqueney, Caddo Indian, 407
Nahueriet, Natchitoches Indian, 143, 960
Nancy (Nansy), 2102, 2108, 2239, 2387-2389, 2502
Nanet, Apalache Indian, 657
Nanet (Nanette, Nano, Annette), 1171, 1318, 1370, 1410, 1540, 1544, 1669, 1902, 2018, 2181, 2187, 2204, 2258, 2271, 2344, 2374, 2514, 2594? *See also Anne.*
Nanny, slave. *See Neni.*
Nararrete, Maria de la Luz (Dna. Ignacio Peña), 872
Narcisse (Narcis, Narcise, Narciso), 1342, 1595, 1908, 2003, 2475, 2499 *See also Julien Marie Narcisse.*

Natchez, 1912-1913
Natchitoches Indians, 138-139, 143, 1211
Navarro, Maria Martina, 2719
Ned (Nete), 2367. *See also Faustin Ned, Francois Nette.*
Negligen (McGlothen),
  Joseph Gregory (Grey), 591
  Michel, 590
  Moris, 590-591
Nelson, Elisabeth (Isabel), 489
Nenchase, Caddo Indian, 1237
Neni, slave, 1565
Neuman, François, 242
Neuville (Nevil), 1681. *See also Francois Neuvill.*
Newman. *See Neuman.*
Nicolas, free Negro. *See Docla, Nicolas.*
Nicolas, slave, 1133, 1503, 1549, 1889, 2049, 2061, 2108, 2245, 2549, 2552. *See also Carlos Nicolas, François Nicolas, Louis Nicolas, Margarite Nicolase, Marie Louise Nicolas.*
Nicolas Apalas, Indian, 675
Nicolas Balien, 1265
Nicolas Capitan, Indian, 2394
Nicolas Celestin, 1283
Nicolas La Palaches, 678
Nina, slave. *See Neni.*
Nivette (Nivet), Francisca, 785, 1777
Noel (Nuel), 1289, 1491, 1957, 2048, 2135, 2161, 2546. *See also Jean Noel, Joseph Noel, Manuel.*
Noffre (Nafry), Adelle, 1320
Nolasco, Apalache Indian, 672. *See Pierre Nolasco Benge*
Noret, slave, 1324, 1409, 1412
Norris (Nores, Nover),
  Marie Juliena (Mrs. William Querk), 500, 2774
  Nathaniel, 770
  Samuel, 768
  Susanne, 757
Noyrit (Norit, Norys), Charles, 336, 452, 742, 750, 787, 796, 999, 1000, 1004-1010, 1015, 1017, 1024-1025, 1105, 1286-1290, 1355, 1521, 2850
Nuel. *See Noel.*
Nugent? *See Naget.*
Nuñez, Maria Josefa (Dna. Francisco Arocha), 1043

Obday?, Marie Josephine (Dna. Juan Joseph Mata, 2884

O'Conor (C'Connor, Oconó)
  Henry, 553
  James, 553
  Loreta Julie (Mme. Remy Christy), 1031
  Pierre (Pedro), 1031
Odisse, slave, 1398-1399
Ohut, slave, 1504
Olday?, Marie Josephine (Dna. Juan Joseph Mata), 2884
Olié. See Holié.
Olivie, Marie (Mme. Jean Couti), 115, 165, 173
Olfenau, Clara, 1281
Olive, slave, 1092
Oliver. See Jean Baptiste Olier.
Olivier (Olivié),
  Anne (Mme. Jean Lugue), 968
  François, 1859
  José, 409
  Perine (Mme. Jean Renaud Aguesse), 364-365, 994
O'Neal (Onil),
  Agusto, I, 629, 633
  Agusto II, 633
  See also Chaconil.
Onesime. See Louis Onezime.
Onye, slave, 1402
Orosco, Maria Jetrudis (Dna. Alberto Morales), 877
Ortiz (Hortis, Hortiz, Ortis),
  Antoine, 2871
  Faustino, 1319, 2785, 2871
  Guillaume?, 494
  Maria del Pilar, 494
  Nasario, 1306
Osilinue, _____ (Dna. Toussaint Sinegal), 919
Ositte, slave, 2056
Ovid, slave. See Aovidon.
Ovil, slave. See Bensan Ovil
Owens, Susana (Mrs. Worner Harmon), 489

P_____y, slave, 1651
Pablo. See Paul.
Pacalé, Yves dit, 1776
Padilla,
  Augustin, 2892
  Josef Antonio, 2892
  Maria (Dna. Joseph Procella), 2898
  Maria, 2477
  Maria Estefania, 679
  Maria Lina, 2588, 2809
  Maria Petra, 467, 2807, 2918?

Paillette (Palliet, Paillet, Pallete),
  Elise Victoire, 487
  George. See Marie Pierre Jorge.
  Germin Spartratte?, 780
  Jean Baptiste Jacques, 233-234, 243, 304, 346, 487, 504, 727, 744, 777, 780, 844, 953, 970, 972, 1025, 1047, 1727-1728, 1865, 1955, 1962, 1997, 1999, 2037-2038, 2057, 2272, 2559
  Jean Jacques William, 346, 2057
  José, 234
  Marie Pierre Jorge, 233, 487, 780, 953, 2037
  Pierre, 2154
  Tranquelline Susanne, 233, 2037
Paissant, Marie Magdelinne (Mme. Etienne Deterville), 1051
Palie, slave, 2519
Palier, Apalache Indian. See Atanasio Palier.
Paloma, Josefa, 463, 2796
Palvado (Palvados),
  Adelayde (Mme. Valery ____), 730
  Carmelita, 1265
  François, 56
  Jean Baptiste, 1, 2762
  Jean François, 1, 56, 262, 982, 1013, 1043, 2762
  Marie, 56
  Marie Adelise, 262, 473
  Marie Josephe, 384, 982, 1013, 1435
  Marie Norin (Dna. Juan Nepomuceno Arocha), 1043
Pancho, Apalache Indian. See François Pancho.
Pannelle, Ant., 2613, 2623
Pantaleon. Dit of Hissoura.
Paret, Jacques, 184
  Laigné 184
Pasiano (Pasano), Maria Asseni, 1570
Pastio, Marie Adelayde, 566
Patience (Pacians), 2477
Patton, Marie (Mrs. Wm. Harris), 2868-2869
Paul (Pablo), 1099, 1171, 1265, 1268, 1290, 1454, 1462, 2077, 2183, 2577
  See also Pierre Paul, Pierre Paul Basil, Pierre Paul Ana.
Paul, Jacques, 766
Pauline, 1708. See also Polinne.
Pavi, Marie, 1101
Pavie,
  _____, Mrs. 251
  Charles Roque, 975, 988-989, 1105, 1521, 2092, 2124, 2869

Pavie (Continued),
  Etienne, 13, 134, 860
  Heleine. *See Marie Louise Heleine Euphrosine.*
  Jean Baptiste, 975
  Jean Baptiste Etienne, 809
  Jean Charles, 134, 177, 203, 280, 370, 375
  Joseph, 1716, 1856
  Marie Louise Heleine Euphrosine, (Mme. Marie Attanasse Poissot), 13, 134, 742, 1018
Payne, slave. *See Joseph Pain.*
Pelagie,
  Canneci Indian, 159
  F.W.C., 58, 148. *See also Marie Pelagie LeCourt.*
  Slave, 1215, 1605, 1715, 1874, 2056, 2077, 2132, 2135, 2148-2149, 2162, 2456, 2504, 2608
Peña (Pena, Pina),
  Ignacio, 872
  Maria Paula (Dna. Juan José Alamillo), 524, 923
Peoro, 2190
Peper, Agata (Mme. Antoine Coton-Maïs), 2461
Peralta, Maria Aroy (Dna. José Luis de la Bega), 2690
Peralta, Rita, 2109
Peré,
  Luc, 952
  Antoine, 952
Pereau (Perau, Perraut, Perot, Peraut, Pereaut, Peraux, Perrot, Piero, Pero, Perrault),
  _____, *fils*, 1042
  _____ne (Mme. François Scopini), 735
  Arcène. *See Marie Aurore Arcene.*
  Casimir. *See Remy Casimir*
  Celestin. *See Jean Celestin Faustin.*
  Charles, 739
  Crisostomé. *See Jean Crisostomé.*
  Damas B., 2791
  Dorothée. *See Marianne Dorothée.*
  Emely (Emé), 1286, 2606
  Euphrosine, 341
  Euresime, 356
  Faustin. *See Jean Celestin Faustin.*
  Felicité (Mme. Jean Pierre Grappe), 739
  Felicité. *See also Marie Felicité Crisostomé.*
  François I, 52, 57, 105, 180, 205
  François II, 75, 237, 287, 735, 756, 941, 955, 963, 971, 1014, 1518, 2020-2021, 2781

Pereau (continued),
  François III, 1659
  François *fils* Louis I, 2793
  François *fils* Louis II, 469
  Jean II, 722, 733, 739-740
  Jean Baptiste, 183, 735, 1049, 1225, 1349, 2126, 2577
  Jean Celestin Faustin, 371, 1012, 1204, 2792, 2894
  Jean Chrisostome, 105, 132, 180, 245, 855, 950, 1009, 1012, 1018, 1029
  Jean François Crisostomé, 245, 732, 2158
  Jean François Crisostomé *fils* Jean, 245
  Jean Louis, 2792
  Jeanne Reine, 245, 436, 478, 480, 521, 1360, 1986, 2782, 2893?
  Joseph Crisostomé, 290, 481, 690, 1029, 2131, 2606, 2820
  Joseph Victor, 690, 2820
  Julien, 740
  Leonard Faustin, 371
  Louis Derzilen, 237, 469, 739, 1014, 2607, 2733, 2893
  Marianne Dorothée (Mme. Jacques Cristy), 960, 1002, 1031
  Marie, 99, 285, 286
  Marie A., 2766
  Marie Aimée (Mme. J. B. Theodore Grillet), 140, 288, 290, 455, 1009
  Marie Aurore Arcine, 180, 855
  Marie Catherine Marcelite (Mme. J. B. Theodore Grillet), 205, 237, 434, 484, 971, 1852, 2722
  Marie Celine, 2894
  Marie de l'Incarnation (Mme. Julien Besson), 848, 955
  Marie Felicité Crisostomé (Mme. Antoine Grillet), 57, 65, 75, 76, 132, 216, 290, 359, 372, 430, 497, 686, 950
  Marie Jeanne Narcisa, 481
  Marie Josephe (Mme. Gaspard Derbanne II), 57, 854, 963, 1024, 1026
  Marie Louis, Sieur, 2074, 2828
  Marie M., 2820
  Marie Magdeleine (Mme. Jean Louis Vascocu), 52, 205, 286-287, 787, 862, 1038
  Marie Marcelinte, 105, 690, 2446, 2894?
  Marie Melanie, 2893
  Marie Modeste, 481
  Marie Zephelin, 688
  Remy, 178, 787, 1230
  Remy Casimir I, 396, 688, 1018, 1231, 1248, 1511, 2575

Pereau (continued),
  Remy Casimir I, Widow, 1573
  Remy Casimir II, 396
  Titis (Tete), 1852
Perez,
  Francisco, 2701
  Juan de dios, 751, 757, 782
  Juana, 2701
Perine (Perin, Perrine), 1132, 1326, 1355, 1367, 1581, 1583-1584, 2056, 2431, 2516. *See also Eleonore Perine.*
Pesebant?, J., 1051
Pessinne, slave, 1089
Phanor, slave. *See Louis Phaneau.*
Phanye, slave. *See Fanny.*
Philibert (Philivert, Filibert, Pheliber, Philiver, Phibbert, Phibert),
  Augustin, 991
  Augustin Gilbert, 460, 2645
  Caroline, 2653
  Gaspart, 259, 325, 460, 492, 745, 756, 991, 2645, 2653, 2895
  Maria, 903
  Marie Caroline, 378
  Marie Clo, 2895
  Marie Ophelie, 325
Philipe (Felipe, Philippe), 1544, 1600, 1608, 1688, 2051, 2056, 2182, 2383, 2389, 2514
Philippe Daunois, f.m.c., 973
Philipot, Thérèse (Mme. Ignace Mailloux), 18, 74, 189, 194, 239, 933
Philippe, Marie Euphrosine, 84
Phoebe (Phebie, Phequi, Phevi), 1329-1331, 1642-1643, 1645
Picard, Marie Anne (Mme. Jacques Botien *dit* St. André I), 51, 121-122
Piedferme?, Ignace (Leger *dit*), 2588
Pierat, Magdeleine (Mme. Jean Charles Gause), 820
Piernas,
  Augustin, 1753, 2127, 2275-2276
  Josephe Augustine, 2127
  Marie Nanet, 1753
Pierre (Pier, Pedro),
  Apalache Indian. *See Jean Pierre.*
  Apalache Indian, 675
  Canneci Indian, 43
  F.M.C., 1939, 1941, 2034, 2056
  Slave, 1075, 1083, 1125, 1147, 1157, 1190, 1197, 1207, 1221, 1224, 1229, 1244, 1253, 1268, 1299, 1328, 1344, 1349, 1448, 1512, 1519, 1581, 1596, 1614, 1620, 1635, 1651, 1725, 1736,

Pierre (continued),
  1821, 1823, 1901, 1927, 1933, 1941-1943, 1945, 1947, 1954, 1975, 1984, 1989-1990, 2035-2036, 2049-2050, 2056, 2066, 2072, 2077, 2119, 2148, 2150, 2164, 2171, 2173, 2231, 2239, 2271-2272, 2327-2331, 2365, 2437, 2441, 2450, 2501, 2504, 2527, 2529, 2566, 2573, 2587, 2592. *See also Julien Jean Pierre*
Pierre Andreson, 1502, 2422
Pierr Briset, 1250
Pierre Capitaine, Canneci Indian, 1970
Pierre Digne, 2476
Pierre Ely, 2486
Pierre Joseph (Pedro Jose), 2130
Pierre Joseph Prince, 1726
Pierre Louis, 1227
Pierre Noel, 2001
Pierre Nolasco Benge, 672
Pierre Paul, 1069, 1307, 1882, 2568
Pierre Paul Ana, 1101
Pier Paul Basil, 1099
Pierre Tensa, Apalache Indian, 676-677
Pierro, Apalache Indian. *See Susanne Pierro.*
Pierrot (Pieró), 1784
Pievert, Marianne (Mme. Jean Baptiste Besson?), 435
Pina. *See Peña.*
Pindro, Ale?, 2736
Pinsouneau,
  François, 1041
  Marie Asencion, 527
  Toussaint, 527, 1041
Plaisance (Plasencia, Plesons, Plesanns),
  Bertrand, 20, 79, 88, 94, 202, 215, 236, 434, 436, 445, 550, 795, 1024, 2485, 2776?, 2891, 2902
  Céline. *See Marie Louise Céline.*
  Edouard, 79
  Faustin. *See Jean Baptiste Faustin.*
  Isaac, 1102
  Jacques, 1986
  Jean Baptiste, 1, 20, 79, 202, 349, 430, 1013, 2119, 2749?, 2762?
  Jean Baptiste Faustin, 20
  Jean Baptiste François, 430
  Jean Baptiste Marguerita, Sieur, 445, 1013
  Marguerite Lise, 445
  Marie Felicité, 2891
  Marie Louise Céline (Mme. Germain/Gervais? Trichel), 202, 2747
  Marie Leucile "Lucie" (Mme. J. B. Derbanne), 683, 1024, 2020, 2776

Plaisance (continued),
  Marie Silvie (Silbye), 348
  Roque Isidore, 436
  Richard, 2749
  Susanne, 683, 1860, 2891
Plo____, Miguel, 881
Poirrier (Poiriet, Poirier, Pearia, Paurriere, Pouarret, Povarrier),
  ____, (Mrs. Samuel Norris), 770
  Anne, 605
  Antoine, 273
  Bersy (Betsy?), 650
  Catherine (Mme. Wm. Berzot), 1047
  Curany? Laurent, 517, 2819
  François I, 272-273, 517-518, 957, 2775, 2819
  François II, 272
  J____, 770
  Jeanne, 649
  Joseph, 614, 617, 638
  Juny, 2381
  Laurent. *See Curany Laurent.*
  Marianne (Mrs. Robin Chaguet), 614, 635-636
  Marie (Mme. François Dorcin Rachal), 605, 678
  Marie Josephine, 617
  Rose, 614
  Vincent, 957
Poirrier. *See also Paret.*
Poissot (Poisot, Puesau, Puaso, Pueso, Puesot, Poisont),
  ____, Mlle., 1740
  Antoine, 97
  Athanase I, 13, 134, 2112, 2118, 2155
  Athanase II. *See Marie Athanase.*
  Athanase (I or II), 1096-1098
  Denize (De Neige), 304
  Damascene. *See Marie Delphine Damascene.*
  Firmin. *See Marie Firmin.*
  Jacques Victor, 2896
  Jean Baptiste Damas, 187
  Manuelle, 233
  Marcelite, 187, 296, 1738, 2037, 2270
  Marcelitte, *fille* Paul, 367
  Marie Agnes (Mme. Augustin Metoyer), 103, 720-721, 1161, 1210, 1470, 1479, 1557, 1625, 1634, 1689, 1698, 2032-2033
  Marie Anne (Mme. Jacques Jacob Lambre) 62-63, 108, 128-129, 191
  Marie Athanase, 13, 134, 396, 742, 1018, 1139, 1141, 1516, 2440, 2527, 2528, 2530

Poissot (continued),
  Marie Celine. *See Marie Zeline.*
  Marie Delphine, 13
  Marie Damascene Delphine (Mme. Casimir Pereau), 396, 1018
  Marie Euphrosine, 97, 1258
  Marie Firmin (male), 13, 688, 742, 2674
  Marie Françoise (Mme. J. B. Brevel II) 37, 55, 66, 80-81, 109, 136, 146, 186, 198, 209, 847, 961, 966
  Marie Louise, 188, 727
  Marie M___ite (Mme. Leon Bruno T<u>ot</u>in?) 756
  Marie Marcelitte (Mme. F. Landreaux), 744
  Marie Merandi, 36
  Marie Victoire, *fille* Athanase, 134
  Marie Victoire (Mme. Jean Denis Buart; Mme. Jean Jacques Paillette), 8, 233, 346, 487, 504, 742, 780, 806, 812, 844, 953, 1016, 1851, 2037, 2057
  Marie Zeline, 689, 1285
  Paul, 36, 187, 243, 304, 367, 744, 836, 959, 1998, 2896
  Remy II, 8, 36, 97, 187-188, 233, 243, 487, 858, 953, 2037
  Roques Remy Silvestre, 13, 194, 422, 1398-1399, 1576?
  Sylvestre, 243, 411, 2795
Polerie, slave, 1534
Polierre, Antonio, 532
Polinau, slave. *See Marie Genevieve Polinair.*
Polinne, slave, 1105
Polonio, slave, 1089
Polonio, Indian. *See Joseph Polonio.*
Pomier (Pommier, Pomié),
  Anne Barbe (Mme. Michel Chelettre), 45, 153, 204
  Euphrosine, (Mrs. James Miller), 111, 339
  Felicité (Mme. Pierre Delouche), 339, 789, 1115, 1218, 2541, 2814
  Jacques, 2541-2542
  Jean, 789, 1872
  Louis, 339
Pompey, slave. *See Jean Pompey; Jean Baptiste Pompey.*
Pompone, 2222. *See also Poupone.*
Pompose, f.w.c., 1610
Pompose, slave, 1290, 1608, 2191
Pompose Celeste Cayacac, 2443
Pontieu (Ponthieu),
  Alexandre I, 716, 2673

Ponthieu (continued),
  Alexandre II, 2673
  Eduardo, 700, 2897
Porcuna (de Porcuna, Nolasco de Porcuna, Porcunne),
  Juan Manuel, 967
  Marie Agathe, 388, 2400
  Marie Florentine, 2483
  Pierre, 388, 569, 672, 764, 967, 1164, 1293, 1566, 2394-2402, 2482-2483
  Pierre, Widow, 1443-1444. *See also Marie Madeleine La Berry.*
Porter, James (Jacques) F., 332, 764, 1445
Posos, Maria Albina (Dna. Francisco Vimenes), 526, 2707
Poupone (Popona, Pouponne), 1898, 1905, 2049
Poupoun, Me. Angelle, 759
Prado (Prada),
  José, 439
  Joseph Martin, 751
  Maria Antonia, 439
  Maria Martina (Dna. Francisco Cardena), 751, 2663, 2664
  Martin, 782
Prevot,
  Jean, 799
  Louis, 799
Prince, 2457. *See also Pierre Joseph Prince*
Procella (Procela),
  Jacinta, 2837
  Jean Baptiste. *See Juan Bautista.*
  José, 2743
  Joseph, 2898
  José (Juan?) Felix, 2768
  José Dionisio, 679
  Joseph Maria, 741, 2477, 2899
  Joseph Polycarpe, 2899
  Juan, 757, 1052
  Juan Bautista, 752, 776, 768, 2768, 2823, 2888
  Juana (Dna. Josef Antonio Padilla), 2892
  Louis, 476, 2778
  Maria, 1507
  Maria A. (Dna. Manuel Menchaco), 2887
  Maria Antonia? (Dna. José Malbourge?) 741
  Maria del Pilar (Dna. Rosalina Alamillo), 1048
  Maria Jetrudis (Dna. Jose Maria Cortinas), 488, 688, 1106, 2772, 2822

Procella (continued),
  Maria Ignacia (Dna. José Flores), 776, 2752
  Maria Petra, 2898
  Pedro, 1106
  Trinidad, 2815-2816
Prou (Pru, Prout),
  Antonio, 748
  Manuel, 776, 1580
  Marie Carmelite, 1580
  Maria Guadalupe (Dna. José Luis de la Bega), 748, 2690
Provot,
  Henry I, 89
  Henry II, 89
  Henry III, 89
Prudard (Prudhomme?), Franca., 2130
Prudence (Proudans, Prudencia, Prudans), 1081, 1253, 2627
Prudhomme (Prudeaon, Pruddeau, Proudhomme),
  _____, 729, 780
  _____, Sieur, 980, 1053
  _____, *fils*, 1046
  Ami, 2609
  Antoine, 62, 108, 130, 191, 250, 337, 548, 729, 811, 962, 974, 980, 1207, 1347, 1408-1415, 1544, 1701, 1903-1905, 2048, 2162-2176, 2393
  Antoine Neuville, 62, 1408, 1418
  Azelie. *See Marie Henriette Azelie.*
  Bastien, 78, 951. *See also Jacques Bastien.*
  Clarisse?, 1701
  Delphine?, 1701
  Desirée. *See Marie Anne Desirée.*
  Dominique, 128
  Eloiza, 2456
  Emanuel, 251, 254, 361, 824, 953, 962, 974, 1046, 1165-1180, 1310-1311, 1426, 1829, 1832, 1874, 1890-1902, 1957, 2002, 2049, 2179-2188, 2583-2584
  Euphrasine, 1267
  François, 231, 269, 385, 734, 1022, 1028, 1267, 1403.
  Gabriel, 255
  Jacques Bastien, 1718
  Jean Baptiste (identity uncertain), 1701
  Jean Baptiste I, 62-63, 108, 128-129, 191, 211
  Jean Baptiste *fils* Antoine, 108
  Jean Baptiste *fils* Bastien, 78, 231, 423, 426, 951, 2900
  Jean Baptiste *fils* Emanuel, (cont'd)

Prudhomme (continued),
129, 191, 253-255, 502, 962, 1114,
1155-1156, 1361, 1421, 1514, 1517,
1565, 2050, 2192-2193, 2427-2428,
2548-2551
Jean Baptiste, *fils* Pierre Sebastien?
749, 1263, 1530
Jean Emanuel, 254
Jean Jacques, 2164
Joseph Jean Baptiste, 78
Louis, 108
Louis Narcisse, 249, 360-361, 502,
742, 974, 1016, 1324-1325, 1563-
1564, 2148-2153, 2207-2212, 2454-
2458, 2529, 2901
Louis Narcisse II, 249
Louise Euphrosine, 269, 2798, 2926
Magdeleine (Mme. Pierre Rublo), 421-
422, 798
Marguerite Bastien, 430
Marguerite Victoire (Mme. Pierre Tristant, Mme. Etienne Ternier *dit* Grenoble, Mme. Pierre Durranton), 868
Marie, identity uncertain, 729
Marie (Mme. Joseph Valentin), 394,
2111
Marie Adele (Mme. Jean Baptiste Le Comte), 108, 502, 1046, 2220, 2468
Marie Adeline, 108, 2048, 2468
Marie Aglae, 360
Marie Anne Desirée (Mme. Jean François Hertzog), 108, 128, 250, 337, 354,
548, 685, 736, 750?, 980, 1413,
2163
Marie Antoinette, 250, 1415
Marie Cephalide, 361
Marie Deneige (Mme. Timothé Adlé),
1022, 2765
Marie Emelie, 2900, 2926?
Marie Henriette Amire Azelie, 191,
1470?, 2164
Marie Louise (Mme. F. Rouquier I),
78, 289, 374, 400, 451, 464, 975,
988-989, 1005
Marie Marguerite (Mrs. David Case),
5, 200, 232, 295, 379, 945, 2006
Marie Modeste (Mme. Andres Adlé),
442, 1028, 1402
Marie Pompose (Mme. Jean Pierre Dolet),
750, 1262, 2798
Marie Rosalie, 426
Marie Thérèse, 2901
Marie Thérèse Victoire (Mme. Joseph Valentin), 129, 2110, 2927
Marie Virginie, 502

Prudhomme (continued),
Narcisse. *See Louis Narcisse.*
Phanor. *See Pierre Phanor.*
Pierre, 251
Pierre Phanor, 454, 2456
Susanne (Mme. Remi Lambre), 63, 128-
129, 211, 252-253, 264, 454, 531,
548, 791, 933, 970, 1027
Susanne "Suzette" (Mme. Bernard Theophile Lafon), 729, 1408, 2484
Susanne Desirée, 1701
Valsin, 1701
Victoire. *See Marguerite Victoire.*

Queenie?, slave. *See Guiny.*
Querk (Quirk, Cuerca),
Anne Marie (Mrs. Thomas Chenoweth),
2843
Guillermo (William), 500, 2774
Henry (Enrique), 500, 2774
Quierry (Queri, Querry, Thierry, Kerry),
Adeline, 1554
Antoine, 9, 71, 157
Jean Baptiste Narcisse, 71
Marie Adeline, 157
Marie Aspasie, 9
Pierre, 9, 71, 157
Quinnelty. *See Conelty, Coreltine.*
Quesada,
José Cayetano, 484, 2902
José Manuel, 2902
Juan Fermin, 484
Quete (Kitty?), female slave, 2367
Quieto, slave. *See Jean Baptiste Quieto.*
Quin (Guin?),
_____ Widow (Mda. Ve.), 1100, 1282
Ana Maria, 496
Charles Antoine, 2903
Miguel (Michel), 496, 2903

Rabalais (Rabalé, Raballé),
Anne Barbe, 16
Joseph I, 16, 64, 163, 1004
Joseph II, 16, 64, 163, 309, 562
Joseph III, 163
Margueritte (Mme. Pierre Charnau II)
310, 1004, 1446
Marie Celeste, 64
Marie Pesin, 562
Marie Rose, 309
Placide, 16
Rachal (Raichal, Richal, Rachalle),
_____, 715

Rachal (continued),
Agathe, 357, 386
André. *See Joseph Maurice André.*
Andresse, 2422
Antoine I, 170, 271, 308, 577, 763, 794, 1017, 1032, 1086, 1978-1980, 2356-2360, 2362, 2470-2472
Antoine I (Widow, 1086. *See also Marie L. LeMoine.*
Antoine II, 794, 1085, 2357
Antoine, identity uncertain, 2910, 2935
Antoine Barthelemy, 55, 152, 959, 995, 2808
Antoine Neres, 1655, 1673, 2511
Aselie. *See Euphrosine Aselie.*
Athanase, 769
Aurore, 344
Barthelemy I, 55, 59, 65, 152, 198-199, 236, 995
Barthelemy II, 59, 152, 215, 786, 911, 948, 961, 1053, 2071, 2271
Barthelemy, Widow, 1147, 1318, 1668, 1669, 1770, 1791, 1795, 1841, 2243-2246, 2370, 2436, 2627, 2640 *See also Marie Magdeleine Grillet.*
Barthelemy, identity uncertain, 84, 436, 1037, 1858
Barthelemy. *See also Antoine Barthelemy; Bernard Barthelemy; Louis Barthelemy.*
Bernard Barthelemy, 68, 1444, 1566, 1934
Clément, 1425
Clément. *See also Théodore Clément.*
Cyprien Julien, 786, 1503
Dominique, 65, 199, 236, 732, 950, 971, 1113, 2122-2123, 2199-2201, 2433, 2450
Edouard, 55
Elisabeth (Dna. Jerome Hernandez), 50, 1835, 1862, 2811-2812
Emanuel, 61, 82, 133, 363, 727, 982, 1085, 1295, 1299, 2359, 2471, 2891
Etienne, *fils* J. B. B., 386
Etienne, *fils* Jacques?, 311, 483, 1272, 2354, 2562, 2622, 2794
Euphrosine Aselie (Mme. Cyprien Julien Rachal), 152, 300, 786, 2243?, 2908
François Dorcin), 605, 678, 1272, 2811
François, 1272
François Ursin, 1272
Hilaire, 344, 386, 773, 1053, 2904

Rachal (continued),
Hilaire Valier, 699, 2904
Honorine, 215
Jacques, 51, 121-122
Jacques Eloy, 65
Jean Baptiste *fils* J. B. Julien), 2907
Jean Baptiste Barthelemy I, 26, 55, 167, 198, 253, 386, 731, 762, 842, 973, 1000, 1037, 1056, 1592-1593, 1921-1922, 1974, 2084-2085, 2414, 2511, 2558?
Jean Baptiste Barthelemy II, 699, 1000, 2414, 2904
Jean Baptiste Barthelemy, Madame, 2424
Jean Baptiste Bolivar, 1666
Jean Baptiste d'Espallier, 762, 1239, 1666, 2085, 2099, 2534, 2564, 2616
Jean Baptiste Julien, 303, 2907
Jean Bill., 2908
Jean Joseph, 51, 313
Jean Louis, 2087
Jeanne, 2811
Joseph, 2395, 2399
Joseph Maurice André, 483, 2794
Julien I, 37, 83, 786, 938, 983, 1001, 1017, 1023, 1025
Julien II, 265, 302, 344, 697-698, 983, 1312-1313, 2003, 1998, 2905-2906
Louis I, 37, 39, 67-68
Louis II, 39, 813, 835
Louis *fils* Louis Barthelemy, 428, 508, 1008, 1431, 2908
Louis III, 39
Louis, identity uncertain, 194, 220, 1678, 2070, 2078
Louis, *fils* Julien II, 265
Louis Barthelemy, 193, 235, 428, 996, 1006, 1008, 1327, 2197-2198, 2546-2547, 2715
Louis Barthelemy *fils* Louis, 68, 794, 995
Louis Gacion, 2910
Louis Julien, 332, 1001, 2909
Louis Raymond, 2909
Louis Simeon, 67, 1445, 2346, 2396, 2400
Louis Solastie, 763, 1086, 2470
Louise, 17
Ludger, 59, 1593
Manette (Mme. Narcisse Rachal), 1017, 1299, 2353, 2360, 2909
Manuel. *See Emanuel.*

Rachal (continued)
  Marcela, 605
  Marie, identity uncertain, 67, 313
  Marie, *fille* Marie Louise, 2718
  Marie Adele, 1164, 1444, 2471
  Marie Adelaïde (Mme. Jean Baptiste Dominique Metoyer), 731, 1240, 1655, 2128, 2406, 2558
  Marie Adelaïde (Adele), (Mme. Pierre Michel-Zoriche), 37, 783, 1292
  Marie Arthemise, 1858, 2197
  Marie Aselie (Esely), *fille* J. B. d'Espallier), 2616
  Marie Aselie, *fille* Louis, 508
  Marie Aspasie (Astasie, etc), f.w.c., 1240, 1397, 1921
  Marie Ausite (Ozite, etc.), (Mme. F. Roubieu), 431, 1025, 2425, 2916-2917
  Marie Céline, 311
  Marie Sidalise, 1239, 2084
  Marie Clysin (Elysin?), 698, 2905
  Marie (del) Pilar, 1671
  Marie Dolet, 966
  Marie Elise, 428
  Marie Emelie, 1595, 2250, 2370
  Marie Euphrosine (Mme. J. B. Chelette), 35, 94, 152, 220, 402, 485, 1006, 2651, 2777
  Marie Euphrosine (Mme. Michel Derbanne), 2659
  Marie Françoise (Mme. Louis Derbanne), 59, 80, 109, 2812
  Marie Jacob (Mme. André St. André), 51, 121-122, 1035
  Marie Josephe, 107, 313
  Marie Josephe Melanie, 32, 39, 66, 89, 835, 1841
  Marie Lana (Laura?), 485, 2777
  Marie Lolette (Mme. Pierre Sebastien Compere), 186, 265, 332, 687, 1023, 2806
  Marie Louise (Mme. Noel Gallien, Mme. Alexis Cloutier I, Mme. Pierre Charpentier), 116, 123-124, 995
  Marie Louise (Mme. Baltasar Brevel), 226, 2794?
  Marie Louise (Metoyer); Mme. Francoise Maurice Melon), 973, 1159, 1395, 2029
  Marie Louise, identity uncertain, 55, 79, 228, 557, 1271, 1593, 2818
  Marie Louise Clarisse, 2085
  Marie Louise Desirée, 198

Rachal (continued),
  Marie Luce (Mme. Alexis Cloutier II), 25, 193, 207, 306, 487, 506, 508, 695, 996, 2410, 2847, 2917, 2929
  Marie Odisse, 1053, 2245, 2255, 2312
  Marie Pelagie, 253
  Marie Robt., 68
  Marie Susanne, *fille* Julien II, "Suzette", 302, 530, 686
  Marie Suzanne (Mme. Jean Crisostome Pereau), 732
  Marie Zelina Andrea, 1239
  Marie Zeline. *See Marie Céline.*
  Maurice. *See Joseph Maurice André.*
  Meline, 2214
  Michel, 2216
  Narcisse, 530, 763, 783, 1017, 1087, 1298-1299, 1980, 2355, 2360, 2908-2909
  Noel Barthelemy, 1134, 1350
  Osite. *See Marie Ausite.*
  Paul, 236
  Pierre, 2425
  Pierre Mission, 1921, 2358, 2616
  Remy, 605
  Silvestre, 160-161, 170, 763, 783, 794, 1032, 1093-1094, 2341, 2356, 2905, 2910
  Simeon I, 67, 967, 1862
  Simeon II. *See Louis Simeon.*
  Solastie. *See Louis Solastie.*
  Théodore Clément, 193, 2547
  Ursin, 2245.
  Ursin. *See also François Ursin.*
  Victor, 697, 2906
  Victor Damas, 199
  Victoria, 2216
  Zulime, 303
Rachel (Rechil, Richel, Recha), slave, 1488-1489, 1501-1502, 1667, 2105, 2238, 2240, 2284, 2610
Racquel, slave. *See Requenne.*
Rafael. *See Raphael.*
Raimond, 1598, 2077
Raimond (Remond, Ramon, Rameaun),
  G____lise (Mme. Etienne Rachal), 483, 2794
  Louis, 2669
  Marie Anne Magdeleine (Mme. André Vascocu), 140, 224, 268, 977, 1055, 1062
  Pierre, 140
Rambin (Rambino),
  ____, Mr., 1714, 1719, 1737, 2008
  A. Jean Baptiste, 2911

Ris (continued),
  Guillermo, 351
  Jean, 30, 98, 131, 181, 210
  Joseph Jean, 98, 263, 274, 285,
    787, 955, 1038
  Marcelitte, 98
  Marie (Mme. Michel Denis Aimé
    Casenave), 131, 247, 391, 1997
  Marie, *fille* Guillermo), 351
  Marie Barbe, 263
  Marie Celeste (Mme. Louis Vascocu)
    263, 1038, 2928
  Pelagie, 278
Roberson (Roverson, Robinson),
  Edward, 495, 558
  Jean Baptiste, 797
  Litch Page, 797
  Marie Margarita, 500, 2774, 2783
  Margaret (Mrs. William Hays), 393,
    471, 500, 554, 2641
Robert (Roverto), 2050, 2290
Robert, Magdeleine, Canneci Indian,
  827
Robin, slave. *See Rovim.*
Robin (Robain, Rovin, Roven),
  Anne (Mme. Jean Pierre Baudouin),
    28, 117, 212, 276, 507, 513-
    514, 1042, 2829
  François, 1845, 2797
  Marie (Mme. Athanase LeCourt), 141,
    309, 520, 1250, 1909, 2087, 2212
  Michel, 28, 212
Roblai, José, 571
Robleau (Roubleau, Roblo, Raublaut,
  Rublo),
  Damascene (Damasia), 422
  Edward Lestan, 1302
  Hélène (Mme. Michel Vincent), 992
  Marie Celeste, 1302
  Marie Susette (Dna. Felipe Flores),
    798, 1238
  Pierre, 421-422, 798, 1238, 1400-
    1401, 1527
  Zeledina, 421
Rochetted?, René, 724
Rocques (Rocque, Roque),
  Charles Nerestan I, 1210, 1440, 1463,
    1479, 1481-1483, 1559, 1621-1622,
    1624, 1632, 1654, 1699
  Charles Nerestan II, 1210
  Elisée (Eliset, Elset), 1456, 1466
    1471, 1557-1560, 1625, 1699, 1700
  Marguerite, 1622
  Marie Claire, 1624
  Marie Elina, 1625
  Marie Elise, 1700

Rocques (continued),
  Marie Elysa, 1699
  See also Roque.
Rodriguez,
  _____ a (Dna. Sanchez?), 916
  Cypriano Augustin, 474, 2795, 2914
  Francisco, 884
  J. A., 2883
  Jose Manuel, 474, 2795
  Juana Francisca, 2914
  Maria A., 2839, 2881
  Maria Cruz (Dna. J. B. Cortes/Cortinas?)
    782
  Maria Guadalupe, 1118
  Maria Teresa (Dna. Juan Toval), 466,
    488, 688, 2822
Rogé
  Magdalene (Mme. Michel LaPrairie), 638
  Marie Egepsiace, 2496
Roger,
  François, 343, 984
  Jean Baptiste, 984
  Marie Reine, 343
  See also Royer.
Rolan, Vicente, 412, 421
Romain, 1547
Romero, Margarita (Dna. Enrique Estrada),
  796
Romuel, 1809
Rondain (Ronde), Marie Julien (Mme.
  Antoine LeNoir), 189, 197)
Rondeau, Adrienne (Mme. Nicolas Bordelon)
  44, 144
Roque, free Negro, 1711
Roque. *See also Rocque.*
Roquigni. *See Rouquier.*
Rosales?, Julien, 466
Rosalie, Indian (Mme. Louis Guillerie),
  312, 1237?, 1238?
Rosalie (Roselene, Rosaline, Rosely, Ro-
  saly, Rosalye, Rosalia), 1144, 1316,
  1516, 1546, 1641, 1692, 1795, 1842-
  1843, 1959, 2016, 2050, 2077, 2192,
  2194, 2297, 2342, 2361, 2495, 2550
Rosas, Marie Celeste (Dna. Joseph An-
  tonio Caro?), 752
Rose, Apalache Indian, 660
Rose (Rosse, Rosa, Roset, Rosete),
  352, 1079, 1083, 1193, 1310, 1351,
  1359, 1499, 1575, 1746, 1828, 1850,
  1920, 1928, 1950, 2049, 2124, 2185,
  2187, 2226, 2535, 2538, 2570-2571,
  2583
Rosales (Rosalis, Rozales),
  Julian, 466
  Maria (Dna. Ignacio Gonzales) 2866

Rambin (continued),
  Adelaïde. *See Marie Françoise Adelaïde.*
  André I, 194
  André, identity uncertain, 694, 2911-2913
  André Antoine, 34, 53, 142, 151, 240, 438, 893, 1020
  André Michel, 497
  André Lestan, 194
  Euphrosine, 1811, 2911
  François Augustin, 151, 438, 1020, 1402-1403, 1823, 2911
  Lestan, 2486
  Marie Barbe (Mme. François Prudhomme), 1022, 1028
  Marie Catherine Damascene, 438
  Marie Dolores, 423
  Marie Françoise Adelaïde (Mme. Christian Hesser), 34, 142, 151, 2813
  Marie Louise Euphrosine (Mme. Michel Chamart), 53, 142, 151
  Marie Osite, 2912
  Michel, 194, 423, 2912, 2927
Rami, Diegue, 173
Ramon. *See Raimond.*
Ramos,
  Ana Maria (Dna. Juan José Vela), 865
  Maria Ignacio, 1505
  Victoriano, 866
Raphael (Rafael), 1153, 1476, 2139, 2151, 2565, 2580. *See also Joseph Raphael.*
Rapicault, Louise (Mme. Jean Archinard), 639-641
Rasaly, Pierre, 2856
Raquel (Requinne, Requin, Requiole), 1088, 1090, 1442, 2363
Rechin, 1286-1288
Reese. *See Ris.*
Reed,
  Anne, 96
  David, 96
  Heleine, 96
  Samuel, 96
Reine, 2050, 2054
Remira, Josephine, 617
Remy (Remi),
  Free Negro, 1232
  Slave, 1121, 1252, 1459, 1530, 1679, 1685, 2357
Renau,
  Andres, 619
  Chatalina, 620

Renau (continued)
  Francisca, 621
  Jean, 25
  Josephine, 622, 635. *See also Aguesse.*
Rendon,
  Jose Manuel, 694, 2913
  Marie Louise, 2913
Renoy. *See Renua.*
Resit, Apalache Indian. *See Joseph Resit.*
Reuben. *See Jacques Reuben.*
Revoil, Antoine, 1384
Reyes, Regina, 1306
Rice. *See Ris.*
Richal,
  Maria Candelaria (Dna. Eduardo Ariola) 521
  Morico, 914
Richal. *See also Rachal, Richard.*
Richard,
  Marie Anne (Mme. Augustin Philibert), 991
  Marie Louise (Mrs. David McClellan), 2886
  Matheo, 738, 2886
Riché (de Riche),
  George Petre, 111
  Manuel (Emanuelle), (Mme. J. B. Gonin, Mme. Guillaume Lestage), 27, 45, 101, 195, 964-965, 1056
  Jeanne (Mme. Vincent Poirrier), 957
  Marie Louise (Mme. Augustin Langlois), 33, 133
Richel. *See Rachel, Richal.*
Richey,
  Ben, 554
  Charles David Yewell, 554
Riesse. *See Ris.*
Rigobert, 2049
Rio (Rios),
  Candida (Mme. Antoine de Mézières), 915
  François, 2933
  José Ignacio, 522
  Maria Catarina, 2915
  Maria Josefa (Dna. Francisco Santos) 2797
  Maria Martina Ignacia, 522
  Victor, 2915
Rio. *See also Del Rio.*
Rio-Ybarbo, Marie El., 2933
Ris (Jean-Ris, Riesse, Risse),
  Eleonore (Mme. J. B. F. Dubois), 30, 181, 210
  Genevieve (Mme. Henry Trichel), 98, 192, 546, 1014, 2094, 2579, 2867
  Guillermo, 351

Rosales,
  Maria del Carmen?, 466
Rosée, Susanne, 629
Rosillon, Louise, 1375?, 1378
Ross, Reuben, 2835, 2895
Rosse,
  Joseph, 5, 76, 185
  Marie Manuel (Mme. Nicolas Duroque) 5, 76
  Sarah, 328
  See also Rosee.
Roubieu (Roubeau, Roubiau, Ruvio, Rubieu),
  _____, female, 2667
  Auguste, 327, 431, 949
  Auguste, Mme. Widow, 2349
  Euphemie, 327
  François Oscar I, 327, 431, 777, 786, 994, 1017, 1025, 1222, 1315, 1500-1502, 1835, 2422-2425, 2667, 2916-2917
  François Oscar II, 431, 1222, 1315
  Françoise Adelaide, 2916, 1222
  Gaspard, 46, 1025
  Marie Luz, 2917
  Pupon?, 1315
Roubleau. *See Robleau.*
Roulou, Susanne (Mme. Amable Cadieu I) 1049
Rouquier (Ruquier, Rouquierre, Rouqui, Rouquié, Ruquie),
  _____, Widow, 1772
  Eugenie (Mme. Joseph Lambre), 260, 333
  François I, 8, 18, 36, 451, 727, 952-953, 974-975, 988-989, 1005, 1729, 1844, 1850-1851, 1866-1867, 1869, 1885, 1962, 1999, 2007, 2014, 2066
  François II. *See Jean Marie François.*
  François III, 400
  Françoise, 2113
  Henriette. *See Marie Josephe Henriette.*
  Jean Marie François, 18, 63, 232, 260, 270, 289, 293, 374, 397-398, 796, 951, 975, 977, 988-990, 1005, 1112, 1285, 1406, 1493-1494, 1608, 2191, 2261, 2266, 2282, 2601
  Joseph, 1098, 1112, 1200, 1284, 1499, 1760, 1956, 2065, 2090, 2123-2124, 2157, 2623, 2642
  Marie, 34, 1828, 1850

Rouquier (continued),
  Marie Aimé (Mrs. James Bludworth), 36, 63, 375, 397-399, 451
  Marie Anne (Mme. Charles Roque Pavie) 248, 268, 280, 293, 335, 345, 373, 399, 975, 1612, 2065, 2764, 2869
  Marie Josephe Henriette (Mrs. John C. Carr), 18, 62, 374-375, 989, 1820, 1867
  Marie Josephine Marcelite (Mme. Jean Cortes), 208, 289, 336, 370, 379, 373, 451-452, 523, 988
  Marie Louise, 397
  V., 791
Rouquillo (Roc), Barbarita (Barbe), 242, 2885
Roussot, Marie (Mme. Gabriel Buart), 8
Rovim (Robin?), slave, 2428
Roy, Thérèse (Mme. J. B. Derbanne), 109, 146
Royer (Royore),
  François Octave, 539
  Pierre I, 539, 1051
  Pierre Vital, 539
  See also Roger.
Rozales. *See Rosales.*
Ruelle,
  Antoine, 791
  François, 791
Ruiz,
  J. J. (female), 2770
  Maria (Dna. Francisco Rodriguez), 884
  Maria Antonia Iniculina, 701, 2918
  Maria Simona (Dna. Juan Antonio Cruz) 2807
  Santiago (Jacquez), 701, 2918
Rutch (Routh?), Maria, 456
Rutin, Jeanne (Mme. Jean Brosset), 25
Ry____olf, Michel, 781
Rysse. *See Ris.*

Saidek (Saydre, Seideik) *dit* LeComte,
  Antoine, 456
  Marie Rose (Mrs. James Teal), 154, 284, 2890, 2921, 2937
  Pierre Clavis François, 154
  Pierre II, 456-457
St. Amand (St. Amans) Bauvard *dit*
  _____, Sieur, 742
  Edward de, 728
  G. B., 689
  Jean Joseph, 369, 730, 1036, 1047, 1060, 1064
  Marie Magdeleine Giraud, 460

St. Amand (continued),
  Prudans, 1309
St. André (Ste. Andres), Botien dit,
  André I, 51, 121-122, 572, 763,
    1035, 1294-1296, 1674-1676,
    1933, 2338-2348
  André II, 122
  Antoine Chata, 1278
  Claire, 1278
  Félicité (Felise), 51
  Felix, 1278, 1675
  Jacques I, 51, 121-122
  Jacques II, 311, 566, 968-969,
    1084, 2338, 2353-2355, 2520
  Janvier, 1278
  Louis Phanor (Phaneau), 1678
  Marie Adrienne (Mme. François St.
    Germaine), 121, 170, 572, 1034,
    1980, 2341
  Marie Ausite (Mme. Alexis Moreau),
    1061, 2338, 2346, 2354, 2357
  Marie Celina, 1678
  Marie Heloise (Mme. Louis Solastie
    Rachal), 121, 574, 763, 1278,
    1295, 1674, 2348, 2355, 2935
  Marie Victoire (Mme. François Baudry), 573-574, 1084, 2340
  Marie Zelia, 1278
  Onezime (Lesime), 573, 763, 1034-
    1035, 1278, 1677-1678
  Seraphin, 1278
St. Cyr. See Louis St. Cir.
St. Denis, Juchereau de
  Louis II, 814
  Louis II, Widow, 1828, 1845. See
    Marie Marguerite Derbanne also.
  Marie DeNeige (Mme. Antonio Manuel
    Bermudez y de Soto), 156
St. Germain (San German, Sant German,
  Ste. Charne, St. Charme, Chan Charmé),
  André, 572
  François, 572, 1035, 1110, 1674,
    1679, 2347
  Michel, 1035
St. Germaine dit Blese, Pierre, 968-
  969
St. Michel, Marguerite (Mme. Michel
  St. Germain), 1035
St. Romes. See Durand de St. Romes.
St. Ville (Sinvil), 2599. See also
  Jean Baptiste St. Ville.
Sali (Saly), 2132-2133, 2427
Salinas,
  José Francisco, 2688
  José Leno, 2688

Sallie, slave. See Sali, Lou Sally,
  Marie Anne Sallie.
Salmon. See Solomon.
Salvados. See Palvados.
Salvant (Clavens, Salvon, Salban),
  Jean, 105, 123-124, 180
  Marie (Mme. Jean Pierre Cloutier),
    122-124, 306, 1701
  Marie Louise (Mme. Jean Crisostomé
    Pereau), 105, 132, 180, 245, 855,
    950, 1009, 1012, 1018
Sampson (Sanson), 2283
Samuel,
  José Guadalupe, 525
  Pablo, 2588
  Santiago, 525
San Carquier,
  José Candido, 492
  Pedro, 492
Sanchez,
  _____, 916
  _____ idad, 703
  José, 1044, 1050
  José Leonardo, 463, 2796
  J. M., 2783
  Ludgard, 2821
  Luis, 1058
  Maria, 2852
  Maria, 463
  Maria Anastasia (Dna. Joseph Lucas
    Chirino), 2844
  Maria Dolores (Dna. J. Domingo Ibarbo), 458, 2786
  Maria Jetrudis (Dna. Jose Faustin
    del Rio), 458, 1044, 2147, 2786
  Maria Josepha (Dna. Ramon Chavana),
    702, 2770, 2842
  Maria Luisa (Dna. Manuel Bustamente),
    2804
  Maria Manuella, 752
  Maria Mauricia, 2821
  Maria Merzed (Dna. Juan Bautista
    Chirino), 1058
  Maria Teresa, 875
  Maria Teresa, hija Jose Leonard, 2796
  Maria Trinidad, 2840
Sandoval, Josef, 2698
Sn. Miguel,
  Cresencio, 1050
  Maria Alexandra, 1033, 2742
  Nepomuceno, 1033
Sansom, Andres, 617, 621, 781
Sta. Coy. See de los Santa Coy.
Sta. Cruz (Crous),
  Maria Micaela Rosalia (Dna. Jn. Laurent Bodin I), 31, 43, 942

Sidrec (continued),
  Ther(ese?), (Mrs. Joseph Clark), 2845
    See also Saydek, Cedars.
Silvain, 1588. See also L. Silvain.
Silvestre, 1963, 1967, 2141, 2388, 2390
Silvie, 2056
Simeon (Simeyon), 1571, 1857, 2279
Simon (Simons),
  Charles, 1406, 1421
  Jean, 992
  Michel, 992
Sims (Chimis, Chinny),
  Marie (Mme. Jean Baptiste Maximilien Arze), 2826, 2887
Sin____, slave, 1364
Sinegal, Toussaint, 919
Sinsin, slave, 1255. See also Manuel Senciel, Sousin.
Siors, slave. See Jose Siors.
Siverino, Juana, 2142
Slocum,
  Charles, 554
  Juliana Josepha (Mme. Firmin Poissot), 2674
  James, 546, 549, 743, 745, 748-749
Socier. See Saucier.
Soco, 1773
Sodelle, 1576
Solés, Theresa (Dna. Luis Thomasino, I), 95
Soli Bellas, Maria Jetrudis (Dna. Louis Was Brom), 615-616
Solomon, slave. See Joseph Solomon.
Solomon, Susanne, 73, 665-6, 662, 669
Sompayrac (Sompairact, Sompayract),
  Ambroise I, 452, 695, 990
  Ambroise II, 292, 296, 369, 685, 728, 777, 795, 987, 990, 1005-1010, 1012-1014, 1018, 1023, 1025, 1037, 1043, 1060, 1064, 1534, 1612, 1749, 1761, 2676
  Ambrose Bernard Theophile, 685
  Charles Emile, 452
  Marc, 742, 777, 780, 794, 1280, 1335, 1555
  Marie, 2676
  Pierre Jean Joseph, 369
Sophie (Sofy, Sophy, Sofi, Sophine), 1141, 1446, 1991, 2010, 2048, 2057, 2152, 2171-2172, 2183, 2192, 2324, 2440, 2548. See also Marguerite Sophie.

Sorel, *dit* Marli,
  Dominique Pierre, 22, 230, 787, 822, 830, 959, 1074, 2830
  Genevieve (Mme. Jean Baptiste Grappe I), 99, 819, 889, 1232
  Louis, 230
  Luc, 22
  Marie Anne Jeanne (Mme. Augustin Fredieu), 6, 125, 1026, 1029
  Marie Felicité (Mme. Jean Vital Vascocu), 787, 1074
  Pierre, 6, 22, 99, 125, 959.
  Pierre. See also Dominique Pierre.
  Stephanie, 22
Sosa (Sose, Soso),
  ____ino de, 709
  Juan, 703
  Juan (Jean) André, 2880
  Guadalupe, 2145
  Joseph Ignace, 2880
  Mauricia (Dna. José Luis Duran), 879
  Pedro, 2607
Sosthene, male slave. See Marie Sosthene.
Sotenel, Cade (Cadet?), 246
Soto,
  Incarnation (Dna. Pedro Garza), 2859-2860
  Juan, 534, 1050
  Maria, 570
  Maria Dolores, 438, 2778
  Maria Jetrudis (Dna. Felipe Mora), 880
  Maria Ignacia, 501
  Maria In(carnacion), 2860
  See also de Soto.
Sousin. See Louis Sousin, Sinsin.
Souly, Apalache Indian, 665-668
Spade,
  Daniel, 282
  John, 282
Stephen, slave. See Etienne.
Stephanie, 1925
Sudie, 2339-2340
Sirigni,
  Catarina, 473
  Luis, 473
Susanne (Susana, Susette, Susene, Susy, Suasin, Suset, Suzette, Susete),
  Free, 1200, 1284, 1660, 1664, 2098
  Slave, 1095, 1111, 1122, 1178, 1300, 1308, 1343, 1400-1401, 1491, 1520, 1527, 1549, 1618, 1677-1678, 1751, 1839-1840, 1861-1862, 1901-1902, 1913, 1916, 1924, 1927, 1936, 1961

Sta. Cruz, (continued),
  Venancia (Berenciana), 714, 1054, 2842
  See also Cruz, de la Cruz.
Santiago, slave. *See Jacques.*
Santos,
  Francisco, 2797, 2818
  Jose Benigno, 552
  Jose Facundo, 486, 2797
  Manuel, 552
  See also de los Santos
Santuche, Ignacio, 2142
Sarah (Sair, Zaire, Sira), 1296, 1675, 1932-1933, 1937, 2050, 2072, 2428. *See also Magdeleine Sarah.*
Sarde, Marguerite (Mme. Joseph Gillard I), 579-580, 583
Sarnac, Sarniac. *See Guisarnac.*
Sarpy (Charpi, Sarpi, Sarpygs, Sarpigs),
  Euphrosie, 1621
  Gerome (Geronimo), Joseph I 1478, 1560, 1562, 1621-1622 1628, 1662, 1698
  Gerome, II, 1698
  Marie Lilette (Ilette), 1628
Saturnin (Saturin), 1798, 1963.
  See also Jean Saturnin.
Saucier (Saucié, Sausciere, Sausier, Saucierre, Sousiere, Socier),
  Félicité (Mme. Andres Chamard) 693?, 712, 726, 2636, 2841
  François, 539, 1051
  François Joseph, 1051
  Henry, 693
  Henriette (Anriette), 539, 693 2841
  Louis I, 550, 1051
  Louis II, 550
  Marie (Mme. Jean Marie Morin), 968
  Marie Louise Victoire, 550
  Marie Rose (Mme. Jacques Simon Theodore Deterville), 1051, 2686, 2744
Sauvage, Marie Catherine (Mme. Philippe Frederick), 9, 71, 87, 206, 958, 993, 2038, 2758
Savoyau, slave. *See Jean Baptiste Savoyau.*
Saydek. *See Saidek.*
Schamps (Scamps, Scemps),
  George, 1201, 2496
  Marie Clare, 706

Schlette. *See Chelette.*
Scopini, François, 735
Sears, slave. *See Joseph Siors.*
Sebastien, 2057. *See also Bastian, Martin Sebastien.*
Seguin (Segound),
  Juan F., 2916
  Juan José, 1054
  Maria Manuela (Dna. Jose Eginio Casanova), 1054, 2839
Seideik. *See Saidek.*
Semiry, slave, 1087.
Senciel, slave. *See Manuel Senciel.*
Sephorin, slave. *See Jean Baptiste Ziphorine.*
Sepulveda,
  ____, 705
  J. Antonio, 765, 2842
  Polonia, 765
  Th.____, 2903
Seraphin (Seraphim), 1319, 2493, 2593
Serena, 1571
Serpault, Marie Anne (Mme. Pierre Badin), 846
Serpentini, François, 377, 797-798
Serria, Maria (Dna. Miguel Plo___), 881
Servantes,
  Marcel, 874, 1039
  Maria de Jesusa (Dna. Hilario Carrasco), 494, 1039, 2785
Sesten, slave, 1492
Severinne, slave, 1213
Sheridan (Seredem),
  ____, Mr., 1107
  See also Cheredem.
Shilé (Chifilef, Lely), Charity (Mrs. Frederic Walker), 542-543, 575, 792
Shlater. *See Chelette.*
Shumas?, Guillaume C., 2874
Sibley,
  Ana Elisa, 392
  Elisabeth, 381
  Henry, 2920
  Henry Hopkins, 2920
  John, Dr., 343, 378, 1019, 1028, 1358, 2692, 2919
  John II, 2692
  Marie Nette, 2919
  Robert, 2919
  Samuel Hopkins, 381, 1523, 2920
Sidalisse, 1568
Sidonie (Sidony), 2361
Sidrec,
  Marianne (Mme. Pierre Tessier), 2924

Susanne (continued),
  1966, 1992, 1999, 2023-2024, 2049-2050, 2054, 2056, 2105, 2144, 2168, 2176, 2204, 2207, 2213, 2234-2235, 2244, 2268, 2282, 2389, 2392, 2427, 2468, 2494, 2500, 2565, 2613, 2632. *See also Marie Anne Susanne.*
Susanne Michel, Apalache Indian, 672
Susanne Pierro, Apalache Indian, 674
Suibuck? (Saideck?), Pedro, 350
Suibuck? (Saideck?), Marie Rose (Mme. Jacques Totin?/Teal?), 350

Tamonet Acoye, Apalache Indian (wife of Meson Blans), 681
Tanson, Rosa, 2476
Taudem (Totin?), Charles, 937
Tausin, slave. *See Toussaint.*
Tauzin (Tausin, Teuzin, Tozin, Tauzen),
  Adelaïde (Mrs. Thomas M. Linnard), 292, 380-381, 533, 1003, 2069, 2864
  Ambroise Velein, 296
  Celeste. *See Mathilde Celeste, Victoire Celeste.*
  Eugene, 241
  Euphrosine (Mme. Alexandré Louis Deblieux), 241, 453, 1064, 2069, 2136, 2435
  Evariste. *See Henri Evariste, Theophile Evariste,* also. 106.
  François Celestin, 38, 1320
  Girard, 38, 106
  Henri Evariste, 106, 750, 1060, 1064, 2641, 2705
  Joseph I, 38, 106, 233, 241, 296, 380, 682, 726, 728, 730, 742, 744, 750, 776, 798, 852, 950-951, 958, 975, 993-998, 1003, 1030, 1060, 1064, 1067, 1320-1321, 1524, 1787, 1788, 2057, 2069, 2076, 2137, 2405, 2442-2443, 2635?, 2639, 2643, 2705, 2868
  Louis Joseph, 453, 533, 744, 756, 991-992, 1003, 1031, 1060, 1064, 1103, 1157-1158, 1243, 1512, 1600-1601, 2443, 2757
  Marcellin, 241
  Marie, identity uncertain, 241
  Marie, *fille* Louis, 2757
  Marie Eliset, 1532
  Matilde Celeste (Mme. Benjamin Dranguet), 106, 533, 728, 2137

Tauzin (continued),
  Theophile Evariste, 106, 2636
  Victoire Celeste (Victoria Selesta), 2189
  Valein. *See Ambroise Valein.*
Teal (Teel),
  Edward, 154
  James (Jacques), 154, 2921, 350?
  Jean Baptiste Alexandre, 154
  Joseph, 570
  Mary Nancy Brown (Mrs. William Ettredge), 457, 2921, 2931
  Pierre, 2921
  Placide, 284
  Susanne (Mme. Pierre Saidek II), 456-457
Tensá, Apalache Indian. *See Louis Tensá, Michel Tensá, Pierre Tensá.*
Ternier *dit* Grenoble,
  Etienne, 868
  Marie, 232
  Marie Cephalide, 385
  Pierre I, 4, 232, 384-385, 442, 733, 735, 747, 750, 1154, 1189, 2574, 2763
  Pierre II, 442
Terrence, slave. *See Joseph Terans.*
Terrié, Jacques, 12.
Terrié. *See also Herrié.*
Tessier *dit* LaVigne (Tecier, Texier),
  Eleonora (Mme. Jean François Palvados), 1, 56, 262, 982, 1013, 1043, 2762
  Joseph, 2760
  Manuel, 2924
  Pierre, 1, 56, 2924
Texada (Texeda, Texedo),
  Juana Francisca, 2902
  Marie F., 2930
  Maria Jetrudis (Dna. Juan Procela, Dna. José Tomas Caro), 1052, 2932
  Mariano, 1052
Theodore, slave, 1587
Theotis, slave?, 2535
Thérèse (Theresse, Teresa),
  Canneci Indian, 998
  Slave, 1147, 1166, 1169, 1291, 1311, 1313, 1328, 1330, 1735, 1873, 1942, 2050, 2052, 2275, 2609, 2527
Thibauth, slave, 2049
Thibodeux. *See Tibodo.*
Thierry. *See Quierry.*
Thomas, Indian. *See C(h)atarine Thomas, Joseph Thomas, Marie Thomas.*
Thomas (Tomas), slave, 352, 2285,

Thomas (continued), 2359, 2385, 2392, 2472. *See also Tom.*
Thomas?, William C. (Guillaume), 2874
Thomassie (Thomassino, Thomacine, Thomassine),
  Cesaire, 518
  Joseph, 517, 2819
  Luis I, 95
  Luis II, 95, 273, 957, 1001
  Marie Françoise, 95, 517, 2819
  Marie Reine (Mme. Louis Julien Rachal), 332, 518, 1001, 2909
  Thérèse (Mme. François Poirier I), 272-273, 517, 957, 2819
Thompson (Thomson),
  Joseph, 2922
  Marie Emeline, 2923
  Marie Sophie, 2922
  Thomas, 2923
Tibido,
  Maria Celeste, 495
  Maria Luisa, 495
Tiery, Marie P., 2889. *See also Quierry.*
Tihoua, Natchitoches, Indian, 143, 960
Tihoua,
  Cesaire, 960
  Louis, Natchitoches Indian, 143, 960
  Marie Euphrosine, 960
  Marie Marguerite, 960
  Marie Deneige (Christy), 12, 960
Titus, slave. *See Joseph Titos.*
Tocour,
  Celeste, 2622
  Felicité, 2621
  Jacques Claver, 2622
  Marie Espasit (Aspasie), 2621
Tom, 2072, 2077.
Tom, Tomas. *See also Thomas.*
Tomacin. *See Thomassine*
Tonton, Apalache Indian, 1804-1805
Toró (Torro),
  Apalache Indians. *See Estevan Toró, Louise Tor(r)o*
  José, 1052. *See also Torres.*
Torres (Taure),
  _____, 796
  Ascencion. *See Marie de l'ascencion*
  Azenor Gabriel, 73
  Francisco, 2716
  Françoise, 1109
  Joseph Cleto?, 757

Torres (continued),
  Joseph Courretant I, 72-73, 84, 90-92, 115, 164-165, 170, 207-208, 969
  Joseph Emanuel, 170
  Joseph Gabriel Marie, 72-73, 170, 600-601, 657, 669, 1979, 2081
  José Ignacio, 2197
  Joseph Jerome, 21
  Joseph Laurent, 72, 664
  Jul(iana?), 2892
  Marcelina, 601
  Marie Antoinette Corretant (Mme. Germain Wallette), 21, 313, 969
  Maria Antonia (Dna. Santiago Arevalo) 2827
  Marie de l'Assumption/Ascencion (Mme. J. B. Varangue/Vallery), 90-92, 207-208, 598-599, 645, 652
  Marie Gertrude (Mme. J. B. Aragon), 21, 84, 164
  Marie Joseph Corré (Mme. Jean Paul Couti), 115, 165, 566-568
  Maria Reine, 600
  Marie Rose, 664
  Matilde (Dna. Franco. Torres), 2716
Totin (Toutin, Totem, Tauttin),
  Celestin, 1062
  Charles, 1044, 2683, 937?
  Honorine. *See Marie Josephe Honorine.*
  Jacques (Teal?), 350
  Leon Brunet, 756
  Margueritte (Mme. Jean Baptiste Plaisance), 20, 57, 79, 202, 1013
  Mariano del Refugio, 349
  Marie Jeanne (Mme. Guillaume Chever), 839
  Marie Josephe Honorine (Mme. J. B. Gagné *fils* Etienne), 88, 93, 199, 215-216, 795
  Marie Louise (Mme. Guillaume Le Brun) 32, 947)
  Morine, 349
  Marin. *See Mariano del Refugio.*
  Remy I, 795, 977, 1062
  Remy II, 93, 349, 977
Touazin, Apalache Indian. *See Joseph Touazin*
Toucaye, Yguanes Indian, 1270
Toups, Marie Barbe (Mme. Antoine Vascocu), 52, 98, 140, 205
Toussaint (Tauzin, Tosin, Toissain, Tousin), slave, 1103, 1165, 1174, 1337, 1519, 1556, 1637, 1639, 1991-

Toussaint (continued), 1992, 2056, 2421. *See also Jean Toussaint, François Toussaint, Joseph Touzin, Joseph Touazin.*
Toutin. *See Totin.*
Touton Celestin, Apalache Indian, 661, 671
Toval (Tovar),
  Francisca de los Dolores, 704
  Francisco Firmin, 488
  Juan, 488, 688, 782, 2822
  Juan Francisco de los Delores, 688, 2822
  Maria Antonio, 704
  See also Joval.
Tranquilin, slave, 2335
Traviezo (Travioso, Travieso),
  ____na (Dna. Francisco Rodriguez), 884
  Guadalupe (Dna. Jose Luis Duran) 879
  Maria Dolores(Dna. Sulas Comes), 2684
Trenier, Marie, slave? *See Marie Trenier.*
Trepanié, Elisabeth (Mme. Louis Alexandré Guerbois), 829.
Tressini (Trechini),
  Jeann, 1127
Trevino, Francisco, 864
Trichel (Trichle, Tris, Trisselle, Trische, Trichette, Tricle, Trist),
  Alexis, 733, 1419, 1510, 1569, 2041, 2088, 2606, 2617, 2620
  Athanase, 735, 1212, 1569, 2459
  Baptiste, 2926. *See also Emanuel Baptiste, Jean Baptiste.*
  Catherine. *See Marie Thérèse Catherine.*
  Emanuel Baptiste, 1883
  Fanchonette (Fansonet). *See Françoise.*
  François, 2265
  François Berthil (Verthil), 2459
  François Henry, 269
  Françoise "Fanchonette", 102, 131, 267, 269, 326, 329, 1226, 1283, 1570, 1951, 2572
  Germain (Gervais?), 2747
  Henri, 268, 368, 546, 722, 733, 735, 740, 769, 985, 1010, 1014, 1036, 1070, 1099, 1269, 1857, 1802, 2000, 2024, 2094, 2097, 2145, 2403, 2487, 2793, 2867

Trichel (continued),
  Henri. *See also François Henry.*
  Jean Baptiste I, 47, 158, 238, 987, 1731?, 1818
  Jean Baptiste, *fils* Athanase, 1212
  Jean Baptiste II, 47, 158, 236-238, 326, 446, 538, 733, 735, 845, 976, 978-979, 982, 1055, 1756, 1951, 2268, 2642, 2717, 2925
  Jean Baptiste III, 158
  Jean Baptiste, Widow, 1323, 1428, 1602-1603, 1809
  Jean Louis, 326
  Joseph, 952
  Julien, 2097
  Lolette, 266
  Manuel, 11, 44, 57, 138-139, 144, 804, 1010, 1854?
  Manuel, 269, 326, 747, 1041, 1854?-1855, 2798, 2926
  Manuel, *fils* Lolette, 266
  Margueritte (Mme. Jean Simons) 992
  Marie Arcene, *fille* Manuel, 2798
  Marie Arcene, *fille* J.B., 47, 845
  Marie Celedina, 2926
  Marie Cilesie (Mme. Celestin Elie Bernard), 144, 368, 548, 1010, 1814, 2792
  Marie Emelie, 238, 1323
  Marie Felicité Modeste, 11, 138, 158-159, 180, 368, 435, 537, 1569, 2041, 2088
  Marie Françoise (Mme. Jean F. Le Vasseur), 329, 355, 537, 987, 2695
  Marie Hiacinthe (Mme. J. B. Davion) 19
  Marie Josephe, 804, 1809
  Marie Louise, 2264
  Marie Melanie (Mme. Louis Derzelin Pereau), 260, 469, 2793, 2893, 1014
  Marie Thérèse Catherine (Mme. Hypolite Bordelon), 44, 144, 222, 267, 371, 1012
  Modeste. *See Marie Felicité Modeste.*
  Pierre, 144, 148, 1040, 2460, 2893
  Sepherin, 446
  Severin, 2925
  Simeon, 1237
  Victor, 1659
  _____, Widow, 1703
  See also Felicité, f.w.c.; Marie Arcise, f.w.c.
Tristant, Pierre, 868
Troquillo? (Roquillo), Barbarita, 242

Trudeau (Troudeau, Trouidou),
  Emery, 2124
  Felix, 728, 742, 779, 782, 970, 1322, 1743, 1762, 1853, 1878, 1987, 2014, 2741
  Marie Adelaïde (Mme. Augustin Piernas), 1753
  Marie Josephe (Mme. François Pinsouneau), 1041
Turjon, Paschal, 843
Turpain, Magdeleine (Mme. Pierre Tessier), 56

Uigangham (Wigington?), Mary (Mrs. Lisky Franklin), 328
Ulalaye. *See Eulalie.*
Unidentified,
  _____ie, Marie Asely, 2729
  _____ie, Carlos, 2729
  _____em, slave, 2561
  _____, Berthelmy, 2497
  _____, Bmy, Widow, 1102
  _____, Euphrosine Celeste, 434
  _____, José, 930
  _____, José Geronimo, 1305
  _____, Juan (Spaniard), 2693
  _____, Juana, 2670
  _____, Marie Auresite (Oresyl), 2329, 2337
  _____, Marie Celesty?, 2497
  _____, Maria Gra_____, 705
  _____, Maria Lucovidi (Loucouvidhe), 1261
  _____, Maria Telesfora (Dna. Antonio Toval), 704
  _____, Pant____, 2604
  _____, Pelagio (Spanish woman) 2678
  _____, Pierre, Mr., 1597
  _____, Portuges, 931
  _____, Victoire, (Victoria), 2249
Untiel, Mari Luise, 756
Urany. *See Marie Ursul Urany.*
Urive, Maria Josefa (Dna. Bernardo Gutierrez), 536
Ursin (Ursen), 1149, 1245, 1343, 1349, 1402, 2500, 2532, 2628. *See also Louis Ursin.*
Ursulle, Caddo *metive*. *See Marie Ursulle.*
Ursulle (Ursula, Ursul), 1198, 1335, 1848, 1993, 2050, 2122, 2278.
Ursuline. *See Felicité Ursuline, Marie Magdalenne Euphrasinne Erselinne.*

Uuily (Wiley? Euly?), Marguerite (Mrs. David Reed), 96
Uuily (Wiley? Euly?), Jacque (James?) 96
Uueb. *See Webb.*

Vachon,
  Francisca, 691
  Rose (Mme. Jean Eugene Mechamps), 788
Vade, slave, 2437
Vailaim. *See Villain.*
Val_____, Jean Baptiste, 1281
Valcour, Apalache Indian, 681
Valentin (Balentin), slave, 1731, 2430, 2455. *See also Francois Valentin.*
Valentine (Valantin, Balantin, Valentin),
  André, 56, 262, 421, 1022, 1190, 1258, 1261-1263, 2110, 2486, 2900.
  André. *See also Jean André.*
  François, 394
  Jean André, 1264
  Joseph, 394, 1263, 2111, 2927
  Marie Louise, 2927
  Marie Thérèse (Mme. Pierre Gagnon), 235
Valery (Valeri, Valerin),
  Free, 1515, 2267, 2304, 2570-2572
  Slave, 1512, 1809, 2050, 2377
Valerin, Leandre, f.m.c., 2098
Vallery (Valery, Valeri, Baleri),
  Antonio, 599
  Barbara, 654
  François, 207, 681
  Jacques (Varangue), 92, 1808
  Jacques, *fils* J. B. (Varangue) I, 92
  Jean Baptiste (Varangue), I, 90-92, 207-208, 595, 598-599, 634, 644, 652, 2477, 2892
  Jean Baptiste II, 90, 647, 673, 2476
  Joseph, 2083
  Marcel (Varangue), 91, 658
  Maria Ascencion, 598
  Marie Des Neiges (Denis), 208, 647, 1089
  Marie Elene, 1808
  Pierre, 651, 656
  Susanne (Varangue), (Mme. Joseph Gabriel Torres), 72-73, 170, 600-601, 1979. *See also Susanne Solomon.*
Valsin (Valsain, Valsem, Balzin, Balsim, Balsine),
  Free. *See Francois Valsin.*
  Slave, 1216, 1614, 1667, 2268 (cont.)

Valsin (continued), 2336, 2397, 2432, 2585.
Vaqari?, Helene, 1586
Varangue (Barranco, de Barange),
   ____, Mr., 1842
   Jean Baptiste, 64, 166
   Jean Baptiste Vallery. *See Vallery.*
   Marie Barbe Joseph LeGrand (wife of Solomon, Apalache Indian), 72-73, 90-92, 170, 207-208, 595, 672
   See also Vallery.
Vargas. *See Barcas, Bargas, Borgas.*
Varrera, Maria Damascena, 522
Vascocu (Bacocu),
   André, 140, 224, 268, 977, 1055, 1062
   André. *See also Jean Baptiste André.*
   André Raimond, 140
   Antoine I, 52, 98, 140, 205, 218
   Antoine II, 841, 965
   Chrisostome, 52
   François, *fils* Louis, 287
   François II, 348, 977
   Heleine, 210, 2485
   Jean Baptiste André, 140, 1055, 2677
   Jean Louis, 52, 205, 286-287, 727, 733, 787, 862, 1038
   Jean Pierre Baptiste, 2677
   Jean Vital, 722, 787, 1038
   Joseph André, 140, 733
   Louis, 1038, 2928
   Louis. *See also Jean Louis, Vital Louis.*
   Marie, 268
   Marie Aimé, 140
   Marie Eulalie (Mme. J. B. Davion), 2691
   Marie Françoise (Mme. Joseph Jean Ris), 98, 1038
   Marie Lolette, 286
   Marie Louise, 2928
   Marie Miramie, 205
   Marie Modeste Raimond (Mme. Celestin Totin), 52, 239, 1062
   Marie Thérèse (Mme. Remy Totin), 140, 349, 977
   Michel, 224
   Vital. *See Jean Vital.*
   Vital Louis, 63, 976
Vega. *See de la Bega*
Vela,
   Juan José, 865
   Salvador, 865
Vely, slave, 2280

Veneuil, ____, Sieur, 781
Venoiy (Veronique?), slave, 1349
Venus, 2077, 2384-2387, 2637
Vercher (Verchere, Bercher, Verschair, Verchaire, Vercere, Verger),
   Adelaÿde Marcelite, 530
   Amelie, 357
   Beloni. *See Jean Baptiste Beloni.*
   Cirian, 912
   Emelie. *See Amelie.*
   Jacques Marcelin, 147
   Jacques Therin (Querin), 60, 116, 147, 314-315, 510, 695, 775, 1338, 2319-2320, 2784, 2799, 2929
   Jean Baptiste, 695, 2929
   Jean Baptiste Beloni, 330, 506, 510, 695, 1007, 2800, 2929
   Jean Louis, 60, 2407
   Jean Pierre, 330, 357, 530, 911, 999
   Joseph, 314, 732
   Joseph Louis, 272, 682, 1047
   Joseph Sorvic, 682
   Louis I, 60, 65, 147, 199, 236, 1007
   Louis II. *See Joseph Louis.*
   Louis, *fils* Jean Pierre, 330
   Lucie Delzie, 506
   Manuel, 314, 2319
   Marie Celine, 2800
   Marcelite. *See Adelaÿde Marcelite.*
   Marie Adelaïde (Mme. Jean LaLande), 20, 291, 510, 2714.
   Marie Louise Agathe, 510
   Marie Laÿsa, 2799
   Marie Rosalie (Mme. Dominique Rachal), 65, 147, 199, 236-237
   Victor, 315
Verger (Vergé, Vergara, Vergau),
   Anne (Mme. Joseph Lattier I), 95, 204, 972
   Etienne, 33, 133, 2516
   Etienne, Widow, 1146. *See also Marie Françoise Dupre.*
   Jeanne (Mme. Jean Baptiste Malbert) 167-169
   Jean Baptiste, 2382
   Marie (Mme. Gaspard Derbanne I), 57, 80, 136
   Marie Celeste (Mme. Augustin Louis Langlois), 33, 133, 301, 587
   Marie Louise (Mme. Pierre Crete, Mme. Pierre LaCour), 35, 81, 209, 2547?
Veroni, slave, 2449
Veronique, slave, 1225, 1349
Verson, Margarita, Madame, 2127
Veve. *See Beebe.*

Via, Cornelius, 778
Vici, slave. *See Jeanne Vici.*
Victoire (Victoria, Victorina),
    Apalache Indian, 644
    Free, 2397, 2412
    Slave, 1112, 1124, 1346, 1361, 1419, 1536, 1792, 1977, 2057, 2061, 2258, 2390, 2444-2445, 2448, 2455. *See also Marie Stephanie Victoire.*
Victor, f.m.c., 1585
Victoria Crisostomé, Apalache Indian, 665, 1806
Victoriana, 1246
Victorin, 1629. *See also Joseph Victorin.*
Victorine, 1835, 2070, 2587
Vidol,
    _____, Mr., 1875
    Dupalier, 1687
Vienne (Bienne),
    François, 499, 524, 727, 780, 791, 795, 1038, 1122, 1345, 1532, 1667, 1773, 1785, 1790, 2493-2494, 2531, 2610, 2724, 2765, 2896
    Jean Baptiste, 2724
    Louis François Maxil, 1532
Viet, slave. *See Joseph Viet.*
Vige, Genevieve (Mme. Jacques Herrié I), 18
Villand, Evariste?, 781
Villain (Vailaim, Vaillem, Bilaim),
    Nicolas, 613
    Nicolas II, 613, 1369
Villareal,
    Lucianne, 2930
    Marie Brigette, 2930
Villefranche. *Dit* of LeDuc.
Villegar. *See Bellegarde.*
Vimenez (Vimonez),
    Francisca (Dna. Franco. Leal), 1033
    Francisco, 526, 2707
    Joseph, 2707
    José de Jesus, 526
    Marie Tomasa (Dna. Fernando Menchaca), 870, 2699
    Pedro, 863
Vincent (Vicente),
    Ciriaco, 2640
    Michel, 992
    Rosalie (Mme. Michel Simons), 992
Violet, slave, 1187

Voltaris,
    Eligio, 570
    Marcelina de Jesus, 570
    Michel, 2598
Vivian, slave. *See Elena Vivian.*

Wallace (Ouales, Wallet, Wales),
    Etienne Maximien (Jacques), I, 4, 2763
    Etienne Maximilian II, 4, 2763
    Joseph, 4, 1030
    Marie Elenne, 2863
    Thomas I, 1030, 1435, 2863-2864
    Thomas II, 2864
Wallett (Wallette, Wallte),
    André, 969
    Charles, 569
    Germain, 313, 969
    Jean Baptiste, 569, 2482
    Louis, 528, 2862
    Louis II, 2862
    Marie Denize, 313
    Marie Odisse, 528
Waltheman. *See Gualtheman.*
Walthers (Walteher),
    Charles F., 542-543, 792-793
    Frederick, 542-543, 575, 792
    Jean Baptiste Frederick, 575
    Marie Celeste (Dna. Hilario Carrasco), 543, 792
Was Brom,
    Jeann Tabitha, 615
    Louis, 615-616
    Marie Louise, 616
Washington, slave, 2229. *See also Joseph Wasinton.*
Webb (Uueb),
    Leonard, 196-197
    Susanne (Mrs. Alexandre Laurence), 196-197
Wells (Well)
    Edith (Mme. Policarp Lamot), 625-628
    Elisabeth, 618
    Oliviet, 618
    Signy, 627
    _____, Mr., 2554
William (Guillermo), slave, 2290 *See also Guillermo.*
William (Willom) George, 1243
Wilson? *See Guilscem.*
Winslow, Maria (Mrs. John Sibley), 1019

Ximenes. *See Vimenez.*
Ybarbo (Ibarbo),
  J. Domingo, 458, 2786
  Joseph Antoine, 2932
  José Ignacio, 477, 1526, 1529, 2866?
  Joseph Manuel, 2934
  Joseph Polonio, 2932
  Juan José Cesario, 477
  Maria Jetrudis (Getrude), 2933
  Marie Luciane (Dna. Joseph Polonio Ybarbo), 2932
  Maria Tomasa, 458, 2786
  Pedro (Pierre), 2934
  Ponciana, 477, 2807
Ydalgo. *See Hidalgo.*
Yeper,
  _____, 908
  Juana, 908
  Luis, 908
Yguanes Indians, 1270
Yiné (Inez?), slave, 1107
Yocase Indians, 1276
Ysabel. *See Isabel.*
Ysidre, 1453
Ystor,
  Harrison, 2935-2936
  Marie, 2936
  Marie Celeste, 2935
Ysurd. *See Hissoura.*
Yudd, Maria Antonia, 395
Yves *dit* Pacalé, 1776
Zalye, slave. *See Marie Sallie.*
Zair, slave. *See Sarah.*
Zariche. *See Michel-Zoriche.*
Zebeda, Concepcione (Dna. Juan Delgado), 2775
Zeli, slave. *See Marie Celezi.*
Zenon (Senon),
  Free, 1390, 1782
  Slave, 1068, 1109, 1141, 1169, 1493, 1605-1606, 1635, 1667, 1685, 2049, 2215, 2436. *See also François Zenon.*
Zephany, slave. *See Marie Stephanie.*
Zoe, slave, 1611
Zoriche. *See Michel-Zoriche.*

www.ingramcontent.com/pod-product-compliance
Lightning Source LLC
Chambersburg PA
CBHW070056020526
44112CB00034B/1408